# CORPORATE TAX RATES

| If taxable income is: | The tax is: |
| --- | --- |
| Not over $50,000 | 15% of taxable income |
| Over $50,000 but not over $75,000 | $7,500 + 25% of the excess over $50,000 |
| Over $75,000 but not over $100,000 | $13,750 + 34% of the excess over $75,000 |
| Over $100,000 but not over $335,000 | $22,250 + 39% of the excess over $100,000 |
| Over $335,000 but not over $10,000,000 | $113,900 + 34% of the excess over $335,000 |
| Over $10,000,000 but not over $15,000,000 | $3,400,000 + 35% of the excess over $10,000,000 |
| Over $15,000,000 but not over $18,333,333 | $5,150,000 + 38% of the excess over $15,000,000 |
| Over $18,333,333 | $6,416,667 + 35% of the excess over $18,333,333 |

# ESTATE AND TRUST INCOME TAX RATES

| If taxable income is: | The tax is: |
| --- | --- |
| Not over $1,900 | 15% of taxable income |
| Over $1,900 but not over $4,500 | $285.00 + 27% of the excess over $1,900 |
| Over $4,500 but not over $6,850 | $987.00 + 30%of the excess over $4,500 |
| Over $6,850 but not over $9,350 | $1,692.00 + 35% of the excess over $6,850 |
| Over $9,350 | $2,567.00 + 38.6% of the excess over $9,350 |

Visit the *Advanced Strategies in Taxation* Online Learning Center at
www.mhhe.com/sjones2005

# Advanced Strategies in Taxation

Fourth Edition

**Sally M. Jones**
*KPMG Professor of Accounting*
*McIntire School of Commerce*
*University of Virginia*

**Shelley C. Rhoades-Catanach**
*College of Commerce and Finance*
*Villanova University*

McGraw-Hill
Irwin

Boston   Burr Ridge, IL   Dubuque, IA   Madison, WI   New York   San Francisco   St. Louis
Bangkok   Bogotá   Caracas   Kuala Lumpur   Lisbon   London   Madrid   Mexico City
Milan   Montreal   New Delhi   Santiago   Seoul   Singapore   Sydney   Taipei   Toronto

ADVANCED STRATEGIES IN TAXATION

Published by McGraw-Hill/Irwin, a business unit of The McGraw-Hill Companies, Inc., 1221 Avenue of the Americas, New York, NY, 10020. Copyright © 2005, 2004, 2003, 2002 by The McGraw-Hill Companies, Inc. All rights reserved. No part of this publication may be reproduced or distributed in any form or by any means, or stored in a database or retrieval system, without the prior written consent of The McGraw-Hill Companies, Inc., including, but not limited to, in any network or other electronic storage or transmission, or broadcast for distance learning.

Some ancillaries, including electronic and print components, may not be available to customers outside the United States.

This book is printed on acid-free paper.

1 2 3 4 5 6 7 8 9 0 CCW/CCW 0 9 8 7 6 5 4

ISBN 0-07-286654-3

Editorial editor: *Brent Gordon*
Publisher: *Stewart Mattson*
Executive editor: *Tim Vertovec*
Managing developmental editor: *Gail Korosa*
Media producer: *Elizabeth Mavetz*
Project manager: *Laura Griffin*
Production supervisor: *Gina Hangos*
Coordinator freelance design: *Artemio Ortiz Jr.*
Senior supplement producer: *Rose M. Range*
Senior digital content specialist: *Brian Nacik*
Cover design: *Asylum Studios*
Typeface: *10/12 Times Roman*
Compositor: *GAC Indianapolis*
Printer: *Courier Westford*

**Library of Congress Cataloging-in-Publication Data**

Jones, Sally M.
    Advanced strategies in taxation / Sally M. Jones, Shelley C. Rhoades-Catanach.—4th ed.
      p. cm
    Includes index.
    ISBN 0-07-286654-3 (acid-free paper)
    1. Business enterprises—Taxation—Law and legislation—United States. 2. Tax
planning—United States. I. Rhoades-Catanach, Shelley C. II. Title.
KF6464.J66 2005
343.7304—dc22

                                          2004042606

www.mhhe.com

In loving memory of our fathers,
Tom Morrow and Ira Rhoades

# Brief Contents

# Contents

# About the Authors

**Sally M. Jones** is the KPMG Professor of Accounting at the McIntire School of Commerce, University of Virginia, where she teaches both graduate and undergraduate tax courses. Before joining the Virginia faculty in 1992, Professor Jones spent 14 years on the faculty of the Graduate School of Business, University of Texas at Austin. She received her undergraduate degree from Augusta College, her MPA from the University of Texas, and her PhD from the University of Houston. She is also a CPA. Professor Jones is the author of *Federal Taxes and Management Decisions* and *Principles of Taxation for Business and Investment Planning* (McGraw-Hill/Irwin) and was the first editor of *Advances in Taxation* (JAI Press) and the *Price Waterhouse Case Studies in Taxation.* She has published numerous articles in the *Journal of Taxation, The Tax Adviser,* and the *Journal of the American Taxation Association.* Professor Jones is a frequent speaker at tax conferences and symposia, a past president of the American Taxation Association, and the 2000 recipient of the Ray M. Sommerfeld Outstanding Tax Educator Award.

**Shelley C. Rhoades-Catanach** is an Associate Professor of Accountancy at Villanova University and a CPA. She teaches a variety of tax courses in Villanova's undergraduate, graduate tax, MBA, and Master of Professional Accounting and Consultancy programs. Before joining the Villanova faculty in 1998, she spent four years on the faculty of Washington University in St. Louis and one semester as a visiting faculty member at the Darden Graduate School, University of Virginia. She received her undergraduate degree in accounting from the University of Nebraska at Lincoln and her PhD from the University of Texas at Austin. Professor Rhoades-Catanach has published articles in numerous journals, including the *Journal of the American Taxation Association*, *The Accounting Review*, *Issues in Accounting Education*, the *Journal of Accounting Education*, and *Review of Accounting Studies*. She is a member of the board of trustees of the American Taxation Association.

In 1997, McGraw-Hill/Irwin published *Principles of Taxation for Business and Investment Planning* to provide tax educators with an innovative alternative to traditional textbooks. *Principles* had its origin in the 1989 White Paper entitled *Perspectives on Education: Capabilities for Success in the Accounting Profession* published jointly by the (then) Big Eight public accounting firms. The White Paper expressed disenchantment with the narrow focus of undergraduate accounting curricula and called for scholastic emphasis on a broad set of business skills that are necessary for a lifetime of professional success. The Accounting Education Change Commission (AECC), operating under the aegis of the American Accounting Association, embraced the philosophy reflected in the White Paper. In September 1990, the AECC published its Position Statement No. 1, *Objectives of Education for Accountants*. This statement reiterated that an undergraduate business education should provide a base on which lifelong learning can be built.

In spite of these calls for reform, many undergraduate tax courses are taught in a traditional manner based on a compliance-oriented paradigm. In today's world, this traditional paradigm is an anachronism. Most business students do not need to learn how to generate tax information. Instead, they must learn to assess the reliability of tax information generated by tax specialists and to use the information to make good business decisions. *Principles* reflects this fundamental shift in the focus of tax education, and instructors who have adopted it for their introductory tax course are enthusiastic about its conceptual approach and emphasis on the role of taxes in the decision-making process. However, many business schools offer both an introductory and an advanced tax course in their accounting curricula. Instructors who use *Principles* have been frustrated by the lack of a follow-up text for the second course. Many instructors have expressed a need for a textbook that reflects the pedagogical philosophy of *Principles* in the coverage of advanced tax topics.

In response to market demand, *Advanced Strategies in Taxation* was developed to provide coverage of advanced tax topics. This book is ideal for students who studied *Principles of Taxation for Business and Investment Planning* in their introductory course. The two textbooks provide an integrated two-semester sequence of topics that represent a complete educational package for tax students. Nevertheless, *Advanced Strategies* is written in a self-contained manner. Although its approach is consistent with that of *Principles,* its technical content builds on knowledge that students should have acquired from their introductory tax course regardless of the textbook used.

## ORGANIZATION AND CONTENT

*Advanced Strategies* explores the tax consequences of many sophisticated business, financial, and personal wealth-planning transactions. Each transaction is presented in an economic or legal context, and the nontax motives of the transacting parties are examined before the tax issues are identified. The discussion of tax issues emphasizes the development and implementation of strategies to make transactions as tax efficient as possible to all parties involved. Many of the tax strategies are analyzed in terms of their impact on net cash flows and on the income statements and balance sheets of the transacting parties.

All technical topics specified in the AICPA's Model Curriculum for the second semester (advanced) tax course are included in *Advanced Strategies*. These topics are not organized in the traditional entity-by-entity manner, however, but are organized functionally, according to the type of transactions characteristic of each stage in the evolution of a business from formation through liquidation. This functional organization provides a context to help students appreciate the rationale behind complicated technical provisions. The functional organization should also help students recognize common themes that unite many apparently unrelated rules and regulations and thereby increase their understanding of the basic structure of the tax law.

The learning approach of *Advanced Strategies* is well suited to preparing accounting students for the changes recently made in the CPA exam. The new exam stresses critical thinking, research and communication skills, and greater focus on conceptual knowledge. Success on the new exam will require less memorization and more application. In addition, the exam now includes case-based simulations designed to more closely replicate the real world while testing integrated knowledge across accounting topical areas and assessing research and analytical skills. The strategic planning focus of *Advanced Strategies* fosters development of analytical reasoning and critical thinking skills reflected in the new exam. The text also stresses conceptual knowledge and application versus memorization. The discussion of the tax research process and related resources in Chapter 2 and the end-of-chapter research problems throughout the text assist in developing research skills, a critical success factor for the new exam. Finally, *Advanced Strategies* fosters integration through its comprehensive cases, discussion of nontax business issues affecting tax strategy, and focus on permanent and temporary differences between financial accounting and tax treatment of common business income and expense items.

*Sally M. Jones*
*Shelley C. Rhoades-Catanach*

# Key Features

Advanced Strategies is designed for use in a one-semester (15-week) advanced tax course at either the undergraduate or graduate level. Instructors can choose which of the 17 chapters in the book deserve a full week's coverage, which can be covered in less time, and which might be omitted on the basis of the particular educational needs of their students. The following summaries of the six parts of the text describe the sequencing and content of the chapters.

**Part One** consists of Chapters 1 and 2. Chapter 1 examines fundamental tax planning ideas and reviews the business decision-making process, net present value concepts, and the impact of taxation on the maximization of after-tax value. Four basic maxims of tax planning are explained and illustrated with examples drawn from topics covered in the typical introductory tax course. Chapter 2 describes the six steps in the tax research process and the variety of available tax research resources. It illustrates each step of the research process with hypothetical tax research questions.

**Part Two** considers tax planning opportunities related to the formation of business entities. Chapter 3 explores the tax aspects of the choice of organizational form and the contribution of cash or property by the owners to their new entity. Chapter 4 focuses on compensation strategies, including the use of fringe benefits and deferred compensation arrangements, and the contribution of services in exchange for corporate stock or partnership interests.

**Part Three** considers tax and accounting issues that affect routine business operations. Chapter 5 focuses on the measurement of annual income and analyzes many of the differences in the computation of book income and taxable income. Chapter 6 examines a variety of tax incentives provided by existing law to encourage specific economic activities. The chapter considers the effect of these incentives on investment decisions as well as the potential alternative minimum tax cost for businesses that take advantage of tax incentives. Chapter 7 addresses tax issues unique to passthrough entities, including the measurement and characterization of income at the entity level and the allocation and reporting of that income to the owners. Chapter 8 examines the tax consequences of distributions of cash or property from both taxable corporations and passthrough entities to their owners.

## PART ONE

### Strategic Tax Planning

1 Introduction

2 Tax Research

## PART TWO

### Tax Strategies for New Businesses

3 Organizational Strategies

4 Employee Compensation Strategies

## PART THREE

### Business Operating Strategies

5 Income Measurement and Reporting

6 Business Incentive Provisions

7 Income and Loss Allocations by Passthrough Entities

   Appendix 7–A    Section 704(c) Remedial Allocation Method

8 Distributions to Business Owners

# PART FOUR

## *Strategies for Business Growth and Expansion*

Part Four concerns the tax issues involved in the growth and expansion of business enterprises. Chapter 9 considers the use of multiple entities to provide the structure for business expansion. The chapter includes a broad overview of the topic of consolidated corporate tax returns. Chapter 10 considers the multistate tax implications of geographic expansion, and Chapter 11 concentrates on tax strategies that facilitate business expansion on an international scale.

# PART FIVE

## *Business Capital Transactions*

Part Five examines the tax consequences of capital transactions that change the ownership structure of business enterprises. Chapter 12 explores the tax consequences of sales and redemptions of corporate stock and partnership interests. Chapter 13 discusses both taxable and tax-deferred corporate acquisitions, mergers, and divisions. Chapter 14 addresses the tax issues faced by financially distressed companies and the tax consequences of business liquidations and terminations.

# PART SIX

## *Personal Wealth Planning*

Part Six focuses on the transfer tax system and its impact on preserving family wealth. Chapter 15 covers the basic concepts and computations of the gift, estate, and generation-skipping transfer taxes. This chapter also discusses the policy rationale for the transfer tax system and the current political debate surrounding the prospective repeal of the estate and generation-skipping transfer taxes in 2010. Chapter 16 describes the use of trusts in personal wealth planning and the income tax treatment of trusts, estates, beneficiaries, and decedents. Chapter 17 applies transfer and income tax concepts to develop strategies for the preservation of family wealth and the transfer of family assets, including closely held businesses.

# New Features

This fourth edition of the text includes a number of exciting new features.

## Chapter 2

The tax research appendix included in previous editions has been expanded and moved to Chapter 2. This change acknowledges the increasing importance of research skills in a complex tax and business environment, as well as the significant research emphasis of the new CPA exam.

### Chapter **Two**

## Tax Research

**Learning Objectives**

*After reading this chapter, you will be able to:*

1. Understand and apply the six steps of the tax research process.
2. Identify primary sources of tax law.
3. Utilize secondary sources of tax law to locate primary authorities.

Tax research is the process of determining the most probable tax consequences of a course of action that an individual or organization undertakes. Because of the complexity of state, local, and federal tax laws, most taxpayers are unable to conduct research on their own behalf. Consequently, they engage professionals such as certified public accountants (CPAs) or attorneys to investigate the tax consequences of their business, investment, and financial . . .

## Tax Talk

Each chapter includes brief examples of "Tax Talk." These items highlight current business and accounting illustrations of new tax planning strategies, tax resources, tax legislative proposals, or innovative transactions with interesting tax implications reported in the business press.

**Tax Talk**
A recent tax practitioner article entitled "Sharpening Decision-Making Skills to Improve Tax Advice" recommends four key considerations for tax advisors when making recommendations to clients: (1) look at the big picture; (2) think outside the box; (3) recognize the time value of money; and (4) consider the flexibility of each alternative.*

could impose additional nontax costs on the firm that negatively impact after-tax value. Potential conflicts between tax and nontax considerations complicate the evaluation of decision alternatives. However, recognition of these trade-offs emphasizes the importance of considering taxation as part of the decision-making process rather than as a set of isolated legal requirements important only for filing tax returns.

When before-tax earnings and nontax costs of decision alternatives are equal, taxation plays a central role in defining value. In these circumstances, the optimal choice is the alternative with the lowest tax costs or greatest tax benefits. Throughout this text, the planning opportunities identified often assume equality of before-tax value and focus on strategies to minimize tax costs or maximize tax benefits. The astute planner should remain alert, however, for differences in nontax factors across decision alternatives. **Tax planning** can thus be defined as the structuring of transactions to reduce tax costs or increase tax savings to maximize the NPV of the transaction.

When decision makers ignore taxation in evaluating potential transactions, they are implicitly assuming that tax costs will be incurred uniformly across each alternative. Our discussion of the tax system throughout this text will illustrate many situations in which this assumption is erroneous. The tax consequences of a business transaction depend on the interaction of four variables common to all transactions:

1. *The entity variable:* Which entity undertakes the transaction?
2. *The time period variable:* During which tax year or years do the transaction and its tax consequences occur?
3. *The jurisdiction variable:* In which taxing jurisdiction does the transaction occur?
4. *The character variable:* What is the tax character of the income from the transaction?

**Objective 3**
Define the four basic maxims of tax planning.

Tax planning seeks to exploit differences in tax treatment across transactions, entities, time periods, jurisdictions, and tax character. These variables create related planning opportunities, which are summarized in the following four basic maxims of tax planning:

1. Tax costs decrease (and cash flows increase) when income is generated by an entity subject to a low tax rate.
2. In present value terms, tax costs decrease (and cash flows increase) when a tax liability is deferred until a later taxable year.

## Comprehensive Cases

Comprehensive cases have been added at the conclusion of Parts Two through Six of the text. These comprehensive cases each provide a rich fact scenario allowing for an integrated consideration of topical issues covered within the several chapters in a given part of the text. Some of these cases require research, while others focus on technical or numeric analysis.

*the tax savings from this series of future deductions is immaterial.*

- Mr. Olmer's discount rate is 7 percent, so the discount factor for computing the N of his after-tax cash from the sale of his investment shares in three years is .816.

**Comprehensive Case for Part Two**

On March 1, 2004, Mr. Shaun, Ms. Bolt, and Ms. Ivy formed a new corporation (SBI I by making the following exchanges.

Mr. Shaun contributed business inventory worth $105,000. His tax basis in the inven was $87,300. He also contributed the licensed trade name of his sole proprietor (Shaun's Services), which the corporation will use as its trade name. The three incorp tors agreed that this name represented $50,000 worth of goodwill. Mr. Shaun had no basis in the trade name. In exchange for the inventory and goodwill, Mr. Shaun rece SBI's short-term note for $35,000 and 1,200 shares of common stock. SBI must pay note (plus 7 percent interest) by December 31, 2004.

Ms. Bolt contributed business equipment worth $150,000. The original cost of equipment was $160,000 and accumulated MACRS depreciation was $113,800. The eq ment was subject to a $25,000 liability, which SBI assumed. Ms. Bolt incurred this lia ity for a bona fide business reason, and SBI's assumption was not for any tax avoida purpose. In exchange, Mrs. Bolt received 1,250 shares of common stock.

Ms. Ivy contributed $40,000 cash and a two-year lease on commercial office space. cause of the favorable lease terms, the three incorporators agreed that the lease was w $15,000. However, Ms. Ivy had no tax basis in the lease. In exchange, Ms. Ivy received shares of common stock.

SBI Inc. adopted the accrual method of accounting and a calendar year for tax purpo On March 4, the three shareholders made a valid subchapter S election for their corp tion. Also on March 4, SBI Inc. entered into a three-year employment contract with Ms. und. . .which the corporation agreed to pay her a $40,000 annual salary plus 600 . . .stock. These . . . . Ms. Ivy's . . .

# Chapter Highlights

## Learning Objectives

**Learning Objectives**

*After reading this chapter, you will be able to:*

1. Compare the tax consequences of conducting business in a passthrough entity or in a corporation.

2. Explain the tax advantage of shareholder debt to a closely held corporation.

3. Describe the requirements for a nontaxable exchange of property for corporate stock.

4. Determine the effect of boot and the assumption of liability in a property-for-stock exchange.

5. Determine the basis of property received by a corporation as a contribution to

### BASIC TAX CONSEQUENCES OF ENTITY CHOICE

**Objective 1**
Compare the tax consequences of conducting business in a passthrough entity or in a corporation.

As a rule of thumb, entrepreneurs prefer passthrough entities to corporations because of the difference in income tax consequences. In the next section of the chapter, we will compare these consequences with respect to both business income and business loss.

**Taxation of Business Income**

*Corporate Income*

Business income generated by a corporation is reported on Form 1120, U.S. Corporate Income Tax Return. The income is taxed at the corporate level, and the after-tax earnings

Each chapter begins with **Learning Objectives** that preview the major concepts to be covered. These objectives also appear in marginal notations throughout the chapter, indicating the specific place where each learning objective is addressed.

## Examples and Cases

fortunately, the process cannot be reversed so cheaply. As we will discuss in Chapter 14, the distribution of corporate assets to shareholders in liquidation of the corporation is a taxable event to *both* the corporation and the shareholders. Thus, if the shareholders of a closely held taxable corporation would prefer to operate the business as a passthrough entity, their only viable option is to make a Subchapter S election.

*Trapped in the Corporate Form*

The 20 members in Myroni LLC planned to "go public" by the end of 2005. In anticipation of their IPO, the members incorporated their LLC into Myroni Inc., a Delaware corporation. A year after the incorporation, Myroni's investment bankers gave the shareholders the disappointing news that an IPO is no longer feasible. The shareholders cannot afford to liquidate the corporation and reorganize their business as a partnership or LLC because of the tax cost. If Myroni meets the eligibility requirements, however, the shareholders can make a Subchapter S election so that their corporation will be a nontaxable passthrough entity for federal tax purposes.[5]

### BASIC TAX CONSEQUENCES OF ENTITY CHOICE

**Objective 1**
Compare the tax consequences of conducting business in a passthrough entity or in a corporation.

As a rule of thumb, entrepreneurs prefer passthrough entities to corporations because of the difference in income tax consequences. In the next section of the chapter, we will compare these consequences with respect to both business income and business loss.

**Taxation of Business Income**

*Corporate Income*

Business income generated by a corporation is reported on Form 1120, U.S. Corporate Income Tax Return. The income is taxed at the corporate level, and the after-tax earnings

[5] According to Section 7704, PTPs that were in existence on December 31, 1987 (grandfathered PTPs), can retain their status as passthrough entities under two conditions. First, the PTP must not add a substantial new line of business after December 31, 1997. Second, the PTP must pay an entity-level federal tax equal to 3.5 percent of annual gross business income.
[6] Partnership must capitalize the costs connected with the marketing and placement of partnership interests. These "syndication costs" include brokerage, underwriting, and placement fees as well as costs

The chapters contain numerous examples illustrating the concept or demonstrating the calculation being discussed.

income by leasing property to an entity?

No, for an S corporation if the shareholder materially participates in the business.

participates in the business.

## Key Terms

| Key Terms | | | |
|---|---|---|---|
| attribution rules  68 | inside basis  64 | publicly traded partnership |
| boot  58 | limited liability company | (PTP)  52 |
| capital account  64 | (LLC)  50 | recourse liability  66 |
| carryover basis  62 | limited liability partnership | related parties  68 |
| corporation  50 | (LLP)  50 | S corporation  50 |
| disregarded entity  51 | limited partnership  50 | self-rental rule  71 |
| fair market value | net operating loss | sole proprietorship  50 |
| (FMV)  57 | (NOL)  54 | Subchapter C  55 |
| general partnership  50 | nonrecourse liability  66 | Subchapter K  55 |
| initial public offering | outside basis  64 | Subchapter S  50 |
| (IPO)  51 | partnership  50 | substituted basis  57 |
| | passthrough entity  50 | |

| Questions and Problems for Discussion | |
|---|---|
| | 1. Compare the extent of the owners' personal liability for debt incurred by general partnerships, limited partnerships, LLPs, and LLCs. |
| | 2. What are the nontax and the tax advantages of operating a business as a single-member LLC rather than as a sole proprietorship? |
| | 3. What are the nontax and tax advantages of operating a business as an LLC rather than as a limited partnership? |
| | 4. If a closely held corporation pays no dividends to its shareholders, are the shareholders avoiding the double tax on corporate income? |
| | 5. Why are constructive dividends a more important issue for individual shareholders than for corporate shareholders of closely held corporations? |

Key terms are indicated in boldface in the text. A list of key terms is also listed at the end of the chapter with page references for easy review. Definitions of key terms from all the chapters are compiled in a Glossary for the text.

# End-of-Chapter Material

## Questions and Problems for Discussion

Challenge students to think critically about conceptual and technical issues covered in the chapter. These problems are often open ended and are intended to promote debate.

**Questions and Problems for Discussion**

1. Compare the extent of the owners' personal liability for debt incurred by general partnerships, limited partnerships, LLPs, and LLCs.
2. What are the nontax and the tax advantages of operating a business as a single-member LLC rather than as a sole proprietorship?
3. What are the nontax and tax advantages of operating a business as an LLC rather than as a limited partnership?
4. If a closely held corporation pays no dividends to its shareholders, are the shareholders avoiding the double tax on corporate income?
5. Why are constructive dividends a more important issue for individual shareholders than for corporate shareholders of closely held corporations?
6. Identify three differences between the nonrecognition rules of Section 351 (exchange of property for stock) and Section 721 (exchange of property for partnership interest).

## Application Problems

Give students practice in applying the material covered in the chapter. Most of these problems are quantitative and require calculations to derive a numeric solution to the problem.

**Application Problems**

Use the tax rates printed on the inside front cover of the text to make any tax calculations required in the following problems.

1. Mrs. Rei, who is in the 35 percent marginal tax bracket, is the sole owner of Rei Company, a delivery business. This year, the company generated $140,000 taxable income (before accounting for any payments or distributions to Mrs. Rei). Compute the total tax cost of this income under each of the following assumptions. Ignore any effect of payroll taxes in making your computations.
   a. Rei Company is a sole proprietorship. The company distributed $100,000 cash to Mrs. Rei.
   b. Rei Company is an S corporation that paid a $75,000 salary to Mrs. Rei.
   c. Rei Company is an S corporation that paid a $75,000 salary and distributed $10,000 cash to Mrs. Rei.

## Issue Recognition Problems

Challenge students to identify tax issues suggested by a set of facts and to state those issues as research questions. The technical issues buried in these problems may not be discussed in the chapter. Students must use their conceptual knowledge to analyze the fact situation, spot the tax problem or opportunity, and formulate the question to be resolved. These problems help students take the first step in the tax research process.

**Issue Recognition Problems**

Identify the tax issue or issues suggested by the following situations and state each issue in the form of a question.

1. Mr. and Mrs. Javon are the sole shareholders in Javon Lawn Ornaments. This year, the corporation hired Mr. Javon's sister to redecorate its corporate offices. Her fee for the redecoration was $48,200.
2. Taggert Inc. owns 700 of the 1,000 shares of SunFarms Inc.'s only class of stock. Mr. and Mrs. Storad own the 300 remaining shares. Taggert plans to contribute appreciated property worth $500,000 to SunFarms in exchange for 100 additional shares. Taggert has requested that Mr. and Mrs. Storad contribute $5,000 cash for one additional share as part of the same transaction. If necessary, Taggert will loan the cash to the Storads.
3. Harris Properties has 1,000 shares of outstanding stock. Mrs. Harris owns 400 shares, and each of her three children owns 200 shares. Mrs. Harris owns investment land that sh____ contribute to the family corporation in ex____ for 50 more shares.

## Research Problems

Provide another opportunity for students to develop their research skills. These problems consist of short scenarios suggesting one or more tax questions. To find the answers, students need access to either a traditional or an electronic tax library. **Chapter 2** can aid students in solving these research problems.

**Research Problems**

1. As part of a Section 351 nontaxable exchange, Mr. Robinson contributed the following business assets to WPL Inc.

| | Tax Basis | FMV |
|---|---|---|
| Accounts receivable | $ 8,000 | $ 8,000 |
| Inventory | 26,300 | 30,000 |
| Office equipment | 15,000 | 15,000 |
| Machinery | 50,000 | 60,000 |
| Long-term lease | –0– | 37,000 |
| | $99,300 | $150,000 |

He received 1,200 shares of common stock ($140,000 FMV) and 10 shares of pre____ ($10,000 FMV) in exchange for his ____. The preferred stock has a ____ation ____ ____ rate. Th____

## Tax Planning Cases

Give students a chance to integrate their tax knowledge into a business or personal wealth-planning situation. Most cases involve taxpayers deciding whether to undertake a transaction or choosing between alternative transactions. Students assume the role of tax adviser by analyzing the case and recommending a choice of action to maximize the after-tax value of the transaction.

**Tax Planning Cases**

1. Mrs. Lucci plans to start a new business venture. According to her five-year projection, the venture will operate at a loss for two years before becoming profitable. Here is the projection.

| | Year 0 | Year 1 | Year 2 | Year 3 | Year 4 |
|---|---|---|---|---|---|
| Net income (loss) | $(75,000) | $(25,000) | $30,000 | $90,000 | $160,000 |

Mrs. Lucci plans to operate the venture through year 4 before disposing of it in year 5. She is undecided whether to organize the venture as a single-member LLC or to incorporate, but she wants to choose the entity that will maximize NPV of her cash flows.

Supplements are difficult to write and require enormous amounts of time. We are thankful to the authors who helped us with these valuable resources. The following materials supplement *Advanced Strategies in Taxation*. All are available on the **Instructor CD-ROM** (ISBN 0072866551) that accompanies the text.

## Instructor's Manual

The **Instructor's Manual,** prepared by the authors, includes a course outline, topics for class discussion, and teaching hints for a one-semester advanced tax course. The Instructor's Manual also provides suggested solutions to all end-of-chapter problems and cases.

## Test Bank

The **Test Bank,** prepared by James Fellows of the University of South Florida, contains multiple choice, true-false, and short problems requiring analysis and written answers. It is available as a Word file and in a computerized version on the Instructors CD-ROM.

## Online Learning Center

The **web page** for the book (www.mhhe.com/sjones2005) provides a wealth of information for instructors and students. Relevant **web links and research projects** for each chapter are included. The **online quizzes** were prepared by James Fellows of the University of South Florida, and the **PowerPoint slides** were done by Richard Leaman of the University of Denver.

# Acknowledgments

We want to thank the many friends and colleagues who shared their ideas for this textbook. Special thanks to Gary Bingel of Smart and Associates, Philadelphia, who provided helpful suggestions on current issues in state and local taxation; Professor Lillian Mills, University of Arizona, who reviewed the coverage of financial accounting for income taxes; Professor Rick Boley, University of North Texas, who reviewed the coverage of consolidated tax returns; and Peter Morrow of Golden Gate Capital, San Francisco, who provided valuable insight on the topic of leveraged buyouts.

We also wish to acknowledge the following individuals who reviewed the text. Their expert comments were invaluable, and this edition is significantly improved because of their involvement.

Caroline Craig
*Illinois State University*

Tim Fogarty
*Case Western Reserve University*

Paul Gutterman
*University of Minnesota*

Taylor Klett
*Sam Houston State University*

Richard Malamud
*California State University, Dominguez Hills*

John Malloy
*University of Memphis*

Edmund Outslay
*Michigan State University*

Susan Porter
*University of Massachusetts*

Paul Shoemaker
*University of Nebraska—Lincoln*

Francis Thomas
*Richard Stockton College of New Jersey*

Wayne Wells
*St. Cloud State University*

Marilyn Young
*Belmont University*

We also want to thank the following people who have reviewed previous editions of the book and have helped the book evolve to its present form.

Hughlene Burton
*University of North Carolina at Charlotte*

Sandra R. Callaghan
*Texas Christian University*

William E. Dellinger
*University of Missouri–Columbia*

Jim DeSimpelare
*University of Michigan*

James A. Fellows
*University of South Florida*

Ramon Fernandez
*University of St. Thomas*

Gregory Geisler
*Georgia State University*

Linda Johnson
*Kennesaw State University*

John E. Karayan
*California State Polytechnic University at Pomona*

*(continued)*

Roberta Klein
*Rochester Institute of Technology*

Kathy Krawczyk
*North Carolina State University*

Sharon Lassar
*Florida Atlantic University*

Richard Leaman
*University of Denver*

Edward Mendola
*California University of Pennsylvania*

Richard Newmark
*Old Dominion University*

Tracy J. Noga
*Suffolk University*

Simon R. Pearlman
*California State University, Long Beach*

Susan Porter
*University of Massachusetts*

Sonja Olhoft Rego
*University of Iowa*

Kent N. Schneider
*East Tennessee State University*

Eugene Seago
*Virginia Poly Institute and State University*

Ron Singleton
*Western Washington University*

Marilynn K. Skinner
*Georgia College and State University*

Brian Spilker
*Brigham Young University*

John L. Stancil
*Florida Southern College*

William Terando
*University of Notre Dame*

Ralph B. Tower
*Wake Forest University*

George Violette
*University of Southern Maine*

We are grateful to the entire McGraw-Hill/Irwin team for the professional support of each member during the development and production of this text. Gail Korosa, our developmental editor, was with us every step of the way, and we couldn't have done it without her.

**Sally M. Jones**
*University of Virginia*

**Shelley C. Rhoades-Catanach**
*Villanova University*

# Strategic Tax Planning

# Introduction

## Learning Objectives

*After reading this chapter, you will be able to:*

1. Describe the primary objective of business decisions and the impact of taxation on achieving that goal.

2. Integrate tax costs and tax savings into net present value calculations of after-tax cash flows.

3. Define the four basic maxims of tax planning.

4. Explain the impact that changes in nontax factors have on the achievement of tax planning goals.

5. Describe the legislative and judicial doctrines used by the IRS and the courts to challenge tax planning strategies.

6. Identify tax-related uncertainties that impact long-term planning and decision making.

**Objective 1**
Describe the primary objective of business decisions and the impact of taxation on achieving that goal.

The objective of business and financial decisions is to maximize after-tax value. Shareholders invest in businesses that provide the greatest after-tax return on their investment. Managers are rewarded for business investment and operating decisions that increase after-tax earnings and stock price. In this context, taxes represent a cost of doing business and must be managed in much the same way as production costs, employee salaries, financing costs, and so on. Our discussion throughout this text will focus on taxes as a strategic planning variable and highlight their role in the business decision-making process.

In this chapter, we describe the basic elements of business decision making and the role of taxation in this process. To facilitate calculations of after-tax value, we review time value of money concepts, including the calculation of present value. We state four basic maxims of tax planning and illustrate each maxim with examples drawn from material covered in many introductory tax courses. The chapter concludes with a discussion of the constraints on tax planning imposed by legislation and the courts, and the risks and uncertainties inherent in all long-term strategic planning endeavors. The ideas covered in this chapter continue to guide tax planning strategies discussed throughout the text.

## THE DECISION-MAKING PROCESS

Business and investment activities involve transactions intended to generate a positive return on invested capital. Business managers and investors evaluate potential transactions by first quantifying the cash inflows and outflows associated with each alternative under consideration. In the simplest case, the decision maker must choose whether or not to engage in a transaction with a single cash inflow or outflow. If an alternative involves multiple cash inflows and outflows, the **net cash flow** from the transaction must be determined. Business costs involve cash outflows that initially reduce firm value. Costs that contribute to revenue-producing activities, however, are a necessary part of business operations. If a manager determines that a particular cost transaction is necessary and will ultimately contribute to revenue generation, the manager should attempt to minimize the net cash outflow associated with the transaction.

Additional complexity arises in evaluating transactions with cash inflows and outflows occurring over several time periods. In this case, decision makers must consider the **time value of money:** A dollar received in the future is not as valuable as a dollar received today because the one received today could be invested to generate a positive return. A dollar received today has a present value of one dollar. Cash inflows and outflows in future periods must be discounted using an appropriate **discount rate** to determine their present values. A transaction's **net present value (NPV)** is the sum of the present values of all cash inflows and outflows associated with the transaction.

The next several paragraphs briefly review the calculation of present value. Readers familiar with this material might skip ahead to the discussion of taxation and present value analysis beginning on page 6.

## Present Value of a Single Cash Flow

The mathematical expression for the present value (PV) of a dollar to be received at the end of $n$ periods based on a constant discount rate ($r$) is:

$$\text{PV}(\$1) = \frac{1}{(1 + r)^n}$$

---

*PV Calculation*

At an annual discount rate of 8 percent, the present value of one dollar to be received at the end of 10 years is:

$$\frac{1}{(1.08)^{10}} = \frac{1}{2.1589} = \$0.4632$$

In other words, $0.4632 invested today to earn 8 percent compounded annually will accumulate to $1 at the end of 10 years.[1]

---

*PV of Future Receipt*

Garnett Corporation sells a piece of property for $100,000, taking back a note under which the purchaser, Crane Inc., will pay the entire sales price at the end of five years. Using a 7 percent discount rate, the present value of this future cash receipt is $71,300, calculated as follows.

$$\$100,000 \times \frac{1}{(1.07)^5} = \$100,000 \times 0.713 = \$71,300$$

---

[1] In Excel, the present value of a single cash flow or a series of unequal cash flows can be calculated using the NPV function. For this example, the formula to be entered in Excel is = NPV(.08,0,0,0,0,0,0,0,0,0,1) where the first value is the specified discount rate and the next 10 values are the amounts to be received in years 1 through 10.

Although Garnett and Crane have agreed to a price of $100,000 for the property, the delay in payment decreases the current value of the transfer to Garnett (and decreases Crane's cost, in current value terms) to $71,300, the present value of the future receipt. For tax purposes, however, the stated sales price is used as the amount realized on the sale in calculating any gain or loss to Garnett.[2] Similarly, Crane's initial tax basis in the asset equals its stated cost of $100,000.

## Present Value of an Annuity

An ordinary **annuity** is a stream of constant equal cash flows to be received at the end of each period for a specified number of periods. The mathematical expression for the present value of an annuity of one dollar to be received at the end of each period for $n$ periods based on a discount rate of $r$ is:

$$\text{PV}(\$1 \text{ for } n \text{ periods}) = \frac{1}{r} - \frac{1}{r(1 + r)^n}$$

It is important to note that this formula works only for a series of *equal* cash flows. Unequal cash flows must each be discounted individually using the approach described earlier for calculating the present value of a single amount.

---

*PV of an Annuity*

At an 8 percent annual discount rate, the present value of $1 to be received at the end of each of years 1 through 10 is $6.71, calculated as follows.[3]

$$\frac{1}{(0.08)} - \frac{1}{0.08(1.08)^{10}} = 12.5 - \frac{1}{0.08(2.1589)} = 12.5 - 5.79 = \$6.71$$

---

*PV of Stream of Future Receipts*

In the previous example involving Garnett Corporation, the purchaser of the property, Crane Inc., also pays Garnett annual interest of $10,000 for the entire five-year term of the note. Using a 7 percent discount rate, the present value of $10,000 to be received at the end of each of these five years is $41,000, calculated as follows.

$$\$10,000 \times \left( \frac{1}{0.07} - \frac{1}{0.07(1.07)^5} \right) = \$10,000 \times 4.10 = \$41,000$$

---

The payment of interest compensates Garnett for the lower NPV it receives by waiting five years to collect the sales price of the asset. Although interest payments total $50,000, Crane's cost of these payments is lower in present value terms since the payments are spread over the five-year term of the note.

Appendix A contains a table of discount factors derived using the formula for the present value of a single cash flow, for a variety of combinations of periods and discount rates. Appendix B contains similar factors for calculating the present value of an annuity.

---

[2] This statement assumes that the contract also bears interest at a market rate.

[3] In Excel, the present value of an annuity can be calculated using the PV function. For this example, the formula to be entered in Excel is =PV(.08,10,1,0,0) where the first value is the discount rate, the second value is the number of periods, the third value is the annual payment, the fourth value is any final payment at the end of the annuity, and the fifth value indicates that payments are made at the end of each period.

## Taxation and Present Value Analysis

**Objective 2**
Integrate tax costs and tax savings into net present value calculations of after-tax cash flows.

The tax consequences of a proposed transaction must also be considered in determining NPV. If a transaction increases the firm's overall tax liability, the incremental tax cost is a cash outflow associated with the transaction. If a transaction reduces the firm's overall tax liability, the tax benefit of the reduction is treated as a cash inflow associated with the transaction. Tax costs and benefits occurring in future time periods must be discounted in the same manner as other future cash flows to determine the transaction's NPV.

*Tax Costs and Benefits*

Halcion Company is considering a transaction that would require a cash outflow of $10,000 and produce a cash inflow of $30,000. The cash inflow would be included in Halcion's federal taxable income, increasing its federal income tax liability by $10,200. If the cash outflow is deductible, it will reduce Halcion's federal taxable income and reduce its federal income tax liability by $3,400. The net after-tax cash inflow from this transaction would be determined as follows.

*[handwritten: have to pay this much more in taxes due to increased inflow]*

| | |
|---|---|
| Revenue (cash inflow) | $30,000 |
| Tax cost of revenue (cash outflow) | (10,200) |
| Expenditure (cash outflow) | (10,000) |
| Tax benefit of expenditure (cash inflow) | 3,400 |
| Net after-tax cash inflow | $13,200 |

This example illustrates the tax cost imposed on earnings as well as the tax benefit produced when expenditures are deductible against positive earnings. The tax cost of the revenue reduces Halcion's after-tax cash flow from this item to $19,800 ($30,000 cash inflow − $10,200 tax cost). The tax benefit produced by Halcion's expenditure reduces the after-tax cost of the expenditure to $6,600 ($10,000 cash outflow − $3,400 tax benefit).

The income tax cost or savings associated with a particular transaction depends on the taxpayer's marginal tax rate. The **marginal tax rate** is the rate that applies to the next dollar of taxable income. In analyzing transactions that would either increase or decrease taxable income, the marginal tax rate is the rate at which that increase or decrease would be taxed. If the marginal tax rate is constant for the entire amount of the increase or decrease, the computation of the **tax cost** or the **tax benefit** from the transaction is simply the amount of the cash inflow or outflow multiplied by the marginal tax rate. If the marginal tax rate is not constant for the entire amount of the increase or decrease, however, the computation of tax cost or benefit is more complex.

*Changing MTR*

Quantum Corporation expects to have annual taxable income of $70,000. Under the U.S. corporation income tax system, Quantum will be taxed at 15 percent on its first $50,000 of taxable income and 25 percent on taxable income between $50,000 and $75,000. Taxable income between $75,000 and $100,000 would be taxed at 34 percent. If Quantum is considering a transaction expected to generate additional taxable income of $10,000, the first $5,000 of this increase will be taxed at 25 percent, and the next $5,000 of this increase will be taxed at 34 percent. Thus, the total tax cost of this transaction will be ($5,000 × 25 percent) + ($5,000 × 34 percent) = $2,950. After-tax cash flow from the transaction will be $10,000 − $2,950 = $6,050.

This example stresses the importance of considering the taxpayer's current income level in determining the marginal tax rate or rates applicable to incremental earnings. In most of the examples in this text, we will assume a constant marginal tax rate.

# BASIC MAXIMS OF TAX PLANNING

Maximizing after-tax value differs fundamentally from minimizing taxes. To understand this difference clearly, note that the simplest way to minimize taxes is to earn no income! However, this approach will certainly not enhance the value of the firm. In addition, the restructuring of business transactions and operations necessary to achieve tax minimization could impose additional nontax costs on the firm that negatively impact after-tax value. Potential conflicts between tax and nontax considerations complicate the evaluation of decision alternatives. However, recognition of these trade-offs emphasizes the importance of considering taxation as part of the decision-making process rather than as a set of isolated legal requirements important only for filing tax returns.

**Tax Talk**

A recent tax practitioner article entitled "Sharpening Decision-Making Skills to Improve Tax Advice" recommends four key considerations for tax advisers when making recommendations to clients: (1) look at the big picture; (2) think outside the box; (3) recognize the time value of money; and (4) consider the flexibility of each alternative.[4]

*Tax Consequences Dependon these four variables*

**Objective 3**
Define the four basic maxims of tax planning.

When before-tax earnings and nontax costs of decision alternatives are equal, taxation plays a central role in defining value. In these circumstances, the optimal choice is the alternative with the lowest tax costs or greatest tax benefits. Throughout this text, the planning opportunities identified often assume equality of before-tax value and focus on strategies to minimize tax costs or maximize tax benefits. The astute planner should remain alert, however, for differences in nontax factors across decision alternatives. **Tax planning** can thus be defined as the structuring of transactions to reduce tax costs or increase tax savings to maximize the NPV of the transaction.

When decision makers ignore taxation in evaluating potential transactions, they are implicitly assuming that tax costs will be incurred uniformly across each alternative. Our discussion of the tax system throughout this text will illustrate many situations in which this assumption is erroneous. The tax consequences of a business transaction depend on the interaction of four variables common to all transactions:

1. *The entity variable:* Which entity undertakes the transaction?
2. *The time period variable:* During which tax year or years do the transaction and its tax consequences occur?
3. *The jurisdiction variable:* In which taxing jurisdiction does the transaction occur?
4. *The character variable:* What is the tax character of the income from the transaction?

Tax planning seeks to exploit differences in tax treatment across transactions, entities, time periods, jurisdictions, and tax character. These variables create related planning opportunities, which are summarized in the following four basic maxims of tax planning:

1. Tax costs decrease (and cash flows increase) when income is generated by an entity subject to a low tax rate.
2. In present value terms, tax costs decrease (and cash flows increase) when a tax liability is deferred until a later taxable year.
3. Tax costs decrease (and cash flows increase) when income is generated in a jurisdiction with a low tax rate.
4. Tax costs decrease (and cash flows increase) when income is taxed at a preferential rate because of its character.

---

[4] Rolf Auster, "Sharpening Decision-Making Skills to Improve Tax Advice," *Practical Tax Strategies,* August 2003.

Tax planning strategies used to reduce tax costs and increase after-tax value typically exploit one or more of these maxims. The following examples illustrate each of the variables with its related planning maxim.

## Entity Variable

*Tax costs decrease (and cash flows increase) when income is generated by an entity subject to a low tax rate.*

This text will focus primarily on individuals and corporations as the two types of taxpaying entities involved in business and investment transactions. In Part Six of the text, we will also discuss tax planning related to trusts and estates as taxpaying entities subject to federal income taxes. Given the progressive nature of federal income tax rates, the marginal tax rate applying to each taxpaying entity will depend on that entity's particular circumstances. Thus, rates are likely to vary across entities. Entity variable tax planning takes advantage of such rate differentials to enhance NPV. Such planning opportunities include a shift of income to an entity subject to a lower tax rate or a shift of deductions to an entity subject to a higher tax rate.

*Entity Variable Tax Savings*

Mr. Clemens is the sole shareholder of Climate Corporation. During 2004, Climate earned $400,000 of taxable income and cash flow. If Climate is a C corporation, it will pay federal income tax of $136,000. If Climate is an S corporation, Mr. Clemens will report the corporation's $400,000 of income on his individual tax return. If Mr. Clemens is in the 35 percent tax bracket, his federal income tax liability will increase by $140,000 as a result of the S corporation's earnings.

Assume that Climate distributes its after-tax cash flow to Mr. Clemens each year. If Climate is a C corporation, Mr. Clemens will report dividend income of $264,000 ($400,000 − $136,000 corporate tax), increasing his individual federal income tax liability by $39,600 given a 15 percent tax rate on dividends. His 2004 after-tax cash flow from this investment is $224,400 ($264,000 − $39,600). Income from the C corporation bears federal income tax at a combined rate of 43.9 percent [($136,000 corporate tax + $39,600 shareholder tax)/$400,000 before-tax earnings].

If Climate is an S corporation, its $400,000 distribution to Mr. Clemens is not taxable since he pays tax on the S corporation's earnings. His after-tax cash flow from this investment is $260,000 ($400,000 − $140,000 shareholder tax on earnings), and the total rate of federal income tax on the S corporation's income is 35 percent. Thus, if Climate intends to distribute available cash flow to Mr. Clemens each year, its annual federal income tax savings from operating as an S corporation is $35,600 ($136,000 + $39,600 − $140,000).

260,000 − 224,400

In this example, entity variable tax savings is achieved by varying the organizational form through which the income is earned. In other cases, income may be shifted between existing entities to be earned by and taxed to an entity with a lower tax rate. Of course, the before-tax cash flow from the transaction must also be shifted to produce tax savings. Thus, entity variable tax planning often occurs between related parties (such as family members) or entities under common control. Our discussion of family wealth planning in Part Six of this text considers many entity variable planning opportunities created by the interaction of the wealth transfer and income tax systems.

## Time Period Variable

*In present value terms, tax costs decrease (and cash flows increase) when a tax liability is deferred until a later taxable year.*

Time period variable planning recognizes that the payment of tax liability in the future is less costly in present value terms than current tax liability. Deferral of tax liability can be obtained either by postponing taxation of income items to the future or by accelerating tax deductions into earlier tax years. Such planning is most effective when taxation of the income can be deferred without deferring the related cash flow from the income. Similarly, an acceleration of deductions without altering the timing of the related cash payments will result in greater tax savings. In many cases, a separation of tax cost (benefit) from the related cash inflow (outflow) is difficult. However, various special tax rules, including the installment sale method for reporting gains, the completed contract method of accounting, the limited expensing election under Section 179, and many of the incentive provisions discussed in Chapter 5, achieve this result.

*review*

## *Time Period Variable Tax Savings*

Mystic Inc. sells a piece of land held for investment on an installment basis. The sales contract provides for an initial payment of $20,000 followed by annual installments of $50,000 for the next two years. Mystic may elect to report any gain on the sale using the installment method or may report the entire gain in the year of the sale. Mystic's tax basis in the land (purchased five years ago) is $40,000. Mystic's marginal tax rate is 34 percent; it has no capital loss carryovers at the time of the sale; and it uses a 10 percent discount rate to determine present value.

### Alternative 1

If Mystic does not elect to report the gain on this sale using the installment method, the federal income tax consequences of the sale are computed as:

| | |
|---|---|
| Amount realized | $120,000   20+50+50 |
| Tax basis | 40,000 |
| Gain realized | $ 80,000 ✻ .34 =(27,200) TaxLiab |

Given Mystic's marginal tax rate, recognition of this long-term capital gain will increase Mystic's current federal income tax liability by $27,200.[5]

The NPV of after-tax cash flows from the sale is computed as:

| | Year 0 | Year 1 | Year 2 |
|---|---|---|---|
| Cash receipt | $20,000 | $50,000 | $50,000 |
| Tax liability | (27,200) | –0– | –0– |
| Net cash flow | $ (7,200) | $50,000 | $50,000 |
| Discount factor | 1.0 | 0.909 | 0.826 |
| Net present value | $ (7,200) | $45,450 | $41,300 |
| Total NPV | $79,550 | | |

### Alternative 2

Mystic could elect to recognize the gain on this sale using the installment sale method.[6] Under this method, Mystic's gross profit percentage on the sale is 0.6667 = $80,000/$120,000. Using this gross profit percentage, Mystic would recognize and pay federal income tax on the following gain amounts each year.

---

[5] Since Mystic is a corporation, its capital gains are taxed at the same rate applicable to ordinary income.
[6] Section 453.

| | Year 0 | Year 1 | Year 2 |
|---|---|---|---|
| Cash receipt | $20,000 | $50,000 | $50,000 |
| Gain recognized (66.67%) | 13,334 | 33,333 | 33,333 |
| Tax liability (34%) | 4,534 | 11,333 | 11,333 |

Under this alternative, the NPV of after-tax cash flows from the sale is:

| | Year 0 | Year 1 | Year 2 |
|---|---|---|---|
| Cash receipt | $20,000 | $50,000 | $50,000 |
| Tax liability | (4,534) | (11,333) | (11,333) |
| Net cash flow | $15,466 | $38,667 | $38,667 |
| Discount factor | 1.0 | 0.909 | 0.826 |
| Net present value | $15,466 | $35,148 | $31,939 |
| Total NPV | $82,553 | | |

*Preferential maximizes NPV*

With the election of the installment sale method, NPV increases by $3,003. As a result, Mystic defers federal income tax liability into future periods with no effect on the cash receipts from the sale. The use of the installment method in this situation represents an effective use of time period variable tax planning.

In the example just completed, note that cash flows associated with the year of the sale are assumed to be immediately available and thus are not discounted, but cash flows associated with subsequent years are discounted back to year 0. The examples throughout this text will assume that year 0 is the present (and therefore requires no discounting), but year 1 cash flows must be discounted for one period, and so forth.

The assumption that current year cash flows are not discounted is clearly a simplification and may not be descriptive of the actual flow of cash. In some cases, it may be more appropriate to treat the initial return on an investment as occurring in year 1 rather than in year 0. More generally, any separation of cash flows into discrete periods ignores value differences between cash flows occurring at the beginning of the period and those occurring in the middle or at the end. By focusing on annual cash flows and annual discount rates, we do not mean to suggest that deferral of tax costs within a given year has no value. For example, taxpayers making quarterly estimated tax payments often seek ways to defer such payments to later quarters. To the extent dollars not deposited in earlier quarters can be invested to earn a positive short-run return prior to payment, intrayear deferral has value. The examples in this text assume annual discounting purely for simplicity. More detailed models of present value might wish to consider biannual, quarterly, or monthly discounting to achieve a more accurate calculation of after-tax return.

## Jurisdiction Variable

*Tax costs decrease (and cash flows increase) when income is generated in a jurisdiction with a low tax rate.*

As discussed in Chapter 11, all U.S. citizens and residents, including all corporations incorporated in the United States, are subject to federal income tax on their worldwide income. In addition, various state and local governments may also claim jurisdiction to tax such income. If a U.S. taxpayer earns income from operations or investments in a foreign country, the taxing authority of that country may also levy a tax. When making business investment and operating decisions, the incremental tax burden imposed by these additional jurisdictions may influence where such investment occurs. As discussed in Chapter 10, state and local jurisdictions offer a variety of incentives to attract new investment to their areas.

*Jurisdiction Variable Planning*

Largo Corporation is planning to build a new manufacturing facility and must decide whether to locate the facility in Delaware or Pennsylvania. Delaware assesses no corporate income tax, but Pennsylvania assesses tax at a 5 percent rate. The facility is expected to commence operations in the year following construction and be productive for at least 10 years. Largo projects $2,400,000 of annual federal taxable income before deduction for state income taxes. Annual state and federal tax liabilities and the cash flow in each alternative location are determined as follows:

|  | Delaware | Pennsylvania |
|---|---|---|
| Taxable income before state taxes | $2,400,000 | $2,400,000 |
| State income tax | –0– | (120,000) |
| Federal taxable income | $2,400,000 | $2,280,000 |
| Federal income tax | (816,000) | (775,200) |
| Annual after-tax cash flow* | $1,584,000 | 1,504,800 |
| NPV over 10 years at 10% (Annuity factor = 6.145, Appendix B) | $9,733,680 | $9,246,996 |

*For simplicity, we ignore differences between annual taxable income and cash flow from operations in this example.

If the new facility costs $8 million to build, its after-tax rate of return on investment in each alternative location is determined as follows.

|  | Delaware | Pennsylvania |
|---|---|---|
| After-tax rate of return | 21.67%† | 15.59%‡ |

†21.67 percent = ($9,733,680 − $8,000,000)/$8,000,000.
‡15.59 percent = ($9,246,996 − $8,000,000)/$8,000,000.

Given the higher rate of return, Largo should build the facility in Delaware. This example illustrates the importance of considering the tax jurisdiction in making decisions regarding the location and scope of business operations.

## Character Variable

*Tax costs decrease (and cash flows increase) when income is taxed at a preferential rate because of its character.*

Most business income is characterized as ordinary income and taxed at the tax rates applicable to the taxpayer earning the income. Several special tax characters may provide for taxation at a lower rate, however. For example, your introductory tax course likely explored the special tax rates available to individual taxpayers earning long-term capital gains and dividend income. You may also recall that municipal bond interest income is tax exempt or equivalently taxed at a preferential rate of zero.

| | |
|---|---|
| *Character Variable Tax Savings* | ALF Inc. is considering investing $100,000 in City of Nashville tax-exempt bonds yielding 4.7 percent interest. Alternatively, ALF could invest in Togota Corporation taxable bonds paying 7 percent interest. If ALF's marginal tax rate is 35 percent, the after-tax return from the taxable bonds is 4.55 percent, computed as 7 percent × (1 − .35 percent). Thus, even though the taxable investment has a much higher before-tax return, ALF would prefer the investment generating tax-exempt interest income over the investment generating taxable interest income.<br><br>However, if ALF's marginal tax rate were 25 percent instead of 35 percent, its investment preferences would be different. In this case, the after-tax return on the taxable bonds would be 5.25 percent, computed as 7 percent × (1 − 25 percent). The lower tax cost no longer absorbs the incremental pretax return on the taxable bond investment. |

The preceding example illustrates an important consideration in applying the fourth maxim for tax planning. When income is taxed at a preferential rate, the before-tax return earned may be lower than the return earned on income subject to a higher tax rate. To understand why this is so, consider the decision process of a municipality issuing tax-exempt bonds. The municipality recognizes that the interest it pays receives preferential tax treatment. Thus, it can offer a lower rate than is paid on comparable taxable bonds and still attract investors. The reduction in pretax return inherent in tax-favored investments is often referred to as an **implicit tax.** Implicit taxes arise in many settings in which preferential tax treatment is granted to certain activities but not to others. For example, the tax law encourages the acquisition of business property by allowing accelerated depreciation of asset costs over recovery lives much shorter than the assets' economic lives. This tax benefit decreases the after-tax cost of purchasing assets relative to leasing comparable property. As a result, the cost of leasing may decline to induce businesses to continue to rent rather than buy assets.

# OTHER FACTORS AFFECTING TAX PLANNING

**Objective 4**
Explain the impact that changes in nontax factors have on the achievement of tax planning goals.

The examples presented in the preceding section illustrate effective tax planning through the use of the basic maxims. However, the next two examples present variations in which results conflicting with the basic maxims could maximize after-tax value. Why do these conflicting results occur? In many cases, tax factors other than the current marginal tax rate (such as tax carryforwards and credits) or nontax factors could differ across the transaction alternatives in ways that require a trade-off of tax costs for other cost savings. Such trade-offs must be considered in analyzing the impact of taxation on each alternative. The following examples serve to emphasize an important point: The basic maxims are most effective when nontax factors can be held constant. If nontax costs and benefits change as the tax treatment of alternative transactions changes, a complete analysis of tax and nontax cash flows is required to determine the value-maximizing decision.

| | |
|---|---|
| *Impact of Other Tax Factors* | Refer to the time period variable example involving Mystic Inc. Although it might seem that the installment sale method would always be desirable, let's consider a change in the facts to illustrate one situation in which Mystic might not wish to make that election. Assume that Mystic has a capital loss carryforward of $50,000 that will expire at the end of year 0. With this additional fact, we must reanalyze each alternative to determine the best choice. |

## Alternative 1

The capital loss carryforward will offset a portion of the $80,000 gain from the sale, reducing the taxable gain to $30,000 with a related tax cost of $10,200. Computation of the NPV of after-tax cash flows from the sale, without the installment sale election, follows.

|  | Year 0 | Year 1 | Year 2 |
|---|---|---|---|
| Cash receipt | $20,000 | $50,000 | $50,000 |
| Tax liability | (10,200) | –0– | –0– |
| Net cash flow | $ 9,800 | $50,000 | $50,000 |
| Discount factor | 1.0 | 0.909 | 0.826 |
| Net present value | $ 9,800 | $45,450 | $41,300 |
| Total NPV | $96,550 | | |

## Alternative 2

Under the installment sale method, Mystic could use the capital loss carryforward to completely offset the year 0 gain of $13,334, reducing the year 0 tax liability from the sale to zero. The remaining capital loss carryforward of $36,666 would expire unused. The following is the computation of the NPV of after-tax cash flows from this alternative.

|  | Year 0 | Year 1 | Year 2 |
|---|---|---|---|
| Cash receipt | $20,000 | $50,000 | $50,000 |
| Tax liability | –0– | (11,333) | (11,333) |
| Net cash flow | $20,000 | $38,667 | $38,667 |
| Discount factor | 1.0 | 0.909 | 0.826 |
| Net present value | $20,000 | $35,148 | $31,939 |
| Total NPV | $87,087 | | |

Under the capital loss carryforward situation, the installment sale election actually reduces the NPV of cash flows from the sale by $9,463. This result might seem to contradict the second tax planning maxim, but it illustrates the trade-off of lowering total tax liability versus deferring a larger liability into the future.

*Impact of Nontax Factors*

Refer to the jurisdiction variable example involving Largo Corporation. Let's alter this scenario to consider differences in the cost of investment in Delaware and Pennsylvania. Suppose that property suitable for the new facility would cost $8.5 million in Delaware in comparison to the $8 million acquisition cost in Pennsylvania. In this case, the after-tax rate of return on investment in Delaware drops to 14.51 percent.[7] Under these revised assumptions, Largo would prefer to construct the new facility in Pennsylvania. The higher investment required in Delaware overcomes the tax cost of the Pennsylvania corporate income tax.

In this example, tax is not the only variable that differs across the two jurisdictions. The difference in nontax factors must be incorporated into the overall NPV analysis to determine the value-maximizing decision.

[7] 14.51 percent = ($9,733,680 − $8,500,000)/$8,500,000.

Although the majority of our focus in this text will be on the federal income tax system, other taxes (such as foreign, state, and local income taxes; sales and use taxes; property taxes; and payroll taxes) might also affect transactions differentially and impose substantial costs that must be incorporated into calculations of after-tax value. Chapter 10 of this text discusses state and local income, sales, use, and property taxes. Chapter 11 addresses foreign taxes, including income and value-added taxes, assessed on multinational taxpayers.

A variety of additional constraints also limit tax planning, including legislative restrictions, judicial doctrines, and economic factors such as risk and uncertainty. In this concluding section of Chapter 1, we briefly discuss each of these constraints and their impact on effective tax planning.

## Legislative Restrictions

**Objective 5**
Describe the legislative and judicial doctrines used by the IRS and the courts to challenge tax planning strategies.

An important presumption underlying business and investment transactions is that parties to the transaction will act in their own self-interests. This **arm's-length transaction** assumption is fundamental to a market economy and ensures that the economic results of transactions negotiated between independent, self-interested parties will be respected by the IRS. When **related-party transactions** take place, however, several legislative restrictions exist to prevent the achievement of favorable tax results that are not consistent with arm's-length behavior.

Section 482 of the Internal Revenue Code gives the IRS broad power to reallocate income, deductions, and credits between related parties to "clearly reflect income." Section 482 is often invoked in situations resulting in a beneficial income shift between related parties. In particular, the IRS has used its authority under Section 482 to challenge transfer pricing arrangements between U.S. corporations and their multinational affiliates that result in a shift of income to low-tax foreign jurisdictions. We will discuss the transfer pricing implications of Section 482 in more detail in Chapter 11.

Section 267 specifically disallows a tax deduction for losses on the sale or exchange of property between related parties. This section also prohibits a deduction for unpaid expenses until the year in which the related payee recognizes income. Both provisions are intended to prevent manipulation of transactions to achieve an accelerated reduction in taxable income before the realization of a true economic decline in value by the related parties.

**Related-Party Losses**

Stein Inc. sold real estate to its wholly owned subsidiary, Higgins Corporation, for $1.5 million. Stein's tax basis in the property was $2.2 million, resulting in a $700,000 realized loss. Because Stein and Higgins are related parties, Stein may not deduct this loss for federal income tax purposes. Its after-tax cash flow from the transaction is $1.5 million.

Had Stein been allowed a tax deduction, the loss would have reduced tax due on gains recognized by Stein. Assuming a 34 percent marginal tax rate, the deduction would have produced a tax benefit of $238,000, increasing after-tax cash flow from the transaction to $1.738 million.

The loss disallowance occurs in this situation regardless of whether the $1.5 million sales price is the arm's-length market value of the property. Advance consideration of the related-party loss rules might have lead Stein to sell the property to an unrelated third party instead of to Higgins to allow a tax deduction for the realized loss.

## Judicial Restrictions

Three important judicial doctrines grant the IRS broad power to rewrite the tax consequences of transactions to reflect its view of the underlying economic reality. The **business**

**purpose doctrine** originated in 1935 as one means to ensure that tax planning strategies adhere not only to the letter of the law but also to its spirit.[8] Under this doctrine, the IRS will disregard the tax results of transactions held to have no substantial business purpose other than tax avoidance.

| | |
|---|---|
| *Lack of Business Purpose* | Kaufman Corporation paid $25,000 to rent a backhoe and deducted the payment as an ordinary and necessary business expense. Kaufman operates a retail clothing store. It had no real need for a backhoe and, in fact, never used the equipment for any purpose. In auditing Kaufman's tax return, the IRS disallowed a deduction for the rental payment, arguing that the expense lacked any business purpose.<br><br>Why would Kaufman rent a backhoe it did not need? The owner of the equipment was a candidate for mayor in the city where Kaufman is located. Kaufman's management believed that the candidate's proposals would benefit its business. Since political contributions are not tax deductible, management arranged the rental scheme in an attempt to deduct the payment. |

The **substance over form doctrine** is a related weapon allowing the IRS to look through the legal form of a transaction to discover its true economic substance and tax the parties involved in accordance with that substance.[9] In the Kaufman Corporation example, the IRS recognized the substance of the transaction as a political contribution, ignoring its form as a rental payment.

Finally, the **step transaction doctrine** allows the IRS to collapse a series of intermediate transactions into a single transaction to determine the resulting tax consequences. This doctrine is applied when it is clear that the parties involved would not have undertaken the initial transactions without believing that the entire series would take place.[10]

| | |
|---|---|
| *Step Transaction Collapsed* | Ms. Carlos and Mr. Dillon each owned 50 percent of the stock of two corporations, A and B. In recent years, Ms. Carlos and Mr. Dillon had argued frequently over shareholder issues and no longer wished to continue their association. Both agreed that Ms. Carlos should own 100 percent of the stock of A and Mr. Dillon should own 100 percent of the stock of B. A direct exchange of shares between the two owners, however, would produce taxable gains. To avoid this result, they contributed their stockholdings in both corporations to a partnership in exchange for partnership interests. Two weeks later, the partnership liquidated, distributing the stock of A to Ms. Carlos and the stock of B to Mr. Dillon in liquidation of their partnership interests. Section 731 in general provides that a distribution of capital gain property in liquidation of a partner's interest produces no current gain or loss. However, the IRS applied the step transaction doctrine to ignore the contribution and distribution of property to and from the partnership. The transaction was treated as a taxable exchange of stock between Ms. Carlos and Mr. Dillon, producing capital gains.[11] |

The substance over form doctrine would also apply to the preceding example. In substance, the transaction is an exchange of stock by two individuals, even though its legal form included intermediary ownership of the stock by the partnership.

A fourth judicial restriction, of particular relevance to the first tax planning maxim discussed earlier, is the **assignment of income doctrine.** This doctrine requires that income

---

[8] The business purpose doctrine was first introduced in *Gregory v. Helvering*, 293 U.S. 465 (1935).

[9] See *Court Holding Company* (S. Ct., 1945) 324 U.S. 331.

[10] See *Helvering v. Alabama Asphaltic Limestone Co.*, 315 U.S. 179 (1942). These three doctrines are discussed in more detail in Chapter 4 of Sally M. Jones, *Principles of Taxation* (New York: McGraw-Hill/Irwin, 2005).

[11] Example based on Rev. Rul. 57-200, 1957-1 CB 205.

be taxed to the taxpayer who provides the services or owns the capital with respect to which the income is paid. As a result, shifting income to a low-tax entity cannot be accomplished by giving away the income without also transferring ownership of the underlying income-producing asset.

| | |
|---|---|
| *Income Shifting versus Assignment of Income* | Mr. Lucas owns rental property generating $30,000 of annual income. He directs his tenants to pay their rent directly to his daughter, Meredith. Mr. Lucas's marginal tax rate is 38.6 percent, and Meredith's is 27 percent. If Mr. Lucas could successfully shift taxation of the rental income to his daughter, this entity-variable planning strategy would save the family unit $3,480, or $30,000 × (38.6 − 27 percent), of tax per year. However, the assignment of income doctrine will tax the rental income to Mr. Lucas, because he retains ownership of the underlying property. The transfer of cash flow to Meredith will be treated as a gift. |

## Uncertainty

**Objective 6**
Identify tax-related uncertainties that impact long-term planning and decision making.

Projections of future cash inflows and outflows are based on a variety of assumptions that incorporate market data, trend analysis, and the advice of business consultants. Managers recognize that these assumptions could be wrong and that the realized cash flows from a particular transaction might differ from their expectations. When future cash flows are highly uncertain, the risk inherent in the transaction might justify the use of a higher discount rate for computing the present value of such cash flows. Transactions with less risk might be evaluated using a lower discount rate. In this text, we will assume that risk is stable over time so that the appropriate discount rate does not change from period to period.

Several uncertainties specific to tax costs and benefits are important to effective tax planning. First, recall that calculation of the tax cost or benefit of a proposed transaction uses the taxpayer's expected marginal tax rate. For taxpayers whose income level fluctuates annually, the marginal rate could be difficult to project. It could also change in the future due to changes in the tax law. Unanticipated tax law changes can affect more than the tax rate applicable to a transaction. If a tax plan depends on specific provisions of existing law, a change in those provisions could have undesirable effects on future cash flows. However, many provisions of the tax law have been relatively stable, reducing the risk associated with reliance on current law for planning purposes.

At times in this text, we will examine areas in which the tax law is unclear or open to interpretation. Taxpayers whose planning exploits these gray areas in the tax law face the risk that the IRS will challenge their interpretations in an audit. A taxpayer losing such a challenge faces additional tax costs and potential interest and penalty assessments. Taxpayers should always consider the likelihood of an IRS challenge to any aggressive tax plan.

## Conclusion

Effective tax planning seeks to exploit differences in taxation across alternative transactions, based on differences in character, entity, jurisdiction, and time period. The planner must always be aware that differences in tax treatment could impact nontax factors, imposing additional costs or implicit taxes that alter investment preferences. Only through careful analysis of the present value of after-tax cash flows can value-maximizing decisions be ensured.

This discussion of fundamental concepts in tax planning coupled with the foundation of tax knowledge from your introductory tax course should provide you the necessary building blocks for our exploration of advanced topics in business taxation and personal wealth planning. In Part Two of the text, we explore tax issues related to the formation of new business entities, including the choice of organizational form and the methods for compensating business owners and employees for their efforts.

**Key Terms**

annuity  *5*

arm's-length
  transaction  *14*

assignment of income
  doctrine  *14*

business purpose
  doctrine  *14–15*

discount rate  *4*

implicit tax  *12*

marginal tax rate  *6*

net cash flow  *4*

net present value
  (NPV)  *4*

related-party
  transaction  *14*

step transaction
  doctrine  *15*

substance over form
  doctrine  *15*

tax benefit  *6*

tax cost  *6*

tax planning  *7*

time value of money  *4*

**Questions and Problems for Discussion**

1. Under what circumstances is the before-tax return on an investment equal to the after-tax return on the investment?

2. Assume that each of the following investments generates the same amount of pretax value. Rank the investments from highest to lowest in terms of their after-tax value. Explain your rankings.

   a. Corporate stock paying an annual dividend. *(5% Dividend taxrate → not deferred)*

   b. Corporate stock paying no dividend but expected to appreciate in value. *Defer gain until*
   *sale stock + then realize ↓ preferential*
   c. Municipal bonds. | *rate at 15%*

3. Under what circumstances might it not be appropriate to assume that the discount rate is stable over time?

4. Mrs. Kanisha is the owner of Kanisha's Sub Shop. In order to lower her taxable income from the shop, Mrs. Kanisha "employs" her three-year-old daughter as a janitor at a salary of $200 per week. *substance over form doctrine*

   a. Does Mrs. Kanisha's employment of her daughter reflect economic reality? *no*

   b. Should Mrs. Kanisha be allowed to deduct the salary paid to her daughter? What tax doctrine(s) might the IRS apply to disallow such a deduction?

   c. Do your conclusions change if Mrs. Kanisha's daughter is 15 and works 20 hours per week in the shop? *yes if that is the arm's length rate*

5. *offset gains 2yrs back or 20 infront.* If a corporation expects to have a tax net operating loss in the current year, what tax benefit, if any, could it derive from additional deductible expenditures?

6. *TVmoney — accelerating deductions* Section 179 allows qualifying taxpayers to take an immediate deduction for up to $100,000 of acquisitions of personal property used in a trade or business. Congress believed that this legislation would provide small businesses an incentive to invest in new business assets. On which tax planning maxim was this belief founded?

7. Consider two investment alternatives with the following projected cash flows.

|  | Year 0 | Year 1 | Year 2 |
|---|---|---|---|
| Investment 1 | $10,000 | $10,000 | $10,000 |
| Investment 2 | –0– | 10,000 | 25,000 |

   Can we assume that Investment 2 is preferable because its total cash flow over the three-year period is higher? What additional information is needed to make an informed choice between these investments?

8. The newly hired assistant controller of Dominion Services Inc. has just completed a capital budgeting analysis of proposed asset acquisitions for the company's long-term planning committee. He has asked you to review his analysis and incorporate any relevant tax considerations. You note that, in computing the return on investment for each

potential acquisition, the assistant controller (1) has used depreciation methods prescribed by Generally Accepted Accounting Principles and (2) has not considered the manner in which these purchases will be financed. Identify and discuss three ways in which existing federal income tax laws will influence the realized rate of return for asset acquisitions. Provide feedback to the assistant controller regarding how he should revise his analysis.

9. Explain how a shift of deductions can accomplish tax savings through entity-variable planning. Should deductions be shifted from a low-tax entity to a high-tax entity or vice versa? *Deductions shifted to higher marginal tax rate entity*

## Application Problems

1. Cantor Corporation is considering an investment that would generate a current tax deduction of $25,000. If Cantor's expected taxable income before this deduction is $110,000, calculate the potential tax benefit attributable to the proposed investment.

*HB,000*
*(10,000 x .39)+ 22, 250*
*=*
*Before Deduction Taxliab = 26,150*

2. Delhi Inc. plans to lease new technology for use in its manufacturing process. The lease calls for annual rental payments of $40,000 over the next five years (years 0 through 4). Delhi projects that the new technology will increase gross profit by $100,000 per year in the first two years of use (years 0 and 1) and $50,000 per year in the next three years of use (years 2 through 4). Delhi's marginal tax rate is 34 percent.

*w/ Deduction = 85,000 Taxable Income*
*13750+ (0,000 x .34) =17,150*
*Tax Savings of 9,000*

   a. Assuming that the rental payments are deductible, calculate Delhi's annual net cash flow associated with the leasing arrangement for the next five years.

   b. Using a 7 percent discount rate, calculate the firm's expected NPV of the rental agreement.

3. Refer to application problem 2. Assume that the increase in gross profit from use of the new technology is expected to be $80,000 annually.

   a. Calculate Delhi's annual cash flow associated with the leasing arrangement for the next five years.

   b. In calculating the NPV of the rental agreement under these assumptions, can you use the present value of an annuity approach? Why or why not? Calculate the expected NPV of the rental agreement using a 7 percent discount rate.

4. Mallory Corporation is a small consulting firm that uses the cash basis of accounting for tax purposes. Mallory is negotiating with a new client on the timing of payment for a lengthy project estimated to cost $50,000. Mallory is considering requesting payment of one-half of its fee now and one-half in one year when the project has been completed versus receiving the entire fee next year.

   a. Using a 10 percent discount rate, compute Mallory's after-tax cash flow from each alternative assuming a 34 percent marginal tax rate for both years.

   b. If Mallory qualified to use the completed-contract method of accounting (so that all income from the project would be taxed when completed), how would your answers to part (a) change?

   c. How would your answers to parts (a) and (b) change if Mallory's marginal tax rate is only 15 percent next year?

5. Ms. Consuelo has $10,000 to invest. She is considering an investment in (1) City of Los Angeles municipal bonds paying 6 percent annual interest, (2) publicly traded corporate bonds paying 9 percent annual interest, or (3) corporate stock expected to increase in value at a rate of 7.5 percent annually. She expects to hold her investment for three years (years 0 through 2) and uses a 6 percent discount rate to calculate present value. Her best guess is that her marginal tax rate on ordinary income for these years will be 28 percent.

a. For Ms. Consuelo's benefit, briefly define the concept of an implicit tax.
b. Based on Ms. Consuelo's guess as to her marginal tax rate, explain to her which investment option is superior. Show supporting calculations.
c. Explain the implications to Ms. Consuelo if her guess is wrong and she ends up in a 35 percent marginal tax bracket.

6. Mrs. Carmen plans to invest $100,000 in corporate stock. She anticipates that the stock will pay annual dividends of $2,000 and that the stock will be worth $140,000 in five years when she plans to sell it. If Mrs. Carmen's tax rate on ordinary income is 28 percent and she uses a 7 percent discount rate, calculate the NPV of after-tax cash flows associated with this investment.

7. Mr. Noel is a self-employed consultant and is preparing bills to clients totaling $10,000 for work performed during October 2004. Prior to these collections, Mr. Noel projected that his taxable income for 2004 would be approximately $140,000. If Mr. Noel collects these billed amounts prior to year-end, how much additional after-tax cash flow will he realize? Assume that he is single and has no dependents. For purposes of this question, you may ignore self-employment taxes.

*(handwritten:)*
1¼00,000 a₍₎
6,750 * .28    Tax liab.
3,250 * .33 = 2,972
inflow  . Aflow
10,000 − 2,972 = 7,038 after tax

8. Consider three investment alternatives with the following projected cash flows:

|  | Year 0 | Year 1 | Year 2 |
|---|---|---|---|
| Investment 1 | $10,000 | $10,000 | $10,000 |
| Investment 2 | –0– | 10,000 | 25,000 |
| Investment 3 | –0– | –0– | 38,000 |

a. Using a 10 percent discount rate and assuming that these cash flows are all taxed as ordinary income at a 30 percent rate, calculate the NPV of after-tax cash flow for each investment alternative.
b. Which investment produces the highest after-tax return?

9. Minelli Corporation is selling an investment asset on an installment basis (year 0). The stated sales price is $300,000, with $100,000 payable at the time of the sale, $100,000 payable one year following the sale, and $100,000 payable two years following the sale. The contract bears interest at a rate of 8 percent on the outstanding balance. Thus, in the year following the sale, Minelli will receive interest income of $16,000; in the final year of the contract, Minelli will receive interest income of $8,000. The firm's tax basis in the property is $165,000, and its marginal tax rate is 35 percent. Minelli uses a 10 percent discount rate to calculate net present value.
a. Assuming that Minelli does not qualify to use the installment method of accounting, calculate its gain realized and recognized on the sale and the NPV of after-tax cash flows from the contract.
b. How would your answers to part (a) change if Minelli qualifies to use the installment method of accounting? Do you recommend that Minelli make the installment method election?

*(handwritten:)*
a)
             1          2
Salary    100,000    110,000
Fed. Tax  (22,627)   (25,427)
State Tax  (5000)    (5,500)
Non Tax Benefits 5000  3000
Aftertax   77,373    82,073 ✓

b)
Aftertax  82,373   82,073 ✓

10. Mr. Linus, a single individual, is considering two job offers. The first offer includes a salary of $100,000 and nontaxable employee benefits worth $5,000. The second offer includes a salary of $110,000 and nontaxable employee benefits worth $3,000.
a. If both offers are for employment in a state with a 5 percent individual income tax, calculate Mr. Linus's after-tax earnings from each offer. (Ignore payroll taxes for purposes of this problem.) Which offer would you recommend that he accept?

      *b.* How would your answer to part (*a*) change if the first offer is in a state with no individual income tax?

11. Ms. Selma is starting a new business. She wishes to operate in corporate form to preserve limited liability but is considering whether to elect S corporation status. She projects that the business will generate the following taxable income (loss) amounts (and related cash flows) during the first five years of operation:

| Year 0 | Year 1 | Year 2 | Year 3 | Year 4 |
|---|---|---|---|---|
| $(20,000) | $(10,000) | $10,000 | $40,000 | $50,000 |

Ms. Selma is single, in a 30 percent marginal tax bracket, and uses a 10 percent discount rate to calculate present value.

    *a.* Calculate the NPV of after-tax cash flows from the business if Ms. Selma elects S corporation status. You may assume that she materially participates in the business activity and thus can deduct the year 0 and year 1 losses on her individual tax return.

    *b.* Calculate the NPV of after-tax cash flows from the business if Ms. Selma does not elect S corporation status.

    *c.* Would you recommend that Ms. Selma elect S corporation status? What other tax and nontax factors should she consider in making this choice?

12. Mr. and Mrs. Cheung wish to help their 22-year-old daughter April pay her graduate school tuition. They could simply give April $5,000 per year, or they could transfer income-producing property to her from which she would earn sufficient after-tax income to match a $5,000 annual gift.

    *a.* If Mr. and Mrs. Cheung's marginal tax rate is 38.6 percent, how much before-tax income must they earn to fund a $5,000 annual gift to April?

    *b.* If April's marginal tax rate is 15 percent, how much before-tax income must she earn from the property gift to generate $5,000 of after-tax cash flow?

    *c.* Given your analysis in parts (*a*) and (*b*), which alternative would you recommend? What nontax factors should the Cheungs consider in making this decision?

13. As part of a wealth-transfer plan, Mr. and Mrs. Wallace transfer income-producing property to their son and his wife as a gift. Mr. and Mrs. Wallace are in the top marginal income tax bracket (currently 38.6 percent); their son and his wife are in the 27 percent income tax bracket.

    *a.* If the property earns $20,000 of net income during 2003, calculate the family's net tax savings from this income shift.

    *b.* Using an 8 percent discount rate, calculate the present value of tax savings from this income shift over a 10-year period.

## Issue Recognition Problems

Identify the tax issue or issues suggested by the following situations and state each issue in the form of a question.

1. Ms. Lunai is single and expects her 2004 taxable income to be $60,000. On October 1, 2004, she purchased 100 shares of Skyrocket Inc. for $10 per share. On December 15, 2004, the stock traded at $15 per share. Ms. Lunai is considering whether to sell the stock before year-end or hold onto it in anticipation of further appreciation.

2. Mrs. Alana transfers income-producing property to her son Adam as a gift.

3. Morgan Corporation is planning to expand its operations into either State J or State K. Property costs are lower in State J, but skilled labor is in greater supply in State K, which would result in lower projected payroll costs.

4. Mr. Tony owns stock that has declined in value. He is considering selling the stock to recognize the tax loss but is reluctant to do so because he believes the stock price will rebound. He arranges to sell the stock to a friend, who then immediately sells it to Stella, Mr. Tony's wife.

5. Ms. Christina owns rental property earning monthly rent of $2,000. On December 1, 2004, she instructs her tenant to pay the rent due directly to her daughter, Joanna.

6. Mr. Gunter owns stock that is appreciating in value at a rate of approximately 5 percent annually. He has considered selling the stock and investing in real estate that would generate a higher rate of ordinary income. However, he believes that the lower tax rate on capital gains justifies holding onto the stock for at least five more years rather than putting his money into an asset whose returns would be taxed as ordinary income.

7. Modern Corporation pays rental fees of $10,000 per month to one of its shareholders, Mr. Anton. The fees are for rental of computer equipment that Modern rarely actually uses.

8. Quality Corporation manufactures products in Ireland for sale in Europe through a subsidiary corporation, Quality-EU. Because the tax rate in Ireland is very low, Quality sets its transfer prices so that most of the profit on European sales is recognized in Ireland rather than in the countries where the sales occur.

9. Rocinante is a new corporation. It expects to grow its business and earnings substantially over the next 10 years but will likely have tax operating losses for the first 2 to 3 years of operations. In projecting after-tax return on investment in new assets, Rocinante's controller has been using a 34 percent marginal tax rate.

**Tax Planning Cases**

1. Mr. Moshe is planning to invest $100,000 in a small business venture expected to generate a 10 percent before-tax return on investment. Given his other sources of income, Mr. Moshe's marginal tax rate on ordinary income is 35 percent. He is considering incorporating his new business to take advantage of the lower marginal tax rate available to the new corporation. Alternatively, he could operate the business as a sole proprietorship. Under each alternative, respond to the following.

   *a.* Compute the after-tax cash flow from this business the first year.

   *b.* If Mr. Moshe reinvests the after-tax earnings of the business each year and the investment continues to earn a 10 percent before-tax return, compute the accumulated value of the business after five years.

   *c.* If Mr. Moshe liquidates the business in five years, compute his total accumulated after-tax earnings assuming the following:
      i. If the investment is made personally, no additional tax is due on liquidation.
      ii. If the investment is made through the corporation, Mr. Moshe is taxed on the liquidated value in excess of his original investment. Note that this excess value would be considered a long-term capital gain.

   *d.* On the basis of your analysis, would you recommend that Mr. Moshe incorporate his new business or operate as a sole proprietorship? What nontax factors should Mr. Moshe consider in making this choice?

2. Ming Corporation wishes to sell a piece of land currently held for investment with an adjusted basis of $80,000. Esposito Inc. has offered to buy the land, and the two parties have

agreed to a purchase price of $200,000. Esposito has asked Ming whether it would consider financing the purchase over a four-year period, with equal payments of $50,000 per year. Esposito would make these payments at the beginning of each year and would at that time also pay simple interest of 11 percent, computed on the unpaid balance each year. (Thus, at the beginning of year 0 [1], Esposito would pay principal of $50,000 and interest on $150,000 [$100,000]. At the beginning of year 2 [3], Esposito would pay principal of $50,000 and interest on $50,000 [$0].) Alternatively, Esposito could borrow money from a third party to make the purchase and pay Ming the entire purchase price now. Ming uses an 8 percent discount rate to calculate present value and expects its marginal tax rate on ordinary income to be 34 percent throughout the next four years.

*a.* Compute Ming's realized gain on the sale of the land.

*b.* Compute the after-tax present value of the sale for Ming, assuming that it agrees to finance the sale. In this case, Ming would use the installment method for reporting gain on the sale.

*c.* Compute the after-tax present value of the sale for Ming, assuming that it does not agree to finance the sale.

*d.* Do you recommend that Ming finance the sale? What nontax factors should it consider in making this decision?

3. Haverford Inc. is a new business planning to establish its operations in either State A or State B. State A assesses corporate income tax at a rate of 10 percent; State B assesses no corporate income tax. However, State B's property tax rates are 15 percent of tangible property value; State A's property tax rates are 8 percent. Haverford expects to invest $1.3 million in tangible property. It projects annual federal taxable income before deduction for state income and property taxes of $250,000 over the next 10 years. Assume that Haverford's property neither increases nor decreases in value during this period and that the corporation uses a 7 percent discount rate to calculate NPV.

*a.* Calculate Haverford's projected annual state income and property tax liabilities in each alternative location.

*b.* Calculate Haverford's projected annual federal taxable income and tax liability in each alternative location.

*c.* Calculate the NPV of after-tax cash flows in each alternative location over the next 10 years.

*d.* Calculate Haverford's rate of return on investment in each alternative location. In which state would you recommend that Haverford locate its operations?

*e.* How would your answer to part (*d*) change if locating in State A required an initial property investment of $1.5 million rather than the investment of $1.3 million required in State B?

# Tax Research

**Learning Objectives**

*After reading this chapter, you will be able to:*

1. Understand and apply the six steps of the tax research process.

2. Identify primary sources of tax law.

3. Utilize secondary sources of tax law to locate primary authorities.

Tax research is the process of determining the most probable tax consequences of a course of action that an individual or organization undertakes. Because of the complexity of state, local, and federal tax laws, most taxpayers are unable to conduct research on their own behalf. Consequently, they engage professionals such as certified public accountants (CPAs) or attorneys to investigate the tax consequences of their business, investment, and financial transactions. Taxpayers expect to receive fair value in return for the substantial fees they pay their tax advisers. Specifically, they expect their advisers to provide accurate, useful, and complete tax information on a timely basis.

A client might engage a tax adviser to research a transaction (or series of transactions) that has already occurred. In this case, the adviser must identify the consequences of the transaction and its proper reporting on the client's tax return. Because the transaction has been completed, the facts surrounding it are a matter of record and are no longer subject to the client's control. The tax consequences of such a closed-fact transaction cannot be changed even if they are not to the client's liking. Thus, the adviser is limited to providing a tax compliance service to the client.

Alternatively, a client may engage a tax adviser to research a transaction that the client proposes to undertake at some future date. In this case, the adviser not only can determine the tax consequences of the prospective transaction but also can suggest ways to modify the transaction to result in a more favorable outcome. The facts surrounding a prospective transaction have yet to be established and, therefore, are subject to the client's control. In such an open-fact transaction, the adviser can help the client create facts that will influence the tax consequences. Clearly, this tax planning service can be extremely valuable to clients who want to maximize the after-tax value of their transactions.

For working tax professionals, tax research is often critical to determining the tax consequences of client transactions. The details of the tax law are so numerous and complex that tax professionals cannot possibly memorize the answers to all tax questions. Thus, the ability to find answers via tax research is a skill developed through training and experience. Men and women who enter the tax profession have completed many hours of formal study as part of their undergraduate and graduate education. During their careers, they will devote many more hours to maintaining the currency of their technical tax knowledge. Tax professionals also learn by doing. As with any skill, proficiency comes with practice, and tax professionals become more proficient with every research project they undertake.

Tax students gain a broad understanding of fundamental concepts in taxation from textbooks but cannot possibly address all tax questions using the material covered in these references. An understanding of the tax research process facilitates the student's quest for additional tax knowledge and provides a deeper familiarity with the sources of tax law. Most graduate accounting and law programs offer a course on tax research. Several textbooks are devoted entirely to the subject. This chapter provides only a brief discussion of the fundamentals of a complex subject.[1] However, after reading this chapter, students should be ready to try their hand at solving the Research Problems provided at the end of the subsequent chapters. Students who do so will enjoy an intellectual challenge that will increase their understanding of the fascinating subject of taxation.

# THE TAX RESEARCH PROCESS

**Objective 1**
Understand and apply the six steps of the tax research process.

The tax research process can be broken down into six steps. This chapter provides a description of each research step, followed by an example of the application of the step to a research case. Students who are just starting to develop their research skills should focus on and complete each distinct step in sequence. By doing so, you will establish good research "habits." As you become more proficient, you will gradually integrate the steps into a seamless research process. Those students who become accomplished researchers will automatically perform the six steps for every research project they undertake.

The six steps of the tax research process are listed below and presented graphically in Exhibit 2.1.

1. Understand the client's transaction and ascertain the facts.
2. Identify the tax issues, problems, or opportunities suggested by the facts and formulate specific research questions.
3. Locate relevant tax law authority.
4. Analyze relevant authority and answer the research questions.
5. Repeat steps 1 through 4 as many times as necessary.
6. Document your research and communicate your conclusions.

## Step 1: Understand the Client's Transaction and Ascertain the Facts

Before a researcher can analyze the tax consequences of a transaction, she must thoroughly understand the transaction itself. Specifically, the researcher should discuss the details of the transaction with her client to ascertain the client's motivation. What are the client's business or financial objectives in undertaking the transaction? What does the client foresee as the desired outcome? What risks has the client identified? By asking these types of questions, the researcher acquaints herself with the nontax features of the transaction before considering any tax implications.

[1] For students familiar with *Principles of Taxation for Business and Investment Planning,* this chapter reviews the basic steps in the tax research process introduced in Appendix C of *Principles* and expands on the discussion of step 3, identifying relevant authorities. For students not familiar with *Principles,* this chapter provides a thorough introduction to the tax research process.

**EXHIBIT 2.1**
**The Tax Research Process**

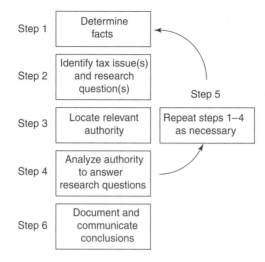

The researcher must discover all the facts concerning the client's transaction. Like a newspaper reporter, the researcher should question the client about the precise "who, when, where, why, and how" of the transaction. The researcher should not assume that the client's initial summary of the transaction is factually accurate and complete. Perhaps the client hasn't determined all the facts that the researcher needs. Or the client may have discounted the significance of certain facts and omitted them from the initial summary. The researcher should encourage the client to be objective in stating the facts. Often a client unwittingly presents the researcher with the client's subjective conclusions about the facts rather than with the facts themselves.

When working with a client to uncover the relevant facts, the researcher must take into account the level of the client's tax knowledge. If the client has some knowledge of the tax law, the researcher can ask questions that presume such knowledge. On the other hand, if the client is unsophisticated in tax matters, the researcher should ask only questions that the client can answer without reference to the tax law.

---

*Applying Step 1*

Sara Colter, a professional photographer, is a new client who has engaged your accounting firm to determine the tax consequences of a proposed transaction: Ms. Colter's sale of a 12-acre tract of land to CCM Inc. She provides the following facts in her initial summary of the transaction.

- Ms. Colter purchased the land from Mr. and Mrs. Bianca in 1994 for $400,000 cash.
- Ms. Colter and CCM Inc. have reached a tentative agreement under which CCM will pay $325,000 cash for the land and all transaction expenses.

As a tax professional, you know that the tax consequences of a transaction may depend on whether the parties involved are "related parties" for federal tax purposes. You also know that the tax consequences of the sale of an asset depend on its classification as capital or non-capital. Because Ms. Colter is unsophisticated in tax matters, you cannot ask her directly if she and CCM Inc. are related parties. Nor can you ask her if the land is a capital asset. Because of her lack of tax knowledge, such questions would be meaningless to your client. Accordingly, you decide to ask Ms. Colter the following series of questions:

- Do you have any personal relationship with Mr. and Mrs. Bianca? Did you know them in any capacity other than as the sellers of the land that you purchased in 1994?

- What was your reason for purchasing the land? Have you made any improvements to the land since 1994? Have you purchased or sold any other real estate during the last 10 years?
- How did you and CCM Inc. reach an agreement that the land is worth only $325,000? Why has the land declined in value since you purchased it?
- Do you own any stock in CCM Inc.? Who are CCM Inc.'s stockholders?

In response to your questions, Ms. Colter provides the following additional facts:

- She has no personal relationship with the Biancas and did not know them prior to her purchase of their land. The purchase was arranged through a professional real estate broker.
- She purchased the land because she thought that its value would increase over time and she could eventually sell it at a profit. She has not made any improvements to the land; it is in exactly the same condition today as the day she purchased it. She has never purchased or sold any other real estate other than her personal residence.
- Two months ago, Ms. Colter obtained two independent appraisals of the value of the land. The appraisals both concluded that the current market value of the land is $325,000. CCM Inc. performed its own appraisal that confirmed this value. The $75,000 decline in value is attributable to local zoning restrictions on the land that were put in place in 1997.
- Ms. Colter does not own any CCM Inc. stock. Twenty-four individual stockholders own the 1,000 outstanding CCM shares. Two of these stockholders are her brother Jack and Jack's son Robert. She is not acquainted with any of the other stockholders.

## Step 2: Identify the Tax Issues, Problems, or Opportunities Suggested by the Facts and Formulate Specific Research Questions

After a researcher is satisfied that she understands her client's transaction and knows all the relevant facts, she can proceed to the second step in the research process. In this step, the researcher identifies the tax issue or issues suggested by the transaction. The ability to recognize tax issues is the product of technical education and professional experience. Consequently, this step is usually the most difficult for students learning tax research skills.

The identification of issues leads to the formulation of tax research questions. The tax researcher should be as precise as possible in formulating questions. A precise question is narrowly stated and provides clear parameters for the remaining steps in the research process. An imprecise question which is vague or overly broad in scope may provide insufficient parameters and result in wasted time and effort.

If the tax issues suggested by a transaction lead to multiple research questions, the researcher must determine the order in which the questions should be answered. In our complex tax system, the answer to one question often depends on the answer to one or more preliminary questions. Tax researchers who understand the hierarchy of their research questions can address each question in the right order and conduct their research with maximum efficiency.

*Applying Step 2*

After studying the facts, you conclude that Ms. Colter's proposed transaction involves one basic tax issue: Will the sale of the land to CCM Inc. result in a loss that she can deduct on her individual income tax return? This issue suggests four research questions, which you decide to address in the following order.

1. Will Ms. Colter realize a loss on the sale of her land to CCM Inc?
2. Can she recognize her realized loss?
3. What is the character of any recognized loss?
4. Given the character of the loss, to what extent can Ms. Colter deduct the loss in the computation of taxable income for the year of sale?

Students should note that the research problems provided at the end of the chapters do not require you to perform the first two steps in the tax research process. These problems are deliberately written to contain all the facts necessary to solve the problem. Moreover, the problems provide the specific research question or questions to be answered. Such is the nature (and weakness) of textbook research problems! But in the real world of tax practice, the first two tasks are not performed by anyone but the researcher herself. If the researcher fails to ascertain the key facts, identify the important issues, and ask the right questions, all her subsequent efforts are futile.

## Step 3: Locate Relevant Tax Law Authority

As the third step in the research project, the researcher heads for a tax library. Her mission is to locate authority providing answers to her research questions. Traditional libraries consist of shelves filled with books, loose-leaf binders, magazines, and other published materials containing the technical minutiae of the tax law. Today, traditional libraries are disappearing as professional tax advisers gain access to the electronic libraries available on CD-ROM or the Internet. One obvious advantage of electronic libraries is the speed at which researchers can access sources of authority and move among the sources. A second advantage is the ease with which electronic databases can be updated to include current developments. A third advantage is that an electronic library is portable. A tax researcher with a laptop computer can access her library at any time and from any location.

Whether working in a traditional or electronic library, a tax researcher must be knowledgeable about the content and organization of the reference materials in that library. The researcher must know how to locate references pertaining to the problem at hand and must be able to distinguish between the two main categories of reference materials: primary authorities and secondary authorities.

### *Primary Authorities*

**Objective 2**
Identify primary sources of tax law.

All sources of tax information can be categorized as either *primary authority* or *secondary authority*. This distinction is important for several reasons. First, only **primary authorities** can be relied on in the final determination of tax issues. In particular, only primary authorities can be cited in court proceedings when arguing the appropriate application of tax law to a particular transaction. Thus, any research conclusions should be supported by available primary authorities. Relevant primary authorities are items written by the government and arise from three sources: statutory authority, administrative authority, and judicial authority.

The original **statutory authority** for tax law is codified in the **Internal Revenue Code** of 1986. Each numerically ordered section of the Code contains an operational, definitional, or procedural rule relating to one of the federal taxes. Each section of the Code is further divided into subsections, paragraphs, subparagraphs, and so on, to provide detailed referencing to the specific legal wording to be cited. For example, Section 461(h)(3)(A) refers to subparagraph A, paragraph 3, subsection h of Section 461. Many Code sections contain precise, legalistic language written in a detail-oriented manner whose meaning challenges even seasoned tax professionals. Other Code sections are broad and brief in nature, delegating the authority to write detailed rules and procedures to the administrative function of the U.S. Department of the Treasury.

The Department of the Treasury provides a variety of **administrative authority** through its interpretation of the Internal Revenue Code. Sources of administrative authority include treasury regulations, revenue rulings, and revenue procedures. **Treasury regulations** are numbered in sequence to match the Code section to which they relate, with the initial number in the sequence indicating the type of tax in question. Income tax regulations begin with the number 1, followed by a period and the related Code section. Thus, Reg. 1.446-1 refers to the first regulation under Section 446. Treasury regulations can be proposed, temporary, or final in nature. *Temporary* regulations are typically issued in cases in which immediate guidance is needed under new statutes; they are often modified before becoming final. *Proposed* regulations are issued for comment and are not considered authoritative until reissued as *final* regulations. Both temporary and final regulations are effective when issued and should be considered as primary authority whose importance is exceeded only by the Code itself.

The Internal Revenue Service (IRS), as an agency within the U.S. Department of the Treasury, also issues a number of authoritative and nonauthoritative types of guidance. For researchers, the most useful of these issuances are revenue rulings and revenue procedures. **Revenue rulings** are issued to address a specific fact pattern and tax issue arising for that set of facts. These rulings are helpful to taxpayers whose facts match those of the ruling in applying tax provisions. Revenue rulings are published in the *Cumulative Bulletin* for the year of issuance and are numbered in the order issued. For example, the citation Rev. Rul. 91-30, 1991-1 CB 61 refers to the 30th revenue ruling issued in 1991, found on page 61 of the first volume of the 1991 *Cumulative Bulletin*.

**Revenue procedures** address taxpayer administrative and procedural issues, such as information requirements for reporting special transactions or how and when to file certain forms. Revenue procedures are also published in the *Cumulative Bulletin* and are cited in the same manner as revenue rulings with Rev. Proc. as the appropriate initial abbreviation.

The IRS also issues two types of administrative guidance that are authoritative only for the specific taxpayer to whom they are issued and cannot be relied on as authority by any other taxpayer. A taxpayer may request a **private letter ruling (PLR)** from the IRS regarding the appropriate tax treatment of a proposed transaction or a completed transaction for which a tax return has not yet been filed. The request must detail all relevant facts surrounding the transaction and requires the payment of a user's fee that could be as high as several thousand dollars. The PLR controls the tax treatment of the transaction for that taxpayer if it is completed in the manner described in the factual statement of the ruling request. A revenue agent or appeals officer can request a **technical advice memorandum (TAM)** during the examination or appeal of a taxpayer's return. The TAM represents the IRS position on a disputed item in the return and applies only to the taxpayer for whom it was issued.

When conflicts between taxpayers and the IRS cannot be resolved administratively, federal courts often hear tax cases. Their decisions represent **judicial authority** that interprets the tax law and often expands it beyond the narrow language of the Code. For researchers, the decisions rendered by these courts are important sources of primary authority in addition to the Code and the administrative pronouncements of the U.S. Department of the Treasury.

In federal tax matters, one of three trial courts has original jurisdiction. A taxpayer may refuse to pay the deficiency determined by the IRS and file a petition with the **U.S. Tax Court** to hear the case. Alternatively, the taxpayer may pay the deficiency, then immediately sue the government for a refund in either the local **U.S. District Court** or the **U.S. Court of Federal Claims** located in Washington, D.C. The losing party at the trial court level (taxpayer or government) may appeal the verdict to one of 13 **U.S. Circuit Courts of Appeals.** The geographic location of the trial court determines which appellate court has jurisdiction. These courts generally do not review findings of fact by a lower court, but they will consider whether the lower court properly applied the relevant law to the facts. After the appellate court has either affirmed or reversed the trial court's decision, the losing party may appeal the case to the **U.S. Supreme Court.** This court may agree to hear the case (*grant certiorari*) or refuse to hear it (*deny certiorari*). When the Supreme Court denies certiorari, the decision of the appellate court is final. During an average term, the Supreme Court hears no more than a dozen federal tax cases, which are selected either because the court believes that the case involves a significant principle of law or because two or more appellate courts have rendered conflicting opinions on the proper resolution of a tax issue.

Exhibit 2.2 provides examples of citations to each type of statutory, administrative, and judicial authority discussed above. Because court cases are published in several different sources, multiple citations are possible for a single case. The exhibit lists alternative cites to sample decisions and the publications in which they appear.

**EXHIBIT 2.2**
**Sample Citations to**
**Primary Authorities**

| Type of Authority | Citation(s) | Explanation |
|---|---|---|
| Internal Revenue Code | Section 1250(d)(1)<br>Sec. 1250(d)(1)<br>§ 1250(d)(1) | Three alternative citations to the first paragraph, subsection (d) of Section 1250. |
| Treasury regulations | Reg. Sec. 1.267-5(b)<br>Reg. 1.267-5(b)<br>Reg. § 1.267-5(b) | Three alternative citations to the fifth subpart of the regulations under Section 267. |
| Revenue rulings | Rev. Rul. 89-257, 1989-1 C.B. 221 | Citation to the 257th revenue ruling issued in 1989, appearing in the 1st volume of the 1989 cumulative bulletin, page 221. |
| Revenue procedures | Rev. Proc. 2002-32, 2002-1 C.B. 959 | Citation to the 32nd revenue procedure issued in 2002, appearing in the 1st volume of the 2002 cumulative bulletin, page 959. |
| U.S. Tax Court memorandum decisions | *Jack D. Carr*, T.C. Memo 1985-19<br>*Jack D. Carr*, PH TCM ¶85019<br>*Jack D. Carr*, 49 TCM 507. | Three alternative citations to a tax court memorandum decision. The first is published by the U.S. government, the second by RIA (formerly Prentice Hall), and the third by CCH. |
| U.S. Tax Court regular decisions | *Teleservice Co. of Wyoming Valley*, 27 T.C. 722 (1957) | Citation to a regular Tax Court decision, published by the U.S. government. |
| U.S. District Court decisions | *Montgomery Engineering Co. v. U.S.*, 64-2 USTC ¶9618 (D.Ct. N.J., 1964)<br>*Montgomery Engineering Co. v. U.S.*, 13 AFTR2d 1747 (D.Ct. N.J., 1964)<br>*Montgomery Engineering Co. v. U.S.*, 230 F. Supp. 838 (D.Ct. N.J., 1964) | Three alternative citations to a 1964 district court case for New Jersey. The first is published by CCH, the second by RIA, and the third by West. |
| U.S. Courts of Appeals | *Lengsfield v. Comm.*, 57-1 USTC ¶9437 (CA-5, 1957)<br>*Lengsfield v. Comm.*, 50 AFTR 1683 (CA-5, 1957)<br>*Lengsfield v. Comm.*, 241 F.2d 508 (CA-5, 1957) | Three alternative citations to a 1957 case before the Fifth Circuit Court of Appeals. The first is published by CCH, the second by RIA, and the third by West. |

*continued on page 30*

| Type of Authority | Citation(s) | Explanation |
|---|---|---|
| U.S. Supreme Court | *U.S. v. The Donruss Co.,* 69-1 USTC ¶9167 (USSC, 1969)<br>*U.S. v. The Donruss Co.,* 23 AFTR2d 69-418 (USSC, 1969)<br>*U.S. v. The Donruss Co.,* 89 S.Ct. 501 (USSC, 1969) | Three alternative citations to a 1969 case before the Supreme Court. The first is published by CCH, the second by RIA, and the third by West. |

**EXHIBIT 2.2**
**Sample Citations to Primary Authorities**
continued

**Objective 3**
Utilize secondary sources of tax law to locate primary authorities.

**Tax Talk**
Several websites provide topical indexes to free tax-related resources, including:
- *Tax Resources on the Web,* at www.taxtopics.net
- *Tax Topics,* at www.taxsites.com
- *Ryan SALT Gateway* at www.ryanco.com/salt.html

### Secondary Authorities

Although primary authorities are required to adequately support tax conclusions and recommendations, they are written in detailed legal and technical language and are often difficult to understand and interpret. **Secondary authorities,** such as textbooks, treatises, professional journals, and commercial tax services, attempt to explain and interpret the tax law. Commercial tax services also organize information about primary authorities in a manner that facilitates tax research. These resources are an excellent *starting point* in the tax research process, but a researcher should always ensure that any conclusions drawn from secondary resources are adequately supported by the underlying primary authority. Our discussion of secondary authorities focuses on the content of the more popular commercial tax services. In the next section, we explore how these services can be used to guide the tax research process.

*Tax Services*    Traditionally, tax services are multivolume publications in loose-leaf form that contain a wealth of tax information. Most services are now also available electronically, either on CD-ROM or over the Internet. Although each service has its own organizational format and special features, the type and scope of information presented are common. In paper format, tax services are organized either topically or by Code section. The popular Code-arranged tax services are *United States Tax Reporter* (published by Research Institute of America [RIA]) and *Standard Federal Tax Reporter* (published by Commerce Clearing House [CCH]). The popular topically arranged tax services are *Federal Tax Coordinator 2d* (published by RIA), *CCH Federal Tax Service* (published by CCH), *Law of Federal Income Taxation* (also called *Mertens,* published by West), and *Tax Management Portfolios* (published by Bureau of National Affairs [BNA]). Electronic format contains each type of tax information in a separate database and provides the ability to search multiple databases, frequently with hyperlinks from items in one database to related items in other databases. The RIA Checkpoint online tax research service includes both the *United States Tax Reporter* and *Federal Tax Coordinator 2d.* The CCH Internet Tax Research Network includes both *Standard Federal Tax Reporter* and *CCH Federal Tax Service.*

Although the format differs, the RIA and CCH Code-arranged services contain similar information. These services reproduce the text of each Code section and related Treasury regulations. Each service also provides some legislative history for each Code section. Following each Code section and its regulations is an editorial explanation written by the publisher. The explanation attempts to clarify application of the Code section. These editorial explanations are often helpful to researchers in locating primary authority, but they do not themselves constitute primary authority and should not be cited. Following the editorial explanation, each service provides a citation listing and brief summary of court cases, revenue rulings, and other primary authorities relevant to the Code section under discussion. These summaries are helpful to the researcher in locating primary authority. Each service also contains a detailed topical index that can be searched for relevant keywords as a way to locate useful material. Finally, each service attempts to highlight current developments and incorporates new information into the text of the service on at least a monthly basis (more frequently in the online versions).

The topically oriented services are organized according to major topic areas with more extensive editorial explanation of the application of tax law to specific topics. These services also provide citations to court cases, revenue rulings, and other primary authority related to the topics under discussion. The organization and content of the major topically oriented services differ considerably; experience working with a particular service increases the researcher's efficiency in finding useful material.

### Strategies for Locating Relevant Authority

The materials used for tax research depend on both the nature of the research question and the experience level of the researcher. A skilled researcher tends to rely on materials she can use most efficiently to find answers to her questions in minimal time. She might bypass a number of the steps suggested here as she finds a research approach that works best for her. The novice researcher tends to examine more materials in a methodical manner to maximize the opportunities to find all relevant information. The strategies suggested here are just that—suggestions!

Suppose that you have completed steps 1 and 2 of the research process as described earlier and are now ready to identify relevant authority. One option is to go directly to the Internal Revenue Code and use its topical index to find the relevant section; this approach is sufficient to answer some research questions. However, what if this approach does not uncover a clear solution? In many cases, more than one Code section might seem to apply, or the Code could be very general, and you might wish to find other authority that seems to match the specific facts at hand and more clearly support the research conclusions. In that case, you can turn to one of the commercial tax services and adopt one or more of the following approaches using (1) the topical index, (2) the table of contents, or (3) a keyword search in an electronic service.

**Using the Topical Index**   Each service provides a detailed topical index that lists hundreds of tax-related terms alphabetically. As with any index, a single term appears in multiple places within the service; thus, it might be necessary to check several referenced locations before finding the relevant use of the term. The researcher should also try several different wordings or related terms to ensure complete coverage of topics related to the issue being researched.

To illustrate this approach, suppose that you are researching an issue related to the deductibility of losses incurred by an individual taxpayer engaged in a horse-breeding activity. You know from your taxation study that such losses should be deductible if the activity is considered a trade or business rather than a hobby. A review of the topical index for the *United States Tax Reporter* reveals the topic "hobby losses and expenses" under the letter *H.* This topic heading lists four references for the general topic and provides eight subtopics, including "horse ranching." Four additional references are listed for this subtopic. You would turn to each of the eight subtopics in your search for additional information.

**Using the Table of Contents**   A researcher might also wish to begin the search for authorities by scanning the table of contents of a tax service to locate an area of discussion that appears relevant. This approach is particularly useful with topically oriented services. This alternative has the additional benefit of helping the novice researcher become familiar with the service's organization.

To illustrate this approach, let's reconsider the example involving horse breeding. The table of contents to the *Federal Tax Coordinator 2d* lists "Chapter M, Deductions: Losses, Bad Debts." Further examination of the table of contents reveals the following subchapter within Chapter M: "M-5800 Activities Not Engaged in for Profit—Hobby Losses." This portion of the service seems a useful starting point in the search for information relevant to the research question.

*Using a Keyword Search*   In an electronic service, the researcher has the option to search the entire database or a specified portion of it for user-defined keywords. This type of search is similar to using a topical index but allows the researcher to combine words and phrases to target the search. Keyword searching can be very efficient, but the researcher must ensure that she does not miss important information because the keywords were defined too narrowly.

Returning to the example, a keyword search could combine the phrase *hobby loss* and the word *horse* to narrow the identification of potential authorities relative to the material found via the use of the topical index or table of contents entries regarding the hobby loss rules. Using the keyword search function in *RIA Checkpoint*, your search *"hobby loss" and horse* identifies 45 documents within the federal income tax database in which the phrase *hobby loss* and the word *horse* appear. You can then examine each of these documents to determine its usefulness in answering the research question.

Once you have located a promising starting point via the topical index, table of contents, or a keyword search, you can examine related material in the service. For example, if you find the search term within an editorial explanation, you should read the related Code section, scan the regulations, and examine any references to court cases or other primary authorities to determine whether that material addresses the tax issue at hand. Cross-references within the material initially examined can also lead you in promising directions for additional exploration. When you have identified primary authorities that appear relevant, you should read those sources carefully.

Returning to our horse breeding example, a review of the documents identified in the RIA Checkpoint keyword search uncovers a reference to a U.S. Tax Court memorandum decision, *Herbert C. Sanderson* T.C. Memo 1964-284. In this case, a doctor and his wife were allowed a deduction for losses incurred in breeding, raising, showing, racing, and selling horses. This case should be examined further as possible authority to support a deduction for horse breeding expenses.

If the first application of the process just described fails to provide an answer to the tax research question, additional iterations are necessary. You might proceed by trying other search terms, defining the search either more broadly or more narrowly, and combining the use of the topical index, the table of contents, and various keywords to discover useful information. You also might consult more than one service.

*Applying Step 3*   To begin your search for authority, you turn to the table of contents of the *Federal Tax Coordinator 2d*. You locate "Chapter I, Sales and Exchanges, Capital Gains and Losses, Cost Recovery Recapture, Depreciation Recapture." Within this chapter, Subchapter I-2500, "Amount of Gain or Loss on Sale or Exchange," refers you to Section 1001 of the Internal Revenue Code. When you examine this section, you determine that subsections (a) and (c) seem relevant.

Section 1001. Determination of amount of and recognition of gain or loss
(a) Computation of gain or loss
The gain from the sale or other disposition of property shall be the excess of the amount realized therefrom over the adjusted basis provided in section 1011 for determining gain, and the loss shall be the excess of the adjusted basis provided in such section for determining loss over the amount realized

(c) Recognition of gain or loss
Except as otherwise provided in this subtitle, the entire amount of the gain or loss, determined under this section, on the sale or exchange of property shall be recognized.

Section 1001(c) reminds you that gain or loss realized on a sale or exchange is not always recognized. Further examination of the subchapters of Chapter I in the *Federal Tax Coordinator 2d* reveals I-3500, "Losses Resulting from Sales and Exchanges between Related Taxpayers." This subchapter points you to Section 267, which provides that a taxpayer cannot recognize a loss realized on a sale to a related party.

## Step 4: Analyze Relevant Authority and Answer the Research Questions

Regardless of whether a researcher is reading from a printed page or a computer screen, she must have the skill to interpret and evaluate the authority at hand. In some cases, the authority may provide an unambiguous answer to the researcher's question. In other cases, the answer may be equivocal because the authority is inconclusive or subject to interpretation. Or perhaps different sources of authority provide conflicting answers. In these cases, the researcher must bring her judgment to bear in analyzing the authority and answering the question.

As part of the analytic process, the researcher should decide if the authority requires her to make a factual judgment or an evaluative judgment. In making a factual judgment, the researcher compares the authority to a set of facts. Assuming that the facts are complete and accurate, the researcher can provide a definitive answer to the research question. For example, consider the following research problem.

Mr. Johnson provides 100 percent of the financial support for Ms. Lewis, who is Mr. Johnson's sister-in-law. Does Ms. Lewis qualify as Mr. Johnson's dependent?

Section 152 provides the relevant statutory authority for this research question.

Sec. 152. Dependent defined

(a)  General definition
For purposes of this subtitle, the term "dependent" means any of the following individuals over half of whose support, for the calendar year in which the taxable year of the taxpayer begins, was received from the taxpayer:
(1)  A son or daughter of the taxpayer, or a descendant of either,
(2)  A stepson or stepdaughter of the taxpayer,
(3)  A brother, sister, stepbrother, or stepsister of the taxpayer,
(4)  The father or mother of the taxpayer, or an ancestor of either,
(5)  A stepfather or stepmother of the taxpayer,
(6)  A son or daughter of a brother or sister of the taxpayer,
(7)  A brother or sister of the father or mother of the taxpayer,
(8)  A son-in-law, daughter-in-law, father-in-law, mother-in-law, brother-in-law, or sister-in-law of the taxpayer, or
(9)  An individual (other than an individual who at any time during the taxable year was the spouse, determined without regard to section 7703, of the taxpayer) who, for the taxable year of the taxpayer, has as his principal place of abode the home of the taxpayer and is a member of the taxpayer's household.

By comparing the facts of this research problem to the relevant authority, a researcher can conclude that Ms. Lewis qualifies as Mr. Johnson's dependent. Therefore, the answer to the research question is an unqualified yes.

Researchers are required to make evaluative judgments when the relevant authority relates to a conclusion inferred from a set of facts, rather than to the facts themselves. By definition, conclusions are subjective; different observers may infer different conclusions from the same facts. A researcher who must draw a conclusion to complete a research project can never be sure that such conclusion will go unchallenged by the IRS. Therefore, the researcher should never give an unqualified answer to a research question requiring an evaluative judgment. To illustrate this point, return to our example involving losses incurred as part of a horse breeding activity. Recall that in the case *Herbert C. Sanderson* T.C. Memo 1964-284 taxpayers were allowed a deduction for losses incurred in breeding, raising, showing, racing, and selling horses. At issue in this case was whether the horse farm activities constituted a trade or business under Section 162. The text of the case states, in part:

> the burden is on petitioners to show that they conducted this horse venture as a business with a genuine intention of earning a profit. . . . Based on the facts which we have outlined in some detail in our Findings of Fact and the record as a whole, and from our observation of petitioners and the other witnesses as they testified at the trial, we have found as an ultimate fact that petitioners' operation of the horse venture in 1957, 1958, and 1959 did constitute a business. . . . (p. 64-1900)

This authority requires the researcher to evaluate the factual circumstances surrounding a taxpayer's horse breeding operations. If the researcher believes that the facts and circumstances support a conclusion that the operation is a trade or business, she could advise the taxpayer to deduct the related losses. But the researcher should qualify her advice by explaining the risk that the IRS might draw the opposite conclusion and disallow the deduction.

When relying on a judicial opinion to support research conclusions, one final step is needed to ensure that the opinion remains a valid interpretation of the law. In particular, has the decision been appealed, and if so, what was the result? The researcher might also wish to determine whether other courts have supported the conclusion of the court in the opinion in question. These issues can be assessed using an important resource called the **Citator.** The Citator may be used to determine the status of tax judicial decisions, revenue rulings, and revenue procedures. Citators are published by RIA, CCH, and Shepard's and are also available through the major computerized tax services. For each case reported, the Citator provides a list of subsequent rulings that have referenced the case and a brief indication of the nature of the subsequent reference. For example, a review of the RIA Citator listing for *Herbert C. Sanderson* T.C. Memo 1964-284 reveals that the case was not appealed (no appellate court decision is listed), the case has been cited favorably in three subsequent cases, and the case has been distinguished (the cited case is distinguished either in law or on the facts) in one subsequent case. The Citator listing provides complete citations to each of these subsequent cases, which the researcher may wish to examine further.

*Applying Step 4*  Based on your reading of Section 1001(a), you determine that Ms. Colter will realize a $75,000 loss if she sells her land to CCM Inc. for $325,000 cash. According to the general rule of Section 1001(c), realized losses are recognized "except as otherwise provided in this subtitle." Therefore, Ms. Colter can recognize the loss and report it on her tax return for the year of sale unless Section 267 disallows the loss. The portions of Section 267 that seem applicable to Ms. Colter's case read as follows:

Sec. 267. Losses, expenses, and interest with respect to transactions between related taxpayers

(a) In general
   (1) Deduction for losses disallowed
     No deduction shall be allowed in respect of any loss from the sale or exchange of property, directly or indirectly, between persons specified in any of the paragraphs of subsection (b).
(b) Relationships
   The persons referred to in subsection (a) are:
   (2) An individual and a corporation more than 50 percent in value of the outstanding stock of which is owned, directly or indirectly, by or for such individual;
(c) Constructive ownership of stock
   For purposes of determining, in applying subsection (b), the ownership of stock—
   (2) An individual shall be considered as owning the stock owned, directly or indirectly, by or for his family;
   (4) The family of an individual shall include only his brothers and sisters (whether by the whole or half blood), spouse, ancestors, and lineal descendants; and
   (5) . . . stock constructively owned by an individual by reason of the application of paragraph (2) or (3) shall not be treated as owned by him for the purpose of again applying either of such paragraphs in order to make another the constructive owner of such stock.

According to Section 267(a)(1), Ms. Colter cannot recognize her realized loss if she and CCM Inc. are related parties. According to Section 267(b)(2), Ms. Colter and CCM Inc. are related parties if Ms. Colter directly or indirectly owns more than 50 percent in value of CCM's outstanding stock. You know that Ms. Colter does not own any CCM stock directly, but you are uncertain as to whether she owns any stock indirectly. Section 267(c)(2) provides that Ms. Colter is considered to own any CCM stock owned by her "family." When your refer to the facts you established during your first meeting with Ms. Colter, you discover that you do not know how many shares of CCM stock are owned by her brother Jack and nephew Robert.

## Step 5: Repeat Steps 1 through 4 as Many Times as Necessary!

At some point in the research process, even an expert researcher may discover that she does not have all the facts necessary to complete her analysis of the client's transaction. In such case, the researcher must repeat step one by obtaining additional information from the client. Oftentimes the additional information suggests additional tax issues and research questions that the researcher must address. A researcher may have to repeat Steps 1 through 4 several times before she is satisfied with her analysis.

*Applying Step 5*

You contact Ms. Colter to ask one more question: How many shares of CCM stock do Jack and Robert each own? She replies that Jack owns 350 shares and Robert owns 200 shares of the 1,000 outstanding shares of CCM stock. With this additional fact, you can complete your analysis of Section 267 as it applies to Ms. Colter's proposed sale.

According to Section 267(c)(2), Ms. Colter's family includes her brother Jack but does not include her nephew Robert. Therefore, she indirectly owns the 350 CCM shares directly owned by Jack. However, Jack also indirectly owns the 200 CCM shares owned by his son Robert. Section 267(c)(5) states that Jack's indirect ownership of these shares is disregarded for the purpose of determining Ms. Colter's ownership. On the basis of these statutory rules, you conclude that she directly and indirectly owns only 350 (35 percent) of CCM's 1,000 outstanding shares of stock. Thus, Ms. Colter and CCM Inc. are not related parties, Section

267(a) will not apply to her sale of the land to the corporation, and Ms. Colter can recognize her $75,000 realized loss.

You continue to analyze sources of information and sources of authority that pertain to your last two research questions. Ms. Colter's recognized loss is considered a capital loss if the land is considered a capital asset under Section 1221. The land is not a capital asset if it is considered property held for sale to customers under Section 1221(a)(1). This determination has been the topic of numerous judicial decisions. One recent case, *James E. Zurcher Jr. v. Commissioner,* TC Memo 1997-203, states in part:

> Whether the Property is a capital asset or was instead held primarily for sale in the ordinary course of petitioner's business is a factual determination. . . . Courts have developed the following nonexclusive factors to assist in this determination: (1) The nature of the taxpayer's business; (2) the taxpayer's purpose in acquiring and holding the property; (3) subdivision, platting, and other improvements tending to make the property more marketable; (4) the frequency, number, and continuity of sales; (5) the extent to which the taxpayer engaged in the sales activity; (6) the length of time the property was held; (7) the substantiality of income derived from the sales, and what percentage the income was of the taxpayer's total income; (8) the extent of advertising and other promotional activities; and (9) whether the property was listed directly or through brokers.

> Ms. Colter's stated purpose in acquiring the land was to hold it as a long-term investment. She has made no improvements to the property, engaged in no other real estate sales (other than of her personal residence), does not derive a substantial portion of her income from such sales, and does not advertise or promote real estate activities. On the basis of these facts, you conclude that Ms. Colter did not hold the land for sale in the ordinary course of business and thus the land is a capital asset and her loss is a long-term capital loss.

> She can deduct this loss in the year of sale to the extent of any capital gain recognized during the year. If the capital loss exceeds her capital gain, Ms. Colter is allowed to deduct $3,000 of the excess in the computation of adjusted gross income. Any nondeductible loss becomes a long-term capital loss carryforward into subsequent taxable years.

## Step 6: Document Your Research and Communicate Your Conclusions

The tax researcher's task is to find an accurate, useful, and complete answer to the research question(s) concerning her client's situation. This task is not finished until the researcher documents her work by preparing a written summary of the research process. Such summary usually takes the form of a research memo that includes (1) a statement of the pertinent facts, (2) an analysis of the relevant sources of authority, (3) an explanation of the researcher's conclusions, and (4) the details of any advice given to the client as part of the research engagement. This memo becomes a permanent record of the research process—a record to which the researcher (or any other professional) can refer at a future date.

The researcher also must communicate her conclusions to the client. Typically, the researcher writes a client letter containing information similar to that in her research memo. In writing the letter, the researcher should tailor both the contents and writing style to accommodate the client. For example, a letter to a client who has extensive tax knowledge may contain technical references that would be inappropriate in a letter to a client with minimal tax knowledge. Similarly, a letter to an individual who has been both a client and friend for many years may be written in an informal style that would be inappropriate for a letter to the chief financial officer of a new corporate client.

*Applying Step 6*

You write the following research memo for your permanent record:

March 5, 2003

TAX FILE MEMORANDUM

**From:**    Bridget McGuffin
**Subject:** Sara Colter
             Engagement Research Conclusions

**Summary of Facts**

Sara Colter is considering a sale of 12 acres of undeveloped land to CCM Inc. at a proposed price of $325,000. The land was purchased in 1994 for $400,000 as a long-term investment from unrelated sellers, Mr. and Mrs. Bianca. Ms. Colter has made no improvements to the land since the date of purchase and has neither purchased nor sold any other real estate with the exception of her personal residence. CCM Inc. is a closely held corporation with 1,000 shares of stock outstanding. Ms. Colter is not a shareholder of CCM; however, her brother Jack Colter and his son Robert Colter own 350 and 200 shares, respectively. Ms. Colter is not acquainted with any other CCM shareholders.

**Law and Analysis**

Under Section 1001 of the Internal Revenue Code of 1986, Ms. Colter will realize a $75,000 loss on the proposed sale of the land equal to the excess of her adjusted basis in the land ($400,000 purchase price) over the amount realized on the sale ($325,000 proposed sales price). However, Section 267(a)(1) provides that no deduction is allowed for a loss from the sale or exchange of property between related parties, as defined in subsection (b) of Section 267. For this purpose, related parties include an individual and a corporation more than 50 percent in value of the outstanding stock of which is owned, directly or indirectly, by or for such individual. Although Ms. Colter does not directly own any stock in CCM Inc., we must consider whether ownership of CCM stock by her brother and nephew constitutes indirect ownership of more than 50 percent of the value of CCM stock.

   Section 267(c)(2) provides that, in determining indirect ownership for purposes of Section 267(b), an individual is considered as owning the stock owned, directly or indirectly, by or for his family. Under Section 267(c)(4), family includes an individual's brothers, sisters, spouse, ancestors, and lineal descendants. Thus, Sara Colter is considered to own indirectly the stock owned by her brother Jack Colter, but not the stock owned by her nephew, Robert Colter. Note that Jack Colter would be considered to indirectly own the stock owned by his son, Robert Colter. However, under Section 267(c)(5), Jack's indirect ownership of these shares is disregarded in determining Sara's ownership. Thus, Sara Colter indirectly owns 350 shares of CCM Inc., equaling 35 percent of its 1,000 outstanding shares of stock. Because Ms. Colter's ownership of CCM is less than 50 percent, the related-party loss disallowance rule of Section 267(a) does not apply.

   Ms. Colter's recognized loss is considered a capital loss if the land is considered a capital asset under Section 1221. The land is not a capital asset if it is considered property held for sale to customers (Section 1221(a)(1)). This determination has been the topic of numerous judicial decisions. One recent case, *James E. Zurcher Jr. v. Commissioner,* TC Memo 1997-203, states in part:

Whether the Property is a capital asset or was instead held primarily for sale in the ordinary course of petitioner's business is a factual determination. . . . Courts have developed the following nonexclusive factors to assist in this determination: (1) the nature of the taxpayer's business; (2) the taxpayer's purpose in acquiring and holding the property; (3) subdivision, platting, and other improvements tending to make the property more marketable; (4) the frequency, number, and continuity of sales; (5) the extent to which the taxpayer engaged in the sales activity; (6) the length of time the property was held; (7) the substantiality of income derived from the sales, and what percentage the income was of the taxpayer's total income; (8) the extent of advertising and other promotional activities; and (9) whether the property was listed directly or through brokers.

Ms. Colter's stated purpose in acquiring the land was to hold it as a long-term investment. She has made no improvements to the property, engaged in no other real estate sales (other than of her personal residence), does not derive a substantial portion of her income from such sales, and does not advertise or promote real estate activities. These facts support the conclusion that Ms. Colter did not hold the land for sale in the ordinary course of business and thus the land is a capital asset.

### Conclusions

Ms. Colter will recognize a $75,000 capital loss. Because she held the land for more than one year, the loss will be a long-term capital loss. If the loss exceeds any recognized capital gains, under Section 1211(b) she may deduct $3,000 of the excess in computing adjusted gross income. Any nondeductible loss may be carried forward into subsequent taxable years.

You also write the following letter to Sara Colter:

March 5, 2003

Ms. Sara Colter
1812 Riverbend Place
Kirkwood, Missouri 62119

Dear Ms. Colter:
   This letter is in response to your inquiry concerning the tax consequences of a proposed sale of 12 acres of undeveloped land to CCM Inc. Before stating my conclusions, I'd like to summarize the facts of your case. You purchased the land in 1994 as a long-term investment. The purchase price was $400,000 and the sellers of the property, Mr. and Mrs. Bianca, are unrelated to you. You have not improved the land in any way since date of purchase, and have neither purchased nor sold any other real estate with the exception of your personal residence. CCM Inc. is a closely held corporation with 1,000 shares of outstanding stock. Although you do not own any shares, your brother Jack Colter and his son Robert Colter own 350 and 200 shares, respectively. You are not acquainted with any other CCM stockholders. The accuracy of my conclusions depends entirely on my understanding of these facts. Consequently, if the statement of facts is in any way incorrect or incomplete, please notify me immediately.
   If you sell your land to CCM Inc. for the proposed contract price of $325,000, you will realize a $75,000 loss. This loss equals the excess of your $400,000 investment in the land over the $325,000 cash you will receive at closing. You are allowed to report this loss on your individual tax return in the year of sale unless you and CCM Inc. are "related parties" within the meaning of the tax law. According to my research, you and CCM Inc. do not meet the statutory definition of "related parties," even though your brother and nephew own an aggregate 55 percent interest in CCM Inc. Therefore, you can report your $75,000 loss for tax purposes. Because you held the land for investment and owned it for more than one year, the loss is classified as a long-term capital loss. You can deduct a long-term capital loss to the extent of your capital gains for the year. If your capital loss exceeds your capital gains, you can deduct only $3,000 of the excess against other sources of income.
   Thank you for giving my firm the opportunity to advise you in this matter. If you have any questions about my conclusions, please don't hesitate to call me. If you proceed with

your plans to sell the land, I would be glad to meet with you to develop a strategy to maximize your deduction for the projected $75,000 capital loss.

Sincerely,

Bridget McGuffin

## Conclusion

Given the length and complexity of existing tax law, tax research is a critical skill for the tax practitioner. Tax research often occurs as part of tax compliance, and is also important to the tax planning process by allowing the researcher to identify and explore the tax consequences of alternative investment and business choices. The six steps reviewed in this chapter provide a guide to the novice tax researcher in formulating research questions, identifying and analyzing relevant authority, and communicating research results. As the tax researcher gains experience and familiarity with the variety of legal resources available, the tax research process will become a natural part of strategic tax planning.

## Key Terms

administrative authority *27*
Citator *34*
Internal Revenue Code *27*
judicial authority *28*
primary authorities *27*
private letter ruling (PLR) *28*

revenue procedures *28*
revenue rulings *28*
secondary authorities *30*
statutory authority *27*
technical advice memorandum (TAM) *28*
Treasury regulations *27*

U.S. Circuit Court of Appeals *28*
U.S. Court of Federal Claims *28*
U.S. District Court *28*
U.S. Supreme Court *28*
U.S. Tax Court *28*

## Questions and Problems for Discussion

1. Why is tax research necessary? In other words, why is it not possible for experienced tax professionals to answer all tax questions without performing tax research?
2. List the primary authorities for federal tax law and identify the source of each type of primary authority.
3. Explain the difference between primary and secondary authorities as sources of tax information.
4. Describe the circumstances under which it is useful and appropriate to use secondary authorities in performing tax research.
5. Explain the difference between a private letter ruling and a technical advice memorandum.
6. Explain why several different citations may be available and appropriate in referring to a single tax judicial decision.
7. Briefly describe the courts of original jurisdiction for tax cases and the appropriate appellate-level courts for these cases.
8. Describe two alternative strategies for using a tax service to locate primary authority.

## Application Problems

1. Mrs. Lulu Banks and Mr. Sonny Jacobs are half sister and brother (same dad, different moms). Are Lulu and Sonny considered family members under Section 318(a)(1)? How about Section 267(b)(1)?
2. For each of the following, use the Internal Revenue Code and Treasury regulations to locate the primary authority that answers the following questions.

a. Mr. and Mrs. Croner borrowed $250,000 to purchase their new personal residence. The debt is secured by the Croner's portfolio of marketable securities and not by the residence itself. Can the Croners deduct the annual interest on this debt?

b. Marty King is a 10-year-old girl whose parents were killed in a plane crash four years ago. She lives with her paternal grandparents. This year, Marty earned $17,800 interest and dividend income from a stock portfolio that she inherited from her parents. Is this income subject to the "kiddie tax" rules?

c. This year, Shelley Liu's corporate employer transferred her from its Phoenix office to its Dallas office. A professional moving company charged $4,100 to move Shelley's household goods from her old home to her new home. The corporation reimbursed Shelley for this entire cost. Must she include this $4,100 reimbursement in gross income?

3. For each of the following, use the Internal Revenue Code and Treasury regulations to locate the primary authority that answers the following questions.

a. John Perez is a self-employed artist. This year, John completed a four-week course of study on portraiture and life drawings that improved his professional skills immensely. The tuition for the course was $1,500. Can John claim this educational expense as a business deduction on his Form 1040?

b. Maria Kline is a successful real estate broker. After meeting with a new client, Maria always sends the client a beautiful basket of fresh fruit. The cost of the fruit itself is usually $50. However, Maria has to pay an additional $7 for the basket, cellophane wrapping, and shipping fee. Can Maria deduct the full $57 cost of these business gifts?

c. The IRS recently audited Robert Sloan's 2001 federal individual income tax return. The revenue agent calculated a $32,000 tax deficiency, and the IRS charged $5,200 interest on this unpaid tax liability. Robert paid the deficiency and interest without protest. Can he deduct the interest payment on his Form 1040?

4. Find the IRC section that requires a personal exemption phaseout for individual filers above a certain income level. Identify the specific Code cite for the phaseout. Be precise in your IRC reference [e.g., Section 61(a)(1), not Section 61].

5. Find the IRC section that defines a long-term capital gain. Be precise in your IRC reference [e.g., Section 61(a)(1), not Section 61].

6. Find the case *Bush Brothers & Co.* 73 TC 424 and answer the following questions. The purpose of these questions is to enhance your skills in reading and interpreting authorities that you locate while doing research.

a. In what year was the case decided?

b. What were the issues being litigated?

c. Who won the case?

d. Was the decision appealed?

e. Has the case been cited in other cases? If so, how many times?

7. Find the case *Biltmore Homes, Inc.,* a 1960 Tax Court memo decision, and answer the following questions. The purpose of these questions is to enhance your skills in reading and interpreting authorities that you locate while doing research.

a. What is the complete citation for this case?

b. How many issues were involved in the trial court litigation? (Hint: refer to the headnote of the case.)

   c. According to the Citator, how many times has the Tax Court decision been cited by other cases on Headnote Number 5?

   d. Did an appellate court hear the case? If so, which court? Provide the complete citation to the appellate court decision.

   e. According to the Citator, how many times has the appeals court decision been cited by other cases on Headnote Number 5?

8. Find the *Rooney* case at 88 TC 523 and answer the following questions. The purpose of these questions is to enhance your skills in reading and interpreting authorities that you locate while doing research.

   a. What is the complete citation to the case?

   b. For what taxable year is the tax liability in dispute?

   c. What code section(s) was at issue?

   d. In whose favor did the court rule?

   e. What is the general controversy being litigated in this case?

   f. Why is the plaintiff in this case the partner (Rooney) instead of the partnership?

   g. Was the decision appealed? How did you determine your answer?

9. Find the case *Corn Products Refining Co. v. Commissioner,* a 1955 Supreme Court decision, and answer the following questions. The purpose of these questions is to enhance your skills in reading and interpreting authorities that you locate while doing research.

   a. What is the complete citation for this case?

   b. What was the issue before the court?

   c. What was the taxpayer's position regarding the issue? Upon what authority was the taxpayer relying?

   d. What was the IRS's position regarding the issue? Upon what authority was the IRS relying?

   e. How did the court hold? What was its reasoning, and upon what authority did it rely?

   f. Is this case still authoritative with respect to similar issues and facts? How did you determine your answer?

10. Find the case *Thomas A. Curtis, M.D., Inc., 1994 TC Memo ¶94,015,* and answer the following questions. The purpose of these questions is to enhance your skills in reading and interpreting authorities that you locate while doing research.

   a. What is the general controversy being litigated in this case?

   b. Which party—the taxpayer or the government—won the case?

   c. Why is the plaintiff the corporation instead of Dr. and/or Mrs. Curtis?

   d. What is the relationship between Ellen Barnett Curtis and Dr. Thomas A. Curtis?

   e. Approximately how many hours a week did Ms. Curtis work, and what were her credentials?

   f. For the fiscal year ended in 1989, how much salary did Ms. Curtis receive from the corporation? What did the court decide was a reasonable amount of compensation for her for that year?

11. Find the IRS revenue procedure that gives the standard deduction amounts for the 2004 tax year. Typically the revenue procedure is released in December of the previous year. Copy the standard deduction amounts and their associated filing statuses into a table in a document file. Include the full citation for your source, in the form of the following example: Rev. Proc. 98-1,1998-1 C.B. 7.

12. Find Revenue Ruling 84-13, 1984-1 C.B. 21.

    a. To which Code section(s) does this revenue ruling relate?

    b. What was the taxpayer's occupation?

    c. Why was the taxpayer required to include the private practice fees in gross income?

    d. Find the most recent case citing that revenue ruling. What was the year of decision of that case?

## Issue Recognition Problems

Identify the tax issue or issues suggested by the following situations and state each issue in the form of a question.

1. In researching a tax question involving deductibility of accrued expenses, a tax researcher identifies a judicial decision that seems to address the issue at hand. However, the decision was rendered in 1964, and the researcher knows that the tax law has changed many times in the last 40 years.

2. Babcock Costumes Inc. operated its small business at a retail outlet located five blocks from the World Trade Center. Since September 11, it has struggled to keep its business afloat but is having trouble meeting its cash flow needs. In January 2002, Willis LLC, one of Babcock's suppliers, forgave a $5,600 account receivable from Babcock. The LLC's owners did so as a patriotic gesture and a tribute to Babcock's entrepreneurial spirit.

3. Mr. Wolford, a single individual, lived in a five-bedroom home in Hawaii from 1960 through 1999. In 2000, he traveled to Santa Fe, New Mexico, to visit an old friend. He liked the high desert so much that he rented an apartment and has spent most of his time there ever since. He visits his Hawaiian home occasionally, and his children and grandchildren use it extensively throughout the year. Two weeks ago, Mr. Wolford signed a contract to sell the Hawaiian home for $1.3 million. His cost basis in the home is $265,000.

4. Last year, Randy and Jean Robertson paid $5,000 to put in a lawn for their personal residence. This month, every blade of grass suddenly turned yellow, and the landscaper concluded that the unprecedented winter and spring draught had killed the root system. He told the Robertsons that the entire lawn would have to be dug out and replaced with new sod.

5. Mrs. Matsuko has severe arthritis. However, she is a Christian Scientist who does not consult licensed physicians or take prescription drugs. Instead, she visits a Christian Science practitioner who also practices acupuncture. Although the practitioner does not charge for the services rendered, Mrs. Matsuko insists on giving her $40 at the end of each visit.

6. Two years ago, WD Corporation sold depreciable realty for $225,000. It purchased the realty 14 years ago for $350,000 and deducted $155,000 MACRS depreciation through date of sale. This year, the IRS audited WD's return for the year of sale and determined that the corporation had incorrectly computed its depreciation with respect to the realty. Correct depreciation through date of sale should have been $200,000.

7. On May 3, 1997, John F. Kennedy, Jr., hosted a dinner party for eight of his friends and family at Maude's Seafood Diner in Martha's Vineyard. He paid the $683 bill by writing a check on his personal bank account. The restaurant's owner did not cash the check, but instead had it framed and mounted next to a photograph of JFK Jr. Last week, the owner sold the framed check for $5,000.

## Research Problems

1. Find the Internal Revenue Code on any website other than a government site and provide the URL. Do you consider the site reliable? Why or why not?

2. Find any tax glossary on the Internet and provide the URL. What is its definition of a capital asset?

3. Using Thomas, at http://thomas.loc.gov/, a legislative information site maintained by the U.S. Congress, find the schedule of hearings held by the House Ways and Means Committee for the current week. Copy the schedule into a document file.

4. Find the website for the U. S. Treasury Department. Who is the current secretary of the Treasury? Find the equivalent of the U.S. Treasury Department for one the following countries: Western Australia, Germany, Japan, or Spain. If you have difficulty finding the foreign countries, start at *The Tax and Accounting Sites Directory* found at http://www.taxsites.com/international.html.

5. Find the IRS website and answer the following questions:

   a. What types of tax-related documents are available on this site?

   b. What tax-rate schedules are available on this site?

   c. Find the IRS publication dealing with moving expenses. What is its publication number?

   d. Find form 4506. What is the title of this form?

   e. Find the form for calculating the corporate alternative minimum tax. What is the form number?

6. Using the Internet, find the use tax imposition rules for Pennsylvania. Briefly explain Pennsylvania's rules for imposition of use tax, including the applicable rates. Hint: The general form for any state's homepage is www.state.xx.us, where xx is replaced with the two-letter postal code.

7. In December 2002, Mr. and Mrs. Berry paid a $4,750 fee to an attorney who specializes in private adoption proceedings. The attorney initiated a series of meetings with several charitable organizations that facilitate adoptions. In February 2004, the Berrys paid an additional $6,000 to the attorney for finalizing the adoption and $3,600 of court costs and other fees related to the adoption. On March 10, 2004, the couple became the legal parents of 18-month-old Noel Lyn Berry.

   The Berrys file a joint federal income tax return. Their 2002 AGI was $112,600, their 2003 AGI was $140,918, and their 2004 AGI was $166,150. With these facts:

   a. Describe and quantify any tax consequence of the Berrys' 2002 and 2004 adoption expenses assuming that baby Noel's birth parents were U.S. citizens. Be sure to note the precise statutory authority for your answer.

   b. Describe and quantify any tax consequence of the Berrys' 2002 and 2004 adoption expenses assuming that baby Noel's birth parents were citizens and residents of Honduras.

8. Susan and Tim Blake file a joint return for federal income tax purposes. Susan is a botany professor at a local university. During the summer months, Susan owns and operates a part-time business as a landscape designer. Susan's participation in the business consists of meeting with clients and designing gardens on paper. In 2004, Susan devoted a total of 134 hours to these business activities. Susan employed Brad Sanders, a college student, to transport and plant the garden materials included in her designs. During 2004, Susan paid Brad $1,932 (161 hours at $12 per hour). Tim Blake, who is a CPA employed by a major accounting firm, performs all the accounting and tax work for his wife's business. During 2004, Tim devoted 45 hours of his time to this task. According to Tim's accounting records, Susan's business generated a $7,619 net loss for 2004. This loss was unusual; the landscaping business generated a net profit from 1994 through 2003.

a. Identify the tax research issue(s) suggested by the facts above and formulate your primary research question(s) accordingly.

b. Locate the statutory or regulatory authority that addresses the research issue(s).

c. Prepare a written memorandum stating the research issue(s), your conclusions concerning the issue(s), and the specific statutory or regulatory authority for your conclusions.

## Tax Planning Cases

1. The First Lady is writing a book about her experiences in the White House and intends to direct any royalties she receives on the book to her favorite charitable organization. She has not yet made any arrangements with a publisher.

   Will the future royalties be includable in the First Lady's gross income? Why or why not? If your answer is yes, is there any alternative arrangement she might make to avoid gross income recognition? Prepare a written memorandum stating the research issue(s), your conclusions concerning the issue(s), and the specific statutory or regulatory authority supporting your conclusions.

2. Akembe, a famous basketball player, is considering the possibility of transferring the sole right to use his name to promote basketball shoes produced and sold by Reboy Corporation. Reboy will pay $10 million to obtain the right to use Akembe's name for the next 20 years. Reboy may use his name on the shoes and as part of any of the company's advertisements for basketball shoes.

   If Akembe signs the contract and receives the $10 million, does he recognize gross income? If so, is the payment considered ordinary income or capital gain? Prepare a written memorandum stating the research issue(s), your conclusions concerning the issue(s), and the specific statutory or regulatory authority supporting your conclusions.

3. Mr. Slater is the sole shareholder and CEO of SMS, a calendar year S corporation. SMS is in financial difficulty, and Mr. Slater has been negotiating with several of SMS's major creditors to obtain debt relief for the corporation. On November 1, 2003, Langley Supplies agreed to discharge a $75,000 account receivable from SMS for $40,000 cash. According to an independent appraisal, the fair market value (FMV) of SMS's assets immediately before its $40,000 cash payment to Langley was $440,000, and its liabilities (including the Langley payable) totaled $470,000.

   For its 2003 taxable year, SMS's deductible operating expenses and depreciation exceeded its gross revenues from sales and services by $81,600. SMS incurred $2,075 of nondeductible meals and entertainment expenses. Mr. Slater has engaged you to determine how much of SMS's loss he can deduct on his 2003 Form 1040 (which has an extended due date of October 15, 2004). He also wants to know how any nondeductible loss will be treated in 2004 and future taxable years, and he wants you to compute the adjusted basis in his SMS stock on January 1, 2004.

   Mr. Slater has kept good tax records showing that the adjusted basis in his SMS stock on January 1, 2003, was $16,150. During 2003, Mr. Slater received a $60,000 salary from SMS, but he did not receive any cash or property distributions with respect to his SMS stock. In fact, Mr. Slater had to loan $20,000 cash to SMS on December 14, 2003, so that SMS could make its December payroll. SMS's bookkeeper recorded the loan on SMS's books as "short-term loan payable—Mr. Deke Slater," but Mr. Slater did not bother to draw up any additional written evidence of SMS's debt to him. For our purposes, assume the loan is bona fide and that Section 7872 does not apply. He has not yet demanded any repayment from his corporation, but he plans to do so before the end of 2004.

Write a letter to Mr. Deke Slater in which you respond to his specific questions concerning SMS's 2003 loss. You should also address any additional tax issues suggested by the facts and bring these issues to Mr. Slater's attention. In writing the letter, assume that Mr. Slater has an MBA degree from Stanford University, 20 years of business experience, and extensive knowledge of the tax law. He is willing to pay top dollar for your professional help and expects you to provide a thorough technical analysis of your conclusions, including complete cites to all relevant authority.

# Tax Strategies for
# New Businesses

# Organizational Strategies

## Learning Objectives

*After reading this chapter, you will be able to:*

1. Compare the tax consequences of conducting business in a passthrough entity or in a corporation.

2. Explain the tax advantage of shareholder debt to a closely held corporation.

3. Describe the requirements for a nontaxable exchange of property for corporate stock.

4. Determine the effect of boot and the assumption of liability in a property-for-stock exchange.

5. Determine the basis of property received by a corporation as a contribution to capital.

6. Compute a partner's capital account and outside basis and a partnership's inside basis in contributed property.

7. Calculate the effect on outside basis when a partnership assumes a partner liability.

8. Identify the tax issues when an owner sells or leases property to an entity.

In Part Two of *Advanced Strategies*, we begin our study of the tax issues facing business entities and their owners. This text takes an evolutionary approach by arranging the issues around the life cycle of a business entity. Part Two, which focuses on the tax strategies involved in starting a new business, consists of two chapters. Chapter 3 examines the initial choice of organizational form and the various methods by which owners can contribute cash or property to their new business organization. Chapter 4 examines the variety of compensation strategies through which new organizations attract and retain valuable employees.

Starting a business is both an exhilarating and a frightening experience. Entrepreneurs are faced with dozens of important decisions that could lead to financial success or failure. One such decision concerns the organization of the business: Which type of entity is best for this particular activity and its owners? To make an informed decision, entrepreneurs must understand both the nontax and tax characteristics of the various entity choices.

Business entities are formed under the statutes of one of the 50 states or the District of Columbia, and the nontax legal characteristics (as well as the state tax characteristics) are determined by the controlling state law. In this chapter, we concentrate on the federal tax characteristics of business entities as determined by the Internal Revenue Code, Treasury regulations, and other sources of tax authority.

# ORGANIZATIONAL FORMS FOR BUSINESS ENTITIES

**Tax Talk**
According to the Congressional Research Service, S corporations are by far the most numerous type of passthrough entity. In 2000, the IRS received 2.7 million S corporation returns as compared to only 1.9 million partnership returns. Because of the increasing popularity of LLCs, the number of partnership filings should soon catch up to the number of S corporation filings.

The federal income tax characteristics of a business entity depend primarily on whether the entity is incorporated or unincorporated under state law. A **corporation** is a taxable entity unless the shareholders make a **Subchapter S** election for the corporation. Subchapter S is the portion of the Internal Revenue Code (Sections 1361 through 1379) governing the operation of S corporations. Taxable corporations are often called *regular* or *C corporations* to distinguish them from nontaxable **S corporations.** *In this textbook, any reference to a corporation means the taxable, rather than the nontaxable, type.* Unincorporated businesses and S corporations are **passthrough entities,** which are not subject to federal income tax. Any profit or loss generated by a passthrough entity flows through the entity to be reported on the owners' income tax returns.

## Unincorporated Entities

The simplest passthrough entity is a **sole proprietorship,** which is an unincorporated business owned by one individual.[1] Sole proprietorships are accounting entities because the owner must maintain adequate books and records to compute business profit or loss. The owner can even have a name for the business (for example, Thomas Blake "doing business as" Blake's Bouquets). However, sole proprietorships are not separate legal entities. The owner has title to the business assets and is personally liable for the repayment of debt incurred in the business name.

**Partnerships** are business entities formed by contractual agreement between two or more partners. Forty-nine states and the District of Columbia have statutes patterned after the Uniform Partnership Act or the Revised Uniform Limited Partnership Act that establish the legal characteristics of partnerships formed under their jurisdiction.[2] Under state law, partnerships are legal entities that can hold title to property and incur debt in the partnership name. In a **general partnership,** all partners have personal liability for repaying partnership debt. In a **limited partnership,** one or more limited partners have no personal liability for repayment of partnership debt. Every limited partnership must have at least one general partner with personal liability. A **limited liability partnership (LLP)** is a specialized form of general partnership in which individual partners are not personally liable for malpractice claims arising from the professional misconduct of another partner. LLPs are often the entity of choice for professional firms in which individual partners and their employees perform personal services for patients or clients.

**Limited liability companies (LLCs)** are formed under state law as unincorporated legal entities. Like partnerships, LLCs can hold title to property and incur debt in the entity name. Unlike partnerships, no member of an LLC has personal liability for repayment of LLC debt. As a result, LLCs provide their members with the same immunity to business risk as that enjoyed by corporate shareholders. Because LLCs offer limited liability for every member, they have become the passthrough entity of choice for U.S. businesses.

---

[1] Sole proprietorships include businesses in which the owner's spouse has an equity interest under state property law.

[2] Louisiana is the exception.

Reg. 301.7701-3 (the check-the-box regulation) allows members of an LLC to elect the entity's classification for federal tax purposes. The members can elect that the LLC be classified as a taxable corporation. While corporate classification offers tax planning opportunities for foreign LLCs, members of domestic LLCs have no reason to elect corporate classification. Overwhelmingly, members in domestic LLCs want their entities to be classified as partnerships for federal tax purposes. The regulation provides that domestic LLCs with at least two members are classified as partnerships by default. Consequently, members in domestic LLCs are not required to file written elections with the IRS for their LLC to be treated as a passthrough entity. The default classification for single-member LLCs (which are permitted in all but 12 states) is a **disregarded entity,** which has no separate federal tax identity. Thus, a single-member LLC owned by an individual is treated as a sole proprietorship, and the LLC's business activities are reported on a Schedule C included in the individual's Form 1040. A single-member LLC owned by a corporation is treated as a division or branch operation, and the LLC's business activities are reported on the corporation's Form 1120.

## State Taxation of Business Entities

Forty-five states and the District of Columbia impose an income or franchise tax on corporations doing business within the state. If the shareholders of a corporation have made a Subchapter S election for federal tax purposes, most states treat the corporation as a nontaxable passthrough entity for state tax purposes. However, some states, such as New York and Pennsylvania, require a separate S election for state tax purposes. Other states, such as New Hampshire and Tennessee, require all corporations subject to their jurisdiction to pay the state's corporate income tax.

The state tax treatment of unincorporated entities varies from state to state. Many states follow the federal model by treating unincorporated businesses as nontaxable passthrough entities. Some states impose entity-level taxes on certain types of unincorporated businesses. For example, the Texas corporate franchise tax applies to regular corporations, S corporations, and LLCs, but not to partnerships. California imposes a franchise tax on limited partnerships and LLCs. Michigan's single-business tax applies to all incorporated and unincorporated entities conducting business within the state. Clearly, tax professionals must pay attention to the state tax consequences when advising clients about the tax characteristics of the different unincorporated entities.

## Incorporating a Growing Business

Many small businesses begin as a sole proprietorship. As a business grows, the proprietor might join forces with other entrepreneurs or investors by forming a partnership or an LLC. Such unincorporated businesses can grow into global enterprises. For example, the Big Four public accounting firms, which generate billions of dollars of annual revenue from their worldwide operations, are organized as LLPs. Other unincorporated businesses may need access to capital markets to finance continued growth. The owners gain access by incorporating the business and making an **initial public offering (IPO)** of stock, thereby sacrificing passthrough entity status.

| *A Sweet IPO* | Krispy Kreme Doughnuts launched one of the more successful IPOs in years. The North Carolina corporation went public in April 2000, and investors snapped up the shares the way that customers snap up the company's mouth-watering products. An investor who bought Krispy Kreme stock at its opening price of $33 per share could have sold the stock for $83 on the last trading day of the year. |

A capital-hungry business cannot avoid the corporate income tax by forming a limited partnership and selling interests to the investing public. The tax law negates this strategy by treating publicly traded partnerships (PTPs) as corporations for federal tax purposes.[3] A **publicly traded partnership (PTP)** is any partnership conducting an active business if interests in such partnership are traded on an established securities market or are readily tradable on a secondary market.

| | |
|---|---|
| *Publicly Traded Partnership* | DFG Partnership, which manufactures computer hardware, decided to raise venture capital by using an underwriter to sell limited interests through a regional securities market. The public placement was a success because it raised $14 million for DFG. However, DFG is now a publicly traded partnership and is treated as a corporation instead of a partnership for federal tax purposes.[4] |

As you will learn later in the chapter, the owners of an unincorporated business can transfer the business assets to a newly formed corporation with no front-end tax cost. Unfortunately, the process cannot be reversed so cheaply. As we will discuss in Chapter 14, the distribution of corporate assets to shareholders in liquidation of the corporation is a taxable event to *both* the corporation and the shareholders. Thus, if the shareholders of a closely held taxable corporation would prefer to operate the business as a passthrough entity, their only viable option is to make a Subchapter S election.

| | |
|---|---|
| *Trapped in the Corporate Form* | The 20 members in Myroni LLC planned to "go public" by the end of 2005. In anticipation of their IPO, the members incorporated their LLC into Myroni Inc., a Delaware corporation. A year after the incorporation, Myroni's investment bankers gave the shareholders the disappointing news that an IPO is no longer feasible. The shareholders cannot afford to liquidate the corporation and reorganize their business as a partnership or LLC because of the tax cost. If Myroni meets the eligibility requirements, however, the shareholders can make a Subchapter S election so that their corporation will be a nontaxable passthrough entity for federal tax purposes.[5] |

# BASIC TAX CONSEQUENCES OF ENTITY CHOICE

**Objective 1**
Compare the tax consequences of conducting business in a passthrough entity or in a corporation.

As a rule of thumb, entrepreneurs prefer passthrough entities to corporations because of the difference in income tax consequences. In the next section of the chapter, we will compare these consequences with respect to both business income and business loss.

## Taxation of Business Income

*Corporate Income*

Business income generated by a corporation is reported on Form 1120, U.S. Corporate Income Tax Return. The income is taxed at the corporate level, and the after-tax earnings

[3] According to Section 7704, PTPs that were in existence on December 31, 1987 (grandfathered PTPs), can retain their status as passthrough entities under two conditions. First, the PTP must not add a substantial new line of business after December 31, 1997. Second, the PTP must pay an entity-level federal tax equal to 3.5 percent of annual gross business income.

[4] Partnerships must capitalize the costs connected with the marketing and placement of partnership interests. These "syndication costs" include brokerage, underwriting, and placement fees as well as costs to print the prospectus and other promotional materials. Unlike organization costs, syndication costs cannot be amortized. Section 709(a).

[5] As we will discuss in Chapter 7, the conversion of a regular corporation into an S corporation exposes the S corporation to several corporate-level taxes.

become the corporation's earnings and profits. (This important term is defined more completely in Chapter 8.) If the corporation's board of directors decides to distribute earnings to the shareholders, the distribution is a dividend taxed at the shareholder level. For both individual and corporate shareholders, dividends are ordinary income. However, individual shareholders compute the tax on their dividends at a 15 percent preferential rate. The rate drops to 5 percent for any dividend income that would be taxed at 15 percent or less under the regular rate structure.[6] Corporate shareholders are allowed a dividends-received deduction that significantly reduces the corporate tax on the dividend.[7]

Individual shareholders who operate a closely held corporate business must understand that the after-tax dollars in the corporation's bank account belong to the corporation, not to them. Shareholders who pay personal expenses with corporate funds could be inadvertently creating a constructive dividend that they must report as income.

| | |
|---|---|
| *Constructive Dividend* | Mr. Hood operated a food service business as a sole proprietorship for 10 years before incorporating the business as Hood's Institutional Foods, Inc. (HIF). Mr. Hood was the sole shareholder and president of HIF. In 1990, Mr. Hood was indicted by the federal government for criminal tax evasion because of his failure to pay individual income tax. During 1991, HIF paid $86,000 of legal fees incurred in Mr. Hood's defense of the indictment. The corporation deducted the payment on its own return as a business expense. When the IRS audited HIF, it reclassified the payment as a nondeductible dividend and assessed additional tax on both HIF and Mr. Hood. The Tax Court upheld the IRS's position, stating, "A constructive dividend arises when a corporation confers an economic benefit on a shareholder without the expectation of repayment, even though neither the corporation nor the shareholder intended a dividend."[8] |

Shareholders in closely held corporations can defer payment of the shareholder-level tax by reinvesting the corporation's after-tax earnings in the business rather than distributing the earnings as dividends. The reinvestment increases the shareholders' equity and the value of their corporate stock. When shareholders dispose of the stock in a future taxable transaction, they will recognize the increase in value as a long-term capital gain. The tax on the gain is the second tax with respect to the corporation's accumulated earnings.[9] Shareholders who adopt this tax planning strategy must be aware that the Internal Revenue Code includes two rather nasty taxes that could apply to corporations that accumulate after-tax earnings rather than pay dividends. These penalty taxes, the accumulated earnings tax and the personal holding company tax, are discussed in more detail in Chapter 8.

### Passthrough Income

Business income generated by a passthrough entity is reported on the entity's annual return (Form 1065 U.S. Partnership Return of Income or Form 1120S U.S. Income Tax Return for an S Corporation). The business income, however, is taxed only once to the entity's owners. For individual owners, the passthrough income is taxed at progressive rates ranging from 10 percent to 35 percent. For corporate owners, the passthrough

---

[6] Section I (h)(3)(B).

[7] Section 248 states that the dividends-received deduction equals 70 percent of dividends received if the recipient corporation owns less than 20 percent of the payor's stock, 80 percent of dividends received if the recipient corporation owns 20 percent or more but less than 80 percent of the payor's stock, and 100 percent of dividends received if the recipient corporation owns 80 percent or more of the payor's stock.

[8] *Lenward C. Hood*, 115 TC 172 (2000).

[9] If an individual shareholder transfers stock at death, the basis of the stock is adjusted to its fair market value (FMV) under Section 1014. Consequently, death can be viewed as an effective strategy for avoiding the second tax on corporate earnings.

income is taxed at the corporate rates. Although the corporate rate schedule is also progressive, the surtaxes in the schedule cause most corporate income to be taxed at a flat rate of 34 or 35 percent. The individual and corporate rate schedules are provided on the inside front cover of the text.

Once the owners of a passthrough entity pay their federal and state tax on the entity's income, the after-tax earnings belong to them. The owners can withdraw earnings from the business to spend for personal consumption or to make other investments. Alternatively, they can reinvest earnings in the business to finance growth. Regardless of the choice, the earnings are not subject to any additional income tax.

*Spending After-Tax Cash*
Ms. Pratt owns and operates a pet grooming service as a single-member LLC. Last year, the LLC generated $55,000 net profit, which Ms. Pratt included in the adjusted gross income (AGI) reported on her Form 1040. During the year, Ms. Pratt withdrew $32,000 from the LLC's bank account. She used $21,000 to pay her federal and state estimated tax and the remaining $11,000 to buy a horse for her granddaughter. These cash withdrawals had no income tax consequences to Ms. Pratt.

## Deduction of Business Loss

### Corporate Loss

A loss generated by a business operated as a corporation is trapped at the entity level as a **net operating loss (NOL).** The corporation can carry the loss back two years and forward 20 years as an NOL deduction against taxable income. The shareholders never receive an ordinary deduction for a corporate NOL. If the NOL causes a decrease in the value of the corporation's stock, the shareholders cannot recognize their loss until they dispose of the stock in a future taxable transaction.[10]

### Passthrough Loss

The fact that a business is losing money is bad economic news to the owners. If they can deduct the loss against other sources of income, however, the resultant tax savings is a positive cash flow. Owners generally can deduct a business loss incurred by a passthrough entity. If the entity is a partnership or LLC, each owner's deduction is limited to the adjusted basis in the owner's partnership or LLC interest.[11] If the entity is an S corporation, each owner's deduction is limited to the adjusted basis in the owner's stock plus the adjusted basis of any S corporation debt held by the shareholder.[12] Owners who have sufficient investment basis to deduct at least some portion of their loss could discover that the deduction is further limited by the at-risk and passive activity loss rules.[13] Any nondeductible portion of a business loss is carried forward for potential deduction in future tax years. The statutory limitations on passthrough loss deductions are reviewed in more detail in Chapter 7. For now, the important point is that the limitations can reduce an owner's current deduction for the passthrough loss, thereby decreasing the tax savings and cash flow from the deduction.

[10] The loss on sale is a capital loss unless Section 1244 converts some portion to an ordinary loss.
[11] Section 704(d).
[12] Section 1366(d).
[13] Sections 465 and 469.

| *Limited Deduction for Passthrough Loss* | Mrs. Boyd owns 25 percent of the outstanding stock of an S corporation. Because she earns so much salary, interest, and dividend income, her marginal tax rate is 35 percent. This year, the S corporation generated a $100,000 business loss. If Mrs. Boyd could deduct her entire $25,000 share of the loss, the deduction would reduce her tax by $8,750 (35 percent × $25,000). Unfortunately, Mrs. Boyd's basis in her stock is only $7,000, and she holds no debt from the corporation. Thus, she can deduct only $7,000 this year and must carry an $18,000 loss into future years. As a result, the current tax savings from her business loss is only $2,450 (35 percent × $7,000). |
|---|---|

Now that we have reviewed the tax consequences of operating a business as either a corporation or a passthrough entity, we are ready to move on to the tax consequences of forming new business entities. As we compare corporate formations with partnership formations, we will use some new terminology. The tax rules pertaining to transactions between shareholders and their corporations are contained in **Subchapter C** of the Internal Revenue Code (Sections 301 through 385). The tax rules pertaining to transactions between partners and partnerships (including LLCs) are contained in **Subchapter K** (Sections 701 through 777). Tax practitioners use these subchapter designations to refer to the corporate rules or the partnership rules, and so will we.

# CORPORATE FORMATIONS

The formation of a corporation is a straightforward legal process in which the organizers (or their attorney) file the requisite articles of incorporation with the state government. Many states require the organizers to pay a filing fee and contribute a minimum amount of capital to the corporation.[14] In return, the state grants a corporate charter to the organizers who become shareholders in the newly formed entity. Once a corporation has been formed, the shareholders can make a Subchapter S election if they want the corporation to be a nontaxable passthrough entity for tax purposes.

**Objective 2**
Explain the tax advantage of shareholder debt to a closely held corporation.

New corporate businesses typically need more working capital than the minimum contribution required by state law. Although a corporation can borrow money in its own name, commercial creditors might be unwilling to lend money to a new corporation (with few assets and an untested business plan) unless the shareholders personally guarantee repayment. As an alternative to third-party financing, the shareholders themselves can lend money to the corporation in return for a debt obligation. In fact, the use of shareholder debt in a corporation's capital structure is an excellent tax strategy. The corporation can deduct the interest payments on the debt, and the corporation's repayment of the principal represents a source of nontaxable cash flow to the investors.

| *Shareholder Debt* | Mr. Wilkins and Mr. Weinberg each invested $50,000 cash to form WW Inc. under Maryland law. Each investor received 50 of the corporation's 100 shares of common stock and a $30,000 note with a 15-year repayment schedule and a 9 percent annual interest rate. Here is WW's initial balance sheet. |
|---|---|

[14] Corporations must capitalize their organization costs and can amortize the costs over 60 months beginning with the month in which the corporation begins business. Section 248.

| | |
|---|---|
| Cash | $100,000 |
| Notes payable to shareholders | $ 60,000 |
| Contributed capital (100 shares) | 40,000 |
| | $100,000 |

Over the next 15 years, WW will make principal repayments and deductible interest payments to Mr. Wilkins and Mr. Weinberg. If the two shareholders had made their entire $100,000 investment in return for capital stock, any distributions from WW with respect to their investment would be nondeductible dividends.

Corporate investors who appreciate the tax advantage of interest payments over dividends might be tempted to overload the corporation's capital structure with shareholder debt. If a closely held corporation is thinly capitalized with an unreasonably high ratio of shareholder debt to equity, the IRS can challenge the debt's validity. If facts and circumstances indicate that a shareholder debt is disguised equity, the IRS can reclassify the corporation's interest and principal payments as constructive dividends.

| | |
|---|---|
| **Shareholder Debt as Disguised Equity** | Assume that Mr. Wilkins and Mr. Weinberg each received a $49,500 note from newly formed WW Inc. In this case, WW's balance sheet shows a debt-to-equity ratio of 99 to 1. |

| | |
|---|---|
| Cash | $100,000 |
| Notes payable to shareholders | $ 99,000 |
| Contributed capital (100 shares) | 1,000 |
| | $100,000 |

Because the corporation is so thinly capitalized, the IRS could conclude that some portion of the purported debt is really a permanent equity investment. On the basis of this conclusion, WW's deduction for interest payments on the disguised equity would be disallowed, and Mr. Wilkins and Mr. Weinberg would recognize both interest and principal payments as dividend income.

## Section 351 Nontaxable Exchanges

**Objective 3**
Describe the requirements for a nontaxable exchange of property for corporate stock.

Investors who contribute property to a corporation in exchange for stock retain an indirect equity interest in the property. The investors have changed the form of their ownership but have not "cashed out" their investment in the property. Subchapter C acknowledges this economic fact by treating certain exchanges of property for stock as nontaxable events. Section 351(a) provides that no gain or loss is recognized if property is transferred to a corporation by one or more persons solely in exchange for stock if the transferors control the corporation immediately after the exchange. *Control* is defined as the ownership of 80 percent or more of (1) the total voting power represented by all classes of voting stock and (2) the shares of each outstanding nonvoting class.[15] If more than one person contributes property (including cash) in the exchange, the control requirement applies in the aggregate.

[15] Section 368(c) and Rev. Rul. 59-259, 1959-2 CB 115.

*Formation of MGL Inc.*

Mr. Mack, Ms. Garcia, and Ms. Lutes formed a new corporation (MGL Inc.) by contributing cash and property in exchange for 100 shares of MGL common stock. Mr. Mack contributed $40,000 cash for 20 shares, Ms. Garcia contributed business inventory worth $80,000 for 40 shares, and Ms. Lutes contributed $10,000 cash and business equipment worth $70,000 for 40 shares. Here is MGL's initial balance sheet for financial reporting purposes. Note that the inventory and equipment are recorded at **fair market value (FMV).**[16]

|  | Book Basis |
| --- | --- |
| Cash | $ 50,000 |
| Inventory | 80,000 |
| Equipment | 70,000 |
|  | $200,000 |
| Contributed capital (100 shares) | $200,000 |

*(handwritten: 100%)*

Immediately after the exchange, the three contributors owned 100 percent of MGL's only class of outstanding stock, and the Section 351(a) control requirement is satisfied.

When Section 351(a) applies, the contributor's gain or loss realized on the exchange of property for stock is not recognized. The contributor's basis in the stock received is a **substituted basis** determined by reference to the basis of the contributed property.[17] This substituted basis ensures that the contributor's unrecognized gain or loss is merely deferred until the contributor disposes of the stock in a taxable transaction.

*Tax Consequences to MGL Shareholders*

*(handwritten: review)*

Refer to the facts concerning the formation of MGL Inc. Because Mr. Mack contributed cash in exchange for his MGL stock, he realized no gain or loss, and the basis in his 20 MGL shares equals his $40,000 cost. Ms. Garcia's tax basis in the contributed inventory was $63,000. Therefore, she realized a $17,000 gain on the exchange ($80,000 FMV of 40 shares received − $63,000 basis surrendered). Ms. Garcia has no recognized gain, but the basis in her 40 MGL shares is only $63,000. Ms. Lutes's tax basis in the contributed equipment was $20,000. Therefore, she realized a $50,000 gain on the exchange ($70,000 FMV of 35 shares received *in exchange for the equipment* − $20,000 basis surrendered). Ms. Lutes has no recognized gain, but the basis in her 40 MGL shares is only $30,000 ($10,000 cash +$20,000 basis of equipment).

### Control Requirement

Taxpayers who are relying on Section 351(a) to avoid a taxable exchange of property for stock must keep a watchful eye on the control requirement. Only the stock received by shareholders who contributed property (including cash) in the exchange is aggregated to determine control. If a shareholder received stock in exchange for services, that stock is not counted toward control.

---

[16] Fair market value is the price at which property would change hands between a willing buyer and a willing seller in an arm's-length transaction in which neither party is under any compulsion to transact and in which both parties have reasonable knowledge of the relevant facts.

[17] Section 358(a).

*Lack of Section 351 Control*

Assume that a fourth individual, Mr. Lattrell, participated in the formation of MGL Inc. While Mr. Mack, Ms. Garcia, and Ms. Lutes contributed property, Mr. Lattrell contributed professional services to the new corporate entity. In exchange for these services, MGL issued 30 additional shares of common stock to Mr. Lattrell (increasing the total number of shares outstanding to 130). Immediately after formation, the three contributors of property owned only 100 shares of MGL stock. Because their aggregate ownership was only 76.9 percent (100 shares/130 shares), Section 351(a) does not apply to their exchanges. As a result, Ms. Garcia must recognize her $17,000 gain, and Ms. Lutes must recognize her $50,000 gain. Both women take an $80,000 cost basis in their 40 MGL shares. Section 351 does not apply to any exchange of services for corporate stock. Consequently, Mr. Lattrell must recognize the FMV of his 30 shares (presumably $60,000) as ordinary income and take a $60,000 cost basis in the shares.

Shareholders that control an existing corporation can use Section 351 to transfer additional property to their corporation at no tax cost. These shareholders must remember that the 80 percent control requirement applies to both voting stock and nonvoting classes of stock.

*Lack of Section 351 Control of a Subsidiary*

At the beginning of the year, Grebee Inc., a publicly held corporation, owned 96 percent of the voting common stock of its operating subsidiary, Turlow Inc. The remaining 4 percent of Turlow's common stock was owned by Turlow employees. Turlow has one class of nonvoting, preferred stock, all of which is owned by a tax-exempt charitable organization. On August 1, Grebee transferred commercial real estate (FMV $2 million, adjusted basis $600,000) to Turlow in exchange for 2,500 shares of newly issued common stock. This exchange increased Grebee's ownership of the total voting power of Turlow's stock to 97.3 percent. Yet because Grebee did not own the requisite 80 percent of Turlow's nonvoting stock, the exchange did not qualify under Section 351, and Grebee recognized a $1.4 million taxable gain on the transfer of property to its subsidiary.

## Tax Consequences of Boot

**Objective 4**
Determine the effect of boot in a property-for-stock exchange.

Section 351(a) applies only to the exchange of property for stock. If a contributor receives cash, the corporation's debt obligation, or any other property, the receipt of such **boot** triggers the recognition of gain (but not loss) on the exchange.[18] The amount of gain recognized equals the amount of cash plus the FMV of any noncash boot. Of course, the gain recognized can never exceed the gain realized on the exchange.

*Receipt of Boot*

Refer to the original facts in which Mr. Mack, Ms. Garcia, and Ms. Lutes each contributed property in exchange for MGL stock. Assume that Ms. Garcia received only 38 shares of MGL stock plus $4,000 cash from the corporation in exchange for her inventory so that MGL's balance sheet immediately after formation showed the following.

|  | Book Basis |
|---|---|
| Cash | $ 46,000 (50-4) |
| Inventory | 80,000 |
| Equipment | 70,000 |
|  | $196,000 |
| Contributed capital (98 shares outstanding) | $196,000 |

[18] Section 351(b). Section 351(g) provides that nonqualified preferred stock (as defined in the subsection) is treated as boot in a Section 351(a) exchange.

*gain recognized is cash up to amount realized but because of deferral*

Because Ms. Garcia exchanged property for both stock and $4,000 boot, she must recognize $4,000 of her $17,000 realized gain on the exchange. Because the property was inventory, the gain is ordinary income. If Ms. Garcia had received only 20 MGL shares and $40,000 cash, she would have recognized her entire $17,000 gain on the exchange of her inventory.

When a shareholder receives boot in a Section 351 exchange, the substituted basis in the corporate stock is decreased by the amount of boot. If the shareholder recognizes some portion of a realized gain because of boot, the stock basis is increased by the gain, and the two adjustments offset each other. In the preceding example, Ms. Garcia's basis in her MGL stock with or without the receipt of $4,000 boot is $63,000. If the shareholder realized a loss on the exchange, the reduction in stock basis for the boot stands alone.

**Stock Basis Reduction for Boot**

Mr. Ott contributed property (FMV $12,000) to Opal Inc. in exchange for 10 shares of Opal stock (FMV $10,500) and $1,500 cash. This exchange qualified under Section 351. The following table shows the computation of Mr. Ott's basis in his 10 shares under two different assumptions. The first column assumes that Mr. Ott had a $3,000 basis in the contributed property; the second column assumes that he had a $13,000 basis in the property.

|  |  |  |
|---|---|---|
| Amount realized by Mr. Ott | $12,000 | $12,000   *FMV property given* |
| **Basis of contributed property** | **(3,000)** | **(13,000)**   *basis of prop given* |
| Gain (loss) realized | $ 9,000 | $ (1,000) |
| Gain (loss) recognized *up to boot amt* | $ 1,500 | $  –0– |
| Gain (loss) deferred  *Diff.* | 7,500 | (1,000) |
| Basis of contributed property | $ 3,000 | $13,000 |
| Less: Boot received | (1,500) | (1,500) |
| Plus: Gain recognized | 1,500 | –0– |
| Substituted basis of stock | $ 3,000 | $11,500 |

*10,500 + 1,500* (annotation beside Amount realized row)

*liability assumed* (handwritten under Plus: Gain recognized)

Note that in both computations, the difference between Mr. Ott's stock basis and the stock's $10,500 FMV is the deferred gain (loss) on the Section 351 exchange.

## Corporate Assumption of Liabilities in a Section 351 Exchange

**Objective 4**
Determine the effect of the assumption of liability in a property-for-stock exchange.

Business owners who contribute their operating assets to a newly formed corporation usually have the corporation assume their business liabilities. In this case, their amount realized on the exchange includes not only the stock received but also the relief of liability. Subchapter C accommodates this situation with a general rule that such relief is not treated as boot received in a Section 351 exchange.[19] The only consequence of the liability relief to the contributor is a reduction in stock basis equal to the relief.[20]

**Incorporating a Sole Proprietorship**

Mr. and Mrs. Tifton were the sole proprietors of Tiftons' Toffees, a candy-making business, for eight years. On June 1, the Tiftons incorporated the business by contributing the operating assets (FMV $985,000) to Tifton Toffees Inc., a New York corporation. In exchange, the corporation assumed $26,300 business accounts payable and a $15,000 long-term debt that the Tiftons incurred to purchase a toffee stretcher. The corporation also issued 100 shares of

[19] Section 357(a).
[20] Section 358(d).

common stock to the Tiftons. Immediately after its formation, Tifton Toffees had the following balance sheet for financial reporting purposes.

| | Book Basis |
|---|---|
| Cash | $ 12,000 |
| Accounts receivable | 73,000 |
| Inventory | 300,000 |
| Equipment | 600,000 |
| | $985,000 |
| Accounts payable | $ 26,300 |
| Long-term debt | 15,000 |
| Contributed capital (100 shares) | 943,700 |
| | $985,000 |

Mr. and Mrs. Tifton's aggregate adjusted tax basis in the operating assets was $700,000. Accordingly, they realized a $285,000 gain on the exchange. This gain equals the $985,000 amount realized ($943,700 FMV of 100 shares + $41,300 relief of liability) less the $700,000 basis. Because the Tiftons controlled the corporation immediately after the exchange, Section 351(a) applies. Because the liability relief is not considered boot, they do not recognize any of their realized gain. The basis in their 100 shares is $658,700 ($700,000 basis of contributed property − $41,300 relief of liability).

### Exceptions to the General Rule

The general rule that the relief of liability does not cause gain recognition in a Section 351 exchange facilitates the incorporation of established businesses with both assets and liabilities on the balance sheet. Business owners should be aware of two major exceptions to this rule. The first exception looks to the reason that the corporation assumed a shareholder liability as part of the exchange. If facts and circumstances suggest that the assumption was principally motivated by the shareholder's desire to avoid tax or that the assumption did not have a bona fide business purpose, the relief of liability is treated as boot.[21] This exception is particularly dangerous because its application to only a portion of the assumption causes the entire assumption to be treated as boot. Thus, the exception is a classic example of one bad apple spoiling the barrel!

**No Business Purpose Exception** — In the previous example, Tifton Toffees assumed $26,300 business accounts payable and a $15,000 business debt as partial payment for the Tiftons' operating assets. The corporation's assumption of these liabilities makes good business sense. Now change the facts by assuming that the Tiftons did not borrow the $15,000 to buy a toffee stretcher. Instead, they used the borrowed funds to buy a sports car. If the IRS audits the Tiftons and their corporation, the revenue agent could conclude that the corporation's assumption of the Tiftons' personal debt had no business purpose. As a result, the assumption of the entire $41,300 of liabilities is treated as boot. The Tiftons must recognize $41,300 of their $285,000 realized gain, and their basis in the 100 shares is $700,000 ($700,000 basis of contributed property − $41,300 relief of liability + $41,300 recognized gain).

The first exception to the general rule is a matter of motivation; the second exception is a matter of arithmetic. When a taxpayer exchanges property for stock under Section 351(a), the taxpayer's substituted basis in the stock is reduced by any liability relief. What is the

[21] Section 357(b).

result if the relief is so great that it would reduce the stock basis below zero? The tax law does not tolerate negative basis in an asset. Consequently, the shareholder must recognize gain to the extent that the liability relief exceeds the total adjusted basis of the properties contributed in the Section 351 exchange.[22]

**Relief of Liability in Excess of Basis**

Maloney LLC contributed two tracts of investment land to PMG Inc. in exchange for PMG stock under Section 351(a). At the date of contribution, tract 1 was worth $100,000, had a $28,000 basis, and was not subject to any liability. Tract 2 was worth $135,000, had a $30,000 basis, and was subject to a $100,000 mortgage. The mortgage holder agreed that PMG would assume this mortgage when title to the land transferred from Maloney to PMG. Maloney realized a $177,000 gain on the exchange: $235,000 amount realized ($135,000 FMV of stock + $100,000 liability relief) less the $58,000 total basis of tracts 1 and 2. Maloney's substituted basis in the PMG stock before reduction for the liability relief is only $58,000. Accordingly, Maloney must recognize a $42,000 gain equal to the excess of liability relief over the total basis. The gain is a capital gain because Maloney held tracts 1 and 2 as investment property. Maloney's substituted basis in its PMG stock is zero ($58,000 basis of contributed property − $100,000 relief of liability + $42,000 recognized gain).

The rule that shareholders must recognize gain to the extent of liability relief in excess of contributed basis could create a trap on the incorporation of a cash basis business. The business owner could be contributing trade accounts receivable, which have not yet been realized as income and therefore have a zero tax basis. The new corporation could be assuming the owner's trade accounts payable, which have not yet resulted in a deduction. Regardless of the relative dollar amounts of the receivables and payables, the excess of the payables over the *zero basis* of the receivables creates the potential for gain recognition. Section 357(c)(3) eliminates this potential by specifying that a liability that will give rise to a deduction when paid is excluded in determining the amount of liabilities assumed in a Section 351 exchange.

**Exclusion of Cash Basis Accounts Payable**

Mr. Deal incorporated his cash basis sole proprietorship by contributing the following business assets to DFK Inc.

| | Tax Basis |
|---|---|
| Accounts receivable ($84,500) | –0– |
| Equipment | $18,700 |
| Leasehold costs | 6,400 |
| Contributed basis | $25,100 |

In exchange for the assets, DFK issued 100 shares of common stock and assumed $24,900 trade accounts payable and a $13,000 long-term note to Union Bank. The note was secured by the equipment.

Mr. Deal was relieved of $37,900 total liabilities in the exchange. However, the trade accounts payable did not result in a deduction when they were incurred and can be excluded from consideration. Thus, the $13,000 remaining liability relief does not exceed the $25,100 basis of contributed property, and Mr. Deal does not recognize gain on the incorporation. His substituted basis in the DFK stock is $12,100 ($25,100 contributed basis − $13,000 relief of liability).

Note that the incorporation of a cash basis business can result in the shift of both income and deductions from the owner to the corporation. In the above example, DFK will recognize $84,500 ordinary income when it collects the accounts receivable contributed by

[22] Section 357(c).

Mr. Deal and will recognize $24,900 ordinary deductions when it pays the trade accounts payable assumed from Mr. Deal.[23]

## Corporate Tax Consequences of Stock Issuance

Section 1032(a) provides that a corporation does not recognize gain or loss on the receipt of money or other property in exchange for its stock (including treasury stock). This nonrecognition rule applies regardless of whether the exchange is taxable or nontaxable to the recipient of the stock. Treasury regulations expand the statutory rule by providing that a corporation does not recognize gain or loss when it uses stock as compensation for services rendered.

*Stock Issued in Exchange for Property and Services*

Mrs. Noel contributed investment property with a $27,000 basis to Farell Inc. in exchange for 1,200 shares of Farell stock. Mrs. Noel also performed consulting services for Farell for an additional 140 shares. On the date of exchange, Farell stock had a FMV of $35 a share. Because Mrs. Noel did not meet the 80 percent control requirement, Section 351(a) did not apply to her exchange of property for stock. As a result, she recognized a $15,000 capital gain on the exchange ($42,000 FMV of 1,200 shares received − $27,000 basis). She also recognized $4,900 ordinary income on the receipt of 140 shares as payment for her services. Farell recognized no gain on the issuance of 1,340 shares in exchange for $46,900 worth of property and services. If Farell's payment for the services was an ordinary business expense, it can deduct the $4,900 FMV in the computation of taxable income.

The corporation's basis in property acquired in exchange for its own stock equals the basis of the property in the hands of the contributor increased by any gain recognized by the contributor on the exchange.[24] In the preceding example, Farell's basis in the property received from Mrs. Noel was $42,000 (her $27,000 basis + $15,000 gain that she recognized). Because of this **carryover basis** rule, a corporation's tax basis in contributed property can be different than its book basis.

*Basis of MGL's Contributed Property*

Refer to the example on page 57 in which Mr. Mack, Ms. Garcia, and Ms. Lutes formed MGL Inc. Mr. Mack contributed $40,000 cash for 20 shares, Ms. Garcia contributed business inventory ($80,000 FMV and $63,000 basis) for 40 shares, and Ms. Lutes contributed $10,000 cash and business equipment ($70,000 FMV and $20,000 basis) for 40 shares. Because of Section 351(a), neither Ms. Garcia nor Ms. Lutes recognized gain on the exchange. MGL's balance sheet showing both the book and tax basis of its assets follows.

|  | Book Basis | Tax Basis |
| --- | --- | --- |
| Cash | $ 50,000 | $50,000 |
| Inventory | 80,000 | 63,000 |
| Equipment | 70,000 | 20,000 |
|  | $200,000 |  |
| Contributed capital | $200,000 |  |

In the above example, MGL will recover the basis in its inventory through cost of goods sold and the basis in its equipment through depreciation. The initial difference between the book basis and the tax basis of these assets will be eliminated over time through book/tax

[23] Rev. Rul. 80-198, 1980-2 CB 113.
[24] Section 362(a).

differences for cost of goods sold and depreciation. (Book/tax differences are discussed in Chapter 5.)

*Contributions to Corporate Capital*

**Objective 5**
Determine the basis of property received by a corporation as a contribution to capital.

Corporations often receive cash or property as a contribution to capital without issuing any stock in exchange. For example, shareholders could agree to invest additional funds in a corporation in proportion to their existing equity interests. In this case, the corporation has no reason to issue additional shares in exchange for the funds. The corporation does not recognize income on the receipt of the contributed funds, and the shareholders increase the basis of their existing shares by the amount of the contribution.[25] Occasionally, a corporation receives a contribution to capital from a nonshareholder. The most common example is a contribution of land or a long-term lease on land by a governmental unit or civic group to induce the corporation to locate its business in a particular community. The corporation's basis in property contributed by a nonshareholder is zero. In the case of a cash contribution by a nonshareholder, the corporation must reduce the basis of the property acquired with the cash by the amount of the contribution.[26]

*Nonshareholder Contribution to Capital*

The City of Nantucket contributed six acres of municipal land worth $275,000 and $2 million cash to Pawnee Inc. in exchange for Pawnee's commitment to build a light industrial plant on the land. Pawnee's total construction cost of the plant was $8.1 million. It did not recognize income on the receipt of the contribution and had the following book and tax basis in the completed property.

|  | Book Basis | Tax Basis |
|---|---|---|
| Building and structure | $8,100,000 | $6,100,000 |
| Land | 275,000 | –0– |

# PARTNERSHIP AND LLC FORMATIONS

Entrepreneurs who organize a partnership or LLC should engage an attorney to prepare a written partnership or membership agreement. This agreement should specify the amount of capital (money or property) that each partner or member will invest in the entity and the ratios in which the partners or members will share profits and losses generated by the entity. The organizers (or their attorney) could be required to file a certificate of partnership or articles of organization with the state and to pay a state filing fee.[27] The following discussion of the tax consequences of partnership formation applies to the formation of general and limited partnerships, LLPs, and LLCs.

## Section 721 Nontaxable Exchanges

**Objective 6**
Compute a partner's capital account and outside basis and a partnership's inside basis in contributed property.

According to Section 721(a), neither a partner nor a partnership recognizes gain or loss when a partner contributes property in exchange for an interest in the partnership. This Subchapter K provision is broader in scope than its Subchapter C counterpart. Unlike Section 351, Section 721 has no control requirement. Consequently, the partner's percentage interest in the partnership is irrelevant to the nontaxable exchange. Unlike Section 351,

---

[25] Reg. 1.118-1.
[26] Section 362(c).
[27] Partnerships and LLCs must capitalize their organization costs and can amortize the costs over 60 months beginning with the month in which the entity begins business. Section 709.

Section 721 creates a nontaxable exchange for the partnership as well as for the contributing partner. Finally, Section 721 makes no provision for the receipt of boot by the contributing partner.

When a partner contributes cash or property to a partnership, the contribution is recorded in the partner's capital account on the partnership books. A **capital account** is the financial record of each partner's equity in partnership assets. A partner's capital account must be credited with the amount of cash and the FMV of any property that the partner contributed.[28]

---

*Formation of MGL Partnership*

(This example is a variation of the example on page 57.) Mr. Mack, Ms. Garcia, and Ms. Lutes formed MGL Partnership by contributing cash and property in exchange for their partnership interests. Mr. Mack contributed $40,000 cash, Ms. Garcia contributed business inventory worth $80,000, and Ms. Lutes contributed $10,000 cash and business equipment worth $70,000. Here is MGL's book balance sheet immediately after formation.

|  | Book Basis |
|---|---|
| Cash | $ 50,000 |
| Inventory | 80,000 |
| Equipment | 70,000 |
|  | $200,000 |
|  |  |
| Capital: Mr. Mack | $ 40,000 |
| Ms. Garcia | 80,000 |
| Ms. Lutes | 80,000 |
|  | $200,000 |

According to their partnership agreement, the three partners have equal interests in MGL's profits and losses, even though Mr. Mack contributed only 20 percent of MGL's initial capital.

---

## Outside and Inside Basis

A partnership interest is an intangible asset representing the partner's equity in the partnership. When a partner acquires an interest as the result of a contribution, the partner's tax basis in the interest (referred to as the partner's **outside basis**) equals the amount of contributed cash plus the adjusted basis of contributed property.[29] Because of this substituted basis rule, the partner's unrecognized gain or loss on the contribution of property is captured as a difference between the partner's outside basis and capital account. The partnership's tax basis in contributed property (referred to as the partnership's **inside basis**) equals the basis of the property in the hands of the contributing partner.[30]

---

*Tax Consequences to MGL Partners and Partnership*

Because Mr. Mack contributed cash in exchange for his partnership interest, he realized no gain or loss, and the outside basis in his interest is $40,000. Ms. Garcia's tax basis in the contributed inventory was $63,000. Therefore, she realized a $17,000 gain on the exchange ($80,000 FMV of partnership interest received − $63,000 basis surrendered), recognized no taxable gain, and has a $63,000 outside basis in her interest. Ms. Lutes's tax basis in the contributed equipment was $20,000. Therefore, she realized a $50,000 gain on the exchange

---

[28] See the capital account maintenance rules in Reg. 1.704-1(b)(2)(iv).

[29] Section 722.

[30] Section 723.

($70,000 FMV of partnership interest received *in exchange for the equipment* − $20,000 basis surrendered), recognized no taxable gain, and has a $30,000 outside basis in her interest ($10,000 cash + $20,000 basis of equipment). MGL's balance sheet showing both the book basis and the tax (inside) basis of its assets follows.

|  | Book Basis | Tax (Inside) Basis |
|---|---|---|
| Cash | $ 50,000 | $ 50,000 |
| Inventory | 80,000 | 63,000 |
| Equipment | 70,000 | 20,000 |
|  | $200,000 | $133,000 |
| Capital: Mr. Mack | $ 40,000 | $ 40,000 |
| Ms. Garcia | 80,000 | 63,000 |
| Ms. Lutes | 80,000 | 30,000 |
|  | $200,000 | $133,000 |

The difference between a partnership's book and tax basis in its contributed property has significant tax consequences once the partnership begins operations. These consequences are explored in Chapter 7 in the section entitled Allocations with Respect to Contributed Property.

## Disguised Sales

A partner who sells appreciated property to a partnership for cash must recognize gain on the sale. In order to avoid such gain recognition, the partner might try to take advantage of the Subchapter K rules regarding property contributions by partners and cash distributions to partners, both of which are nontaxable transactions. Instead of selling the property to the partnership, the partner could contribute the property in exchange for an increased partnership interest. Then in a second transaction, the partnership could distribute cash to the partner in an amount equal to the FMV of the property. Provided that the amount of the distribution does not exceed the partner's outside basis, the partner would not recognize gain on receipt of the cash.[31]

Subchapter K counters this tax avoidance strategy with a **disguised sale** rule. If a partner contributes property to a partnership and the partnership makes a *related* cash distribution to the partner, the contribution and distribution are treated as a sale of the property.[32] If the related distribution is less than the FMV of the entire property, the partner must treat the transaction as a sale of a portion of the property and a contribution of the rest. The basis of the portion sold is computed by multiplying the total basis of the property by the ratio of the cash distribution to the FMV of the entire property.

*Disguised Sale to MGL Partnership*

Assume that MGL Partnership agreed that Ms. Garcia should receive a $4,000 cash distribution when she contributed her inventory to the partnership. Because the contribution and distribution were related, Ms. Garcia must treat this transaction as a sale of a portion of the inventory to MGL. Her amount realized on the sale equals the $4,000 distribution, and the basis in the inventory deemed sold is $3,150 [$63,000 total basis × ($4,000/$80,000 total FMV of

---

[31] Sections 731(a)(1) and 733.

[32] Section 707(a)(2)(B). According to Reg. 1.707-3(c), if a contribution by a partner and a distribution to that partner occur within a two-year period, they are presumed to be a disguised sale. The partnership can rebut this presumption if facts and circumstances clearly establish that the contribution and distribution were unrelated, independent transactions.

inventory)]. Ms. Garcia must recognize $850 ordinary gain on the disguised sale ($4,000 amount realized – $3,150 basis), and MGL has a $4,000 cost basis in the inventory purchased in the disguised sale. MGL's balance sheet reflecting Ms. Garcia's part sale/part contribution of inventory follows.

|  | Book Basis | Tax (Inside) Basis |
| --- | --- | --- |
| Cash | $ 46,000 | $ 46,000 |
| Inventory | 80,000 | 63,850 |
| Equipment | 70,000 | 20,000 |
|  | $196,000 | $129,850 |
| Capital: Mr. Mack | $ 40,000 | $ 40,000 |
| Ms. Garcia | 76,000 | 59,850 |
| Ms. Lutes | 80,000 | 30,000 |
|  | $196,000 | $129,850 |

Although the book basis of MGL's inventory is $80,000, Ms. Garcia's capital account reflects only the $76,000 FMV of the inventory that she contributed. The partnership's $63,850 inside basis in its inventory equals the $59,850 carryover basis of the *contributed* inventory ($63,000 total basis − $3,150 basis of purchased inventory) plus the $4,000 cost of the *purchased* inventory. Ms. Garcia's outside basis in her MGL interest is $59,850 (basis of contributed inventory).

## Partnership Assumption of Liabilities in a Section 721 Exchange

**Objective 7**
Calculate the effect on outside basis when a partnership assumes a partner liability.

When a partner contributes property in exchange for a partnership interest and the partnership assumes a liability of the partner as part of the transaction, the assumption is treated as a cash distribution to the partner.[33] If the assumption has a bona fide business purpose, this deemed cash distribution does not trigger the disguised sale rule and simply decreases the partner's outside basis in the interest.[34]

All partnership liabilities, including those assumed from a partner, are shared among the partners for purposes of determining outside basis. Specifically, each partner's share of partnership liabilities is treated as a cash contribution that increases basis in the partnership interest. Thus, when a partnership assumes a partner's liability, the partner's outside basis is simultaneously decreased (by the amount of the assumption) and increased (by the partner's share of partnership liabilities). The other partners' outside bases are increased or decreased by the net change in their respective shares of partnership liabilities.

A partner's share of partnership liabilities is determined under a formidable set of rules contained in the Section 752 regulations. These rules distinguish between recourse and nonrecourse liabilities. A partnership liability is **recourse** to the extent that any partner has personal liability for repayment. The simplified rule is that recourse liabilities are shared among the *general* partners based on their relative loss-sharing ratios.[35] A partnership liability is **nonrecourse** to the extent that no partner has personal liability for repayment. In other words, a nonrecourse liability is secured only by specific partnership assets pledged

---

[33] Section 752(b).
[34] Reg. 1.707-5(a)(6) defines "qualified" partner liabilities that a partnership can assume without triggering the disguised sale rules.
[35] Reg. 1.752-2(b)(1).

as collateral. The simplified rule is that nonrecourse liabilities are share<br>
ners based on their profit-sharing ratios.[36]

---

*Partnership Assumption of Partner Liability*

Riley Inc. contributed land ($200,000 FMV and $160,000 basis) to Cheyne Partnership in ex<br>
change for a general partnership interest. Riley's profit and loss–sharing ratio is 40 percent.<br>
The land was subject to a $150,000 recourse mortgage, which Cheyne assumed (with per-<br>
mission of the mortgage holder). Immediately before the contribution, Cheyne had $48,000<br>
recourse liabilities and no nonrecourse liabilities. Cheyne's assumption of the mortgage is<br>
treated as a $150,000 cash distribution to Riley, while Riley's $79,200 share of Cheyne's total<br>
liabilities (40 percent × $198,000) is treated as a cash contribution to the partnership. Con-<br>
sequently, Riley's outside basis in its Cheyne interest is $89,200, computed as follows.

| | |
|---|---|
| Basis of contributed land *Carryover* | $160,000 |
| Deemed cash distribution | (150,000) *liab. assumed* |
| Deemed cash contribution | 79,200 *his liab. resp.* |
| Outside basis | $ 89,200 |

*$150,000 Riley Contr.*<br>
*+ 48,000 already had*

Remember that Riley's admission to Cheyne Partnership affected the other partners' out-<br>
side bases in their partnership interests. Before Riley's admission, their aggregate share of<br>
Cheyne liabilities was $48,000 (100 percent × $48,000). After Riley's admission, their aggre-<br>
gate share increased to $118,800 [60 percent × ($48,000 + $150,000 assumed mortgage)].<br>
Consequently, the other partners' aggregate outside bases increased by $70,800 ($118,800<br>
postadmission share − $48,000 preadmission share of Cheyne liabilities).

Cash distributions from a partnership cannot decrease the partner's outside basis below<br>
zero. Therefore, a partner who receives either an actual or a deemed cash distribution that<br>
exceeds outside basis must recognize the excess as capital gain.[37] This arithmetic creates a<br>
problem if a partner's basis in contributed property is less than the *net* relief of liability re-<br>
sulting from the contribution.

---

*Relief of Liability in Excess of Basis*

Assume that in the previous example, Riley's basis in the contributed land was only $45,000.<br>
In this case, Riley's $70,800 net relief of liability ($150,000 mortgage assumed − $79,200<br>
share of total liabilities) exceeds the contributed basis by $25,800.

| | |
|---|---|
| Basis of contributed land | $ 45,000 |
| Deemed cash distribution | (150,000) *Loss ration* |
| Deemed cash contribution | 79,200 *40% × total partnership liab. assumed* |
| Distribution in excess of basis | $ (25,800) |

As a result, Riley must recognize a $25,800 capital gain and take a zero basis in its Cheyne<br>
interest.

If a partner contributes property subject to a liability for which no partner is personally<br>
liable (nonrecourse liability), the Section 752 regulations contain a special sharing rule to

---

[36]Reg. 1.752-3(a)(3).<br>
[37]Section 731(a).

protect the partner from gain recognition.[38] The contributing partner is allocated a preemptive share of the nonrecourse liability equal to any excess of the liability over the basis of the property. Only the remainder of the nonrecourse liability is shared among the partners according to their profit-sharing ratios.

| *Sharing of Nonrecourse Liability on Contributed Property* | Assume that in the previous example, Cheyne is an LLC rather than a general partnership so that no member has personal liability for any of Cheyne's debts. In this case, the mortgage on the contributed land becomes a nonrecourse liability. Riley's preemptive share of the mortgage under the special sharing rule is $105,000 ($150,000 mortgage − $45,000 basis). Riley's share of the $45,000 remainder of the mortgage and $48,000 of other liabilities is $37,200 (40 percent × $93,000). Consequently, Riley recognizes no gain because of Cheyne's assumption of the mortgage and has a $37,200 outside basis in its Cheyne interest. |
|---|---|

| | |
|---|---:|
| Basis of contributed land | $ 45,000 |
| Deemed cash distribution | (150,000) |
| Deemed cash contributions: | |
| Preemptive share of mortgage | 105,000 |
| Share of remaining liabilities | 37,200 |
| Outside basis | $ 37,200 |

# OTHER STRATEGIES FOR TRANSFERRING PROPERTY TO CONTROLLED ENTITIES

The nontaxable exchange provisions of Sections 351 and 721 are extremely useful to shareholders and partners who want to avoid recognizing gain on the transfer of appreciated property to their business entity. Unfortunately, both sections also prevent the recognition of loss on the transfer of property with an adjusted basis in excess of FMV. As a result, shareholders and partners should consider other ways to make devalued property available for business use by their entity.

## Sales of Property to Controlled Entities

**Objective 8**
Identify the tax issues when an owner sells or leases property to an entity.

The sale of property by an owner to an entity is a taxable transaction. Even so, if the owner recognizes a loss on the sale, the loss may or may not be allowed as a deduction, depending on the extent of the owner's control of the entity.

### Sales of Devalued Property to Corporations

Section 267(a)(1) disallows the deduction of losses recognized on sales or exchanges between related parties. The term **related parties,** as defined in Section 267(b), includes an individual shareholder and a corporation if the shareholder owns, directly or indirectly, more than 50 percent of the FMV of the outstanding stock.[39] An individual's indirect ownership is determined under a set of **attribution rules.** For example, any stock owned by an individual's family (brothers and sisters, spouse, ancestors, and lineal descendants) is attributed to (indirectly owned by) that individual.[40] Shareholders who plan to sell devalued

---

[38] Reg. 1.752-3(a)(2).

[39] Section 267(f) has a special rule that defers, rather than disallows, a loss realized on the sale of property by a *corporate* shareholder to a 50 percent or more controlled subsidiary.

[40] Section 267(c) has the complete set of attribution rules for determining indirect ownership for purposes of Section 267(a).

property to a closely held corporation to avoid the Section 351 nonrecognition rule should make sure that Section 267(a) does not defeat their purpose.

| *Sale of Devalued Property to Corporation* | Mrs. Wong, Mrs. Hehmann, and Mr. Troy formed WHT Inc. Each contributed $15,000 cash for 50 shares of WHT's common stock. Mrs. Wong also sold an investment asset ($20,000 FMV and $27,600 adjusted basis) to WHT, which paid for the asset by issuing its $20,000 note to Mrs. Wong. WHT's balance sheet immediately after formation showed the following. |
|---|---|

|  | *Book/Tax Basis* |
|---|---|
| Cash | $45,000 |
| Business asset | 20,000 |
|  | $65,000 |
| Notes payable to Mrs. Wong | $20,000 |
| Contributed capital (150 shares) | 45,000 |
|  | $65,000 |

Mrs. Wong realized a $7,600 loss on the asset sale. Assuming that the three WHT shareholders have no family ties, Mrs. Wong owns only 33.3 percent of WHT's stock, and she can deduct the loss. But what if Mrs. Wong and Mrs. Hehmann are sisters? In this case, Mrs. Wong directly and indirectly owns 66.7 percent of WHT's stock, and she and the corporation are related parties. As a result, Mrs. Wong can never deduct her $7,600 loss.

Regardless of whether Mrs. Wong and WHT are related parties, WHT's tax basis in the asset is its $20,000 cost. If Mrs. Wong and WHT are related parties, WHT can use Mrs. Wong's $7,600 disallowed loss to offset any gain recognized on a future disposition of the asset.[41] For example, if WHT sells the asset for $28,000, it will recognize only a $400 tax gain ($8,000 realized gain − $7,600 previously disallowed loss).

### Sales of Devalued Property to Partnerships

It should come as no surprise that the Section 267 loss disallowance rule has a counterpart in Subchapter K. Section 707(b)(1) disallows the deduction of losses recognized on sales or exchanges of property between a partner and partnership if the partner owns, directly or indirectly, more than 50 percent of either the capital or profits in the partnership. Indirect ownership of capital or profits is determined by reference to the Section 267 attribution rules. If a partner has a disallowed loss on the sale of property to a partnership, the partnership can use the disallowed loss to offset any gain recognized on a future disposition of the property.

### Sales of Capital Assets to Controlled Entities

If an owner recognizes a gain on sale of property to an entity, the gain is taxable without exception. Generally, the character of the gain depends on the character of the property (capital asset, noncapital asset, or Section 1231 property) in the hands of the seller. In the case of a sale to a controlled entity, the character of the *seller's* gain depends on the character of the property in the hands of the *purchaser*.

Section 1239 provides that gain recognized from the sale or exchange of property to a related person is ordinary income if the property is depreciable or amortizable in the hands

[41] Section 267(d).

of the purchaser. The definition of related party is basically the same as the definition in Section 267.

| | |
|---|---|
| *Sale of Section 1231 Property to Controlled Corporation* | Mrs. and Mrs. Zeff sold a commercial building ($266,000 basis) to ZVP Inc. for $500,000 cash. The Zeffs recognized a $234,000 taxable gain on this sale. If they do not own, directly or indirectly, more than 50 percent of the FMV of ZVP's outstanding stock, the character of their gain is determined by reference to their use of the building. Because the Zeffs used the building as depreciable realty subject to straight-line depreciation, the entire gain is a Section 1231 gain. If this is the Zeffs' only Section 1231 gain for the year, it is treated as long-term capital gain taxed at a 15 or 25 percent preferential rate.[42] If the Zeffs own more than 50 percent of the FMV of ZVP's stock, the character of their $234,000 gain is ordinary because the building is depreciable realty to ZVP. |

Section 707(b)(2) is an *almost* identical characterization rule for gains recognized on sales of property between a partner and a controlled partnership. Such gains are characterized as ordinary income if the property is *not a capital asset* in the hands of the purchaser. (Such subtle discrepancies among rules fascinate tax professors and dismay everyone else.)

| | |
|---|---|
| *Sale of Capital Asset to Controlled Partnership* | Mr. and Mrs. Zoloff sold investment land ($266,000 basis) to ZVP Partnership for $500,000 cash. The Zoloffs recognized a $234,000 taxable gain on this sale. If they do not own, directly or indirectly, more than a 50 percent capital or profits interest in ZVP, their gain is a capital gain because they held the land as a capital asset. If they own more than 50 percent of ZVP's capital or profits, the character of their $234,000 gain depends on how the partnership holds the land. If ZVP holds the land as a long-term investment, it is a capital asset to the partnership, and the Zoloffs have their capital gain. If, however, ZVP subdivides and develops the land for sale to customers, the land is inventory to the partnership, and the Zoloffs' gain is ordinary. |

## Leases of Property to Controlled Entities

If an owner holds property that the entity could use in its business, the owner can avoid any tax issues associated with a sale or exchange of the property by simply leasing it to the entity. The rent paid by the entity represents a source of cash flow (and ordinary income) to the owner and is deductible by the entity. If the entity is a corporation, the rent should reflect the fair rental value of the property (the rent that an unrelated lessor would charge in an arm's-length lease). If the rent paid is unreasonably high, the IRS might reclassify some portion as a nondeductible constructive dividend.

| | |
|---|---|
| *Constructive Dividend for Unreasonable Rent* | Mr. and Mrs. Eckel are the sole shareholders of DoubleE Inc. They own commercial real estate that they rent to DoubleE for use in the corporate business. The corporation pays $35,000 annual rent to the Eckels, which it deducts as an ordinary business expense. The IRS agent who audited DoubleE's most recent tax return determined that the annual fair rental value of the property was only $22,500. Therefore, the agent disallowed $12,500 of DoubleE's rent deduction and increased its tax accordingly. |

---

[42] The portion of the gain that does not exceed the accumulated depreciation on the building is unrecaptured Section 1250 gain taxed at 25 percent. Section 1(h)(7).

*Rent Income as Passive Activity Income*

As a general rule, a rental activity conducted by a person subject to the passive activity loss rules (individuals, estates, trusts, closely held corporations, and personal service corporations) is a passive activity. Consequently, income from rental activities is passive activity income, which allows the recipient to deduct an equal amount of loss from other passive activities. Reg. 1.469-2(f)(5) contains an important exception to this general rule: Rental income does not qualify as passive activity income if the property is rented for use in a business in which the owner of the property materially participates. This **self-rental rule** prevents the owners of passthrough entities from creating passive activity income by leasing property to the entity.

| Self-Rental Rule | Ms. Small is a meber of Asherwood LLC, which operates a chain of retail stores. Ms. Small owns commercial real estate that she leases to the LLC for $19,500 annual rent. The LLC deducts the rent payment in the computation of ordinary business income. If Ms. Small materially participates in Asherwood's business, her share of the LLC's business income (or loss) is active (rather than passive). Because of the self-rental rule, her rental income from Asherwood is also active. On the other hand, if Ms. Small does not materially participate in Asherwood's business, both her share of the LLC's business income (or loss) and her rental income are passive. |
|---|---|

## Conclusion

In Chapter 3, we explored the tax consequences of the decision to organize a new business as a corporation or as a passthrough entity. These tax consequences are generally benign. Taxpayers can contribute appreciated property to a new entity in exchange for equity at no tax cost, and the entity can assume the contributor's business liabilities as part of the exchange. The chapter also evaluated alternatives to property contributions, such as the sale or lease of property by owners to their entity. Exhibit 3.1 provides a chart that summarizes the major tax issues introduced in Chapter 3 and compares the answers pertaining to corporations with the answers pertaining to partnerships and LLCs. In Chapter 4, we will continue to explore tax strategies for new businesses as we turn our attention to compensation issues for both owners and employees.

**EXHIBIT 3.1 Comparison Chart**

| Tax Issue | Corporation | Partnership/LLC |
|---|---|---|
| Can owners transfer appreciated property in exchange for equity without recognizing gain? | Yes, if transferors have 80% or more control of the corporation after the exchange. | Yes. |
| What is the owner's basis in equity received in a nontaxable exchange? | Basis of contributed property (substituted basis). | Basis of contributed property (substituted basis). |
| Can owners receive property other than equity in a nontaxable exchange? | Yes, but receipt of boot triggers gain recognition. | Yes, but disguised sale rule may cause gain recognition. |
| Can the entity assume an owner's liability in a nontaxable exchange without triggering gain recognition? | Yes, if no tax avoidance motive and a business purpose. | Yes. |
| Does an owner's relief of liability in excess of transferred basis trigger gain recognition? | Yes. | Yes. |

*continued on page 72*

**EXHIBIT 3.1 Comparison Chart**—continued

| Tax Issue | Corporation | Partnership/LLC |
| --- | --- | --- |
| Does an entity recognize gain on the exchange of equity for property? | No. | No. |
| What is the entity's basis in property received in a nontaxable exchange? | Carryover basis. | Carryover basis. |
| Can owners recognize a loss on sale of property to an entity? | No, if the shareholder owns more than 50% of the FMV of the corporate stock. | No, if the partner owns more than 50% of the partnership profits or capital. |
| Can owners recognize capital gain on sale of a capital asset to an entity? | No, if the shareholder owns more than 50% of the FMV of the corporate stock and the asset is depreciable or amortizable by the corporation. | No, if the partner owns more than 50% of the partnership profits or capital and the asset is not a capital asset to the partnership. |
| Can owners generate passive activity income by leasing property to an entity? | Yes, for a C corporation. No, for an S corporation if the shareholder materially participates in the business. | No, if the partner materially participates in the business. |

## Key Terms

| | | |
| --- | --- | --- |
| attribution rules  *68* | inside basis  *64* | publicly traded partnership |
| boot  *58* | limited liability company | (PTP)  *52* |
| capital account  *64* | (LLC)  *50* | recourse liability  *66* |
| carryover basis  *62* | limited liability partnership | related parties  *68* |
| corporation  *50* | (LLP)  *50* | S corporation  *50* |
| disguised sale  *65* | limited partnership  *50* | self-rental rule  *71* |
| disregarded entity  *51* | net operating loss | sole proprietorship  *50* |
| fair market value | (NOL)  *54* | Subchapter C  *55* |
| (FMV)  *57* | nonrecourse liability  *66* | Subchapter K  *55* |
| general partnership  *50* | outside basis  *64* | Subchapter S  *50* |
| initial public offering | partnership  *50* | substituted basis  *57* |
| (IPO)  *51* | passthrough entity  *50* | |

## Questions and Problems for Discussion

1. Compare the extent of the owners' personal liability for debt incurred by general partnerships, limited partnerships, LLPs, and LLCs.
2. What are the nontax and the tax advantages of operating a business as a single-member LLC rather than as a sole proprietorship?
3. What are the nontax and tax advantages of operating a business as an LLC rather than as a limited partnership?
4. If a closely held corporation pays no dividends to its shareholders, are the shareholders avoiding the double tax on corporate income?
5. Why are constructive dividends a more important issue for individual shareholders than for corporate shareholders of closely held corporations?
6. Identify three differences between the nonrecognition rules of Section 351 (exchange of property for stock) and Section 721 (exchange of property for partnership interest).

7. Explain the difference between a substituted basis and a carryover basis in an asset.

8. In a closely held corporation in which shareholders have loaned substantial sums to the business, what factors might suggest to the IRS that the shareholder debt should be treated as disguised equity?

9. What is the difference between a partner's capital interest and the partner's interest in profit and loss?

10. Distinguish between the terms *outside basis* and *inside basis* in the partnership context.

11. Compare the consequences of the receipt of boot in connection with the exchange of property for corporate stock with the receipt of a distribution in connection with the exchange of property for a partnership interest.

12. Thames LLC needs to borrow $50,000 to meet its immediate working capital needs. A commercial lender has agreed to make the loan if Ms. Ames, who owns a 20 percent interest in the LLC, will personally guarantee it. If Ms. Ames agrees, what effect should the new LLC liability have on her basis in her LLC interest?

13. Which tax planning maxim might apply to a transaction in which a shareholder leases property to a controlled corporation?

## Application Problems

Use the tax rates printed on the inside front cover of the text to make any tax calculations required in the following problems.

1. Mrs. Rei, who is in the 35 percent marginal tax bracket, is the sole owner of Rei Company, a delivery business. This year, the company generated $140,000 taxable income (before accounting for any payments or distributions to Mrs. Rei). Compute the total tax cost of this income under each of the following assumptions. Ignore any effect of payroll taxes in making your computations.
   a. Rei Company is a sole proprietorship. The company distributed $100,000 cash to Mrs. Rei.
   b. Rei Company is an S corporation that paid a $75,000 salary to Mrs. Rei.
   c. Rei Company is an S corporation that paid a $75,000 salary and distributed $10,000 cash to Mrs. Rei.
   d. Rei Company is a corporation that paid no salary or dividend to Mrs. Rei.
   e. Rei Company is a corporation that paid a $75,000 salary and distributed a $10,000 dividend to Mrs. Rei.

2. Mr. And Mrs. O'Tool are the sole shareholders of Tolera Inc., a public relations business. Their youngest daughter was married this year, and they invited Tolera's entire staff and clientele to the lavish reception. Because the reception provided so much business goodwill, Tolera paid the $73,000 cost and deducted 50 percent as business entertainment.
   a. Determine the effect on Tolera's taxable income if the IRS reclassifies the $73,000 payment as a constructive dividend.
   b. Determine the effect on Mr. and Mrs. O'Tool's taxable income if the IRS reclassifies the $73,000 payment as a constructive dividend.

3. Edlin Company incurred a $500,000 loss this year (year 0). Compute the NPV of the tax savings from the loss under each of the following assumptions.
   a. Edlin Company is a corporation that expects to generate $200,000 net profit in years 1, 2, and 3. It uses an 8 percent discount rate to compute NPV.
   b. Edlin Company is a single-member LLC owned by Randolph Inc., which generated $30 million taxable income this year.

*disregarded → sole prop.*

c. Edlin Company is a single-member LLC owned by Mr. Townsend, whose taxable income before consideration of the Edlin loss is $942,000. → 35%.

d. Edlin Company is an S corporation owned by Mr. and Mrs. Loew. Before consideration of the Edlin loss, they have $190,000 taxable income this year. On their Form 1040 filed two years ago, their taxable income exceeded $1 million (35 percent marginal tax rate).

4. Mr. Smith and Ms. Litwin formed SL Inc. by contributing business property in exchange for 50 shares each of SL's stock. Mr. Smith's property had a $45,000 FMV and a $31,000 basis; Ms. Litwin's property had a $45,000 FMV and an $18,000 basis.
   a. What is the FMV of the 50 shares received by each contributor?
   b. How much gain does each contributor realize and recognize on the exchange?
   c. What is the basis of each contributor's 50 SL shares?
   d. What is SL's book and tax basis in the contributed property?

5. Prelude Inc. contributed commercial real estate ($900,000 FMV and $370,000 adjusted basis) to PRT Inc. in exchange for 5,000 shares of PRT's only class of stock. Determine Prelude's tax basis in the 5,000 shares and PRT's book and tax basis in the real estate under the following assumptions.
   a. Before the contribution, PRT had 60,000 shares of outstanding stock, 53,000 of which Prelude owned.
   b. Before the contribution, PRT had 60,000 shares of outstanding stock, 30,000 of which Prelude owned.
   c. Before the contribution, PRT had 1,000 shares of outstanding stock, none of which Prelude owned.

6. Mrs. Sims, Mrs. Tan, and Mr. Underhill formed STU Inc. by making the following property contributions.

*$1200 per share*

|  | Tax Basis | FMV |  |
|---|---|---|---|
| Mrs. Sims | $26,000 | $30,000 | 25 shares |
| *10,000 cash* Mrs. Tan | 53,000 | 50,000 | 50 shares |
| Mr. Underhill | 12,000 | 30,000 | 25 |

Mrs. Tan also contributed $10,000 cash. Mrs. Sims received 25 STU shares, Mrs. Tan received 50 shares, and Mr. Underhill received 25 shares.
   a. What is the FMV of each share of STU stock?
   b. How much gain or loss does each contributor realize and recognize on the exchange?
   c. What is the basis of each contributor's STU stock?
   d. What is STU's book and tax basis in the contributed property?

7. Refer to the facts in the preceding problem, but assume that Mr. Underhill received only 21 shares and $4,800 cash in exchange for his contributed property.
   a. How much gain does Mr. Underhill realize and recognize on the exchange?
   b. What is the basis of Mr. Underhill's 21 shares?
   c. What is STU's book and tax basis in Mr. Underhill's contributed property?

8. Refer to the facts in the two preceding problems, but assume that it was Mrs. Sims who received only 21 shares and $4,800 cash in exchange for her contributed property.
   a. How much gain does Mrs. Sims realize and recognize on the exchange?
   b. What is the basis of Mrs. Sims's 21 shares?
   c. What is STU's book and tax basis in Mrs. Sims's contributed property?

9. Mr. Badgett plans to incorporate his accrual basis landscaping business. The aggregate adjusted basis in his business assets is $312,000, and the FMV is $500,000. He has $40,000 business liabilities.

   a. If Mr. Badgett contributes his business assets and liabilities to a new corporation in exchange for 100 shares of stock, calculate his realized and recognized gain on the exchange.  *FMV stock = 460,000 (Net assets)*

   b. Determine Mr. Badgett's basis in the 100 shares and the corporation's tax basis in the assets immediately after the exchange.

   c. How would your answers to parts (a) and (b) change if Mr. Badgett's aggregate adjusted basis in the assets was only $27,750?

   *when lia exceeds aggregate basis, gain should be recognized*

10. Ms. Olan incorporated her accrual basis sole proprietorship by transferring the following assets and liabilities to Spring Day Inc. in exchange for 100 percent of Spring Day's stock.

|  | Tax Basis | FMV |
|---|---|---|
| Cash | $ 35,000 | $ 35,000 |
| Inventory | 48,000 | 55,000 |
| Furniture and fixtures | 112,000 | 112,000 |
| Real property | 379,000 | 600,000 |
|  | $574,000 | $802,000 |
| Unsecured debt | $ 12,000 | $ 12,000 |
| Mortgage on real property | 75,000 | 75,000 |
|  | $ 87,000 | $ 87,000 |

   Ms. Olan incurred the unsecured debt seven months ago when she borrowed $12,000 to invest in a dot-com business that went bankrupt.

   a. Compute Ms. Olan's realized and recognized gain assuming that Spring Day's assumption of both the unsecured debt and the mortgage has a business purpose and was not motivated by tax avoidance.

   b. Compute Ms. Olan's realized and recognized gain assuming that Spring Day's assumption of the unsecured debt had no bona fide business purpose.

11. Mr. Pride incorporated his sole proprietorship by transferring the following assets and liabilities to PPX Inc. in exchange for 100 percent of PPX's stock.

|  | Tax Basis |
|---|---|
| Accounts receivable ($96,100) | –0– |
| Tangible business assets | $53,200 |
|  | $53,200 |
| Rent payable | $ 7,300 |
| Interest payable | 2,500 |
| Note payable | 50,000 |
|  | $59,800 |

   *ignore cuz cash basis*

   Because he is a cash basis taxpayer, Mr. Pride has not taken a deduction for the rent or interest payable. He borrowed the $50,000 to meet the working capital needs of his business.

a. Compute Mr. Pride's gain recognized on the incorporation.

b. What is the tax basis in his PPX stock?

12. NHK Inc. transferred the following operating assets to West Inc. in exchange for 100 percent of West's stock.

| | Tax Basis | FMV |
|---|---|---|
| Accounts receivable | $ 404,000 | $ 404,000 |
| Inventory | 834,000 | 950,000 |
| Equipment | 275,000 | 200,000 |
| Plant and land | 5,000,000 | 8,600,000 |
| | $6,513,000 | $10,154,000 |

The plant and land are subject to a mortgage that West assumed in the incorporation.

a. Compute NHK's realized and recognized gain, its basis in the West stock, and West's aggregate tax basis in its assets if the mortgage was $5,250,000.

b. How would your answers in part (a) change if the mortgage was $7,000,000?

13. Midland Meat Packing plans to build a new beef-processing plant in the Midwest. Phelps County, Nebraska, has offered Midland 100 acres of land valued at $75,000 plus $500,000 cash if it will locate the plant in the county. What are the tax consequences to Midland if it accepts this offer and builds a plant costing $3 million on the contributed land?

14. Ms. Lowinsky and Mrs. Kormera formed LK Partnership as equal partners. Ms. Lowinsky contributed equipment ($30,000 FMV and $40,000 adjusted basis) and land ($70,000 FMV and $20,000 adjusted basis) in exchange for her 50 percent interest. Mrs. Kormera contributed $100,000 cash in exchange for her 50 percent interest.

a. Prepare a beginning balance sheet that shows LK's book and tax (inside) basis in its assets and each partner's capital account.

b. Compute Ms. Lowinsky's realized and recognized gain or loss and determine the outside basis in her partnership interest.

c. Determine the outside basis in Mrs. Kormera's partnership interest.

15. Ms. Dale contributed $40,000 cash and investment land ($35,000 FMV and $22,000 adjusted basis) and Ms. Ervin contributed business equipment ($50,000 FMV and $60,000 adjusted basis) to form DE Partnership.

a. Determine each partner's capital account balance.

b. Determine each partner's outside basis in her DE interest.

c. Determine DE's inside basis in the contributed land and equipment.

16. Toby Inc. contributed investment land ($600,000 FMV and $210,000 adjusted basis) to Harrison LLC in exchange for a 10 percent membership interest. Immediately after the contribution, Harrison mortgaged the land for $350,000 and distributed $200,000 of the borrowed funds to Toby. The mortgage is Harrison's only liability. Assuming that Toby's contribution and distribution must be treated as a disguised sale, compute the following.

a. Toby's recognized gain on sale.

b. Toby's outside basis in its LLC interest immediately following its receipt of the cash distribution.

c. Harrison's book and tax basis in the investment land.

17. Refer to the facts in problem 16. Assume that Toby and Harrison LLC can establish that Toby's contribution and Harrison's subsequent cash distribution were unrelated and independent events. On this assumption, compute the following.

  *a.* Toby's recognized gain on the contribution of land.

  *b.* Toby's outside basis in its LLC interest immediately following its receipt of the cash distribution.

  *c.* Harrison's book and tax basis in the investment land.

18. Mr. Habib contributed real estate ($400,000 FMV and $250,000 adjusted basis) to Mega Partnership in exchange for a 20 percent general interest. The property was transferred subject to a $100,000 recourse mortgage. Mega has $32,000 other recourse liabilities and no nonrecourse liabilities.

  *a.* Calculate Mr. Habib's realized and recognized gain on the contribution.

  *b.* Determine Mr. Habib's outside basis in his Mega interest.

  *c.* How would your answers to parts (*a*) and (*b*) change if Mr. Habib's adjusted basis in the real estate was $45,000?

  *d.* How would your answers to parts (*a*) and (*b*) change if Mega is an LLC?

19. Mrs. Barker contributed business assets ($150,000 FMV and $62,000 adjusted basis) to Major Partnership. These assets were subject to a $90,000 recourse liability that Major assumed. How much gain must Mrs. Barker recognize on the contribution, and what is the outside basis in her partnership interest under each of the following assumptions?

  *a.* The liability assumed from Mrs. Barker is Major's only liability, and Mrs. Barker's share as a partner is $75,000.

  *b.* The liability assumed from Mrs. Barker is Major's only liability, and Mrs. Barker's share as a partner is $10,000.

  *c.* Major has other liabilities in addition to the liability assumed from Mrs. Barker, and Mrs. Barker's share of the total liabilities is $112,000.

20. Mr. Lauer contributed investment land ($200,000 FMV and $111,300 adjusted basis) to Isaax LLC in exchange for a 25 percent membership interest. The land was subject to a mortgage that became the LLC's only liability. Determine Mr. Lauer's outside basis in his LLC interest under each of the following assumptions.

  *a.* The principal amount of the mortgage was $100,000.

  *b.* The principal amount of the mortgage was $160,000.

21. Mr. Trent owns a 35 percent interest in TV Partnership. He recently sold investment land to TV for $100,000 cash. His basis in the land was $140,000. Determine the tax consequences of the sale to Mr. Trent and to TV, assuming the following.

  *a.* Mr. Trent is not related to any other partner.

  *b.* Mr. Trent's daughter, Alma, owns a 30 percent interest in TV.

  *c.* Assuming the facts in part (*b*), compute TV's book gain and tax gain if it sells the land purchased from Mr. Trent for $161,500.

22. Conroe LLC owns an undeveloped tract of land with a $400,000 cost basis. The land is an investment (capital) asset. Conroe is planning to sell the land to CFG, a real estate development partnership, for $1,200,000. CFG will improve and subdivide the land (i.e., convert it to inventory) and sell it in one-half acre residential lots. Determine the tax consequences of the sale to Conroe and CFG assuming the following.

  *a.* No partner in Conroe owns any direct or indirect interest in CFG.

  *b.* Mr. and Mrs. Conroe own a 75 percent interest in Conroe and a 10 percent interest in CFG.

  *c.* Mr. and Mrs. Conroe own a 75 percent interest in Conroe and a 55 percent interest in CFG.

23. Mr. and Mrs. Bush, the sole shareholders of Rose Corporation, own real estate that they lease to Rose for use in the corporate business. The annual rental is $24,000. Rose pays tax at a 34 percent marginal rate, while the Bushes pay tax at a 35 percent marginal rate.

    *a.* Calculate Rose's after-tax cost and the Bushes' after-tax cash flow from the rental arrangement.

    *b.* Given that the Bushes pay tax at a higher tax rate than Rose, is the rental arrangement an effective tax planning strategy? Identify the possible tax reasons that the Bushes prefer to own the rental property rather than transferring ownership to their corporation.

## Issue Recognition Problems

Identify the tax issue or issues suggested by the following situations and state each issue in the form of a question.

1. Mr. and Mrs. Javon are the sole shareholders in Javon Lawn Ornaments. This year, the corporation hired Mr. Javon's sister to redecorate its corporate offices. Her fee for the redecoration was $48,200.

2. Taggert Inc. owns 700 of the 1,000 shares of SunFarms Inc.'s only class of stock. Mr. and Mrs. Storad own the 300 remaining shares. Taggert plans to contribute appreciated property worth $500,000 to SunFarms in exchange for 100 additional shares. Taggert has requested that Mr. and Mrs. Storad contribute $5,000 cash for one additional share as part of the same transaction. If necessary, Taggert will loan the cash to the Storads.

3. Harris Properties has 1,000 shares of outstanding stock. Mrs. Harris owns 400 shares, and each of her three children owns 200 shares. Mrs. Harris owns investment land that she wants to contribute to the family corporation in exchange for 50 more shares.

4. Mr. and Mrs. Matsuko contributed business assets ($675,000 FMV and $411,000 basis) to newly formed Matsuko Inc. Their son contributed $15,000 cash to Matsuko Inc. The corporation issued 300 shares of stock: 100 shares to Mr. Matsuko, 100 shares to Mrs. Matsuko, and 100 shares to their son.

5. Ms. Morton and Mr. Gide were sole proprietors who pooled their resources by forming a corporation. On March 12, Mr. Gide transferred title to his business assets to MG Inc. in exchange for 500 shares of stock. Ms. Morton was out of the country on an extended vacation until September 18. On October 1, she finally transferred title to her business assets to MG in exchange for 500 shares of stock. Immediately after her transfer, MG had 1,000 shares outstanding.

6. Mr. Nielsen owns 25 percent of Highland's outstanding stock. Two years ago, Highland borrowed $15,000 from a commercial lender, and Mr. Nielsen gave his personal guarantee that the loan would be repaid. This year, Highland defaulted on the loan, and Mr. Nielsen had to pay $17,800 ($15,000 principal plus $2,800 accrued interest) to the commercial lender.

7. Nizny Inc. plans to transfer property ($18 million FMV and $2.3 million adjusted basis) that it currently uses in its Florida division to a new corporation formed under the laws of Mexico. Immediately after the transfer, Nizny will own 100 percent of the stock in the Mexican subsidiary.

8. Mrs. Collier's investment portfolio includes $13,000 worth of tax-exempt municipal bonds and $392,000 worth of stock in her corporate employer. She wants to diversify her portfolio and is considering joining an investment LLC. She could become a member by exchanging her bonds and stock for an LLC interest. The only assets that the LLC owns are marketable securities, and its only activity is collecting the interest and dividends and distributing them to its members.

9. Shea Inc. owns 75 percent of the stock in RSQ. Last year, Shea sold an asset with a $710,000 adjusted basis to an unrelated party for $400,000 cash. This year, the unrelated party sold the asset to RSQ for $410,000 cash.

10. Mr. and Mrs. Terry, who are in the highest marginal tax bracket, own a 75 percent interest in the Terry Family Partnership. The partnership is planning to lease commercial office space from Terry Inc., which is closely held by the Terry family. In recent years, the corporation's business activities have been unprofitable, and it has large NOL carryforwards.

## Research Problems

1. As part of a Section 351 nontaxable exchange, Mr. Robinson contributed the following business assets to WPL Inc.

|  | Tax Basis | FMV |
|---|---|---|
| Accounts receivable | $ 8,000 | $ 8,000 |
| Inventory | 26,300 | 30,000 |
| Office equipment | 15,000 | 15,000 |
| Machinery | 50,000 | 60,000 |
| Long-term lease | –0– | 37,000 |
|  | $99,300 | $150,000 |

He received 1,200 shares of common stock ($140,000 FMV) and 10 shares of preferred stock ($10,000 FMV) in exchange for his assets. The preferred stock has a $1,000 per share liquidation value and an 8 percent cumulative dividend rate. The preferred stockholders have the right to require WPL to redeem the stock on demand. What is Mr. Robinson's tax basis in his common and preferred shares? What is WPL's basis in each of the assets received from Mr. Robinson?

2. Mr. Tucker owns investment land ($690,000 FMV and $228,000 adjusted basis) that he is interested in selling. Several prospective purchasers have offered to pay cash, but Mr. Tucker wants to avoid recognizing his entire gain in the year of sale. Accordingly, he is considering selling the land to the Tucker Family Corporation in return for a 20-year, 9 percent corporate debt obligation. The corporation could then sell the land to an unrelated party for cash. Will Mr. Tucker's strategy be effective in deferring gain recognition on sale of the land?

3. Six years ago, Ms. Fuentes borrowed $75,000 as a personal loan from First Union Bank and used the money to form Fuentes Architects LLP. Ms. Fuentes is a practicing architect and managing partner of the LLP. This year, she paid $4,500 interest on the loan. To what extent can Ms. Fuentes deduct the interest payment, and where should she report the deduction on her Form 1040?

## Tax Planning Cases

1. Mrs. Lucci plans to start a new business venture. According to her five-year projection, the venture will operate at a loss for two years before becoming profitable. Here is the projection.

|  | Year 0 | Year 1 | Year 2 | Year 3 | Year 4 |
|---|---|---|---|---|---|
| Net income (loss) | $(75,000) | $(25,000) | $30,000 | $90,000 | $160,000 |

Mrs. Lucci plans to operate the venture through year 4 before disposing of it in year 5. She is undecided whether to organize the venture as a single-member LLC or to incorporate, but she wants to choose the entity that will maximize NPV of her cash flows.

a. If Mrs. Lucci creates a single-member LLC, she can deduct the business losses without limitation and will pay tax on the business income. Her marginal tax rate (federal and state) over the five-year period will be 40 percent. She will not withdraw any cash from the LLC until year 5 when she will withdraw all accumulated net income at no tax cost. Compute the NPV of Mrs. Lucci's cash flows (tax savings, tax costs, cash withdrawal) using a 7 percent discount rate.

b. If Mrs. Lucci incorporates, the corporation will pay tax on its annual income based on the corporate rate schedule and will pay no dividends over the five-year period. In year 5, Mrs. Lucci will sell her stock for an amount of cash equal to the corporation's accumulated after-tax earnings through year 4. She will recognize the entire amount as capital gain taxable at 15 percent. Compute the NPV of her year 5 after-tax cash flow using a 7 percent discount rate.

On the basis of your computations in parts (*a*) and (*b*), should Mrs. Lucci organize the venture as an LLC or a corporation?

2. Mr. Gardner is in a group of unrelated entrepreneurs who plan to contribute cash and property to form a new corporation. After the incorporation, the group (in the aggregate) will own 100 percent of the stock. According to the plan of incorporation, Mr. Gardner will contribute business equipment with a $296,000 adjusted tax basis. The equipment is worth $225,000, which is about 8 percent of the total FMV of the property that the group will contribute. Mr. Gardner must decide what type of payment to receive from the new corporation in exchange for his equipment. Which of the following alternatives would you recommend, and why?

a. Mr. Gardner could receive $225,000 worth of stock.

b. Mr. Gardner could receive $100,000 worth of stock and $125,000 cash.

c. Mr. Gardner could receive $225,000 cash.

d. Mr. Gardner could receive an interest-bearing note representing the corporation's promise to pay him $225,000 at a future date.

# Chapter **Four**

# Employee Compensation Strategies

**Learning Objectives**

*After reading this chapter, you will be able to:*

1. Explain the issue of unreasonable compensation.

2. Describe the tax consequences of guaranteed payments.

3. Explain the nontax and tax advantages of employee fringe benefits.

4. Distinguish between the tax consequences of qualified and nonqualified retirement plans.

5. Compare the general timing rule and the elective rule for income recognition on receipt of restricted stock.

6. Distinguish between the tax consequences of a nonqualified stock option and an ISO.

7. Describe how phantom stock and SARs measure deferred compensation.

8. Determine the tax consequences when a person performs services in exchange for a partnership interest.

In today's economy, the toughest challenge that many companies face is attracting and retaining a skilled workforce. The era in which a "full day's pay for a full day's work" could fill a company's staffing needs is long gone. Start-up companies must be particularly creative in designing compensation packages to entice employees. In Chapter 4, we examine a variety of compensation strategies and analyze the tax consequences for both employers and employees. The chapter begins with an overview of the methods by which business owners compensate themselves for services performed in the business. The discussion then moves to the topics of employee fringe benefits, deferred compensation, and equity-based compensation strategies through which employers can share profits with employees by making them owners of the business. Chapter 4 concludes by considering the tax consequences when an individual performs services in exchange for an equity interest in a partnership.

# OWNER COMPENSATION

Individuals who organize a new business venture usually work long hours to get the venture off the ground and make it a success. Such individuals should heed the business adage of "pay yourself first." If a venture does not generate enough cash flow to fairly compensate the owners for their time and effort, they should reevaluate their commitment to the venture.

## Shareholder/Employees

**Objective 1**
Explain the issue of unreasonable compensation.

Individual shareholders who work for their corporations are entitled to reasonable compensation for the work performed. For payroll tax purposes, salaries earned by shareholder/employees are treated in exactly the same way as salaries and wages earned by other employees. The corporation must pay the employer portion of FICA (Social Security and Medicare) tax on the salary and withhold the employee portion (as well as federal and state income tax) from the paychecks of the shareholder/employees.

Shareholder/employees of closely held corporations are inclined to pay themselves generous salaries while avoiding the payment of dividends with respect to their stock. Although both salary and dividends are taxable income to the payee, the corporate payer can deduct the salary as a business expense but not the dividend payment. Closely held corporations that adopt this strategy should be prepared to defend it against an IRS allegation that the salary is unreasonably high. If a revenue agent concludes that the compensation for a shareholder/employee exceeds the amount that an unrelated employer would pay in an arm's-length transaction, the agent can classify the excess compensation as a nondeductible constructive dividend.

*Unreasonable Compensation*

Mr. and Mrs. Paxton are the sole shareholders of Paxton Pub Inc., which operates a profitable microbrewery. As the only corporate officers, Mr. and Mrs. Paxton each received a $375,000 salary last year. Paxton Pub has never paid a dividend. The IRS agent who audited the corporate return compared the Paxton's salaries with those paid by similar corporations to officers who were not controlling shareholders. The agent concluded that a reasonable salary for each officer was only $275,000. Consequently, he reclassified $100,000 of each officer's salary as a nondeductible dividend, increased the corporation's taxable income by $200,000, and assessed corporate tax on the increase.

Shareholder/employees of S corporations adopt quite a different strategy with respect to their corporate salaries. Because S corporations are passthrough entities, shareholders pay individual income tax on both their salaries and their pro rata shares of the corporation's ordinary business income. In contrast, employer/employee payroll tax is imposed only on the shareholders' salaries.[1] By minimizing their salaries, shareholders also minimize their payroll tax burden. Revenue agents who audit S corporations are on the alert for shareholder/employee salaries that are unreasonably *low* rather than unreasonably high. If

---

[1] Unlike general partners or LLC members, S corporation shareholders do not pay self-employment tax on their shares of ordinary business income.

an agent concludes that an S corporation has underpaid its shareholder/employees, the agent can assess additional employer/employee payroll tax based on the underpayment.[2]

| *Unreasonable Compensation Revisited* | Mr. and Mrs. Polidoris are the sole shareholders and officers of Polidoris Produce Inc., an S corporation that operates a profitable farming business. In 2002, the Polidorises each drew a $50,000 salary from their corporation. Polidoris Produce's ordinary business income (after deduction of the salaries) was $800,000, which Mr. and Mrs. Polidoris included in their 2002 gross income. The IRS agent who audited the corporate return compared the officers' salaries to those paid by similar corporations and concluded that a reasonable salary for Mr. and Mrs. Polidoris was $125,000 each. On the basis of the $75,000 constructive increase in each salary, the agent assessed additional FICA tax on both the Polidorises and Polidoris Produce, Inc. |
|---|---|

Currently, the Social Security tax for both employers and employees is 6.2 percent of a base amount of annual compensation. In contrast, the 1.45 percent Medicare tax applies to total annual compensation.[3] The annual cap on the Social Security tax limits the IRS's incentive to challenge the reasonableness of S corporation salaries in excess of the annual base. In the Polidoris example, the constructive increase in Mr. and Mrs. Polidoris's 2002 salaries over the $84,900 base for that year yielded no additional Social Security tax for the government. In future years, the Social Security system will come under increasing financial pressure as the "baby boom" generation retires. Congress could respond to this pressure by eliminating the annual cap on Social Security tax. In other words, the 6.2 percent tax would apply to an employee's total annual compensation. Such a dramatic payroll tax increase would prompt S corporation shareholder/employees at every compensation level to minimize salaries, which would cause the IRS to consider more carefully the question of reasonable compensation.

## Partners and LLC Members

**Objective 2**
Describe the tax consequences of guaranteed payments.

Individual partners (including LLC members) who work on a regular basis in their partnership (or LLC) business certainly expect to be compensated. However, for federal tax purposes, these individuals are not considered employees of the passthrough entity. The regular paycheck that they receive is not a salary but a **guaranteed payment.** Section 707(c) provides that guaranteed payments are ordinary income to the partners and an ordinary business deduction for the partnership.[4] The partnership does not pay employer payroll tax on guaranteed payments, nor does it withhold income tax and employee payroll tax from the payment. Guaranteed payments are reported on each partner's Schedule K-1, along with the partner's distributive share of ordinary business income and any separately stated items. The partner reports both guaranteed payments and ordinary business income on Schedule E, Form 1040, for income tax purposes, and on Schedule SE, Form 1040, for self-employment tax purposes.[5]

[2] *Spicer Accounting, Inc. v. Commissioner*, 918 F.2d 90 (CA-9, 1990). See also *J. Michael Joly v. Commissioner*, 211 F.3d 1269 (CA-6, 2000).

[3] Section 3101.

[4] According to Reg. 1.707-1(c), guaranteed payments are deductible only if they qualify as Section 162 ordinary and necessary business expenses and are not capital expenditures under Section 263 and related sections.

[5] This statement assumes that partners who receive guaranteed payments are general partners. Limited partners, who are prevented by law from taking an active role in the partnership business, do not typically receive guaranteed payments for services.

*Self-Employment Income*

Mr. Cheung is the managing member of Roundtop LLC. In 2004, he received a $10,000 monthly guaranteed payment as compensation for his services. Because Mr. Cheung is not an employee, the LLC did not withhold any income or payroll tax from his monthly payments. Mr. Cheung's 2004 share of LLC ordinary business income was $95,200, his share of interest income was $4,015, his share of long-term capital gain was $12,600, and his share of charitable contributions was $1,600.

Mr. Cheung included his guaranteed payments and his shares of ordinary business income, interest income, and long-term capital gain in his 2004 adjusted gross income and reported his share of the charitable contribution as an itemized deduction. He also reported $215,200 ($120,000 guaranteed payments + $95,200 ordinary business income) as self-employment income on Schedule SE and paid self-employment tax accordingly.

## Cash Flow Management for Business Owners

Individuals whose major source of income is their salary or wage can rely on the imposed discipline of employer withholding to pay their state and federal taxes. The only action required of these taxpayers is to file annual income tax returns and pay any balance of tax due. Individuals who operate a business as a passthrough entity are responsible for paying their own taxes. Specifically, these individuals must make all required estimated tax payments on a timely basis throughout the year and must manage their cash flow to fund these payments.

Partners and S corporation shareholders quickly (and sometimes painfully) learn the difference between cash flow and taxable income. These business owners must pay income tax (and in the case of partners, self-employment tax) on their share of the entity's income, regardless of the amount of cash the entity distributed during the year. Because cash flow management is such a crucial issue, owners of passthrough entities should understand how decisions concerning cash distributions are made.

*Cash Flow Woes*

Mr. Damïon is a new partner in Fairchild Partnership. His 2004 Schedule K-1 showed that his distributive share of taxable income was $39,000, but his year-end cash distribution was only $7,500. Because Mr. Damon did not have enough cash to pay federal and state taxes on his partnership income, he telephoned Fairchild's managing partner to request an additional distribution. The partner suggested that Mr. Damon reread the partnership agreement, which clearly states that any year-end cash distribution must be allocated among the partners on the basis of profit-sharing ratios but that the managing partner has sole discretion to determine the total amount of the distribution. As the managing partner explained to Mr. Damon, the partners' funding of their individual tax liability is their personal responsibility.

# EMPLOYEE FRINGE BENEFITS

**Objective 3**
Explain the nontax and tax advantages of employee fringe benefits.

Employee **fringe benefits** include any indirect or noncash form of compensation in addition to the employee's salary or wage. In spite of their name, fringe benefits are an integral part of most compensation arrangements. Even small businesses typically provide health insurance, life insurance, and some type of retirement savings plan to their employees. One reason that fringe benefits are so popular is that they are cost efficient; employers can purchase benefits for a group of employees at a lower cost than each employee would pay for the benefit on an individual basis. Because of this economy of scale, the cost to the employer is less than the monetary value of the benefit to the employee.

| | |
|---|---|
| *Cost versus Value of Fringe Benefit* | Sutherland Lumber-Southwest Inc. owned a jet that it used for business-related employee travel and for flying the corporate president and vice president to and from their personal vacation destinations. Sutherland valued the personal use of the jet according to the Treasury's own valuation rules [Reg.1.61-21(g)] and reported the value as a taxable fringe benefit to the two executives. Sutherland deducted the actual expenses related to the vacation flights. These expenses exceeded the value of the executive's fringe benefit by $169,000. The IRS disallowed the deduction for the excess expenses, arguing that the excess should be classified as nonbusiness (and therefore nondeductible) entertainment expense. The Tax Court rejected the IRS's argument and allowed the deduction, observing that the law does not require a perfect match between the employer's cost of a compensatory fringe benefit and the imputed value of the benefit to the employee.[6] |

The general rule is that the value of fringe benefits is taxable compensation to the employee.[7] However, the Internal Revenue Code includes many major exceptions to this rule. These exceptions permit employers to provide health insurance, life insurance, child care, adoption services, educational programs, and numerous other fringe benefits to their employees on a tax-free basis. Employers must be careful not to run afoul of any nondiscrimination rule that applies to a particular nontaxable benefit. These rules generally require employers to provide the benefit to all employees on substantially the same terms as the benefit is provided to highly compensated employees (a group that includes the shareholder/employees of a closely held corporation). If an employer provides a fringe benefit that discriminates in favor of highly compensated employees, the value of the benefit is taxable to those employees.

| | |
|---|---|
| *Nondiscriminatory Fringe Benefit* | Mr. and Mrs. Fletcher are the sole shareholders and officers of Fletcher Flights, which operates a regional commercial airline. Fletcher Flights has a policy under which employees can fly free on a stand-by basis. Last year, the Fletchers took nine free flights. The value of the flights (the cost that a passenger would normally pay) was $13,600. If the corporate policy applies to all employees on a nondiscriminatory basis, the free flights qualify as a nontaxable fringe benefit under Section 132(b). But if the corporate policy applies only to highly compensated employees, Mr. and Mrs. Fletcher must include the $13,600 value of the fringe benefit in gross income. |

## Fringe Benefits for Partners and S Corporation Shareholders

A number of important fringe benefits that are nontaxable when provided by employers to their employees (including shareholder/employees) are taxable when provided to partners (including LLC members). For example, coverage under group term life insurance and group health insurance plans is nontaxable to employees but is treated as a taxable guaranteed payment to partners.[8] Other fringe benefits are nontaxable to both employees and partners. Partnerships must refer to the governing statutory or regulatory authority to determine whether a particular benefit can be provided tax-free to its partners.

---

[6] *Sutherland Lumber-Southwest, Inc., v. Commissioner*, 255 F.3d 495 (CA-8, 2002).

[7] Section 61(a)(1).

[8] Rev. Rul. 91-26, 1991-1 CB 184. Section 162(1) provides that self-employed individuals, partners, and S corporation shareholders can deduct 100 percent of their health insurance costs in the computation of AGI.

| | |
|---|---|
| *Partner Fringe Benefits* | Nickols Partnership provides both employees and partners with unlimited access to an on-premises exercise and weight room and free parking in a commercial garage located next to the partnership's office. The value of the athletic facility is nontaxable to both employees and partners per Reg. 1.132-1(b)(3). The value of the parking is nontaxable to employees but is taxable to the partners per Section 132(f)(5)(E). |

For fringe benefit purposes, any shareholder owning more than 2 percent of an S corporation's outstanding stock is treated as a partner.[9] As a result, S corporations face the same restraints as partnerships in providing nontaxable fringe benefits to their owners.

# DEFERRED COMPENSATION

Employers can use many different strategies to provide **deferred compensation** to employees. This term encompasses any arrangement in which an employee performs current services in exchange for the promise of future payment. Even though the employee has earned the right to the compensation, he or she does not recognize current income. Instead, the employee defers income recognition until the future year in which payment is actually or constructively received. The tax consequences to the employer depend on whether the deferred compensation arrangement is a qualified plan or a nonqualified plan.

## Qualified Plans

**Objective 4**
Distinguish between the tax consequences of qualified and non-qualified retirement plans.

**Qualified plans** include both defined-benefit plans and defined-contribution plans through which participating employees can defer income until retirement. **Defined-benefit plans** provide employees with a targeted amount of future income, usually in the form of an annual pension. Each year, employers contribute money or property to the plan to fund the pensions to which participating employees are entitled when they retire. **Defined-contribution plans** require employers to make annual contributions to separate investment accounts for each participating employee. Defined-contribution plans come in many varieties, including profit-sharing plans, employee stock ownership plans (ESOPs), Section 401(k) plans, SEP IRAs, and SIMPLE IRAs. Self-employed individuals (sole proprietors, partners, and LLC members) who want to provide a qualified retirement plan for both themselves and their employees must use a **Keogh plan.** Keogh plans, which can be either defined-benefit or defined-contribution plans, offer the same opportunity for deferred compensation as their corporate counterparts.

Qualified plans must be administered by an independent trustee who manages and invests the plan assets for the exclusive benefit of employees and their families. Qualified plans are tax-exempt organizations that do not pay tax on the earnings generated by their investments.[10] As a result, plan assets can grow at a before-tax rate of return.

| | |
|---|---|
| *Tax-Free Growth in a Qualified Retirement Account* | Bullard Inc. offers a qualified profit-sharing plan to its employees. At the beginning of each of the past 10 years, Bullard contributed $5,000 to Mr. McCarthy's plan account. The plan trustee invested the contributed funds in a portfolio of marketable securities. Mr. McCarthy did not pay tax on the $5,000 annual contribution to his account or on the investment income earned in the account. The account earned 10 percent per year, so the balance in the account at the end of year 10 was $87,657. |

[9] Section 1372.
[10] Section 501(a).

If Mr. McCarthy had received $5,000 additional salary each year, he would have paid income tax on it. If he had invested the after-tax salary in an account earning 10 percent per year, he would have also paid tax on the annual investment income. Assuming a 28 percent tax rate, Mr. McCarthy could have invested only $3,600 each year ($5,000 salary − $1,400 tax), and the investment would have earned only 7.2 percent after tax (10 percent − 2.8 percent). The balance in the account at the end of year 10 would be only $53,827.

Participants in qualified retirement plans do not recognize ordinary income until they begin receiving their pensions or withdrawing funds from their investment accounts. Tax law discourages employees from withdrawing funds before retirement by imposing a 10 percent penalty on **premature withdrawals.** Generally, a withdrawal is premature if the employee has not reached age 59½ by the date of withdrawal.[11]

*Qualified Plan Withdrawals*

At age 52, Mr. McCarthy withdrew $10,000 cash from his Bullard retirement account to meet an immediate financial need. If his marginal tax rate is 28 percent, his after-tax cash from his premature withdrawal from the qualified plan is $6,200.

| | |
|---|---|
| Taxable withdrawal from qualified plan | $10,000 |
| Income tax at 28 percent | (2,800) |
| Premature withdrawal penalty | (1,000) |
| After-tax cash | $ 6,200 |

If Mr. McCarthy can avoid withdrawing more funds from his retirement account until he reaches age 59½, he will pay income tax on the withdrawals but will not incur the 10 percent penalty.

### Employer Tax Consequences

Employers are required by law to fund their qualified retirement plans. In other words, they must make their annual contributions by paying cash or transferring property to the plan trustee. Employers can deduct these payments currently, even though the employees do not recognize the contributions as current income.[12] With reference to our example, Bullard deducted its annual $5,000 payments to Mr. McCarthy's qualified retirement account even though the payments were deferred compensation to him.

## Nonqualified Plans

Qualified retirement plans offer a terrific combination to employers and employees: a current deduction for the employers and deferred income to the employees. However, qualified plans are subject to two constraints. First, the plans cannot discriminate in favor of highly compensated employees or self-employed owners. In other words, all employees must have the right to participate in the plan on an equal footing. Second, the annual amount of employer contributions to qualified plans is limited. For example, the maximum 2004 defined contribution to an employee's account is $41,000. Because of these constraints, qualified

[11] According to Section 72(t)(2), distributions are not subject to the premature withdrawal penalty if they are made because of the employee's disability or death or made to an employee who resigns or is discharged from the job (separated from service) and who has reached age 55.

[12] Section 404(a)(1), (2), and (3).

plans are often inadequate to defer a meaningful amount of compensation for highly paid employees.

Employers can supplement their qualified plans with some type of **nonqualified plan.** Employers can offer these plans to an exclusive group of employees and can defer an unlimited amount of compensation until a future year. In their simplest form, nonqualified plans are nothing more than the employer's promise to pay some portion of an employee's compensation at a future date. Employees do not recognize income until the year in which they receive payment.

---

*Deferred Compensation*

Ms. Potinski's 2004 compensation from her corporate employer was $500,000. The corporation paid $380,000 in salary and credited the $120,000 balance to Ms. Potinski's deferred compensation account. The corporation will pay the deferred compensation (adjusted for an inflation factor) to her over a five-year period beginning in 2010. Ms. Potinski must include her $380,000 salary in 2004 gross income, but she will not recognize any deferred compensation until she actually receives it.

---

Nonqualified plans can be *unfunded:* The employer accrues its liability for the deferred compensation but does not set aside cash or property to secure the liability. The employee becomes an unsecured creditor and bears the risk that the employer will fail to pay the liability. The employee's risk is somewhat reduced in an arrangement called a **Rabbi trust** (the employer that came up with the idea was a Jewish synagogue). In this arrangement, the employer funds the deferred compensation by transferring cash or property to a trust. The employer is legally prohibited from reclaiming the trust assets, but the assets are subject to claim by the employer's creditors. The employee has no vested interest in the trust assets and does not recognize income until the trust pays the deferred compensation.

### Employer Tax Consequences

Regardless of whether the arrangement is funded or unfunded, employers cannot deduct nonqualified deferred compensation until the year in which the compensation is included in the employee's gross income.[13] With reference to our example, the corporate employer can deduct the $380,000 salary paid to Ms. Potinski in 2004 but cannot deduct any deferred compensation until the year in which payment is made.

## Deferred Compensation for Partners

Nonqualified plans are effective deferral strategies for corporations and their shareholder/employees. These plans are much less effective for partnerships and their partners. A partner who is entitled to a compensatory guaranteed payment can arrange for a portion of the payment to be deferred into a future year. In such cases, the partnership must defer a corresponding deduction, partnership taxable income increases, and the partner's deferral is partially offset by an increase in his share of taxable income.

---

*Deferred Guaranteed Payments*

Mr. Gilmore is a 25 percent partner in GMX Partnership. This year, GMX compensated him with a $100,000 guaranteed payment, $65,000 of which was paid during the year and $35,000 of which was credited to a deferred compensation account. GMX's ordinary business income (after deduction of Mr. Gilmore's $65,000 current payment) was $167,000, and Mr. Gilmore's distributive share was $41,750. Thus, his total taxable income from GMX was

---

[13] Section 404(a)(5).

$106,750 ($65,000 guaranteed payment + $41,750 share). If GMX had not deferred any of Mr. Gilmore's guaranteed payment, its ordinary income would have been $132,000 ($167,000 − $35,000 additional deduction), and his 25 percent share would have been $33,000. His total taxable income would have been $133,000 ($100,000 guaranteed payment + $33,000 share). Accordingly, deferral of a $35,000 guaranteed payment resulted in deferral of only $26,250 taxable income for Mr. Gilmore.

Note that Mr. Gilmore's deferred compensation plan with GMX accelerated the recognition of taxable income *to the other partners* because it increased GMX's ordinary business income from $133,000 to $167,000. If all GMX partners deferred some portion of their guaranteed payments, their aggregate deferral would be completely offset by an increase in GMX income, and the deferred compensation plan would have no aggregate benefit.

# EQUITY-BASED COMPENSATION

Compensation arrangements in which employees receive equity in the employer's business are increasingly popular. These arrangements align the economic interests of both parties by giving the employees an incentive to increase the value of the business. The next sections describe a variety of equity-based compensation strategies and highlight the tax consequences to both employer and employee. Let's begin by considering the various ways in which corporate employers use their own stock to reward employees.

## Corporate Stock as Payment for Services

### Employer Perspective

From a corporate employer's perspective, the payment of stock for services is advantageous because the payment requires no cash outflow. The disadvantage is that the payment dilutes corporate equity, so that existing shareholders are surrendering some portion of their right to future dividends and future appreciation in the value of the corporate business. In the case of a closely held corporation, existing shareholders who are willing to dilute their equity typically do not want to lose control of corporate policy. These shareholders can avoid diluting their control by issuing nonvoting stock as compensation to corporate employees.

*Use of Nonvoting Stock as Compensation*

Heathrow Inc. has 30,000 shares of voting common stock, all of which is owned by members of the Heathrow family. It also has 4,100 shares of nonvoting common stock, all of which is owned by Heathrow employees who received the stock as compensation. The Heathrow family has the exclusive right to elect members of the board of directors, who control the corporation's dividend-paying policy. This year, the board declared a $105 dividend per share on common stock. The Heathrow family received $3,150,000 in dividends, and Heathrow employees received $430,500 in dividends.

The tax consequences to a corporation that uses its stock as payment for services are very favorable. The corporation does not recognize gain on the transaction and is allowed a deduction as if it paid cash equal to the FMV of the services.[14]

[14] Reg. 1.1032-1(a).

| Tax Consequences to Corporation | This year, Heathrow Inc. issued 387 new shares of nonvoting common stock as bonuses to various employees. The FMV of the shares was $419,300. Heathrow did not recognize gain on the issuance of the shares and deducted $419,300 compensation expense in the computation of taxable income. |
| --- | --- |

### Employee Perspective

Corporate employees can be dazzled by the prospect of joining the capitalist ranks by receiving stock as compensation for their labor. Business lore is rich with tales of rank-and-file employees who are now millionaires because they owned stock in start-up companies that went on to greatness. Nonetheless, employees should carefully consider the financial implications before accepting employer stock as part of their compensation package. One primary consideration is the risk associated with stock ownership. Employees must understand that there is no guarantee that the value of the stock will increase over time or even that it will hold its current value.

| Risk of Stock Ownership | Seven years ago, Mr. Jacob received a bonus of 3,900 shares of publicly traded stock worth $25,000 from his corporate employer. He planned to use the stock to fund his daughter's education. This year, the daughter was accepted at Oberlin College. Unfortunately, the value of Mr. Jacob's 3,900 shares has declined to $5,000, and the family must find an additional source of funds to pay the tuition. |
| --- | --- |

An individual who performs services for a corporation and receives stock as payment recognizes ordinary income equal to the stock's FMV on the date of receipt. If the individual is a corporate employee, the income is subject to employer/employee payroll tax. If the individual performed the services as an independent contractor, the income is subject to self-employment tax. In either case, the individual needs cash to pay both the income and employment taxes attributable to the noncash compensation. The individual's tax basis in the stock equals the income recognized on its receipt.

| Tax Consequences to Employee | Seven years ago, Mr. Jacob's Form W-2 from his corporate employer reported $98,000 gross income ($73,000 salary + $25,000 FMV of 3,900 shares of employer stock). The employer withheld income tax and employee payroll tax based on $98,000 compensation. This year, Mr. Jacob sold the stock for $5,000 cash, thereby recognizing a $20,000 long-term capital loss ($5,000 amount realized − $25,000 basis in stock). He can deduct this loss against his capital gains but can deduct only $3,000 of net capital loss per year to reduce his ordinary income.[15] |
| --- | --- |

## Restricted Stock

**Objective 5**
Compare the general timing rule and the elective rule for income recognition on receipt of restricted stock.

In theory, corporate employees who are also shareholders have added incentive to work toward the corporation's long-term success. These employees should be more loyal to their employers and less inclined to leave their jobs to work for a competitor. Corporate employers can strengthen this commitment even more by compensating the employee with **restricted stock.** Stock is restricted if the employee's right to the stock is nontransferable or subject to a substantial risk of forfeiture. Usually, the right to stock is subject to a substantial risk of forfeiture because the employee must return the stock if she quits the job

---

[15] Section 1211(b).

within a specified period of time. At the end of the period, the risk of forfeiture lapses, and the employee's right to the stock vests (becomes unrestricted).

| *Restricted Stock* | This year, Mrs. Walton received 500 shares of her corporate employer's stock as part of her annual compensation. If she quits her job before July 1, 2008, she must return the shares. If she is still working for the corporation on July 1, 2008, the risk of forfeiture lapses, and she will have unrestricted ownership of the shares. |
|---|---|

According to the general rule of Section 83(a), employees who receive restricted stock as compensation for the performance of services do not recognize the FMV of the stock as income until the year in which the risk of forfeiture lapses. Section 83(b) offers employees an alternative to this timing rule. An employee who receives restricted stock may elect to recognize the FMV as income in the year of receipt.[16] Note that this Section 83(b) election is detrimental in that it accelerates the employee's recognition of income. An employee would consider the election only if she expects the FMV of the stock to increase significantly during the restriction period.

| *Income Recognition for Restricted Stock* | On the day that Mrs. Walton received her 500 restricted shares, their FMV was $19,300. She believes that the FMV could increase to as much as $75,000 by 2008. If she waits until the year in which the restriction lapses, she will recognize as much as $75,000 ordinary income. If she makes a Section 83(b) election, she recognizes only $19,300 ordinary income this year and no additional income in 2008. |
|---|---|

Employees who make a Section 83(b) election are gambling that the tax on the current FMV of the stock is less than the discounted present value of the future tax on the FMV in the year of lapse. These employees are also gambling that they will not quit their jobs and forfeit their restricted stock. If they do so, they are not allowed any deduction for their tax basis in the stock.

| *Tax Consequences of Forfeiture* | Assume that Mrs. Walton made a Section 83(b) election to recognize $19,300 ordinary income this year. Consequently, her tax basis in the 500 shares is $19,300. In 2005, she quits her job because of irreconcilable differences with her supervisor and returns the shares to the corporation. Mrs. Walton is not allowed to deduct her $19,300 unrecovered basis in the forfeited shares. If she had not made the Section 83(b) election, she would have recognized no income on receipt of the stock and would have a zero basis in the forfeited shares. |
|---|---|

When a corporation compensates an employee with restricted stock, it is allowed a deduction in the year in which the employee recognizes income with respect to the stock. The amount of the deduction equals the amount of recognized income.

| *Corporate Deduction for Restricted Stock* | Because Mrs. Walton elected to recognize $19,300 income in the year she received restricted stock, her corporate employer deducted $19,300 compensation expense for that year. If she had chosen to defer income recognition until 2008 (the year in which the restriction lapses), the employer's deduction would be deferred as well, and the amount of the deduction would equal the FMV of the stock on the date of lapse. |
|---|---|

[16] The employee has only 30 days after receipt to make the election.

# EMPLOYEE STOCK OPTIONS

As an alternative to unrestricted or restricted stock, corporate employers can compensate their employees by granting them stock options. A **stock option** is the right to purchase a stated number of shares of the employer's stock for a stated price (option or **strike price**) for a stated period of time. The strike price is typically equal to or higher than the market price of the stock at the date of grant. Accordingly, the employer's cost in granting the option is zero, and the option has no ascertainable value at the date of grant. The option does entitle the employee to any future appreciation in the value of the optioned shares over the option period. The compensation element in the option is purely prospective and a function of the stock's market price over time.

**Stock Options as Compensation**

Mr. Benet works for Dudly Inc., and Mrs. O'Brien works for EWQ Inc. Five years ago, each employee received an option to purchase 10,000 shares of employer stock for $12 per share. Both options are about to expire. The market price of Dudly stock is $40. By exercising his option, Mr. Benet will pay $120,000 ($12 per share for 10,000 shares) to Dudley for stock worth $400,000. His compensation element in his option is $280,000. The market price of EWQ stock is $18 per share. By exercising her option, Mrs. O'Brien will pay $120,000 to purchase 10,000 shares of EWQ stock. Because the market value of these shares is $180,000, Mrs. O'Brien's compensation element is only $60,000.

In the preceding example, both Mr. Benet and Mrs. O'Brien did, in fact, receive compensation because of their stock options. Such outcome is by no means certain. If the market price of the stock does not climb above the strike price during the option period, the option never develops a compensation element (remains "underwater") and is worthless to the employee. In such case, the employee will simply let the option lapse.

**Underwater Stock Options**

The year 2000 was tough on many publicly traded corporate stocks. Lucent Technologies was one of the most prominent losers. On December 20, 1999, Lucent stock was selling at $79.16 per share, but by December 29, 2000, the price had plunged to $13.50. Because of this decline, Lucent announced that at least 74 percent of the stock options held by its employees had become worthless.

Employees who receive stock options recognize no income on the date of grant, nor is the corporate employer allowed any deduction. If and when the employee exercises the option by purchasing the shares, the employee must recognize ordinary income equal to the **bargain element:** the excess of FMV of the shares over the strike price. This income is treated as employee compensation for tax purposes. As a result, the corporate employer must withhold both income and payroll tax, must report the income on the employee's Form W-2, and is allowed a deduction in the computation of corporate taxable income. The employee's basis in the purchased shares equals the cost of the shares plus the recognized income.

**Income Recognition on Option Exercise**

If Mr. Benet and Mrs. O'Brien exercise their stock options this year, Mr. Benet will recognize $280,000 ordinary income, Mrs. O'Brien will recognize $60,000 ordinary income, and their respective employers will deduct an equivalent amount of compensation. Mr. Benet's basis in his 10,000 Dudly shares will be $400,000, and Mrs. O'Brien's basis in her 10,000 EWQ shares will be $180,000.

## Stock Options as Financial Assets

**Tax Talk**

Microsoft is now awarding restricted stock instead of stock options to its employees. Microsoft's compatriots in the technology sector have not been enthusiastic about this new compensation strategy. Cisco Systems announced that it would continue to award stock options, saying, "Broadbased employee stock option plans are the best way to align shareholder and employee goals because employees benefit only when shareholder value is created."

The benefit of a stock option as a financial asset is that the holder is entitled to any increase in value in the optioned shares over the option period but is not required to purchase the shares until the end of the period. Thus, the longer the option period, the more valuable the option. To maximize the value of an option, the holder should not exercise it until the end of the option period. This important rule is demonstrated in the following comparison of the financial situations of two individuals, one who acquires stock through an option and the other who acquires the same stock without an option.

Ms. Ward is an employee of Parquet Inc. On July 1, 2001, Parquet granted her an option to purchase 1,000 shares for $50 per share, which was the market price. Ms. Ward must exercise the option by June 30, 2011. On the same day that Ms. Ward received her option, Mr. Zantow purchased 1,000 Parquet shares for $50,000. Let's compare the NPV of these two financial assets under two different assumptions about the future value of Parquet stock.

Our first assumption is that Parquet stock is selling at $200 per share on June 30, 2011. Both Ms. Ward and Mr. Zantow cash in their investments on that date. Ms. Ward must exercise her option by paying $50,000 cash to Parquet. She must also pay tax on her $150,000 bargain element ($200,000 FMV − $50,000 strike price). The following calculation assumes that her combined income and payroll tax rate on the bargain element is 40 percent. Because Ms. Ward's basis in her 1,000 shares is $200,000, she recognizes no gain when she immediately sells the shares for $200,000. Mr. Zantow's basis in his 1,000 shares is his $50,000 cost. Therefore, he recognizes a $150,000 capital gain when he sells the shares for $200,000. The calculation assumes that this gain is taxed at a 15 percent preferential rate. With these assumptions in place, let's calculate the NPV of cash flows for Ms. Ward and Mr. Zantow using an 8 percent discount rate.

**First Assumption**

|  | Ms. Ward | Mr. Zantow |
|---|---|---|
| **2001** | | |
| Cost of 1,000 shares | –0– | $ (50,000) |
| **2011** | | |
| Cost of 1,000 shares | $(50,000) | –0– |
| Cash received on sale | 200,000 | 200,000 |
| Tax costs: | | |
| Bargain element × 40 percent | (60,000) | –0– |
| Capital gain × 15 percent | –0– | (22,500) |
| Net cash from sale | $ 90,000 | $177,500 |
| **NPV of cash flows** | | |
| 2001 | –0– | $ (50,000) |
| 2011 net cash from sale (0.463 discount factor) | 41,670 | 82,183 |
| | $ 41,670 | $ 32,183 |

Both Ms. Ward and Mr. Zantow must pay tax on the $150,000 appreciation in value of 1,000 Parquet shares between 2001 and 2011. Because the appreciation is compensation income rather than capital gain to Ms. Ward, her tax rate is much higher than Mr. Zantow's. Even with this rate differential, the NPV of her investment in Parquet stock exceeds the NPV of his investment because Ms. Ward is not required to fund her investment until 2011.

Our second assumption is that Parquet stock is selling at only $60 per share on June 30, 2011, so that Ms. Ward and Mr. Zantow realize only $60,000 on sale of their 10,000 shares.

**Second Assumption**

| | Ms. Ward | Mr. Zantow |
|---|---|---|
| **2001** | | |
| Cost of 1,000 shares | –0– | $ (50,000) |
| **2011** | | |
| Cost of 1,000 shares | $ (50,000) | –0– |
| Cash received on sale | 60,000 | 60,000 |
| Tax costs: | | |
|   Bargain element × 40 percent | (4,000) | –0– |
|   Capital gain × 15 percent | –0– | (1,500) |
| Net cash from sale | $ 6,000 | $ 58,500 |
| **NPV of cash flows** | | |
| 2001 | –0– | $ (50,000) |
| 2011 net cash from sale (0.463 discount factor) | 2,778 | 27,086 |
| | $ 2,778 | $ (22,914) |

In this case, Mr. Zantow's $22,914 *negative* NPV represents a significant financial loss on his investment in Parquet stock. Ms. Ward's $2,778 *positive* NPV represents a small financial gain from her stock option. Because Ms. Ward did not have to fund her investment until 2011, she did not expose her $50,000 to the market risk that caused such a poor financial result for Mr. Zantow.

## Incentive Stock Options

**Objective 6**
Distinguish between the tax consequences of a nonqualified stock option and an ISO.

The tax law creates a special type of stock option called an **incentive stock option (ISO).** (Stock options that do not qualify as ISOs are called *nonqualified options.*) ISOs offer an extremely favorable tax result: An employee who exercises an ISO does not recognize the bargain element as compensation income.[17] The employee's basis in the purchased shares equals the cost of the shares, and the employee recognizes the bargain element as capital gain on sale of the stock. To illustrate the benefit of this conversion of ordinary income to capital gain, let's return to our first assumption in which Ms. Ward exercises a stock option by purchasing 1,000 Parquet shares for $50,000 and later sells the shares for $200,000. The following calculation compares her after-tax cash flow from a nonqualified option with the after-tax cash flow from an ISO.

**Nonqualified Option versus ISO**

| | Nonqualified Option | Incentive Stock Option (ISO) |
|---|---|---|
| **Tax consequences** | | |
| Ordinary income on exercise | $150,000 | –0– |
| Tax cost at 40 percent | 60,000 | –0– |
| Amount realized on sale | $200,000 | $200,000 |
| Basis of shares | (200,000) | (50,000) |
| Capital gain on sale | –0– | $150,000 |
| Tax cost at 15 percent | –0– | 22,500 |

[17] Section 421(a)(1). The bargain element, however, is an individual AMT adjustment added to taxable income in the computation of AMTI. Section 56(b)(3).

**Cash flows**

| | | |
|---|---:|---:|
| Cost of 1,000 shares | $ (50,000) | $ (50,000) |
| Cash received on sale | 200,000 | 200,000 |
| Tax cost | (60,000) | (22,500) |
| After-tax cash | $ 90,000 | $127,500 |

Although this comparison quantifies the tax advantage from the conversion of ordinary income to capital gain, it does not reflect the entire advantage of ISOs over nonqualified options. Employees who exercise nonqualified options must recognize the bargain element as income in the year of exercise. In contrast, employees who exercise ISOs do not recognize the bargain element as income until the year in which they sell the stock. Thus, ISOs offer employees the opportunity to defer any tax cost by holding their purchased stock as a long-term investment. In fact, the favorable tax treatment for ISOs applies *only* if the employee does not sell the stock within one year after exercising the option.[18] The downside to this enforced deferral is that employees must bear the market risk associated with ownership of their employer's stock for at least one year to take advantage of their ISOs.

Given the powerful tax benefit of ISOs, why do corporate employers use any nonqualified options to compensate their employees? One reason is that the ISO qualification requirements limit the FMV of the stock that employees can purchase through ISOs to $100,000 annually.[19] A second reason is that employers receive no tax deduction when employees exercise their ISOs.[20] In our example in which Mrs. Ward exercises her stock option, Parquet is allowed a $150,000 tax deduction if the stock option is nonqualified (and Mrs. Ward recognizes $150,000 ordinary income). Parquet is not allowed any deduction if Mrs. Ward's option is an ISO.

## Phantom Stock and SARs

**Objective 7**
Describe how phantom stock and SARs measure deferred compensation.

Employees who are compensated with stock options must eventually come up with the money to exercise their options and commit to an investment in their employer's stock. Corporations have devised alternative forms of deferred compensation that do not require employees to actually buy stock. However, the amount of compensation is measured by reference to the stock's FMV at some future point in time.

In a **phantom stock plan,** employees earn deferred compensation that is hypothetically invested in shares of the employer's stock. At the end of the deferral period, the corporation pays the employee for the FMV of the phantom shares. Therefore, the value of the deferred compensation is indexed to the appreciation in the market value of the employer's stock.

*Phantom Stock*

Eight years ago, Vizor Inc. awarded a $50,000 year-end bonus to Mrs. Lynley, who elected to defer the compensation until retirement through Vizor's phantom stock plan. Because Vizor stock was selling for $50 per share, the corporation credited her deferred compensation account with 1,000 hypothetical shares. This year, Mrs. Lynley retired. On the date of her retirement, Vizor stock was selling for $92 per share. Consequently, Vizor paid $92,000 cash to Mrs. Lynley in fulfillment of its deferred compensation obligation. She must recognize the payment as compensation income, and Vizor can deduct the payment as compensation expense.

[18] Section 422(a)(1).
[19] Section 422(d).
[20] Section 421(a)(2).

In a **stock appreciation right (SAR)** plan, employees are granted the right to receive a cash payment from their corporate employer for a certain period of time. The payment equals the appreciation in value of one share of employer stock between the date of grant and the date of exercise. The IRS has ruled that employees recognize income only when they exercise their SARs.[21]

**SARs**

Four years ago, Ingleside Inc. granted 5,000 SARs to Mr. Carena, who could exercise the rights at any time during the following 10 years. At the date of grant, Ingleside stock was selling on Nasdaq for $18 per share. Mr. Carena exercised 2,000 SARs this year because he wanted the cash to build a family swimming pool. At the date of the exercise, Ingleside stock was selling at $39 per share. Consequently, Ingleside paid $42,000 cash [2,000 SARs × ($39 − $18)] to Mr. Carena. He must recognize the cash payment as compensation income, and Ingleside can deduct the payment as compensation expense.

Note that both phantom stock and SAR plans are simply devices that correlate the amount of deferred compensation to the increase in value of the employer's stock. In neither case does the employee receive or purchase actual shares of stock. These plans can be quite useful to closely held corporations that do not want their employees to become shareholders. For example, S corporations, which are limited to 75 shareholders owning a single class of common stock, can use phantom stock and SARs to give their employees a stake in the corporation's future without endangering the corporation's Subchapter S election.[22]

## PARTNERSHIP INTEREST AS PAYMENT FOR SERVICES

**Objective 8**
Determine the tax consequences when a person performs services in exchange for a partnership interest.

Corporations have used stock, stock options, and other equity-based arrangements as compensation for decades, and the tax consequences to both employer and employee are well established. The use of equity-based compensation by unincorporated entities (partnerships and LLCs) is much less common, and the tax consequences to both the entity and the person who receives the compensation are uncertain. One reason for the uncertainty is that a partner cannot be an employee of the partnership. As a result, the familiar employee/employer framework for analyzing compensatory transactions does not fit. A second reason is the ambiguous nature of an equity interest in a partnership for tax purposes. In some respects, Subchapter K treats a partnership interest as an ownership interest in the partnership entity. Under this **entity theory of partnerships,** partners are separate and distinct from the partnership in the same way that shareholders are separate and distinct from their corporations. In other respects, Subchapter K treats a partnership interest as an ownership interest in the assets and liabilities of the partnership. Under the **aggregate theory of partnerships,** the partnership itself is transparent, with no separate identity from its partners. Many partnership experts believe that the aggregate theory should apply when a person performs services for a partnership and is compensated with a partnership interest.

The tax consequences to both the *service partner* and the partnership depend on the legal nature of the compensatory interest as specified in the partnership agreement. One possibility is that the interest entitles the service partner to a share of future partnership income but *not* to any share of existing partnership capital. In such case, the service partner's beginning capital account balance is zero. The service partner does not recognize income on

[21] Rev. Rul. 80-300, 1980-2 CB 165.
[22] According to Reg. 1.1361-1(b)(4), phantom stock and SARs are not considered a second class of outstanding stock that violates the single class of stock requirement for an S corporation.

the receipt of the **profits interest** and takes a zero tax (outside) basis in the interest.[23] When the partnership generates taxable income, the service partner will recognize his or her distributive share of such income and pay tax accordingly.

---

*Services in Exchange for a Profits Interest*

On June 1, Mr. Lake, Ms. Potter, and Ms. Terrel formed Eastland LLC. Mr. Lake and Ms. Potter contributed their equal interests in commercial real estate. At the date of contribution, the real estate had a $450,000 tax basis and FMV. Ms. Terrel contributed no money or property but agreed to manage the real estate in exchange for her LLC interest. According to the LLC operating agreement, Mr. Lake and Ms. Potter each have a $225,000 capital account, and Ms. Terrel has a zero capital account. However, each member has an equal interest in the LLC's future profits and losses. Immediately after formation, Eastland had the following tax balance sheet.

|  | Tax Basis |
|---|---|
| Real estate | $450,000 |
| Capital: Mr. Lake | $225,000 |
| Ms. Potter | 225,000 |
| Ms. Terrel | –0– |
|  | $450,000 |

Even though Ms. Terrel received an interest in Eastland LLC as compensation for services, she recognized no income on the receipt of the interest. The outside basis in her interest is zero.

---

A partnership interest received as compensation for the performance of services could entitle the recipient not only to a share of future profits but also to an ownership interest in existing partnership capital. In this case, the service partner's capital account is credited with the FMV of his compensatory capital interest. The service partner must recognize the FMV as ordinary income and take an outside basis equal to the FMV.[24]

---

*Services in Exchange for a Capital Interest*

Assume that the Eastland LLC operating agreement provides that Mr. Lake, Ms. Potter, and Ms. Terrel have equal interests in LLC capital, profits, and losses. Immediately after formation, Eastland had the following tax balance sheet.

|  | Tax Basis |
|---|---|
| Real estate | $450,000 |
| Capital: Mr. Lake | $150,000 |
| Ms. Potter | 150,000 |
| Ms. Terrel | 150,000 |
|  | $450,000 |

---

According to the aggregate theory, Eastland LLC is transparent, and the compensation transaction is between Ms. Terrel and the other partners. In other words, *Mr. Lake and*

[23] Rev. Proc. 93-27, 1993-2 CB 343, and Rev. Proc. 2001-43, 2001-2 CB 191.
[24] Reg. 1.721-1(b)(1).

*Ms. Potter* transferred a one-third interest *in their real estate* as compensation for Ms. Terrel's services. Ms. Terrel recognized the $150,000 FMV of the real estate interest as ordinary income, and then contributed it back to the LLC to establish her $150,000 capital account and $150,000 outside basis in her LLC interest. Because the compensatory payment to Ms. Terrel was an ordinary business expense, the LLC is allowed a $150,000 ordinary deduction *that should be allocated equally between Mr. Lake and Ms. Potter.*[25]

When a partnership transfers a compensatory capital interest to an individual who will perform ongoing services, the partnership can restrict the individual's right to the interest in some way. The restriction usually requires the individual to work for a specified period of time. If the individual fails to do so, he must forfeit the capital interest back to the partnership. Section 83 (which we discussed in the corporate context earlier in the chapter) allows the individual to defer income recognition with respect to the restricted interest until the year in which the risk of forfeiture lapses.[26] Alternatively, the individual could make a Section 83(b) election to recognize income in the year of receipt of the restricted interest.

---

*Services in Exchange for a Restricted Interest*

Assume that the Eastland LLC agreement requires Ms. Terrel to manage the real estate for two years before her interest is vested. If she quits before the end of the two-year period, she must forfeit her interest back to the LLC. Ms. Terrel does not make a Section 83(b) election. Consequently, she does not recognize income in the year she receives the restricted LLC interest, nor does she establish any tax basis in the interest.

Immediately before the end of the two-year period, Eastland LLC has the following balance sheet.

|  | Tax Basis | FMV |
|---|---|---|
| Cash | $ 60,000 | $ 60,000 |
| Real estate (net of depreciation) | 420,000 | 600,000 |
|  | $480,000 | $660,000 |
|  |  |  |
| Capital: Mr. Lake | $240,000 | $330,000 |
| Ms. Potter | 240,000 | 330,000 |
| Ms. Terrel (restricted) | –0– | –0– |
|  | $480,000 | $660,000 |

The three members amend their operating agreement to provide that Ms. Terrel's one-third interest is now fully vested. According to Section 83(a), Ms. Terrel must recognize the $220,000 FMV of this interest (33.33 percent × $660,000) as ordinary income.

Under the aggregate theory, *Mr. Lake and Ms. Potter* transferred $20,000 cash and a one-third interest in their real estate ($200,000 FMV and $140,000 adjusted basis) as compensation for Ms. Terrel's services. Therefore, the LLC can deduct $220,000 compensation expense and must recognize a $60,000 taxable gain. *Both the deduction and the gain should be allocated equally between Mr. Lake and Ms. Potter.* After receiving her compensation, Ms. Terrel contributed the cash and real estate back to the LLC to establish her $220,000 capital account and $220,000 outside basis in her LLC interest. The amended balance sheet follows.

---

[25] Reg. 1.721-1(b)(2) states that the transfer of a compensatory capital interest is treated as a guaranteed payment by the partnership.

[26] The weight of authority suggests that Section 83 applies in the partnership context, but the issue is not without doubt.

|                              | Tax Basis | FMV      |
|------------------------------|-----------|----------|
| Cash                         | $ 60,000  | $ 60,000 |
| Real estate (net of depreciation) | 480,000   | 600,000  |
|                              | $540,000  | $660,000 |
|                              |           |          |
| Capital:  Mr. Lake           | $160,000  | $220,000 |
| Ms. Potter                   | 160,000   | 220,000  |
| Ms. Terrel                   | 220,000   | 220,000  |
|                              | $540,000  | $660,000 |

The inside basis of the real estate increased to $480,000 ($420,000 beginning basis − $140,000 basis of transferred one-third interest + $200,000 basis of contributed one-third interest). Note that the $60,000 net increase in basis equals the gain recognized by Mr. Lake and Ms. Potter. Mr. Lake's and Ms. Potter's capital accounts decreased to $160,000 ($240,000 beginning balance − $110,000 deduction + $30,000 gain).[27]

As our example should suggest, the application of the aggregate theory to a partner's performance of services in exchange for a capital interest can be extremely complicated. In subsequent chapters, we will encounter other partnership transactions that must be analyzed according to the aggregate theory. Determining the correct tax consequences of these transactions can be a formidable challenge even to tax professionals.

## Conclusion

Chapter 4 has provided an overview of compensation strategies by which employers reward and motivate their employees. By using fringe benefits, employers can provide valuable compensation that is exempt from both income and payroll tax. They can offer deferred-compensation plans so that employees will not recognize income until a future year. Corporations can use equity-based compensation to give employees a stake in the corporation's prosperity. Chapter 4 has also discussed the problems faced by partnerships and LLCs, which can use many tax efficient strategies to compensate their employees but relatively fewer strategies to benefit the partners and LLC members themselves. Exhibit 4.1 provides a chart that summarizes the major tax issues introduced in Chapter 4 and compares the answers pertaining to corporations with the answers pertaining to partnerships and LLCs.

**EXHIBIT 4.1** Comparison Chart

| Tax Issue | Corporation | Partnership/LLC |
|-----------|-------------|-----------------|
| Can an owner be an employee of the entity? | Yes. | No. However, partners can receive guaranteed payments for services provided to the partnership. |
| Is owner compensation subject to federal payroll taxes? | Yes. | No. However, partners may be subject to self-employment tax. |

*continued on page 100*

[27] For book purposes only, the LLC can revalue its assets upon the admission of Ms. Terrel by writing up both the book basis of the real estate and Mr. Lake's and Ms. Potter's capital accounts to FMV. See the capital account maintenance rule in Reg. 1.704-1(b)(2)(iv)(f). As a result, the LLC's book basis balance sheet (written up to FMV) would be different from its tax basis balance sheet.

**EXHIBIT 4.1 Comparison Chart—*continued***

| Tax Issue | Corporation | Partnership/LLC |
|---|---|---|
| Does an entity face IRS challenge concerning the reasonableness of compensation paid to owner/ employees? | Yes. Unreasonably high compensation for C corporations; unreasonably low compensation for S corporations. | No (with the exception of certain family partnerships). |
| Can an entity compensate owners with nontaxable fringe benefits? | Yes, on a nondiscriminatory basis. Two-percent shareholders of S corporations are treated as partners. | To a more limited extent than corporations. |
| Can owners participate in entity-sponsored qualified retirement plans? | Yes, on a nondiscriminatory basis. | Yes, through a nondiscriminatory Keogh plan. |
| Can an entity provide nonqualified deferred compensation? | Yes. | Yes. |
| Can an entity provide equity-based compensation? | Yes, including resticted stock, stock options, phantom stock, SARs. | Yes, including profits interests, capital interests, restricted capital interests. |

**Key Terms**

aggregate theory of partnerships  96
bargain element  92
deferred compensation  86
defined-benefit plan  86
defined-contribution plan  86
entity theory of partnerships  96

fringe benefit  84
guaranteed payment  83
incentive stock option (ISO)  94
Keogh plan  86
nonqualified plan  88
phantom stock plan  95
premature withdrawal  87

profits interest  97
qualified plan  86
Rabbi trust  88
restricted stock  90
stock appreciation right (SAR)  96
stock option  92
strike price  92

**Questions and Problems for Discussion**

1. One year ago, Mr. and Mrs. Kovach quit their jobs to start a new business venture. In its first year, the business collected $194,000 revenues and disbursed $170,000 to pay for various operating expenses, including $12,000 to a part-time employee. Discuss whether or not this business can be considered successful for Mr. and Mrs. Kovach.

2. Compare the tax issue of unreasonable compensation for shareholder/employees of taxable corporations and shareholder/employees of S corporations.

3. Can general partners reduce their self-employment tax by minimizing their annual guaranteed payments from a partnership?

4. Mrs. Muncy receives a $10,000 monthly salary from her corporate employer, and Mr. Muncy receives a $10,000 monthly guaranteed payment from his partnership. Discuss the difference in cash flow represented by these two payments.

5. Ms. Marc, an employee of a professional service partnership for six years, was recently admitted as a partner. How does this change in status affect her responsibility for paying state and federal income tax?

6. Mr. Reba's corporate employer recently opened an on-site child care facility for its employees. The employees pay only $30 per month to enroll a child. What factors should Mr. Reba consider in evaluating this fringe benefit as part of his total compensation package?

7. Discuss the reasons that corporations usually offer both qualified and nonqualified retirement plans to their employees.

8. Highly paid corporate employees can use nonqualified deferred compensation arrangements to defer income. Are similar types of arrangements available to sole proprietors, partners, or LLC members?

9. Ms. Nowacki is an employee of Sentinex Inc. Six years ago, she received a stock option to purchase 500 shares of Sentinex stock for $18 per share at any time over the next seven years. At the date of grant, the stock was selling on Nasdaq for $17.30 per share. Two years ago, she exercised her option when the market price of Sentinex stock was $34 per share. Just yesterday, the stock closed at a price of only $20. Discuss whether Ms. Nowacki's decision to exercise her option was a smart financial move.

10. Identify the financial differences between equity-*based* compensation such as restricted stock and stock options and equity-*flavored* compensation such as stock appreciation rights and SARs.

11. Contrast the entity theory with the aggregate theory of partnerships. Which theory applies to transactions between a shareholder and a corporation?

**Application Problems**

1. Mr. Bern, who is in the 35 percent marginal tax bracket, is the sole shareholder and CEO of Bern Products. His salary this year was $345,000, and the corporation's taxable income was $1,211,000.
   a. What are the income tax and FICA tax consequences to Mr. Bern if the IRS determines that $100,000 of his salary is unreasonable compensation?
   b. What are the income tax and FICA tax consequences to Bern Products if the IRS determines that $100,000 of Mr. Bern's salary is unreasonable compensation?

2. Mr. Hope is the managing partner of Stanhope Services and has a 20 percent interest in partnership profits and losses. This year, Stanhope made him a $62,000 guaranteed payment. Its ordinary business income before consideration of this payment was $412,000.
   a. How much ordinary income does Mr. Hope recognize because of his participation in Stanhope Services?
   b. How much of this income is self-employment income?
   c. How would your answers change if Stanhope's ordinary business income before consideration of the guaranteed payment was only $50,000?

3. In his first year as a partner with Jenkle Legal Services, Mr. Fallon received a $2,000 monthly guaranteed payment. His share of Jenkle's ordinary business income was $55,000. If his combined income and SE tax rate on his earned income is 30 percent, compute his after-tax cash flow from Jenkle assuming the following.
   a. In addition to his guaranteed payments, Mr. Fallon received a $10,000 cash distribution from Jenkle.
   b. In addition to his guaranteed payments, he received a $50,000 cash distribution from Jenkle.

4. Ms. Paul is a 25 percent shareholder in PTC and is employed as chief financial officer. She participates in PTC's group life insurance and health insurance plans. The annual value of these fringe benefits to Ms. Paul is $6,900. Assuming that her marginal tax rate is 35 percent, compute the tax cost of her fringe benefits, assuming these facts.

    *a.* PTC offers its life and health insurance plans to all employees on a nondiscriminatory basis.

    *b.* PTC offers its life and health insurance plans only to the corporate officers and top-level management.

5. This year, Mrs. Kurata's corporate employer made a $8,300 cash contribution to her retirement savings plan. Her interest in the plan is fully vested, so she has the legal right to withdraw the contribution at any time. Describe the tax consequences of the contribution to Mrs. Kurata and to the corporate employer assuming the following.

    *a.* The plan is a qualified defined-contribution plan.

    *b.* The plan is a nonqualified savings plan.

6. On December 20, 2004, Youngblood Inc.'s board of directors authorized a $45,000 bonus to Mr. Abeta. The corporation and Mr. Abeta agreed that payment of the bonus (plus an inflation adjustment) would be deferred until the year of his retirement. Youngblood uses the accrual method of accounting for both book and tax purposes.

    *a.* Does Mr. Abeta have any 2004 tax consequences from the deferred bonus?

    *b.* Does the deferred bonus result in either a permanent or a temporary difference in Youngblood's book and tax income? Explain your conclusion.

7. This year, Mr. Owens received a $125,000 salary from his corporate employer plus the employer's obligation to pay him an additional $15,000 in 2008, the year of his mandatory retirement.

    *a.* How much compensation income does Mr. Owens recognize this year, and how much compensation expense can the corporation deduct?

    *b.* Assume that by 2008, the corporation's deferred compensation obligation to Mr. Owens totals $87,000. The corporation is experiencing severe financial problems and offers to satisfy this obligation by paying him only $40,000 cash. What are the tax consequences to him and to the corporation if he accepts this offer?

8. On December 20, 2004, Tyrone Inc. transferred 100 shares of treasury stock (which Tyrone had redeemed from the estate of a deceased shareholder for $83,500) as a bonus to Mrs. Stitt. The FMV of the 100 shares was $125,000. Her ownership of the shares was unrestricted.

    *a.* What were the 2004 tax consequences to Tyrone of the payment of appreciated treasury stock to compensate an employee?

    *b.* What were the 2004 tax consequences to Mrs. Stitt of receipt of the stock bonus?

    *c.* What are the tax consequences to Mrs. Stitt if she sells the 100 Tyrone shares on January 8, 2006, for $61,000?

9. Mr. Meeks is employed by Runyon Inc. On January 1, 2004, he received a bonus of 4,000 shares of Runyon stock with a $40,000 FMV. If he quits his job before January 1, 2008, he must forfeit the shares to Runyon. After this restriction lapses, his ownership of the stock is fully vested.

    *a.* What are the 2004 tax consequences to Mr. Meeks and Runyon if he does not make a Section 83(b) election with respect to the restricted stock?

    *b.* What are the 2004 tax consequences to Mr. Meeks and Runyon if he makes a Section 83(b) election?

    *c.* By what date must Mr. Meeks make the election?

    *d.* What is Mr. Meeks's tax basis in his 4,000 shares if he does not make the election? What is his basis if he makes the election?

10. Refer to the facts in problem 9. Determine the tax consequences to Mr. Meeks and Runyon in each of the following independent cases.

    *a.* Mr. Meeks made a Section 83(b) election. On January 1, 2008, he is still employed by Runyon, and his 4,000 shares are worth $67,200.

b. He did not make a Section 83(b) election. On January 1, 2008, he is still employed by Runyon, and his 4,000 shares are worth $67,200.

c. He made a Section 83(b) election, and he quit his job with Runyon on August 19, 2005, forfeiting his 4,000 shares.

d. He did not make a Section 83(b) election, and he quit his job with Runyon on August 19, 2005, forfeiting his 4,000 shares.

11. Six years ago, Rollo Inc. granted a nonqualified stock option to Mrs. Jacques to buy 5,000 shares of Rollo stock at $15 per share for six years. At the date of grant, Rollo stock was selling on the AMEX for $14.75 per share. This year, Mrs. Jacques exercised the option when the price was $45.10 per share.

a. How much compensation income did Mrs. Jacques recognize in the year the option was granted?

b. How much compensation income did Mrs. Jacques recognize in the year she exercised the option?

c. Did Rollo have any tax consequences from the option in the year of grant or in the year of exercise?

12. Four years ago, Star Inc. granted an ISO to Mr. Ingram to buy 2,500 shares of Star stock at $4 per share for six years. At the date of grant, Star stock was selling on Nasdaq for $3.90 per share. This year, Mr. Ingram exercised the ISO when the price was $27.10 per share.

a. How much compensation income did Mr. Ingram recognize in the year the ISO was granted?

b. How much compensation income did Mr. Ingram recognize in the year he exercised the ISO?

c. Did Star have any tax consequences from the ISO in the year of grant or in the year of exercise?

13. Two years ago, Mr. Cappoci exercised a stock option by purchasing 2,000 shares of XYZ stock for $9 per share. The market price was $24.88 per share. This year, he sold the stock for $35 per share.

a. Compute Mr. Cappoci's capital gain on sale if the stock option was nonqualified.

b. Compute Mr. Cappoci's capital gain on sale if the stock option was an ISO.

14. Three years ago, Werner Inc. granted 500 SARs to Ms. Hudson as a year-end bonus. Werner's stock was worth $44 a share on the date of grant. Ms. Hudson exercised her SARs this year when Werner's stock was worth $78 per share. Her marginal tax rate in both years was 33 percent.

a. How much compensation income did Ms. Hudson recognize in the year she received the SARs?

b. How much compensation income did Ms. Hudson recognize in the year she exercised the SARs?

c. Compute Ms. Hudson's after-tax cash flow from the exercise of her SARs.

15. Ms. Clark and Ms. Opal, the two equal members of Garnet LLC, persuaded Mrs. Todesco to join them in their business. The three women amended the LLC agreement to admit Mrs. Todesco as a member on January 1, 2004, with a 20 percent interest in profits and losses from that date forward. Mrs. Todesco has no interest in any LLC property existing on the date of her admission. For 2004, Garnet LLC generated $119,300 ordinary business income.

a. How much income did Mrs. Todesco recognize on receipt of her LLC interest?

b. Compute Mrs. Todesco's capital account at the end of 2004 if she received $16,000 cash distributions during the year.

    *c.* Compute Mrs. Todesco's outside basis in her LLC interest at the end of 2004 if the LLC had $8,700 in liabilities on its balance sheet.

16. Mrs. Francisco performed consulting services for BT Partnership in exchange for a 10 percent interest in BT's capital and profits. BT had the following balance sheet immediately before her admission.

|  | Inside Basis |
| --- | --- |
| Operating assets | $380,000 |
| Capital: Mr. Bajorek (30 percent interest) | $114,000 |
| Ms. Thon (70 percent interest) | 266,000 |
|  | $380,000 |

Mrs. Francisco and the two partners agreed that the FMV of BT's business equaled its $380,000 book value.

    *a.* How much income did Mrs. Francisco recognize on receipt of her partnership interest?

    *b.* What is the initial outside basis in her partnership interest?

    *c.* Assuming that BT's payment for her services was an ordinary business expense, what is the partnership deduction for the services, and how should that deduction be allocated among the partners?

    *d.* Adjust BT's tax basis balance sheet to reflect Mrs. Francisco's admission as a 10 percent partner.

17. Refer to the facts in the preceding problem but assume that Mrs. Francisco and the two partners agreed that the FMV of BT's operating assets was $380,000 and BT had $50,000 unrecorded goodwill.

    *a.* How much income did Mrs. Francisco recognize on receipt of her partnership interest?

    *b.* Do Mr. Bajorek and Ms. Thon recognize any gain because of Mrs. Francisco's admission as a partner? Explain your conclusion.

    *c.* On the assumption that BT's payment for Mrs. Francisco's services was an ordinary business expense, what is the partnership deduction for the services? How should that deduction be allocated among the partners?

    *d.* Adjust BT's tax basis balance sheet to reflect Mrs. Francisco's admission as a 10 percent partner.

## Issue Recognition Problems

Identify the tax issue or issues suggested by the following situations and state each issue in the form of a question.

1. Darby Inc. sponsors a group health insurance plan for its employees, their spouses, and their dependent children. Mr. Richey, who is employed by Darby as an chemical engineer, requested that his same-sex domestic partner, Mr. Lord, be covered under the plan, and Darby agreed. The annual value of Mr. Lord's coverage is $4,150.

2. Ms. Teague retired from her job with CMP Inc. this year and is legally entitled to receive $49,000 of deferred compensation. She does not need the money right now and requested that CMP defer payment for three more years.

3. Mr. Gonzalez, age 49, has a $146,000 account balance in his corporate employer's qualified profit-sharing plan. He and his wife are divorcing, and he has agreed to give her a one-half interest in this account as part of the property settlement.

4. Tollway is a publicly held corporation that owns 100 percent of the stock of Tollway South. Mrs. Hopper is an employee of Tollway South. This year, Tollway South distributed 1,000 shares of Tollway stock (FMV $12,500) to Mrs. Hopper as a bonus. Tollway South's basis in its parent corporation's stock was zero.

5. Last year, Mr. Lorson received 500 shares of restricted stock as a bonus from his corporate employer. He did not make a Section 83(b) election to recognize the FMV of the stock as income. This year, the corporation paid a $951 dividend with respect to his stock.

6. Two years ago, Ms. Kenneth received a bonus of 3,000 restricted shares of stock from her corporate employer. She did not make a Section 83(b) election to recognize the FMV of the stock as income, and the restrictions on the stock were not scheduled to lapse for seven years. This year, Ms. Kenneth was killed in an automobile accident. The corporation's board of directors voted to waive any legal claim to the 3,000 shares of stock.

7. On February 1, Mrs. Curtiz received restricted stock worth $33.41 per share from her corporate employer. She believed that the market price of the stock would skyrocket over the next several years, so she made a Section 83(b) election on February 3. By late December, the market price of the stock had dropped to $8.02 per share, and Mrs. Curtiz had changed her mind about recognizing current income with respect to her restricted shares.

8. Three years ago, Miss Vinson was granted a stock option from her corporate employer that entitled her to buy 500 shares of employer stock for $45 per share over the next six years. At the date of grant, the stock was selling on the NYSE for $43 per share. This year, the stock split, so that every outstanding share was converted into two shares. Immediately after the split, the stock price was $35.

9. Last year, Mr. Byle performed services in exchange for a restricted capital interest in CMRT General Partnership. Until the interest vests in 2007, he cannot dispose of it and will receive no distributions from CMRT. Because he did not make a Section 83(b) election, he had no tax consequences on the receipt of the interest. This year, CMRT defaulted on a liability to a major creditor, which has sued all general partners to recover the unpaid liability.

## Research Problems

1. Ms. Cisco recently accepted a position as an analyst with an investment banking firm. One of the recruiting inducements that convinced her to accept the position is a $30,000 loan from her employer. She will receive the loan proceeds on her first day of work and must sign a note to repay the loan plus accrued interest in five equal annual installments. The employer will forgive any amount of the unpaid debt if Ms. Cisco dies, becomes disabled, or is terminated from employment through no fault of her own. Her employment contract provides that the employer will pay an annual bonus equal to each annual loan payment. The contract stipulates that the bonus must be applied to the payment of her loan. Does this loan-bonus arrangement allow Ms. Cisco to defer income recognition with respect to her up-front $30,000 cash receipt?

2. Mr. Whit is the sole shareholder and CEO of newly incorporated Talawanda Concepts. He plans to pay himself a reasonable $100,000 annual salary. However, the corporation will pay his first-year salary on a monthly basis and the entire second-year salary on December 31. The corporation will pay nothing to him during the second calendar year, and then it will repeat the payment cycle in the third calendar year. Talawanda will fund each year-end salary prepayment through short-term loans from a local bank. The purpose of this odd payment schedule is to avoid Social Security tax on Mr. Whit's base salary in alternating years. Will this strategy to minimize his payroll tax actually work?

# Tax Planning Case

Mr. Olmer owns a nonqualified option to purchase 10,000 shares of his corporate employer's publicly traded stock for $11.75 per share. The option is about to expire, and the current market price of the stock is $20. Mr. Olmer is considering two alternatives. He could exercise the option, then immediately sell enough shares to generate the cash necessary to pay his income tax on the bargain element and hold the remaining shares as an investment. His other alternative is to use other funds to pay the income tax and hold all 10,000 shares for investment. In either case, he intends to hold the investment shares for three years before selling them for cash.

1. Compare the NPV of Mr. Olmer's cash flows (from exercise of the option and subsequent sale of stock) under both alternatives if the market price of the stock is $30 per share in three years.
2. Compare the NPV under both alternatives if the market price of the stock is $15 per share in three years.

Base your computations on the following assumptions.

- Mr. Olmer's marginal tax rate on ordinary income is 35 percent.

- The employer stock will be Mr. Olmer's only investment asset. If he recognizes a gain on sale, he can use a 15 percent rate to compute the tax cost. If he recognizes a loss on sale, he can deduct the loss only at the rate of $3,000 per year. *Assume that the NPV of the tax savings from this series of future deductions is immaterial.*

- Mr. Olmer's discount rate is 7 percent, so the discount factor for computing the NPV of his after-tax cash from the sale of his investment shares in three years is .816.

# Comprehensive Case for Part Two

On March 1, 2005, Mr. Shaun, Ms. Bolt, and Ms. Ivy formed a new corporation (SBI Inc.) by making the following exchanges.

Mr. Shaun transferred business inventory worth $105,000. His tax basis in the inventory was $87,300. He also transferred the licensed trade name of his sole proprietorship (Shaun's Services), which the corporation will use as its trade name. The three incorporators agreed that this name represented $50,000 worth of goodwill. Mr. Shaun had no tax basis in the trade name. In exchange for the inventory and goodwill, Mr. Shaun received SBI's short-term note for $35,000 and 1,200 shares of common stock. SBI must pay the note (plus 7 percent interest) by December 31, 2005.

Ms. Bolt transferred business equipment worth $150,000. The original cost of the equipment was $160,000, and accumulated MACRS depreciation was $113,800. The equipment was subject to a $25,000 liability, which SBI assumed. Ms. Bolt incurred this liability for a bona fide business reason, and SBI's assumption was not for any tax avoidance purpose. Ms. Bolt received 1,250 shares of common stock.

Ms. Ivy transferred $40,000 cash and a two-year lease on commercial office space. Because of the favorable lease terms, the three incorporators agreed that the lease was worth $15,000. However, Ms. Ivy had no tax basis in the lease. Ms. Ivy received 550 shares of common stock.

SBI Inc. adopted the accrual method of accounting and a calendar year for tax purposes. On March 4, 2005, the three shareholders made a valid subchapter S election for their corporation. Also on March 4, SBI Inc. entered into a three-year employment contract with Ms. Ivy under which the corporation agreed to pay her a $40,000 annual salary plus 600 additional shares of common stock. These shares are restricted because Ms. Ivy's ownership is subject to the following vesting schedule.

| Number of Shares | Vesting Date |
|---|---|
| 200 | December 31, 2005 |
| 200 | December 31, 2006 |
| 200 | December 31, 2007 |

If she quits her job with SBI at any time before December 31, 2007, she must forfeit the nonvested shares back to the corporation.

1. Determine the gain realized, the gain recognized, and the tax character of any gain recognized by Mr. Shaun, Ms. Bolt, and Ms. Ivy on their transfers of property to SBI, Inc.
2. Determine each shareholder's tax basis in their SBI stock.
3. Prepare a beginning book basis and a tax basis balance sheet for SBI Inc.
4. Assume that Ms. Ivy does not make a Section 83(b) election with respect to her 600 restricted SBI shares. How much 2005 taxable income must she recognize with respect to these shares?

Suggested research aid: Rev. Rul. 68-55, 1968-1 CB 140.

# Business Operating Strategies

# Chapter Five

# Income Measurement and Reporting

## Learning Objectives

*After reading this chapter, you will be able to:*

1. Determine the taxable year that a business entity can use.

2. Identify corporations that are prohibited from using the cash method.

3. Differentiate between a permanent and a temporary difference between book income and taxable income.

4. Prepare a Schedule M-1 reconciliation of book income with taxable income.

5. Explain how corporations compute income tax expense for GAAP financial statement purposes.

6. Determine whether a temporary difference results in a deferred tax asset or a deferred tax liability.

7. Describe the corporate tax payment and return-filing requirements.

Part Three of *Advanced Strategies* consists of four chapters on the tax issues surrounding routine business operations. Chapter 5 concerns the measurement of annual taxable income and the reporting of that income to the federal government. Chapter 6 focuses on business tax incentives and the corporate alternative minimum tax that can limit the value of the incentives. Chapter 7 discusses the allocation of taxable income to the owners of passthrough entities. Chapter 8 considers the tax consequences of distributions by corporations, partnerships, and LLCs to their owners.

Chapter 5 begins by considering the taxable years and accounting methods available to business entities. The chapter identifies a number of differences between income for financial statement purposes and taxable income. It also analyzes how the differences must be reconciled on the entity's tax return. The analysis of book/tax differences leads to a discussion of Generally Accepted Accounting Principles (GAAP) under which corporations account for current and deferred tax expense. The chapter concludes with an explanation of the federal income tax payment requirements for corporate taxpayers.

Reg. 1.6001-1(a) provides that taxpayers who engage in any business activity must keep permanent accounting records sufficient to establish the gross income, deductions, credits, or other items reported on their tax returns. Even taxpayers who have no obligation to share their financial information with any other party must share the information with the IRS. Thus, the owners of a new business must establish an accounting system, if for no other reason than to compute taxable income or loss from the business. An accounting system has two elements: a specific time period over which to measure income and an accounting method by which to perform that measurement.

# THE ENTITY'S TAXABLE YEAR

**Objective 1**
Determine the taxable year that a business entity can use.

A business entity must measure its operating income or loss on an annual basis. This annual accounting period can be a calendar year, a fiscal year ending on the last day of any month other than December, or a **52–53 week year** (an annual period consisting of either 52 or 53 weeks and ending on the same day of the week each year). For the most accurate income measurement, an entity's accounting period should correspond to its business operating cycle. For example, a landscaping company might have an operating cycle in which revenues, payroll costs, and inventories are highest during the peak spring and summer seasons and lowest during the slack winter season. If this company uses a fiscal year ending on October 31 for accounting purposes, its annual income will reflect the financial results from one complete operating cycle.

Section 441(a) states that taxable income is computed on the basis of the taxpayer's taxable year, and Section 441(b)(1) provides that the term **taxable year** refers to the taxpayer's annual accounting period. This correlation between taxable year and accounting period holds true for corporate taxpayers. Corporations can use their accounting year as their taxable year without any special permission from the IRS.[1]

| | |
|---|---|
| *Corporate Taxable Year* | Monument Products Inc. keeps its financial books and records and files its Form 1120 on the basis of a fiscal year ending January 31. For the 12-month accounting period ended on January 31, 2004, Monument's taxable income was $4 million, and its federal income tax was $1,360,000 (34 percent × $4 million). |

## Taxable Years for Passthrough Entities

Although passthrough entities (partnerships, LLCs, and S corporations) do not pay federal income tax, they must compute annual income on the basis of their own taxable year. The owners report their share of income for their taxable year in which the *entity's* year ends.[2] If the owner's taxable year is different from the entity's taxable year, the owner's tax on some portion of the entity's income is deferred.

| | |
|---|---|
| *Different Taxable Years for Entity and Owner* | Assume that Monument Products is a passthrough entity instead of a taxable corporation. It is owned equally by four individuals who are calendar year taxpayers. If Monument's taxable year ends on January 31, each owner reports a 25 percent share of Monument's income for that fiscal year on the Form 1040 for the calendar year that includes January 31. If Monument's taxable income for fiscal year-end (FYE) January 31, 2004, was $4 million, each owner reported a $1 million share on his or her 2004 Form 1040. Consequently, the owners paid tax in 2004 on 11 months of income earned in 2003 plus one month of income earned in 2004. |

[1] This statement does not apply to personal service corporations, which must use a calendar year unless the IRS agrees that the corporation has a valid business purpose for a different taxable year. Section 441(i)(1). A *personal service corporation* is a corporation whose principal activity is the performance of personal services, and such services are substantially performed by employee/owners.

[2] Sections 706(a) and 1366(a).

Owners have an incentive to adopt a taxable year for their entity that maximizes the deferral of tax on the entity's income. The law hampers this strategy with a set of restrictions on the choice of taxable year. The essence of these restrictions is that a passthrough entity must use the same taxable year as its owners *unless* the entity can establish a business purpose for a different year to the satisfaction of the IRS.[3] The circumstances in which the IRS will grant an entity's request for a different taxable year are quite limited. Generally, the entity must demonstrate that the requested year coincides with its "natural business year," a 12-month operating cycle in which the entity recognizes at least 25 percent of its gross receipts in the final two months.[4] An entity that cannot meet this mechanical 25 percent test must have an unusual and compelling business purpose to justify a different taxable year.[5]

*tax avoidance strategies*

| *Natural Business Year Test* | Bonding LLC, which is owned by four calendar year individual taxpayers, operates a swimming pool maintenance business. The business is closed from December through February, and its busiest months are June, July, and August. Bonding's accounting records show that it recognizes 40 to 50 percent of its annual gross receipts in July and August. Because Bonding meets the 25 percent test, it has a natural business year ending on August 31, which it can use as its taxable year. |
|---|---|

### Partnerships Restrictions

If a partnership has no business purpose for a particular taxable year, it must use the **majority interest taxable year,** which is the taxable year of one or more partners who own more than 50 percent of capital and profits.[6]

| *Majority Interest Taxable Year* | Cohn Partnership has five equal partners: four individuals who are calendar year taxpayers and one corporation with a fiscal year ending March 31. Because the calendar year partners in the aggregate own more than 50 percent of Cohn's capital and profits, Cohn Partnership must use a calendar year as its taxable year unless it can establish a business purpose for a different year. |
|---|---|

If a partnership does not have a majority interest taxable year, it must use the taxable year of all its principal partners. A **principal partner** is any partner who owns at least 5 percent of capital or profits.[7]

| *Principal Partner Taxable Year* | Worthen Partnership has three corporate general partners, each of which owns a 15 percent interest in capital and profits. All three corporations use a fiscal year ending September 30. Worthen has 40 limited partners, each of whom owns less than a 5 percent interest. No group of partners with the same taxable year owns a majority interest in Worthen. However, the three principal partners do have the same taxable year. Therefore, Worthen Partnership must use a fiscal year ending September 30 unless it can establish a business purpose for a different taxable year. |
|---|---|

A partnership that does not have either a majority interest taxable year or a principal partner taxable year must use the taxable year resulting in the least aggregate deferral of

---

[3] Section 444 allows a passthrough entity to elect a taxable year resulting in no more than three months of income deferral to the owners if the entity makes a noninterest-bearing deposit with the IRS approximating the amount of the owners' tax on the deferred income.

[4] Notice 2001-35, 2001-1 CB 1314 provides the computational details of the 25 percent test.

[5] Notice 2001-34, 2001-1 CB 1302.

[6] Section 706(b)(1)(B)(i). Majority interest taxable year is defined in Section 706(b)(4).

[7] Section 706(b)(1)(B)(ii). Principal partner is defined in Section 706(b)(3).

income to its partners.[8] The income deferral from a *particular* taxable year for a *particular* partner is computed by multiplying the partner's months of deferral by the partner's profit-sharing percentage. The *months of deferral* are the months between the partnership year-end and the partner's year-end. For instance, a partnership fiscal year ending January 31 results in 11 months of deferral for a calendar year partner but only four months of deferral for a partner with a fiscal year ending May 31. The easiest way to understand the concept of least aggregate deferral is through a numeric example.

*Least Aggregate Deferral Taxable Year*

CPR Partnership has three partners, Mr. Cobb, Payne Inc., and Rollin Inc. Mr. Cobb has a 20 percent interest in CPR's profits. Payne and Rollin both have a 40 percent interest. Mr. Cobb is a calendar year taxpayer, Payne's taxable year ends on April 30, and Rollin's taxable year ends on August 31. CPR Partnership has no business purpose for any taxable year and no majority interest or principal partner taxable year. As a result, it must determine which of the three different years used by its partners results in the least aggregate deferral of income to those partners. The aggregate deferral from each different year is computed in the following tables.

| | Months of Deferral from December 31 Year-End | Profit Percentage | Months × Profit Percentage |
|---|---|---|---|
| **Calendar year** | | | |
| Mr. Cobb (12/31 year-end) | –0– | 20% | –0– |
| Payne Inc. (4/30 year-end) | 4 months | 40 | 1.6% |
| Rollin Inc. (8/31 year-end) | 8 months | 40 | 3.2 |
| Aggregate deferral | | | 4.8% |

| | Months of Deferral from April 30 Year-End | Profit Percentage | Months × Profit Percentage |
|---|---|---|---|
| **Fiscal year ending April 30** | | | |
| Mr. Cobb (12/31 year-end) | 8 months | 20% | 1.6% |
| Payne Inc. (4/30 year-end) | –0– | 40 | –0– |
| Rollin Inc. (8/31 year-end) | 4 months | 40 | 1.6 |
| Aggregate deferral | | minimized | 3.2% |

| | Months of Deferral from August 31 Year-End | Profit Percentage | Months × Profit Percentage |
|---|---|---|---|
| **Fiscal year ending August 31** | | | |
| Mr. Cobb (12/31 year-end) | 4 months | 20% | 0.8% |
| Payne Inc. (4/30 year-end) | 8 months | 40 | 3.2 |
| Rollin Inc. (8/31 year-end) | –0– | 40 | –0– |
| Aggregate deferral | | | 4.0% |

On the basis of the data from these three tables, CPR Partnership must adopt a taxable year ending April 30 because this fiscal year results in the least aggregate deferral of income for CPR's partners.

[8] Reg. 1.706-1T.

### S Corporation Restrictions

S corporations that have no business purpose for a particular taxable year generally must use a calendar year.[9] The shareholders in an S corporation must be individuals, trusts, estates, or tax-exempt organizations. Because the shareholders who pay tax on S corporation income are, with rare exceptions, calendar year taxpayers themselves, they cannot defer their tax by using a fiscal year for their S corporation.[10]

# TAX ACCOUNTING METHODS

Section 446(a) provides that taxable income shall be computed under the method of accounting by which the taxpayer regularly computes income in keeping its books. A business entity "keeps its books" by recording transactions in paper or electronic journals of accounts. When the entity closes its books at the end of the taxable year, it uses the cumulative data from its journals to prepare its annual income statement and its balance sheet of assets and liabilities.

An entity that is not required to prepare financial statements for any external user can keep its books solely for tax accounting purposes. These **tax basis books** reflect the statutory and regulatory rules governing the computation of taxable income. In keeping its tax basis books, the entity may adopt an accounting method that is best suited to its needs.[11] Moreover, an entity engaged in more than one line of business can adopt different methods of accounting for each line.[12] The entity's discretion in adopting a method of accounting is subject to an important constraint: The method is acceptable only if the IRS agrees that it clearly reflects the entity's taxable income.[13]

Once an entity has adopted a tax accounting method, it must request the IRS's permission to change to another method. The entity must make the request during the taxable year for which the change is to be effective.[14] The IRS will give its permission only if the entity agrees to make any adjustments that the IRS deems necessary to prevent an omission of income or duplication of deductions because of the change in method.[15] The IRS will grant automatic consent to many common accounting method changes (such as the change from cash to accrual) if the entity follows the procedures outlined in Rev. Proc. 99-49.[16]

*Change of Accounting Method for Aircraft Overhaul Costs*

The Federal Aviation Administration requires commercial airlines to completely overhaul each aircraft every eight years. The purpose of the overhaul is to maintain the aircraft's safety and reliability. Any cracks, dysfunctional equipment, or interior damage is repaired, and the aircraft is repainted. The overhaul does not increase the aircraft's value or extend its useful life. The IRS recently ruled that airlines can deduct the cost of the overhaul in the year in which it was incurred. Airlines that have been capitalizing the cost to the basis of each aircraft can request an automatic change in accounting method to expense the cost for their taxable years ending after January 16, 2001.[17]

---

[9] Section 1378. S corporations can elect a taxable year ending September 30, October 31, or November 30 under Section 444. See footnote 3.

[10] While estates are free to adopt any taxable year, Section 644 requires all trusts to be calendar year taxpayers.

[11] Reg. 1.446-1(a)(2).

[12] Section 446(d).

[13] Section 446(b).

[14] The request is made on Form 3115.

[15] Reg. 1.446-1(e)(3).

[16] 1999-2 CB 725. Taxpayers requesting automatic consent to an accounting method change can file Form 3115 by the extended due date of their federal tax return for the year of change.

[17] Rev. Rul. 2001-4, 2001-1 CB 295.

## Cash Basis Businesses

Small businesses that do not prepare financial statements for external reporting purposes typically use the **cash method of accounting**. A cash basis business records revenue when payment for goods or services is actually or constructively received, regardless of when the revenue was earned, and records an expense when payment is made, regardless of when the liability for the expense was incurred. Under the cash method, taxable income corresponds closely to net cash flow from operations. Consequently, the method is simple, objective, and requires a minimum of record keeping.

Cash basis businesses cannot expense payments that create an asset having a useful life extending substantially beyond the close of the taxable year.[18] If a payment creates a benefit that extends less than one year beyond the year of payment, the courts have allowed the payment to be expensed (and deducted) rather than capitalized.[19] But if the benefit extends beyond this one-year period, the payment must be capitalized to an asset account and recovered through depreciation, amortization, or depletion deductions.

---

*Prepaid Rent*

Osterman Company uses the calendar year and the cash method of accounting for tax purposes. On November 28, 2004, Osterman prepaid $9,700 rent for the use of equipment. The equipment lease runs from January 2005 through June 2006. On December 1, 2004, Osterman prepaid $36,000 rent for the use of an office building. The building lease runs for 36 months beginning on December 1, 2004. Because the benefit of the equipment lease expires within the following year, Osterman can expense the entire payment in 2004. However, it can expense only one month ($1,000) of the prepaid building rent and must capitalize the remaining $35,000 to an asset account. Osterman can amortize this capitalized cost over the remaining 35 months of the lease.

---

A similar accounting rule applies to payments for supplies. Reg. 1.162-3 provides that businesses can expense the cost of *incidental* materials or supplies in the year of purchase. Businesses that purchase substantial (nonincidental) quantities of supplies, however, can expense only the cost of supplies actually consumed during the taxable year. The cost of supplies on hand at year-end must be capitalized to an asset account.

---

*Payments for Supplies*

On November 22, 2004, Osterman paid $220 for coffee, paper towels, dishwashing liquid, and other supplies used in the employee lounge. It also paid $18,100 for industrial supplies used in its manufacturing business. On the basis of a physical inventory, Osterman had $15,500 of industrial supplies on hand at year-end. It can expense the $220 payment for the incidental supplies and the $2,600 cost of the industrial supplies actually consumed during the year.

---

Cash basis businesses have no leeway at all with respect to prepaid interest. Section 461(g) requires interest payments allocable to any period after the close of the taxable year to be capitalized and expensed over such period.

---

[18] Reg. 1.461-1(a).
[19] *Zaninovich v. Commissioner*, 616 F.2d 429 (CA-9, 1980).

| *Prepaid Interest* | On December 13, 2004, Osterman paid $12,000 interest on a loan from First Union Bank. The interest was for the one-year period beginning on April 1, 2004, through March 31, 2005. Osterman can expense the $9,000 payment allocable to 2004 but must capitalize the $3,000 payment allocable to 2005. It will expense the $3,000 capitalized interest in the computation of 2005 taxable income. |
| --- | --- |

### Accounting for Merchandise Inventories

The tax law includes two long-standing accounting rules pertaining to merchandise inventories. First, businesses must account for inventory on hand at the beginning and end of each taxable year if the production, purchase, or sale of merchandise is an income-producing factor.[20] Second, businesses that maintain inventories must use the accrual method of accounting for both sales and purchases of inventory.[21] Because of these two rules, many businesses use the hybrid accounting method in which inventory transactions are reported on an accrual basis and all other transactions are reported on a cash basis.[22]

| *Hybrid Method of Accounting* | CuddlyCoat LLC manufactures protective clothing for small dogs and sells the clothing at retail. The LLC uses the hybrid method of accounting under which it accounts for sales and purchases of inventory under the accrual method. Thus, the LLC recognizes gross income when a sales transaction is complete, reduces gross income by cost of goods sold, and carries its ending inventory as a balance sheet asset. However, it accounts for all other business transactions under the cash method. |
| --- | --- |

### Prohibition of Use of Cash Method by Corporations

**Objective 2**
Identify corporations that are prohibited from using the cash method.

Congress and the IRS are chronically worried that businesses can manipulate the cash method of accounting to understate taxable income. Section 448 was enacted to prohibit the use of the cash method by corporations, partnerships with corporate partners, and tax shelters (loosely defined as arrangements with a significant purpose to avoid or evade federal income tax).[23] This sweeping prohibition is subject to a *de minimus* exception for small businesses.[24] Specifically, a corporation or partnership can use the cash method for a taxable year if it meets a $5 million gross receipts test for *all prior taxable years*. An entity meets this test for a particular year if its average annual gross receipts for the three-year period ending with that year do not exceed $5 million. If the entity was not in existence for the entire three-year period, the test is based on the number of years it did exist.

| *Gross Receipts Test* | Kobi Inc. was incorporated on January 1, 2000, and adopted the calendar year and the cash method for tax purposes. It operates a plumbing service business that generated the following annual gross receipts through 2004: |
| --- | --- |

[20] Reg. 1.471-1.

[21] Reg. 1.446-1(c)(2)(i).

[22] Rev. Proc. 2002-28, 2002-18 IRB 815, allows *service* businesses with average annual gross receipts of $10 million or less to use a simplified cash method under which they account for merchandise sales under the cash method. This accounting method is not available to businesses that are principally engaged in manufacturing, wholesaling, or retailing activities.

[23] Based on the definition of tax shelter in Section 6662(d)(2)(C)(iii).

[24] Section 448(b) also excepts farming businesses and personal service corporations in which the shareholders perform professional services for the corporation's clients.

| | |
|---|---|
| 2000 | $ 743,000 |
| 2001 | 1,849,000 |
| 2002 | 3,620,000 |
| 2003 | 5,340,000 |
| 2004 | 6,010,000 |

Kobi could use the cash method for 2000 through 2004 because it met the gross receipts test for 2000 through 2003. It can continue to use the cash method for 2005 because it meets the gross receipts test for 2004: average annual gross receipts for 2002–2004 are only $4,990,000 ([$3,620,000 + $5,340,000 + $6,010,000]/3 years).

Kobi estimates that its 2005 gross receipts will be $6,800,000. In this case, it will fail the gross receipts test for 2006 because average annual gross receipts for 2003–2005 will be $6,050,000 ([$5,340,000 + $6,010,000 + $6,800,000]/3 years). Accordingly, Kobi will be required to change to the accrual method of accounting for its 2006 taxable year.

The cash method of accounting is usually discussed in the context of small businesses. However, the tax rules limiting the use of the cash method do not apply to individuals who operate a service business (in which inventories are not an income-producing factor) as a passthrough entity, regardless of the size of the business. Numerous large professional service partnerships, LLPs, LLCs, and S corporations operating on a global scale use the cash method of accounting for federal tax purposes.

## Accrual Basis Businesses

**Tax Talk**
According to the Institute on Taxation and Economic Policy, the gap between the profit that companies report to shareholders and their taxable income has been widening steadily for a decade. "When investors hear only of rosy earnings while at tax time Uncle Sam only hears of regrets and red ink, something is very wrong," said U.S. Representative Lloyd Doggett.

Many businesses that adopt the cash method of accounting in their first taxable year eventually change to the accrual method. Some are forced to make the change because of Section 448. Others simply outgrow the cash method. A business often develops to the point at which the owners are required to share financial information with third parties, such as commercial lenders, potential investors, or regulatory agencies. These third parties typically demand income statements and balance sheets based on **Generally Accepted Accounting Principles (GAAP)** established by the Financial Accounting Standards Board (FASB). According to GAAP, only the **accrual method of accounting** results in the correct measurement of income. Thus, the business converts to an accrual basis accounting system to generate financial statements that reflect GAAP and, for the sake of consistency, converts to the accrual method to compute taxable income.[25]

The accrual method for GAAP purposes and the accrual method for tax purposes are not identical. Both methods are based on the same theory of income measurement: A business should record revenue when the earnings process with respect to the sale of goods or services is complete, regardless of when payment is received. Conversely, a business should record an expense when the liability for the expense is incurred, regardless of when the expense is paid. The GAAP accrual method and the tax accrual method vary as to the way this theory is applied to specific transactions. The GAAP method is applied to prevent a business from overstating revenue or understating expense from a transaction. As a result, the GAAP method results in a conservative measurement with the *least* positive effect on net income for external reporting purposes. In contrast, the tax method is applied to prevent a business from understating gross income or overstating deductions from a transaction. The

[25] Businesses that use the accrual method for financial statement purposes can use the cash method for tax purposes if the cash method clearly reflects taxable income. Rev. Rul. 68-35, 1968-1 CB 190.

tax method also results in a conservative measurement with the *most* positive effect on taxable income reported to the federal government.

| *Same Transaction— Different Perspectives* | The GAAP accrual method and the tax accrual method take different perspectives on income measurement. The difference is reflected in the way that financial accountants and tax accountants describe the consequences of business transactions. If a transaction involves a financial benefit or gain, the financial accountant says that the business "is allowed to" report revenue, but the tax accountant says that the business "must" recognize gross income. If the transaction involves a financial detriment or loss, the financial accountant says that the business "must" report an expense, but the tax accountant says that the business "is allowed to" claim a deduction. |
|---|---|

# DIFFERENCES BETWEEN BOOK INCOME AND TAXABLE INCOME

**Objective 3**
Differentiate between a permanent and a temporary difference between book income and taxable income.

The majority of business transactions are accounted for in exactly the same way under the GAAP accrual method and the tax accrual method. Most transactions that generate revenue for financial statement (book) purposes generate the same amount of gross income for tax purposes. Most transactions that generate a book expense generate a corresponding deduction for tax purposes. Transactions that are accounted for differently for book and tax purposes are the exception rather than the rule. Nevertheless, businesses must be aware of these differences to provide accurate information on both their financial statements and their tax return. In the next section, we discuss the two types of book/tax differences: permanent differences that affect only the current year and temporary differences that affect more than one year.

## Permanent Differences

The tax rules governing the recognition of income or gain and the deduction of expense or loss can create a **permanent difference** between book income and taxable income. Let's review two common examples. A business that earns interest on an investment in long-term bonds issued by the City of Chicago includes the interest in book income. However, Section 103(a) provides that gross income does not include interest on any state or local bond. Because of this tax rule, the municipal bond interest is permanently excluded from taxable income and has no tax cost to the business. A business that incurs a fine from the City of Chicago for breach of a local zoning ordinance includes the fine as an expense in computing book income. However, Section 162(f) provides that no deduction is allowed for any fine or similar penalty paid to a government for the violation of any law. Because of this tax rule, the fine never reduces taxable income and never yields a tax savings to the business.

In many cases, a tax rule that causes a permanent difference was not enacted to improve the measurement of taxable income. Instead, it was enacted to implement an economic or social policy. Congress enacted the Section 103 exclusion to enhance the ability of state and local governments to borrow money and the Section 162(f) disallowance rule to enhance the punitive impact of fines and penalties. The following are other common permanent book/tax differences and the statutory authority for each.

- Nontaxable life insurance proceeds [Section 101(a)].
- Dividends-received deduction [Section 243].
- Nondeductible bribes, kickbacks, and other illegal payments [Section 162(c)].
- Nondeductible lobbying and political expenses [Section 162(e)].

- Nondeductible premiums on key-person life insurance policies [Section 264(a)].
- Nondeductible expenses and interest relating to tax-exempt income [Section 265].
- Nondeductible 50 percent of business meals and entertainment [Section 274(n)].

In Chapter 4, we discussed a compensation technique that can cause a permanent book/tax difference: employee stock option plans. For financial accounting purposes, corporations that pay their employees with stock options are not required to record compensation expense unless the market price of the optioned shares is more than the strike price at the date of grant.[26] In the typical case in which the strike price is equal to or slightly higher than the market price, the corporation never records compensation expense for the option. For tax purposes, corporations can deduct the bargain element (excess of market value of the shares over the strike price) when an employee exercises a nonqualified option. Consequently, the compensation deduction is a permanent difference between book income and taxable income in the year of exercise.[27]

| | |
|---|---|
| *Permanent Difference: Exercise of Nonqualified Stock Options* | Six years ago, Farlie Inc. granted a nonqualified stock option to Mrs. Coombs, entitling her to buy 500 shares of Farlie stock for $70 per share at any time during the next six years. At the date of grant, Farlie stock sold on the Nasdaq for $68.55 per share. Because the $70 strike price exceeded the market price, Farlie did not record any compensation expense in the year of grant. This year, Mrs. Coombs exercised her option when the market price of Farlie stock was $114 per share. Farlie deducted the $22,000 bargain element ($57,000 market value of 500 shares − $35,000 strike price), resulting in a permanent $22,000 excess of book income over taxable income. |

## Temporary Differences

The financial accounting rules and the tax accounting rules have many inconsistencies concerning the timing of income measurement. Because of these inconsistencies, items of income, gain, expense, or loss are included in the computation of book income for one year and taxable income for another year. A book/tax difference resulting from a timing inconsistency is only a **temporary difference.** An excess of book over taxable income originating in the current year will reverse as an excess of taxable over book income in some future year (and vice versa). Our first example of a temporary difference involves an item of income that must be recognized for tax purposes in an earlier year but cannot be reported as book income until a later year.

| | |
|---|---|
| *Temporary Difference: Advanced Rentals* | Lionel LLC uses the calendar year and the accrual method of accounting for book and tax purposes. It owns a commercial office building and leases three floors to a tenant for $1,300 a month. On November 1, Lionel received a $15,600 check from the tenant in prepayment of rent for the period November 1 through October 31. For book purposes, Lionel recorded $2,600 revenue on its income statement and $13,000 unearned revenue as a balance sheet liability. For tax purposes, Lionel was required to recognize the entire $15,600 advanced rental as gross income, even though $13,000 had not been earned by year-end.[28] Because of this |

[26] *APB No. 25,* "Accounting for Stock Issued to Employees" (1972). This approach to valuing stock options is called the *intrinsic value method. SFAS No. 12,* "Accounting for Stock–Based Compensation" (1995) encourages (but does not require) corporations to record compensation expense equal to the FMV of the stock option under an asset-pricing model such as the Black-Scholes model.

[27] The tax saving from this deduction does not reduce tax expense per books. Instead, the saving is credited directly to paid-in capital. Donald E. Kieso and Jerry J. Weygandt, *Intermediate Accounting,* 9th ed. (New York: John Wiley & Sons, Inc., 1998), p. 1038.

[28] Reg. 1.61-8(b).

book/tax difference, taxable income exceeded book income by $13,000. This difference will reverse next year when Lionel records $13,000 rent revenue for book purposes but no rent income for tax purposes.

In Chapter 4, we discussed a compensation strategy that causes a classic temporary book/tax difference: nonqualified deferred compensation. When an employer defers the payment of employee compensation until a future year, the employer must accrue an expense for income statement purposes and a liability on its balance sheet. For tax purposes, however, the employer is not allowed a deduction until the year in which the deferred compensation is actually paid.[29]

| *Temporary Difference: Deferred Compensation* | In 1994, Efras Inc. and its CEO, Ms. Furr, agreed to a deferred compensation arrangement in which Efras delayed payment of Ms. Furr's 1994 year-end bonus until 2005. In computing 1994 book income, Efras accrued a $100,000 bonus expense and a $100,000 liability to Ms. Furr. It could not deduct the accrued expense on its 1994 tax return. Therefore, 1994 taxable income exceeded book income by this $100,000 book/tax difference. Efras paid its $100,000 liability to Ms. Furr in 2005 and deducted the payment. Its 2005 taxable income was $100,000 less than book income because of the reversal of the 1994 book/tax difference. |
|---|---|

### Accrued Liabilities

The book/tax difference in the Efras example is characteristic of book/tax differences created by accrued liabilities. For book purposes, a business must record a liability in the year when it was most probably incurred and the dollar amount can be reasonably estimated. This GAAP rule accelerates the corresponding expense into the *earliest* feasible year. For tax purposes, a business cannot account for a liability until "the taxable year in which (1) all the events have occurred that establish the fact of the liability, (2) the amount of the liability can be determined with reasonable accuracy, and (3) economic performance has occurred with respect to the liability."[30] The combination of these three requirements, called the **all-events test,** delays the corresponding deduction into the *latest* feasible year. An estimated expense arising from an anticipated or contingent liability fails the all-events test because the fact of the liability has not been established by the end of the taxable year. Thus, an accrued expense resulting from an increase in an accounting reserve or allowance is not deductible.

| *Temporary Difference: Reserve for Environmental Cleanup* | Smythson Inc. operates a manufacturing plant that generates chemical waste as an industrial by-product. The state government is considering new legislation to require manufacturers to meet much tougher environmental standards for waste disposal sites. Because of Smythson's probable liability for future environmental cleanup, it recorded a $1 million reserve for the estimated cost of the cleanup and a corresponding $1 million expense on its income statement. Smythson cannot deduct the addition to the reserve because the fact of its liability for any environmental cleanup has yet to be established. |
|---|---|

### Economic Performance

Even an expense resulting from an unconditional liability for an exact amount is not deductible if **economic performance** has not occurred. Section 461(h)(2) provides three rules for determining the year in which economic performance occurs. The first rule applies to a

---

[29] Section 404(a)(5).

[30] Reg. 1.461-1(a)(2)(ii).

liability related to the provision of services, property, or the use of property to a business by another person. Economic performance occurs in the year or years in which the person actually provides the services, property, or use of property to the business.

| | |
|---|---|
| *Provision of Services to a Business* | Early this year, Libby Inc. contracted with a consulting firm to provide marketing services for Libby's business. The contract obligates Libby to pay a $90,000 fee when the consulting firm completes the engagement. By the end of the year, the firm had provided only 50 percent of the services described in the contract. Even though Libby has a $90,000 liability under a binding contract, it can deduct only a $45,000 expense because economic performance has occurred with respect to only $45,000 of the liability. |

The second rule applies to a liability related to the provision of services, property, or the use of property to another person by a business (the reverse of the transaction in the first rule). Economic performance occurs in the year or years in which the business incurs costs to satisfy the liability.[31]

| | |
|---|---|
| *Provision of Services by a Business* | Ottarino Inc. sells janitorial services and cleaning supplies to commercial customers. This year, it offered a free "basement-to-roof" office cleanup to any customer that purchased at least $50,000 of supplies. At the end of the year, Ottarino was obligated to provide this future service to 18 local businesses. Its cost for each cleanup will be about $3,000. Even though Ottarino is committed to provide future services at an estimated cost of $54,000, it has no deduction with respect to this liability because economic performance has not occurred. Economic performance will occur in a subsequent taxable year to the extent that Ottarino incurs actual costs in performing the services. |

The third rule for determining economic performance applies to specific liabilities identified in Reg. 1.461-4(g). Economic performance occurs only when, and to the extent that, payment is made to satisfy the liability. These so-called **payment liabilities** include the following.

- A liability arising under any workers' compensation act or any tort, breach of contract, or violation of law.
- A liability to pay a customer a rebate or refund.
- A liability to provide an award, prize, or jackpot.
- A liability to pay any tax *other* than a real property tax. (Section 461(c) provides that real property taxes can be accrued ratably over the period of time to which the property tax relates.)

| | |
|---|---|
| *Liability for Breach of Contract* | This year, Monroe Inc. was sued for breach of contract by a former business associate. In an out-of-court settlement, it committed to pay $35,000 of damages to the associate. Monroe paid $15,000 on the date of settlement and has a $20,000 year-end liability for the remainder. Even though both the fact and the amount of this liability are certain, Monroe has no deduction with respect to the $20,000 liability because economic performance (payment) has not occurred. |

The economic performance requirement has the potential to defer the deduction of a variety of accrued expenses on the income statement. For payment liabilities, the requirement effectively puts the business on the cash method by deferring the deduction until the

[31] Reg. 1.461-4(d)(4)(i).

liability is paid. To moderate the effect of the economic performance requirement on normal business and accounting practices, Section 461(h)(3) provides an exception for accrued liabilities that recur on a routine basis. This **recurring item exception** applies to accrued liabilities that meet the first two requirements of the all-events test and for which economic performance occurs within 8.5 months after the close of the year. The business can deduct the corresponding expense in the earlier year (of accrual) instead of the later year (of economic performance) if the earlier deduction results in a more proper match against income.[32]

| | |
|---|---|
| *Recurring Item Exception* | Yarrow, a calendar-year LLC, manufactures digital cameras. Under a long-standing policy, it refunds the full purchase price of any camera within 90 days of sale. At the end of 2004, Yarrow had 139 requests for refunds totaling $83,400. It routinely pays a refund within 60 days after receiving a request. Yarrow's $83,400 liability for the refunds meets the first two requirements of the all-events test because the fact and the amount of the liability are established. Because economic performance (i.e., payment) will occur within 8.5 months after year-end, Yarrow can deduct its $83,400 accrued refund expense in computing its 2004 taxable income under the recurring item exception. |

### Cost Recovery Book/Tax Differences

A rich source of temporary differences between book income and taxable income are the inconsistent accounting rules governing the capitalization of certain business expenditures. Two common examples of inconsistent capitalization rules involve start-up costs and inventory costs.

| | |
|---|---|
| *Temporary Difference: Start-Up Costs* | Imagex Inc. incurred $119,300 start-up costs during the preoperating phase of a new venture. For book purposes, Imagex expensed the costs on its income statement. For tax purposes, Imagex was required to capitalize the start-up costs and amortize them over a 60-month period beginning with the month in which the venture became operational.[33] |

| | |
|---|---|
| *Temporary Difference: Inventory Costs* | Imagex operates a wholesaling business in which it purchases manufactured goods and sells them to retailers. It incurs warehousing costs that it records as a period expense on its income statement. For tax purposes, Imagex is required to capitalize the warehousing costs to inventory under the Section 263A UNICAP rules. |

Temporary differences also arise when the capitalized cost of a depreciable, amortizable, or depletable asset is recovered at a different rate for book and tax purposes. A difference occurs each year until the cost is fully recovered for both book and tax purposes or until the business disposes of the asset.

| | |
|---|---|
| *Temporary Difference: Depreciation* | On the first day of the year, Darling LLC purchased depreciable equipment for $100,000. For book purposes, it is depreciating the cost over 10 years on a straight-line basis. Thus, its depreciation expense this year is $10,000. For tax purposes, Darling uses MACRS to calculate depreciation. The equipment is 7-year recovery property, and Darling's depreciation deduction this year is $14,290 (14.29 MACRS percentage × $100,000). |

---

[32] The recurring item exception is not available for any liability arising under any workers' compensation act, tort, breach of contract, or violation of law, or any liability incurred by a tax shelter. Reg. 1.461-5(c).
[33] Section 195.

<table>
<tr><td rowspan="6">*Temporary Difference: Disposition of Depreciated Asset*</td><td colspan="3">Darling sold an operating asset for $51,000. The computation of its book and tax gain on sale is as follows.</td></tr>
</table>

|  | Book | Tax |
|---|---|---|
| Original cost | $65,000 | $65,000 |
| Accumulated depreciation | (34,000) | (41,200) |
| Adjusted basis | $31,000 | $23,800 |
| Amount realized on sale | $51,000 | $51,000 |
| Adjusted basis | (31,000) | (23,800) |
| Gain on sale | $20,000 | $27,200 |

## Schedule M-1 Reconciliation

**Objective 4**
Prepare a Schedule M-1 reconciliation of book income with taxable income.

Business entities must reconcile their net income for financial statement purposes with their taxable income as part of the annual return filed with the IRS. This reconciliation is shown on **Schedule M-1,** page 4 of Form 1120, 1120S, or 1065.[34] The beginning number in the reconciliation is net income per books. Net income is increased by **unfavorable M-1 adjustments** (taxable income or gain items not included in book income or nondeductible expense or loss items included in book income). Unfavorable adjustments are entered on the left side of Schedule M-1. Net income is decreased by **favorable M-1 adjustments** (book income or gain items not included in taxable income or deductible items not included in book income). Favorable adjustments are entered on the right side of Schedule M-1.

*Book/Tax Reconciliation*

Shawnee is a corporate taxpayer that uses the accrual method of accounting for both book and tax purposes. This year, its income statement (prepared in accordance with GAAP) showed $5,611,000 net income after $1,900,000 federal income tax expense. Shawnee had two unfavorable M-1 adjustments: $24,700 unearned revenue recognized as taxable income and $11,800 nondeductible meals and entertainment expense. It had two favorable M-1 adjustments: $15,900 tax-exempt interest income and $20,900 excess MACRS over book depreciation. These adjustments are entered on the following Schedule M-1.

| Schedule M-1 | Reconciliation of Income (Loss) per Books With Income per Return (See page 20 of instructions.) | | | |
|---|---|---|---|---|
| 1 | Net income (loss) per books | 5,611,000 | 7 Income recorded on books this year not included on this return (itemize): | |
| 2 | Federal income tax | 1,900,000 | Tax-exempt interest $ 15,900 | |
| 3 | Excess of capital losses over capital gains | | | |
| 4 | Income subject to tax not recorded on books this year (itemize): | | | 15,900 |
| | unearned revenue | 24,700 | 8 Deductions on this return not charged against book income this year (itemize): | |
| 5 | Expenses recorded on books this year not deducted on this return (itemize): | | a Depreciation $ 20,900 | |
| a | Depreciation $ | | b Contributions carryover $ | |
| b | Contributions carryover $ | | | |
| c | Travel and entertainment $ meals and entertainment | 11,800 | | 20,900 |
| 6 | Add lines 1 through 5 | 7,547,500 | 9 Add lines 7 and 8 | 36,800 |
| | | | 10 Income (line 28, page 1)—line 6 less line 9 | 7,510,700 |

For corporate taxpayers, the final number on Schedule M-1 is taxable income or loss *before* any dividends-received deduction or NOL carryforward deduction. After subtracting these deductions, the corporation computes its federal income tax payable on Schedule J, page 3, Form 1120. For passthrough entities (partnerships, LLCs, and S corporations), the final

[34] Corporations with total assets of less than $25,000 and partnerships with total assets of less than $600,000 and total receipts of less than $250,000 are not required to complete Schedule M-1.

number on Schedule M-1 is the total taxable income or loss allocated to the owners. The tax rules governing the allocation of income or loss among the owners are covered in Chapter 7.

# ACCOUNTING FOR INCOME TAXES

**Objective 5**
Explain how corporations compute income tax expense for GAAP financial statement purposes.

Tax consultants with corporate clients certainly must master the state, federal, and international rules governing the computation of their clients' tax liability. They should also understand the accounting rules governing the computation of the income tax expense reported in the clients' financial statements.

## Income Tax Expense per Books

For financial statement purposes, corporate taxpayers must report state and federal income taxes as current expenses.[35] Tax expense per books is computed as follows:

| |
|---|
| Income tax payable |
| + Net increase in deferred tax liabilities |
| − Net increase in deferred tax assets |
| Tax expense per books[36] |

*temp. differences*

Deferred tax assets and liabilities (which we address a bit later) are the result of temporary book/tax differences. Permanent book/tax differences have the same effect on the computation of income tax payable and tax expense per books. Because permanent differences have no deferred tax consequences, tax expense per books can also be computed by the following calculation:

| |
|---|
| Book income before tax |
| ± Permanent book/tax differences |
| Book income adjusted for permanent differences |
| × Tax rate |
| Tax expense per books[37] |

Domestic corporations use the familiar 34 or 35 percent rate to compute federal tax expense per books. Corporations with multistate businesses pay state income tax at varying rates and usually use an average rate to compute state income tax expense per books.

*Computation of Tax Expense*

Yount Inc.'s 2004 book income before tax was $3,700,000. There were three permanent differences between book income and taxable income.

| | |
|---|---|
| Book income before tax | $3,700,000 |
| Nondeductible expenses: | |
| Key-person life insurance premium | 23,000 |
| Meals and entertainment (50 percent) | 41,400 |
| Dividend-received deduction | (173,700) |
| Income adjusted for permanent differences | $3,590,700 |

[35] Foreign income taxes paid by U.S. corporations are discussed in Chapter 11.
[36] *SFAS No. 109,* "Accounting for Income Taxes" (1992).
[37] This is the approach under *APB No. 11,* which was superseded by *SFAS No. 109.*

Yount pays state income tax in eight states at rates varying from 4 percent to 7 percent. It uses a 5 percent average rate to compute state tax expense per books.

*(handwritten margin note:)*
1) Book
+/- Permanent Diff
Income Adj Perm
* State tax rate
State income tax exp

| | |
|---|---|
| Income adjusted for permanent differences[38] | $3,590,700 |
| State tax rate | .05 |
| State income tax expense | $ 179,535 |

State income taxes are deductible in the computation of federal taxable income. Therefore, Yount subtracts state income tax expense from book income before computing federal tax expense.

*(handwritten margin note:)*
2) Income Adj Perm
- State income tax exp
After state tax adj
* federal tax rate
fed. income tax exp

| | |
|---|---|
| Income adjusted for permanent differences | $3,590,700 |
| State income tax expense | (179,535) |
| | $3,411,165 |
| Federal tax rate | .34 |
| Federal income tax expense | $1,159,796 |

Yount's 2004 book income after federal and state tax is computed as follows.

*(handwritten margin note:)*
3) Book Income
- State income tax
- fed. income tax exp
Book income after tax

| | | |
|---|---|---|
| Book income before tax | | $3,700,000 |
| Income tax expense: | | |
| State | $ 179,535 | |
| Federal | 1,159,796 | |
| | | (1,339,331) |
| Book income after tax | | $2,360,669 |

### State Tax Expense versus Deduction

As the Yount example demonstrates, corporate state income tax expense per books is just an estimate. Because of the all-events test, corporations can deduct only the amount of state income tax *actually paid* during the year. The difference between state income tax expense per books and the deduction for state income tax is a temporary book/tax difference.

| | |
|---|---|
| **State Income Tax Deduction** | Yount made the following state income tax payments in 2004. |

| | |
|---|---|
| Balance due of 2003 state taxes | $ 12,790 |
| Estimated payments of 2004 state taxes | 180,000 |
| | $192,790 |

Even though Yount's 2004 state income tax expense on its financial statements was $179,535, its deduction for state income tax on its Form 1120 was $192,790. The $13,255 difference is a favorable Schedule M-1 adjustment.

---

[38] The computations of taxable income for state purposes and for federal purposes are consistent enough that corporations typically calculate state tax expense on the same base as federal tax expense.

### Effective Tax Rate

One of the important items of information that corporations report in the footnotes to their financial statements is their effective tax rate for the year. **Effective tax rate** equals total income tax expense divided by pretax book income. According to GAAP, the tax footnote must reconcile the effective tax rate with the federal statutory tax rate (34 or 35 percent).

| *Tax Rate Reconciliation* | The tax footnote to Yount's 2004 financial statements reported that its effective tax rate was 36.2 percent ($1,339,331 total tax expense/$3,700,000 pretax book income). This rate was reconciled to the 34 percent federal statutory rate as follows: |
|---|---|

| | |
|---|---|
| Federal statutory rate | 34.0% |
| State income tax (net of federal tax benefit) | 3.2  $(4.85 \times (1 - .34)$ |
| Rate increase from nondeductible expenses | 0.6 |
| Rate decrease from dividends-received deduction | (1.6) |
| Effective tax rate | 36.2% |

The rate increase for state income tax equals the 4.85 percent effective state tax rate ($179,535/$3,700,000 pretax book income) multiplied by (1.00 − 0.34).

The rate increase or decrease from the permanent book/tax differences equals the tax cost or savings from each difference divided by pretax book income.

$64,400 nondeductible expenses × 34% = $21,896 tax cost
$21,896 tax cost/$3,700,000 = 0.6% rate increase

$173,700 dividends-received deduction × 34% = $59,058 tax savings
$59,058 tax savings/$3,700,000 = 1.6% rate decrease

## Deferred Tax Assets and Liabilities

**Objective 6**
Determine whether a temporary difference results in a deferred tax asset or a deferred tax liability.

Temporary differences do not affect the computation of tax expense per books, effective tax rate, or the reconciliation of the effective rate with the statutory rate. Instead, temporary differences result in either a deferred tax asset or a deferred tax liability. A **deferred tax asset** resembles an overpayment of tax that the corporation will recoup in a future year when the temporary difference reverses.[39] Conversely, a **deferred tax liability** resembles an underpayment of tax that the corporation will pay in a future year when the temporary difference reverses.

*Deferred Tax Asset*

Hoffman Inc. pays federal income tax at a 35 percent rate. This year, it recorded a $250,000 expense based on an accrued liability for an estimated legal settlement. The expense was nondeductible for tax purposes. Because of this unfavorable temporary difference, Hoffman's book income was $250,000 less than its taxable income, and its tax expense per books was $87,500 less than its federal tax payable. Hoffman recorded the $87,500 "extra" tax payable as a deferred tax asset. In the future year when Hoffman pays the $250,000 settlement and claims a tax deduction, the temporary difference will reverse. Hoffman's book income will be $250,000 more than its taxable income, its tax expense will be $87,500 more than its tax payable, and it will credit its $87,500 deferred tax asset to make up the difference.

[39] If the realization of a deferred tax asset is questionable, the asset may be reduced by a valuation allowance on the balance sheet. See *SFAS No. 109,* "Accounting for Income Taxes" (1992).

| | |
|---|---|
| *Deferred Tax Liability* | Marliss Inc. pays federal income tax at a 35 percent rate. This year, it recorded a $792,000 depreciation expense per books and deducted $988,000 MACRS depreciation on its Form 1120. Because of this favorable temporary difference, its book income was $196,000 more than its taxable income, and its tax expense per books was $68,600 more than its federal tax payable. Marliss recorded the $68,600 "extra" tax expense as a deferred tax liability. Over the future years in which this difference reverses, Marliss's aggregate taxable income will be $196,000 more than its book income, its tax payable will be $68,600 more than its tax expense, and it will charge its $68,600 deferred tax liability to make up the difference. |

A corporation can have any number of temporary book/tax differences during a year, some of which affect its deferred tax assets and some of which affect its deferred tax liabilities. A net increase in deferred tax assets causes a decrease in the corporation's tax expense; a net increase in deferred tax liabilities causes an increase in the corporation's tax expense. To illustrate, let's return once more to Yount Inc. and compute its 2004 federal tax payable and the net change in its deferred tax accounts.

| | |
|---|---|
| *Current and Deferred Federal Tax* | In 2004, Yount had $160,000 unfavorable and $400,000 favorable temporary differences (in addition to the favorable difference for state income tax) between book and taxable income. Yount's Form 1120 showed the following Schedule M-1 reconciliation and calculation of federal income tax. |

| Schedule M-1 | |
|---|---|
| Book income after tax | $2,360,669 |
| Plus: | |
| State tax expense | 179,535 |
| Federal tax expense | 1,159,796 |
| Nondeductible expenses (permanent) | 64,400 |
| Unfavorable temporary differences | 160,000 |
| Less: | |
| State income tax paid | (192,790) |
| Favorable temporary differences | (400,000) |
| Taxable income before special deductions | $3,331,610 |
| Taxable income from Schedule M-1 | $3,331,610 |
| Less: Dividends-received deduction (permanent) | (173,700) |
| Taxable income | $3,157,910 |
| | .34 |
| Federal income tax | $1,073,689 |

Yount's temporary differences resulted in a net increase in deferred tax liability.

| | |
|---|---|
| Additional state income tax deduction | $ 13,255 |
| Other favorable differences | 400,000 |
| Unfavorable differences | (160,000) |
| Net favorable differences | $253,255 |
| | .34 |
| Deferred tax liability | $ 86,107 |

Yount's federal tax payable plus the increase in its deferred tax liability equals the federal tax expense reported on its income statement.

| | |
|---|---:|
| Federal tax payable | $1,073,689 |
| Deferred tax liability (net DTA or DTL) | 86,107 |
| Federal income tax expense | $1,159,796 |

*reconcile*

### Deferred Income Tax as Bad Politics

Although the provision of deferred tax with respect to temporary book/tax differences is good accounting theory, it can also be bad politics for the corporate community. The general public has difficulty understanding why corporations are not required to actually pay the federal income tax expense reported on their financial statements. The following news item from *USA Today* is a perfect example of the negative publicity that can result from perfectly routine book/tax differences.

*Study: Companies Pay Less in Taxes*

Many major companies pay far less income tax than the standard 35 percent federal corporate rate. The 250 biggest companies among the *Fortune* 500 paid a federal tax rate of just 20.1 percent in 1998 vs. 26.5 percent for a similar sized group of companies in 1988, according to the Institute on Taxation and Economic Policy. Companies can cut taxes under a variety of methods, including accelerating depreciation write-offs and deducting employee stock-option profits. They also receive credits for research and other specialized activities . . . [The study] called General Electric the "champion tax evader" with $6.9 billion in tax breaks over the three-year study period. GE spokesman Gary Sheffer says the study is misleading. "Their methodology ignores significant amounts of deferred taxes that will be paid by GE as a result of our current operation," he says.[40]

## CORPORATE TAX PAYMENT REQUIREMENTS

**Objective 7**
Describe the corporate tax payment and return-filing requirements.

Corporations are required to make quarterly installment payments of their state and federal income taxes. For federal purposes, they must pay 25 percent of their estimated tax for the year on the 15th day of the fourth, sixth, ninth, and twelfth months of the year.[41] Most states conform to the federal schedule for quarterly tax payments. Corporations that fail to prepay 100 percent of the tax shown on the Form 1120 may be liable for an underpayment penalty. The law relaxes this strict requirement for small corporations (with less than $1 million taxable income in each of the three preceding taxable years). A small corporation avoids the underpayment penalty if its installment payments total at least 100 percent of the tax shown on Form 1120 for the *preceding* taxable year.

*Small Corporation Exception*

Rogerson, a calendar year corporation, had taxable income for 2001, 2002, and 2003 of $750,000, $690,000, and $910,000, respectively, and therefore qualifies as a small corporation for 2004. During 2004, it made timely installment payments totaling $310,000. Rogerson's tax on its 2004 Form 1120 was $357,000, and it paid the $47,000 balance due when it filed its return. Even though Rogerson failed to prepay 100 percent of its 2004 tax, it does not owe an underpayment penalty because the tax shown on its 2003 Form 1120 was only $307,200.

[40] Strauss, "Study: Companies Pay Less in Taxes," *USA Today,* October 20, 2000, p. B-2.
[41] Section 6655(c), (d), and (i). Corporations do not send tax payments to the IRS. Instead, they deposit payments in a qualified depositary, such as a commercial bank, or make their deposits electronically through the Electronic Federal Tax Payment System (EFTPS).

Quarterly installments represent a significant cash outflow. Corporations can manage this cash flow advantageously by paying the minimum required each quarter to avoid penalty. Generally, quarterly installments must be equal (25 percent of estimated tax). However, corporations with seasonal businesses with less income in the first months and more income in the last months of the year can use one of several annualization methods to reduce their quarterly installments without penalty. This next example illustrates the computation of a corporation's required installments under the basic annualization method.[42]

*Required Installments*

At the beginning of 2005, Breyer Inc. forecasts that it will earn the following amounts of quarterly income.

| | |
|---|---:|
| First quarter (January–March) | $ 150,000 |
| Second quarter (April–June) | 275,000 |
| Third quarter (July–September) | 675,000 |
| Fourth quarter (October–December) | 900,000 |
| | $2,000,000 |

Based on this forecast, Breyer's taxable income will be $2,000,000, and its federal tax will be $680,000. Under the general rule, it must pay a $170,000 installment on April 15, June 15, September 15, and December 15. Breyer can reduce its installments by electing the following computational procedure.

• Its first two installments can equal 25 percent of the tax on annualized income *based on actual income for the first three months.* If Breyer's actual first quarter income is $150,000, its April and June installments are only $51,000.

$$\$150,000 \text{ three-month income} \times \frac{12 \text{ months}}{3 \text{ months}} = \$600,000 \text{ annualized income}$$

 $\$600,000 \text{ taxable income} \times 34\% = \$204,000 \text{ tax} \times 25\% = \underline{\underline{\$51,000}}$

• Its third installment can equal 75 percent of the tax on annualized income *based on its actual income for the first six months* less the first two installments. If Breyer's actual six-month income is $425,000, its September installment is only $114,750.

$$\$425,000 \text{ six-month income} \times \frac{12 \text{ months}}{6 \text{ months}} = \$850,000 \text{ annualized income}$$

$\$850,000 \text{ taxable income} \times 34\% = \$289,000 \text{ tax} \times 75\% = \$216,750$

$\$216,750 - \$102,000 \text{ April and June installments} = \underline{\underline{\$114,750}}$

• Its fourth installment can equal 100 percent of the tax on annualized income *based on its actual income for the first nine months* less the first three installments. If Breyer's actual nine-month income is $1,100,000, its December installment is only $281,917.

$$\$1,100,000 \text{ nine-month income} \times \frac{12 \text{ months}}{9 \text{ months}} = \$1,466,667 \text{ annualized income}$$

$\$1,466,667 \text{ taxable income} \times 34\% = \$498,667 \text{ tax} \times 100\% = \$498,667$

$\$498,667 - \$216,750 \text{ April, June, and September installments} = \underline{\underline{\$281,917}}$

[42] Section 6655(e)

If Breyer's actual 2005 taxable income is $2,000,000, its federal tax is $680,000. A comparison of Breyer's payments of this tax under the general rule and the annualization method emphasizes the cash-flow advantage of the latter.

*deferr tax expense*

| | General Rule | Annualization Method |
|---|---|---|
| April 15 | $170,000 | $ 51,000 |
| June 15 | 170,000 | 51,000 |
| September 15 | 170,000 | 114,750 |
| December 15 | 170,000 | 281,917 |
| Balance due paid with return | –0– | 181,333 |
| | $680,000 | $680,000 |

The statutory due date by which corporations must file their tax returns and pay any balance due of their tax is the 15th day of the third month following the close of the taxable year.[43] Corporations may request an automatic six-month extension of time to file their Form 1120. This extension of the filing deadline does not extend the *payment* deadline. Corporations must pay the estimated balance due of their tax with a timely filed extension request (Form 7004). Corporations that fail to file their return or pay the balance due on a timely basis must pay a late filing or late payment penalty.[44]

## Conclusion

In Chapter 5, we have examined the accounting period and method issues faced by every business entity. Both corporations and passthrough entities must maintain accounting systems that clearly reflect their taxable income. Corporations must take an additional step by computing the tax expense reported to their shareholders and the tax payable to the state and federal governments. In Chapter 6, we will take a closer look at this tax computation as we focus on the topic of business incentive provisions.

## Key Terms

accrual method of accounting   *118*
all-events test   *121*
cash method of accounting   *116*
deferred tax asset   *127*
deferred tax liability   *127*
economic performance   *121*
effective tax rate   *127*

favorable M-1 adjustments   *124*
52–53 week year   *112*
Generally Accepted Accounting Principles (GAAP)   *118*
majority interest taxable year   *113*
payment liabilities   *122*
permanent difference   *119*

principal partner   *113*
recurring item exception   *123*
Schedule M-1   *124*
taxable year   *112*
tax basis books   *115*
temporary difference   *120*
unfavorable M-1 adjustments   *124*

[43] Sections 6072(b) and 6151(a).
[44] Section 6651.

## Questions and Problems for Discussion

1. Why does the tax law restrict the choice of taxable years available to passthrough entities but not the choice available to corporations?

2. Identify five business activities with distinct operating cycles that suggest the use of a taxable year other than the calendar year.

3. Mr. Toshi recently started his own business as a sole proprietor. Because he will use the cash method of accounting, he plans to deduct every cash disbursement made from his business bank account. Identify the flaw in this plan.

4. Compare and contrast the principle of conservatism under GAAP and the principle of conservatism under the tax accounting rules.

5. Explain the difference between a permanent difference and a temporary difference in book and taxable income.

6. Discuss the possible tax policy reasons for the following permanent book/tax differences.
   a. Nondeductible lobbying expenses.
   b. Nondeductible meals and entertainment expense.
   c. Dividends-received deduction.

7. Four years ago, HotSpot granted stock options with a $15 strike price to a key employee. On the date of grant, HotSpot stock sold for $13.92 per share. The stock price has steadily declined, and this year the employee allowed the options to lapse. Discuss the effect of this compensatory transaction on HotSpot's book and tax income in the year of grant and in the year of lapse.

8. Major Inc. deducted an $18 million NOL carryforward deduction on its 2004 corporate tax return. Does this deduction represent a permanent or a temporary difference in Major's 2004 book/tax income?

9. Does the all-events test apply to cash basis businesses, accrual basis businesses, or both?

10. Identify the three requirements of the all-events test.

11. Discuss the difference in the computation of a corporation's marginal tax rate, average tax rate, and effective tax rate as presented in the footnotes to its financial statements.

## Application Problems

1. Steffin LLC is composed of six members with the following taxable years and interests in its capital and profits.

| | Taxable Year Ending | Percentage Interest |
|---|---|---|
| Carolyn Hicks | December 31 | 8% |
| Gayle Spears | December 31 | 19 |
| Robert Rizzo | December 31 | 5 |
| Hycrest Inc. | June 30 | 28 |
| PKL Inc. | June 30 | 25 |
| TopFrame Inc. | October 31 | 15 |

Assuming that the LLC has no natural business year, what is its required taxable year?

2. Quarto Partnership has four partners. Mega Inc. owns a 40 percent interest, Bishop Inc. owns a 45 percent interest, Mr. Dawson owns a 6 percent interest, and Simpson Inc. owns a 9 percent interest in Quarto's capital and profits. Mega and Mr. Dawson use a calendar year, Bishop uses a fiscal year ending March 31, and Simpson uses a fiscal year ending May 31. Which taxable year for Quarto results in the least aggregate deferral of income to the four partners?

3. Stovall LLC uses the calendar year and the cash method of accounting for tax purposes. It made the following rent payments on December 31, 2004. In each case, determine Stovall's 2004 deduction for the payment.
   a. $30,000 for the use of equipment under a six-month lease that began on May 1, 2004.
   b. $1,750 rent for warehouse space for the month of January 2005.
   c. $48,000 rent for office space for the 24-month period beginning on January 1, 2005.

4. Fishback Company uses the calendar year and the cash method of accounting for tax purposes. It made the following payments in December 2004. In each case, determine Fishback's 2004 deduction for the payment.
   a. $2,400 interest on a bank loan for the 12-month period that began on November 1, 2004.
   b. $1,000 for supplies that are incidental to Fishback's business. At year-end, it had $900 of supplies still on hand.
   c. $2,000 for supplies that are nonincidental to Fishback's business. At year-end, it had $1,350 of supplies still on hand.
   d. $1,400 for a six-month contract with a janitorial service that will clean Fishback's office. The contract begins on February 1, 2005.

5. Singh LLC, a retail clothing store, uses the calendar year and the hybrid method of accounting for tax purposes. Describe the correct 2004 tax consequences of each of the following transactions.
   a. On October 9, 2004, Singh paid $6,800 cash to purchase winter hats for resale to customers.
   b. On December 14, 2004, Singh received its $1,720 utility bill for November. It paid the bill on January 12, 2005.
   c. On December 16, 2004, Singh sold eight dresses to a regular customer on credit. The total sales price was $2,200. Singh received payment from the customer on January 3, 2005.
   d. On October 1, 2004, Singh made a short-term loan to an employee. The employee repaid the loan plus $400 (four months) interest on January 31, 2005.

6. Which of the following entities can use the cash method of accounting for tax purposes?
   a. An LLC with eight individual members and average annual gross receipts of $12 million.
   b. An LLC with two individual members and three corporate members and average annual gross receipts of $900,000.
   c. An LLC with 20 individual members and one corporate member and average annual gross receipts of $8.5 million.

7. Palmer Inc. was incorporated on January 1, 1999, and adopted the calendar year and the cash method of accounting for tax purposes. For 1999 through 2005, Palmer had the following annual gross receipts from its manufacturing business.

| | |
|---|---|
| 1999 | $  612,000 |
| 2000 | 1,924,000 |
| 2001 | 3,067,000 |
| 2002 | 7,443,000 |
| 2003 | 4,019,000 |
| 2004 | 5,992,000 |
| 2005 | 4,233,000 |

Determine the first taxable year that Palmer must change to the accrual method of accounting.

8. Shorter is a calendar year, accrual basis corporation. On December 31, 2004, Shorter accrued the following liabilities. In each case, determine its 2004 deduction for the accrual.

   *a.* Accrued interest payable of $34,000 on a long-term note for the four-month period that began on September 1, 2004.

   *b.* Accrued reward payable of $10,000. Shorter is offering the reward to anyone who can provide information concerning vandalism to its corporate office that occurred on October 31, 2004.

   *c.* Accrued rent payable of $5,000 for the 17-day period from December 14 through December 31.

   *d.* Accrued damages payable of $75,000 to a rival business in projected settlement of a patent infringement suit.

9. Zedco LLC uses the calendar year and the accrual method of accounting. On December 1, it signed a contract with a software consultant to pay the consultant $125,000 to undertake a complete review of Zedco's internal software. The consultant will begin work on January 15 and should complete the engagement in four months. Zedco has been in business since 1988 and has never used an external consultant for any of its computing needs. In which year can Zedco deduct the $125,000 consulting expense?

10. Vernon Photography, a calendar year, accrual basis LLC, sells photography equipment and services. As part of a marketing campaign, it mailed 1,500 gift certificates to its recent customers entitling each one to a free studio portrait. As of December 31, only 413 customers had used their certificates. Vernon's cost for each studio portrait is $50.

    *a.* Does Vernon have a fixed liability for a reasonably determinable amount on December 31? Explain briefly.

    *b.* Compute Vernon's current deduction with respect to the accrued liability.

11. Rypon's 2004 compensation package to its CEO included a $500,000 base salary, a $35,000 contribution to a qualified retirement plan, and $180,000 unfunded deferred compensation. In addition, Rypon granted a nonqualified stock option to the CEO to buy 10,000 shares of stock for $62 per share for five years. During 2004, the CEO exercised a 1998 nonqualified option and purchased 5,000 Rypon shares for $41 per share. The market price at date of exercise was $60. Identify Rypon's 2004 permanent or temporary book/tax differences resulting from the:

    *a.* Base salary.

    *b.* Qualified retirement plan contribution.

    *c.* Unfunded deferred compensation.

    *d.* Stock option grant.

    *e.* Stock option exercise.

12. Extronic, a calendar-year, accrual basis corporation, made the following state income tax payments during 2004.

| | | |
|---|---|---|
| March 15 | Estimated 2004 state tax | $58,000 |
| April 8 | Balance due of 2003 state tax | 41,900 |
| June 12 | Estimated 2004 state tax | 58,000 |
| September 9 | Estimated 2004 state tax | 58,000 |
| December 15 | Estimated 2004 state tax | 58,000 |

Extronic's 2004 book income before tax (and adjusted for permanent differences) was $4,821,000, and its actual state income tax for 2004 was $227,300.

   a. Assuming that Extronic's state tax rate is 5 percent, compute its 2004 state income tax expense per books.

   b. Compute Extronic's 2004 state income tax deduction.

13. Al Najjar, a calendar year, accrual basis corporation, reported $3,820,000 net income before tax on its audited financial statements. Its records reveal the following information:

   - Bad debt expense was $52,300, and its direct write-offs of bad debts was $45,900.
   - Book depreciation expense was $912,500, and MACRS depreciation was $1,083,000.
   - The corporation recorded a $67,500 book gain on the exchange of developed real estate for investment land. The like-kind exchange was nontaxable.
   - The corporation contributed $25,000 to the Democratic National Party and $70,000 to the United Way.

   a. Compute Al Najjar's taxable income.

   b. Compute Al Najjar's federal tax expense per books and federal tax payable.

14. Ludlew, a calendar year, accrual basis corporation, reported $8,354,000 net income before tax on its audited financial statements. Its records reveal the following information.

   - Book depreciation expense was $793,000, and MACRS depreciation was $707,000.
   - Ludlew sold equipment for $50,000. Its book basis was $7,800, and its tax basis was zero.
   - Ludlew accrued $2,400 interest expense for the last five months of the year on a short-term note to First Mountain Bank.
   - Ludlew recorded $33,200 meals and entertainment expenses.
   - Ludlew earned $11,290 interest on City of Philadelphia bonds and $21,000 dividends from its 2 percent stock interest TJK, a taxable Delaware corporation.

   a. Compute Ludlew's taxable income.

   b. Compute Ludlew's federal tax expense per books and federal tax payable.

15. Geraldo, a calendar year, accrual basis corporation, reported $931,000 net income before tax on its audited financial statements. Its records reveal the following information.

   - On February 1, Geraldo purchased a business and capitalized $500,000 of the cost to goodwill.
   - Book depreciation expense was $66,100, and MACRS depreciation was $77,800.
   - Geraldo paid an $18,500 premium for its employee group term life insurance plan and a $5,900 premium for its key-person life insurance policies.
   - Geraldo accrued a $35,000 expense for the estimated settlement of a breach-of-contract suit that should go to court next year.

   a. Compute Geraldo's taxable income.

   b. Compute Geraldo's federal tax expense per books and federal tax payable.

16. XZM Corporation's tax department prepared the following reconciliation (in thousands of dollars) between its book and taxable income.

| | |
|---|---|
| Book income before tax | $22,975 |
| Permanent differences | 839 |
| Unfavorable temporary differences | 1,800 |
| Favorable temporary differences | (1,471) |
| Taxable income | $24,143 |

 *a.* Compute XZM's federal tax payable.
 *b.* Compute the net change in XZM's deferred tax accounts.
 *c.* Compute XZM's federal income tax expense per books.
 *d.* Compute XZM's effective tax rate.

17. The CPA for Budo Inc. prepared the following reconciliation of book and taxable income.

| | |
|---|---:|
| Book income before tax | $900,200 |
| Permanent differences | (1,200) |
| Unfavorable temporary differences | 25,600 |
| Favorable temporary differences | (44,100) |
| Taxable income | $880,500 |

 *a.* Compute Budo's federal tax payable.
 *b.* Compute the net change in Budo's deferred tax accounts.
 *c.* Compute Budo's federal income tax expense per books.
 *d.* Compute Budo's effective tax rate.

18. LaMark Corporation's 2004 federal income tax was $319,000. Assuming that it does not use any annualization method, compute its required installments payments of 2005 tax, assuming these facts.
 *a.* LaMark qualifies as a small corporation, and its 2005 taxable income is $875,400.
 *b.* LaMark qualifies as a small corporation, and its 2005 taxable income is $1,240,100.
 *c.* LaMark does not qualify as a small corporation, and its 2005 taxable income is $1,240,100.

## Issue Recognition Problems

Identify the tax issue or issues suggested by the following situations and state each issue in the form of a question.

1. Spencer Inc. has used a calendar year for reporting purposes since 1979 but has a good business reason for changing to a fiscal year that ends April 30. Its annual taxable income averages $200,000, so it derives a yearly benefit from the progressivity in the corporate tax rates.

2. Bedford Corporation, which has used a fiscal year ending August 31 since 1993, owns a 60 percent interest in BGT Partnership. Bedford received permission from the IRS to change to a calendar year for tax purposes.

3. Norton LLC engaged a new CPA to prepare its financial statements and tax return. The CPA discovered that Norton was using an incorrect method to account for its inventories. The LLC agreed to change to the proper method beginning in the next taxable year.

4. Three years ago, TRP paid $300,000 to purchase investment land from Mrs. Calley. When the IRS audited her return for the year of sale, it discovered that TRP and Mrs. Calley were related parties. As a result, the IRS disallowed Mrs. Calley's deduction for her $39,200 loss realized on the sale. This year, TRP sold the land for $350,000.

5. Toomey is a calendar year, accrual basis corporation. At year-end, Toomey accrued $41,700 employer FICA tax payable with respect to salaries and wages paid during the last two weeks of December. Toomey paid the accrued tax in January.

6. Five years ago, Reynolds incurred a $48,000 nondeductible net capital loss. The corporation's carryforward of the loss expired this year.

7. Coogan Corporation's regular income tax rate is 35 percent. However, it also paid about $15 million of alternative minimum tax (AMT) in each of the past four taxable years.

8. Kaystar's balance sheet on December 31, 2004, included a $172,300 deferred tax liability. In 2005, Congress enacted a tax reform bill that replaced the existing corporate tax rate structure with an 18 percent gross receipts tax.

9. Denzel, a calendar year corporation, paid a $1 million installment of its 2005 tax on April 15 and June 15. In July, a hurricane completely destroyed its manufacturing facility. As a result, Denzel forecasts that it will operate at a loss for 2005.

10. MPW is a small corporation that makes quarterly installment payments of federal tax totaling 100 percent of its preceding year's tax. Its 2002 tax was $88,278, and its 2003 installments totaled $90,000. Upon audit, the IRS determined that MPW's correct 2002 tax was $102,423.

**Research Problems**

1. Northeast Products manufactures video equipment that it sells through a distributor. The distributor provides a warranty to its retailers and the final consumers who buy the equipment. The warranty provides that the distributor will make any repairs necessary to correct any problem with the operation of the equipment. Northeast reimburses the distributor for all warranty claims. For book purposes, Northeast records an estimated warranty liability when the equipment is sold by the distributor to its retailers. For tax purposes, Northeast deducts a warranty expense equal to its actual payments to the distributor during the last 3.5 months of the year and the first 8.5 months of the following year. Is Northeast using a proper method of accounting to compute its deduction?

2. Jefferson Floors is an S corporation that installs customized fine wood flooring. It includes the cost of the wood in the price of the installation but does not sell any wood directly to customers. Jefferson's average annual gross receipts are $15 million. The value of the wood that Jefferson stores in its warehouse can be as high as $2,250,000 on any given day. Can Jefferson use the cash method of accounting to compute taxable income?

**Tax Planning Case**

Three individuals, who are calendar year taxpayers with a 40 percent marginal state and federal tax rate, plan to start a new business as an LLC on July 1, 2005. They project that the business will generate $200,000 taxable income for its first 12-month operating period and that annual income will increase by 20 percent each year for the next four years. Here is the projected income stream.

| 12-Month Period Ending June 30 | Taxable Income |
|---|---|
| 2006 | $200,000 |
| 2007 | 240,000 |
| 2008 | 288,000 |
| 2009 | 345,000 |
| 2010 | 415,000 |

The LLC has a compelling business reason to keep its books on a fiscal year ending June 30. Compute the NPV of the individual tax savings that result if the IRS permits the LLC to use this fiscal year as its taxable year. Base your calculations on the five *calendar* years from 2005 through 2009 and use an 8 percent discount rate to compute NPV.

## Comprehensive Book/Tax Reconciliation Cases

The following two cases include information on both permanent and temporary differences between the computation of book income and taxable income. Not all of the differences are identified in Chapter 5, but these differences should be familiar from the introductory tax course and can be easily researched. Not every item of information represents a book/tax difference; these red herrings are accounted for in the same way for financial statement and tax return purposes.

1. Easling Inc., an accrual basis, calendar year corporate taxpayer, reported $516,227 net income before income tax on its 2004 audited financial statements. Easling's records reveal the following information for 2004:

   a. Easling's revenues included $1,290 interest on its investment in City of Pittsburgh bonds and $3,616 interest on its investment in Coca-Cola corporate bonds.

   b. Easling's revenues included a $50,000 legal settlement paid to Easling by a rival corporation that Easling had threatened to sue over an alleged patent infringement. The rival corporation preferred to settle out of court.

   c. Easling paid a $4,350 attorney's fee in connection with the legal action described in (b).

   d. On October 29, Easley received a $14,800 cash payment from a tenant who leases warehouse space from Easling. The prepaid rent was for the four-month period beginning on November 1, 2004, and ending on February 28, 2005.

   e. On December 31, Easley accrued $5,900 rent income from a different tenant. The accrual was for the five-month period beginning on August 1 and ending on December 31, 2004.

   f. Easling made only one purchase of tangible personalty in 2004: an item of new equipment costing $82,400. The corporation made a Section 179 election with respect to the equipment. Its book depreciation on the equipment was $6,900.

   g. Book depreciation for all Easling's other tangible assets (acquired before 2004) was $75,100, and MACRS depreciation was $29,170.

   h. Business meal and entertainment expense was $23,614.

   i. Easling expensed a $1,200 payment to Mahoney & Associates, a lobbying firm that represents the corporation's interests with the Virginia state government in Richmond.

   j. Easley expensed a $16,700 annual premium on its property insurance policy.

   k. Research and experimentation expense was $92,800.

   l. Bad debt expense per books was $13,699. Easley wrote off $17,468 uncollectible accounts receivable during the year.

   m. On December 31, Easling accrued $19,200 wages payable. Easling paid these wages to its clerical employees on January 14, 2005.

   n. Easling was formed in 2002. During the preoperating phase of its business, Easling incurred $25,200 of start-up costs that it had to capitalize for tax purposes. Easling expensed these costs on its 2002 income statement.

   Based on the above facts, compute Easling's 2004 federal taxable income.

2. Singer Inc.'s 2004 income statement (prepared in accordance with GAAP and audited by a national accounting firm) showed the following:

| | |
|---|---:|
| Net income before income tax | $3,097,000 |
| Federal income tax expense per books | (916,141) |
| State income tax expense per books | (207,438) |
| Foreign income tax paid during 2004 | (5,934) |
| Net income after income tax | $1,967,487 |

Singer's records reveal the following information for 2004.

a. Singer paid corporate income tax to the 12 states in which it conducted its interstate business. It uses a 7 percent average rate to compute state income tax expense per books. During 2004, Singer actually paid $268,000 state income tax.

b. Singer received the following dividend income:

| | |
|---|---|
| Zenot Inc. (New York corporation; Singer owns a 6% interest) | $ 44,921 |
| Riola Inc. (Florida corporation; Singer owns a 39% interest) | 127,700 |
| Strudal (Swedish corporation; Singer owns a 4% interest) | 59,340 |

c. The foreign income tax paid was the 10 percent withholding tax collected by Sweden on the Strudal dividend.

d. In 1999, Singer sold six acres of land used as an off-site storage area for heavy equipment and materials used in its business. The original cost of this land was $646,500, and the selling price was $900,000. The purchaser paid $180,000 cash and gave Singer a long-term note for the $720,000 balance of the price. Singer used the installment sale method to compute its taxable gain on sale. In 2004, it received a $140,000 note payment from the purchaser ($95,000 principal plus $45,000 interest).

e. Singer had only one asset sale in 2004. It sold 1,300 shares of Zenot stock (basis $250,000) for $212,250 to an unrelated party.

f. Vandals destroyed a minivan that Singer used in its business. Singer's book basis in the van was $6,370, and its tax basis was zero. Unfortunately, Singer's casualty insurance policy does not cover vandalism.

g. MACRS depreciation totaled $66,300, and book depreciation totaled $38,000.

h. Singer contributed $325,000 to various qualified charitable organizations.

i. Singer paid $400,000 cash dividends to its shareholders and $98,700 interest to its bondholders during 2004.

j. Singer is entitled to a $14,950 general business credit in computing its 2004 federal income tax.

On the basis of the above information, compute Singer's 2004 federal taxable income and federal income tax payable and prepare a Schedule M-1, Form 1120, reconciling Singer's 2004 book income and taxable income.

# Business Incentive Provisions

## Learning Objectives

*After reading this chapter, you will be able to:*

1. Describe tax incentives currently in place to motivate business investment in specific assets and activities and calculate their impact on taxable income, tax liability, and after-tax return on investment.

2. Calculate the general business credit limitation and identify those credits included as part of the general business credit.

3. Describe the purpose of the alternative minimum tax and the common preferences and adjustments required to calculate the corporate alternative minimum tax.

4. Calculate the adjusted current earnings (ACE) adjustment, alternative minimum taxable income, and the corporate alternative minimum tax.

5. Explain the purpose of the minimum tax credit and calculate the amount of the credit generated and used each year.

Although taxation is primarily a means of raising revenue, governments also use it to influence behavior. Some tax provisions are punitive in nature, designed to increase the cost of engaging in behaviors that government wishes to discourage. Other provisions seek to encourage actions the government believes will have desirable economic or social consequences. In this chapter, we detail a number of business incentive provisions currently provided by federal income tax law and describe the impact of tax incentives on the after-tax value of tax-favored activities. Various state and local income tax incentives are discussed in Chapter 10. We also consider the policy implications of provisions that many regard as *corporate welfare* rather than encouragement of desirable economic behavior. Finally, we detail the provisions of the corporate alternative minimum tax (AMT) and examine this hidden cost to taxpayers engaging in multiple activities with preferential regular tax consequences. Initially, it may seem out of place to discuss the AMT in a chapter entitled "Business Incentive Provisions." However, the AMT often negates or reduces the regular-tax benefits of many of the incentive provisions described here. Thus, planning involving tax incentives should always consider the possible imposition of the AMT and its impact on after-tax returns.

# TAX INCENTIVES AND AFTER-TAX VALUE

**Tax incentives** are provided in a variety of forms, including (1) exemptions of special types of income from taxation, (2) increased or accelerated deductions, (3) tax credits, and (4) preferential tax rates. Most incentives are targeted at specific behaviors and seek to encourage taxpayers to engage in those behaviors to obtain the tax savings. Tax incentives are often straightforward applications of the tax planning variables discussed in Chapter 1. For example, tax incentives that exempt certain types of income from taxation illustrate the power of the character variable; tax incentives that increase or accelerate deductions illustrate the value of the time-period variable; and tax credits and preferential tax rates may be related to either the character variable or the entity variable. These incentives have the potential to alter business and investment decisions by reducing tax costs and increasing after-tax return on investment. In some cases, tax incentives encourage taxpayers to undertake, and investors to fund, activities that might not otherwise be economically feasible.

The next section of this chapter describes a number of tax incentives and the types of investors, business activities, and industries most likely to benefit from them. It would be impossible to discuss every available incentive in this text, so we have chosen to focus on those with applicability to the broadest range of taxpayers, producing the greatest amount of tax savings.

## Popular Tax Incentives

### Limited Expensing Election

**Objective 1**
Describe tax incentives currently in place to motivate business investment in specific assets and activities and calculate their impact on taxable income, tax liability, and after-tax return on investment.

Section 179 provides an incentive for small businesses to invest in business assets other than real property through the **limited expensing election.**[1] In 2004, the election permits qualifying taxpayers to deduct up to $102,000 of the acquisition cost of such property in the year of acquisition rather than capitalizing and depreciating this cost.[2] The taxpayer is allowed to choose which of its qualifying acquisitions will be subject to the election. The limited expensing election provides taxpayers an opportunity to use the time period variable to accelerate into the current year deductions that would otherwise occur in the future. In general, assets with the longest MACRS lives provide the greatest potential acceleration and would be the best choice for applying the election. The full amount of the deduction is available only to taxpayers whose qualifying acquisitions during the tax year do not exceed $410,000 in 2004. The available deduction amount is reduced dollar for dollar when total acquisitions exceed $410,000. Thus, the ability to take a Section 179 deduction is eliminated when acquisitions exceed $512,000.

---

[1] The limited expensing election was introduced in Chapter 6 of *Principles*. Because of its popularity and its relationship to the enterprise zone increased expensing election discussed later in this chapter, the limited expensing election is reviewed here. Several other popular incentive provisions were discussed in *Principles* and will not be examined further in this text. For example, the reader is referred to Chapter 6 of *Principles* for a discussion of the election to deduct environment cleanup costs at targeted contamination sites and the deduction for removal of barriers to handicapped access. See Sally M. Jones, *Principles of Taxation* (New York: McGraw-Hill/Irwin, 2005).

[2] The Jobs and Growth Tax Relief Reconciliation 0f 2003 increased the Section 179 deduction to $100,000 for tax years beginning after December 31, 2002, and before December 31, 2005. This limitation is indexed for inflation. Rev. Proc. 2003-85 sets the 2004 indexed amount at $102,000. Beginning in 2006, the maximum deduction under Section 179 will be reduced to $25,000, available to taxpayers whose qualifying property acquisitions do not exceed $200,000.

*Application of Section 179 Deduction*

Cartwright Corporation made three property acquisitions during 2004.

| Asset | Cost | MACRS Life |
|---|---|---|
| Office furniture | $170,000 | 7 years |
| Truck | 40,000 | 5 |
| Computer equipment | 165,000 | 5 |

The greatest potential for acceleration of deductions occurs with the furniture since it has the longest MACRS depreciable life. Cartwright should elect to immediately deduct $102,000 of the cost of the furniture. This deduction reduces Cartwright's tax basis in the furniture to $68,000. This remaining basis and the cost of the other two assets will be depreciated under normal MACRS rules.

*Limitation on Section 179 Deduction*

In the previous example, Cartwright was not limited in its ability to take the Section 179 deduction because its total property acquisitions of $375,000 were less than the $410,000 cap. Now assume that Cartwright made a fourth acquisition of fixtures costing $40,000. As a result, its acquisitions total $415,000. Its available Section 179 deduction is reduced by $5,000 to $97,000.[3]

**Tax Talk**
The limited expensing election is not available for purchases of passenger automobiles but does apply to trucks weighing at least 6,000 pounds. As a result, many larger sport utility vehicles qualify. Following the increase in the deduction amount of $100,000, SUV dealers began using the tax break to pitch their product to small business owners. In late 2003, Congress proposed legislation to limit application of the deduction to SUVs, beginning in 2004 (as of the date this book went to press, such proposals had not yet been enacted).

### Additional First-Year Depreciation

Following the terrorist attacks of September 11, 2001, Congress enacted the Job Creation and Worker Assistance Act of 2002. The act contains a variety of economic stimulus and taxpayer relief provisions. Of these provisions, the allowance of additional first-year depreciation on acquisitions of new nonrealty property is applicable to the largest number of taxpayers.

The 2002 act provides for 30 percent additional first-year depreciation on acquisitions of qualified property placed in service after September 10, 2001, and before September 11, 2004.[4] Qualified property includes depreciable property with a MACRS class life of 20 years or less, certain types of computer software, and leasehold improvements to nonresidential real property placed in service more than three years after the date the building was first placed in service. The original use of qualified property must begin with the taxpayer claiming the additional first-year depreciation. In other words, the property must be new property rather than previously used property acquired by the taxpayer.

The Jobs and Growth Tax Relief Reconciliation Act of 2003 increased the additional first-year depreciation allowance to 50 percent for qualifying property placed in service after May 5, 2003, and before January 1, 2005. To be eligible for the 50 percent allowance, a written binding contract to acquire the property must not have been in effect before May 6, 2003. Taxpayers can elect to apply the 30 percent rate of the 2002 act rather than the 50 percent rate of the 2003 act if desired. Such an election might be appropriate if the taxpayer has expiring net operating losses or expects to be in a higher tax bracket in the future.

After claiming the additional first-year depreciation, the remaining adjusted basis of the property is depreciated under the normal MACRS rules. Thus in the year qualified property

---

[3] $5,000 ($415,000 − $410,000) equals the excess of total acquisitions over the limitation threshold.
[4] Section 168(k).

is placed in service, the taxpayer will claim both 50 percent first-year depreciation and MACRS depreciation using the applicable MACRS percentage and half-year or midquarter depreciation convention required by Section 168.

| *Additional First-Year Depreciation* | During 2004, Lamont Corporation acquired machinery costing $300,000 with a MACRS class life of seven years subject to the half-year convention. The normal first-year depreciation percentage for such property is 14.29 percent. Lamont is entitled to claim the following 2004 depreciation deductions for this property. |
|---|---|

| | |
|---|---:|
| Additional first-year depreciation ($300,000 × 50%) | $150,000 |
| MACRS depreciation allowance [($300,000 − $150,000) × 14.29%] | 21,435 |
| Total first-year depreciation allowance | $171,435 |

In many cases, property eligible for the limited expensing election of Section 179 will also be subject to additional first-year depreciation. In this case, the 50 percent additional first-year depreciation is computed after the limited expensing deduction.

| *Section 179 and Additional First-Year Depreciation* | In the previous example, if the machinery acquired by Lamont Corporation also qualifies for the limited expensing election, Lamont is entitled to claim the following 2004 depreciation deductions for this property. |
|---|---|

| | |
|---|---:|
| Section 179 deduction | $102,000 |
| Additional first-year depreciation [($300,000 − $102,000) × 50%] | 99,000 |
| MACRS depreciation allowance | |
| [($300,000 − $102,000 − $99,000) × 14.29%)] | 14,147 |
| Total first-year recovery deductions | $215,147 |

Are tax savings really sufficient to alter business decisions? Let's use the Lamont example to illustrate how the availability of tax incentives dramatically increases the return on investment in business property. The broad availability of tax incentives for many types of investment in diverse industries suggests that tax savings of this type can have a substantial impact on after-tax value.

| *The Value of Tax Incentives* | Continuing with the example, suppose that as a result of reduced operating costs and production efficiencies associated with the new machinery, Lamont estimates that this purchase will increase operating profit by $65,000 per year for eight years. Lamont's marginal tax rate is 34 percent, and it uses an 8 percent discount rate for computing present value. Without any investment tax incentives, the NPV of after-tax cash flows and return on investment from this purchase can be computed as follows. |
|---|---|

| | Year 0 | Year 1 | Year 2 | Year 3 | Year 4 | Year 5 | Year 6 | Year 7 |
|---|---|---|---|---|---|---|---|---|
| Operating profit | $ 65,000 | $65,000 | $65,000 | $65,000 | $65,000 | $65,000 | $65,000 | $65,000 |
| MACRS depreciation* | (42,870) | (73,470) | (52,470) | (37,470) | (26,790) | (26,760) | (26,790) | (13,380) |
| Taxable income | $ 22,130 | $ (8,470) | $12,530 | $27,530 | $38,210 | $38,240 | $38,210 | $51,620 |
| Tax (cost) benefit | (7,524) | 2,880 | (4,260) | (9,360) | (12,991) | (13,002) | (12,991) | (17,428) |

| | | | | | | | | |
|---|---|---|---|---|---|---|---|---|
| After-tax cash flow[†] | $ 57,476 | $67,880 | $60,740 | $55,640 | $52,009 | $51,998 | $52,009 | $47,572 |
| PV factors | 1.0 | .917 | .842 | .772 | .708 | .650 | .596 | .547 |
| Present value | $ 57,476 | $62,246 | $51,143 | $42,954 | $36,822 | $33,799 | $30,997 | $26,022 |
| Total NPV | $341,459 | | | | | | | |
| Rate of return[‡] | 13.8% | | | | | | | |

* MACRS recovery percentages for 7-year property are 14.29%, 24.49%, 17.49%, 12.49%, 8.93%, 8.92%, 8.93%, and 4.46% from recovery years 1 through 8.

[†] After-tax cash flow = Operating profit – Tax cost + Tax benefit.

[‡] 13.8% = ($341,459 − $300,000)/$300,000.

In this example, a return on investment of 13.8 percent is achieved without any special tax incentives for the acquisition. While this return might be sufficient to attract some investors, the company might find other more attractive uses for its available cash flow. However, let's consider the impact on NPV and rate of return if this purchase qualifies for the $102,000 limited expensing election under Section 179.

| | Year 0 | Year 1 | Year 2 | Year 3 | Year 4 | Year 5 | Year 6 | Year 7 |
|---|---|---|---|---|---|---|---|---|
| Operating profit | $ 65,000 | $65,000 | $65,000 | $65,000 | $65,000 | $65,000 | $65,000 | $65,000 |
| Limited expensing | (102,000) | | | | | | | |
| MACRS depreciation* | (28,294) | (48,490) | (34,630) | (24,730) | (17,681) | (17,662) | (17,687) | (8,832) |
| Taxable income (loss) | $ (65,294) | $16,510 | $30,370 | $40,270 | $47,319 | $47,338 | $47,319 | $56,168 |
| Tax (cost) benefit | 22,200 | (5,613) | (10,326) | (13,692) | (16,088) | (16,095) | (16,088) | (19,097) |
| After-tax cash flow[†] | $ 87,200 | $59,387 | $54,674 | $51,308 | $48,912 | $48,905 | $48,912 | $45,903 |
| PV factors | 1.0 | .917 | .842 | .772 | .708 | .650 | .596 | .547 |
| Present value | $ 87,200 | $54,458 | $46,036 | $39,610 | $34,630 | $31,788 | $29,152 | $25,110 |
| Total NPV | $347,984 | | | | | | | |
| Rate of return[‡] | 16% | | | | | | | |

* MACRS recovery percentages for 7-year property are 14.29%, 24.49%, 17.49%, 12.49%, 8.93%, 8.92%, 8.93%, and 4.46% from recovery years 1 through 8, applied to recovery basis of $198,000, equal to equipment cost ($300,000) reduced by limited expensing deduction ($102,000).

[†] After-tax cash flow = Operating profit – Tax cost + Tax benefit.

[‡] 16% = ($347,984 − $300,000)/$300,000.

This single tax incentive has increased the return on investment in this machinery by more than two percentage points, from 13.8 percent to 16 percent. Finally, consider the impact on NPV and return on investment if this acquisition also qualifies for the 50 percent additional first-year depreciation allowance.

| | Year 0 | Year 1 | Year 2 | Year 3 | Year 4 | Year 5 | Year 6 | Year 7 |
|---|---|---|---|---|---|---|---|---|
| Operating profit | $ 65,000 | $65,000 | $65,000 | $65,000 | $65,000 | $65,000 | $65,000 | $65,000 |
| Limited expensing | (102,000) | | | | | | | |
| Addt'l first year depr.* | (99,000) | | | | | | | |
| MACRS depreciation[†] | (14,147) | (24,245) | (17,315) | (12,365) | (8,841) | (8,831) | (8,841) | (4,415) |
| Taxable income (loss) | $(150,147) | $40,755 | $47,685 | $52,635 | $56,159 | $56,169 | $56,159 | $60,585 |

*continued on page 146*

| continued | Year 0 | Year 1 | Year 2 | Year 3 | Year 4 | Year 5 | Year 6 | Year 7 |
|---|---|---|---|---|---|---|---|---|
| Tax (cost) benefit | 51,050 | (13,857) | (16,213) | (17,896) | (19,094) | (19,097) | (19,094) | (20,599) |
| After-tax cash flow[‡] | $ 116,050 | $51,143 | $48,787 | $47,104 | $45,906 | $45,903 | $45,906 | $44,401 |
| PV factors | 1.0 | .917 | .842 | .772 | .708 | .650 | .596 | .547 |
| Present value | $ 116,050 | $46,898 | $41,079 | $36,364 | $32,501 | $29,837 | $27,360 | $24,287 |
| Total NPV | $ 354,376 | | | | | | | |
| Rate of return[§] | 18.1% | | | | | | | |

[*] Additional first-year depreciation equals 50% of $198,000, equal to equipment cost ($300,000) reduced by limited expensing deduction ($102,000).

[†] MACRS recovery percentages for 7-year property are 14.29%, 24.49%, 17.49%, 12.49%, 8.93%, 8.92%, 8.93%, and 4.46% from recovery years 1 through 8, applied to recovery basis of $99,000, equal to equipment cost ($300,000) reduced by limited expensing deduction ($102,000) and additional first year depreciation ($99,000).

[‡] After-tax cash flow = Operating profit − Tax cost + Tax benefit.

[§] 18.1% = ($354,376 − $300,000)/$300,000.

The addition of this second tax incentive has raised the rate of return on investment to 18.1 percent. Together, these two tax incentives have increased the return on investment in this machinery from 13.8 percent to 18.1 percent, an increase of over 4.3 percentage points. Note that no changes have occurred in the before-tax cash flows related to this investment— all of the increased return is due to lower tax costs (greater tax benefits) in the year of the investment. Through the combination of the Section 179 deduction, additional first-year depreciation, and regular MACRS depreciation, over two-thirds of the cost of the machinery has been deducted in the first year of service. These investment incentives represent a valuable application of the time period variable discussed in Chapter 1: *In present value terms, tax costs decrease (and cash flows increase) when a tax is deferred until a later taxable year.*

### Research Provisions

The tax law currently provides two tax incentives to encourage research activities. First, research and experimentation expenditures may be *deducted* currently or capitalized and amortized over 60 months.[5] Second, a *credit* is available for research expenditures during the current year.[6] The research activities credit has two parts, a basic research credit and an incremental research activities credit. The **basic research credit** equals 20 percent of cash payments to a qualified basic research organization, such as a college or university, to support basic research.[7] Basic research is defined as an original investigation for the advancement of scientific knowledge *without* a specific commercial objective. The **incremental research activities credit** equals 20 percent of qualified current expenditures in excess of a base amount that considers the taxpayer's prior history of research expenditures. Thus, the credit is available only for increases in research activity during the taxable year.

A taxpayer that chooses to take advantage of both the deduction and incremental activity credit incentives for research is subject to some limitations. Three alternatives exist that restrict the combination of benefits available.

1. The taxpayer may use the full credit and reduce the expense deduction by 100 percent of the credit amount.

[5] Section 174.

[6] Section 41.

[7] Corporations taking the basic research credit cannot also take a charitable contribution deduction related to the research payment.

2. The taxpayer may take the full expense deduction and reduce the credit by a percentage equal to the maximum corporate tax rate (currently 35 percent).
3. The taxpayer may choose to capitalize research expenditures and amortize them over 60 months. In this case, the capitalized amount is reduced by 100 percent of the credit only if the credit exceeds the current amortization deduction.

| | | Credit | Deduction |
|---|---|---|---|
| **Alternative 1** | | | |
| | Full credit ($500,000 × 20%) | $100,000 | |
| | Deduction ($500,000 − $100,000 credit) | | $400,000 |
| **Alternative 2** | | | |
| | Reduced credit ($100,000 − $100,000 × 35%) | 65,000 | |
| | Full deduction | | 500,000 |
| **Alternative 3** | | | |
| | Full credit | 100,000 | |
| | Capitalize and amortize expenses over 60 months; amortization deduction ($500,000/5) | | 100,000 |

*Research Incentive*

Harvard Inc. incurred $500,000 of incremental research expenditures qualifying for the research activities credit. Under each of these alternatives, Harvard's available deduction and credit allowable would be calculated as follows.

Which alternative is most beneficial to Harvard? If its current marginal tax rate is less than 35 percent *and* the general business credit limitations (discussed later in this chapter) do not limit its ability to use the credit to reduce current tax liability, it would generally prefer Alternative 1, a full credit and reduction of its deduction. To see this, consider the total tax benefits under Alternatives 1 and 2 if Harvard's marginal tax rate is 31 percent.

| | Alternative 1 | Alternative 2 |
|---|---|---|
| Reduction in tax liability from | | |
| Credit | $100,000 | $ 65,000 |
| Benefit of deduction at 31% | 124,000 | 155,000 |
| Total tax benefits | $224,000 | $220,000 |

However, if Harvard's ability to use additional credits currently and in the near future is limited, it might prefer Alternative 2, to reduce the credit and take a full deduction. Alternative 3 would most likely be beneficial to a taxpayer in a net operating loss position or in expectation of paying tax at a much higher rate in the coming years than in the present.

For purposes of the research deduction and incremental research activities credit, qualified research expenditures include costs incurred in the development of new products, processes, inventions, patents, or formulas. A broad range of industries, such as technology development, pharmaceuticals, chemicals, and many consumer products, can qualify for these incentives. For 2004, the U.S. Department of the Treasury projects that the credit for incremental research activities will save qualifying taxpayers $4.99 billion of income tax, and the election to deduct research and experimentation costs will produce an additional $2.76 billion of tax savings. Together, these research provisions will save businesses nearly $8 billion of income tax in one year, a powerful incentive for investment.[8]

[8] See Budget of the U.S. Government, fiscal year 2004.

*Renewal Communities, Empowerment Zones, and Enterprise Communities*

A group of special tax provisions benefits distressed urban and rural areas designated as **renewal communities, empowerment zones,** and **enterprise communities.** Areas are nominated for designation by state and local governments and must meet a variety of criteria related to population and conditions of pervasive poverty, unemployment, and general distress. Designations generally remain in effect for 10 years. Currently, 40 renewal communities, 41 empowerment zones, and 95 enterprise communities have been authorized.[9] Available tax incentives include (1) an increased limited expensing election for depreciable property acquisitions by enterprise zone and renewal community businesses, (2) an empowerment zone employment credit, and (3) tax-exempt bonds to finance facilities used by enterprise zone businesses in empowerment zones or enterprise communities.

*Increased Limited Expensing Election*   If a qualified business places tangible personal property in service in a renewal community or an empowerment zone, that business could be eligible for a $35,000 immediate **increased limited expensing election** in addition to the normal expensing amount allowed under Section 179.[10] This election is subject to the same annual investment limit of $410,000 (2004) generally applicable to the limited expensing election. However, only one-half of the cost of qualified property is considered for reducing the maximum expensing amount.

| | |
|---|---|
| *Enterprise Zone Expensing Election* | During 2004, an enterprise zone business placed in service qualified zone property costing $840,000. For this year, the maximum normal limited expensing amount under Section 179 is $102,000. The empowerment zone increase brings the maximum expensing amount to $137,000. Since all of the property is qualified zone property, only $420,000 (50 percent of cost) is used to compute the investment limit. Because $420,000 is $10,000 more than the $410,000 annual limit, the maximum expensing amount is reduced to $127,000. Had this taxpayer not been considered an enterprise zone business, its available limited expensing amount would be reduced to zero since its property acquisitions exceed $512,000.[11] |

*Empowerment Zone Employment Credit*   The **empowerment zone employment credit** provides an incentive to hire employees who both live and work in an empowerment zone.[12] Both full-time and part-time employees can qualify for the credit, which can be as much as $3,000 per qualified employee per year. The amount of the available credit varies across empowerment zones. In addition, the employer's tax deduction for salary and wages is reduced by the amount of the credit taken. A similar credit of up to $1,500 is available for hiring employees who live and work in renewal communities.

*Tax-Exempt Bond Financing*   State and local governments can issue tax-exempt bonds to raise funds to provide qualified zone property to enterprise zone businesses. To qualify, a business must be located within an empowerment zone or enterprise community, and at least 80 percent of its gross income must be from the active conduct of business within the zone or community. Although interest income earned by purchasers of these bonds is tax exempt, a qualified enterprise zone business is allowed to deduct interest paid on a loan of bond proceeds from the issuing government to the business.

---

[9] A complete list of designated renewal communities, empowerment zones, and enterprise communities is available in IRS Publication 954.

[10] See Sections 1397A, 1397B, and 1397C.

[11] $410,000 + $102,000 Section 179 amount for 2004.

[12] Section 1396.

| *Tax-Exempt Bond Financing for an Enterprise Zone Business* | Sioux Corporation wishes to relocate its business to an enterprise community. To finance construction of its new facilities, the state in which the enterprise community is located issues enterprise zone facility bonds. The proceeds of the bond issuance are then loaned to Sioux to finance construction of its facilities. The terms of the loan agreement between it and the state provide that Sioux must repay the loan if at any point it fails to meet enterprise zone qualification requirements. |
|---|---|

Note that the increased expensing deduction and the employment credit apply only to businesses in renewal communities and empowerment zones, although tax-exempt bond financing is available for businesses in both empowerment zones and enterprise communities. The group of tax incentives related to renewal communities, empowerment zones, and enterprise communities is expected to generate $1.17 billion of tax savings during 2004.

### New Markets Tax Credit

The Community Renewal Tax Relief Act of 2000 enacted the **new markets tax credit** to provide an incentive for investment in low-income communities.[13] Specifically, the credit applies to equity investments after 2000 in **community development entities (CDEs).** A CDE is a corporation or partnership whose primary mission is serving or providing investment capital for low-income communities or low-income individuals. The entity's governing body must include residents of low-income communities, and it must be certified by the IRS as a qualified CDE. Taxpayers holding an equity investment in a CDE receive a 5 percent tax credit in the year of purchase and the first two years following the year of purchase. A 6 percent credit is then available in each of the next four years. In total, credits equal to 39 percent of the qualified investment are claimed over a seven-year period. The new markets tax credit is expected to generate $290 million of tax savings in 2004.

| *Investment in CDE* | During 2004, Staple Inc. invests $100,000 in the stock of Horizon Corporation, a qualified CDE. Assuming that Staple continues to own this investment for the next seven years, it will claim new markets tax credits as follows: |
|---|---|

| Year | Credit |
|---|---|
| 2004 | $ 5,000 |
| 2005 | 5,000 |
| 2006 | 5,000 |
| 2007 | 6,000 |
| 2008 | 6,000 |
| 2009 | 6,000 |
| 2010 | 6,000 |
| Total | $39,000 |

Assuming an 8 percent discount rate, the NPV of this stream of tax benefits is $30,954.[14]

---

[13] Section 45D.

[14] Note that the 2004 credit amount will not be discounted in calculating NPV since it occurs in year 0.

### Low-Income Housing Credit

The **low-income housing credit** provides a tax incentive to construct or substantially renovate multi-unit buildings housing low-income residents.[15] A building qualifies if either (1) 20 percent of the units are occupied by individuals whose income is 50 percent or less of area median income or (2) if at least 40 percent of the units are occupied by individuals whose income is 60 percent or less of area median income. In addition, the rent charged to tenants cannot exceed 30 percent of an imputed income limitation. The occupancy requirements must be met for 15 years or the credit will be recaptured. The credit is claimed annually over a 10-year period. For new buildings that are not federally subsidized, the credit percentages are set so that during the 10-year period the credits equal the present value of 70 percent of the tax basis of the building. For an existing building or a federally subsidized new building, credits equal the present value of 30 percent of tax basis.

An important limitation affects the total amount of credits available for buildings not financed with tax-exempt bonds. Each state is permitted to annually allocate low-income housing credits with a ceiling amount equal to the greater of $2 million or $1.50 per resident of the state. Tax-exempt bond financing for low-income housing is also subject to annual volume limits. The details of each of these limits is beyond the scope of this text, but any taxpayers considering an investment in low-income housing should investigate them. In spite of these limits, the low-income housing credit is projected to produce $3.64 billion in tax benefits for 2004.

### Disabled Access Credit

An incentive for small businesses to remove existing barriers to handicapped access is provided by the **disabled access credit**.[16] The credit equals 50 percent of qualified expenditures in excess of $250, with a maximum annual credit of $5,000. An eligible small business is any business that either (1) had gross receipts of $1 million or less in the preceding year or (2) had no more than 30 full-time employees in the preceding year. The depreciable basis of the qualified property is reduced by the amount of the credit taken. The disabled access credit is projected to provide $50 million of tax benefits in 2004.

| | |
|---|---|
| *Disabled Access Credit* | Joshua Inc. spent $20,000 to install handicapped access ramps during 2003. During 2002, the company had $1.5 million of gross receipts and 15 full-time employees. Joshua meets the employee test to be a qualified small business. Its available credit is $5,000 [the lesser of $5,000 or 50% × ($20,000 − $250)]. The depreciable tax basis of the property addition is reduced to $15,000 ($20,000 cost − $5,000 credit). |

### Incentives for Alternative-Fuel Vehicles

The **tax credit and deduction for clean-fuel-burning vehicles** acknowledge the pollution caused by standard combustion engines and attempt to encourage the use of vehicles powered by alternative energy sources. These incentives are not limited to vehicles used for business purposes and thus are available to individuals for personal use vehicles. These two incentives together are expected to provide $70 million of tax savings during 2004. The tax credit equals 10 percent of the cost of electric vehicles, with a maximum credit of $4,000 per vehicle.[17] The full credit is available for vehicles placed in service before December 31,

---

[15] Section 42.
[16] Section 44.
[17] Section 30.

2003. The credit begins to phase out in 2004 and will be eliminated completely after 2006. The credit is reduced 25 percent for each year in the phaseout period. Thus, the maximum credit for 2004 is $3,000 per vehicle.

A deduction is also available for a portion of the cost of clean-fuel-burning vehicles in the year placed in service. The amount of the deduction depends on the type of vehicle as follows:

| Type of Vehicle | Maximum Deduction |
| --- | --- |
| Large trucks and buses | $50,000 |
| Medium trucks and vans | 5,000 |
| Smaller passenger vehicles | 2,000 |

Property used to store or deliver clean-burning fuel also qualifies for the deduction up to a maximum of $100,000 for all such property placed in service during the taxable year. Clean-burning fuels include natural gas, liquefied natural and petroleum gases, hydrogen, electricity, and alcohol or ether-based fuels such as ethanol. The deduction is subject to phaseout over the same period as the credit for electric vehicles.

*Clean-Fuel Burning Vehicles Incentives*

Maxwell Corporation purchased three electric buses at a cost of $200,000 per vehicle. It will take a current tax deduction for $150,000 ($50,000 × 3) of the cost of the buses and will capitalize and depreciate the remaining $450,000 cost under the normal cost recovery rules for such vehicles. In addition, Maxwell is entitled to $12,000 (3 times the lesser of $200,000 × 10 percent or $4,000) of tax credits.

## CRITICISMS OF TAX INCENTIVES AND RESTRICTIONS ON THEIR BENEFITS

Although tax incentives for businesses have a long history as part of the federal income tax, their existence is frequently criticized by political candidates and tax reform advocates. Such provisions are labeled as **corporate welfare**—providing tax savings to special interests and large corporations at the expense of middle- and working-class families. Tax reform has played a role in virtually all modern presidential elections. During the 2000 presidential contest, GOP presidential candidate John McCain stated the following:

> Every tax dollar now wasted on special breaks for oil companies, ethanol giants, insurance giants and the multitude of other powerful special interests . . . is now at risk. We are going to take the money back, end the corporate welfare bonanza and give tax relief to the American people.[18]

Although such calls for reform result in frequent changes in the type and form of tax incentives, their complete elimination seems unlikely. However, two important elements of the tax law operate to restrict and sometimes indirectly eliminate tax benefits from these incentive provisions. The remainder of this chapter discusses the general business credit limitation and the alternative minimum tax and their impact on tax savings from business incentive provisions.

[18] "McCain's Tax Plan Would Kill Breaks for Firms, Provide Middle-Class Relief," *Wall Street Journal*, January 12, 2000, p. A4.

## General Business Credit Limitation

**Objective 2**
Calculate the general business credit limitation and identify those credits included as part of the general business credit.

A number of the tax credits described earlier are grouped collectively as part of the **general business credit.** All credits in this group are subject to an important annual limitation. The total **general business credit limitation** in any tax year cannot exceed the lesser of (1) net regular tax liability minus tentative minimum tax or (2) net regular tax liability minus 25 percent of net regular tax liability in excess of $25,000. If total general business credits exceed this limit, the excess can be carried back one year and forward 20 years, subject to the same limit in the carryback/carryover years.

*Basics of the General Business Credit Limitation*

Conifer Corporation is entitled to total general business credits of $120,000. If its net regular income tax before these credits is $500,000 and tentative minimum tax is $410,000, the maximum general business credit usable in the current year is the lesser of

$90,000 = $500,000 − $410,000

or

$381,250 = $500,000 − 25% X ($500,000 − $25,000)

Thus, Conifer may reduce regular tax liability by $90,000 of general business credits, producing net regular tax liability of $410,000 ($500,000 − $90,000). The remaining $30,000 ($120,000 − $90,000) of general business credits may be carried back 1 year and forward 20 years, subject to the credit limitation in these years.

The following credits are part of the general business credit for purposes of this limitation:[19]

- Research credit
- Low-income housing credit
- Disabled access credit
- Rehabilitation credit
- Work opportunity credit
- Welfare-to-work credit
- Empowerment zone employment credit
- New markets tax credit
- Alcohol fuels credit
- Enhanced oil recovery credit
- Renewable electricity production credit
- Indian employment credit
- Employer Social Security credit
- Orphan drug credit

*Applying the Credit Limitation*

Before applying the general business credit limitation, Grayson Corporation qualifies for the following tax credits for the 2004 taxable year.

---

[19] Given their limited applicability, the rehabilitation credit, work opportunity credit, welfare-to-work credit, alcohol fuels credit, enhanced oil recovery credit, renewable electricity production credit, Indian employment credit, employer Social Security credit, and orphan drug credit are not discussed further.

| Research credit | $140,000 |
| Low-income housing credit | 300,000 |
| Clean-fuel burning vehicle credit | 200,000 |

Grayson's taxable income totals $2,500,000. Regular tax liability before credits is $850,000. Of the three tax credits for which Grayson qualifies, the research credit and the low-income housing credit are part of the general business credit; the clean-fuel burning vehicle credit is not. Its regular tax before the general business credit is $650,000 ($850,000 regular tax − $200,000 clean-fuel burning vehicle credit). If Grayson's tentative minimum tax is $260,000, the maximum general business credits usable in 2004 equals the lesser of

$390,000 = $650,000 − $260,000

or

$473,750 = $650,000 − 25% × ($650,000 − $25,000)

Thus, Grayson may reduce tax liability by $390,000 at most for those credits included in the general business credit. Grayson's final tax liability for 2004 is determined as follows:

| Regular tax | $850,000 |
| Less:  General business credit | (390,000) |
| Clean-fuel burning vehicle credit | (200,000) |
| Net tax liability | $260,000 |

Grayson's excess general business credit of $50,000 can be carried back one year and forward 20 years, subject to the credit limitation in these years.

Although the general business credit limitation can reduce the current period benefit available from many credit-based tax incentives, it has no impact on incentives provided in the form of special deductions or exclusions from taxability. The alternative minimum tax, however, can reduce the attractiveness of many such incentives.

## Alternative Minimum Tax

**Objective 3**
Describe the purpose of the alternative minimum tax and the common preferences and adjustments required to calculate the corporate alternative minimum tax.

The **alternative minimum tax (AMT)** is a second tax system paralleling the regular federal income tax. It was enacted primarily in response to perceptions that loopholes in the tax code allowed large, economically profitable corporations to escape their share of the tax burden. Indeed, a firm that arranges its business operations to take advantage of a large number of incentive deductions, exclusions, and tax credits could substantially reduce or eliminate regular tax liability. However, the AMT ensures that the firm will pay tax under this alternative system. In many cases, AMT results because the acceleration of tax benefits under many incentive provisions reduces regular tax currently at a cost of future tax increases. Thus, the AMT accelerates tax payments into the present. Because of the AMT credit provisions discussed at the end of this section, the AMT rarely creates larger total tax payments over longer time horizons. However, the acceleration of tax payments caused by the AMT reduces the present value of after-tax returns on tax-favored investments.

Our discussion of this alternative tax system focuses on the corporate AMT and its impact on business investment incentives. A similar set of provisions subjects individual taxpayers to the AMT, although differences exist in the specifics of the two calculations and in the applicable AMT tax rates.

The corporate AMT is calculated as follows.

|  |
|---|
| Taxable income for regular tax purposes before net operating loss (NOL) deduction |
| + AMT preferences |
| ± AMT adjustments |
| − AMT net operating loss (NOL) deduction |
| Alternative minimum taxable income |
| − AMT exemption |
| AMT base |
| × AMT rate |
| Tentative minimum tax |
| − Regular tax |
| Alternative minimum tax |

To the extent that a corporation engages in activities producing AMT preferences and positive AMT adjustments, alternative minimum taxable income increases and AMT liability is more likely. If tentative minimum tax is less than regular tax, no AMT is due.

### AMT *Preferences*

**AMT preferences** always increase **alternative minimum taxable income (AMTI),** exposing otherwise nontaxable income items to the AMT. The four most common preference items are:

1. Tax-exempt interest from private activity bonds
2. Excess percentage depletion
3. Excess intangible drilling costs
4. Accelerated depreciation of real property

*Tax-Exempt Interest from Private Activity Bonds*   Interest earned on municipal bonds is not taxable for regular tax purposes. However, if the proceeds of the bond issuance are used to benefit private businesses, the interest earned on such **private activity bonds** is subject to the alternative minimum tax. Included in this category are bonds issued by a municipality to fund construction costs for private industry as an incentive for businesses to locate in the municipality. Other examples include bonds issued by city governments to provide construction financing for professional sports facilities. The preference item is reduced by any expenses associated with the bonds.

| *Private Activity Bond Preference* | Conifer Corporation earned $6,000 of tax-exempt interest on Cobb County Industrial Development bonds. The bond proceeds were used to provide construction financing for private businesses relocating to Cobb County. Conifer also incurred $1,000 of carrying costs for these bonds, which were not deductible for regular tax purposes. Conifer's AMT preference amount for these private activity bonds is $5,000 ($6,000 interest income − $1,000 costs). |
|---|---|

*Excess Percentage Depletion*   To the extent that a corporation deducts percentage depletion exceeding the tax basis of the related property, such excess is a preference item for AMT purposes. In other cases, percentage depletion does not generate a tax preference as long as the property's ending adjusted tax basis (after reduction for depletion taken) is positive.

| *Percentage Depletion Preference* | Cassandra Corporation owns a royalty interest in one gas well. During 2004, it deducted $10,000 of percentage depletion related to this property. At the beginning of 2004, the company had an adjusted tax basis in the property of $3,000. Its percentage depletion deduction reduces its tax basis to zero. The $7,000 of percentage depletion in excess of tax basis is an AMT preference item. |
|---|---|

*Excess Intangible Drilling Costs*   Qualifying oil and gas producers may elect to take a current tax deduction for intangible drilling costs (IDCs). For AMT purposes, a tax preference item occurs to the extent that the excess of such deductions over the deduction allowed if the costs had been amortized over 120 months exceeds 65 percent of the net income from the property.

| *IDC Preference* | Anasazi Inc. incurred $1,000,000 of IDC on Property X, which it elected to deduct currently. Net income for the property for the year (before any deduction for IDC) totaled $600,000. If the IDC had been amortized over 120 months, annual amortization would equal $100,000. Anasazi's IDC preference amount for Property X is $510,000 ([$1,000,000 − $100,000] − 65 percent × $600,000). |
|---|---|

*Accelerated Depreciation of Real Property*   Real property placed in service prior to 1987 is depreciated using accelerated methods. For AMT purposes, depreciation on such property is recomputed using the straight-line method, and the excess of regular tax depreciation over AMT depreciation is a tax preference item.

### AMT Adjustments

**AMT adjustments** typically represent items whose regular tax treatment results in either an accelerated deduction or a deferral of income recognition. AMT adjustments can be positive or negative, depending on the nature of the adjustment and its timing. The following are the more common adjustments required in calculating the corporate AMT:

Depreciation adjustment

Amortization adjustments for (1) certified pollution control facilities and (2) mining exploration and development costs

Adjusted gain/loss on property dispositions

Adjustment for long-term contracts using the completed-contract method

Installment sales adjustment

Adjusted current earnings (ACE) adjustment

*Depreciation and Amortization Adjustments*   Most business taxpayers have an AMT adjustment related to depreciation of assets under the MACRS system. In essence, the adjustment equals the difference between depreciation calculated for regular tax purposes and depreciation calculated under an alternate set of AMT rules (alternative depreciation system or ADS) using longer lives and less accelerated methods.[20] The adjustment for amortization of pollution control facilities is similar in that regular tax amortization occurs on a

---

[20] An AMT adjustment is not required for the additional first-year depreciation allowed by Section 168 (k).

straight-line basis over 60 months while AMT amortization is computed using the alternate depreciation system required for depreciable assets.

| AMT Depreciation Adjustment | Glassware Corporation deducted MACRS depreciation of $550,000 in calculating regular taxable income. If depreciation calculated under the ADS system totaled $500,000, Glassware has a $50,000 positive adjustment in calculating its AMT. If depreciation under the ADS system totaled $580,000 instead, a $30,000 negative adjustment is required in calculating AMT. |
| --- | --- |

For regular tax purposes, corporations engaged in mining exploration and development can expense qualifying costs of these activities as incurred.[21] For AMT purposes, however, such costs must be capitalized and amortized over a 10-year period.

| AMT Amortization Adjustment | During 2004, Stripper Inc. incurred $2,500,000 of mining exploration and development costs. Deductible amounts for regular tax and AMT purposes as well as AMT adjustments related to these deductions are as follows: |
| --- | --- |

|  | Regular Tax Deduction | AMT Deduction | AMT Adjustment |
| --- | --- | --- | --- |
| 2004 | $2,500,000 | $250,000 | $2,250,000 |
| 2005–2013 (each year) | –0– | 250,000 | (250,000) |

In 2004, the required adjustment increases the corporation's potential exposure to the AMT. In the subsequent 9 years, the AMT adjustments will reduce potential AMT. Over the 10-year amortization period, the positive and negative AMT adjustments will net to zero.

**Adjusted Gain or Loss on Property Dispositions**   Under general tax principles, gain or loss on property dispositions is calculated as follows.

Amount realized
Less: Adjusted tax basis
Gain or loss realized

Adjusted tax basis is reduced by depreciation, amortization, or other deductions related to the cost of the property. For AMT purposes, gain or loss must be recomputed using the property's AMT adjusted tax basis. Such basis will differ to the extent that AMT and regular tax depreciation and amortization differ. The difference between regular tax gain or loss and the AMT gain or loss on property dispositions is an AMT adjustment.

| AMT Gain (Loss) Adjustments | Lyman Corporation sold two assets for which adjusted basis differs for regular tax and AMT purposes. |
| --- | --- |

|  | Regular Tax Gain (Loss) | AMT Gain (Loss) | AMT Adjustment |
| --- | --- | --- | --- |
| Asset 1 |  |  |  |
| Amount realized | $100,000 | $100,000 |  |
| Adjusted basis | (65,000) | (50,000) |  |
| Gain (Loss) | $ 35,000 | $ 50,000 | $15,000 |

[21] Sections 616(a) and 617(a).

| Asset 2 | | | |
|---|---|---|---|
| Amount realized | $200,000 | $200,000 | |
| Adjusted basis | (250,000) | (225,000) | |
| Gain (Loss) | $ (50,000) | $ (25,000) | 25,000 |
| Total adjustment | | | $40,000 |

Lyman has a positive AMT adjustment for the excess of AMT gain over regular tax gain on asset 1 and a positive AMT adjustment for the excess of regular tax loss over AMT loss on asset 2. The aggregate positive adjustment of $40,000 will increase Lyman's AMTI.

*Adjustment for Long-Term Contracts*   For AMT purposes, corporations earning income from long-term contracts generally must use the percentage-of-completion method to report contract income. If the completed-contract method is used for regular tax purposes, an AMT adjustment will be required.[22]

*Long-Term Contract Adjustments*

Daletski Inc. uses the completed contract method of accounting for income from office construction contracts. One such contract began in 2004, was completed in 2005, and earned $1,300,000. At the end of 2004, 40 percent of the work on the contract had been completed. Daletski's income from the contract for regular tax purposes and AMT purposes as well as the required AMT adjustments are as follows:

| | Regular Tax Income | AMT Income | AMT Adjustment |
|---|---|---|---|
| 2004 | –0– | $520,000 | $520,000 |
| 2005 | $1,300,000 | 780,000 | (520,000) |

Daletski has a positive AMT adjustment in 2004 and an equal negative adjustment in 2005.

*Adjustment for Installment Sales*   A limited number of taxpayers are allowed to use the installment sale method for regular tax purposes to defer gain recognition on qualifying transactions. However, the method is not permitted for AMT purposes. Instead, all gain must be reported as part of AMTI in the year of the sale.

*Installment Sale Adjustments*

Bohwali Corporation sold land held for investment on an installment basis. It realized $400,000 of gain on the sale and collected 50 percent of the proceeds of the sale in 2004 and the remaining 50 percent in 2005. Its recognized gain from the sale for regular tax purposes and AMT purposes as well as the required AMT adjustments are as follows:

| | Regular Tax Income | AMT Income | AMT Adjustment |
|---|---|---|---|
| 2004 | $200,000 | $400,000 | $200,000 |
| 2005 | 200,000 | –0– | (200,000) |

[22] Only certain home construction contractors and small contractors with gross receipts under $10 million whose contracts are completed within two years are not required to use the percentage-of-completion method for regular tax purposes. Section 460(e).

**Objective 4**

Calculate the adjusted current earnings (ACE) adjustment, alternative minimum taxable income, and the corporate alternative minimum tax.

*Adjusted Current Earnings*  The most challenging adjustment in the calculation of corporate AMTI is based on the corporation's **adjusted current earnings (ACE)** for the taxable year. The ACE adjustment equals 75 percent of the difference between ACE and the corporation's AMTI before both the ACE adjustment and the AMT NOL. The ACE adjustment can be positive or negative. However, any current negative ACE adjustment may not exceed the positive cumulative total of prior year ACE adjustments.

*Negative ACE Adjustment*

For 2004, Munoz Inc. has computed a negative ACE adjustment of $(400,000). It has been in existence for three previous years and computed ACE adjustments in those years as follows:

| | |
|---|---|
| 2001 | $200,000 |
| 2002 | (50,000) |
| 2003 | 190,000 |

Cumulative prior year ACE adjustments total $340,000. Munoz can reduce current AMTI by only $(340,000). The excess $(60,000) negative adjustment does not carry forward but is simply lost.

Adjusted current earnings is conceptually similar to a corporation's economic income for the year. In this sense, the ACE adjustment is consistent with the goal of ensuring that all corporations with significant economic income pay some minimum level of tax. The starting point for calculating ACE is AMTI before the ACE adjustment and the AMT NOL. A number of additional adjustments are then required to reflect differences between economic income and those items already included in AMTI. The following is a partial list of common adjustments required in the computation of ACE.

+ Tax-exempt income net of expenses (other than private activity bond income already included as a tax preference item)
+ 70 percent dividends-received deduction
+ Key-employee life insurance proceeds
+ Increase in cash surrender value of life insurance policies
+ Amortization of organization expenses
± Difference between LIFO and FIFO cost of good sold for taxpayers using LIFO for regular tax purposes
− Nondeductible losses on sales between related parties

*ACE Adjustment*

Fairmont Inc. calculates the ACE adjustment for 2004 as follows:

| | |
|---|---|
| AMTI before ACE | $6,000,000 |
| Plus | |
| Public-activity municipal bond interest | 100,000 |
| 70 percent dividends-received deduction | 220,000 |
| Organization expense amortization | 25,000 |
| Adjusted current earnings | $6,345,000 |
| Less: AMTI before ACE | (6,000,000) |
| Excess | $ 345,000 |
| Multiplied by | 0.75 |
| ACE adjustment (positive) | $ 258,750 |

### AMT NOL *Deduction*

The last item that must be considered in calculating AMTI is the AMT NOL deduction. Recall that a taxpayer will have a net operating loss for regular tax purposes when allowable business deductions exceed taxable business income. The AMT NOL deduction is calculated by considering those items of income and deduction included in AMTI. As a result, the amount of a taxpayer's AMT NOL in any given year can differ substantially from the regular tax NOL.

In addition to these calculation differences, the deductibility of the AMT NOL is limited to 90 percent of AMTI before the NOL deduction. This limit ensures that a minimum of 10 percent of AMT is potentially taxable in keeping with the goal of assessing some tax liability on taxpayers with current economic income. For example, if AMTI before the NOL deduction is $100,000, the maximum allowable AMT NOL deduction is $90,000.

### AMT *Exemption, Rate, and Credits*

The corporate **AMT exemption** amount is $40,000 for corporations whose AMTI does not exceed $150,000. Above this threshold, the AMT exemption is phased out at a rate of 25 cents for every dollar of excess AMTI. At this rate, the exemption phases out completely when AMTI reaches $310,000.

The corporate AMT is calculated using a 20 percent rate applied to the AMT base (AMTI − AMT exemption amount). The product of the AMT rate and the AMT base determines the corporation's tentative minimum tax. This amount is then compared to regular tax liability to determine whether the corporation owes alternative minimum tax. If tentative minimum tax exceeds the regular tax, such excess is considered an AMT liability and is paid in addition to the regular tax. If regular tax exceeds the tentative minimum tax, the taxpayer owes no AMT and pays the regular tax.

The only tax credit allowed against the AMT is the foreign tax credit (FTC), and its use is limited to 90 percent of tentative minimum tax.

---

| *Comprehensive AMT Example* | Loveland Corporation has regular taxable income of $3,000,000, resulting in regular tax liability before credits of $1,020,000. Loveland qualifies for general business tax credits totaling $250,000 before applying the general business credit limitation. The following additional information is available: |
|---|---|

- Loveland earned $90,000 of municipal bond interest income, $25,000 of which is considered private activity bond interest.

- In computing taxable income, Loveland deducted $200,000 of depreciation on real property placed in service before 1987. On a straight-line basis, depreciation on this property would be $120,000.

- Loveland also deducted $1,500,000 of depreciation on personal property computed under MACRS. Under the alternate depreciation system (ADS), depreciation on this property would be $950,000.

- Loveland reported $40,000 of gain on asset dispositions. These assets had an AMT adjusted basis $10,000 greater than their regular tax adjusted basis.

- In computing taxable income, Loveland reported $300,000 of dividend income and took a 70 percent dividends-received deduction of $210,000.

- Loveland received $2 million of life insurance proceeds following the death of its vice president.

Loveland computes AMT as follows:

| | | |
|---|---|---|
| Regular taxable income | $ 3,000,000 | |
| AMT preferences | | |
|    Private activity bond interest | 25,000 | |
|    Excess real property depreciation | 80,000 | |
| AMT adjustments | | |
|    Excess of MACRS over ADS depreciation | 550,000 | |
|    Gain adjustment | (10,000) | |
| AMTI before the ACE adjustment | $ 3,645,000 | $ 3,645,000 |
| Plus | | |
|    Public activity bond interest | 65,000 | |
|    Life insurance proceeds | 2,000,000 | |
|    Dividends-received deduction | 210,000 | |
| Adjusted current earnings | $ 5,920,000 | |
| Less: AMTI before ACE | (3,645,000) | |
| Excess | $ 2,275,000 | |
| | 0.75 | |
| ACE adjustment | $ 1,706,250 | 1,706,250 |
| AMTI | | $ 5,351,250 |
| AMT exemption | | –0– |
| AMT base | | $ 5,351,250 |
| AMT rate | | 0.20 |
| Tentative minimum tax | | $1,070,250 |
| Regular tax before credits | | 1,020,000 |
| Alternative minimum tax | | $    50,250 |

Loveland owes alternative minimum tax of $50,250. Its total tax due is $1,070,250 ($1,020,000 regular tax + $50,250 AMT). Loveland cannot use any of its general business credits to reduce current tax liability.

## Minimum Tax Credit

**Objective 5**
Explain the purpose of the minimum tax credit and calculate the amount of the credit generated and used each year.

As previously discussed, AMT adjustments can be either positive or negative. Thus, many differences between regular taxable income and AMTI, in any given year, are a matter of timing. A taxpayer can owe AMT in some years but not in others. To avoid unnecessarily penalizing taxpayers whose AMT liability is timing related and who do pay substantial regular tax in some years, that regular tax liability can be reduced by accumulated minimum tax credits.

A **minimum tax credit** is *generated* in any year in which tentative minimum tax exceeds regular tax. The amount of the minimum tax credit is equal to the excess of tentative minimum tax over regular tax liability. The credit is carried forward for use in future periods. A minimum tax credit can be *used* in any year in which regular tax exceeds tentative minimum tax to reduce tax liability at most by the amount of such excess. The labeling of this credit often creates confusion, since the "minimum tax credit" is not a credit against minimum tax liability but is a credit against regular tax liability to the extent that a taxpayer previously has paid AMT.

| *Generation and Use of Minimum Tax Credits* | For 2002, Desantis Inc. calculated regular tax liability of $300,000 and tentative minimum tax liability of $340,000. As a result, it paid total tax liability of $340,000, equal to regular tax plus $40,000 of AMT. This payment generated a minimum tax credit of $40,000, which Desantis carried forward. In 2003, it calculated regular tax liability of $380,000 and tentative minimum tax liability of $350,000. It can use $30,000 of its minimum tax credit carryforward to reduce regular tax liability to $350,000. Its remaining $10,000 of minimum tax credit will carry forward to 2004 and beyond. |
|---|---|

### Impact of AMT on Tax Incentives

As previously discussed, tax incentives attempt to influence behavior by reducing the after-tax cost of targeted investments. However, the AMT can negate such tax savings in several ways. First, some tax incentives, such as percentage depletion and expensing of IDC, increase AMT exposure directly by creating tax preference items. The effect of the AMT on tax savings from other incentives is indirect but is just as costly. Recall that many incentive credits described here are part of the general business credit. The limitation on the general business credit prevents reduction of regular tax liability below tentative minimum tax. The greater the tentative minimum tax, the lower the current benefit received from these incentive credits and the higher the after-tax cost of the targeted behavior. Finally, to the extent that tax incentives provide accelerated deductions (such as the increased limited expensing deduction for empowerment zone property and the deduction for the cost of clean-fuel-burning vehicles), the gap between AMTI and adjusted current earnings widens, increasing the ACE adjustment with a corresponding increase in AMT. The following simplified example quantifies the effect of the AMT on the value provided by one tax incentive, the percentage depletion deduction.

| *AMT Incentive Impact* | Myer Corporation has $1,000,000 of taxable income after deduction of $900,000 of percentage depletion in excess of the tax basis of its oil-producing properties. Its regular tax liability is $340,000. Given Myer's regular marginal tax rate of 34 percent, its regular tax savings as a result of the percentage depletion incentive provision is $306,000.<br><br>For AMT purposes, assume that Myer has no other preferences or adjustments. Its AMTI is $1,900,000, and its tentative minimum tax is $380,000. Myer will pay AMT of $40,000 in addition to its regular tax liability of $340,000. The AMT has reduced Myer's tax savings from percentage depletion by $40,000, a 13 percent reduction. |
|---|---|

The impact of the ACE adjustment on after-tax return is more subtle. ACE captures items receiving preferential tax treatment that are not directly included in AMTI as tax preferences or adjustments. The following example illustrates the indirect tax cost of the AMT on "tax-exempt" municipal bond interest as a result of the ACE adjustment.

| *ACE Adjustment and Return on Municipal Bonds* | Clock Corporation has regular taxable income of $320,000, resulting in $180,800 of regular tax liability. In addition, it earned $200,000 of municipal bond interest income on an investment of $3.3 million in public activity bonds. AMT preferences and adjustments (before the ACE adjustment) totaled $150,000, resulting in AMTI before the ACE adjustment of $470,000[23] and an ACE adjustment of $150,000.[24] AMT is thus $620,000, and tentative minimum tax is $124,000.[25] Resulting AMT liability is $15,200.[26] |
|---|---|

[23] $320,000 + $150,000.
[24] $200,000 × 75 percent.
[25] AMTI = $470,000 + $150,000. Tentative minimum tax = $620,000 × 20 percent.
[26] $124,000 − $108,800.

Without the municipal bond interest, Clock would owe no AMT.[27] Thus, the total AMT owed is a tax cost of the bond investment. Total current after-tax cash flow from the bonds is $184,800 ($200,000 − $15,200). On an investment of $3.3 million, this cash flow represents a 5.6 percent current rate of return, a 0.46 percent reduction related to the AMT.[28]

The possible interaction of tax incentive provisions and the AMT introduces considerable complexity into the tax planning process. How should the effective tax planner proceed? Projections of tax costs and benefits of any tax-favored investment should consider the possible imposition of the AMT and its impact on the timing of tax payments. The generation and use of minimum tax credits will also impact timing and should be considered in these projections. Taxpayers investing in only a few tax-favored activities producing relatively small AMT adjustments and preferences will likely not be subject to this tax. However, taxpayers investing in many activities eligible for tax incentives should carefully calculate the resulting AMT impact. In many cases, the acceleration of tax payments caused by the AMT will reduce the benefits of tax incentive provisions when AMT is owed. Finally, taxpayers that routinely pay AMT must consider their AMT marginal tax rate (20 percent) rather than their regular tax marginal rate in making investment decisions.

## Conclusion

Various business tax incentives provide an opportunity for taxpayers to reduce the after-tax cost for tax-favored investments with corresponding increases in after-tax return. Although these provisions are available only to qualifying taxpayers engaging in targeted behaviors, the incentives examined in this chapter are expected to generate over $14 billion of tax savings for 2004 alone. In determining the short- and long-term benefits provided by these incentives, taxpayers must be aware of the potential limitations imposed on incentive credits included as part of the general business credit, as well as the additional tax burden of the alternative minimum tax.

## Key Terms

adjusted current earnings (ACE) *158*
alternative minimum tax (AMT) *153*
alternative minimum taxable income (AMTI) *154*
AMT adjustments *155*
AMT exemption *159*
AMT preferences *154*
basic research credit *146*
community development entities (CDEs) *149*
corporate welfare *151*

disabled access credit *150*
empowerment zone *148*
empowerment zone employment credit *148*
enterprise community *148*
general business credit *152*
general business credit limitation *152*
increased limited expensing election *148*
incremental research activities credit *146*

limited expensing election *142*
low-income housing credit *150*
minimum tax credit *160*
new markets tax credit *149*
private activity bonds *154*
renewal community *148*
tax credit and deduction for clean-fuel-burning vehicles *150*
tax incentives *142*

[27] AMTI would be $470,000, resulting in tentative minimum tax of $94,000, which is less than regular tax.
[28] 5.6 percent = $184,800/$3.3 million versus 6.06 percent = $200,000/$3.3 million.

## Questions and Problems for Discussion

1. Critics argue that many business tax incentives are corporate welfare, providing tax benefits at the expense of individuals. Name three possible ways that corporate welfare indirectly provides economic benefits to individual taxpayers.

2. Municipal bonds are widely regarded as being tax exempt. Discuss two ways in which corporate ownership of municipal bonds increases exposure to the alternative minimum tax.

3. What conceptual rationale indicates the need for an AMT adjustment related to the tax treatment of long-term contracts? In other words, in what way is the regular tax treatment preferential?

4. What conceptual rationale indicates the need for an AMT adjustment related to the tax treatment of installment sales? In other words, in what way is the regular tax treatment preferential?

5. Since the AMT rate is considerably lower than the highest corporate regular tax marginal rate, what conditions must occur for a firm to be subject to the AMT?

6. Which tax planning maxim discussed in Chapter 1 explains the incentive effects of the Section 179 limited expensing election? Discuss how this tax planning maxim also explains the choice of assets to which the election should apply.

7. As discussed in the chapter, many tax incentive provisions exist to motivate taxpayer behavior that Congress finds desirable but for which before-tax returns are insufficient to attract investment. Which of the specific provisions of the low-income housing credit ensure that the projects to which it applies require additional incentive in order to generate sufficient return to investors?

8. Hamilton Corporation has owed AMT nearly every year for the last 10 years. As a result, it has accumulated substantial minimum tax credit carryforwards. On the basis of current projections, Hamilton's tax director does not believe it will be able to use these credits at any time in the next 5 years. What does Hamilton's AMT situation tell you about the composition of its alternative minimum taxable income? About other factors that could be reducing its regular tax liability?

## Application Problems

1. Denali Corporation acquired the following business assets during 2004.

| | Cost | MACRS Life |
|---|---|---|
| Building | $250,000 | 39 years |
| Equipment | 150,000 | 7 |
| Vehicles | 70,000 | 5 |

None of these assets is located in an empowerment zone or enterprise community.

a. Does Denali qualify for the Section 179 limited expensing election for 2004? If so, to which assets could the election be applied?

b. Calculate Denali's allowable Section 179 deduction, allowable 2004 MACRS depreciation, and any additional first-year depreciation on these assets, assuming that Denali applies the Section 179 election to the equipment. Note that the year 1 depreciation rates for each MACRS class of assets (assuming a midyear convention for the equipment and vehicles and that the real estate was acquired in the sixth month) are 39 years, 1.97 percent in year 1; 7 years, 14.29 percent in year 1; 5 years, 20 percent in year 1.

c. Calculate Denali's allowable Section 179 deduction, allowable 2004 MACRS depreciation, and any additional first-year depreciation on these assets, assuming that Denali applies the Section 179 election to the vehicles.

d. To which asset should Denali apply the Section 179 election? Explain why.

2. Mission Inc. acquired new business assets during 2004 with a total acquisition cost of $420,000. All of these assets have a five-year depreciable life under MACRS.

   a. If Mission does not elect to take the Section 179 limited expensing deduction, calculate its total first-year depreciation deduction with respect to these assets (assuming the midyear convention, the MACRS depreciation rate for the first year of five-year property is 20 percent).

   b. If Mission elects to take the Section 179 limited expensing deduction, calculate the amount of such deduction allowed, Mission's total current depreciation deduction under MACRS with respect to these assets, and Mission's total cost recovery under both Section 179 and MACRS.

   c. How would your answer to part (b) change if Mission Inc. is an enterprise zone business, and the assets acquired are zone property qualifying for the increased limited expensing election?

3. Beltway Inc. is an enterprise zone business. During 2004, Beltway acquired $850,000 of new equipment. Calculate its total allowable deductions under Section 179.

4. Langtree Corporation is considering investing in a large low-income housing project. Langtree has a history of stable profits in real estate development. During recent years, its marginal tax rate has ranged from 31 to 34 percent. It has not previously paid AMT.

   a. What tax factors should Langtree consider in projecting its after-tax return on investment in this project?

   b. Suppose that Langtree projects 2004 regular taxable income of $1 million and alternative minimum taxable income of $1.2 million. Calculate Langtree's regular tax before credits and tentative minimum tax. How large would Langtree's low-income housing credit need to be before it would owe alternative minimum tax?

   c. At the level of credit calculated in part (b), would Langtree be subject to the general business credit limitation? Calculate Langtree's maximum 2004 general business credit.

5. Waterview Inc. was incorporated in 2002. For its first three taxable years, Waterview's AMTI before the ACE adjustment and its adjusted current earnings were as follows.

|       | AMTI before ACE | Adjusted Current Earnings |
| ----- | --------------- | ------------------------- |
| 2002  | $190,000        | $250,000                  |
| 2003  | 460,000         | 511,000                   |
| 2004  | 900,000         | 600,000                   |

   Compute Waterview's 2004 ACE adjustment and AMTI after the ACE adjustment.

6. Comtec Inc. qualifies for the following tax credits before considering any limitations.

| | |
| --- | --- |
| Low-income housing credit | $100,000 |
| Welfare-to-work credit | 50,000 |
| Credit for electric vehicles | 30,000 → *Not* |

   Comtec's regular tax liability before credits is $250,000, and its tentative minimum tax is $100,000. Calculate Comtec's general business credit limitation and its final tax liability.

7. Moriconi Corporation has taxable income of $500,000. Included in its taxable income is $60,000 of dividend income from other domestic corporations. It owns less than a

5 percent interest in these corporations. Its MACRS depreciation exceeds ADS depreciation by $120,000; other tax preferences total $29,000. During the year, Moriconi realized a $230,000 gain on the sale of investment land. Under the installment method of accounting, only $45,000 of the gain was included in current taxable income. Based on these facts, compute Moriconi's AMT.

8. During the current year, Driller Corporation deducted $900,000 of IDC and $200,000 of percentage depletion. Income earned by the related wells totaled $1,000,000. Driller's tax basis in the property before percentage depletion was $120,000. Calculate Driller's AMT preferences for IDC and percentage depletion.

9. Forkfull Inc. deducted $1,500,000 of mining exploration costs during 2003 and an additional $1,000,000 of such costs during 2004. Calculate Forkfull's AMT adjustment amounts for 2003 and 2004 related to these expenditures.

10. During 2004, Genesis Inc. sold the following assets.

| | Amount Realized | Original Cost | Regular Tax Accumulated Depreciation | AMT Accumulated Depreciation |
|---|---|---|---|---|
| Asset 1 | $10,000 | $15,000 | $12,000 | $10,000 |
| Asset 2 | 200,000 | 220,000 | 50,000 | 35,000 |
| Asset 3 | 45,000 | 60,000 | 20,000 | 12,000 |

Compute the gain or loss recognized on each disposition for regular tax purposes and AMT purposes, and compute the required AMT adjustment for 2004.

11. Kudos Inc. constructs customized equipment under long-term contracts. During 2003, it entered into two contracts to be completed in 2004. Information on each contract is as follows.

| | Expected Profit | Percent Completed during 2003 |
|---|---|---|
| Contract 1 | $500,000 | 40% |
| Contract 2 | 900,000 | 50 |

If Kudos uses the completed-contract method for regular tax purposes, calculate the amount of profit it recognized on each contract during 2003 and 2004 and the required AMT adjustments for each year.

12. During 2002, Elm Corporation sold property held for investment on an installment basis. Elm realized a gain on the sale of $400,000. The proceeds of the sale will be collected in equal annual installments in 2002, 2003, 2004, and 2005. Calculate the requirement AMT adjustments for each of these four years.

13. Odegard Inc. has calculated AMTI totaling $175,000. Determine its allowable AMT exemption amount.

14. Coco Inc. has regular taxable income of $100,000 for 2004. It deducted MACRS depreciation totaling $200,000. Under the ADS system, depreciation on these assets would be $140,000. Coco also earned $100,000 of tax-exempt interest income during 2004. The interest income is from a $1.25 million public activity municipal bond yield-

ing 8 percent. During 2004, Coco received $75,000 proceeds from a key-man life insurance policy on the death of one of its executives.

*a.* Compute Coco's regular tax liability.
*b.* Compute Coco's AMT liability.
*c.* What would Coco's tax liability be if it did not have the interest income?
*d.* Compute Coco's after-tax rate of return on the bond, assuming that the bond price is constant.

15. Assume the following tentative minimum tax and regular tax amounts calculated for Krolick Corporation.

|  | Year 1 | Year 2 | Year 3 | Year 4 |
|---|---|---|---|---|
| Tentative minimum tax | $150,000 | $130,000 | $110,000 | $150,000 |
| Regular tax | 110,000 | 150,000 | 150,000 | 130,000 |

*[handwritten]* AMT  40,000  (20,000)  (40,000)  (20,000)

Complete the following table by calculating any minimum tax credit generated, any such credit usable, and the final tax liability for Krolick Corporation for each year.

*[handwritten margin notes: Tentative min tax – regular tax. any yr which TMT < regular tax]*

|  | Year 1 | Year 2 | Year 3 | Year 4 |
|---|---|---|---|---|
| Minimum tax credit generated | 40,000 | 0 | 0 | 20,000 |
| Minimum tax credit used | 0 | 20,000 | 20,000 | 0 |
| Total tax liability | 150,000 | 130,000 | 130,000 | 150,000 |
| Minimum tax credit carryforward | 40,000 | 20,000 | 0 | 20,000 |

16. Botosan Corporation had the following items of income and expense for regular tax, AMT, and ACE purposes in the current year.

|  | Regular Tax | AMT | Adjusted Current Earnings |
|---|---|---|---|
| Sales revenue | $ 2,300,000 | $ 2,300,000 | $ 2,300,000 |
| Cost of goods sold | (1,500,000) | (1,500,000) | (1,500,000) |
| Operating expenses | (400,000) | (400,000) | (400,000) |
| Depreciation | (150,000) | (100,000) | (100,000) |
| Gain on installment sale | 100,000 | 500,000 | 500,000 |
| Key-man life insurance proceeds | –0– | –0– | 300,000 |

*a.* Compute Botosan's regular taxable income and tax liability.
*b.* Compute Botosan's tentative alternative minimum tax liability and determine its final U.S. tax liability and any minimum tax credit carryforward.
*c.* Botosan is considering investing in public activity municipal bonds with a stated yield of 8 percent annual interest income. In comparing this investment to other alternatives, is 8 percent the appropriate after-tax rate of return to use in this comparison? What factors must be considered to determine the expected future after-tax return from this investment?

17. For 2004, Kappa Inc. had regular taxable income of $40,000. ACRS depreciation (deducted in calculating taxable income) totaled $5,000, and ADS depreciation totaled $3,000. Kappa's regular taxable income included $5,000 of gain on a sale of equipment; AMT gain on the sale was $15,000. Kappa earned $30,000 of municipal bond interest from private activity bonds. It also had a minimum tax credit carryforward of $3,000 from 2003. On the basis of these facts, compute Kappa's regular and AMT tax liabilities for 2004, any minimum tax credit generated or used, and the minimum tax credit carryforward to 2005.

18. During 2004, Lorenzo Corporation incurred $1 million dollars of qualified research and experimentation costs.
    *a.* Calculate Lorenzo's allowable research credit and research deduction for 2004 under each of the three alternatives for combining these incentives.
    *b.* If Lorenzo's 2004 marginal tax rate is 35 percent, which of the alternatives in part (*a*) produces the largest current tax savings? Provide calculations to support your answer.

19. Falcon Inc. incurred $85,000 of incremental research expenditures during 2004. If Falcon's expected taxable income before any research deduction is $500,000, which alternative combination of research deduction and credit would produce the greatest tax savings for Falcon? Would your answer change if Falcon's expected taxable income before the research deduction is $100,000?

20. During 2004, Ordwell Corporation invested $50,000 in qualified equity of a community development enterprise. Calculate the amount of its allowable new markets credits for 2004 through 2010.

## Issue Recognition Problems

Identify the tax issue or issues suggested by the following situations and state each issue in the form of a question.

1. Urban Environments Inc. is evaluating the possible purchase and major renovation of a large apartment complex located near the center of a large city.

2. Lambert Corporation makes electronic toys. Its new product development group is experimenting with a solar-powered scooter designed for children under the age of 12.

3. Given recent instability in the stock market, Schwarzrock Inc. has invested most of its excess cash in tax-exempt municipal bonds.

4. In 2003, DrugCo Inc.'s profits substantially declined. For 2004, it has cut its research budget but plans to increase research activity in the future when it expects profits to rebound.

5. NewPharm Corporation is incurring significant research expenses. For 2004, it projects that it will have a net operating loss but it expects to be profitable within the next 5 to 10 years.

6. Growth Co. has opened a new business in a designated empowerment zone. It expects to spend $100,000 on new equipment for the business and hire 100 new employees in 2004.

7. Mr. Lundstrom is considering investing in a limited partnership that builds and manages low-income housing. He has substantial salary income and wants to reduce his tax liability using the low-income housing credits allocated to him from the partnership.

8. Greedy Inc. has aggressively sought tax-favored investments. For 2004, it expects to qualify for seven different tax credits and hopes to reduce its tax liability to near zero.

9. Natural Gas Inc. is an independent producer qualifying for percentage depletion. Its properties are mature and its depletion deductions in prior years have reduced the tax

basis of these properties to zero. Natural Gas continues to deduct substantial percentage depletion.

10. Hall Corporation wishes to contribute to economic development in a number of low-income and distressed regions in its state of operations. Currently, it is considering investing in stock of several businesses involved in community development activities.

## Research Problems

1. As a result of terminating an unprofitable line of business, Kohala Inc. incurred a net operating loss of $(400,000) for its 2004 taxable year. During 2002 and 2003, its taxable income was relatively low and it paid little tax liability. Kohala is considering an election to forgo the carryback period with respect to its 2004 net operating loss, thus carrying the entire loss forward into future taxable periods in which it hopes to generate substantial taxable income in its streamlined operating form. If Kohala relinquishes the carryback period for its regular tax net operating loss, must it also relinquish carryback for alternative minimum tax purposes? Is a separate election required to relinquish carryback of its AMT NOL?

2. Mango Corporation is a technology company involved in the development of new computer technology. It is a publicly traded corporation whose stock is traded on the Nasdaq. Several years ago, Mango instituted a nonqualified stock option plan for mid- and upper-level management personnel. Under the terms of the plan, qualifying employees are granted options to acquire Mango stock. The option exercise price is set equal to 130 percent of market price on the date any options are granted. As a result, the options have no readily ascertainable value on the date of grant and thus result in no compensation income to the employees when granted. During 2001, 2002, and 2003, the following options were granted.

| Year | Number of Options Granted | Option Life | Exercise Price |
|------|--------------------------|-------------|----------------|
| 2001 | 200,000 | 5 years | $12 |
| 2002 | 250,000 | 5 | 15 |
| 2003 | 400,000 | 5 | 15.50 |

During 2004, employees exercised 100,000 of the 2000 options. At the time of exercise, the company's stock was trading for $17 per share. Under the rules discussed in Chapter 4, these employees recognized ordinary compensation income of $5 per share ($17 FMV − $12 exercise price) for total compensation income of $500,000. Mango reported such income to these employees on their 2004 Form W-2 wage statements. The company deducted $500,000 of compensation expense in computing its 2004 taxable income. Mango is also involved in research activities qualifying for the incremental research activities credit. Can it include any of the $500,000 of compensation expense attributable to employee exercise of stock options in computing its qualified research expenses for 2004?

## Tax Planning Cases

1. Norald Corporation, owner of several small hotels, is planning to purchase three medium-sized commercial vans to transport guests between its hotels and the airport. Norald projects that providing van transportation will increase annual revenue (net of operating costs) by $150,000. It is considering two alternatives: (1) purchase of conventional vans at a cost of $25,000 each or (2) purchase of electric vans at a cost of $30,000 each. The vans are expected to last six years and have a salvage value at the

end of that time of $3,000 each (regardless of fuel type). Note that such assets are five-year property under MACRS with annual depreciation rates equal to 20 percent, 32 percent, 19.2 percent, 11.52 percent, 11.52 percent, and 5.76 percent for years 1 through 6, respectively. Norald expects its marginal tax rate to be 34 percent for the duration of this investment and uses a 7 percent discount rate to calculate present value.

a. Determine the NPV of Norald's after-tax return on each investment alternative over the six-year life of the vans, ignoring the special tax incentives available for purchase of the electric vans.

b. Recalculate the NPV of Norald's after-tax return on investment, taking into account the special tax incentives applicable to purchase of the electric vans.

c. Given the available tax incentives, which alternative do you recommend?

d. What nontax factors should Norald consider in making this decision?

2. Leonidas Corporation projects the following regular tax, AMT, and current earnings figures for 2004:

| | Regular Tax | AMT | Adjusted Current Earnings |
|---|---|---|---|
| Sales revenue | $2,800,000 | $2,800,000 | $2,800,000 |
| Cost of goods sold | (2,200,000) | (2,200,000) | (2,200,000) |
| Operating expenses | (300,000) | (300,000) | (300,000) |
| Depreciation | (250,000) | (200,000) | (200,000) |

Leonidas is considering three investments: a $1 million corporate bond yielding 11 percent, a newly issued $1 million private activity municipal bond yielding 9 percent, and a $1 million public activity municipal bond yielding 8 percent. Rank these three investments in terms of their after-tax return on investment. Provide supporting calculations.

# Chapter Seven

# Income and Loss Allocations by Passthrough Entities

## Learning Objectives

*After reading this chapter, you will be able to:*

1. Apply the capital account maintenance rules to determine a partner's capital interest.

2. Explain the substantial economic effect requirement for partnership tax allocations.

3. Allocate a built-in gain or loss under the traditional Section 704(c) method.

4. Compute a shareholder's pro rata share of S corporation items.

5. Explain the purpose of the built-in gains tax and excess net passive income tax on S corporations.

6. Make the annual basis adjustments to a partnership interest and S corporation stock.

7. Apply the at-risk and passive activity loss limitations.

Passthrough entities (partnerships, LLCs, and S corporations) do not pay federal income tax at the entity level. Even so, these entities must keep the accounting records necessary to measure their items of income, gain, deduction, and loss and to characterize the items for tax purposes. Passthrough entities must have their own taxable year and method of accounting and must make any elections concerning the computation of taxable income.[1] They must file an annual return (Form 1065 for partnerships and LLCs and Form 1120S for S corporations) with the IRS. These returns report the ordinary income or loss from the

---

[1] Sections 703(b) and 1363(c). The major exception to the rule that partnerships and S corporations make their own tax elections is the Section 901 election to credit (rather than deduct) foreign income tax. This election is made separately by each partner or shareholder.

**EXHIBIT 7.1**
Information Flow on Form 1065 or Form 1120S

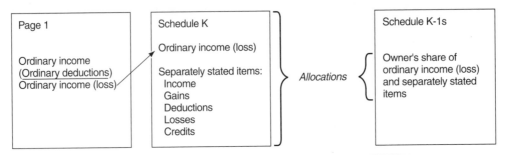

entity's business activities and all **separately stated items** of income, gain, deduction, or loss.[2] A separately stated item is any item that the owners must account for independently to compute their correct tax.

| *Separately Stated Item* | Ramsey Inc., an S corporation, purchased business equipment in 2004 and elected to expense $102,000 of the cost (the maximum allowed). According to Section 179(d)(8), the maximum applies to both the entity and each owner. Consequently, Ramsey cannot deduct its $102,000 expense in the computation of ordinary business income or loss but must report it as a separately stated item.<br><br>Mrs. Ramsey, a 65 percent shareholder, was allocated $66,300 of the corporation's Section 179 expense. She was also allocated an $80,000 Section 179 expense from Munro LLC. Because of the owner-level limitation, Mrs. Ramsey can deduct only $102,000 of the $146,300 total allocation as a business expense on her Form 1040. |
|---|---|

Page 1 of Form 1065 and Form 1120S provides the details of the computation of ordinary business income or loss. Schedule K (page 3) lists this ordinary income or loss and all separately stated items that were not included in the page 1 computation. The entity must allocate each Schedule K item among the owners and report each owner's share on a Schedule K-1. The Schedule K-1s provide the information the owners need to prepare their tax returns and pay tax on the entity's income. The information flow through a passthrough entity's tax return is illustrated in Exhibit 7.1.

Chapter 7 focuses on the tax rules governing the allocation of income and loss from passthrough entities to their owners. The chapter begins with the Subchapter K rules for partnership allocations and then discusses the Subchapter S rules for S corporation allocations. The chapter addresses the situations in which S corporations must pay a special entity-level tax, and it ends with a discussion of the tax consequences of income and loss allocations to partners and shareholders.

# PARTNERSHIP CAPITAL ACCOUNTS

The balance sheet of every business entity has three main components: assets, liabilities, and owners' equity. In a corporation, owners' equity consists of paid-in capital (direct investments by shareholders in exchange for stock) and retained earnings (cumulative after-tax

[2] Sections 703(a) and 1363(b).

income reduced by dividend distributions). The shareholders have a claim on retained earnings through their ownership of the corporation's outstanding stock. However, no shareholder has the right to a segregated amount of retained earnings. In a partnership (or LLC), owners' equity consists of the partners' (or members') capital accounts. A **capital account** is the segregated record of each partner's equity. It includes both the value of the partner's initial investment and the partner's share of cumulative undistributed income. The dollar balance in the capital account represents the partner's *capital interest* in the partnership.

The income or loss generated by partnership activities is allocated among the partners according to the terms of their partnership agreement. This agreement is a legal contract that the partners can renegotiate as business circumstances dictate.

*Partnership Agreement*

Ms. Tower and Ms. Stroh each contributed $50,000 cash to form Towstro Partnership. Because Ms. Tower has more business experience than Ms. Stroh, the original partnership agreement provided that income or loss would be allocated 65 percent to Ms. Tower and 35 percent to Ms. Stroh. After two years of operations, Ms. Stroh considered leaving the partnership. To induce her to stay, Ms. Tower consented to amend their agreement to provide that future income and loss would be allocated equally between them.

## Capital Account Maintenance Rules

**Objective 1**
Apply the capital account maintenance rules to determine a partner's capital interest.

Reg. 1.704-1(b)(2)(iv) provides a detailed set of accounting rules by which partnerships must "determine and maintain" the partners' capital accounts throughout the life of the partnership. The capital accounts computed under these **capital account maintenance rules** are referred to throughout the Subchapter K regulations as *book capital accounts*, and the credits and charges to the accounts are referred to as *book items*. This terminology is confusing to accounting students who think of book accounts as those on financial statements prepared in accordance with GAAP. In the Subchapter K lexicon, book accounts are prepared in accordance with the capital account maintenance rules.

Under the basic maintenance rules, each capital account is credited with (increased by) the partner's share of income and gain items and charged with (decreased by) the partner's share of expense and loss items. If the partnership distributes cash, each capital account is charged with the partner's share of the distribution.

*Capital Account Maintenance*

Towstro Partnership generated a $12,000 operating loss in its first year, $27,400 income in its second year, and $59,300 income in its third year. Towstro made no cash distributions during its first two years. In its third year, it distributed $10,000 cash each to Ms. Tower and Ms. Stroh. Each partner's capital account at the end of the third year is computed as follows.

|  | Ms. Tower | Ms. Stroh |
|---|---|---|
| Initial cash contribution | $50,000 | $50,000 |
| Year 1 loss (65% and 35%) | (7,800) | (4,200) |
| Year 2 income (65% and 35%) | 17,810 | 9,590 |
| Year 3 income (50% and 50%) | 29,650 | 29,650 |
| Cash distribution | (10,000) | (10,000) |
| Capital account balance | $79,660 | $75,040 |

Towstro's balance sheet at the end of its third year shows the following:

| | |
|---|---|
| Assets | $172,700 |
| Liabilities | $ 18,000 |
| Capital: Ms. Tower | 79,660 |
| Ms. Stroh | 75,040 |
| | $172,700 |

As the example demonstrates, capital accounts reflect the partners' respective claims on the net book value of partnership assets and their economic interests in the business entity. Partnerships include a reconciliation of the annual change in a partner's capital account on Schedule K-1, line J.

# PARTNERSHIP TAX ALLOCATIONS

After a partnership closes its books and allocates its annual income or loss to the partners' capital accounts, it must prepare a Form 1065, which includes a Schedule K-1 for each partner. The Schedule K-1s report each partner's **distributive share** of ordinary business income or loss and all separately stated items of income, gain, deduction, loss, or credit. Section 704(a) provides that "a partner's distributive share of income, gain, loss, deduction, or credit shall, except as otherwise provided in this chapter, be determined by the partnership agreement." This general rule gives partners the flexibility to decide how partnership items are allocated for tax purposes. This flexibility is restrained by Section 704(b), which warns that the IRS will disregard any tax allocation that lacks substantial economic effect. In this case, the IRS will determine the partners' distributive shares in accordance with the economic arrangement suggested by the facts and circumstances.

## Substantial Economic Effect

**Objective 2**
Explain the substantial economic effect requirement for partnership tax allocations.

The essence of the **substantial economic effect** requirement is that tax allocations reported on the partners' Schedule K-1s must be consistent with book allocations recorded in their capital accounts. According to Treasury regulations, this consistency guarantees that "in the event that there is an economic benefit or economic burden that corresponds to an allocation, the partner to whom the allocation is made must receive such economic benefit or bear such economic burden."[3]

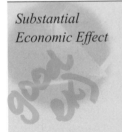

*Substantial Economic Effect*

Refer to the Towstro Partnership with its two partners, Ms. Tower and Ms. Stroh. In its third year, Towstro generated $59,300 income that was allocated equally between the partners' capital accounts. Suppose that the partners' individual tax situations were such that Ms. Tower was in the 35 percent tax bracket, and Ms. Stroh was in the 15 percent tax bracket. Could the partners take advantage of the difference in their marginal rates by agreeing that Ms. Tower's distributive share of income *reported on her Schedule K-1* would be zero, while Ms. Stroh's distributive share of income *reported on her Schedule K-1* would be $59,300? The partners could split the resulting income tax savings between them, and only the federal government would be worse off. This tax strategy does not work, however, because a zero/100

---

[3] Reg. 1.704-1(b)(2)(ii). A tax allocation has substantial economic effect only if the partnership agreement provides that: (1) the capital account maintenance rules will be applied; (2) liquidating distributions will be based on positive capital account balances; and (3) partners either have a deficit restoration obligation upon liquidation or cannot be allocated deductions/losses that result in a negative capital account balance.

percent tax allocation lacks substantial economic effect. For book purposes, Ms. Tower and Ms. Stroh's capital accounts were each credited with $29,650, an economic benefit that *must* correspond to a $29,650 taxable income allocation to each partner.

## Loss Allocations

Under the capital account maintenance rules, each account must be charged with the partner's allocation of loss. If a partnership generates enough losses, a partner's capital account could be negative. In the case of a general partner, a negative (deficit) capital account often represents a financial obligation to the partnership's creditors.

|                       |                   |
|-----------------------|-------------------|
| *Loss Allocations— General Partnership* | Micron Inc., Mr. Borum, and Mrs. Land all contributed $25,000 to form MBL General Partnership. The MBL agreement provides that each general partner is allocated an equal share of income or loss. After three years, MBL has the following balance sheet. |

| | |
|---|---:|
| Assets | $105,000 |
| Unsecured liabilities | $150,000 |
| Capital: Micron Inc. | (15,000) |
| Mr. Borum | (15,000) |
| Mrs. Land | (15,000) |
| | $105,000 |

The deficits in the capital accounts resulted from allocations of MBL's operating losses. At this point, each partner has lost a $25,000 initial investment, and each is personally liable for MBL's liabilities, which exceed its assets by $45,000. Thus, if MBL immediately liquidated, each partner is obligated to contribute an additional $15,000 to satisfy MBL's creditors. Because of this **deficit restoration obligation,** the three general partners bear the economic burden of all losses allocated to their capital accounts, and the corresponding tax allocation of the losses has substantial economic effect.

In a limited partnership, the limited partners are not personally liable for partnership liabilities. They can certainly lose their initial investment, but they have no obligation to make any additional contributions to satisfy partnership creditors. In other words, limited partners have no deficit restoration obligation. Therefore, partnerships generally cannot allocate losses to limited partners that result in a negative capital account because the limited partners do not bear the economic burden of such losses.

|                       |                   |
|-----------------------|-------------------|
| *Loss Allocations— Limited Partnership* | Assume that MBL is a limited partnership in which Micron Inc. is the general partner and Mr. Borum and Mrs. Land are limited partners. The MBL agreement provides that each partner is allocated an equal share of income or loss, but loss allocations to the two limited partners cannot cause or increase a deficit balance in their capital accounts. After three years, MBL has the following balance sheet. |

| | |
|---|---:|
| Assets | $105,000 |
| Unsecured liabilities | $150,000 |
| Capital: Micron Inc. | (45,000) |
| Mr. Borum | –0– |
| Mrs. Land | –0– |
| | $105,000 |

MBL's operating losses were allocated equally *until* each capital account was reduced to zero. All additional losses were allocated to Micron because it has a deficit restoration obligation and therefore bears the economic burden of these additional losses. If the tax allocation of MBL's losses is consistent with the book allocation, the tax allocation has substantial economic effect.

In an LLC, no member is personally liable for LLC liabilities, so no member bears the economic burden of losses that result in a negative capital account. Consequently, the tax allocation of these losses lacks substantial economic effect. In this case, Treasury regulations require that the tax allocation be consistent with the members' economic arrangement suggested by the facts and circumstances.

*Loss Allocations— LLCs*

Assume that MBL is an LLC in which Micron Inc., Mr. Borum, and Mrs. Land have equal interests in capital and profits. After three years, MBL has the following balance sheet.

| | |
|---|---|
| Assets | $105,000 |
| Unsecured liabilities | $150,000 |
| Capital: Micron Inc. | (15,000) |
| Mr. Borum | (15,000) |
| Mrs. Land | (15,000) |
| | $105,000 |

The deficit balances in the capital accounts resulted from allocations of MBL's operating losses. The loss allocations that reduced each capital account to zero have an economic effect because all members lost their $25,000 initial investment. If the LLC immediately liquidated, however, *no member* has a deficit restoration obligation, and the creditors would receive only $105,000 in satisfaction of the $150,000 liabilities. Accordingly, the creditors bear the economic burden of the $45,000 loss that resulted in the deficit capital accounts. The tax allocation of that $45,000 loss to the members lacks substantial economic effect. Nevertheless, the MBL operating agreement clearly stipulates that Micron Inc., Mr. Borum, and Mrs. Land have equal economic interests. Because the tax allocation of the $45,000 loss is consistent with this economic arrangement, the tax allocation is permissible.

### Loss Allocation versus Deduction

In the preceding example, the tax allocation of a $45,000 business loss to LLC members who do not bear the economic burden of the loss seems too good to be true. However, the loss reported on each member's Schedule K-1 is not automatically deductible in the computation of the member's taxable income. In fact, the tax allocation is just the first step toward a deduction. As we discuss in the final section of this chapter, a series of statutory limitations can reduce or even eliminate an owner's deduction for an entity's business loss.

## Allocations with Respect to Contributed Property

According to the capital account maintenance rules, property contributed by a partner must be recorded on the partnership's books at fair market value (FMV).[4] In contrast, the partnership's inside tax basis in the property is a carryover basis from the partner.[5] The difference

[4] Reg. 1.704-1(b)(2)(iv)(d)(1).
[5] Section 723.

between contributed FMV and contributed basis is called the property's **built-in gain or loss.** According to the aggregate theory of partnerships, the contributing partner remains responsible for the built-in gain or loss, even though the partnership owns the property. Section 704(c) implements this theory by requiring partnerships to allocate income, gain, loss, and deduction with respect to contributed property to take account of the difference between the basis of the property and its FMV at date of contribution.

| | *Section 704(c) Allocation* | | | |

*Section 704(c) Allocation*

Two years ago, Rawling Inc. contributed undeveloped land to RTP Limited Partnership in exchange for a 20 percent interest. At the date of contribution, the land was worth $800,000, so RTP recorded an $800,000 book basis and credited Rawling's capital account with $800,000. Rawling's basis in the land was only $500,000, which carried over as RTP's inside tax basis. The $300,000 excess of contributed FMV over basis was a built-in gain.

This year, RTP sold the land for $1 million, resulting in a $200,000 book gain and a $500,000 tax gain. It must allocate $40,000 book gain (20 percent × $200,000) to Rawling's capital account and $160,000 book gain to the capital accounts of the other (noncontributing) partners. For tax purposes, it must allocate $40,000 *plus* the entire $300,000 built-in gain to Rawling and $160,000 gain to the noncontributing partners. These book/tax allocations are presented in the following table.

| | Rawling (20%) | | Other Partners (80%) | |
|---|---|---|---|---|
| | Book | Tax | Book | Tax |
| Gain on sale | $40,000 | $340,000 | $160,000 | $160,000 |

Treasury regulations prescribe the different methods by which partnerships can make their Section 704(c) allocations.[6] We will discuss just one of these methods (the traditional method) in this chapter. A second method (the remedial method) is discussed in Appendix 7–A.

**Objective 3**
Allocate a built-in gain or loss under the traditional Section 704(c) method.

The Rawling/RTP example reflects the **traditional Section 704(c) method** under which the entire difference between a book allocation and a tax allocation caused by a built-in gain or loss must be allocated to the contributing partner. The tax allocations to the noncontributing partners should equal their book allocations. However, the traditional method includes a **ceiling rule:** The tax allocation of income, gain, deduction, or loss to any partner cannot exceed the *actual* taxable income, gain, deduction, or loss. The consequence of the ceiling rule is that the book/tax allocations to the noncontributing partners are unequal.

*Traditional Method—Ceiling Rule Application*

Assume that RTP sold the land contributed by Rawling for $750,000 instead of $1 million. It has a $50,000 book *loss* on the sale ($750,000 − $800,000 book basis) but a $250,000 tax *gain* ($750,000 − $500,000 tax basis). For book purposes, RTP allocates a $10,000 loss to Rawling's capital account and a $40,000 loss to the other partners' capital accounts. The difference between the book and tax allocations is $300,000. This difference (the built-in gain) should be allocated to Rawling so that its tax allocation is a $290,000 gain ($10,000 book loss *plus* $300,000 built-in gain). Because of the ceiling rule, the allocation to Rawling is limited to the actual $250,000 tax gain. As a result, the other partners' $40,000 book loss allocation is not matched by a $40,000 tax loss allocation.

[6] Reg. 1.704-3.

*[handwritten: less of actual or 290,000 but in the book]*

| | Rawling (20%) | | Other Partners (80%) | |
|---|---|---|---|---|
| | *Book* | *Tax* | *Book* | *Tax* |
| Loss/gain on sale | $(10,000) | $250,000 | $(40,000) | –0– |

### Depreciation Allocations

A partnership may be allowed to deduct depreciation (or amortization) with respect to contributed property. It computes tax depreciation by "stepping into the shoes" of the contributing partner.[7] In other words, the partnership depreciates the carryover basis of the property according to the *partner's* remaining depreciation schedule. If the partnership elects the traditional Section 704(c) allocation method, it must compute book depreciation according to the same schedule, but based on the FMV of the property instead of carryover basis. (Note that this book depreciation has nothing to do with GAAP depreciation for financial statement purposes.) Book depreciation is allocated to the partners' capital accounts. Tax depreciation is allocated to the partners' Schedule K-1s with the entire difference between book and tax depreciation allocated to the contributing partner.

*Depreciation Allocation— Traditional Method*

On January 1, 2002, Ms. Stovall contributed equipment ($25,000 FMV and $20,000 adjusted basis) to Leeway LLC, which uses the calendar year for tax purposes. Ms. Stovall has a 35 percent LLC interest. According to her MACRS depreciation schedule, the equipment is five-year recovery property with three years left in its recovery period.[8] The LLC will depreciate the property according to Ms. Stovall's schedule as follows.

*[handwritten: capital gain allocated to partners]*

| | Book | Tax |
|---|---|---|
| Depreciable basis | $25,000 | $20,000 |
| Depreciation 2002 | (10,000) | (8,000) |
| Depreciation 2003 | (10,000) | (8,000) |
| Depreciation 2004 | (5,000) | (4,000) |
| Adjusted basis | –0– | –0– |

*[handwritten left margin: Book allocated deprec. based on FMV — goes to partners capital acts. Tax deprec. allocated to other members based on book turnover methods w/ difference going to contrib. partner]*

Each year, 35 percent of book depreciation is allocated to Ms. Stovall's capital account, and 65 percent is allocated to the other members' capital accounts. Tax depreciation is allocated to the other members in an amount equal to their book depreciation. Only the remaining tax depreciation is allocated to Ms. Stovall. These book/tax depreciation allocations are presented in the following table.

| | Ms. Stovall (35%) | | Other Members (65%) | |
|---|---|---|---|---|
| | *Book* | *Tax* | *Book* | *Tax* |
| Depreciation 2002 | $(3,500) | $(1,500) | $ (6,500) | $ (6,500) |
| Depreciation 2003 | (3,500) | (1,500) | (6,500) | (6,500) |
| Depreciation 2004 | (1,750) | (750) | (3,250) | (3,250) |
| | $(8,750) | $(3,750) | $(16,250) | $(16,250) |

---

[7] Section 168(i)(7).

[8] Because of the half-year or midquarter conventions, the recovery period for five-year recovery property spans six taxable years.

Over the remaining life of the equipment, the difference between Ms. Stovall's book and tax depreciation is $5,000, which was her built-in gain on the date of contribution. At the end of the recovery period, the equipment's book basis and tax basis are both zero, and the built-in gain has been eliminated.

If a built-in gain or loss on contributed property is large enough, the ceiling rule can distort the tax allocations under the traditional method. Let's change the facts in the preceding example to illustrate this distortion.

*Depreciation Allocation— Ceiling Rule*

Assume that the adjusted basis of Ms. Stovall's equipment was only $13,000, so that Leeway has the following depreciation schedule.

|  | Book | Tax |
|---|---|---|
| Depreciable basis | $25,000 | $13,000 |
| Depreciation 2002 | (10,000) | (5,200) |
| Depreciation 2003 | (10,000) | (5,200) |
| Depreciation 2004 | (5,000) | (2,600) |
| Adjusted basis | –0– | –0– |

Because Ms. Stovall's contributed basis is so much less than contributed FMV, Leeway simply does not have enough tax depreciation to allocate to the other members. The best the LLC can do is to allocate 100 percent of tax depreciation to the other members and none to Ms. Stovall.

|  | Ms. Stovall (35%) | | Other Members (65%) | |
|---|---|---|---|---|
|  | Book | Tax | Book | Tax |
| Depreciation 2002 | $(3,500) | –0– | $ (6,500) | $ (5,200) |
| Depreciation 2003 | (3,500) | –0– | (6,500) | (5,200) |
| Depreciation 2004 | (1,750) | –0– | (3,250) | (2,600) |
|  | $(8,750) | –0– | $(16,250) | $(13,000) |

Over the remaining life of the equipment, the difference between Ms. Stovall's book and tax depreciation is only $8,750, which is $3,250 less than her $12,000 built-in gain. The other members have been allocated only $13,000 tax depreciation, which is $3,250 less than their book depreciation.

If a partnership uses the traditional Section 704(c) method, the noncontributing partners can be shortchanged with respect to their tax allocations because of the ceiling rule. Partnerships can avoid this inequity by using one of the other allocation methods designed by the Treasury to avoid the ceiling rule. Unfortunately, the other allocation methods are more complicated to apply than the traditional method.

### Character of Gain or Loss on Dispositions of Contributed Property

When an entity recognizes a gain or loss on the disposition of property, the tax character of the gain or loss is generally determined by reference to the entity's use of the property. Subchapter K has several exceptions to this characterization rule with respect to contributed property. If property was an inventory item in the hands of the contributing partner, the partnership must recognize ordinary income or loss if it disposes of the property within five years of the date of contribution.[9]

| | | |
|---|---|---|
| **Sale of Contributed Inventory** | Mr. Marc is a dealer in real estate. Three years ago, he contributed a tract of land ($160,000 FMV and $125,000 basis) held in his inventory to Mirror LLC in exchange for a 10 percent interest. Mirror held the land as an investment asset. This year, it sold the land for $200,000. Under the general rule, Mirror's $75,000 tax gain ($200,000 amount realized − $125,000 carryover basis) is characterized as a capital gain because it held the land as a capital asset. But because the land was an inventory item to Mr. Marc and the sale occurred within five years of contribution, the $75,000 gain is ordinary income. This taxable income is allocated between Mr. Marc and the other LLC members as follows. | |

| | Mr. Marc (10%) | Other Members (90%) |
|---|---|---|
| Built-in ordinary income | $35,000 | –0– |
| Additional ordinary income | 4,000 | $36,000 |
| | $39,000 | $36,000 |

The ordinary characterization of Mr. Marc's built-in gain seems reasonable and consistent with the aggregate theory of partnerships. In contrast, the ordinary characterization of the additional gain (attributable to the appreciation in the land's value while it was owned by the LLC) seems to be a trap for the other unwary members.

A second exception to the general characterization rule applies to contributed property with a built-in capital loss. If the partnership recognizes a loss on the disposition of the property within five years of the date of contribution, it must characterize the loss as a capital loss to the extent of the built-in loss.[10] Any additional loss is characterized by reference to the partnership's use of the property.

| | | |
|---|---|---|
| **Sale of Capital Loss Property** | Two years ago, Hogart Inc. contributed a tract of investment land ($230,000 FMV and $245,000 basis) to PHJ Partnership in exchange for a 40 percent interest. PHJ used the land in its business. This year, it sold the land for $220,000. Under the general rule, PHJ's $25,000 tax loss ($220,000 amount realized − $245,000 carryover basis) would be characterized as a Section 1231 loss because it held the land as a business asset. But because the land was a capital asset to Hogart and the sale occurred within five years of contribution, $15,000 of the loss is a capital loss. The $25,000 tax loss is allocated between Hogart and the other partners as follows. | |

| | Hogart (40%) | Other Partners (60%) |
|---|---|---|
| Built-in capital loss | $(15,000) | –0– |
| Additional Section 1231 loss | (4,000) | $(6,000) |
| | $(19,000) | $(6,000) |

In this case, the other members are not adversely affected by the capital loss characterization of Hogart's built-in loss recognized on sale of the contributed land.

[9] Section 724(b).
[10] Section 724(c).

## Allocations Based on Varying Partnership Interests

When a partnership makes its tax allocations to determine each partner's share of partnership items, it must consider any changes in the partners' equity interests during the year.[11] If a new partner is admitted during the year, this **varying interest rule** means that the partner can be allocated a share of partnership items attributable only to the period *after* the partner's admission.

| *Varying Interest Rule* | Hightide is a calendar year, accrual basis LLC. On September 1, Exeter Inc. contributed $200,000 to Hightide in exchange for a 20 percent interest. According to an August 31 interim closing of its books, Hightide's taxable income for the first eight months was $114,900. Its taxable income for the entire year was $228,000. The distributive share of Hightide's income reported on Exeter's Schedule K-1 is $22,620 (20 percent × $113,100 income for the four months after Exeter's admission). |
| --- | --- |
| | If Hightide wanted to avoid an interim closing on August 31, it could base its income allocation to Exeter on the number of days during which Exeter was a member.[12] In this case, Exeter's distributive share of LLC income is $15,242 (20 percent × [122 days/365 days] × $228,000 annual income). |

# S CORPORATION ALLOCATIONS

**Objective 4**
Compute a shareholder's pro rata share of S corporation items.

Compared with partnership allocations, S corporation allocations are a simple matter. As passthrough entities, S corporations must allocate their income or loss to their shareholders, but they do not maintain separate capital accounts for each shareholder. The balance sheet reports paid-in capital and retained earnings for the entity as a whole, and the shareholders have a claim on this equity only through their ownership of the S corporation's stock. Therefore, an S corporation makes its allocations with respect to each share of stock rather than with respect to specific shareholders.

According to Section 1366(a), each shareholder must take into account a pro rata share of the S corporation's **nonseparately computed income or loss** (ordinary business income or loss) and any separately stated items. Section 1377(a) explains how a shareholder's **pro rata share** of an item is determined. First, an equal portion of the item is assigned to each day of the year and allocated among the shares outstanding on such day. Each shareholder's pro rata share is the sum of the daily allocations to the stock for the shareholder's period of ownership.[13]

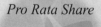

| *Pro Rata Share* | Sloan, a calendar year S corporation, had 750 shares of outstanding stock during 2003. Its 2003 nonseparately computed income was $729,270. The portion assigned to each day of the year is $1,998 ($729,270/365 days), and the daily portion assigned to each share is $2.664 ($1,998/750 shares). Mr. Dobrinin received 110 Sloan shares as a gift from another shareholder on May 11 and owned them for the remainder of the year. His pro rata share of Sloan's 2003 income was $68,571 ($2.664 × 110 shares × 234 days.)[14] |
| --- | --- |

[11] Section 706(d)(1).

[12] Reg. 1.706-1(c)(2)(ii).

[13] Section 1377(b) provides that if an S corporation shareholder terminates his or her interest during the corporation's taxable year, the corporation can elect to perform an interim closing of its books to determine its actual income and loss items through the date of termination. The pro rata shares of these items are computed separately from the pro rata shares of the items incurred during the remainder of the taxable year.

[14] According to Reg. 1.1377-1(a)(2)((ii), a shareholder who disposes of S corporation stock is treated as the shareholder for the day of disposition. Thus, Mr. Dobrinin's first day as a shareholder was May 12.

On September 1, 2004, Mrs. Vaughn contributed $500,000 to Sloan in exchange for 250 newly issued shares of stock, increasing the number of outstanding shares to 1,000. Sloan's 2004 nonseparately computed income was $982,710. The portion assigned to each day of the year is $2,685 ($982,710/366 days). The daily portion assigned to the 750 shares outstanding from January 1 through August 31 is $3.58 ($2,685/750 shares). The daily portion assigned to the 1,000 shares outstanding from September 1 through December 31 is $2.685 ($2,685/1,000 shares). Mr. Dobrinin's pro rata share of Sloan's 2004 income is computed as follows.

| | |
|---|---:|
| $3.58 × 110 shares × 244 days | $ 96,087 |
| $2.685 × 110 shares × 122 days | 36,033 |
| | $132,120 |

Because the determination of pro rata shares is mechanical, shareholders have no flexibility to make special allocations of any item of income, gain, deduction, loss, or credit. If a shareholder contributes property with a built-in gain or loss to an S corporation, responsibility for the gain or loss shifts to all shareholders. If the S corporation disposes of the property, the character of any recognized gain or loss is determined strictly by reference to its use of the property.

*Corporate Recognition of Built-in Gain*

Two years ago, Ms. Rodrigo contributed undeveloped land to RTP, an S corporation, in exchange for 200 shares of stock. After the contribution, RTP had 1,000 outstanding shares. At date of contribution, the land was worth $800,000, so RTP recorded an $800,000 book basis and credited paid-in capital with $800,000. Ms. Rodrigo's basis in the land was only $500,000, which carried over as RTP's tax basis. This year, RTP sold the land for $1 million, resulting in a $200,000 book gain and a $500,000 tax gain. The tax gain was characterized as a capital gain because RTP held the land as a capital asset. Each shareholder's pro rata share of the tax gain is based on stock ownership. If Ms. Rodrigo owned 20 percent of RTP's outstanding shares for the entire year, her pro rata share of the tax gain is $100,000.

# STING TAXES ON S CORPORATIONS

**Objective 5**
Explain the purpose of the built-in gains tax and excess net passive income tax on S corporations.

Under the U.S. tax system, corporations are taxable entities separate and distinct from their shareholders. Corporations pay tax on their earnings, and when the after-tax earnings are distributed as dividends, the shareholders pay tax again. Shareholders can escape this double-tax regime by making a Subchapter S election for an eligible corporation.[15] Because an S corporation is a passthrough entity, its earnings *generally* escape tax at the entity level and are taxed just one time to the shareholders. This statement is qualified because Subchapter S includes two taxes that can be imposed on S corporations. In the next section, we will consider the built-in gains tax and the excess net passive income tax, which have been nicknamed the "sting taxes" because of their painful effect at the entity level.

---

[15] If a taxable corporation that uses the LIFO method of accounting for inventories is converted to an S corporation, it must recognize its "LIFO recapture amount" (excess of FIFO inventory cost over LIFO inventory cost) as ordinary income on its final Form 1120. The corporate tax on this income can be paid over four years. Section 1363(d).

## Built-in Gains Tax

Congress enacted Subchapter S to accommodate individuals who wanted to do business in the corporate form without paying a corporate-level income tax. However, Congress was concerned that individuals could abuse this privilege by making an S election solely to avoid the corporate tax on gains that were economically accrued while the business was operating as a C corporation. (The term *C corporation* refers to a corporation that is not an S corporation for the taxable year.[16]) Congress enacted Section 1374 to prevent this abuse. This section requires S corporations to pay a 35 percent tax on certain built-in gains. The most important point about this **built-in gains tax** is that it does not apply to corporations that have always been S corporations. The tax is of concern only to S corporations that were once C corporations.

An S corporation is exposed to the built-in gains tax to the extent of its **net unrealized built-in gain,** defined as the excess of the FMV of the corporation's assets over their aggregate adjusted basis on the first day of the corporation's first year as an S corporation. If the corporation recognizes any portion of this gain in its first 10 years as an S corporation, it must pay a 35 percent tax on such **net recognized built-in gain.** The following examples demonstrate the basic computation of net unrealized built-in gain, net recognized built-in gain, and the built-in gains tax.

*Net Unrealized Built-in Gain*

Jackson Trucking was a calendar-year, accrual basis C corporation from 1988 through 1996. Its shareholders made a Subchapter S election effective for the year beginning January 1, 1997. On this date, an independent appraisal of the value of the corporate business resulted in the following balance sheet data.

|  | Adjusted Basis | FMV |
|---|---|---|
| Accounts receivable | $  500,000 | $  500,000 |
| Transportation equipment | 2,350,000 | 3,000,000 |
| Other depreciable equipment | 1,840,000 | 1,500,000 |
| Business realty | 2,100,000 | 3,000,000 |
| Unrecorded goodwill | –0– | 500,000 |
|  | $6,790,000 | $8,500,000 |

Jackson's net unrealized built-in gain was $1,710,000, the excess of FMV of its assets over aggregate adjusted basis. Note that this net gain included built-in gains on Jackson's transportation equipment, realty, and goodwill, and a built-in loss on its other equipment.

*Net Recognized Built-in Gain, 1997*

In 1997, Jackson sold two items of equipment for their January 1 appraised values. The recognized gain on the first sale was $135,000, and the recognized loss on the second sale was $20,000. Consequently, Jackson recognized $115,000 of its net unrealized built-in gain and paid a $40,250 tax (35 percent × $115,000 net recognized built-in gain). By 1998, its net unrealized built-in gain was reduced to $1,595,000 ($1,710,000 original unrealized gain − $115,000 recognized gain in 1997).

[16] Section 1361(a)(2).

| *Net Recognized Built-in Gain, 2000* | Jackson did not sell any assets or incur any built-in gains tax in 1998 or 1999. In 2000, it recognized a $1,100,000 gain on sale of its business realty, which was its only asset disposition. Jackson's financial records showed that the built-in gain on the realty on January 1, 1997, was only $900,000. Therefore, its net recognized built-in gain for 2000 was $900,000, and its built-in gains tax was $315,000 (35 percent × $900,000). By 2001, Jackson's net unrealized built-in gain was reduced to $695,000 ($1,710,000 original unrealized gain − $115,000 recognized gain in 1997 − $900,000 recognized gain in 2000). |
|---|---|

| *Net Recognized Built-in Gain, 2004* | Jackson did not sell any assets or incur any built-in gains tax in 2001, 2002, or 2003. In 2004, it recognized a $1.3 million gain on sale of its entire trucking business (including goodwill). Jackson's net recognized built-in gain was limited to $695,000, its remaining net unrealized built-in gain. Its built-in gains tax for 2004 was $243,250 (35 percent × $695,000). Because Jackson's net unrealized built-in gain was reduced to zero, it has no further exposure to the built-in gains tax. |
|---|---|

In the preceding series of examples, Jackson Trucking eventually paid the Section 1374 tax on the entire net built-in gain that existed on the day it converted from a C corporation to an S corporation. If Jackson had no net built-in gain on the date of conversion, it would have no exposure to this sting tax. Similarly, if Jackson did not dispose of any assets with built-in gain during the 10-year period following the conversion, the sting tax would never apply.

### Effect of Tax on Shareholder Allocations

An S corporation that pays a built-in gains tax treats the tax as a loss item. The loss has the same tax character as the recognized built-in gain that triggered the tax.[17] The loss is allocated among the shareholders on the same pro rata basis as all other corporate items.

| *Tax Allocation to Shareholders* | Refer to Jackson's 1997 taxable year in which it paid a $40,250 built-in gains tax. Its recognized built-in gain from the sale of equipment was characterized as ordinary income. As a result, the built-in gains tax is treated as an item of ordinary loss and allocated as such on the shareholders' Schedule K-1s. |
|---|---|

## Excess Net Passive Income Tax

Individuals who do business through a C corporation can defer the shareholder-level tax by accumulating the corporation's after-tax earnings instead of distributing the earnings as dividends. This tax strategy works as long as the corporation has reasonable business needs for the accumulation. If the corporation reaches a point at which it has no need to accumulate more earnings, the IRS can impose a penalty in the form of the accumulated earnings tax or the personal holding company tax. (These taxes are discussed in more detail in Chapter 8.) A closely held corporation is vulnerable to these penalty taxes when its balance sheet is overloaded with investment assets, such as certificates of deposit, marketable securities, rental real estate, or loans to shareholders.

S corporations are not subject to either the accumulated earnings tax or the personal holding company tax. When a C corporation's balance sheet becomes heavy with investment assets, the shareholders might be tempted to make a Subchapter S election solely to avoid these taxes. Congress enacted Section 1375 to help shareholders resist this temptation. This section requires S corporations to pay a 35 percent tax on any excess net passive income for the year. The **excess net passive income tax** is similar to the built-in gains tax

[17] Section 1366(f)(2).

because it does not apply to corporations that have always been S corporations. Furthermore, the passive income tax applies only to corporations with accumulated earnings and profits at the close of the taxable year.

The passive income tax is imposed on income from investment assets, such as royalties, rents, dividends, interest, annuities, and capital gains from sales of marketable securities. Section 1375 gives S corporations leeway to earn a moderate amount of passive income because the tax is imposed only on *excess* passive income. Basically, an S corporation has excess passive income only to the extent that its passive income exceeds 25 percent of gross receipts for the year.

| *Excess Net Passive Income Tax* | Himmel operated as a calendar-year, accrual basis C corporation from 1984 through 2003. Its shareholders made a Subchapter S election effective for the year beginning January 1, 2004. On the date of conversion, Himmel had $8.9 million accumulated earnings and profits. Himmel's 2004 gross receipts totaled $500,000 ($331,700 gross receipts from business services + $168,300 dividends from its portfolio of marketable securities). Himmel's excess passive income was $43,300 [$168,300 passive income − $125,000 (25 percent × $500,000 gross receipts)], and its passive income tax was $15,155 (35 percent × $43,300 excess passive income). |
|---|---|

### Effect of Tax on Shareholder Allocations

An S corporation that pays a passive income tax reduces each item of passive income by a proportionate amount of tax.[18] The passive income item *net of tax* is allocated to the shareholders.

| *Tax Allocation to Shareholders* | Himmel reduced its $168,300 dividend income by $15,155 passive income tax. Thus, only $153,145 dividend income was allocated to its shareholders in 2004. |
|---|---|

**Tax Talk**
A General Accounting Office report requested by Senator Olympia Snowe confirmed that the IRS is working to correct errors in the program whereby the agency matches Schedule K-1 forms to taxpayers' individual tax returns and identify those who might be underreporting their income. "The success of the K-1 Matching Program depends on the IRS's ability to develop a program that identifies taxpayers who are not meeting their tax obligations while imposing the least inconvenience possible on compliant taxpayers and small business owners," said Snowe.

Shareholders in closely held corporations that own substantial investment assets might be willing to tolerate the Section 1375 tax as the cost of maintaining their S election. This strategy, however, works for just three years. If an S corporation with accumulated earnings and profits has excess passive income for three consecutive taxable years, its S election terminates, effective on the first day of the fourth year.[19] As a result, the corporation reverts to C corporation status and is ineligible to make a new S election for five years.[20] Remember that S corporations with no history as C corporations are immune to both the sting tax and the termination of their election because of excess passive income. Such S corporations can earn unlimited investment income for an unlimited period of time.

## TAX CONSEQUENCES OF ALLOCATIONS TO PARTNERS AND SHAREHOLDERS

At the end of each taxable year, a passthrough entity measures its items of income, gain, deduction, and loss, characterizes the items for tax purposes, and allocates the items to its owners on their Schedule K-1s. The owners are responsible for correctly reporting the Schedule K-1s items on their tax returns. If an owner in a passthrough entity is itself a passthrough entity, the items continue to be allocated until they are finally allocated to an individual or a corporate taxpayer.

[18] Section 1366(f)(3).
[19] Section 1362(d)(3).
[20] Section 1362(g).

| *Allocations to Passthrough Entities* | This year, Chiles LLC allocated $22,000 ordinary business income to Kovac LP, which owns a 15 percent interest in the LLC. Kovac LP included the Chiles allocation in its ordinary business income, $15,000 of which was allocated to WPN, an S corporation. WPN included the Kovac allocation in its ordinary business income, which was allocated among WPN's four individual shareholders. |
|---|---|

Individual taxpayers report their share of a passthrough entity's ordinary business income or loss on Schedule E, Form 1040. Corporate taxpayers report their share as other income or loss on page 1, Form 1120.

| *New Matching Program for Schedule K-1s* | The IRS has initiated a program to match information from business entities that pass through approximately $700 billion in taxable income to individual and corporate taxpayers. The program will allow the IRS to determine whether partners, LLC members, and S corporation shareholders are paying tax on the income reported on their Schedule K-1s. The IRS believes that "there may be a 5 percent to 10 percent dip in reporting of passthrough income, compared to the reporting of wage, interest, and dividend income," and that the new matching program will "level the compliance playing field" for passthrough income.[21] |
|---|---|

## Partner and Shareholder Basis Adjustments

**Objective 6**
Make the annual basis adjustments to a partnership interest and S corporation stock.

In addition to reporting Schedule K-1 items on their tax returns, partners and S corporation shareholders must adjust the tax basis in their equity interests at the end of each taxable year. Specifically, the basis in a partnership interest or S corporation stock must be:

- Increased by any contribution to the entity.
- Increased by any allocation of taxable or nontaxable income and gain.
- Decreased by any distribution from the entity.
- Decreased by any allocation of deduction, nondeductible expense, and loss.

Because of these annual adjustments, the tax basis in a partnership interest or S corporation stock provides a record of the owner's ongoing investment in the entity. If the owner disposes of the interest in a taxable transaction, the basis adjustments prevent the double counting of the entity's accumulated income as part of the owner's gain or loss recognized on the disposition.

| *Basis Adjustments* | Six years ago, Ms. Pogue contributed $20,000 cash in exchange for 200 shares of stock in Shadwell, an S corporation. At the beginning of this year, her adjusted stock basis was $26,800. |
|---|---|

| | |
|---|---|
| Initial basis (cash contribution) | $20,000 |
| Allocations of income and gain | 41,200 |
| Cash distributions | (25,600) |
| Allocations of deduction and loss | (8,800) |
| Adjusted basis | $26,800 |

[21] 244 Daily Tax Report G-3 (December 19, 2000).

The adjusted stock basis reflects the fact that Ms. Pogue has not withdrawn $6,800 corporate income on which she has paid tax. If she sells her stock at this point, she will recover both her original $20,000 investment and her $6,800 accumulated income without further tax cost.

If we change the preceding example by making Shadwell a partnership or an LLC, the computation of Ms. Pogue's adjusted basis in her interest would change in only one respect. Her outside basis would include her share of Shadwell's liabilities. Partnerships must provide information concerning a partner's share of liabilities on Schedule K-1, line F.

## Owner-Level Limitations on Loss Deduction

**Objective 7**
Apply the at-risk and passive activity loss limitations.

Earlier in the chapter, we made the point that a loss allocation on Schedule K-1 does not necessarily result in a deduction for the partner or shareholder. Partners can deduct their allocated losses only to the extent of their year-end outside basis in their partnership interest. Shareholders can deduct their allocated losses only to the extent of their year-end stock basis plus their basis in any debt obligation from the S corporation.[22] In both cases, the year-end basis is determined after the adjustments for income and gain items and distributions.

---

*Basis Limitation on Deductible Loss*

Ms. Pogue's Schedule K-1 from Shadwell for this year reported a $30,400 ordinary business loss, a $1,300 long-term capital gain, and a $2,000 cash distribution. Ms. Pogue holds no debt from Shadwell. Because of the basis limitation, her deduction for the loss is only $26,100.

| | |
|---|---:|
| Adjusted basis at beginning of year | $26,800 |
| Allocation of long-term capital gain | 1,300 |
| Cash distribution | (2,000) |
| Limitation on loss deduction | $26,100 |
| Deductible loss | (26,100) |
| Adjusted basis at end of year | –0– |
| Nondeductible loss ($30,400 − $26,100) | $ 4,300 |

---

When the basis limitation applies, the partner's outside basis or the shareholder's stock basis is decreased to zero. Nondeductible losses are carried forward into future taxable years. The partner or shareholder can deduct a loss carryforward to the extent of future increases in basis.

---

*Future Restoration of Basis*

Assume that next year, Ms. Pogue is allocated $5,000 of Shadwell's ordinary business income, and Shadwell makes no cash distributions. Because the income allocation increases her stock basis from zero to $5,000, she can deduct her entire $4,300 loss carryforward and report only $700 ordinary income. Ms. Pogue's stock basis at the end of the year is $700.

| | |
|---|---:|
| Adjusted basis at beginning of year | –0– |
| Allocation of ordinary income | $5,000 |
| Deduction of loss carryforward | (4,300) |
| Adjusted basis at end of year | $ 700 |

---

[22] Sections 704(d) and 1366(d).

The basis limitations on loss deduction have been integral components of Subchapter K and Subchapter S since those subchapters became part of the tax law. Because of concern that the basis limitations did not prevent the deduction of certain artificial losses from abusive tax shelters, Congress enacted the at-risk limitation in 1976 and the passive activity loss limitation in 1986. These two limitations, which are applied in sequence *after* the basis limitation, can significantly reduce an owner's deduction for allocated losses from a passthrough entity.

### At-Risk Limitation

Section 465(a) provides that individuals and certain closely held corporations engaged in any business or income-producing activity can deduct losses only to the extent of their at-risk amount. Conceptually, the **at-risk amount** equals the dollars the taxpayer would lose if the business failed. In the S corporation context, the at-risk amount usually equals the shareholder's combined basis in stock and debt. Thus, the at-risk limitation on loss deductions is no more binding than the basis limitation. In the partnership context, however, the at-risk amount can be less than the partner's outside basis in the partnership interest. In such cases, the at-risk limitation further reduces the partner's deduction for allocated loss.

The singular difference between a partner's outside basis and his at-risk amount relates to the partner's share of partnership liabilities. Outside basis and at-risk amount include the partner's share of recourse liabilities (for which the partner bears the economic risk of loss) and the partner's share of qualified nonrecourse financing. **Qualified nonrecourse financing** is any nonrecourse liability incurred with respect to the holding of real property, secured by such real property, and borrowed from a commercial lender (a bank or credit union) or from the federal, state, or local government.[23] A partner's share of any other nonrecourse liability is included in outside basis but is *not* included in his at-risk amount.

**At-Risk Limitation** Mr. Aber and Telax Inc. are the two equal members in Abrax LLC. At the beginning of the year, Abrax had the following balance sheet.

| | |
|---|---|
| Assets | $200,000 |
| Unsecured accounts payable | $170,000 |
| Nonrecourse mortgage | 20,000 |
| Capital:  Mr. Aber | 5,000 |
|   Telax Inc. | 5,000 |
| | $200,000 |

Both Mr. Aber and Telax had a $100,000 outside basis in their LLC interests. The outside basis included each member's $95,000 share of Abrax's liabilities. Abrax's accounts payable are nonrecourse because no member bears the economic risk of loss for any LLC liability. Abrax's nonrecourse mortgage, which is secured by real property and held by a state bank, is qualified nonrecourse financing.

Abrax's operating loss for the year was $42,000, which was allocated equally between the two members in accordance with their economic arrangement. As a result, the two members had deficit balances in their capital accounts at year-end.

[23] Section 465(b)(6).

| Assets | $175,000 |
|---|---|
| Unsecured accounts payable | $189,000 |
| Nonrecourse mortgage | 18,000 |
| Capital:  Mr. Aber | (16,000) |
|           Telax Inc. | (16,000) |
| | $175,000 |

*[handwritten annotation: BASIS - 8hareIncome (51000 - 21,000)]*

Both Mr. Aber and Telax received a Schedule K-1 reporting a $21,000 distributive share of ordinary business loss. Each member had sufficient outside basis to deduct the loss, which reduced each member's basis to $87,500.

| Adjusted basis at beginning of year | $100,000 |
|---|---|
| Increase in share of LLC liabilities | 8,500 |
| Allocation of loss | (21,000) |
| Adjusted basis at end of year | $87,500 |

Telax is not a closely held corporation, so the at-risk limitation is inapplicable, and its $21,000 loss is deductible. The at-risk rules do apply to Mr. Aber. Consequently, the deduction for his $21,000 loss is limited to his $14,000 at-risk amount immediately before the deduction.

| Adjusted basis at beginning of year | $100,000 |
|---|---|
| Increase in share of LLC liabilities | 8,500 |
| Liabilities for which Mr. Aber is not at risk | (94,500) |
| At-risk amount | $14,000 |

The difference between Mr. Aber's outside basis and at-risk amount is his $94,500 share of the LLC's unsecured accounts payable. His $9,000 share of the qualified nonrecourse financing is included in his at-risk amount.

| At-risk amount before loss deduction | $14,000 |
|---|---|
| Deductible loss | (14,000) |
| At-risk amount at end of year | –0– |
| Nondeductible loss ($21,000 − $14,000) | $ 7,000 |

When the at-risk limitation applies, the taxpayer's at-risk amount is decreased to zero. Nondeductible losses are carried forward into future taxable years and can be deducted to the extent that the at-risk amount in the business increases.

**Future Increase in At-Risk Amount**

At the beginning of the next year, Mr. Aber's at-risk amount in Abrax LLC is zero, and he has a $7,000 loss carryforward because of the at-risk limitation. Assume that next year, Mr. Aber is allocated $10,000 ordinary business income, Abrax makes no cash distributions, and there is no change in the amount of the LLC's qualified nonrecourse financing. Because the income allocation increases both Mr. Aber's outside basis *and his at-risk amount* to $10,000, he can deduct his entire $7,000 loss carryforward and report only $3,000 ordinary income. Mr. Aber's at-risk amount at the end of the year will be $3,000.

| | |
|---|---|
| At-risk amount at beginning of year | –0– |
| Allocation of income | $10,000 |
| Loss carryforward deduction | (7,000) |
| At-risk amount at end of year | $ 3,000 |

### Passive Activity Loss Limitation

Section 469(a) provides that individuals and certain closely held corporations cannot deduct a passive activity loss. A **passive activity loss** is the excess of aggregate losses over aggregate income from passive activities. If a taxpayer is allocated a loss from a pass-through entity and his interest in the entity is a passive activity, the taxpayer can deduct the loss only to the extent of passive activity income from other sources. Nondeductible losses are carried forward into future taxable years.

An interest in a business partnership or an S corporation is passive if the owner does not materially participate in the business. **Material participation** means that the owner is involved in the business's operation on a regular, continuous, and substantial basis.[24]

| | |
|---|---|
| *Passive Activity Loss Limitation* | This year, both Mr. Aber and Telax were allocated a $21,000 business loss from Abrax LLC. Both members had sufficient basis in their LLC interest to deduct the allocated loss. The at-risk rules limited Mr. Aber's deduction to $14,000. Because Telax is not a closely held corporation, the passive activity loss limitation is inapplicable, and it can deduct its $21,000 business loss on Form 1120. |

If Mr. Aber materially participates in the LLC's business, his LLC interest is not a passive activity. In this case, he can deduct his $14,000 business loss on Schedule E, Form 1040. If Mr. Aber does not materially participate, his LLC interest is a passive activity, and his $14,000 loss is deductible only to the extent that he has income from other passive activities. To complete this example, assume that Mr. Aber does not materially participate in Abrax's business and has only $1,800 income from another passive activity. Thus, he can deduct only $1,800 of his $14,000 loss this year and has a $12,200 carryforward into future years.

Mr. Aber now has *two* loss carryforwards: a $7,000 carryforward because of the at-risk limitation and a $12,200 carryforward because of the passive activity loss limitation. Exhibit 7.2 is an illustrative summary of the sequence of limitations that reduced Mr. Aber's $21,000 allocated loss from the LLC to a $1,800 deductible loss on his Schedule E.

**EXHIBIT 7.2**
**Sequence of Loss Limitations**

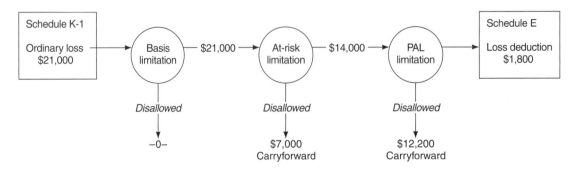

[24] Reg. 1.469-5 provides a complete definition of material participation.

Passive activity loss carryforwards are deductible to the extent of future passive activity income or in the year in which the taxpayer disposes of the passive activity interest in a taxable transaction. The tax consequences of the disposition of partnership interests and S corporation stock are discussed in more detail in Chapter 12.

| *Future Generation of Passive Activity Income* | Assume that next year, Mr. Aber is allocated $10,000 of Abrax's ordinary business income. This allocation increases his at-risk amount and allows him to deduct his $7,000 carryforward under the at-risk limitation. Even so, he still faces the passive activity loss limitation with respect to his combined $19,200 loss carryforwards. Assume that Mr. Aber has $2,500 income from his other passive activity, so that his total passive activity income is $12,500 ($10,000 from Abrax + $2,500 from the other passive activity). Consequently, Mr. Aber can deduct $12,500 of his $19,200 loss carryforwards and has a $6,700 carryforward because of the passive activity loss limitation. |
|---|---|

| | | |
|---|---:|---:|
| Income from Abrax | | $10,000 |
| Income from other passive activity | | 2,500 |
| Total passive activity income | | $12,500 |
| At-risk loss carryforward | $ 7,000 | |
| PAL carryforward | 12,200 | |
| Total carryforward | $19,200 | |
| Deductible loss | | (12,500) |
| | | –0– |
| Loss carryforward under PAL limitation | | $ 6,700 |

## Conclusion

Chapter 7 introduced the tax rules governing the annual allocation of income and loss from a passthrough entity to the entity's owners. These rules are extraordinarily complex for partnerships and LLCs but much less so for S corporations. Exhibit 7.3 provides a chart that summarizes the major allocation issues and compares the answers pertaining to partnerships and LLCs with the answers pertaining to S corporations. Chapter 7 also discussed the sting taxes (built-in gains tax and excess net passive income tax) that plague S corporations that were formerly C corporations. The chapter concluded with a review of the basis, at-risk, and passive activity loss limitations that can prevent owners from deducting losses from their partnerships, LLCs, and S corporations.

**EXHIBIT 7.3 Comparison Chart**

| Tax Issue | Partnership/LLC | S Corporation |
|---|---|---|
| Does a passthough entity keep a segregated record of each owner's equity interest? | Yes, in the form of partner capital accounts. | No. |
| Can a passthrough entity make special allocations of different items of income, gain, deduction, or loss to its owners? | Yes, if the allocation has substantial economic effect. | No, all allocations are based strictly on stock ownership. |
| Does a passthrough entity make special allocations to account for built-in gain or loss on contributed property? | Yes, partnerships must make special allocations with respect to contributed property. | No. |
| Do annual allocations reflect any changes in owners' equity interests during the year? | Yes, according to the varying interest rule. | Yes, allocations are based on daily stock ownership. |

## Key Terms

at-risk amount  *188*
built-in gain or loss  *177*
built-in gains tax  *183*
capital account  *173*
capital account
  maintenance rules  *173*
ceiling rule  *177*
deficit restoration
  obligation  *175*
distributive share  *174*
excess net passive income
  tax  *184*

material
  participation  *190*
net recognized built-in
  gain  *183*
net unrealized built-in
  gain  *183*
nonseparately computed
  income or loss  *181*
passive activity loss  *190*
pro rata share  *181*

qualified nonrecourse
  financing  *188*
remedial method  *199*
separately stated
  items  *172*
substantial economic
  effect  *174*
traditional Section 704(c)
  method  *177*
varying interest rule  *181*

## Questions and Problems for Discussion

1. Discuss the reasons that the following items must be separately stated on a passthrough entity's tax return.
   *a.* Charitable contribution.
   *b.* Dividend income.
   *c.* Net long-term capital gain.
   *d.* Section 1231 loss.
   *e.* Investment interest expense.

2. NNP Partnership spent $12,300 on business meals and entertainment this year. Ms. Nyari owns a 22 percent interest in NNP. What is the effect of the $12,300 expenditure on her capital account, share of ordinary business income, and outside basis in her NNP interest?

3. Three unrelated individuals each contributed $50,000 cash to form Trio Partnership. Must the three individuals be allocated equal shares of Trio's profits and losses?

4. Mr. Moses and Mr. Helm are the two owners in MH Enterprises. MH owns two retail stores, one that Mr. Moses manages and the other that Mr. Helm manages.
   *a.* Could the two owners agree to allocate 100 percent of net profits from each store to the owner who manages it if MH is a partnership?
   *b.* Could the two owners agree to allocate 100 percent of net profits from each store to the owner who manages it if MH is an S corporation?

5. If a partner's outside basis and capital account balance both represent her investment in the partnership, why are the two numbers different?

6. Why do book allocations to partner capital accounts represent a benefit or burden with substantial economic effect?

7. Discuss the nontax reasons that a partnership would prefer to avoid an interim closing of its books when a new partner joins the partnership.

8. Compare and contrast the tax consequences of built-in gains and losses for property contributed to a partnership and property contributed to an S corporation.

9. Section 275(a)(1) disallows any deduction for federal income tax. Discuss how Subchapter S bends this rule with respect to any sting tax paid by an S corporation.

10. Mr. Wychenski owns a 10 percent equity interest in a passthrough business entity. Identify the difference in the amount of his tax basis in the interest if the entity is an LLC or an S corporation.

11. Explain why the at-risk limitation is considered a nonissue for S corporation losses allocated to shareholders.

**Application Problems**

1. On June 1, Mrs. Marlow contributed $15,000 cash to TSL Partnership for a limited interest. Her first Schedule K-1 reported the following items.

| | |
|---|---|
| Ordinary business income | $2,800 |
| Tax-exempt interest income | 400 |
| Section 179 expense | 500 |
| Nondeductible meals and entertainment | 72 |
| Cash distributions | 1,000 |

The Schedule K-1 reported that Mrs. Marlow's share of TSL's liabilities at year-end was $1,100. She owns no interest in any other business activity.

a. How much ordinary income should Mrs. Marlow report on her Schedule E, Form 1040?
b. Compute her capital account at year-end.
c. Compute her outside basis in her TSL interest at year-end.

2. On September 1, Mr. Grimes contributed undeveloped land ($400,000 FMV and $290,000 basis) to Dulescu LLC for an LLC interest. His first Schedule K-1 reported the following items.

| | |
|---|---|
| Ordinary business income | $33,600 |
| Interest income | 3,100 |
| Long-term capital gain | 2,400 |
| Charitable contribution | (775) |
| Investment interest expense | (900) |
| Cash distributions | 6,700 |

The Schedule K-1 reported that Mr. Grimes's share of Dulescu's liabilities at year-end was $35,200.

a. How much ordinary income should Mr. Grimes report on his Schedule E, Form 1040?
b. Compute his capital account at year-end.
c. Compute his outside basis in his Dulescu interest at year-end.

3. Mr. Adam, Ms. Lui, Mr. Oliver, and Mrs. Helmig are the four equal partners in calendar year Aloha Partnership. On January 1, each partner's capital account balance was $50,000. Aloha incurred a $300,000 operating loss for the year.

a. If Aloha is a general partnership, how much loss is allocated to each partner, and what is each partner's ending capital account balance?
b. How would your answers to part (a) change if Aloha is a limited partnership, and Mr. Adam is the sole general partner?
c. How would your answers to part (a) change if Aloha is an LLC?

*[handwritten: bult ingain 138,000]*

4. In 1995, Ms. Janelle contributed investment land ($1 million FMV and $862,000 basis) to Jayco Company for a 40 percent equity interest. This year, Jayco sold the land for $1.25 million.
   a. Compute Jayco's book and tax gain on the land sale. *[handwritten: book 250,000 tax 388,000]*
   b. Allocate the tax gain between Ms. Janelle and the other owners, assuming that Jayco is an LLC. *[handwritten: big Janelle 138,000]*
   c. Allocate the tax gain between Ms. Janelle and the other owners, assuming that Jayco is an S corporation.

5. Refer to the facts in problem 4 but assume that Jayco sold the land for only $900,000.
   a. Compute Jayco's book and tax gain on the land sale.
   b. Allocate the tax gain between Ms. Janelle and the other owners, assuming that Jayco is an LLC that uses the traditional Section 704(c) method. *[handwritten: 38,000]*
   c. Allocate the tax gain between Ms. Janelle and the other owners, assuming that Jayco is an S corporation.

6. Jatczk Inc. and Mr. Dial formed calendar year JD Partnership on January 1. Jactzk contributed $50,000 cash, and Mr. Dial contributed a patent (FMV $50,000 and adjusted basis $40,000) for their equal interests. Mr. Dial had been amortizing the basis of the patent at the rate of $10,000 per year.
   a. Prepare a schedule showing JD's book and tax amortization of the patent for the remaining four years of the amortization period.
   b. Apply the traditional method to allocate the annual tax amortization between Jatczk and Mr. Dial.
   c. How would your answers to part (*a*) and part (*b*) change if Mr. Dial's contributed basis in the patent was only $22,000, which he was amortizing at the rate of $5,500 per year?

7. Refer to the original facts in the preceding problem. JD Partnership used the patent for two years, then sold it on January 1 of the third year for $28,000 cash.
   a. Compute JD's book and tax gain on the sale.
   b. Allocate the tax gain between Jatczk and Mr. Dial.

8. Dylan LLC sold a work of art that it had displayed in its New York office for $145,000. It acquired the artwork as a contribution from Mrs. Ainsworth, who owns a 30 percent interest in the LLC. Mrs. Ainsworth is an art dealer, and the artwork was inventory in her hands. At the date of contribution, the artwork had a $90,000 FMV and a $66,400 basis to Mrs. Ainsworth.
   a. Compute Dylan's tax gain on sale, and characterize it as either capital gain or ordinary income, assuming that Mrs. Ainsworth contributed the artwork 10 years ago.
   b. How would your answer to part (*a*) change if Mrs. Ainsworth contributed the artwork three years ago?
   c. Allocate the tax gain between Mrs. Ainsworth and the other LLC members.

9. WestWind LLP operates an art gallery in Santa Fe. This year, it sold a work of art for $139,000. WestWind acquired the artwork as a contribution from Mr. Chitkara, who owns a 25 percent interest in the LLP. He held the artwork as an investment. At the date of contribution, the artwork had a $160,000 FMV and a $200,000 basis to Mr. Chitkara.
   a. Compute WestWind's tax loss on sale, and characterize it as either capital loss or ordinary loss, assuming that Mr. Chitkara contributed the artwork two years ago.
   b. How would your answer to part (*a*) change if Mr. Chitkara contributed the artwork eight years ago?

c. How would your answer to part (*a*) change if WestWind sold the artwork for $180,000 instead of $139,000?

d. On the basis of your answer in part (*a*), allocate the capital and ordinary loss between Mr. Chitkara and the other partners.

10. At the beginning of the year, Mrs. Gary and Mr. Hudson were the two equal owners of calendar year Longwood Company. On April 1, Mrs. Travis was admitted as a equal owner. Longwood's ordinary income for the year was $338,600. Determine each owner's share of this income under the following assumptions.

a. Longwood is a partnership that did not perform an interim closing of its books on March 31.

b. Longwood is a partnership that closed its books on March 31. Based on the closing, its ordinary income for the first three months was $122,200.

c. Longwood is an S corporation.

11. Trimble was formed in 1995 and operated as a calendar year C corporation from 1995 through 2002. Its shareholders made a Subchapter S election effective for 2003. On January 1, 2003, Trimble's business consisted of the following assets.

|  | Tax Basis | FMV |
| --- | --- | --- |
| Accounts receivable | $ 100,000 | $ 100,000 |
| Marketable securities | 175,000 | 120,000 |
| Equipment | 710,000 | 700,000 |
| Real estate | 1,000,000 | 1,500,000 |
| Unrecorded goodwill | –0– | 250,000 |
|  | $1,985,000 | $2,670,000 |

a. Compute Trimble's net unrealized built-in gain on January 1, 2003.

b. In November 2003, Trimble recognized a $300,000 gain on sale of a one-half interest in the real estate. Compute its built-in gains tax for 2003.

c. Assume that in 2004, Trimble recognizes a $315,000 gain on sale of its remaining interest in the real estate and a $75,000 loss on sale of its marketable securities. Compute its built-in gains tax for 2004.

d. Assume that in 2009, Trimble recognizes a $400,000 gain on the sale of its entire business (including goodwill). Compute its built-in gains tax for 2009.

12. This year, Hilo Inc. earned $168,200 interest and dividend income from its portfolio of marketable securities and collected $419,400 gross receipts from its consulting business. Compute Hilo's excess net passive income tax under each of the following assumptions.

a. Hilo has always been an S corporation.

b. Hilo was a C corporation through last year. On January 1, Hilo had $7,300 accumulated earnings and profits.

c. Hilo was a C corporation until last year. On January 1, Hilo had an accumulated earnings and profits deficit.

13. Mr. Zenfro owns a 10 percent interest in Roosa Company. This year, Roosa incurred a $78,000 debt to a business supplier and borrowed $25,000 from Mr. Zenfro. Neither debt is secured by company property. What is the effect of each debt on Mr. Zenfro's at-risk amount under each of the following assumptions?

a. Roosa is a general partnership.

  b. Roosa is an LLC.

  c. Roosa is an S corporation.

14. Mrs. Painter's outside basis in her BJD Partnership interest is $80,000. This basis includes a $2,800 share of recourse liabilities, a $17,200 share of nonrecourse liabilities, and a $30,000 share of qualified nonrecourse financing. Compute Mrs. Painter's at-risk amount in BJD.

15. Partner P's share of ordinary business loss from CRX Partnership was $100,000. P's outside basis before consideration of the loss was $112,000. The basis included a $25,000 share of CRX's nonrecourse liabilities (none of which were qualified nonrecourse financing). How much loss can Partner P deduct in each of the following cases?

  a. Partner P is a publicly held corporation.

  b. Partner P is an individual who materially participates in CRX's business.

  c. Partner P is an individual who does not materially participate in CRX's business.

16. On July 12, Mr. Yang contributed $10,000 cash to XYZ Partnership for a general interest. He materially participates in XYZ's business, and his first Schedule K-1 reported the following items.

| | |
|---|---|
| Ordinary business loss | $19,000 |
| Tax-exempt interest income | 840 |
| Dividend income | 1,700 |
| Long-term capital gain | 2,200 |
| Cash distributions | 4,500 |

The Schedule K-1 showed that Mr. Yang had the following shares of XYZ's liabilities.

| | |
|---|---|
| Recourse liabilities | $3,600 |
| Qualified nonrecourse financing | 2,000 |
| Other nonrecourse liabilities | 1,200 |

  a. How much ordinary business loss can Mr. Yang deduct on his Form 1040?

  b. Compute his outside basis and at-risk amount in XYZ on January 1 of the next year.

  c. Compute his loss carryforward under the basis limitation and the at-risk limitation.

17. Refer to the facts in problem 16. Assume that Mr. Yang does not materially participate in XYZ's business and does not own an interest in any other passive activity.

  a. How much ordinary business loss can he deduct on his Form 1040?

  b. Compute his outside basis and at-risk amount in XYZ on January 1 of the next year.

  c. Compute his loss carryforward under the basis limitation, the at-risk limitation, and the passive activity loss limitation.

18. Mr. Thomas is a partner in calendar year Marion Partnership. In November, he learns that his share of Marion's current ordinary business loss will be approximately $15,000. His CPA informs him that his deduction for the loss will be limited to $2,900. Identify any year-end tax planning strategies that might increase his deduction under each of the following assumptions.

  a. The deduction is limited because Mr. Thomas has an insufficient basis in his Marion interest.

  b. The deduction is limited because Mr. Thomas has an insufficient at-risk amount in Marion.

  c. The deduction is limited because Mr. Thomas's interest in Marion is a passive activity.

| | |
|---|---|
| **Issue Recognition Problems** | Identify the tax issue or issues suggested by the following situations and state each issue in the form of a question. |

1. On March 1, five investors formed Madison LLC to operate a manufacturing business. The original operating agreement provided that each investor would be allocated 20 percent of profit or loss. Shortly after the end of the LLC's first taxable year, the members amended their agreement to provide that two investors would each be allocated 30 percent, and the remaining three investors would each be allocated 13.33 percent of profit or loss. The amendment was retroactive to March 1.

2. Ms. Chaiken and Ms. Shugart have equal profit and loss interests in CS Partnership. Ms. Chaiken's marginal tax rate is 35 percent, and Ms. Shugart's marginal tax rate is 25 percent. This year, CS purchased $20,000 of municipal bonds, and the partners amended their agreement to allocate 100 percent of the tax-exempt bond interest to Ms. Chaiken. Ms. Shugart will receive a special allocation of ordinary business income equal to the bond interest, and the remaining ordinary income will be allocated equally between Ms. Chaiken and Ms. Shugart.

3. Karo LLC uses the calendar year and the cash method of accounting for tax purposes. On November 15, RRT Inc. contributed $500,000 cash for a 60 percent LLC interest. On December 12, Karo paid $82,500 of overdue interest on a bank loan. The interest was for the one-year period ending November 30. Immediately after the payment, Karo's members amended their agreement to allocate 100 percent of the interest payment to RRT for both book and tax purposes.

4. Mr. and Mrs. Trevedi are the sole shareholders of calendar year High Concepts, which was a C corporation from 1993 through 2003. The Trevedis made a Subchapter S election effective on January 1, 2004. They hired a professional appraiser to determine the FMV of each item of tangible corporate property. The aggregate FMV was $219,600, and the excess of FMV over the aggregate tax basis of the property was $69,200. Eighteen months after High Concepts converted from a C to an S corporation, it sold its entire business to an unrelated third party for $800,000.

5. Yarrow had $11,000 accumulated earnings and profits on the day that it converted from a C to an S corporation. Because it had excess net passive income, it paid a $4,800 sting tax for its first S year. The next year, the IRS audited the last two Form 1120s that Yarrow filed as a C corporation and concluded that $100,000 of officers' salaries were unreasonable.

6. Nabil Inc. is a member of Chandler LLC. Nabil's chief financial officer carefully reviews the annual Schedule K-1 from the LLC. This year, the CFO discovered what appeared to be an error on the Schedule K-1. Rather than contacting the LLC, she corrected the error by recording a different number on Nabil's Form 1120.

7. Mr. and Mrs. Visnu are the sole shareholders of Visnu Products, an S corporation. The corporation has a $75,000 debt to First State Bank, which Mr. and Mrs. Visnu personally guaranteed. This year, the corporation generated a $49,000 operating loss. Mr. and Mrs. Visnu's basis in their stock before consideration of this loss was only $23,000.

8. Tolbert LLC recently borrowed $15,000 from a commercial lender. The debt is not secured by any specific LLC asset, but Ms. Gregson, who owns a 40 percent interest in Tolbert, personally guaranteed repayment of the debt.

9. Mr. and Mrs. Loos each own 15 of the 100 shares of stock in BTB, an S corporation. Mr. Loos is not involved in BTB's business, but Mrs. Loos is employed full-time as BTB's in-house attorney. This year, Mr. and Mrs. Loos each received a Schedule K-1 showing a $13,900 pro rata share of ordinary business loss.

10. Howard LLC operates a bowling alley and two ice cream shops at three different locations. Mrs. O'Brien, who owns a 15 percent interest in Howard, manages the bowling alley but has no involvement with the ice cream shops. This year, Mrs. O'Brien's share of Howard's business loss was $19,000.

## Research Problems

1. Gambali, a calendar year, accrual basis S corporation, makes regular and substantial contributions to local tax-exempt charitable organizations. On December 20, its board of directors authorized a $175,000 contribution to the Calvin Home for Abused Children. The corporation paid the contribution on January 25. Gambali's ordinary business income for the year in which the contribution was authorized was $1,286,200. Can it accrue a $175,000 separately stated charitable contribution for the year?

2. Four individuals formed St. Francis Properties as a C corporation in 1995. St. Francis invested in commercial rental properties that generated passive activity losses. The shareholders made a Subchapter S election for St. Francis, effective on January 1 of this year. On the date of conversion, St. Francis had $118,000 of suspended passive activity losses from its commercial rental properties. This year, the properties generated $44,000 net rental income. Can St. Francis deduct the suspended losses incurred when it was a C corporation against the rental income earned while it is an S corporation?

## Tax Planning Cases

1. Harmon Company leases small airplanes and other transportation equipment. The aggregate FMV of its equipment is $900,000, and the aggregate adjusted basis is $500,000. According to Harmon's tax depreciation schedule, its $500,000 basis will be recovered over the next three years as follows.

| | |
|---|---|
| Remaining depreciable basis | $500,000 |
| Year 1 depreciation | (200,000) |
| Year 2 depreciation | (200,000) |
| Year 3 depreciation | (100,000) |
| | –0– |

PLZ Inc. is interested in acquiring a one-half interest in Harmon's leasing business. One alternative is for PLZ to purchase a one-half interest in Harmon's equipment for $450,000. PLZ's interest in the equipment would be seven-year recovery property, so it would recover the cost through MACRS depreciation in years 1 through 8. A second alternative is for PLZ and Harmon to form a partnership. PLZ would contribute $900,000 worth of income-producing investment assets, and Harmon would contribute its equipment. The two partners would have equal interests in the new partnership's profits, losses, and cash flows.

a. Compare the NPV of PLZ's tax savings from its depreciation deduction with respect to the equipment under both alternatives. Base your computations on the following assumptions.
   • PLZ's marginal tax rate is 35 percent, and it uses a 5 percent discount rate to compute NPV.
   • The new partnership would use the traditional method to make its Section 704(c) allocations with respect to the contributed equipment.

b. Discuss any tax or nontax issues that PLZ should consider before agreeing to either alternative.

2. Sussex LLC operates an active business (a chain of music stores) and also owns commercial real estate. The average annual income from its music business is $950,000, and the average annual rent income from its real estate is $50,000. Ms. Reynolds, who actively participates in the music business, owns a 10 percent interest in Sussex. This January, she invested in a limited partnership in Chicago. She recently learned that her loss from this passive activity will be $25,000 annually for four years (years 0, 1, 2, and 3). Her only passive activity income is her 10 percent share of Sussex's annual rent income. The excess of the Chicago loss over the rent income will be a nondeductible passive activity loss.

   Ms. Reynolds has requested that Sussex amend its operating agreement to allocate 50 percent of its rent income to her for four years (years 0, 1, 2, and 3). The other members will agree to this amendment only if her allocation of business income is decreased to 7 percent over the four-year period. Determine whether Ms. Reynolds should accept this offer by comparing the NPV of her cash flows with and without the change in her allocation percentages. When making your computations, assume the following.

   - Sussex members receive annual cash distributions equal to their shares of LLC income.
   - Ms. Reynolds has a 35 percent marginal tax rate and uses an 8 percent discount rate to compute NPV.
   - Ms. Reynolds will dispose of her entire Chicago partnership interest (and deduct any suspended passive activity loss) in year 4. The gain or loss recognized and any cash flows from the sale are neutral factors in her decision.

## Appendix **7–A**

# Section 704(c) Remedial Allocation Method

The remedial method of Section 704(c) allocations is designed to eliminate distortions caused by the ceiling rule under the traditional method. When the ceiling rule applies, the **remedial method** allows the partnership to create a fictitious tax item (a *notional* item) to allocate to the noncontributing partners. This notional item equalizes the noncontributing partners' tax and book allocations with respect to the contributed property. The partnership simultaneously creates an offsetting notional item to allocate to the contributing partner. The net effect of the notional items to the partners in the aggregate is zero.

The following is the example from page 175 in which the ceiling rule distorted the book/tax allocations to the noncontributing partners.

### Traditional Method—Ceiling Rule Application

Assume that RTP sold the land contributed by Rawling for $750,000 instead of $1 million. It has a $50,000 book *loss* on the sale ($750,000 − $800,000 book basis) but a $250,000 tax *gain* ($750,000 − $500,000 tax basis). For book purposes, RTP allocates a $10,000 loss to Rawling's capital account and a $40,000 loss to the other partners' capital accounts. The difference between the book and tax allocations is $300,000. This difference (the built-in gain) should be allocated to Rawling so that its tax allocation is a $290,000 gain ($10,000 book loss *plus* $300,000 built-in gain). Because of the ceiling rule, the allocation to Rawling is limited to the actual $250,000 tax gain. As a result, the other partners' $40,000 book loss allocation is not matched by a $40,000 tax loss allocation.

| | Rawling (20%) | | Other Partners (80%) | |
|---|---|---|---|---|
| | **Book** | **Tax** | **Book** | **Tax** |
| Loss/gain on sale | $(10,000) | $250,000 | $(40,000) | –0– |

The following is the revised example illustrating the remedial method.

## Remedial Method

If RTP elects to use the remedial method of Section 704(c) allocations, it creates a $40,000 notional item of loss to report on the other partners' Schedule K-1s and a $40,000 notional item of gain to report on Rawling's Schedule K-1.

|  | Rawling (20%) | | Other Partners (80%) | |
|---|---|---|---|---|
|  | **Book** | **Tax** | **Book** | **Tax** |
| Loss/gain on sale | $(10,000) | $250,000 | $(40,000) | –0– |
| Notional items on K-1s | –0– | 40,000 | –0– | $(40,000) |
|  | $(10,000) | $290,000 | $(40,000) | $(40,000) |

Because of the remedial notional items, Rawling's combined tax allocations reflect the property's entire built-in gain, and the other partners' book and tax allocations are equal.

The remedial method also eliminates distortions of depreciation or amortization allocations with respect to contributed property. The example from page 177 illustrates how the ceiling rule distorts the allocation of tax depreciation to noncontributing partners.

## Depreciation Allocation—Ceiling Rule

Assume that the adjusted basis of Ms. Stovall's equipment was only $13,000, so that Leeway has the following depreciation schedule.

|  | **Book** | **Tax** |
|---|---|---|
| Depreciable basis | $25,000 | $13,000 |
| Depreciation 2002 | (10,000) | (5,200) |
| Depreciation 2003 | (10,000) | (5,200) |
| Depreciation 2004 | (5,000) | (2,600) |
| Adjusted basis | –0– | –0– |

Because Ms. Stovall's contributed basis is so much less than contributed FMV, Leeway simply does not have enough tax depreciation to allocate to the other members. The best that the LLC can do is to allocate 100 percent of tax depreciation to the other members and none to Ms. Stovall.

|  | Ms. Stovall (35%) | | Other Members (65%) | |
|---|---|---|---|---|
|  | **Book** | **Tax** | **Book** | **Tax** |
| Depreciation 2002 | $(3,500) | –0– | $ (6,500) | $(5,200) |
| Depreciation 2003 | (3,500) | –0– | (6,500) | (5,200) |
| Depreciation 2004 | (1,750) | –0– | (3,250) | (2,600) |
|  | $(8,750) | –0– | $(16,250) | $(13,000) |

Over the remaining life of the equipment, the difference between Ms. Stovall's book and tax depreciation is only $8,750, which is $3,250 less than her $12,000 built-in gain. The other members have been allocated only $13,000 tax depreciation, which is $3,250 less than their book depreciation.

Unfortunately, the remedial method adds complexity to the computation of book depreciation for contributed property with built-in gain. The portion of the partnership's book basis equal to the tax basis (carryover portion) is depreciated according to the contributing partner's remaining depreciation schedule. The additional book basis (built-in gain portion) is treated as newly purchased property to be depreciated over its own recovery period.

## Depreciation Allocation—Remedial Method

If Leeway LLC elects to use the remedial method to allocate depreciation on Ms. Stovall's contributed equipment, the computation of book depreciation changes dramatically. Book depreciation on $13,000 of the $25,000 book basis (carryover portion) is computed according to Ms. Stovall's depreciation schedule. The $12,000 additional book basis (built-in gain portion) is treated as newly purchased five-year recovery property depreciated at the MACRS rate. The revised book depreciation schedule follows.

|  | **Carryover Portion** | **Built-in Portion** | **Total** |
|---|---|---|---|
| Depreciable basis | $13,000 | $12,000 | $25,000 |
| Depreciation 2002 | (5,200) | (2,400) | (7,600) |
| Depreciation 2003 | (5,200) | (3,840) | (9,040) |
| Depreciation 2004 | (2,600) | (2,304) | (4,904) |
| Depreciation 2005 | — | (1,382) | (1,382) |
| Depreciation 2006 | — | (1,382) | (1,382) |
| Depreciation 2007 | — | (692) | (692) |
| Adjusted basis | –0– | –0– | –0– |

Annual book depreciation is allocated 35 percent to Ms. Stovall and 65 percent to the other members. In 2002, tax depreciation is sufficient to match the book allocation to the other members with an equal amount of tax depreciation, with the $260 remaining tax depreciation allocated to Ms. Stovall. In 2003 through 2007, annual tax depreciation is insufficient to match the book allocation to the other members, and notional income and deduction items must be used to correct the disparity.

| | Ms. Stovall (35%) | | Other Members (65%) | |
|---|---|---|---|---|
| | **Book** | **Tax** | **Book** | **Tax** |
| Depreciation 2002 | $(2,660) | $(260) | $(4,940) | $(4,940) |
| Depreciation 2003 | (3,164) | –0– | (5,876) | (5,200) |
| **Notional items** | | **676** | | **(676)** |
| Depreciation 2004 | (1,716) | –0– | (3,188) | (2,600) |
| **Notional items** | | **588** | | **(588)** |
| Depreciation 2005 | (484) | | (898) | |
| **Notional items** | | **898** | | **(898)** |
| Depreciation 2006 | (484) | | (898) | |
| **Notional items** | | **898** | | **(898)** |
| Depreciation 2007 | (242) | | (450) | |
| **Notional items** | | **450** | | **(450)** |
| | $(8,750) | $3,250 | $(16,250) | $(16,250) |

Leeway's use of the remedial allocation method accomplishes two objectives: The cumulative difference between Ms. Stovall's book and tax allocations equals her $12,000 built-in gain ($8,750 book depreciation − $3,250 taxable income), and the other members' book and tax allocations are equal. Remember that the notional items appear *only* as ordinary income on Ms. Stovall's Schedule K-1 and as ordinary deductions on the other members' Schedule K-1s. Although the notional items have the same effect as actual tax items on the members' tax liabilities and outside basis in their LLC interests, they have no effect on Leeway's book income and no effect on the adjusted book basis or tax basis of the equipment.

# Chapter **Eight**

# Distributions to Business Owners

## Learning Objectives

*After reading this chapter, you will be able to:*

1. Define the term *earnings and profits*.

2. Determine the extent to which a corporate distribution is a dividend.

3. Explain the tax consequences of a return of capital.

4. Describe the tax consequences of corporate property distributions.

5. Describe the tax consequences of stock dividends.

6. Recognize when a corporation is vulnerable to the accumulated earnings tax and personal holding company tax.

7. Summarize the tax consequences of partnership cash and property distributions.

8. Determine the tax consequences of S corporation distributions.

**Tax Talk**

The Jobs and Growth Tax Relief Reconciliation Act of 2003 reduced the maximum tax rate on dividends to 15 percent. According to the Securities Industries Association, more than 400 corporations reacted by increasing their 2003 dividend payments by at least 10 percent, and more than 130 corporations that had never paid a dividend announced that they would start doing so.

Business owners must routinely decide how to use the earnings generated by their business. They can reinvest the earnings to finance business growth and expansion, thus reducing the need for external financing. Alternatively, they can withdraw the earnings to invest in other ventures or to spend on personal consumption. In the tax lexicon, *withdrawals from business entities* are referred to as distributions. In Chapter 8, we examine the tax consequences of distributions at both the entity and the owner levels. The first half of the chapter deals with the Subchapter C rules governing corporate distributions; the differences between cash, property, and stock dividends; and the potential penalty taxes on corporations that avoid dividend payments. The second half of the chapter deals with the Subchapter K and Subchapter S rules that determine the tax consequences of cash and property distributions by partnerships and S corporations.

## CORPORATE DISTRIBUTIONS

The predominant feature of the corporate income tax system is the double taxation of earnings. The corporation itself pays tax on its income. If the corporation then distributes after-tax earnings as a dividend to its shareholders, the shareholders must include the dividend in gross income and pay a second tax. Section 316(a) defines a **dividend** as any distribution of cash or property made by a corporation to its shareholders to the extent the distribution is paid out of earnings and profits.

## Earnings and Profits

**Objective 1**
Define the term *earnings and profits*.

In theory, **earnings and profits (E&P)** measures a corporation's financial capacity to pay a return on invested capital without returning the capital itself. The term *earnings and profits* is not comprehensively defined in either the Internal Revenue Code or the Treasury regulations. The computation of annual E&P customarily begins with corporate taxable income reduced by federal income tax. This after-tax income number is subject to a series of statutory adjustments that result in **current E&P.**[1] This series of adjustments is intended to fine-tune E&P to approximate the corporation's capacity to pay a dividend.

*Current E&P*

Roider Inc.'s taxable income for the year was $20 million, and its federal tax was $7 million. Roider earned $28,900 tax-exempt interest, which increased its capacity to pay a dividend. It also realized a $95,000 nondeductible capital loss, which decreased its capacity to pay a dividend. If the tax-exempt interest and capital loss were Roider's only E&P adjustments, current E&P is $12,933,900.

| | |
|---|---:|
| Taxable income | $20,000,000 |
| Federal income tax | (7,000,000) |
| Adjustments:  Tax-exempt interest | 28,900 |
|   Nondeductible capital loss | (95,000) |
| Current E&P | $12,933,900 |

Many (but not all) of the adjustments to taxable income in the E&P computation are the reverse of the adjustments on the Schedule M-1 reconciliation of book/tax income. As a result, current E&P is usually closer to after-tax *book* income than after-tax *taxable* income. For the remainder of the text, we ignore any fine-tuning and assume that current E&P equals corporate taxable income reduced by federal income tax. If a corporation generates a net operating loss, the loss (net of any tax refund from an NOL carryback deduction) equals an E&P deficit for the year.[2]

If a corporation makes a distribution during a year in which it has current E&P, the distribution is a dividend to the extent of the E&P.

*Dividend Payment: Current E&P*

BRJ, a calendar year corporation, distributed $500,000 to its shareholders on June 30 and on December 31, 2004. BRJ's 2004 taxable income was $4,480,000, its federal tax was $1,523,200, and its current E&P was $2,956,800 (taxable income − federal tax). Because BRJ's $1,000,000 total distribution was less than current E&P, the entire distribution was a dividend to the shareholders.

### Accumulated E&P

After the close of the year, current E&P, reduced by dividends paid during the year, is added to the corporation's **accumulated E&P,** which measures undistributed E&P for all prior taxable years. If a corporation has a current E&P deficit, the deficit is subtracted from

---

[1] Section 312 lists the effects of specific transactions on E&P.

[2] For accrual basis corporations, the refund increases E&P for the year of loss. For cash basis corporations, the refund increases E&P for the year in which the corporation receives the refund.

accumulated E&P. The concept of accumulated E&P is similar to the concept of retained earnings on a balance sheet. Both numbers represent a running total of after-tax earnings that were reinvested in the corporate business rather than distributed to shareholders. Nevertheless, retained earnings is a financial accounting number, accumulated E&P is a tax number, and the two numbers are not necessarily the same.[3]

*Accumulated E&P*

On January 1, 2004, BRJ's accumulated E&P was $6,920,500. Its accumulated E&P on January 1, 2005, is computed as follows.

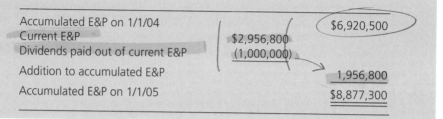

| | | |
|---|---|---|
| Accumulated E&P on 1/1/04 | | $6,920,500 |
| Current E&P | $2,956,800 | |
| Dividends paid out of current E&P | (1,000,000) | |
| Addition to accumulated E&P | | 1,956,800 |
| Accumulated E&P on 1/1/05 | | $8,877,300 |

**Objective 2**
Determine the extent to which a corporation distribution is a dividend.

If corporate distributions during the year exceed current E&P, the excess distribution is a dividend to the extent of accumulated E&P. In other words, a corporation can pay a dividend out of either current or accumulated E&P.

*Dividend Payment: Accumulated E&P*

During 2005, BRJ distributed $875,000 to its shareholders. Its 2005 taxable income was $988,000, its federal tax was $335,920, and its current E&P was $652,080. Consequently, $652,080 of the $875,000 distribution was a dividend paid out of current E&P. The $222,920 excess distribution was a dividend paid out of accumulated E&P. BRJ's accumulated E&P on January 1, 2006, is computed as follows.

| | | |
|---|---|---|
| Accumulated E&P on 1/1/05 | | $8,877,300 |
| Current E&P | $652,080 | |
| Dividend paid out of current E&P | (652,080) | |
| | | –0– |
| Dividend paid out of accumulated E&P | | (222,920) |
| Accumulated E&P on 1/1/06 | | $8,654,380 |

*Dividend Payment: Accumulated E&P*

During 2006, BRJ distributed $100,000 to its shareholders. It incurred a $45,000 net operating loss for the year. The carryback of the NOL resulted in a $15,300 federal tax refund. Because BRJ had a $29,700 E&P deficit ($45,000 NOL − $15,300 refund), none of the $100,000 distribution was a dividend paid out of current E&P. However, the entire distribution was a dividend paid out of accumulated E&P. BRJ's accumulated E&P on January 1, 2007, is computed as follows.

| | |
|---|---|
| Accumulated E&P at 1/1/06 | $8,654,380 |
| Current E&P deficit | (29,700) |
| Dividend paid out of accumulated E&P | (100,000) |
| Accumulated E&P at 1/1/07 | $8,524,680 |

[3] See *Estate of Vincent DeNiro*, TC Memo 1990-398.

Even if a corporation has a deficit in accumulated E&P at the beginning of the year, it has the capacity to pay a dividend out of current E&P.

*Accumulated E&P Deficit*

On January 1, 2004, Toolson Inc. had a $450,000 deficit in accumulated E&P. On June 30, it distributed $75,000 cash to its shareholders. Toolson's 2004 taxable income was $400,000, its federal tax was $136,000, and its current E&P was $264,000. Consequently, the $75,000 distribution was a dividend paid out of current E&P. Toolson's accumulated E&P deficit on January 1, 2005, is computed as follows.

| | | |
|---|---:|---:|
| Accumulated E&P deficit on 1/1/04 | | $(450,000) |
| Current E&P | $264,000 | |
| Dividend paid out of current E&P | (75,000) | |
| Addition to accumulated E&P | | 189,000 |
| Accumulated E&P deficit on 1/1/05 | | $(261,000) |

Profitable corporations that routinely distribute only a fraction of their annual earnings as dividends might not bother to keep a tax record of their accumulated E&P. These corporations do, however, update the retained earnings on their balance sheet when they prepare year-end financial statements. The balance in retained earnings is usually the best *approximation* of accumulated E&P. In a situation in which the dividend component of a distribution is questionable, however, the corporation must make an accurate calculation of its E&P.

**Objective 3**
Explain the tax consequences of a return of capital.

### Returns of Capital

Any portion of a corporate distribution not paid out of E&P (and therefore not a dividend) is a return of paid-in capital and has no effect on E&P. Accordingly, a corporation creates an E&P deficit *only* by operating at a loss, not by distributing capital to its shareholders.

*Return of Capital*

Havelka Inc. was formed on March 15, 2003, and operated at a $37,300 loss for its first taxable year. As a result, it had a $37,300 deficit in accumulated E&P on January 1, 2004. On September 30, 2004, Havelka distributed $900,000 to its shareholders. Its current E&P for 2004 was $810,000, so only $810,000 of the distribution was a dividend. The $90,000 remainder was a return of capital with no effect on Havelka's E&P. Its accumulated E&P deficit on January 1, 2005, remained at $37,300.

| | | |
|---|---:|---:|
| Accumulated E&P deficit on 1/1/04 | | $(37,300) |
| Current E&P | $810,000 | |
| Dividend paid out of current E&P | (810,000) | |
| Addition to accumulated E&P | | –0– |
| Accumulated E&P deficit on 1/1/05 | | $(37,300) |

Shareholders that receive a return of capital do not recognize ordinary income but apply the return against the basis in their stock. If the return of capital exceeds their stock basis, they must recognize the excess as capital gain.[4]

[4] Section 301(c).

### Summary

The tax treatment of distributions from C corporations to shareholders is summarized in the diagram in Exhibit 8.1. This diagram depicts the equity section of the corporate balance sheet as a beaker of funds out of which the corporation can make distributions. The top layer in the beaker consists of current E&P, which the corporation must completely distribute before dipping into the second layer of accumulated E&P. If the corporation has distributed all current and accumulated E&P, it can dip into the bottom layer in the beaker, which consists of paid-in capital. Distributions out of the two E&P layers are taxable dividends to the recipient shareholders, while distributions out of the bottom layer are nontaxable to the extent of the recipient shareholder's basis in the C corporation stock.

**EXHIBIT 8.1**
**C Corporation Shareholder's Equity**

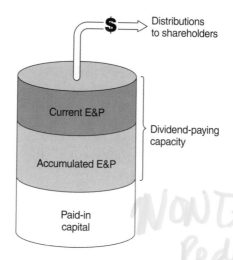

### Property Distributions

**Objective 4**
Describe the tax consequences of corporate property distributions.

Although corporations usually make their distributions in cash, they occasionally distribute other assets as a dividend or return of capital. Such property distributions have significant tax consequences to the corporation. If the fair market value (FMV) of the distributed property exceeds its tax basis, the corporation must recognize gain as if it had sold the property for FMV.[5] The recognized gain on the constructive sale is included in taxable income, and current E&P increases by the after-tax amount of the gain. The distribution itself decreases current E&P by the FMV of the property.[6]

[5] Section 311(b).
[6] Section 312(b).

| | |
|---|---|
| *Distribution of Appreciated Property* | Munro Inc. distributed a tract of land as a dividend to its shareholders. The FMV was $240,000, and Munro's tax basis in the land was $200,000. Munro must treat the distribution as a constructive sale on which it recognized a $40,000 gain. Its tax on the gain was $14,000. The distribution itself decreased current E&P by $240,000. The net decrease in current E&P is computed as follows. |

| | |
|---|---|
| Taxable gain on property distribution | $ 40,000 |
| Tax on gain | (14,000) |
| Increase in E&P | $ 26,000 |
| Decrease in E&P for distribution | (240,000) |
| Net decrease in E&P | $(214,000) |

If the FMV of the distributed property is less than its basis, the corporation cannot recognize a loss.[7] The distribution decreases current E&P by the adjusted basis of the property.[8]

| | |
|---|---|
| *Distribution of Devalued Property* | Assume that Munro's basis in the distributed land was $250,000 instead of $200,000. Even though the FMV of the land is only $240,000, Munro could not recognize a loss because of the distribution. The distribution itself decreased current E&P by the $250,000 basis in the land. |

Shareholders that receive a property distribution must account for the FMV of the property as either a dividend or a return of capital.[9] Regardless of the corporation's basis in the distributed property, the recipient shareholder's basis equals the property's FMV.[10]

| | |
|---|---|
| *Shareholder Consequences* | Mrs. Maloney, who owns 25 percent of the stock in Munro, received a one-fourth undivided interest in the tract of land distributed as a dividend. The FMV of this interest is $60,000. Consequently, Mrs. Maloney recognized a $60,000 dividend, and her tax basis in the one-fourth interest is $60,000. |

## Stock Dividends

**Objective 5**
Describe the tax consequences of stock dividends.

Instead of cash or property, a corporation can distribute shares of common or preferred stock to its shareholders. For financial accounting purposes, a stock dividend represents a capitalization of retained earnings through an increase in the number of outstanding shares. Corporations pay **stock dividends** for a variety of business reasons, one of which is to reduce the selling price per share to make the stock more marketable.

| | |
|---|---|
| *Accounting for a Stock Dividend* | At the beginning of the year, BeniHam, a publicly held corporation, had 100,000 shares of $100 par value common stock outstanding. The stock was selling for $200 per share. BeniHam's board of directors believed that this price was too high and was discouraging small, online investors. The board authorized a dividend of one share of common stock for every four shares outstanding (a 25 percent pro rata stock dividend). BeniHam recorded the stock dividend |

[7] Section 311(a).
[8] Section 312(a)(3).
[9] Section 301(b)(1).
[10] Section 301(d).

by increasing its capital stock account by $2,500,000 (25,000 new shares × $100 par value) and by decreasing retained earnings by the same amount. Because of the increased number of shares outstanding, the market price of BeniHam common dropped to $160 per share.

### Tax Consequences of Stock Dividends

For tax purposes, a stock dividend is treated in one of two ways: either a nonevent to the shareholders or a property distribution resulting in dividend income. A stock dividend is a nonevent only if it has no potential for a differential effect on the equity interests of the shareholders. In other words, each shareholder is in the same relative financial position before and after the dividend. The stock dividend merely increases the number of shares representing each shareholder's investment.

| | |
|---|---|
| *Nontaxable Stock Dividend* | Ms. Hicks owned 2,300 shares of BeniHam stock with a basis of $110 per share, representing a total investment of $253,000. She received a stock dividend of 575 additional shares. Because the stock dividend had no differential effect on BeniHam's shareholders, it had no tax consequences to any of them. Ms. Hicks recognized no income on receipt of the 575 shares.[11] After the receipt, her basis in each share is $88 ($253,000 investment/2,875 shares).[12] |

Corporations can structure stock dividends to change the shareholders' relative financial positions. For instance, a corporation could give its shareholders the option to receive a dividend in either cash or additional shares of stock. Shareholders that choose the stock dividend increase their equity interest relative to the shareholders who choose cash. Because the stock dividend could have a differential effect on the shareholders, it is treated as a property distribution.[13] The shareholders must recognize the FMV of their new shares as a dividend (to the extent of corporate E&P) and take a basis in the new shares equal to their FMV.

| | |
|---|---|
| *Taxable Stock Dividend* | On December 15, MCX declared a $5 dividend on each share of its outstanding common stock. Shareholders had the choice of taking their dividend in cash or in additional shares of stock, which were valued at $125 per share. Mrs. Rob, who owned 14,200 MCX shares, was entitled to a $71,000 dividend (14,200 shares × $5), which she chose to take as 568 additional shares ($71,000/$125 value per share). Mrs. Rob recognized $71,000 dividend income and took a $125 basis in each new share of MCX stock. Her receipt of the taxable stock dividend did not affect the basis of her original 14,200 shares. |

The payment of a nontaxable stock dividend has no effect on corporate E&P. In contrast, the payment of a taxable stock dividend decreases E&P by the FMV of the stock.[14]

| | |
|---|---|
| *Effect of Stock Dividends on E&P* | During this taxable year, MCX declared the following dividends out of retained earnings: |

| | | |
|---|---|---|
| March 15 | Cash dividend | $1,500,000 |
| June 30 | Pro rata stock dividend (nontaxable) | 1,000,000 |
| December 15 | Cash/stock dividend (taxable) | 750,000 |

---

[11] Section 305(a).

[12] Section 307(a).

[13] Section 305(b)(1). Section 305(b) and the regulations thereunder identify the variety of stock dividends that must be treated as property distributions.

[14] Reg. 1.312-1(d).

The March 15 and the December 15 dividends reduced corporate E&P by a total of $2,250,000. The nontaxable June 30 dividend had no effect on E&P, even though it reduced MCX's retained earnings by $1 million.

## Constructive Dividends

Shareholders of closely held corporations typically want to defer the second tax on corporate earnings by avoiding dividends for as long as possible. This strategy often prompts shareholders to find other ways to extract cash from the corporate business. As we discussed in Chapter 4, shareholders who are also corporate employees can receive reasonable compensation for their services. Shareholders and corporations can engage in other transactions that create cash flow to the shareholders. For instance, shareholders can lease property to their corporations for a reasonable rent or can lend money at a reasonable rate of interest. Because corporations can deduct the rent or interest payments, these payments are not double taxed.

Shareholders who control the corporate purse strings must be cautious to avoid constructive dividend payments. If a corporate payment confers an economic benefit that primarily advances the shareholder's personal interest instead of the corporation's business interest, the IRS could classify the payment as a nondeductible dividend.

*Corporate Payment as Constructive Dividend*

Mr. Gow was both an enthusiastic big game hunter and a principal shareholder in Williamsburg Vacations Inc., which operated a luxury resort in Virginia. Over a four-year period, the corporation spent $750,000 for travel, food, lodging, professional guide fees, and taxidermy expenses to enable Mr. Gow to acquire a world-class animal trophy collection. The collection purportedly was used for corporate marketing purposes. The IRS concluded that the corporate payments were constructive dividends to Mr. Gow, and the Tax Court agreed, stating, "We do not believe the display of exotic animals such as elk, caribou, or Armenian red sheep furthers the historical colonial theme that was in place as a marketing strategy."[15]

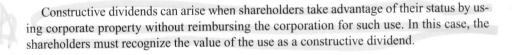

Constructive dividends can arise when shareholders take advantage of their status by using corporate property without reimbursing the corporation for such use. In this case, the shareholders must recognize the value of the use as a constructive dividend.

*Use of Corporate Property as Constructive Dividend*

Mr. Baird was the sole shareholder in Offshore Operations Inc. The corporation owned several oceangoing yachts that it leased to customers throughout the year. When the IRS audited Offshore's 1997 tax return, it discovered that Mr. Baird used the yacht *Crows Nest IV* to make two family trips to Bermuda. He did not reimburse his corporation for any expenses associated with the two trips. The IRS determined that the fair rental value of *Crows Nest IV* for the trips was $26,000 and required Mr. Baird to include a $26,000 constructive dividend in his 1997 income.[16]

# PENALTY TAXES ON CORPORATE ACCUMULATIONS

Shareholders with no immediate need for cash can defer a second tax by having their corporation accumulate earnings instead of paying dividends. The increase in retained earnings should be mirrored by an increase in the value of the corporate stock. The shareholders

[15] *Robert T. Gow*, TC Memo 2000-93.
[16] *Offshore Operations Tr.*, TC Memo 1973-212.

will not recognize the increase in value as income until they dispose of the stock in a taxable transaction. This next example shows how such deferral dramatically reduces the cost of the shareholder tax in present value terms.

| | |
|---|---|
| *Deferral of Second Tax* | Mr. and Mrs. Reiver are the sole shareholders in RRR Inc. This year, RRR's current E&P was $500,000. If RRR distributed the E&P as a dividend, Mr. and Mrs. Reiver's tax cost would be $75,000 (15 percent × $500,000). If RRR accumulates the E&P, the value of its stock will increase by $500,000. If Mr. and Mrs. Reiver hold the stock for 10 years and then recognize a $500,000 long-term capital gain on sale, their future tax cost will be $75,000 (15 percent × $500,000). However, the NPV of this tax cost at an 8 percent discount rate is only $34,725 ($75,000 × 0.463 discount factor). |

## Accumulated Earnings Tax

**Objective 6**
Recognize when a corporation is vulnerable to the accumulated earnings tax.

Corporations who implement an earnings accumulation strategy must be prepared to defend themselves against the **accumulated earnings tax.** The IRS can impose this penalty tax on any corporation that accumulates earnings for the purpose of avoiding the shareholder-level tax on dividends.[17] The law presumes that this forbidden purpose exists when a corporation accumulates earnings beyond the reasonable needs of its business.[18] If a corporation can demonstrate a bona fide business purpose for its accumulations, it is invulnerable to the accumulated earnings tax. The first place to look for evidence of such business purpose is the balance sheet, which provides information about the corporation's use of its retained earnings.

| | |
|---|---|
| *Reasonable Business Needs* | Ragged Mountain Inc. has the following balance sheet. |

| | |
|---|---|
| Cash on hand | $ 13,000 |
| Trade accounts receivable | 1,488,000 |
| Merchandise inventory | 4,020,500 |
| Supplies inventory | 600,000 |
| Machinery and equipment | 7,690,000 |
| Furniture and fixtures | 1,370,000 |
| Leasehold costs | 276,000 |
| | $15,457,500 |
| | |
| Accounts payable | $ 681,100 |
| Long-term debt | 1,400,000 |
| Shareholders' equity: | |
| Paid-in capital | 200,000 |
| Retained earnings | 13,176,400 |
| | $15,457,500 |

The equity section of the balance sheet shows that Ragged Mountain has about $13 million undistributed earnings. (Remember that retained earnings only approximate accumulated E&P.) The asset section of the balance sheet shows that the corporation reinvested these earnings in inventory, supplies, and other essential operating assets. Ragged Mountain can offer its balance sheet as proof that it accumulated earnings to finance its business needs and not for the forbidden purpose of tax avoidance.

[17] Section 532(a).

[18] Section 533(a).

A corporation's reasonable business needs include both present needs and reasonably anticipated future needs for capital. According to Treasury regulations, corporations must have "specific, definite, and feasible plans" that justify accumulations of earnings for future needs.[19] Ideally, these plans should be documented and formally approved by the board of directors. A plan can involve a long-term project that the corporation might not undertake in the immediate future. Even so, the regulations warn that if the execution of a plan is postponed indefinitely, the plan will no longer justify an accumulation of earnings.

| *Reasonably Anticipated Future Need* | Lombardi Inc. has the following balance sheet. | |
|---|---|---|
| | Cash on hand | $ 65,000 |
| | Certificate of deposit | 250,000 |
| | U.S. government securities | 390,000 |
| | Trade accounts receivable | 419,200 |
| | Merchandise inventory | 897,000 |
| | Furniture and fixtures | 1,502,900 |
| | | $3,524,100 |
| | Accounts payable | $ 53,500 |
| | Shareholders' equity: | |
| | Paid-in capital | 600,000 |
| | Retained earnings | 2,870,600 |
| | | $3,524,100 |

The balance sheet shows that Lombardi reinvested $640,000 of retained earnings in *nonbusiness* assets ($250,000 certificate of deposit + $390,000 U.S. government securities). According to the minutes of the last board of directors meeting, Lombardi plans to use these earnings to fund the acquisition of a competitor's business. Negotiations between Lombardi and the competitor are well under way, and the acquisition is scheduled to take place early in 2007. Thus, Lombardi can justify its accumulation of earnings to finance a reasonably anticipated future business need.

When the IRS audits a corporation, the revenue agent routinely inspects the balance sheet and other financial records to determine the corporation's use of retained earnings. An agent who concludes that the corporation is accumulating earnings for the prohibited purpose of tax avoidance can assess an accumulated earnings tax for the years under examination. The tax equals 15 percent of accumulated taxable income for the year.[20] Essentially, accumulated taxable income equals after-tax income reduced by (1) dividends paid during the year and (2) the accumulated earnings credit.[21] This credit (which properly should be called a *deduction*) equals the amount of current earnings retained to meet business needs. If the corporation lacks any business need, it is entitled to a $250,000 minimum credit ($150,000 for personal service corporations) less accumulated E&P at the beginning of the year.[22] The minimum credit allows new corporations to retain a *de minimis* amount of earnings without any business justification.

---

[19] Reg. 1.537-1(b)(1).
[20] Section 531.
[21] Section 535 provides the complete definition of accumulated taxable income.
[22] Section 535(c)(2).

*Computation of Accumulated Earnings Tax*

Mr. and Mrs. Vernon incorporated their plumbing business as VKZ Products in 1999. The IRS just completed an audit of VKZ's Form 1120 for 2002 and 2003. The relevant data from the corporate records follow.

|  | 2002 | 2003 |
|---|---|---|
| Accumulated E&P on January 1 | $142,600 | $224,010 |
| Taxable income reported on return | 106,000 | 123,000 |
| Corporate income tax paid | (24,590) | (31,220) |
| Dividends paid to shareholders | –0– | –0– |

The revenue agent concluded that the returns were correct as filed. She also noticed that VKZ reinvested most of its after-tax earnings in mutual fund shares. Consequently, the agent assessed an accumulated earnings tax computed as follows.

|  | 2002 | 2003 |
|---|---|---|
| Taxable income | $106,000 | $123,000 |
| Corporate income tax paid | (24,590) | (31,220) |
| Dividends paid | –0– | –0– |
| Minimum accumulated earnings credit ($250,000 − accumulated E&P on 1/1) | (107,400) | (25,990) |
| Accumulated taxable income | –0– | $ 65,790 |
|  |  | .15 |
| Accumulated earnings tax | –0– | $ 9,869 |

VKZ had no business reason to retain any 2002 or 2003 after-tax earnings, but it was entitled to a minimum accumulated earnings credit because it had not yet accumulated $250,000. On January 1, 2004, its accumulated E&P was $305,921.

| | |
|---|---|
| Accumulated E&P on January 1, 2003 | $224,010 |
| Taxable income | 123,000 |
| Federal income tax | (31,220) |
| Accumulated earnings tax | (9,869) |
| Accumulated E&P on January 1, 2004 | $305,921 |

Consequently, VKZ has no minimum accumulated earnings credit for 2004 and future taxable years. If the corporation continues to needlessly accumulate its after-tax earnings, it will continue to be vulnerable to the accumulated earnings tax.

The accumulated earnings tax can apply to any domestic taxable corporation, regardless of the nature of its business or the identity and number of its shareholders. However, this ubiquitous tax does not apply to personal holding companies.[23] Instead of the accumulated earnings tax, a corporation that qualifies as a personal holding company must concern itself with its own specialized penalty tax.

---

[23] Section 532(b)(1).

# Personal Holding Company Tax

**Objective 6**
Recognize when a corporation is vulnerable to the personal holding company tax.

The personal holding company tax is an anachronism dating back to the era when individual tax rates were drastically higher than corporate tax rates. Individuals were tempted by the rate differential to hold their investment assets in closely held corporations that never paid dividends. Congress enacted the **personal holding company tax** to discourage this abusive use of corporations as shelters from the individual income tax. Today, the top individual rate and the top corporate rate are both 35 percent, and wealthy individuals have no incentive to form personal holding companies as tax shelters. The personal holding company tax is alive and well, however, and applies to every personal holding company regardless of the shareholder motivation for forming the corporation.[24]

The classification of a corporation as a personal holding company is made on a year-by-year basis. A corporation is a personal holding company for any taxable year in which it meets two requirements.[25] The first requirement relates to the type of income earned. A corporation meets this requirement if at least 60 percent of its ordinary gross income consists of personal holding company income. While the technical definition of personal holding company income is tortuous, the term generally refers to investment income, such as interest, dividends, rents, and royalties.[26] The second requirement relates to the corporate ownership. A corporation meets this requirement if five or fewer individuals directly or indirectly owned more than 50 percent of the FMV of the outstanding stock at any time during the last half of the year.[27]

| | |
|---|---|
| *Classification as Personal Holding Company* | NPH Inc., a calendar year taxpayer, operates a retail business and owns a sizable portfolio of marketable securities. For the last several years, about 75 percent of its ordinary gross income consisted of dividends and interest (personal holding company income). Nonetheless, NPH has not been a personal holding company because only 15 percent of its outstanding stock was owned by individual shareholders. On August 31, 2004, Mr. Benton and Mrs. Smith each purchased a 30 percent stock interest. As a result, NPH met both the income and the stock ownership requirements and was a personal holding company for 2004. |

The personal holding company tax equals 15 percent of undistributed personal holding company income.[28] The term *undistributed personal holding company income* is misleading because it includes more than just undistributed investment income. Instead, undistributed personal holding company income equals *total* after-tax ordinary income reduced by dividends paid during the year.[29] Personal holding companies must compute their personal holding company tax on Schedule PH, Form 1120, and pay the tax by the due date of the return.[30]

---

[24] Reg. 1.541-1(a).

[25] Section 542(a).

[26] Section 543 provides the complete definition of personal holding company income.

[27] Section 544 provides the attribution rules for determining an individual's indirect ownership.

[28] Section 541.

[29] Section 545. A corporation's net capital gains are excluded from personal holding company income.

[30] Corporations are not required to make quarterly installment payments of personal holding company tax. Section 6655(g)(1).

*Computation of Personal Holding Company Tax*

Because NPH was a personal holding company for 2004, it was liable for a personal holding company tax computed as follows.

| | |
|---|---:|
| Ordinary taxable income | $287,300 |
| Federal income tax on ordinary income | (95,297) |
| Dividends paid during the year | (150,000) |
| Undistributed personal holding company income | $ 42,003 |
| | .15 |
| Personal holding company tax | $ 6,300 |

If a corporation is aware that it is a personal holding company, it can avoid the penalty tax by paying enough dividends to reduce its undistributed after-tax income to zero.[31] This opportunity is lost if a corporation is unaware that it was a personal holding company until several years after the fact when the IRS audits its Form 1120. Even in this case, the corporation can avoid the penalty tax by paying a **deficiency dividend,** which is a cash distribution made within 90 days after the determination that the corporation is liable for the personal holding company tax for a previous year.[32] The distribution is treated as a dividend paid during the previous year for purposes of computing undistributed personal holding company income.

*Deficiency Dividend*

Assume that the shareholders did not realize that NPH was a personal holding company, and NPH did not file a Schedule PH or pay the personal holding company tax in 2004. Several years later, the IRS determined that NPH had been a personal holding company and calculated a $6,300 personal holding company tax deficiency. Immediately after the determination, NPH paid a $42,003 deficiency dividend (which the recipient shareholders included in gross income). This dividend retroactively reduced its 2004 undistributed personal holding company income to zero and eliminated the personal holding company tax deficiency.[33]

We have now concluded our discussion of the issues faced by shareholders who must contend with the troublesome double tax on corporate distributions as well as the potential penalty taxes on undistributed earnings. In the next section, we turn to the topic of partnership distributions. As you will see, the Subchapter K rules governing distributions of partnership earnings are much simpler than their counterparts in Subchapter C.

# PARTNERSHIP DISTRIBUTIONS

In the partnership context, the decision to either reinvest earnings in the business or distribute them to the partners has no effect on the taxation of those earnings. In either case, the earnings are taxed only once at the partner level. Partnerships certainly are under pressure to

[31] Section 563 provides that dividends paid within 2.5 months after the close of a taxable year may be considered paid during that year for purposes of both the accumulated earnings tax and the personal holding company tax.

[32] Section 547.

[33] A deficiency dividend does not abolish interest and penalties computed with respect to the personal holding company tax deficiency.

distribute enough cash so that the partners have the wherewithal to pay the tax on their share of income, but partnerships are under no pressure from the tax law to distribute earnings.

Each partner's share of earnings is credited to the partner's capital account, and any distribution of those earnings is charged against the capital account. Partnership distributions can be classified as either current or liquidating distributions. A **current distribution** decreases a partner's capital account *but does not* extinguish the partner's equity interest in the partnership. A **liquidating distribution** decreases the partner's capital account to zero and extinguishes the partner's equity interest. This chapter addresses the tax consequences of current distributions; Chapter 12 addresses the tax consequences of liquidating distributions.

## Cash Distributions

**Objective 7**
Summarize the tax consequences of partnership cash distributions.

As a general rule, partners do not recognize gain on receipt of a current cash distribution. The distribution is a nontaxable return of investment that simply decreases the partner's outside basis (but not below zero) in the partnership interest.[34] If a cash distribution exceeds outside basis, the partner must recognize the excess as a capital gain.[35] Routine distributions of earnings made throughout the partnership year are taken into account on the last day of the year.[36] The basis decrease for the distributions is made *after* the basis increase for income items but *before* the basis decrease for loss items.[37] These timing and ordering rules minimize the possibility that a cash distribution will result in a gain to the recipient partner.

---

*Nontaxable Cash Distributions*

On January 1, Ms. Warford's basis in her TFT Partnership interest was $15,800. TFT's business was extremely profitable during the first half of the year, so the managing partner authorized a midyear cash distribution. Ms. Warford received her $21,200 share of this distribution on July 1. On December 15, TFT made a second cash distribution, $28,100 of which went to Ms. Warford. Her Schedule K-1 for the year showed that her share of ordinary business income was $60,900. The outside basis in her TFT interest on December 31 is computed as follows.

| | |
|---|---|
| Outside basis on January 1 | $15,800 |
| Increase for share of income | 60,900 |
| Decrease for cash distributions | (49,300) |
| Outside basis on December 31 | $27,400 |

Ms. Warford included her $60,900 share of TFT's income in her taxable income. The cash distributions were nontaxable because they did not exceed her outside basis adjusted for her share of income.

---

*Gain Recognized on Cash Distribution*

On January 1, Mr. Butler's outside basis in his Ingleside LLC interest was $3,400. On August 31, Ingleside made its annual cash distribution to its members. Mr. Butler's distribution was $12,750, and his Schedule K-1 for the year showed that his share of ordinary business income was $9,000. The outside basis in his Ingleside interest on December 31 is computed as follows.

---

[34] Section 733.
[35] Section 731(a)(1).
[36] Reg. 1.731-1(a)(1)(ii).
[37] Reg.1.705-1.

| | |
|---|---:|
| Outside basis on January 1 | $ 3,400 |
| Increase for share of income | 9,000 |
| Decrease for cash distribution | (12,400) |
| Outside basis on December 31 | –0– |

Mr. Butler included his $9,000 share of Ingleside's income in his taxable income. He also included a $350 capital gain, which equaled the excess of his $12,750 cash distribution over his $12,400 outside basis adjusted for his share of income.

## Property Distributions

**Objective 7**
Summarize the tax consequences of partnership property distributions.

When a partnership distributes property to a partner, the capital account maintenance rules require the partnership to record the distribution as if it had sold the property for FMV. The book gain or loss on the constructive sale is allocated among all partners' capital accounts, and the recipient partner's capital account is reduced by the property's FMV. This accounting rule ensures that the economic effect of the property distribution is reflected on the partnership books.

*Accounting for a Property Distribution*

Gerado Partnership distributed Greenacre, a tract of undeveloped land, to Mr. Perez, who has a 20 percent interest in profit and loss. Immediately before the distribution, Gerado had the following balance sheet:

| | Book/Tax Basis |
|---|---:|
| Greenacre | $ 115,000 |
| Other assets | 1,050,000 |
| | $1,165,000 |
| | |
| Liabilities | $ 100,000 |
| Capital:  Mr. Perez | 340,000 |
| Other partners | 725,000 |
| | $1,165,000 |

The partners agreed that Greenacre's FMV is $200,000. For book purposes, Gerado recorded an $85,000 gain on the distribution ($200,000 FMV − $115,000 book basis), which it allocated among the partners according to their profit-sharing ratios. The partnership then decreased Mr. Perez's capital account by $200,000.

| | Mr. Perez (20%) | Other Partners (80%) |
|---|---:|---:|
| Predistribution capital account | $340,000 | $725,000 |
| Book gain on constructive sale | 17,000 | 68,000 |
| FMV of distributed property | (200,000) | |
| Postdistribution capital account | $157,000 | $793,000 |

Gerado's balance sheet after the distribution shows the following.

|  | Book/Tax Basis |
|---|---|
| Other assets | $1,050,000 |
| Liabilities | $ 100,000 |
| Capital: Mr. Perez | 157,000 |
| Other partners | 793,000 |
|  | $1,050,000 |

### Tax Consequences of Property Distributions

Even though a partnership may record a book gain or loss on a property distribution, it *never* recognizes a taxable gain or loss.[38] Moreover, the receipt of a current property distribution is generally nontaxable to the partner.[39] For tax purposes, the property simply transfers from the partnership's balance sheet to the partner's balance sheet. The partnership's inside basis in the property carries over to become the partner's basis, and the partner's outside basis in the partnership interest is reduced by the carryover basis.[40] These general rules reflect the aggregate theory under which the partnership entity is transparent, with no separate identity from its partners.[41]

| | |
|---|---|
| *Tax Consequences of a Property Distribution* | Gerado Partnership did not recognize a taxable gain on the distribution of Greenacre to Mr. Perez. Immediately before the distribution, Mr. Perez's outside basis in his partnership interest was $360,000, which equaled his $340,000 capital account plus his $20,000 share of partnership liabilities. Gerado's $115,000 inside tax basis carried over to become Mr. Perez's basis in Greenacre, and Mr. Perez decreased the outside basis in his interest to $245,000 ($360,000 outside basis − $115,000 carryover basis in Greenacre). Note that after this property transaction, Mr. Perez's outside basis *no longer equals* his capital account balance plus his share of Gerado's liabilities. |

If the partnership's basis in distributed property is more than the recipient partner's outside basis, the recipient's basis in the property is limited to the outside basis.[42] In this case, the partner's outside basis in the partnership interest after the distribution is zero.

| | |
|---|---|
| *Limited Basis in Distributed Property* | Assume that Mr. Perez's outside basis in his Gerado interest immediately before the property distribution was only $100,000. In this case, the partnership's $115,000 basis in Greenacre cannot carry over to Mr. Perez. Instead, Mr. Perez's basis in Greenacre is limited to $100,000, and the outside basis in his partnership interest is decreased to zero. |

---

[38] Section 731(b).

[39] Section 731(a). Distributions of marketable securities or property distributions involving a partner who contributed property to the partnership can result in gain or loss recognition at the partner level. See Sections 731(c), 704(c)(1)(B), and 737.

[40] Sections 732(a)(1) and 733.

[41] If a partnership distributes an inventory item to a partner and the partner disposes of the item within five years, the gain or loss recognized on the disposition is characterized as ordinary gain or loss regardless of the partner's use of the distributed item. Section 735(a)(2).

[42] Section 732(a)(2).

# S CORPORATION DISTRIBUTIONS

**Objective 8**
Determine the tax consequences of S corporation distributions.

Business income earned by an S corporation is taxed only once at the shareholder level. As in the case of partnerships, the extent to which the S corporation reinvests or distributes these earnings is irrelevant. S corporations are under pressure to distribute cash so that shareholders can pay the individual tax on their pro rata share of corporate income. But because S corporations are not subject to either the accumulated earnings tax or the personal holding company tax, they are under no pressure from the tax law to make distributions to their shareholders.

An S corporation's undistributed earnings are reflected in the retained earnings account on the balance sheet. However, these undistributed earnings do not create E&P because they represent income that has already been taxed to the shareholders.[43] Each share of outstanding stock has an identical right to retained earnings, so any distribution of earnings must be pro rata with respect to the stock.[44]

## Distributions of S Corporation Earnings

As a general rule, a distribution from an S corporation is treated as a nontaxable return of investment that decreases the shareholder's stock basis (but not below zero).[45] If a cash distribution exceeds stock basis, the shareholder must recognize the excess as a capital gain.[46] The effect of a cash distribution is determined at the close of the corporation's taxable year, *after* the basis increase for income items but *before* the basis decrease for loss items.[47]

*Nontaxable Cash Distributions*

Pym has been an S corporation since it was formed in 1990. On January 1, Mr. Chuan's basis in his Pym stock was $119,400. On July 1, he received a $150,000 cash distribution from Pym. His pro rata share of income for the year was $169,200. The basis in his Pym stock on December 31 was computed as follows.

| | |
|---|---|
| Stock basis on January 1 | $119,400 |
| Increase for pro rata share of income | 169,200 |
| Decrease for cash distribution | (150,000) |
| Stock basis on December 31 | $138,600 |

Mr. Chuan included his $169,200 share of Pym's income in his taxable income. The cash distribution was nontaxable because it did not exceed his stock basis adjusted for his share of income.

## S Corporations with Accumulated E&P

The general rules governing the distribution of S corporation earnings are identical to the rules governing partnership distributions. A complication arises in the special case of an S corporation with a history as a C corporation. The corporation could have retained earnings (accumulated E&P) from the years that it operated as a taxable entity. A distribution of

[43] Section 1371(c)(1). This rule applies to S corporation taxable years beginning after December 31, 1982.
[44] Reg. 1.1361-1(l)(1).
[45] Section 1368(b)(1).
[46] Section 1368(b)(2).
[47] Reg. 1.1367-1(d) and (f)

these C corporation earnings must be treated as a dividend even if the distribution is made after the conversion to a passthrough entity. When the corporation distributes cash to its shareholders, it must determine to what extent the distribution consists of S corporation earnings (nontaxable return of investment) or accumulated E&P (dividend).

### Accumulated Adjustments Account

Subchapter S contains a favorable ordering rule that allows S corporations to distribute S corporation earnings before any accumulated E&P. To implement this ordering rule, S corporations must keep track of undistributed S corporation earnings in an **accumulated adjustments account (AAA).**[48] When the corporation distributes cash, the distribution is nontaxable to the extent of the AAA. If the distribution exceeds the AAA, the excess is a dividend to the extent of accumulated E&P. If the distribution exceeds both the AAA and accumulated E&P, the excess is not a distribution of earnings at all but a nontaxable return of paid-in capital.[49]

*AAA*

Varney converted from a C corporation to an S corporation effective January 1, 2003. It had $971,000 accumulated E&P on the date of conversion. Varney's taxable income for 2003 was $206,000, and it distributed $165,000 to its shareholders. This entire distribution was paid out of Varney's AAA and was nontaxable to the shareholders. Varney's AAA at the end of the year was computed as follows:

|  | AAA |
| --- | --- |
| Balance on 1/1/03 | –0– |
| Taxable income[50] | $206,000 |
| Distribution | (165,000) |
| Balance on 12/31/03 | $ 41,000 |

*Next Year*

Varney's taxable income for 2004 was $95,000, and it distributed $200,000 to its shareholders. Only $136,000 of the distribution was paid from its AAA. The $64,000 excess distribution came from accumulated E&P.

|  | AAA | Accumulated E&P |
| --- | --- | --- |
| Balance on 1/1/04 | $41,000 | $971,000 |
| Taxable income | 95,000 | |
| Distribution ($200,000 total) | (136,000) | (64,000) |
| Balance on 12/31/04 | –0– | $907,000 |

Accordingly, $136,000 was nontaxable to the shareholders (and reduced their stock basis), and $64,000 was a taxable dividend (with no effect on stock basis).

[48] Schedule M-2, Form 1120S includes an annual reconciliation of the AAA.
[49] Section 1368(c).
[50] According to Section 1368(e)(1)(A), the AAA does not include tax-exempt income or nondeductible expenses related to the tax-exempt income. These items are recorded in an "other adjustments account," which is part of the S corporation's retained earnings. However, an S corporation can distribute these earnings only after it distributes all accumulated E&P. In other words, the "other adjustments account" is treated as paid-in capital.

## Effect of Losses on AAA

In the preceding example, Varney's AAA on December 31, 2004, was zero. Distributions to shareholders do not create a negative AAA. In contrast, if an S corporation operates at a loss for a taxable year, the loss can cause a negative AAA. If the corporation makes distributions during a loss year, they are made from the AAA *before* the account is decreased for the loss.

### Negative AAA

On January 1, 2003, Mitrex, an S corporation with a history as a C corporation, had a $28,900 AAA and $337,000 accumulated E&P. On May 31, it distributed $50,000 cash to its shareholders. Mitrex's business generated a $37,500 loss for 2003. Consequently, only $28,900 of the distribution was nontaxable to the shareholders, and $21,100 was a taxable dividend.

|  | AAA | Accumulated E&P |
| --- | --- | --- |
| Balance on 1/1/03 | $28,900 | $337,000 |
| Distribution ($50,000 total) | (28,900) | (21,100) |
| Loss | (37,500) | |
| Balance on 12/31/03 | $(37,500) | $315,900 |

### Next Year

Mitrex's business generated a $3,900 loss for 2004, and it distributed $5,000 cash to its shareholders. The entire distribution was a taxable dividend.

|  | AAA | Accumulated E&P |
| --- | --- | --- |
| Balance on 1/1/04 | $(37,500) | $315,900 |
| Distribution | | (5,000) |
| Loss | (3,900) | |
| Balance on 12/31/04 | $(41,400) | $310,900 |

### Next Year

Mitrex's taxable income for 2005 was $59,000, and it distributed $20,000 cash to its shareholders. Because the income resulted a positive balance in the AAA, $17,600 of the distribution was nontaxable, and $2,400 was a taxable dividend.

|  | AAA | Accumulated E&P |
| --- | --- | --- |
| Balance on 1/1/05 | $(41,400) | $310,900 |
| Taxable income | 59,000 | |
| Distribution ($20,000 total) | (17,600) | (2,400) |
| Balance on 12/31/05 | –0– | $308,500 |

The purpose of the AAA is to segregate undistributed S corporation earnings from accumulated E&P. If an S corporation has no accumulated E&P (which is the case if it was never a C corporation), it has no need to maintain an AAA.[51] In this case, all distributions of earnings are nontaxable returns of the shareholders' investment.

---

[51] In the case of certain corporate mergers, S corporations must be able to calculate their AAA. Consequently, the instructions to Form 1120S recommend that all S corporations maintain this account.

## S Corporation Earnings Distributed from a C Corporation

At some point in the life of an S corporation, the shareholders can encounter a legal or financial reason to convert to a C corporation. Perhaps they want to increase the number of shareholders to more than 75, or they want to issue preferred stock. On the date of conversion, the corporation could have undistributed earnings on which the shareholders have already paid tax. Subchapter S includes a favorable rule that allows the shareholders to withdraw these earnings as a nontaxable distribution during the one-year period beginning on the date of conversion.[52] The nontaxable distribution, which is limited to the balance in the AAA immediately before the conversion, reduces the shareholders' basis in their stock.[53] If they fail to withdraw their S corporation earnings during this one-year grace period, subsequent distributions will be taxed as dividends under the normal Subchapter C rules.

*AAA at Date of Conversion*

Jenette has been an S corporation for every taxable year since it was formed in 1990. The shareholders have decided to revoke their S election and convert Jenette to a C corporation effective January 1 of next year. They estimate that its undistributed earnings on December 31 (all of which are included in the AAA) will be about $112,000, but Jenette does not have enough cash to distribute these earnings before year-end.

*Last Chance for Nontaxable Distributions*

Assume that Jenette's taxable income for its first year as a C corporation is $489,000 on which it pays $166,260 tax. Therefore, it has $322,740 current E&P ($489,000 taxable income − $166,260 tax). During the year, it distributes $125,000 cash to its shareholders. The actual balance in Jenette's AAA on December 31 of the previous year was $109,240, so $109,240 of the cash distribution is nontaxable; only the $15,760 remainder is a taxable dividend.

On January 1, Jenette shareholders had an aggregate stock basis of $550,000. They must reduce this basis by the $109,240 nontaxable distribution from their C corporation. Their receipt of the taxable dividend has no effect on the stock basis.

*Summary*

The tax treatment of distributions from S corporations to shareholders is summarized in the diagram in Exhibit 8.2. This diagram is comparable to the diagram in Exhibit 8.1 because it depicts the equity section of the corporate balance sheet as a beaker of funds out of which the corporation can make distributions. However, the top layer in the beaker consists of the S corporation's AAA, which represents undistributed earnings on which the shareholders have already paid income tax. If the S corporation has a history as a C corporation, the second layer is accumulated E&P, which the corporation can distribute as taxable dividends. If the corporation has no accumulated E&P, it can dip into the bottom layer in the beaker, which consists of paid-in capital. Distributions out of the top AAA layer or the bottom layer are nontaxable to the extent of the recipient shareholder's basis in the S corporation stock.

## Property Distributions

Because S corporations are passthrough entities, many of the Subchapter S operating rules are identical to the Subchapter K operating rules. However, if Subchapter S is silent as to the tax consequences of a transaction between an S corporation and its shareholders, the

[52] This one-year period is described as the posttermination transition period in Section 1377(b).
[53] Section 1371(e).

**EXHIBIT 8.2**
S Corporation
Shareholder's Equity

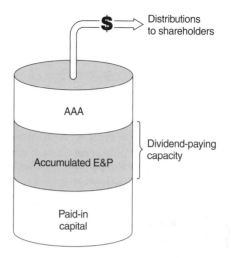

rules of Subchapter C apply to the transaction.[54] Subchapter S does not address the tax consequences of property distributions, so the Subchapter C rules discussed earlier in this chapter apply by default.[55] Namely, if the FMV of distributed property exceeds its tax basis, the corporation must recognize a gain as if the property had been sold for FMV. If the FMV of distributed property is less than its basis, the corporation cannot recognize a loss. In either case, the amount of the distribution to the shareholders and their basis in the property equals the property's FMV.

| *Property Distribution* | O'Dale has been an S corporation since it was formed in 1994. On August 15, it distributed a tract of land to Mr. Daley, the sole shareholder. The land's FMV was $180,000, and its tax basis was $120,000. O'Dale recognized a $60,000 long-term capital gain on the distribution, which it reported as a separately stated item on Mr. Daley's Schedule K-1. He included this gain on his Schedule D, Form 1040. The $180,000 FMV of the land was included in the total amount of O'Dale's distributions for the year. The distributions were nontaxable to Mr. Daley and decreased the basis in his stock. His basis in the distributed land is $180,000. |
|---|---|

## Conclusion

This chapter concludes Part Three of *Advanced Strategies* in which we explored the tax issues pertaining to the routine operation of a business entity. The chapter identified the major issues involved in the decision to reinvest or distribute business earnings. For taxable corporations, the major issues are the double taxation of dividends and the penalty taxes on corporate accumulations. For partnerships, the major issue is the effect of distributions on the partners' capital accounts and outside bases. For S corporations, the issues depend on whether the corporation accumulated earnings as a C corporation. If an S corporation does not have accumulated E&P, the major issue is the effect of distributions on the shareholders' stock basis. If an S corporation has accumulated E&P, the major issue is the extent to which distributions are taxable dividends.

Exhibit 8.3 provides a chart that summarizes the tax issues introduced in Chapter 8 and compares the answers pertaining to corporations with the answers pertaining to partnerships and LLCs.

---

[54] Section 1371(a).

[55] See the text at footnote 5.

**EXHIBIT 8.3 Comparison Chart**

| Tax Issue | Corporation | Partnership/LLC |
|---|---|---|
| Are distributions of earnings from an entity to an owner taxable to the owner? | Yes, for distributions of C corporation E&P. No, for distributions from S corporation AAA. | No. |
| Do dividend distributions affect a shareholder's stock basis? | No. | Inapplicable. |
| Do nontaxable distributions affect an owner's investment basis? | Yes, distributions reduce stock basis (but not below zero). | Yes, distributions reduce outside basis (but not below zero). |
| How is a distribution in excess of investment basis treated? | Excess distribution over stock basis is capital gain. | Excess distribution over outside basis is capital gain. |
| Does an entity recognize gain or loss on a property distribution? | Gain is recognized as if the property were sold for FMV. Loss is not recognized. | No. |
| What is the owner's tax basis in distributed property? | FMV. | Carryover basis (limited to outside basis). |
| Is the entity exposed to penalty tax on accumulated earnings? | Yes, C corporations are exposed to the accumulated earnings tax and the personal holding company tax. S corporations are not exposed. | No. |

**Key Terms**

accumulated adjustments account (AAA) *220*
accumulated E&P *204*
accumulated earnings tax *211*
current distribution *216*

current E&P *204*
deficiency dividend *215*
dividend *204*
earnings and profits (E&P) *204*

liquidating distribution *216*
personal holding company tax *214*
stock dividend *208*

**Questions and Problems for Discussion**

1. Midland Inc. paid $7,400 nondeductible premiums on key-person life insurance policies and incurred $50,600 nondeductible meals and entertainment expense. Should these transactions have any effect on Midland's current E&P?

2. Differentiate between the terms *retained earnings* and *accumulated E&P*.

3. Noland Inc. was formed on January 1 and adopted a calendar year for tax purposes. It distributed $15,000 to its shareholders on August 1. Does this distribution have any effect on the computation of current E&P for the first taxable year?

4. KPL Inc. owns a 40-acre tract of investment land (FMV $200,000 and $283,000 tax basis). Compare the tax consequences to KPL and its shareholders if KPL distributes the land as a dividend or if it sells the land to an unrelated purchaser and distributes the sales proceeds as a dividend.

5. Addams Family Corporation has 100 shares of outstanding stock. Grandpa and Grandma Addams each owns 30 shares, and the four Addams children each owns 10 shares. The six shareholders want to begin transferring corporate ownership to 14 grandchildren. Discuss how a pro rata nontaxable stock dividend could help the Addams family with its financial planning.

6. If an IRS revenue agent suspects that a corporation is accumulating earnings to avoid the shareholder-level tax on dividends, will the agent be more interested in the corporation's income statement or balance sheet? Explain briefly.

7. Why are closely held corporations more vulnerable to the accumulated earnings tax than publicly held corporations?

8. Discuss the nontax reasons that a family might want to create a personal holding company to manage its investments.

9. Explain the logic of the tax rate for both the accumulated earnings tax and the personal holding company tax.

10. Does the rule that a partnership does not recognize gain or loss on the distribution of property reflect the entity theory or the aggregate theory of partnerships? Explain briefly.

11. Explain the purpose of an S corporation's accumulated adjustment account (AAA). Does an S corporation with no history as a C corporation need to maintain an AAA? Explain briefly.

## Application Problems

Assume that the entities in the following problems use the calendar year for federal tax purposes.

1. On January 1, Janus Inc. had $230,000 accumulated E&P. On October 1, it distributed $300,000 cash to its shareholders. Its current E&P was $168,400.
   a. How much of the distribution was a dividend?
   b. Compute accumulated E&P on January 1 of the next year.

2. On January 1, Magruder Inc. had $642,000 accumulated E&P. On June 30, it distributed $1 million cash to its shareholders. Magruder's current E&P was $255,600.
   a. How much of the distribution was a dividend?
   b. Compute accumulated E&P on January 1 of the next year.

3. On January 1, Sansoni Inc. had a $489,000 deficit in accumulated E&P. On May 15, it distributed $140,000 cash to its shareholders. Its current E&P was $90,000.
   a. How much of the distribution was a dividend?
   b. Compute accumulated E&P on January 1 of the next year.

4. Mr. Vojas is the sole shareholder of Vantage Corporation. On January 1, Vantage had $45,000 accumulated E&P, and Mr. Vojas had a $72,000 tax basis in his stock. Vantage had $20,000 current E&P and distributed $100,000 to Mr. Vojas on June 30.
   a. How much income does Mr. Vojas recognize because of the distribution?
   b. What is Mr. Vojas's basis in his stock on January 1 of the next year?
   c. Compute Vantage's accumulated E&P on January 1 of the next year.

5. Mrs. Lake is the sole shareholder of LGL. On January 1, LGL had a $36,900 deficit in accumulated E&P, and Mrs. Lake had a $17,000 tax basis in her stock. LGL had $41,000 current E&P and distributed $50,000 to Mrs. Lake on February 28.
   a. How much income does Mrs. Lake recognize because of the distribution?
   b. What is Mrs. Lake's basis in her stock on January 1 of the next year?
   c. Compute LGL's accumulated E&P on January 1 of the next year.
   d. How would your answers to parts (a), (b), and (c) change if Mrs. Lake's stock basis on January 1 was only $2,900?

6. Shareholder K received a $160,000 distribution from Barrons Inc. According to the Form 1099, $141,000 was a dividend, and $19,000 was a return of capital. Calculate the effect of the distribution on K's taxable income under each of the following assumptions.
   a. Shareholder K is a corporate taxpayer that owns 4 percent of Barron's stock. K's basis in the stock at the beginning of the year was $70,000.

b. Shareholder K is a corporate taxpayer that owns 35 percent of Barron's stock. K's basis in the stock at the beginning of the year was $15,000.

c. Shareholder K is an individual taxpayer who owns 69 percent of Barron's stock. K's basis in the stock at the beginning of the year was zero.

7. For each of the following independent situations, complete the table by computing the dividend payment and accumulated E&P at the beginning of year 2.

| | Accumulated E&P 1/1/ Year 1 | Cash Distribution | Current E&P | Dividend Payment | Accumulated E&P 1/1/ Year 2 |
|---|---|---|---|---|---|
| Situation 1 | $190,000 | $100,000 | $150,000 | 100,000 | 240,000 |
| Situation 2 | 55,000 | 100,000 | 80,000 | 100,000 | 35,000 |
| Situation 3 | (50,000) | 100,000 | 133,700 | 100,000 | (16,300) |
| Situation 4 | (18,000) | 100,000 | (48,000) | 0 | (66,000) |
| Situation 5 | 160,000 | 100,000 | (22,900) | 100,000 | 37,100 |
| Situation 6 | –0– | 100,000 | (72,500) | 0 | (72,500) |

8. Herzig Inc. had $369,100 accumulated E&P on January 1. On May 19, Herzig distributed property ($75,000 FMV and $50,000 basis) to its sole shareholder, Mr. Morton. Corporate taxable income before consideration of the property distribution was $500,000.

   a. Calculate Herzig's current E&P and accumulated E&P on January 1 of the next year.

   b. How much dividend income does Mr. Morton recognize? What is his tax basis in the distributed property?

   c. How would your answers to parts (a) and (b) change if Herzig's tax basis in the distributed property was $90,000?

9. Badger LLC owned 1,230 shares of LJR stock with a basis of $16.50 per share. It received a stock dividend of 615 additional LJR shares. Immediately after the dividend, LJR stock was selling at $33 per share.

   a. Compute Badger's basis in each of its 1,845 LJR shares, assuming that the stock dividend was taxable.

   b. Compute Badger's basis in each of its 1,845 LJR shares, assuming that the stock dividend was nontaxable.

10. On January 1, Honu Inc. had 1 million shares of $10 par value common stock outstanding. On June 30, it issued a pro rata dividend of one share of common stock for every five shares outstanding. Immediately after the issue of the 200,000 new shares, the stock's market price was $65 per share. Determine the effect of this stock dividend on Honu's retained earnings and current E&P.

11. Yosey Inc. declared a $13 per share dividend on its common stock. The shareholders had the option to receive the dividend in cash or in additional shares. Denton LLP owned 5,800 Yosey shares ($31 basis per share) and elected to receive its $75,400 dividend as 1,450 additional shares.

    a. How much dividend income does Denton recognize on receipt of the 1,450 shares?

    b. Compute Denton's basis in its 1,450 additional shares.

12. The revenue agent who audited Energex's tax return decided that the corporation was accumulating income to avoid the shareholder-level tax on dividends and had no business purpose for retaining any more earnings. Energex's taxable income reported on the return was $367,000, and it paid a $35,000 dividend during the year. Compute Energex's accumulated earnings tax under each of the following assumptions.

    a. Accumulated E&P on January 1 was $119,000.

    b. Accumulated E&P on January 1 was $588,200.

13. The four members of the Paserelli family are equal shareholders in EastBay. This year, EastBay's business generated $4,215,000 ordinary gross income, and its portfolio of investment securities generated $5,185,000 dividends and interest. Its ordinary taxable income was $5,590,000, on which it paid $1,900,600 federal income tax. EastBay paid a $1,500,000 dividend for the year.

    *a.* Is EastBay a personal holding company this year?

    *b.* Regardless of your answer to part (*a*), assume that EastBay is a personal holding company, and compute its personal holding company tax.

14. Mrs. Import owns an interest in Leighton, which is a passthrough entity for federal tax purposes. On January 1, her adjusted basis in her interest was $30,700. On July 15, she received a $12,000 cash distribution. She was allocated a $14,200 share of Leighton's ordinary business income and a $2,900 share of long-term capital loss for the year. Compute Mrs. Import's adjusted basis in her interest on January 1 of next year under each of the following assumptions.

    *a.* Leighton is an LLC, and Mrs. Import's share of its liabilities did not change during the year.

    *b.* Leighton is an S corporation.

15. Mr. Kidd's Schedule K-1 from KLN Partnership reported the following information.

    | | |
    |---|---|
    | Ordinary business income | $80,200 |
    | Tax-exempt interest income | 4,100 |
    | Section 1231 loss | 7,600 |
    | Cash distribution | 112,500 |

    His share of KLN's liabilities did not change during the year.

    *a.* What is the tax consequence of the cash distribution to Mr. Kidd if his outside basis on January 1 was $50,000?

    *b.* What is the tax consequence of the cash distribution to Mr. Kidd if his January 1 outside basis was only $10,000?

    *c.* How much of the Section 1231 loss can Mr. Kidd deduct if his January 1 outside basis was $50,000? How much can he deduct if his outside basis was only $10,000?

16. Duran LLC distributed an asset (FMV $35,000 and $22,000 book/tax basis) to Mr. Rehr, who owns a 40 percent interest in capital and profits. Immediately before the distribution, his capital account was $86,000, and the outside basis in his LLC interest was $93,200.

    *a.* How much book and tax gain did Duran report on the distribution?

    *b.* How much income did Mr. Rehr recognize on receipt of the distribution?

    *c.* What is Mr. Rehr's tax basis in the distributed asset?

    *d.* Compute Mr. Rehr's capital account and outside basis immediately after the distribution.

17. Refer to the facts in problem 16. How would your answers change if Mr. Rehr's outside basis in his LLC interest immediately before the distribution was only $15,000?

18. Skylark has been an S corporation since its formation. On January 1, Mrs. Dunbar's basis in her Skylark stock was $24,800. Her Schedule K-1 showed the following allocations.

    | | |
    |---|---|
    | Ordinary business income | $35,400 |
    | Dividend income | 2,000 |
    | Long-term capital gain | 8,690 |
    | Cash distribution | 55,000 |

 *a.* How much income does Mrs. Dunbar recognize on receipt of her cash distribution?

 *b.* Compute Mrs. Dunbar's basis in her stock on January 1 of the next year.

 *c.* How would your answers to parts (*a*) and (*b*) change if Mrs. Dunbar's January 1 basis in her stock was only $6,000?

19. Goldberry converted from a C corporation to an S corporation on January 1, when its accumulated E&P was $248,700. This year, Goldberry earned $230,000 taxable income and distributed $275,000 cash to its shareholders.

 *a.* How much of the distribution was a dividend?

 *b.* Compute Goldberry's accumulated E&P and AAA on January 1 of the next year.

 *c.* How would your answers to parts (*a*) and (*b*) change if Goldberry had distributed only $105,000 cash to its shareholders?

20. Mishra converted from a C corporation to an S corporation on January 1, when its accumulated E&P was $161,000. This year, Mishra generated an $11,000 operating loss and distributed $25,000 cash to its shareholders.

 *a.* How much of the distribution was a dividend?

 *b.* Compute Mishra's accumulated E&P and AAA on January 1 of the next year.

21. Refer to the facts in problem 20. In Mishra's second year as an S corporation, it earned $64,000 taxable income and distributed $60,000 cash to its shareholders.

 *a.* How much of the distribution was a dividend?

 *b.* Compute Mishra's accumulated E&P and AAA on January 1 of the next year.

22. JoJo converted from an S corporation to a C corporation on January 1, when its AAA was $56,000. On March 31, it distributed $70,000 cash to its shareholders. JoJo's taxable income for the year was $500,000, and it paid $170,000 corporate tax.

 *a.* On January 1, Mr. Bjorn had a $65,000 basis in his 50 percent interest in JoJo's stock. What are his tax consequences on receipt of his $35,000 distribution?

 *b.* How would your answer to part (*a*) change if JoJo made no cash distributions during its first year as a C corporation but distributed $70,000 to its shareholders on February 1 of its second year as a C corporation?

## Issue Recognition Problems

Identify the tax issue or issues suggested by the following situations and state each issue in the form of a question.

1. On July 2, Tomburn Inc. exchanged investment land for commercial real estate. Although the transaction was a nontaxable like-kind exchange for tax purposes, it resulted in an $800,000 gain included in book income. Tomburn, which had an accumulated E&P deficit at the beginning of the year, distributed $200,000 cash to its shareholders in September.

2. Ott's accumulated E&P on January 1 was $166,000. It distributed $100,000 cash to its shareholders on May 15. Ms. Schuete sold her 35 percent interest in Ott's stock to Mrs. Mayner on August 1. Ott distributed $200,000 cash to its shareholders on September 15. Its current E&P was $44,000.

3. On January 31, Laslo distributed investment land as a dividend to Ms. Rutherford. Laslo reported the FMV of the land at $250,000. On November 12, Ms. Rutherford sold the land to an unrelated party for $219,000.

4. Toomis declared a nontaxable stock dividend of one share of nonvoting, nonparticipating preferred stock ($1,000 redemption value, 8 percent annual interest) for every 100 shares of voting common stock. Mr. Sigrun, who owned 20,000 shares of common stock (aggregate basis $720,000), received 200 preferred shares.

5. Mr. Bourse is the sole shareholder of Bourse Inc. The corporation owns undeveloped land on which Mr. Bourse wants to build a vacation home. Of course, he plans to finance the construction of the home with his personal funds.

6. Mr. Maroney, who is disruptive and bad-tempered, owns 28 percent of the stock in HPT Corporation. The other shareholders want to get rid of him. For the last four years, HPT has been accumulating cash to finance a redemption of Mr. Maroney's shares. In two more years, it should have enough cash to pay him the FMV of his equity interest.

7. Mrs. Chow has a 15 percent interest in both the capital and profits of Keelo LLC. She wants to substantially reduce her investment in Keelo's business and has requested that it distribute $80,000 cash to reduce her capital account balance from $100,000 to $20,000.

8. Nyerland is an S corporation that was formerly a C corporation. This year, the IRS audited Nyerland's Form 1120 for its last taxable year as a C corporation. As a result of the audit, Nyerland was assessed $14,900 additional corporate tax plus $3,600 interest on the deficiency.

9. Haflen converted from a C corporation to an S corporation. On the date of conversion, it had a $16,000 NOL carryforward from 1998. In its first S corporation taxable year, it generated $52,900 ordinary business income.

10. The 12 members of the Kawasuto family are both the shareholders and the board of directors of KWS, an S corporation. This year, the board authorized KWS to distribute commercial real estate to Lily Kawasuto as a special token of their esteem on the occasion of her 70th birthday.

## Research Problems

1. Two weeks ago, the IRS completed an audit of Porter Inc.'s 2003 tax return. Because the IRS determined that Porter was a personal holding company, it assessed personal holding company tax on $67,500 undistributed personal holding company income. Mr. and Mrs. Porter, the sole shareholders, want the corporation to declare a $67,500 deficiency dividend to eliminate the penalty tax for 2003. However, Porter has only $3,051 cash on hand and no investments that it can liquidate without incurring a loss. Can Porter declare a taxable dividend without any corresponding cash flow to its shareholders? What would be the tax consequences of such a dividend to Mr. and Mr. Porter?

2. Ticonderoga converted from a C corporation to an S corporation on January 1. On the date of conversion, it had only $1,200 accumulated E&P. Its shareholders anticipate that the corporation will generate at least $45,000 investment income and only $80,000 ordinary business income this year. Because Ticonderoga has accumulated E&P, it will have to pay the excess net passive income tax on some portion of its investment income. The shareholders want to eliminate the corporation's accumulated E&P (and exposure to the sting tax) by declaring a dividend, but they do not want to drain the corporation's bank account to do so. Is there a way for Ticonderoga to distribute its E&P without distributing the balance in its AAA?

## Tax Planning Cases

1. Curlew Inc. and Gregson Corporation are equal members in Curlson LLC. Both members have a 35 percent marginal tax rate. Curlew has a $425,000 capital loss carryforward that will expire at the end of this year. The LLC owns a tract of investment land worth $1.2 million. Its book basis and tax basis in the land is $700,000. Curlew wants the LLC to sell the land to generate capital gain, but Gregson does not want it to sell because Gregson does not want to accelerate recognition of the unrealized gain. Curlew has suggested that the LLC distribute the land to Curlew and $1.2 million cash

to Gregson. Curlew can then sell the land and recognize capital gain accordingly. Prior to any distribution, each member's capital account is $2 million, and each member's outside basis (including an equal share of LLC liabilities) is $2.21 million.

a. Discuss the tax consequences to both members if the LLC distributes the land to Curlew, which subsequently sells the land for FMV.

b. Is Gregson giving up its 50 percent economic interest in the unrealized appreciation in the land by agreeing to the distribution? Discuss briefly.

2. Mr. Zinser is the sole shareholder of ZK, a calendar year S corporation with $131,000 accumulated E&P. In every year since ZK converted to an S corporation, Mr. Zinser has withdrawn cash equal to ZK's taxable income. Consequently, ZK's AAA has a zero balance. In February, Mr. Zinser discovered that he had overestimated ZK's taxable income for last year and had withdrawn $11,000 too much cash. Here is his initial calculation of ZK's income for last year.

| | |
|---|---:|
| Gross receipts from sales and services | $790,200 |
| Cost of goods sold | (443,000) |
| Gross income | $347,200 |
| Mr. Zinser's salary | (135,000) |
| Operating expenses | (62,000) |
| Cost recovery deductions: | |
| Section 179 expense | (24,000) |
| MACRS depreciation | (3,200) |
| Ordinary business income | $123,000 |

Mr. Zinser really does not want to recognize a dividend (for the excess cash withdrawals) on his Form 1040. He is not required to file ZK's Form 1120S for several more weeks. Can you suggest a way to solve his tax problem?

## Comprehensive Case for Part Three

Dumas Inc. was organized in 1991 and operated as a calendar year, accrual basis C corporation through 2003. Its shareholders elected to convert Dumas to an S corporation effective January 1, 2004. Here is Dumas's balance sheet and an independent appraisal of the FMV of its assets on the date of conversion.

| | Tax Basis | FMV |
|---|---:|---:|
| Cash | $ 4,400 | $ 4,400 |
| Accounts receivable | 32,000 | 30,000 |
| Merchandise inventory | 84,250 | 95,000 |
| Furniture and fixtures | 51,800 | 51,800 |
| Long-term lease | -0- | 10,000 |
| | $172,450 | $191,200 |
| | | |
| Note payable to bank | $ 15,000 | |
| Shareholders' equity: | | |
| Paid-in capital (1,000 shares) | 10,000 | |
| Retained earnings | 147,450 | |
| | $172,450 | |

For taxable year 2004, Dumas reported $38,200 ordinary business income on page 1 of Form 1120S. It had only two separately stated items: a $21,000 Section 179 expense deduction and a $1,000 charitable contribution. During 2004, Dumas sold all the merchandise inventory reported on its beginning balance sheet for a total retail price of $99,400. It also collected $29,000 of the $32,000 accounts receivables reported on its beginning balance sheet and took a bad debt deduction for the $3,000 uncollectible receivables. Dumas made only one distribution to its shareholders during 2004: a $17,500 cash distribution on December 29.

For taxable year 2005, Dumas reported a $16,900 ordinary loss on page 1, Form 1120S. It had no separately stated items and made no distributions to shareholders during the year.

1. Dwayne Pretzer was one of the two original Dumas shareholders and is employed full time by the corporation. Dwayne had a $5,000 basis in his 500 shares of stock on January 1, 2004.

   a. On December 29, Dwayne received an $8,750 cash distribution from Dumas. What are the tax consequences of the distribution to Dwayne, and what is his basis in his Dumas stock on January 1, 2005?

   b. How much of his 2005 allocated loss from Dumas can Dwayne deduct on his Form 1040, and what is his basis in his Dumas stock on January 1, 2006?

2. Rebecca Wills purchased 125 Dumas shares from another shareholder on May 19, 2004, for $20,000 cash. She is employed full time by the corporation.

   a. On December 29, Rebecca received a $2,188 cash distribution from Dumas. What are the tax consequences of the distribution to Rebecca, and what is her basis in her Dumas stock on January 1, 2005?

   b. How much of her 2005 allocated loss from Dumas can Rebecca deduct on her Form 1040, and what is her basis in her Dumas stock on January 1, 2006?

Suggested Research Aid: Section 1374(d)(5)(B)

# Part **Four**

# Strategies for Business Growth and Expansion

# Multiple-Entity Business Structures

## Learning Objectives

*After reading this chapter, you will be able to:*

1. Explain the limitations on tax benefits for controlled groups of corporations.

2. Determine which corporations are members of an affiliated group.

3. Compute the consolidated taxable income of a consolidated group.

4. Describe the premise of the intercompany transaction accounting rules.

5. Explain the purpose of the basis adjustments to subsidiary stock.

6. Determine the tax consequences of a Section 338(h)(10) election.

7. Explain how QSubs and single-member LLCs can achieve the same tax result as consolidated filing.

Part Four of *Advanced Strategies* concerns the tax issues involved in the growth and expansion of business enterprises. Chapter 9 explores the use of multiple entities to provide the structure for business expansion. Chapter 10 considers the multistate tax implications of geographic expansion, and Chapter 11 concentrates on tax strategies that facilitate business expansion on an international scale.

This chapter begins by considering the nontax reasons that owners use multiple legal entities to operate a business. It continues with a discussion of the tax treatment of controlled groups of corporations and then considers the topic of consolidated corporate tax returns. It analyzes the regulatory rules governing the computation of consolidated taxable income and introduces the consolidated stock basis adjustments. The chapter ends with a discussion of new types of multiple-entity structures that offer an alternative to consolidated corporate groups.

## BUSINESS REASONS FOR MULTIPLE-ENTITY STRUCTURES

Many owners operate their business as a single legal entity for the entire life of the business. Other owners discover that the use of multiple entities can be helpful, or even essential, for business growth and expansion. The transformation of one business entity into a multiple-entity structure can be motivated by legal, political, financial, accounting, or even personal reasons. Here are a few examples.

- An entity plans to embark on a venture that will create new financial risks. It can limit its exposure to the risk by operating the venture through a separate corporate entity or LLC.
- An entity formed under California law plans to expand its business into Oregon. Management believes that the local governments and civic organizations will react more favorably if the expansion is organized as an Oregon corporation with local residents on its board of directors.
- An entity plans to finance its development of a new line of business by issuing stock to a consortium of investors. The entity can avoid the dilution of the original owners' equity by forming a subsidiary corporation to develop the business and then transferring subsidiary stock in exchange for new venture capital.
- An entity plans to diversify into an industry that uses a specialized method of accounting for financial reporting purposes. The entity can avoid complicating its own accounting system by operating the new activity through a separate reporting entity.
- An entity is closely held by nine members of the same family. The younger owners want to introduce a new line of products, but the older owners have no interest in the innovation. The family can solve the problem by creating a separate entity to introduce the new product line with managerial control in the hands of the younger owners.

Owners have considerable flexibility in designing multiple-entity structures to meet the needs of a growing enterprise. As you learned in Chapter 3, owners can contribute cash or property to form new corporations, LLCs, and partnerships at no front-end tax cost. They can combine these new entities to achieve the desired outcome for the enterprise as a whole. Of course, the owners must understand that a transaction undertaken by one entity can create a ripple of tax consequences throughout the structure. They must also understand that multiple-entity structures create their own set of tax planning opportunities and challenges.

## CONTROLLED CORPORATE GROUPS

According to Section 11(b), every corporation computes its tax according to a schedule consisting of four income brackets with rates of 15, 25, 34, and 35 percent. (The corporate rate schedule is printed on the inside of the front cover of the text.) The rate schedule also includes two surtaxes, 5 percent on income between $100,000 and $335,000 ($11,750 maximum) and 3 percent on income between $15 million and $18.333 million ($100,000 maximum). The 5 percent surtax recoups the benefit of the 15 percent and 25 percent rates on the first $75,000 of taxable income. The 3 percent surtax recoups the benefit of the 34 percent rate on the first $10 million of taxable income. If a corporation's taxable income is low enough that it does not pay the maximum amount of both surtaxes, it derives some benefit from the progressive rates.

*Benefit of Progressive Corporate Rates*

Mondale Inc.'s taxable income was $9.831 million. Because this income exceeded $335,000, Mondale paid the maximum 5 percent surtax ($11,750). Consequently, its $3,342,540 regular tax equaled a flat 34 percent of taxable income. Because Mondale's income was less than $15 million, it did not pay any of the 3 percent surtax. If its income had been taxed at a flat 35 percent rate, its regular tax would have been $3,440,850. Therefore, Mondale's tax benefit from the progressive rates was $98,310 ($3,440,850 − $3,342,540).

Without some preventive rule, the owners of a growing business could avoid the higher corporate tax rates by partitioning the business into multiple corporate entities. Although this strategy would not affect business operations, it would reduce the average tax rate on income.

| | |
|---|---|
| *Potential Tax Avoidance through Multiple-Corporate Structure* | The May family operates a restaurant as LeMay Inc. The restaurant generates $100,000 annual income on which the corporation pays $22,250 tax (22.25 percent average rate). The family plans to open a second restaurant that should be as profitable as the first. If LeMay Inc. owns and operates the new restaurant, its tax on the additional $100,000 income will be $39,000 (34 percent + 5 percent surtax). If the second restaurant is organized as a new corporate entity, its tax on $100,000 income would be only $22,250 (22.25 percent average rate). |

**Objective 1**
Explain the limitations on tax benefits for controlled groups of corporations.

Of course, the tax law *does* prevent this tax avoidance strategy. Section 1561(a)(1) provides that members of a **controlled group** of corporations must share the amounts of income in each tax bracket. In other words, only the first $50,000 of the group's aggregate income is taxed at 15 percent, only the next $25,000 of the group's aggregate income is taxed at 25 percent, and so forth. Other tax benefits expressed in dollar amounts are also limited to one amount per controlled group. For instance, a controlled group is entitled to only one of the following.

- A $250,000 minimum accumulated earnings credit for computing the accumulated earnings tax.[1]
- A $40,000 exemption for computing the alternative minimum tax.[2] *AMT*
- An annual dollar limitation on the cost of tangible business personalty that can be expensed under Section 179.[3]
- Gross receipts of $5,000,000 for purposes of qualifying for the cash method of accounting under the gross receipts test in Section 448.[4]

| | |
|---|---|
| *Limitations on Tax Benefits for Controlled Groups* | Assume that the May family had a good nontax reason for organizing its second restaurant as a new corporation named North LeMay Inc. LeMay Inc. and North LeMay Inc. each earns $100,000 taxable income this year. If the two corporations meet the definition of a controlled group, they must share the tax brackets in the corporate tax rate schedule. In this case, their combined tax on the $200,000 income generated by the restaurants is $61,250 [$22,250 + (39 percent × $100,000)], and the average tax rate on the income is 30.63 percent. |

## Types of Controlled Group

A controlled group can be a **brother-sister group:** two or more corporations in which five or fewer shareholders who are individuals, estates, or trusts meet two ownership tests. Under the first test, the shareholders collectively own at least 80 percent of the voting power or value of each corporation's stock. Under the second test, the shareholders collectively own more than 50 percent of the voting power or value based on each shareholder's identical ownership of each corporation's stock.[5] *Identical ownership* refers to a shareholder's lowest ownership percentage in any corporation in the group.

[1] Section 1561(a)(2).

[2] Section 1561(a)(3).

[3] Section 179(d)(6).

[4] Section 448(c)(2).

[5] Section 1563(a)(2). A shareholder's ownership is based on both direct and indirect ownership. The attribution rules for determining indirect stock ownership are provided in Section 1563(e).

| | | | |
|---|---|---|---|
| ***Brother-Sister*** *Group* | | | |

The percentage ownership information for the four unrelated individuals who own the stock in Lennox Inc. and Jacobi Inc. follows.

| | *Lennox* | *Jacobi* | *Identical Ownership* |
|---|---|---|---|
| Mr. Casey | 20% | 40% | 20% |
| Mrs. Falcini | 30 | 5 | 5 |
| Ms. Thorsen | 25 | 35 | 25 |
| Ms. Woo | 25 | 20 | 20 |
| | 100% | 100% | 70% |

The first two columns show that the four shareholders meet the first test (at least 80 percent ownership) for both corporations. The third column shows that they also meet the second test (more than 50 percent based on identical ownership) for both corporations. Because the shareholders meet both tests, Lennox and Jacobi are a brother-sister controlled group.

Now consider the percentage ownership information for a different set of unrelated individuals who own the stock in Marin Inc. and WLT Inc.

| | *Marin* | *WLT* | *Identical Ownership* |
|---|---|---|---|
| Mr. Leigh | 20% | 10% | 10% |
| Mr. Tsu | 55 | 10 | 10 |
| Ms. Weinstein | 25 | 80 | 25 |
| | 100% | 100% | 45% |

The three shareholders meet the first ownership test for both corporations, but they fail the second ownership test. Because the three individuals do not have enough common ownership of Marin and WLT, the two corporations are not a brother-sister controlled group.

A controlled group can also be a **parent-subsidiary group:** a chain of corporations headed by a parent in which at least 80 percent of either the voting power or the value of each subsidiary's stock is owned within the chain.[6]

***Parent-*** *Subsidiary* *Group*

Trenton, a publicly held corporation, owns 100 percent of the stock in Garfield, which owns 91 percent of the stock in HBZ. The three corporations are a parent-subsidiary controlled group.

Finally, a controlled group can be a **combined group:** three or more corporations with one corporation as both the parent of a parent-subsidiary group and a member of a brother-sister group.[7]

***Combined Group***

Mr. and Mrs. Darling own 100 percent of the stock in both DMK and Darling Properties. DMK owns 100 percent of the stock in Dar-Tex. The three corporations are a combined group.

[6] Section 1563(a)(1).
[7] Section 1563(a)(3).

The tax benefit–sharing rules that apply to controlled groups are based on the presumption that each member of the group files a separate Form 1120. As we will discuss in the next section, this presumption does not hold for parent-subsidiary groups that file a consolidated tax return. Because a consolidated Form 1120 reflects only one set of tax benefits, no benefit-sharing rules are needed for the separate corporations participating in the return.

# CONSOLIDATED CORPORATE TAX RETURNS

Section 1501 allows an affiliated group of corporations to file a consolidated income tax return for the group instead of separate returns for each member. An affiliated group is not required to file a consolidated return but may "exercise its privilege" to do so. However, once it files a consolidated return, it must continue to file on a consolidated basis for all future taxable years in which the group remains in existence.[8] Filing a consolidated return is generally advantageous for the tax reasons identified in this chapter. Consolidated filing is also advantageous because it enables the parent corporation to centralize the tax reporting, payment, and planning processes for the entire group, thereby improving the efficiency of the corporate tax function.

## Affiliated Group

**Objective 2**
Determine which corporations are members of an affiliated group.

An **affiliated group** is a chain of corporations headed by a common parent. The parent must *directly* own at least 80 percent of the stock in one subsidiary. Once this parent-subsidiary core is established, other subsidiaries are included in the affiliated group if at least 80 percent of the subsidiary's stock is *collectively* owned within the group. The stock ownership test for affiliated groups is based on both the total voting power and the total value of the outstanding stock.[9]

*Identifying an Affiliated Group*

Gunner, a publicly held corporation with thousands of shareholders, is the head of a chain of corporations. The following diagram shows each corporation's percentage ownership of the stock in other corporations in the chain.

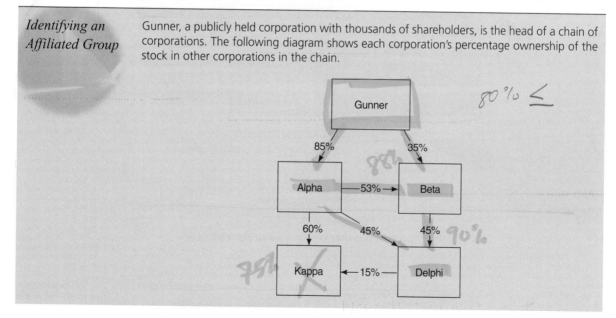

[8] Reg. 1.1502-75(a)(2). An affiliated group can request permission from the IRS to discontinue filing a consolidated return for "good cause," but the IRS rarely grants such permission. It does occasionally grant blanket permission for all groups to discontinue consolidated filing when a change in the tax law has a substantial adverse effect on the tax liabilities of consolidated groups. Reg. 1.1502-75(c)(1).

[9] Section 1504(a). For purposes of this definition, the term *stock* does not include pure preferred stock (nonvoting, nonparticipating, and nonconvertible).

Gunner directly owns 85 percent of Alpha. Therefore, Gunner and Alpha form the core of an affiliated group of which Gunner is the common parent. Beta is included in the group because Gunner and Alpha collectively own 88 percent of Beta. Delphi is also included in the group because Alpha and Beta collectively own 90 percent of Delphi. Kappa is not included in the group because the group collectively owns only 75 percent of Kappa.

The statutory definition of an affiliated group is narrower than the definition of a parent-subsidiary controlled group, so not every parent-subsidiary group can elect to file a consolidated tax return. Moreover, the members of an affiliated group must be **includible corporations,** which the statute defines by listing the types of corporations that are not includible. For instance, tax-exempt corporations, foreign corporations, life insurance companies, and S corporations are not includible corporations.[10]

Assuming that Gunner, Alpha, Beta, and Delphi are all includible corporations, they form an affiliated group with Gunner as its common parent. Note that all three of Gunner's subsidiaries have minority shareholders. The presence of minority shareholders can be troublesome because of their claim on earnings and assets and their right to participate in certain management decisions. Consequently, affiliated groups are often structured to avoid or "squeeze out" minority shareholders. In our discussion of consolidated returns, we assume that all the subsidiaries are 100 percent owned within the consolidated group unless otherwise stated.

## Consolidated Filing for Financial Statement Purposes

According to GAAP, corporations and their controlled subsidiaries are required to file consolidated financial statements.[11] The Securities and Exchange Commission (SEC) has supported this requirement by stating that consolidated statements provide more meaningful financial information than separate company statements do. The general control requirement for consolidated financial reporting is a "majority interest" defined as more than 50 percent of the voting power of a subsidiary's stock. This control requirement is much less stringent than the 80 percent control requirement for consolidated tax return filing. As a result, many corporate groups that prepare consolidated financial statements are not permitted to file a consolidated tax return. Consolidated financial statements usually include the controlling parent's domestic and foreign subsidiaries. Only domestic subsidiaries can be included in the parent's consolidated tax return.

*Consolidated Financial Statements and Tax Returns*

Smiley, a publicly held Delaware corporation, owns the following percentages of stock of its four subsidiaries.

| | |
|---|---|
| Towhee (New York corporation) | 60% |
| Underhill (New Jersey corporation) | 83 |
| Versife (French corporation) | 100 |
| Warford (Florida corporation) | 75 |

Under GAAP, Smiley is required to file consolidated financial statements that include the financial data for all four of its controlled subsidiaries. For tax purposes only Smiley and Underhill constitute an affiliated group. Smiley and Underhill can file a consolidated tax return, but Towhee and Warford must each file a separate Form 1120. Because Versife is a French corporation that does not conduct any business in the United States, it is not required to file a Form 1120.

[10] Section 1504(b).
[11] *SFAS No. 94,* "Consolidation of All Majority-Owned Subsidiaries" (1987).

# Consenting to the Consolidated Return Regulations

In Section 1502, Congress gives the Treasury the authority to write regulations governing the computation of consolidated taxable income and the filing of consolidated tax returns. Because of this statutory delegation of authority, the consolidated return regulations are *legislative* regulations with the full force and effect of law. For the first year in which an affiliated group files a consolidated return, each subsidiary must consent to be included in the consolidation.[12] A subsidiary consents by completing a Form 1122, which is attached to and filed with the group's Form 1120. An affiliated group that files a consolidated return is referred to as a **consolidated group.**

The identity of a consolidated group is determined by reference to the common parent. A group remains in existence for every year in which the common parent directly owns at least one subsidiary, so subsidiaries can join and leave without terminating the group's existence.[13] Subsidiaries that join a group after the first consolidated year are not required to file a Form 1122.

*Consolidated Filing*

Refer back to the example on page 239 in which Gunner is the common parent of an affiliated group of four corporations. The Gunner group filed its first consolidated return for calendar year 2002. Each of the three subsidiaries (Alpha, Beta, and Delphi) filed a Form 1122 with the return.

In 2003, Alpha formed Theta as a new controlled subsidiary, and Beta sold its 45 percent interest in Delphi to an LLC. The fact that Theta joined and Delphi left the group did not affect the Gunner group's existence. Thus, it was required to file a 2003 consolidated tax return.

In 2004, Gunner purchased 100 percent of the stock in Zeta and sold its 85 percent interest in Alpha to a French investment consortium. Because Gunner directly owned an 80 percent controlled subsidiary (Zeta) in 2004, the Gunner group remained in existence, although Alpha, Beta, and Theta left the group that year. Thus, the Gunner group was required to file a 2004 consolidated tax return.

A consolidated tax return must include the common parent's income or loss for the entire taxable year and each subsidiary's income or loss for the portion of the year that it was a member of the group. The subsidiary's income for the portion of the year that it was not a member must be reported on a separate return or the consolidated return of another group.[14]

*Income Included on a Consolidated Tax Return*

Refer back to the previous example in which the Gunner group filed a consolidated return for 2002, 2003, and 2004. In 2002, Alpha, Beta, and Delphi were members of the Gunner group from January 1 through December 31, and the group's 2002 consolidated tax return included the income of each of the four corporations for the entire taxable year.

The Gunner group's 2003 consolidated return included the entire year's income for Gunner, Alpha, Beta, and Theta (which was a member of the group from the day of its incorporation through December 31). The consolidated return included Delphi's income from January 1 through the day it left the group.[15]

The Gunner group's 2004 consolidated return included Gunner's income for the entire taxable year and the income for Alpha, Beta, and Theta from January 1 through the date that they left the group. The return also included Zeta's income from the day after it joined the group through December 31.

---

[12] Reg. 1.1502-75(b).

[13] Reg. 1.1502-75(d).

[14] Reg. 1.1502-76(b)(1)(i).

[15] Reg. 1.1502-76(b)(1)(ii) provides an "end-of-the-day rule" under which subsidiaries are considered to join or leave a consolidated group at the end of the day.

The next section discusses the computation of consolidated taxable income reported on a consolidated return. To avoid the computational complexities that occur when a subsidiary joins or leaves a group during a year, the discussion presumes that all subsidiaries are members of the group for the entire taxable year.

# CONSOLIDATED TAXABLE INCOME

**Objective 3**
Compute the consolidated taxable income of a consolidated group.

A consolidated Form 1120 must be filed on the basis of the common parent's taxable year, which each subsidiary must adopt.[16] In contrast, each corporation in the group maintains its own set of accounting records and generally can adopt its own accounting methods for tax purposes. The members must aggregate their accounting information to compute the group's consolidated taxable income. This process involves four steps.

Step 1.  Each member determines its items of taxable income, gain, deduction, and loss on a separate entity basis.

Step 2.  Each member adjusts its separate items to account for transactions with other members of the consolidated group (intercompany transactions).

Step 3.  Each member excludes those items that must be computed on a consolidated basis (see Step 4) and calculates its net income or loss. The regulations refer to this net income or loss as the member's **separate taxable income.**[17]

Step 4.  The separate taxable incomes of all members are totaled, and those income or deduction items that must be computed on a consolidated basis (consolidated items) are taken into account. These are the more common consolidated items.

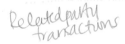

- Capital gain net income
- Section 1231 net loss
- Charitable contributions deduction
- Net operating loss (NOL) deduction
- Dividend-received deduction

The total of the members' separate taxable incomes adjusted for consolidated items equals the group's **consolidated taxable income (CTI).**[18]

The parent corporation reports CTI on the Form 1120 used by every corporate taxpayer. Each line item of income or deduction on page 1 is either the total of the line items included in each member's separate taxable income or the group's consolidated item. The details of the computation of the line items are shown on supporting schedules included with the return.

Before developing a comprehensive example of the CTI computation, let's look more closely at Step 2.

## Intercompany Transactions

An **intercompany transaction** occurs between corporations that are members of the same consolidated group immediately after the transaction.[19] Such transactions include:

---

[16] Reg. 1.1502-76(a)(1).
[17] Reg. 1.1502-12.
[18] Reg. 1.1502-11.
[19] Reg. 1.1502-13(b)(1)(i).

- The performance of services by one member for compensation received from another member
- The rental of tangible property by one member to another
- The license of intangible property by one member to another
- The loan of money by one member to another
- The sale or exchange of property between members

**Objective 4**
Describe the premise of the intercompany transaction accounting rules.

The consolidated return regulations contain a voluminous set of accounting rules for intercompany transactions. Their purpose is to prevent these transactions from distorting the taxable income of the group as a whole. Their fundamental premise is that the effect of an intercompany transaction on CTI should be determined as if the transaction had occurred between the divisions of a single corporate entity. If the effect of the transaction based on each member's separate method of accounting (separate-entity treatment) is inconsistent with this single-entity treatment, one member must adjust its accounting for the transaction to achieve consistency.[20]

For many intercompany transactions, separate-entity treatment and single-entity treatment have the same effect on CTI. In this case, adjustments to the members' accounting methods are unnecessary.

*No Adjustments for Intercompany Transactions*

Stanzak and NGK are members of a calendar year consolidated group. This year, Stanzak and NGK engaged in two intercompany transactions.

- Stanzak performed $100,000 worth of consulting services for NGK. On the basis of their separate accounting methods, Stanzak recorded $100,000 ordinary income from the transaction, and NGK recorded a $100,000 deductible expense.
- NGK leased equipment to Stanzak for $37,500 annual rent. On the basis of their separate accounting methods, NGK recorded $37,500 ordinary income from the transaction, and Stanzak recorded a $37,500 deductible expense.

In both transactions, the ordinary income that one entity recognizes corresponds to the ordinary deduction allowed to the other entity. Therefore, the intercompany transactions on a separate-entity basis have no effect on CTI. If Stanzak and NGK were divisions of a single corporation, the transactions between them would not affect corporate taxable income. Because the separate-entity treatment matches the single-entity treatment, neither Stanzak nor NGK must make an accounting adjustment for the intercompany transactions.[21]

### Matching Rule

If the effect of an intercompany transaction on a separate-entity basis does not match the effect on a single-entity basis, one member must adjust its income, gain, deduction, or loss from the transaction to result in a proper matching.[22] This **matching rule** often affects only the timing of the member's recognition of income, gain, deduction, or loss. Here are three examples of its application.

[20] Reg. 1.1502-13(a).

[21] In contrast, intercompany transactions are generally eliminated in the preparation of consolidated financial statements.

[22] Reg. 1.1502-13(c).

Refer back to the first intercompany transaction described in the previous example in which Stanzak performed $100,000 worth of consulting services for NGK. Assume that NGK was required to capitalize its payment for the services as an intangible asset amortizable over five years ($20,000 per year). The following chart shows the effect of this transaction on CTI on both a separate-entity and a single-entity basis and the adjustment necessary to achieve consistency between the two.

|  | Stanzak | NGK | Effect on CTI |
|---|---|---|---|
| Separate-entity treatment | $100,000 income | $20,000 deduction | $80,000 |
| Single-entity treatment | no income/no deduction | | –0– |
| **Matching rule adjustment** | **(80,000) income** | | |
| Adjusted separate-entity treatment | $ 20,000 income | $20,000 deduction | –0– |

Note that application of the matching rule affects only the timing of Stanzak's recognition of income from the intercompany transaction. In each of the next four years, Stanzak will have a $20,000 positive income adjustment to match NGK's $20,000 amortization deduction.

*Matching Rule: Intercompany Sale of Land*

MKO and Lenski are members of a calendar year consolidated group. In 2002, MKO sold land (basis $361,000) to Lenski for $500,000. According to the matching rule, MKO does not recognize gain on this intercompany sale unless and until Lenski disposes of the land outside of the consolidated group. The following chart shows the effect of MKO's sale on 2002 CTI on both a separate-entity and a single-entity basis and the adjustment necessary to achieve consistency between the two.

|  | MKO | Lenski | Effect on CTI |
|---|---|---|---|
| Separate-entity treatment | $139,000 gain | $500,000 cost basis in land | $139,000 |
| Single-entity treatment | no gain/no basis step-up | | –0– |
| **Matching rule adjustment** | **(139,000) gain** | | |
| Adjusted separate-entity treatment | no gain | | –0– |

In 2005, Lenski sold the land to an unrelated party for $600,000, thereby recognizing a $100,000 gain ($600,000 amount realized – $500,000 cost basis). This disposition of the land outside the consolidated group also triggered recognition of MKO's $139,000 gain deferred on the 2002 intercompany sale. The following chart shows the effect of Lenski's sale on 2005 CTI on both a separate-entity and a single-entity basis and the adjustment necessary to achieve consistency between the two.

|  | MKO | Lenski | Effect on CTI |
|---|---|---|---|
| Separate-entity treatment | no gain | $100,000 gain | $100,000 |
| Single-entity treatment | $239,000 gain | | $239,000 |
| **Matching rule adjustment** | **$139,000 gain** | | |
| Adjusted separate-entity treatment | $139,000 gain | $100,000 gain | $239,000 |

Note again that the application of the matching rule affects only the timing of MKO's gain recognition on the intercompany transaction.

| *Matching Rule: Intercompany Sale of Depreciable Property* | SpeedWork and Westley are members of a calendar year consolidated group. This year, SpeedWork sold an inventory item with a $40,000 basis to Westley for $75,000. Westley placed the item in service as seven-year recovery property and deducted $10,718 MACRS depreciation ($75,000 × 14.29 percent). On a single-entity basis, MACRS depreciation on inventory converted to depreciable property would be $5,716 ($40,000 × 14.29 percent). The following chart shows the effect of the transaction on CTI on both a separate-entity and a single-entity basis and the adjustment necessary to achieve consistency between the two. |
|---|---|

|  | *SpeedWork* | *Westley* | *Effect on CTI* |
|---|---|---|---|
| Separate-entity treatment | $35,000 gain | $10,718 deduction | $24,282 |
| Single-entity treatment | no gain | $5,716 deduction | $ (5,716) |
| **Matching rule adjustment** | **(29,998) gain** | | |
| Adjusted separate-entity treatment | $ 5,002 gain | $10,718 deduction | $ (5,716) |

Because of the matching rule, SpeedWork recognizes only 14.29 percent of its $35,000 gain in the year of the intercompany sale. This amount of gain matches Westley's first-year MACRS deduction on $35,000 of its cost basis in the purchased property. Next year, SpeedWork will have an $8,572 positive income adjustment to match Westley's second-year MACRS deduction on $35,000 basis ($35,000 × 24.49 percent). Over the full recovery period of the property, SpeedWork will recognize its entire $35,000 intercompany gain at the same rate that Westley deducts $35,000 of MACRS depreciation.

In each of the three examples, income or gain realized by one member on an intercompany transaction was recognized in a later taxable year. This deferral of intercompany profit is one of the tax advantages of consolidated filing.

### Intercompany Dividends

The payment of a dividend by one member to another member of a consolidated group is an intercompany transaction that the members must account for on a single-entity basis. As a result, the recipient does not include the **intercompany dividend** in gross income.[23] As we will discuss later in the chapter, the recipient treats an intercompany dividend as a return of investment that decreases its basis in the stock of the corporation that paid the dividend.

## Comprehensive Example

Now that we have presented the basic accounting rules for intercompany transactions, we can develop a comprehensive example of the CTI computation.

| *The Laughlin Group: Consolidated Taxable Income* | The Laughlin consolidated group includes Laughlin, the common parent, and its two subsidiaries, McGlam and Nolan. The group uses a calendar year, and each member uses the accrual method of accounting. The Laughlin group's CTI is computed as follows. |
|---|---|

**Step 1**

Each member determines its items of taxable income, gain, deduction, and loss on a separate-entity basis. The records of the three corporations provide this tax information (in thousands of dollars).

[23] Reg. 1.1502-13(f)(2). If a corporation receives a dividend from another corporation and the recipient and payer are members of an affiliated group that does not file a consolidated return, the recipient is allowed a 100 percent dividends-received deduction per Section 243(a)(3) and (b).

|                               | Laughlin  | McGlam  | Nolan     |
| ----------------------------- | --------- | ------- | --------- |
| Gross receipts                | $27,000   | $3,000  | $19,200   |
| Cost of goods sold            | (14,900)  | –0–     | (10,000)  |
| Gross income from operations  | $12,100   | $3,000  | $ 9,200   |
| Interest income               | 1,600     | –0–     | –0–       |
| Dividend income               | 1,200     | –0–     | 330       |
| Section 1231 gain (loss)      | –0–       | 200     | (470)     |
| Capital gain (loss)           | (300)     | 740     | –0–       |
| Deductible operating expenses | 4,100     | 3,900   | 5,300     |
| MACRS depreciation            | 1,600     | 700     | 840       |
| Interest expense              | 110       | 6       | 750       |
| Charitable contributions      | –0–       | 25      | –0–       |

### Step 2

Each member adjusts its separate items to account for intercompany transactions. The Laughlin group had three intercompany transactions this year.

- Nolan deducted $750,000 interest paid on a long-term loan from Laughlin, and Laughlin included the interest in gross income. Because the separate-entity treatment of the intercompany interest payment matches the single-entity treatment (no effect on taxable income), no adjustment is necessary.
- Nolan paid a $1,000,000 dividend to Laughlin. In accordance with single-entity treatment, Laughlin does not take the intercompany dividend into account. Thus, its *adjusted* dividend income is $200,000 ($1,200,000 dividend income − $1,000,000 intercompany dividend).
- McGlam recognized a $210,000 capital gain on the sale of investment land to Nolan, and Nolan capitalized the cost as its basis in the land. According to the matching rule, McGlam must adjust its gain to zero to reflect the single-entity treatment of the intercompany sale (no effect on taxable income). Thus, McGlam's *adjusted* capital gain is $530,000 ($740,000 capital gain − $210,000 intercompany gain).

### Step 3

Each member calculates its separate taxable income. This calculation excludes each member's consolidated items (Section 1231 and capital gain or loss, charitable contribution deduction, and dividends-received deduction). Here is the calculation (in thousands of dollars).

|                              | Laughlin  | McGlam    | Nolan     |
| ---------------------------- | --------- | --------- | --------- |
| Gross receipts               | $27,000   | $ 3,000   | $19,200   |
| Cost of goods sold           | (14,900)  | –0–       | (10,000)  |
| Gross income from operations | $12,100   | $ 3,000   | $ 9,200   |
| Interest income              | 1,600     | –0–       | –0–       |
| *Adjusted* dividend income   | 200       | –0–       | 330       |
| Gross income                 | $13,900   | $ 3,000   | $ 9,530   |
| Deductible operating expense | (4,100)   | (3,900)   | (5,300)   |
| MACRS depreciation           | (1,600)   | (700)     | (840)     |
| Interest expense             | (110)     | (6)       | (750)     |
| Separate taxable income      | $ 8,090   | $(1,606)  | $ 2,640   |

### Step 4

The separate taxable incomes of the members are totaled, and consolidated items are taken into account.

|  | Laughlin | McGlam | Nolan | Consolidated |
|---|---|---|---|---|
| Separate taxable income | $8,090 | $(1,606) | $2,640 | $9,124 |
| Consolidated items |  |  |  |  |
| Section 1231 gain (loss) | –0– | 200 | (470) | (270) *Ordinary* |
| *Adjusted* capital gain (loss) | (300) | 530 | –0– | 230 |
| Charitable contributions | –0– | 25 | –0– | (25) |
| Dividends-received deduction | NA | NA | NA | (371) |
| Consolidated taxable income | NA | NA | NA | $8,688 |

- The consolidated Section 1231 net loss is deductible as an ordinary loss.
- The consolidated net capital gain is included in taxable income. *To extent subtract losses*
- The consolidated dividends-received deduction equals 70 percent of the $530,000 dividends received by the group ($200,000 Laughlin's adjusted dividend income + $330,000 Nolan's dividend income).

This comprehensive example demonstrates the most important tax advantage of consolidated filing: losses generated by members of the group reduce income generated by other members. Note that McGlam's $1,606,000 separate loss reduced CTI and resulted in an immediate tax benefit to the Laughlin group. If McGlam had reported a net operating loss on a separate return, the NOL would have resulted in an immediate benefit only to the extent that McGlam could carry it back as a deduction against prior year taxable income. The tax benefit would have been postponed to the extent that McGlam had to carry the NOL forward as a deduction against future taxable income. Similarly, Laughlin's $300,000 separate capital loss was completely deductible against McGlam's $530,000 capital gain. If Laughlin had filed a separate tax return, its net capital loss would have been nondeductible and would have resulted in a tax benefit only as a carryback or carryforward against Laughlin's capital gains.

The Laughlin group enjoyed still another advantage from filing a consolidated return. Note that McGlam was the only member that made a charitable contribution this year. The deduction for charitable contributions is limited to 10 percent of corporate taxable income (computed without regard for the deduction).[24] Because McGlam operated at a loss for the year, it could not have deducted this $25,000 charitable contribution on a separate return. McGlam would have carried the nondeductible contribution forward for five years as a future deduction, but because the 10 percent limitation is based on CTI, the Laughlin group was allowed to deduct the entire contribution.

## Consolidated Payment and Filing Requirements

The federal tax liability of a consolidated group is determined on a consolidated basis.[25] In other words, the group's regular income tax is based on CTI, its alternative minimum tax is based on consolidated alternative minimum taxable income, its accumulated earnings tax

---

[24] Section 170(b)(2).
[25] Reg. 1.1502-2.

is based on the group's accumulated taxable income, and so forth. Any tax credits generated by the activities of any member of the group (including the foreign tax credit) are also computed on a consolidated basis.[26]

The common parent acts as the group's agent for purposes of paying federal tax and filing the consolidated Form 1120.[27] Even so, each corporation that was a member of the group during any part of the consolidated return year is liable for the entire federal tax for that year.[28]

| | |
|---|---|
| *Consolidated Corporate Income Tax* | In our comprehensive example, the Laughlin group's CTI was $8,688,000, and its federal income tax before credits was $2,953,920 (CTI × 34 percent). The group had a $14,000 consolidated Section 38 general business credit. During the year, Laughlin made quarterly estimated tax payments totaling $3,000,000. It filed a Form 1120 for the group that showed a $2,939,920 consolidated tax liability and a $60,080 refund due. The Treasury will pay the refund to Laughlin as the common parent. |

# BASIS ADJUSTMENTS TO SUBSIDIARY STOCK

*CTI - consolidated taxable income*

**Objective 5**
Explain the purpose of the basis adjustments to subsidiary stock.

According to the consolidated return regulations, CTI is computed as if each member were a division of a single corporate entity. On the basis of this single-entity approach, each member's income or loss should be included only one time in CTI. The income or loss should not be indirectly included a second time in the form of gain or loss recognized by one member on the disposition of another member's stock. To prevent this double inclusion, the regulations require each member that owns stock in a subsidiary member to adjust its tax basis in the subsidiary's stock.[29] Here are the principal **stock basis adjustments.**

- A member's basis in subsidiary stock is increased or decreased by the stock's proportionate share of the subsidiary's (1) income or loss included in CTI, (2) tax-exempt income, and (3) nondeductible expenses.[30]
- A member's basis in subsidiary stock is decreased by any distributions (including dividends) from the subsidiary with respect to the stock.

These adjustments are made at the close of each consolidated return year or when a member must determine its basis in the stock of a subsidiary member.

| | |
|---|---|
| *Net Positive Basis Adjustments* | On January 1, 2003, Prairie formed Sunset by contributing $50,000 in exchange for 100 percent of Sunset's stock. Prairie is the common parent of a calendar year consolidated group. For 2003, Sunset generated $179,000 taxable income included in the Prairie group's CTI. Sunset had no tax-exempt income or nondeductible expenses and paid no dividends. At year-end, Prairie made the following adjustment to its Sunset stock basis. |

[26] Regs. 1.1502-3 and 1.1502-4.

[27] Reg. 1.1502-77.

[28] Reg. 1.1502-6. A member's contingent liability for any tax deficiency of the group is particularly relevant in the negotiation of a sale of the member to a purchaser outside the group.

[29] Reg. 1.1502-32.

[30] Nondeductible expenses include the subsidiary's allocated share of the group's federal income tax. Reg. 1.1502-32(b)(3)(iii)(A).

| | |
|---|---|
| Initial basis on January 1, 2003 | $ 50,000 |
| Increase for Sunset's income included in CTI | 179,000 |
| Adjusted basis on December 31, 2003 | $229,000 |

**Second Year**

For 2004, Sunset generated $230,000 taxable income included in the Prairie group's CTI. Sunset had no tax-exempt income or nondeductible expenses and paid a $150,000 dividend to Prairie. At year-end, Prairie made the following adjustments to its Sunset stock basis.

| | |
|---|---|
| Adjusted basis on January 1, 2004 | $229,000 |
| Increase for Sunset's income included in CTI | 230,000 |
| Decrease for distributions from Sunset | (150,000) |
| Adjusted basis on December 31, 2004 | $309,000 |

**Third Year**

On January 1, 2005, Prairie sold its Sunset stock to a Florida partnership for $309,000. Because the FMV of Sunset's assets equaled their tax basis, this price equaled the shareholders' equity on Sunset's tax basis balance sheet.

| | *Tax Basis* |
|---|---|
| Accounts receivable | $ 27,000 |
| Inventory | 130,000 |
| Operating assets | 183,000 |
| | $340,000 |
| Liabilities | $ 31,000 |
| Shareholders' equity: | |
| Paid in capital | 50,000 |
| Retained earnings | 259,000 |
| | $340,000 |

The retained earnings resulted from Sunset's accumulation of $259,000 income that was included in CTI. Because Prairie's adjusted basis in the Sunset stock was $309,000, the sale did not generate any gain for inclusion in CTI. If Prairie had not adjusted its initial $50,000 basis in the Sunset stock, the sale would have generated a $259,000 gain that duplicated Sunset's retained earnings. Thus, the stock basis adjustments prevented the double inclusion of $259,000 income in CTI.

Now let's change the facts of the example to demonstrate the effect of negative stock basis adjustments.

**Net Negative Basis Adjustments**

Assume that for its first and second taxable years, Sunset generated $36,000 of operating losses that were included in the Prairie group's 2003 and 2004 CTI. Sunset had no tax-exempt income or nondeductible expenses and paid no dividends in either year. At the end of 2004, Prairie had the following basis in its Sunset stock.

| | |
|---|---|
| Initial basis on January 1, 2003 | $50,000 |
| Decrease for Sunset's losses included in CTI | (36,000) |
| Adjusted basis on December 31, 2004 | $14,000 |

On January 1, 2005, Prairie sold its Sunset stock to a Florida partnership for $14,000. Because the FMV of Sunset's assets equaled their tax basis, this price equaled the shareholders' equity on Sunset's tax basis balance sheet.

| | Tax Basis |
|---|---|
| Accounts receivable | $ 27,000 |
| Inventory | 90,000 |
| Operating assets | 183,000 |
| | $300,000 |
| | |
| Liabilities | $286,000 |
| Shareholders' equity: | |
| Paid in capital | 50,000 |
| Retained earnings | (36,000) |
| | $300,000 |

The negative retained earnings resulted from Sunset's $36,000 of losses included in CTI. Because Prairie's adjusted basis in the stock was $14,000, the sale did not generate any loss for inclusion in CTI. If Prairie had not adjusted its initial $50,000 basis in the Sunset stock, the sale would have generated a $36,000 loss that duplicated Sunset's negative retained earnings. Thus, the stock basis adjustments prevented the double inclusion of $36,000 of losses in CTI.

## Excess Loss Account

Losses generated by a subsidiary member of a consolidated group can be included in the CTI computation even if the losses exceed the basis of the subsidiary's stock in the hands of the other members. In this case, the negative stock basis adjustment creates an **excess loss account** with respect to the subsidiary's stock. An excess loss account is a unique phenomenon in the tax law, a negative tax basis in an asset.[31] Because the regulations sanction this negative basis, current losses generated by group members can be applied *without limit* to offset current income generated by other members. If the owner of subsidiary stock with an excess loss account disposes of the stock outside the group, the owner must recapture the excess loss account as additional gain from the disposition.

| | |
|---|---|
| *Recapture of Excess Loss Account* | On March 1, Primo formed Solaris by contributing $300,000 in exchange for 100 percent of Solaris stock. Primo and Solaris are members of a calendar year consolidated group. For its first taxable year, Solaris generated a $419,000 operating loss included in CTI. At year-end, Primo made the following adjustment to its Solaris stock basis: |

[31] Reg. 1.1502-19(a)(2)(ii).

| | |
|---|---|
| Initial tax basis on March 1 | $ 300,000 |
| Decrease for Solaris loss included in CTI | (419,000) |
| Excess loss account on December 31 | $(119,000) |

On January 1 of the next year, Primo sold its Solaris stock to a Brazilian corporation for $37,500. Primo's gain on sale included in CTI is $156,500 [$37,500 amount realized − $(119,000) negative basis in Solaris stock].

## Section 338(h)(10) Election

**Objective 6**
Determine the tax consequences of a Section 338(h)(10) election.

Positive stock basis adjustments prevent a double inclusion of income in CTI when a subsidiary's stock is sold outside the consolidated group. If the selling price includes payment for any unrealized appreciation in the FMV of the subsidiary's assets, the sale could trigger a gain that must be included in CTI.

*Recognized Gain on Sale of Subsidiary Stock*

Yazoo and WFL are members of a consolidated group. Yazoo owns 100 percent of WFL's stock. According to a recent appraisal, WFL's business (including unrecorded goodwill) is worth $1 million. WFL's balance sheet including the FMV of its separate assets follows.

| | Tax Basis | FMV |
|---|---|---|
| Accounts receivable | $ 50,000 | $ 50,000 |
| Inventory | 250,000 | 300,000 |
| Operating assets | 400,000 | 500,000 |
| Goodwill | –0– | 150,000 |
| | $700,000 | $1,000,000 |
| | | |
| Shareholders' equity: | | |
| Paid in capital | $ 50,000 | |
| Retained earnings | 650,000 | |
| | $700,000 | |

An unrelated corporation has offered to purchase the WFL stock for $1 million cash. Yazoo's basis in the stock (including adjustments) is $700,000. Thus, Yazoo would recognize a $300,000 gain that would be included in CTI.

Yazoo's recognition of the $300,000 gain on sale of WFL stock would have no effect on WFL's balance sheet. The purchasing corporation will take a $1 million cost basis in the WFL stock, but the cost will not be reflected in a step-up in the basis of WFL's assets. Consequently, the purchaser acquires a corporate business with a $300,000 built-in gain in its assets that duplicates the taxable gain on sale of Yazoo's stock.

The tax law includes a very useful provision to prevent the duplication of gain on sale of subsidiary stock by a member of a consolidated group. According to Section 338(h)(10), the member corporation selling the stock and the corporation purchasing the stock can jointly elect to treat the transaction as a sale of the subsidiary's assets. The group's CTI includes the gain recognized from the constructive asset sale. The seller's actual gain on the stock sale is disregarded. The purchaser's cost basis in the stock is allocated to the subsidiary's assets. Therefore, the subsidiary (after its acquisition by the purchaser) has a stepped-up basis (and no built-in gain) in its assets.

*Subsidiary Stock Sale Treated as Asset Sale*

Assume that Yazoo and the purchasing corporation elect to treat the sale of WFL stock as a sale of WFL's assets for $1 million. The constructive asset sale generates a $300,000 gain ($1 million amount realized — $700,000 aggregate tax basis in WFL's assets) for inclusion in CTI. Yazoo's actual $300,000 gain on the stock sale is disregarded. After the acquisition of its stock by the purchasing corporation, WFL will have the following tax basis in its assets.

|  | Tax Basis | FMV |
|---|---|---|
| Accounts receivable | $ 50,000 | $ 50,000 |
| Inventory | 300,000 | 300,000 |
| Operating assets | 500,000 | 500,000 |
| Goodwill | 150,000 | 150,000 |
|  | $1,000,000 | $1,000,000 |

WFL recovers the stepped-up basis in its inventory and operating assets through increases in cost of goods sold and MACRS depreciation. It can amortize the $150,000 capitalized cost of goodwill over 15 years.

In the Yazoo example, the **Section 338(h)(10) election** clearly benefits the purchasing corporation by stepping up the tax basis of WFL's assets. Where is the benefit to Yazoo and the consolidated group? With or without the election, Yazoo's sale of WFL stock increases CTI by $300,000. The answer is that the availability of the election gives Yazoo a stronger negotiating position as a seller. By agreeing to the election, Yazoo can reduce the after-tax cost of the transaction to the purchasing corporation. In return, Yazoo can demand a higher price for the WFL stock, thereby capturing a share of the tax savings from the election.

# ALTERNATIVES TO CONSOLIDATED CORPORATE GROUPS

**Objective 7**
Explain how QSubs and single-member LLCs can achieve the same tax result as consolidated filing.

Consolidated corporate returns have been a feature of the federal tax law since 1918. According to the Senate Finance Committee,

> The principle of taxing as a business unit what in reality is a business unit is sound and equitable and convenient to the taxpayer and the government. The permission to file consolidated returns by affiliated corporations merely recognizes the business entity as distinguished from the legal corporate entity of the business enterprise.[32]

The business community considers consolidated filing a mixed blessing. The single-entity treatment reflected in the consolidated return regulations does offer many tax advantages, and the majority of affiliated groups do file consolidated returns. Nevertheless, these groups must contend with the length and complexity of the regulations, which certainly add to their tax compliance costs. Because of recent developments in the tax law, multiple-entity businesses now have two alternatives to consolidated corporate filing: qualified Subchapter S subsidiaries and single-member LLCs.

## Qualified Subchapter S Subsidiaries

For taxable years beginning before 1997, a corporation could not be an S corporation for federal tax purposes if it had a corporate shareholder. Because of this prohibition, business

---

[32] S. Rpt. No. 617, 65th Cong., 3rd Sess. (1918) and S. Rpt. No. 960, 70th Cong., 1st Sess. (1928).

owners could not use parent-subsidiary groups of S corporations. In 1997, Congress changed the law by creating a new type of entity, a **qualified Subchapter S subsidiary (QSub).** A QSub is a corporation that meets all Subchapter S eligibility requirements *except* that it is wholly owned by an S corporation parent.[33] For federal tax purposes, a QSub is not treated as a separate corporate entity but as an operating division of its parent. The QSub's items of income, gain, deduction, and loss are included in the parent's computation of its items, which flow through to the parent's individual shareholders.

| | |
|---|---|
| *Operating a Multiple-Entity Business through QSubs* | Members of the Munro family are the sole shareholders of M&M, an Oklahoma corporation that manufactures leather goods. M&M is an S corporation for federal tax purposes. Last year, the family expanded its business into Texas and Arkansas by having M&M form a corporate subsidiary in each state. Because M-Tex and M-Ark are QSubs, they are treated as federal tax "nothings." The Form 1120S filed by M&M includes all tax items generated by M-Tex and M-Ark, and the total items (from all three corporations) are allocated to the Munro family for inclusion on their individual Form 1040s. |

**Tax Talk**

An S corporation cannot have a partnership as a shareholder. However, the IRS recently announced that an LLC owned by one individual is allowed to own stock in an S corporation. Because single-member LLCs are disregarded entities for federal tax purposes, the LLC's shares are treated as directly owned by the individual member.

## Single-Member LLCs

The main historic reason for the organization of parent-subsidiary corporate groups was the segregation of financial risk. Although a corporate group represents a single economic enterprise, each corporate member is liable only for its own debts. Today, business owners can achieve the same legal protection by forming LLCs. Many states allow the formation of **single-member LLCs** that have only one owner. Unless the owner elects for the LLC to be classified as a corporation for federal tax purposes, a single-member LLC is a disregarded entity.[34] If the owner is a corporation, the LLC is treated as a division. As a result, the LLC's activities are combined with those of the corporate owner and reported on the owner's Form 1120. This tax treatment achieves a result similar to that of consolidated filing by a parent and subsidiary—without the necessity of consenting to the consolidated return regulations.

| | |
|---|---|
| *Operating a Multiple-Entity Business through a Single-Member LLC* | Rouan Inc. is planning to start a new business with a high degree of risk. It can protect its own assets by organizing the business as a single-member LLC. Although the LLC will be a separate legal and accounting entity, it will be a federal tax "nothing." The LLC's items of income, gain, deduction, and loss will be included in the computation of Rouan's taxable income and federal tax liability. This tax outcome mirrors the outcome that Rouan could have achieved by organizing the new business as a corporate subsidiary and filing a consolidated tax return. |

## Conclusion

Many businesses grow and expand through the use of a multiple-entity organizational structure. If the structure is a controlled corporate group, the group shares certain benefits that the tax law provides for single corporate entities. Affiliated corporate groups can choose to file a consolidated tax return. By doing so, these groups can compute their taxable income and tax liability as if the members were divisions of a single corporation. Consolidated filing has been a dominant characteristic of the business landscape for 80 years, but with the recent advent of QSubs and single-member LLCs, a consolidated corporate tax return is no longer the only game in town.[35]

[33] Section 1361(b)(3). The parent must elect to treat its subsidiary as a QSub.
[34] See the discussion of single-member LLCs under the check-the-box regulations in Chapter 3.
[35] See Lawrence M. Axelrod, "Are Consolidated Returns Obsolete?" *Tax Notes Today* 97, pp. 3–78.

## Key Terms

affiliated group  *239*

brother-sister group  *237*

combined group  *238*

consolidated group  *241*

consolidated taxable
  income (CTI)  *242*

controlled group  *237*

excess loss account  *250*

includible
  corporations  *240*

intercompany
  dividend  *245*

intercompany
  transaction  *242*

matching rule  *243*

parent-subsidiary
  group  *238*

qualified Subchapter S
  subsidiary (QSub)  *253*

Section 338(h)(10)
  election  *252*

separate taxable
  income  *242*

single-member LLC  *253*

stock basis
  adjustments  *248*

## Questions and Problems for Discussion

*[handwritten: 18,333,333 < taxable income  35% flat rate]*

1. The Wu family owns 100 percent of the stock in two corporations: Winston Manufacturing and Winston Development. This year, each corporation's taxable income is approximately $20 million. Will the combined regular tax liability of the two corporations be affected by the fact that they are a brother-sister controlled group?

*[handwritten: Brother sister can't file consolidated]*

2. Why are the tax benefit limitations for controlled groups more of an issue for brother-sister corporations than for parent-subsidiary corporations? *[handwritten: → file consolidated]*

3. Discuss the reasons that affiliated groups are structured to avoid minority shareholders.

4. If a calendar year corporation becomes a member of a consolidated group on July 15, identify two different methods it can use to compute the portion of its annual income included in CTI.

5. Compare and contrast the four-step CTI computation described in the Treasury regulations with the presentation of CTI on the consolidated Form 1120.

6. Culver Inc. owns 90 percent of the stock in ELZ Inc. This year, it received a $100,000 dividend from ELZ. Discuss Culver's tax treatment of this dividend, assuming that: *[handwritten: control 80%]*
   a. Culver and ELZ file a consolidated return. *[handwritten: 100,000 related party eliminated]*
   b. Culver and ELZ file separate returns. *[handwritten: 100% DRD]*

7. Rumpole is the common parent of a consolidated group that includes 20 subsidiaries. This year, eight members generated operating losses included in CTI. Consolidated tax liability for the year was $89 million. To what extent is each member of the group liable for the tax? *[handwritten: Consolidated tax group are personally liable]*

8. Identify any similarities or differences between the stock basis adjustments under the consolidated return regulations and the stock basis adjustments under Subchapter S.

9. Nordlund owns 100 percent of the stock in Orion, and the two corporations file a consolidated tax return. Nordlund wants to expand into another state by forming an LLC. However, that particular state does not permit single-member LLCs. Can you suggest a solution to Nordlund's problem?

*[handwritten: Increased  ← Decreased]*
*[handwritten: -pro rata share  -deductible  taxable income  nondeductible  tax exempt income  expenses  losses]*
*[handwritten: excess loss account        no negative basis]*

## Application Problems

Unless otherwise stated, the business entities in the following problems are calendar year taxable corporations.

1. This year, ZRT's taxable income was $163,000, and Gregson's taxable income was $219,000.
   a. Assuming that ZRT and Gregson are not a controlled group, compute each corporation's regular tax.
   b. Assuming that ZRT and Gregson are a controlled group, compute their combined regular tax. *[handwritten: flat 34%]*

2. Four unrelated individuals collectively own 100 percent of the stock in Acme and Sigma. Their ownership percentages follow.

| | Acme | Sigma |
|---|---|---|
| Ms. Moses | 50% | 25% |
| Mr. Nero | 32 | 5 |
| Mrs. Oberlane | 8 | 50 |
| Ms. Pratt | 10 | 20 |
| | 100% | 100% |

*48% not B-S*

a. Are Acme and Sigma a brother-sister controlled group?

*yes 58% to* b. Would your answer change if Mrs. Rodman purchased the Acme and Sigma stock owned by Mr. Nero and Ms. Pratt?

*B/*

3. Three unrelated individuals collectively own 100 percent of the stock in Lucas, Marvel, and NDKY. These are their ownership percentages.

*2 or more corps where 5 or few shareholders pass two test*

| | Lucas | Marvel | NDKY |
|---|---|---|---|
| Mr. Tenorio | 35% | 80% | 5% |
| Ms. Reece | 10 | 10 | 65 |
| Ms. Tarver | 55 | 10 | 30 |
| | 100% | 100% | 100% |

*brother sister*
*– 80% controlling given corp*
*– 50% least ownership*

a. Are Lucas, Marvel, and NDKY a brother-sister controlled group? *no 80%✓ 50%✗*

b. Are any two of the corporations a brother-sister controlled group? *Lucas, Marvel*

4. Mr. Perez, Mr. Bertog, and Mrs. Bertog own 33.3 percent of the stock in PBB and 33.3 percent of the stock in Breeley. PBB owns 100 percent of the stock in PB Tech, and Breeley owns 100 percent of the stock in WestBree. How many controlled groups are included in this group of corporations?

5. Identify any affiliated groups included in the following chain of domestic taxable corporations: *80% chain*

*P          S*
*CNS → TD > 1 group*
*Sulli, Chloe, Beeson, Chloebee > group 2*

a. Sulli is a publicly held corporation.
b. Sulli owns 100 percent of Chloe.
c. Chloe owns 75 percent of Natchez and 85 percent of Beeson.
d. Chloe and Beeson both own 50 percent of ChloBee.
e. Chloe owns 60 percent and Natchez owns 25 percent of CNS.
f. CNS owns 90 percent of TopDown.

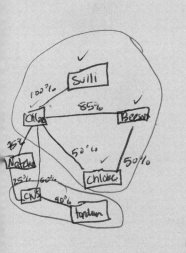

6. Devonshore, a publicly held Pennsylvania corporation, owns the following percentages in the stock of five other corporations.

*book tax*

| | | |
|---|---|---|
| Gosset (New Jersey corporation) | 100% ✓ | ✓ |
| HPV (Delaware corporation) | 75% ✓ | ✗ |
| Martel (Swiss corporation) | 100% ✓ | ✗ foreign |
| BTPS (Missouri corporation) | 38% ✗ | ✗ |
| Asiago (Texas corporation) | 90% ✓ | ✓ |

*a.* Which corporations must be included in Devonshore's consolidated financial statements?

*b.* Which corporations must be included in Devonshore's consolidated federal tax return?

7. Juliat has filed a separate tax return since it was incorporated in 1988. This year, it purchased 100 percent of the stock in BRW on March 1 and 85 percent of the stock in Penzance on August 1. The taxable income (in thousands of dollars) earned by each corporation during the year follows.

|  | Juliat | BRW | Penzance |
|---|---|---|---|
| January 1–February 28 | $225 | $ 53 | $102 |
| March 1–July 31 | 408 | 221 | 358 |
| August 1–December 31 | 692 | 256 | 400 |

Juliat and its two subsidiaries filed a consolidated tax return this year. On the basis of these data, compute CTI.

8. Puma, Sloan, and TriState are members of a consolidated group. Puma and Sloan use the accrual method of accounting; TriState uses the cash method. The following intercompany transactions occurred this year. In each case, determine the accounting adjustment (if any) that a member must make under the matching rule.

*a.* Sloan sold marketable securities to Puma that it purchased through its broker three years earlier for $93,000. The selling price was $120,000.

*b.* TriState performed management services for Puma and billed it for $25,000 but did not receive payment before year-end. Puma properly accrued its $25,000 liability to TriState as a deductible expense.

*c.* TriState performed services for Sloan pursuant to its incorporation. Sloan paid TriState $8,000 for the services and capitalized the payment as an organization cost. Sloan amortized $1,300 of the cost this year.

*d.* Sloan rented business equipment from Puma and deducted $50,000 accrued rent expense.

9. Beaumont and Bimiji are members of a consolidated group. This year, Beaumont sold tangible property to Bimiji for $75,000. The property was an inventory item with a $50,000 cost basis to Beaumont. Bimiji will use the property in its business.

*a.* Bimiji's first-year depreciation with respect to the property was $15,000 (20 percent × $75,000 depreciable basis). How much ordinary income should Beaumont recognize this year because of the intercompany sale?

*b.* Assume that Bimiji sells the property for $6,000 to an unrelated party in a future consolidated year. The property is fully depreciated (zero basis), so Bimiji recognizes a $6,000 gain. Will Beaumont recognize any income because Bimiji sold the property? Briefly explain your answer.

10. The Catanach consolidated group includes Catanach and its subsidiary, ATX. Both members use the accrual method. The accounting records provide the following information (in thousands of dollars) for this taxable year.

|  | Catanach | ATX |
|---|---|---|
| Gross receipts | $691,000 | $215,000 |
| Cost of goods sold | (378,000) | –0– |
| Gross income from operations | $313,000 | $215,000 |

| | | |
|---|---|---|
| Interest income | 17,000 | –0– |
| Section 1231 gain (loss) | ~~59,000~~ 1,600 | –0– |
| Capital gain (loss) | –0– | (47,400) |
| Deductible operating expenses | 174,500 | 242,700 |
| MACRS depreciation | 22,800 | 6,400 |

Compute CTI, assuming that no intercompany transactions occurred during the year.

11. The Laremy consolidated group includes Laremy, the common parent, Devon (100 percent owned by Laremy), and Largo (85 percent owned by Devon). The three members use the accrual method. The accounting records provide the following information (in thousands of dollars) for this taxable year.

| | Laremy | Devon | Largo | *Consolid* |
|---|---|---|---|---|
| Gross receipts | $102,300 | $65,000 | $21,100 | |
| Cost of goods sold | (74,900) | (38,700) | –0– | |
| Gross income from operations | $ 27,400 ✓ | $26,300 ✓ | $21,100 ✓ | |
| Interest income | –0– | 18 | –0– | |
| Dividend income | ~~100~~ 0 | ~~360~~ 0 | –0– | |
| Section 1231 gain (loss) | –0– | (180) | 265 | |
| Capital gain (loss) | 320 | (900) | –0– | |
| Deductible operating expenses | 13,100 | 30,500 | 6,100 | |
| MACRS depreciation | 3,700 | 12,000 | –0– | |
| Interest expense | 48 | –0– | 73 | |
| Charitable contributions | 500 | 25 | –0– | |

*(handwritten annotations: "Limited to the gain.", "10,552", "(16,182)", "14,927", "#9,297", "Seperate tax line.", "1231 gain 85", "(cap loss 85)", "Contr. 525", "8,772")*

Compute CTI assuming that the only intercompany transactions for the year were (1) payment of a $360,000 dividend by Largo to Devon and (2) payment of a $100,000 dividend by Devon to Laremy.

12. Heuer formed MRH in 1990 and has owned 100 percent of its stock since the formation. This year, the two corporations filed their first consolidated return. Heuer had separate taxable *income* of $933,200. MRH had a separate taxable *loss* of $157,000 and a $267,890 NOL carryforward into the year. On the basis of this information, compute CTI.

13. On January 1, Khombu purchased 100 percent of Kiatta's stock for $100,000, making it a member of the Khombu consolidated group. This year, Kiatta's tax records showed the following.

| | |
|---|---|
| Separate taxable income | $69,200 |
| Tax-exempt interest | 1,800 |
| Nondeductible expenses | 3,350 |
| Dividend paid to Khombu | 40,000 |

*(handwritten left margin:)*
10,000 cash basis in stock
(17,300) 100% of taxable loss
1,400 Capital gain
(5,900) excess loss account ael

Compute Khombu's adjusted basis in its Kiatta stock at the close of the year.

14. On January 1, Oswego contributed $10,000 cash in exchange for 100 percent of Newton's stock, and Oswego and Newton became members of the same consolidated group. This year, Newton generated a $17,300 operating loss and a $1,400 long-term capital gain.

a. How much of Newton's operating loss can be included in the computation of CTI?

b. Compute Oswego's adjusted basis in its Newton stock at the close of the year.

15. Garvon sold its 85 percent interest in Urtanis to an unrelated purchaser for $250,000. Garvon and Urtanis were members of the same consolidated group, and Garvon had a $33,850 excess loss account with respect to its Urtanis stock. Compute Garvon's gain on sale included in CTI.

16. Rylander sold its 100 percent interest in OED stock to Olafson Corporation for $2 million cash. Rylander and OED were members of the Rylander consolidated group. Immediately before the sale, Rylander had a $1,070,000 adjusted basis in its OED stock, and OED had the following balance sheet.

|  | Tax Basis | FMV |
|---|---|---|
| Accounts receivable | $    85,000 | $    85,000 |
| Inventory | 500,000 | 600,000 |
| Operating assets | 715,000 | 1,045,000 |
| Unrecorded goodwill | –0– | 500,000 |
|  | $1,300,000 | $2,230,000 |
| Liabilities | $  230,000 |  |
| Shareholders' equity: |  |  |
| Paid in capital | 100,000 |  |
| Retained earnings | 970,000 |  |
|  | $1,300,000 |  |

a. What is the effect on CTI if Rylander and Olafson do not make a Section 338(h)(10) election with regard to the OED stock sale?
b. What is the effect on CTI if Rylander and Olafson make a Section 338(h)(10) election with regard to the OED stock sale?
c. Describe the tax consequences to OED if Rylander and Olafson make a Section 338(h)(10) election.
d. Compute Olafson's basis in its OED stock with and without a Section 338(h)(10) election.

17. Centralia sold its 100 percent interest in MJC stock to O'Flynn Inc. for $383,000 cash. Centralia and MJC were members of the Centralia consolidated group. Immediately before the sale, Centralia had a $633,000 adjusted basis in its MJC stock, and MJC had the following balance sheet.

|  | Tax Basis | FMV |
|---|---|---|
| Accounts receivable | $  13,000 | $  13,000 |
| Operating assets | 800,000 | 550,000 |
|  | $813,000 | $563,000 |
| Liabilities | $180,000 |  |
| Shareholders' equity: |  |  |
| Paid in capital | 25,000 |  |
| Retained earnings | 608,000 |  |
|  | $813,000 |  |

a. Should O'Flynn agree to make a Section 338(h)(10) election with respect to its purchase of MJC stock? Briefly explain your conclusion.
b. What is the effect of the MJC stock sale on CTI?

18. In which of the following cases is Swehanna eligible to be a QSub for federal tax purposes?

    a. Swehanna is an Illinois corporation. Toulouse, an S corporation, owns 95 percent of its stock, and Mr. Tousend, who is Toulouse's sole shareholder, owns the 5 percent minority interest. *NO, it's not 100% owned by an S Corp.*

    b. Swehanna is a wholly owned Canadian subsidiary of Toulouse, an S corporation. *No, it's not a domesti[c] corp.*

    c. Swehanna is an Alaskan corporation. Toulouse, an S corporation, owns 100 percent of the common stock and 100 percent of the preferred stock in Swehanna. *No:*

    *Cuz has a preferred class of outstanding stock.*

    d. Swehanna is an Alabama corporation. Toulouse, an S corporation, owns 100 percent of its voting and nonvoting common stock. *Yes.*

## Issue Recognition Problems

Identify the tax issue or issues suggested by the following situations, and state each issue in the form of a question.

1. Martell, a New York corporation, owns 100 percent of Brennan, a German corporation. Brennan owns 90 percent of HillTop, a Delaware corporation.

2. TopCo has been the common parent of the TopCo consolidated group since 1990. TopCo was publicly held until three months ago when HighTower, a Pennsylvania corporation, purchased 90 percent of TopCo's stock.

3. In 1998, Kellogg sold investment land (basis $41,000) to Brady for $200,000. Because they were members of the same consolidated group, Kellogg did not recognize gain on the intercompany sale. Brady still owns the land. However, Brady's stock was sold this year, and it left the consolidated group.

4. Marko and Betona are members of the same consolidated group. Three years ago, Marko realized a $300,000 gain on the sale of investment land to Betona, which subdivided and developed the land and will begin selling the subdivided tracts to its customers next year.

5. Grizez filed a tax return as a single corporate entity from 1982 through 2003. Early in 2004, it formed two subsidiaries, and the three corporations filed a 2004 consolidated tax return. Although Grizez was profitable, the two subsidiaries both generated sizable operating losses. Consequently, the 2004 return showed an $840,300 consolidated net operating loss.

6. Last year, Durstan, which was a member of the Benjamin consolidated group, recognized a $475,000 capital loss. As a result of Durstan's loss, the Benjamin group has a $285,000 capital loss carryforward into this year. On June 30, Durstan's stock was sold, and it left the Benjamin group.

7. Micah, the common parent of a consolidated group, owns 100 percent of the stock in Regal, and Regal owns 100 percent of the stock in Waydown. Both subsidiaries have been very profitable but have paid minimal dividends to Micah. Micah is planning to sell its Regal stock to an unrelated purchaser.

8. VeriTech, a member of the Agape consolidated group, is hopelessly insolvent, and its stock is worthless. The Agape group member that owns the VeriTech stock has an $835,000 excess loss account with respect to the stock.

9. Since its incorporation in 1990, Lombardi has been a member of the DFT consolidated group. It has always been profitable and generated more than $15 million separate taxable income included in CTI. Last year, Lombardi's stock was sold, and it left the group. In its first year as a separate corporation, it had $916,000 current E&P and distributed $1.2 million cash to its shareholders.

## Research Problems

1. Four individuals own 100 percent of the stock in Maxfield and Dana. These are the ownership percentages for each individual in each corporation.

|  | Maxfield | Dana |
|---|---|---|
| Mr. Maxfield | 55% | 55% |
| Mrs. Maxfield | 45 | –0– |
| Ms. Lane | –0– | 20 |
| Mr. Aciello | –0– | 25 |
|  | 100% | 100% |

Are Maxfield and Dana a brother-sister controlled group for federal tax purposes?

2. In 1998, Stargaze, an S corporation, contributed $25,000 cash in exchange for 100 percent of the stock in Sherrell, a QSub. Stargaze has received an offer from an unrelated party to purchase Sherrell's stock for $5 million cash. According to its financial records, Sherrell has assets with an aggregate tax basis of $2.35 million but no liabilities. What are the tax consequences to Stargaze if it sells Sherrell's stock?

## Tax Planning Case

Last year, Wehby Corporation, an extremely profitable calendar year taxpayer, diversified into two new lines of business (business A and business Z). Wehby's legal department has strongly advised that the two new businesses should be organized as separate legal entities to protect Wehby's core assets from creditor claims against either business. Business A is already profitable and should generate at least $15 million annual income. Business Z is still in the start-up phase, and Wehby expects it to operate at a substantial loss for several more years. Wehby's financial department has observed that business A is very seasonal with an operating cycle ending in late spring. Consequently, a fiscal year ending June 30 would be a much better fit than a calendar year for financial reporting purposes. Business Z is not seasonal, and a calendar year is appropriate for financial reporting purposes.

Design an organizational structure for Wehby, business A, and business Z that accomplishes these three goals.

1. Wehby is protected from legal liability with respect to both businesses.
2. Business Z's operating losses result in the maximum tax benefit.
3. Business A can adopt a fiscal year ending June 30.

# Chapter **Ten**

# Multistate Business Expansion

### Learning Objectives

*After reading this chapter, you will be able to:*

1. Describe the general form of sales and use tax imposition.

2. Discuss the importance of nexus in determining sales tax collection requirements for out-of-state sellers.

3. Define nexus for the imposition of state income tax on multistate businesses and distinguish between economic and physical presence nexus.

4. Describe the relation between federal and state taxable income and the common adjustments to federal taxable income required in calculating state taxable income.

5. Explain the formula recommended for apportionment of business income across states under the Uniform Division of Income for Tax Purposes Act. Calculate the sales, payroll, and property factors and the apportionment of income for state purposes under alternative weighting systems.

6. Explain the unitary business approach that related corporations may be required to follow in filing state income tax returns.

7. Describe the important tax issues that a business conducting operations over the Internet must address.

8. Describe the objectives of state tax incentive programs and the types of incentives they commonly offer.

The first nine chapters of this text have focused on planning opportunities associated with the U.S. federal tax system. The burden imposed by this system can be substantial, but these are not the only taxes assessed on the business and investment activities of U.S. taxpayers. In this chapter, we discuss the plethora of state and local taxes that could apply to even the smallest business activity. As businesses expand operations into multiple state and local jurisdictions, their tax burdens similarly expand. We describe the conditions under which these taxes are owed and identify planning strategies to reduce state and local tax

**TABLE 10.1**
State and Local Government Tax Collections for 1999 (in millions)

| Type of Tax | Total | State | | Local | |
|---|---|---|---|---|---|
| Property tax | $240,107 | $ 11,654 | (2%) | $228,453 | (72%) |
| General sales tax | 200,627 | 164,378 | (33) | 36,249 | (12) |
| Selective sales taxes[a] | 90,366 | 74,989 | (15) | 15,377 | (5) |
| Individual income tax | 189,309 | 172,764 | (35) | 16,545 | (5.2) |
| Corporate income tax | 33,922 | 30,766 | (6) | 3,157 | (1) |
| License taxes | 16,632 | 15,372 | (3) | 1,260 | (0.4) |
| Death and gift taxes | 7,519 | 7,493 | (1) | 26 | (0.1) |
| Other | 37,295 | 22,527 | (4) | 14,766 | (4.3) |
| Total | $815,777 | $499,943 | (100%) | $315,833 | (100%) |

[a]Includes motor fuel, alcoholic beverages, tobacco products, and public utilities sales taxes.

Source: U.S. Census Bureau, *Statistical Abstract of the United States,* 2002.

burden and to qualify for incentive programs offered by local jurisdictions to encourage desirable business activities. Chapter 11 focuses on the impact of foreign tax systems on U.S. companies that have expanded globally.

Table 10.1 presents data on tax revenue collected by state and local governments in 1999. Note that although sales tax collections represent 49 percent of tax revenue at the state level, property taxes are the most significant source of tax revenue for local jurisdictions. At both levels, the individual income tax is a more significant revenue generator than the corporate income tax. In fact, the corporate income tax accounts for only 6 percent of state tax collections and a mere 1 percent of local tax revenue. Although these data might suggest otherwise, traditional approaches to tax education have focused the discussion of state and local taxation on the mechanics of the corporate income tax.

This chapter begins with a discussion of sales and use taxation, including the transactions to which it applies and the exemption opportunities available to many business transactions. Next it discusses issues related to corporate income taxation including apportionment of the income of multistate businesses. The chapter then describes sales and income tax issues related to the Internet with an update on the status of Congressional actions to limit taxation of e-commerce. A variety of other taxes—property, transfer, licensing, and franchise—assessed at the state and local levels are examined briefly. The chapter concludes with a discussion of the planning opportunities created by state and local tax incentive programs. These programs seek to induce businesses to locate and expand their operations within the locality providing the incentives.

# SALES AND USE TAXATION

## Sales Tax

**Objective 1**
Describe the general form of sales and use tax imposition.

Forty-five states and many county and city governments impose a **sales tax** on purchases of tangible personal property for consumer use or consumption.[1] A few states also impose a sales tax on personal services and intangible assets. The tax is assessed as a percentage of the purchase price of goods or services, with average sales tax rates varying from 3 to 11 percent. Although the tax is typically imposed on the purchaser of goods or services, the seller collects it and is responsible for remitting the tax to the taxing authority. Thus, businesses selling products or services in multiple jurisdictions must determine which sales are

[1] Alaska, Delaware, Montana, New Hampshire, and Oregon do not assess state sales and use tax.

subject to sales tax and how much must be remitted to each taxing jurisdiction. Generally, businesses file sales tax reports and pay required remissions to state and local taxing authorities on a quarterly basis. Businesses should take extra care in complying with these reporting and remission requirements; penalties for failing to do so on a timely basis are often severe and could even jeopardize the future of the business.

**Objective 2**
Discuss the importance of nexus in determining sales tax collection requirements for out-of-state sellers.

The mere sale of a product or service to residents of a particular jurisdiction does not necessarily obligate the seller to collect sales tax. This obligation is enforceable only if the seller has nexus within the jurisdiction. **Nexus** is defined as the degree of contact between a business and a jurisdiction necessary to permit taxation. Each jurisdiction has its own statutory definition of nexus. The courts traditionally have held that some physical presence by the seller is a precondition to establishing sales and use tax jurisdiction over an out-of-state vendor. Physical presence can be established if a company locates retail outlets, employees, or equipment or owns other property in the state. In a recent decision, the U.S. Supreme Court stopped short of endorsing physical presence as a condition of nexus but stated that a vendor whose only connection with customers in a taxing state is by U.S. mail or common carrier cannot be required to collect sales tax.[2] As discussed later in this chapter, nexus issues related to Internet sales activities have generated considerable scrutiny by taxpayers, state taxing authorities, the courts, and Congress.

| *Nexus for Collecting Sales Tax* | Hollywood Looks is a clothing boutique located in Santa Monica, California. It rents retail space in downtown Santa Monica, has 15 employees, buys products from a wholesale distributor, and sells them primarily to customers visiting the store. Hollywood also distributes a mail order catalog. It accepts orders by mail or telephone and ships them to customers via U.S. mail. Hollywood clearly has a physical presence in the jurisdictions of the city of Santa Monica and the state of California. It must collect and remit sales tax on sales made in the store and by catalog anywhere in the state of California. However, Hollywood is not required to collect sales tax on catalog sales to customers outside California. |
| --- | --- |

## Use Tax

Most states with sales tax statutes also impose a complementary **use tax** on goods purchased out of state but brought into the state for use or consumption. Use tax typically applies only when no sales tax has been paid to the jurisdiction in which the goods were purchased. Thus, the goal of the use tax is to thwart consumer efforts to avoid tax in their jurisdiction of residence by purchasing goods in a jurisdiction in which sales tax is not assessed. Such purchases include those made via the Internet or through mail-order catalogs as well as via physical travel across state lines. In reality, however, many such purchases escape taxation. The U.S. Supreme Court has held that out-of-state vendors cannot be required to collect use tax from customers residing in a taxing state.[3] Use tax is generally a self-compliance system, yet few consumers are aware of their responsibilities for reporting and paying it. Most jurisdictions do not aggressively pursue use tax collection on smaller purchases. As the magnitude of unreported use tax increases, however, states are beginning to consider new enforcement strategies. A number of states now ask individual taxpayers to report out-of-state purchases of goods subject to use tax on their individual income tax returns. The tax is then calculated and paid when the individual income tax return is filed. Although still a self-reported amount, this approach informs taxpayers of their liability for use tax.

---

[2] *Quill v. North Dakota*, 112 S. Ct. 1904 (1992).
[3] Ibid.

**Tax Talk**

South Carolina has launched a taxpayer education campaign to inform residents of their responsibilities for use tax, particularly on Internet or mail-order purchases. The state also participates in a program with 11 other southeastern states to exchange information on interstate sales. As a result of this program, South Carolina shoppers who did not pay use tax on out-of-state purchases could receive a bill from the South Carolina Department of Revenue. Currently, the state estimates that unreported use tax in South Carolina exceeds $40 million annually.[4]

Given the implicitly regressive burden of sales and use taxes, many jurisdictions exempt necessities such as food and prescription drugs. However, the nature and scope of such exemptions vary by jurisdiction. Most sales and use tax statutes also apply only to goods purchased by the final consumer. As a result, goods purchased for resale or used in manufacturing products for resale are often exempt from sales and use tax.

To obtain a **reseller exemption** from sales tax, most jurisdictions require that the reseller or manufacturer obtain an exemption certificate or reseller code number. The holder provides the certificate or number to its suppliers of goods when making purchases that are exempt from sales tax. If proof of exemption is not provided, the supplier should refuse to make sales without collecting sales tax. Failure to document the purchaser's qualification for exemption makes the supplier liable for the unpaid tax.

In summary, multistate businesses should consider the following sales and use tax issues:

- Nexus requirements for collection of sales tax for each jurisdiction in which the businesses make consumer sales or provides services

- Establishment of procedures to ensure that the proper amount of tax is collected and that reporting and remission requirements are met for each jurisdiction in which the businesses have nexus for sales tax collection

- Sales tax exemption requirements with the proper documentation for each jurisdiction in which the businesses purchase products for resale or use in manufacturing

- Establishment of procedures to ensure obtaining proof of exemption from every qualifying purchaser for businesses that sell products to manufacturers or resellers

# STATE AND LOCAL INCOME TAXATION

Determining liability for sales tax is only one jurisdictional tax issue affecting multistate businesses. Forty-six states and the District of Columbia currently impose a tax based on a state-defined measure of corporate taxable income.[5] Our discussion of multistate corporate income tax will focus on four main issues.

1. Determination of the state(s) that has jurisdiction to tax a multistate business.

2. Impact of state taxation on federal income tax liability.

3. State-level definitions of taxable income.

4. Income apportionment among the states with jurisdiction to tax a multistate business.

Throughout this discussion, we highlight areas in which planning opportunities exist to maximize after-tax value.[6]

---

[4] "South Carolina Taxpayer Education Seeks Greater Use Tax Compliance," *Journal of Multistate Taxation* 10 (45), July 2000.

[5] Nevada, South Dakota, Washington, and Wyoming are the four exceptions. Although some states call their corporate tax a *franchise tax, business tax,* or *profits tax,* all are based on a measure of taxable income.

[6] Many state income tax issues discussed in this chapter were introduced in Chapter 12 of *Principles.* Students familiar with that text can use this chapter to review issues that it introduced and to identify additional ones to consider. For those students not familiar with *Principles,* the coverage here should be sufficient to introduce the important issues in state taxation.

# State Taxing Jurisdiction

**Objective 3**
Define nexus for the imposition of state income tax on multistate businesses and distinguish between economic and physical presence nexus.

Federal law grants each state the right to levy income tax on all businesses incorporated in it. For nonresident businesses, taxing jurisdiction depends on the level of business activity conducted in the state. Specifically, the business activity must be sufficient to establish nexus in the state. Once nexus has been created, the state can tax that business activity.

What types of activities create nexus for income tax purposes? In general, nexus requires a physical presence within the state; manufacturing, sales, distribution, and administrative facilities would certainly create nexus. However, a temporary physical presence, such as sending company personnel to install or maintain equipment for customers, also creates nexus. Service businesses that send consultants or other service providers to states where their customers are located create nexus. Some states consider the maintenance of a home office by in-state resident personnel to be sufficient presence to create nexus. The definition of nexus varies across states, making the determination complex but also creating opportunities for businesses to avoid state taxation when their presence in the state is insufficient to create nexus.

Federal law provides clear limits on the ability of the states to subject certain transactions to income tax. **Public Law 86-272** prohibits each state from taxing businesses whose only connection with it is the sale of tangible personal property to customers in the state whose orders are filled and shipped outside the state.[7] However, this exemption does not extend to sales of services or intangible property. Several states have taken the aggressive position that the use of intangible assets, such as trademarks or licenses, within a state establishes **economic nexus** in the state. Under this approach, the state has the jurisdiction to tax business activity that has no physical presence in it.[8] As a result, businesses not subject to taxation under the traditional **physical presence nexus** standards may be taxed when the economic nexus standard is applied.

*Economic Nexus versus Physical Presence Nexus*

Conifer Chemicals Inc., a Delaware corporation, has developed a patented process to extract impurities from etching chemicals used in computerized manufacturing. Conifer has licensed the rights to use this process to 20 manufacturers in 15 different states. If Conifer conducts no other business activity in these states, the licensing agreements do not establish physical presence nexus; however, they do establish economic nexus. As a result, Conifer could be subject to income tax reporting and payment requirements in some states in which it licenses its patent but not in others.

Certainly, using the same definition of nexus for income tax purposes and sales tax purposes would greatly simplify compliance with state tax requirements. Unfortunately, such conformity currently does not exist.[9] A business could have sufficient nexus to require the collection and remission of sales tax, but not be subject to income tax reporting requirements. The reverse could also be true, with income tax reporting required when sales tax collection is not. Clearly, professional advice in this practice area is well worth the investment!

[7] 15 U.S.C. 381-384 (1959).

[8] South Carolina was the first state to successfully argue the economic nexus approach in *Geoffrey, Inc. v. South Carolina Tax Commission*, 437 S.E. 2d 13 (1993), cert. denied, 510 U.S. 992 (1993). Since the court decision in *Geoffrey*, other states have adopted the economic presence test for nexus.

[9] Some uncertainty in this area arises because P.L. 86-272 applies to income tax nexus but not sales and use tax nexus. The *Quill* decision (see footnote 2) applies only to sales and use tax; the *Geoffrey* decision (see footnote 8) applies to income tax.

**Objective 4**
Describe the relation between federal and state taxable income and the common adjustments to federal taxable income required in calculating state taxable income.

## Impact of State Taxes on Federal Taxable Income

State and local income taxes incurred in connection with business activities are generally deductible in calculating federal taxable income. For corporate taxpayers, these taxes are considered an ordinary and necessary business expense. For individual taxpayers, state income taxes associated with business activities are deductible in arriving at adjusted gross income, typically on Schedule C of Form 1040. State income taxes paid on wage income are deductible as an individual itemized deduction.

*Deducting State Income Taxes*

Hungate Corporation conducts business in three states—Illinois, Iowa, and Missouri. During the current year, it incurred the following state income taxes.

| | |
|---|---|
| Illinois | $130,000 |
| Iowa | 210,000 |
| Missouri | 180,000 |
| Total | $510,000 |

If Hungate's taxable income before income tax payments is $9 million, its federal taxable income and tax liability is computed as follows:

| | |
|---|---|
| Taxable income before state income tax deduction | $9,000,000 |
| State income tax deduction | (510,000) |
| Federal taxable income | $8,490,000 |
| Federal tax liability at 34% | $2,886,600 |

Hungate's total state and federal income tax liability is $3,396,600 ($510,000 + $2,886,600), producing a combined state and federal tax burden of 37.7 percent ($3,396,600/$9,000,000).

## State Definitions of Taxable Income

Of the 46 states imposing an income tax, each has its own unique statutes defining its tax system. Calculation of tax liability for any particular state should consider its unique requirements; however, some commonalities exist across the state systems. We briefly consider typical differences between federal and state taxable income. Most states calculate state-level taxable income by starting with federal taxable income or federal taxable income before special deductions (net operating loss deduction and dividends-received deduction). Then a series of modifications is made to arrive at state taxable income. Common modifications include the following:

- Adding back the federal deduction for state income taxes, which are typically not deductible at the state level.
- Adding tax-exempt income earned on municipal bonds. Such income is not taxed at the federal level, but is often taxed by the state.[10] Any expenses related to such income that are not deducted for federal purposes are deductible in computing state taxable income.

[10] Some states tax interest on municipal bonds issued by jurisdictions outside the taxing state; others tax all municipal bond interest income regardless of jurisdiction.

- Subtracting interest income earned on federal bonds, which is subject to tax for federal purposes but often not at the state level.
- Adding or subtracting differences due to different depreciation methods required at federal and state levels.

This list is by no means all-inclusive but does illustrate some common differences in calculating state-level taxable income. For planning and compliance purposes, multistate businesses must recognize that each state system is unique and that the result of these calculations—state-level taxable income—varies from state to state.

| *State-Level Taxable Income* | Simmons Corporation is domiciled in Kansas. For 2003, it reported federal taxable income of $650,000. To calculate Kansas taxable income, Simmons made the following modifications: |
|---|---|

| | |
|---|---:|
| Federal taxable income | $650,000 |
| Plus | |
| State and municipal interest income | 8,000 |
| State and local income taxes | 20,000 |
| Less: Interest on U.S. government obligations | (4,000) |
| Kansas taxable income before apportionment | $674,000 |

Note that in this example, state-level taxable income is greater than federal taxable income, which likely increases the company's state income tax burden.

## Apportioning Income of a Multistate Business

**Objective 5**
Explain the formula recommended for apportionment of business income across states under the Uniform Division of Income for Tax Purposes Act. Calculate the sales, payroll, and property factors and the apportionment of income for state purposes under alternative weighting systems.

Once a business has determined which states have nexus to tax its activities and how each taxing state defines taxable income, it must determine the extent of taxation in each state. Nexus permits a state to tax only the income attributable to activities in it. Thus, the overall income of a multistate business must somehow be divided among the states in which it operates. One option for accomplishing this division is to trace the income and deductions associated with each state. However, this approach is problematic in allocating indirect and administrative costs. Some states use this type of tracing (often referred to as allocation) for nonbusiness income. The definition of nonbusiness income varies from state to state but typically includes interest, dividend, rent, and royalty income. In some states, nonbusiness income also includes gains and losses from the sale of business assets; other states include only gains and losses on the sale of investment assets in nonbusiness income but include gains and losses on business assets in business income.[11]

State tax laws typically require the **apportionment** of business income, according to a formula, among states in which the business has nexus. In applying this **apportionment formula,** some states consider only business income and allocate nonbusiness income directly to the state of origin. Other states apportion all income, business and nonbusiness. Allocating and apportioning income across states are two alternative methods of achieving the same goal: dividing the income of a multistate business among the states in which it operates. While allocation may seem intuitively appealing in its attempt to identify the

[11] For example, Kansas includes as nonbusiness income only items that are unusual or infrequent in occurrence, while Illinois includes all interest and dividend income of corporations domiciled there, rents and royalties from property located there, gains and losses on sales of real property located there, and gains and losses on sales of personal property and intangible assets by corporations domiciled in Illinois.

specific income and deductions associated with operations in each state, apportionment requires considerably less record keeping. Allocation of nonbusiness income and apportionment of business income is a popular compromise between these two methods of dividing income.

| *Allocated versus Apportioned Income* | McPherson Corporation is located in Illinois, which allocates nonbusiness income to the state of domicile and apportions business income. It had $1 million of total income during 2004, including $100,000 of nonbusiness income. All of its nonbusiness income is subject to Illinois corporate income tax. The remaining $900,000 of McPherson's income is apportioned among the states in which it conducts business. |
|---|---|

In 1957, a group of state representatives seeking to standardize the apportionment of business income across states created the Uniform Division of Income for Tax Purposes Act (UDITPA) as a model of income apportionment. UDITPA provides apportionment of income by measuring the degree of business activity within a state using three factors: sales, payroll, and property. Each factor is a ratio, defined as follows:

$$\text{Sales factor} = \frac{\text{Sales within the state}}{\text{Total sales}}$$

$$\text{Payroll factor} = \frac{\text{Payroll within the state}}{\text{Total payroll}}$$

$$\text{Property factor} = \frac{\text{Property within the state}}{\text{Total property}}$$

Once each factor has been calculated, the factors are combined to determine the total percentage of taxable income to be reported in the state. The factors are combined using the following formula:

$$\text{Percentage of taxable income reported in the state} = \text{Sales factor} \times \text{Sales weight}$$
$$+ \text{Payroll factor} \times \text{Payroll weight}$$
$$+ \text{Property factor} \times \text{Property weight}$$

UDITPA recommends equal weighting of the three factors, meaning that one-third of the weight is assigned to each. Currently, about 40 percent of the states use equal weighting. However, over 50 percent double weight the sales factor, applying the formula with 50 percent weight on sales and 25 percent weight on both payroll and property factors. Double weighting the sales factor is beneficial to firms with a high level of property and payroll within a state but increases tax liability to firms that sell in the state but have most of their property and payroll outside the state. States generally double-weight the sales factor as an incentive to attract additional investment in the state by multistate businesses. As a more extreme investment incentive, three states apportion income using 100 percent of the sales factor (a single-factor approach rather than a three-factor apportionment) to apportion income.[12] Finally, some states allow taxpayers a choice of apportionment methods. For example, Kansas allows qualifying corporations to choose either an equally weighted three-factor approach or a two-factor apportionment based on sales and property factors.

---

[12] Texas, Nebraska, and Iowa currently use single-factor apportionment.

*Apportioned Income under Alternative Weighting Schemes*

Nolke Inc. has total taxable income of $464,000 computed under Kansas state law. This total includes $10,000 of nonbusiness income taxable in Kansas, the firm's state of domicile. Its $454,000 business income must be apportioned among the states in which it does business. Nolke has calculated the following apportionment factors related to its Kansas activities:[13]

| Sales factor | 35% |
| Payroll factor | 80% |
| Property factor | 50% |

Under equally weighted three-factor apportionment, 55 percent ([35 + 80 +50]/3) of Nolke's apportionable income is taxed in Kansas. Its total taxable income in Kansas would be:

| | |
|---|---|
| Nonbusiness income | $ 10,000 |
| Apportioned business income ($454,000 × 55%) | 249,700 |
| Total Kansas taxable income | $259,700 |

If Nolke qualifies for the optional two-factor apportionment, only 42.5 percent [(35 + 50)/2] of its apportionable income is taxed in Kansas. Its total taxable income in Kansas would then be:

| | |
|---|---|
| Nonbusiness income | $ 10,000 |
| Apportioned business income ($454,000 × 42.5%) | 192,950 |
| Total Kansas taxable income | $202,950 |

Finally, suppose that Nolke conducts business in a state such as Arkansas that double-weights the sales factor. Under this alternative apportionment system (assuming the same factors just presented), 50 percent [(35 +35 + 80 + 50)/4] of Nolke's apportionable income is taxed in Arkansas. Its total taxable income in Arkansas would be:[14]

| | |
|---|---|
| Nonbusiness income | $ 10,000 |
| Apportioned business income ($454,000 × 50%) | 227,000 |
| Total Arkansas taxable income | $237,000 |

Note that Nolke's apportioned state income is lower under the double-weighted sales formula than under the equally weighted three-factor formula because the firm is heavily invested in Arkansas (via its payroll and property factors) and sells products inside and outside the state. Thus, the Arkansas apportionment approach rewards Nolke for this investment by reducing its state income tax burden.

---

[13] For purposes of this example, we do not describe the calculation of these apportionment factors in order to focus on the impact of alternative formula weightings. Details regarding the calculation of the apportionment factors are discussed in the next section with additional examples.

[14] Note that this example ignores any differences that occur in the way Kansas and Arkansas calculate state-level income before apportionment and any differences in the treatment of nonbusiness income.

### Sales Factor

To calculate apportionment factors, we must determine what is considered as sales, payroll, and property. Of course, each state has its own definitions, not necessarily consistent with those of other states. Our discussion here focuses on the most common rules, beginning with the sales factor. The **sales factor** is typically defined as gross sales revenue less returns, allowances, and discounts. Interest, service, and carrying charges incidental to the sale are also included. The sales factor generally includes only sales of inventory or services, but excludes occasional sales of business assets or intangible property.

In determining the numerator of the sales factor for a particular state, most states apply the *ultimate destination concept* that considers the source of each sale to be the point of delivery to the customer. For determining the source of sales, about 50 percent of states have adopted the **throwback rule** that considers the sales source to be the state where the sale originated if the state of destination does not assess an income tax.[15]

The throwback rule frustrates some tax planning opportunities associated with business activity in states with no income tax. As demonstrated in the following example, without throwback, income attributable to sales in states with no income tax escapes taxation, but the throwback rule captures the income on sales in such states and taxes it in the state where the sale originates. Multistate businesses selecting new locations for manufacturing and distribution facilities should investigate whether the states considered have adopted throwback in determining the sales factor.

*Calculating the Sales Factor with and without Throwback*

Bowden Inc. operates in two states. Its production and distribution facilities are located in State A. Sales-related information for both states and in total follows.

|  | State A | State B | Total |
|---|---|---|---|
| Gross sales | $500,000 | $300,000 | $800,000 |
| Returns and allowances | (5,000) | (4,000) | (9,000) |
| Interest charges on accounts receivable | 2,000 | 1,000 | 3,000 |
| Discounts allowed | (3,000) | (5,000) | (8,000) |

The denominator of Bowden's sales factor is $786,000 ($800,000 gross sales − $9,000 returns and allowances + $3,000 interest earned on accounts receivable − $8,000 discounts allowed). Assume that State B is Wyoming with no corporate income tax. Without a throwback rule for State A, income apportioned to Wyoming escapes taxation. To illustrate the impact of the throwback rule on the calculation of the numerator of the sales factor for State A, first assume that State A is Ohio, which does not apply throwback. In this case, Bowden's Ohio sales factor is 62.8 percent [($500,000 − $5,000 + $2,000 − $3,000)/$786,000].

Now assume that State A is Indiana, which applies throwback. As a result, Bowden's Indiana sales factor is 100 percent since all sales are either sourced in Indiana or thrown back to it from a state with no income tax.

To quantify the impact of the throwback rule on overall state apportionment, assume that all of Bowden's payroll and property are located in State A. Both Ohio and Indiana apportion income by double-weighting the sales factor, so Bowden's percentage of income apportioned to each state is calculated as follows:

---

[15] Alabama, Alaska, Arizona, California, Colorado, Idaho, Illinois, Indiana, Kansas, Maine, Massachusetts, Michigan, Mississippi, Missouri, Montana, Nebraska, New Hampshire, New Mexico, North Dakota, Oklahoma, Oregon, Texas, Utah, Vermont, and Wisconsin apply some form of throwback rule in calculating the sales factor.

| State A (Ohio) | $(62.8 + 62.8 + 100 + 100)/4 = 67.3\%$ |
| State A (Indiana) | $(100 + 100 + 100 + 100)/4 = 100\%$ |

Thus, without throwback (i.e., if Bowden's primary operations are in Ohio), 32.7 percent of its income escapes state taxation. However, application of the throwback rule negates this savings, subjecting 100 percent of its income to Indiana state taxation.

Finally, note that if Bowden's distribution operations were in State B, the throwback rule would have no impact since State B sales did not originate in State A. The State A sales factor is 62.8 percent regardless of whether State A is Ohio or Indiana.

## Payroll Factor

Next let's consider measures of payroll cost for purposes of the **payroll factor.** This factor typically includes wages, salary, commissions, and other compensation paid or accrued to employees for personal services but generally excludes payments to independent contractors. Some states also exclude compensation to corporate officers. In the numerator of the payroll factor, compensation for any particular employee is generally sourced to the state in which the employee primarily performs services. If the employee performs services in more than one state, compensation might be sourced to the employee's base of operations, the state from which the services are directed, or to the employee's state of residency, depending on circumstances and state law.

**Calculating the Payroll Factor**

Delancey Corporation, located in Columbia, South Carolina, conducts business in both South Carolina and Georgia. Payroll-related information for both states and in total follows.

|  | South Carolina | Georgia | Total |
| --- | --- | --- | --- |
| Officer compensation | $ 500,000 | –0– | $ 500,000 |
| Other compensation | 1,000,000 | $800,000 | 1,800,000 |
| Total compensation | $1,500,000 | $800,000 | $2,300,000 |

In calculating the payroll factor, Georgia includes all business-related compensation, but South Carolina specifically excludes officer compensation from both the numerator and denominator of the payroll factor. As a result, Delancey's payroll factor for each state is computed as follows.

| South Carolina | $1,000,000/$1,800,000 = 55.6\% |
| Georgia | $800,000/$2,300,000 = 34.8\% |

Note that as a result of the differences in defining the payroll factor for the two states in which Delancey operates, payroll apportionment factors total less than 100 percent.

## Property Factor

The **property factor** is the single largest influence on the apportionment of state income for many businesses. The property factor numerator is the average value of real and tangible personal property a firm owns or rents and uses within the state. This factor includes land, buildings, machinery, inventory, and equipment. The corporation's property is usually valued at its historical cost, plus improvements, without reduction for accumulated depreciation. A few states use net book value or adjusted tax basis. In computing the apportionment factor, value is typically the average of the value at the beginning and the end of the tax year. Many states also include leased or rented property in the property factor at eight times annual rental cost.

## Calculating the Property Factor

Refer to the example involving Delancey Corporation. Property-related information for both states in which Delancey operates and in total follows.

| | South Carolina | | | Georgia | | |
|---|---|---|---|---|---|---|
| | Beginning of Year | End of Year | Average | Beginning of Year | End of Year | Average |
| Land | $ 200,000 | $ 200,000 | $ 200,000 | 0 | 0 | 0 |
| Buildings | 1,000,000 | 1,000,000 | 1,000,000 | 0 | 0 | 0 |
| Equipment | 100,000 | 120,000 | 110,000 | $ 50,000 | $ 60,000 | $ 55,000 |
| Accumulated depreciation | (300,000) | (320,000) | (310,000) | (10,000) | (15,000) | (12,500) |
| Inventory | 400,000 | 350,000 | 375,000 | 150,000 | 200,000 | 175,000 |

Delancey also leases warehouse space in Georgia at an annual rental cost of $75,000.

In calculating the property factor, both Georgia and South Carolina use the average of the gross book value of assets (not reduced by depreciation) at the beginning and the end of the year plus eight times the annual rental cost of leased property. The average gross book value for both states is computed as follows.

| | Total Property in Both States | | |
|---|---|---|---|
| | Beginning of Year | End of Year | Average |
| Land | $ 200,000 | $ 200,000 | $ 200,000 |
| Buildings | 1,000,000 | 1,000,000 | 1,000,000 |
| Equipment | 150,000 | 180,000 | 165,000 |
| Inventory | 550,000 | 550,000 | 550,000 |
| Total | $1,900,000 | $1,930,000 | $1,915,000 |

The denominator of the property factor is calculated as follows.

$1,915,000 + (8 \times $75,000) = $2,515,000$

The numerator of Delancey's property factor in each state is then computed:

South Carolina $200,000 + $1,000,000 + $110,000 + $375,000 = $1,685,000

Georgia $55,000 + $175,000 + (8 \times $75,000) = $ 830,000

Delancey's final property factor for each state is computed as follows.

South Carolina $1,685,000/$2,515,000 = 67%

Georgia $830,000/$2,515,000 = 33%

## State Apportionment Factors—Putting It All Together

Refer to the two previous examples involving Delancey Corporation, in which its payroll and property factors were calculated as:

| | South Carolina | Georgia |
|---|---|---|
| Payroll factors | 55.6% | 34.8% |
| Property factors | 67.0% | 33.0% |

Delancey's net sales apportionment factors in each state are:

|  | South Carolina | Georgia |
|---|---|---|
| Net sales | $5,000,000 | $3,000,000 |
| Sales factors | 62.5% = | 37.5% = |
|  | $5,000,000/$8,000,000 | $3,000,000/$8,000,000 |

In combining its apportionment factors, note that both South Carolina and Georgia double-weight the sales factor. The apportionment formula for each state is:

Percentage of income taxable in South Carolina: 61.9% = (62.5%+62.5%+55.6%+67%)/4

Percentage of income taxable in Georgia: 38.1% = (37.5%+37.5%+34.8%+33%)/4

## State Income Tax Liability

After a firm has apportioned its income to a state using the prescribed system, it can determine its state income tax liability. State income tax rates vary among the states. Some states use progressive income tax rate structures, but most assess income tax at a flat rate from 1 to 10 percent. Final liability might be reduced by state-level tax credits and increased by additional assessments such as state alternative minimum tax.

*State Tax Liability*

Shiprock Inc. conducts business in States A and B. After apportionment, its total income taxable in each state is:

| | |
|---|---|
| State A taxable income | $300,000 |
| State B taxable income | 500,000 |

The income tax in State A is a flat 8 percent rate and in State B is determined using a progressive rate structure of 2 percent for the first $100,000 of a corporation's taxable income and 4 percent for additional income. Shiprock's state tax liability in each jurisdiction and in total is:

| | | |
|---|---|---|
| State A tax | $24,000 | ($300,000 × 8 percent) |
| State B tax | 18,000 | [($100,000 × 2 percent) + ($400,000 × 4 percent)] |
| Total state tax | $42,000 | |

Note that although Shiprock's total income taxable in both states is $800,000, this sum might differ considerably from Shiprock's federal taxable income because of differences in the calculation and the apportionment of income in both states. Assume that Shiprock's federal taxable income before any deduction for state taxes is $785,000. After deducting its $42,000 of state tax liability, Shiprock's federal taxable income is $743,000, and its federal tax liability is $252,620. Its total income tax liability of $294,620 ($42,000 + $252,620) represents a combined tax burden of 37.5 percent.

## State Treatment of Net Operating Losses

If a multistate business incurs a net operating loss in the current year, its NOL is typically apportioned across the states in which the business operates in the same manner in which its net income is apportioned. This process identifies the amount of the loss attributable to operations in each state. After the state-level NOL has been determined, its deductibility against prior or future income is subject to state rules.

| | |
|---|---|
| *Calculating and Using a State NOL* | During 2004, Hosta Inc. incurred a federal NOL of $(1,000,000). After adjustment for state-level differences in the definition of taxable income, a loss of $(950,000) remains to be apportioned between the two states in which Hosta has nexus. Using formulary apportionment as defined in each state, Hosta's loss is apportioned 46 percent to State A and 51 percent to State B.[16] Thus, Hosta's 2004 income tax report in State A shows a net operating loss of $(437,000) and in State B is a net operating loss of $(484,500).<br><br>For federal reporting purposes, assume that Hosta carries back its 2004 net operating loss to 2002, and files a refund claim. The applicable carryback or carryforward rules for States A and B determine when Hosta can use its state NOLs to claim refunds of prior state tax or future NOL deductions against income apportioned into these states. |

## State Income Tax Reporting by Affiliated Corporations

**Objective 6**
Explain the unitary business approach that related corporations may be required to follow in filing state income tax returns.

A final issue on which states also vary considerably is the business unit whose income is measured, apportioned, and subject to state income tax. Many corporations are part of affiliated groups that file consolidated federal income tax returns. Several states allow consolidated state filing; only a few mandate it.[17] State-level consolidated returns usually include only the income of group members that have nexus within the state. In most states, however, separate corporations file separate state tax returns.

A number of states have adopted a unitary approach to state taxation that requires a combined or consolidated state tax return including the results of operations of all related corporations, not just those having nexus within the state.[18] This theory applies when the related corporations are found to be part of a **unitary business** whose operations are integrated and interdependent.

| | |
|---|---|
| *Defining a Unitary Business* | Schmidt Corporation provides security personnel to businesses in six western states. Its operations in each state are conducted through a controlled subsidiary. Each subsidiary reports all income and expenses related to state-specific contracts. Schmidt's management directs subsidiary operations, sets prices, controls personnel hiring, and licenses the Schmidt name to each subsidiary. Because of the subsidiaries' economic dependence on the parent corporation, Schmidt and its six subsidiaries are considered a unitary business. |

Other examples of unitary businesses include corporate groups that conduct manufacturing, distribution, and marketing functions through separate subsidiaries. The use of unitary reporting tends to increase tax liability in high-tax states and negates planning techniques aimed at sheltering income in low-tax states.

[16] If States A and B use different definitions of the three factors or different weighting schemes in combining the factors, total apportionment percentages are unlikely to equal 100 percent.

[17] The following states either require or allow consolidated or combined filing: Alabama, Arkansas, Connecticut, Florida, Georgia, Hawaii, Indiana, Iowa, Kentucky, Massachusetts, Michigan, Missouri, New Mexico, Ohio, Oklahoma, Rhode Island, South Carolina, Vermont, Virginia, and West Virginia.

[18] These states either require or allow unitary filing: Alaska, Arizona, California, Colorado, Idaho, Illinois, Indiana, Kansas, Maine, Minnesota, Montana, Nebraska, New Hampshire, New Mexico, New York, North Dakota, Oregon, and Utah.

*Unitary versus Nonunitary Filing for a Consolidated Group*

Josiah Inc. is the parent corporation of two wholly owned subsidiaries, Tux Corporation and Unit Inc. The three corporations file a consolidated federal income tax return. Josiah and Tux have nexus solely in State A, and Unit has nexus solely in State B. Sales, payroll, and property information for the three corporations follows.

| | Josiah | Tux | Unit | Total |
|---|---|---|---|---|
| Sales | $ 500,000 | $1,000,000 | $1,000,000 | $2,500,000 |
| Payroll | 400,000 | 250,000 | 250,000 | 900,000 |
| Property | 2,000,000 | 500,000 | 1,500,000 | 4,000,000 |

State-level income before apportionment for each corporation and the group as a whole follows.

| | Josiah | Tux | Unit | Total |
|---|---|---|---|---|
| Net income | $100,000 | $300,000 | $400,000 | $800,000 |

If States A and B require each corporation to file separate state income tax returns, each company reports income as follows: Josiah, $100,000 to State A; Tux, $300,000 to State A; and Unit, $400,000 to State B. If State A allows consolidated reporting for group members with activity in State A, a combined return for Josiah and Tux reports $400,000 income to State A. Unit would continue to file a separate return in State B, reporting $400,000 of income.

Now suppose that State A requires unitary reporting and that the three corporations are considered part of a unitary business. In this case, the total group income of $800,000 is apportioned to State A as follows (using an equally weighted three-factor apportionment formula).

Sales factor    ($500,000 + $1,000,000)/$2,500,000 = 60%

Payroll factor    ($400,000 + $250,000)/$900,000 = 72.2%

Property factor  ($2,000,000 + $500,000)/$4,000,000 = 62.5%

The percentage of unitary income apportioned to State A is:

(60% + 72.2% + 62.5%)/3 = 64.9%

The group pays taxes in State A on $519,200 ($800,000 × 64.9 percent) of taxable income. If State B is not a unitary state, Unit reports its $400,000 of separate income there. Thus, the group reports total state income of $919,200 to the two taxing regimes ($519,200 in State A + $400,000 in State B) versus the $800,000 actual income for the three corporations. As a result, $119,200 is double taxed. If the State A tax rate is 10 percent, this double taxation costs the group $11,920 this year.

For a business operating in numerous states, the complexity introduced by unitary reporting requirements in some, but not all, states in which it reports can be bewildering. The corporations included in a unitary business might not be the same corporations filing a consolidated federal income tax return. In particular, states can require foreign subsidiaries that are part of a U.S. parent corporation's unitary business to be included in the unitary state return. (As we discuss in Chapter 11, such subsidiaries are not includible in the federal consolidated tax return.) Although the U.S. Supreme Court has upheld the constitutionality of worldwide unitary reporting requirements,[19] many states now permit a **water's edge election** by which multinational corporate groups confine their unitary state reporting to activities occurring within the border of the United States.

## State Taxation of Partnerships, LLCs, and S Corporations

The partnership form of business is generally treated in the same way for state and federal income tax reporting purposes. Thus, the partnership itself does not pay state income tax, but the partners are responsible for reporting their share of partnership income on their individual state income tax returns. Note that partners must file state income tax returns in each state in which the partnership's business has nexus. Thus, a partner in a multistate business could be required to file a number of state income tax returns on a nonresident basis. To reduce compliance burden, some states allow large partnerships to file on behalf of their nonresident partners. Partnership income is generally apportioned among the states in which the partnership does business using the same formulary apportionment approach applied to corporations.

| | |
|---|---|
| *Partner State Income Tax Reporting of Partnership Income* | Mrs. Jahn is a partner in Condor Partnership, which conducts business in 15 states. In addition to filing an individual state income tax return in her state of residence, she is subject to the reporting and tax payment requirements in each state in which Condor conducts business. Her state of residence might allow her a tax credit for taxes paid in other states, but the burden of filing numerous state tax returns is significant. |

Virtually all states that assess an income tax now have statutes recognizing limited liability companies (LLCs). In most cases, the state income tax treatment of these entities follows the federal income tax treatment chosen by the members. Thus, if the LLC has chosen to be taxed as a partnership for federal tax purposes, it also will be taxed as a partnership for state income tax purposes. A few states automatically tax LLCs as partnerships regardless of their federal income tax treatment.

Most states that impose a corporate income tax have provisions similar to federal law that address the tax treatment of S corporations. In these states, an S corporation files a state information return, and its shareholders report and are taxed on its income. As discussed for partners, S corporation shareholders generally are required to file a state return in each state in which the corporation has nexus. A few states (Louisiana, Michigan, New Hampshire, Tennessee, and Texas) subject S corporations to state corporate income tax.[20] In addition, many states assess franchise tax on partnerships, LLCs, and S corporations.

## Summary of State Income Tax Issues

In summary, multistate businesses should consider the following planning and compliance issues related to state income tax.

- Nexus requirements for payment of income tax in each state in which the businesses make sales or have property or personnel

---

[19] *Container Corporation of America v. Franchise Tax Board*, 103 S. Ct. 2993 (1983).

[20] Some states require state-level elections to be treated as an S corporation for state purposes. In addition, a few states impose additional eligibility requirements. Any new S corporation should determine its state filing status in every state in which it does business.

- State income tax filing requirements, including computation, apportionment, and payment requirements for each state in which the businesses have nexus
- Requirements for consolidated or unitary reporting in each state in which controlled groups of corporations have nexus
- Filing and tax payment requirements in each state in which partnerships, LLCs, and S corporations do business
- The states in which nexus should be avoided, in which throwback is required, and in which a favorable tax environment for expansion is provided when planning operations

# INTERNET TAX ISSUES

**Objective 7**
Describe the important tax issues that a business conducting operations over the Internet must address.

**Tax Talk**
In a policy ruling issued in May 2000, the Texas comptroller's office asserted that digitally downloaded music is subject to Texas sales tax. The ruling concluded that digital products meet the definition of tangible personal property because downloading stores the product on a tangible physical medium.[23] Conversely, recent Iowa legislation specifically exempts such digital products from Iowa sales and use tax.[24]

The growth of commercial activity on the Internet[21] creates unique questions regarding the application of traditional sales and income tax concepts. In addition to online sales to consumers, businesses are engaging in online purchasing, logistics management, software and data transmission, and marketing activities. In what jurisdictions might these value-creating activities be taxed? How can traditional concepts of nexus be applied to e-commerce, or are new concepts required? Although many states are addressing these questions on a case-by-case basis, little consensus has emerged.

With respect to sales tax, the physical presence standard described previously also applies to Internet sales. For example, if the seller has retail locations, warehouses, or service personnel in the same jurisdiction in which it makes sales electronically, it must collect sales tax. However, does the location of a server housing the seller's website constitute a physical presence?

Other difficult issues involve the definition of *tangible personal property* subject to sales tax. Is computer software transmitted electronically rather than on diskette considered tangible personal property? What about digital music or video downloaded from the Internet? Several states have issued conflicting rulings on these issues.

For income tax purposes, the economic nexus concept previously discussed could easily be extended to Internet activity. Although the court decision establishing the economic nexus concept dealt with intangible assets, several jurisdictions have extended this concept to the licensing of computer software.[22]

To avoid both sales and income tax nexus related to Internet sales, many bricks-and-mortar retailers have established separate legal entities (typically affiliated corporations) to conduct Internet sales activities. The courts have generally declined to attribute nexus from one entity to the other so long as all transactions between the affiliated entities are at arm's length, each company has substance, and each is legally distinct. Note that the avoidance of tax collection responsibility by Internet retailers does not negate the customer's legal requirement to pay use tax on purchases through catalogs or the Internet.

---

[21] Given the rapid development of state and federal law related to Internet taxation, the information in this section will likely be out of date shortly after publication! Our goal here is to identify issues and sources of potential controversy rather than provide the most current rulings. See the end-of-chapter research problems for ideas in searching for updates on the status of these issues.

[22] See, for example, New Jersey Admin. Code Sec. 18:7-1.9. These rules are discussed in G. Neary, "New Jersey: Proposed Regulations seek to Broaden Taxing Powers," *Journal of Multistate Taxation* 5 (260), January/February 1996.

[23] Texas Ltr. Rul. 200005359L, 5/30/00.

[24] Iowa legislation H.F. 2562, 5/16/00.

**Tax Talk**

The retailing giant Bloomingdale's conducts both catalog and Internet sales through a separate subsidiary corporation. The Pennsylvania Department of Revenue unsuccessfully argued that the parent corporation's physical presence in Pennsylvania created nexus for sales by the subsidiary corporation.[27]

The Internet Tax Freedom Act, passed on October 1, 1998, and extended on November 21, 2001, imposed a moratorium on the imposition of *new* taxes on Internet commerce. However, the moratorium does not affect the application of tax laws already in existence prior to the act. As a result, the act does not restrict sales and income taxation of Internet activity if nexus exists.

A Congressional Advisory Commission on Electronic Commerce has identified a variety of tax issues related to Internet activity that require clarification.[25] In response to the commission's findings and the expiration of the Internet Tax Freedom Act scheduled on November 1, 2003, several pieces of legislation have been offered in Congress.[26] Although the details of these bills differ, all seek to extend the moratorium on new Internet taxes while encouraging states to simplify and unify their sales and use tax systems. If simplification by a sufficient number of states occurs, these proposals also offer Congressional authorization to require sellers without nexus to collect sales and use tax on sales of goods and services delivered into a state regardless of the seller's location. Supporters of this proposal argue that requiring online retailers to collect sales tax would "level the playing field" between traditional and online sellers.[28]

These recent Congressional proposals provide increased support for an ongoing effort by 40 states. The **Streamlined Sales Tax Project** is a joint effort to simplify and integrate the assessment and collection of sales and use taxes.[29] The project's goals are to design, test, and implement a simplified, modernized system that incorporates technology into the tax collection process. On November 12, 2002, representatives of 33 states and the District of Columbia approved a multistate agreement to simplify sales tax laws by establishing one uniform system to administer and collect sales taxes. The simplified system reduces the number of tax rates, provides uniformity in defining the tax base, reduces paperwork for retailers, and uses technology to modernize administration of the system. Under the agreement, state legislatures must now act to pass implementing legislation. The agreement does not take effect until appropriate legislation is approved by a minimum of 10 states constituting at least 20 percent of the total population of states with a sales tax. As of late 2003, the project appears to have met this threshold, and its governing board is taking action to certify the compliance of each state's legislation with the multistate agreement. For a number of states, the effective date of related legislation is mid-2004. The agreement does not require sellers without nexus under current law to begin collecting sales or use tax. However, some participants in the project expect these businesses may voluntarily agree to collect taxes under the simplified system.

# OTHER STATE AND LOCAL TAXES

The variety of other taxes assessed by state and local jurisdictions appears limited only by the imagination of the elected officials serving these locales. Although many jurisdictions

---

[25] The commission's report is discussed in K. Silverberg and M. Foster, "ACEC's Report to Congress on Electronic Commerce—Mission Accomplished?" *Journal of Multistate Taxation* 10 (6), August 2000.

[26] See H.R. 49 and S. 150 among others. At the date this book went to press, H.R. 49 had passed in the House, but its companion bill, S. 150, was tabled by the Senate.

[27] *Bloomingdale's by Mail, Ltd. v. Department of Revenue*, 567 A.2d 773 (Pa. Commonwealth Court, 1989).

[28] Eugene F. Corrigan, "How Congress Can Help Remote Sellers and States," *Readings in State Tax Policy, Tax Analysts* (2001), STT 53-28.

[29] Information on the project can be found at its website, www.streamlinedsalestax.org.

seek to provide "business-friendly" environments to attract new business operations, these governments need tax collections for the revenue lifeblood to operate and provide services to both residents and businesses. The variety of tax bases and rates on which such levies occur increases both the tax and the compliance burden on multijurisdictional businesses.

**Tax Talk**

Since 1998, an estimated 3,900 companies have used a simple planning strategy to eliminate Texas franchise tax liability. The strategy works as follows: a public corporation doing business in Texas forms two or more out-of-state subsidiaries to which it transfers all of its business assets. The corporation and its subsidiaries then form an LLC to conduct business in Texas. Because LLCs are not subject to Texas franchise tax, and the corporation is no longer actively conducting business in Texas, the prior liability is completely eliminated.

As noted in the discussion of state and local government tax collections, property taxes are a primary revenue source for local governments. These taxes are assessed on real and personal property based on value as determined by the taxing jurisdiction. Property tax rates vary considerably across jurisdictions and can impose substantial costs on business activities. Planning options to reduce property tax focus on two issues: (1) determining whether the correct tax rate has been applied to the property in question and (2) challenging the property valuation established by the taxing authority. In terms of property tax rates, many jurisdictions apply different rates to different classes of property, but the burden often falls to the taxpayer to prove eligibility for lower rates. Local tax authorities periodically revise property tax valuations, often resulting in substantial valuation and tax increases. A taxpayer who believes that the new property valuation is too high might need the assistance of professional appraisers to challenge the tax authority's valuation and provide evidence of a more appropriate value. Finally, jurisdictions often offer property tax rate reductions and exemptions to attract new business investment as part of a state's tax incentive programs discussed in the next section.

Many local jurisdictions assess transaction taxes on sales or other transfers of title on real property located within the jurisdiction. State and local jurisdictions also assess a variety of licensing taxes on individuals and businesses engaged in commercial activity. In addition, a number of states assess franchise or capital stock taxes on corporations domiciled or operating within the state. These taxes might be assessed on stock value or an alternative value measure such as gross revenue.

| *Texas Corporation Franchise Tax* | A corporation doing business in Texas computes both a tax on net income and a franchise tax on net capital. *Capital* for this purpose includes both the corporation's stated capital stock and its retained earnings. The Texas Corporation Franchise Tax equals the *greater* of the income tax or the capital tax. As a result, a corporation with operating losses for income tax purposes still pays Texas franchise tax. |
| --- | --- |

# STATE TAX INCENTIVE PROGRAMS

**Objective 8**

Describe the objectives of state tax incentive programs and the types of incentives they commonly offer.

As the U.S. economy has grown and prospered, successful businesses have sought opportunities to expand their operations across the nation and the globe. Fierce competition has developed between state and local jurisdictions to attract new business facilities or promote the expansion of existing ones. In many cases, jurisdictions offer tax incentives as an enticement. Although direct costs of such programs negatively impact the jurisdiction's revenue stream, the indirect benefits can be substantial.

Location incentives vary across jurisdictions as to type, magnitude, and qualification requirements. They also are often transitory; state legislatures enact them for limited time periods subject to benefits caps. Some benefits are available simply by claiming income tax credits and exemptions when filing annual tax returns; others require advance negotiation to obtain. A business must meet paperwork and documentation requirements to claim promised benefits and perhaps obtain annual certifications. Finally, incentive legislation often contains recapture provisions that require companies to repay claimed benefits if they do not meet investment targets or other incentive requirements.

**Tax Talk**

Infineon Technologies has negotiated an incentive package with the state of Virginia to build a $1 billion-plus circuit board fabrication facility. The state offered an incentive package that totals $60 million in performance-based grants to the company over approximately six years. The project is expected to create more than 1,100 new jobs and generate $127 million in additional tax revenues for the state over the next 20 years.[30]

Many large companies employ internal economic development specialists or hire external consultants to ensure that available benefits are identified, negotiated, and properly claimed. While a variety of resources can locate incentive information, the assistance of experienced negotiators familiar with personnel in the state industrial development office can be helpful.

The following is a brief list of some incentive categories available in various jurisdictions.

- Investment tax credits as a percentage of new tangible property placed in service.
- Job credits based on the number of new employees hired.
- Property tax abatements.
- Low-interest financing often through industrial development bonds.
- Sales tax exemptions on purchases of tangible property used in a new facility.
- Exclusions related to property typically included in the property factor for income tax apportionment.
- Exemption from throwback in calculating the sales factor for income tax apportionment.
- Grants or credits for payroll tax paid.
- State enterprise zones.

---

*Pennsylvania's Keystone Opportunity Zones*

Pennsylvania introduced this state-level program in 1999. It offers a virtual tax holiday in which companies pay no taxes at all with respect to a new facility located in a designated opportunity zone. Although the zones are in very economically depressed areas, the value of the incentive program has made them attractive to industry. In addition to tax incentives, zone companies can also receive training grants, infrastructure improvement grants, and low-interest financing.[31]

---

State and local jurisdictions use **tax increment financing (TIF)** as one technique to link the incentive they grant a business directly to the benefits its investment provides to the locality. A TIF arrangement provides an incentive payment based on the increase in a specific tax base as a result of the firm's investment. For example, suppose that a retailer is considering moving to a location with a 1 percent local sales tax. If the retailer has sales of $50 million, the resulting increase in sales tax revenue would be $500,000. The locality could give a portion of the increased sales tax revenue back to the retailer as a location incentive. Similar approaches also apply to property taxes when a business moves into an economically depressed area and the resulting development increases property values for other taxpayers in the surrounding area.

State and local incentive programs have proliferated since the 1980s. Such programs are not without their critics, however; some claim that incentive programs give away tax benefits for investment that would have occurred without any tax break.[32] Others argue that the long-term benefits envisioned for economically depressed areas have not been realized and competition from businesses relocated as a result of incentive programs has hurt existing businesses.

---

[30] The *Site Selection Online Insider,* "Incentives Deal of the Month," January 31, 2001, www.conway.com/insider/incentive/.

[31] D. Durigon and F. Winn, "State Unveils Tax-Free 'Keystone Opportunity Zones,'" *Journal of Multistate Taxation* 9 (44), June 1999.

[32] "Interview with Greg LeRoy on Incentives and Accountability," *Readings in State Tax Policy*, Tax Analysts (1999), STT 186-19.

## Conclusion

This chapter briefly examined issues associated with a variety of taxes and tax incentives that might apply to multistate businesses. A business expanding its operations across state lines must consider whether the move creates nexus for sales and income tax purposes and liability for property, licensing, and franchise taxes. The myriad state and local tax systems can create a reporting and compliance nightmare for multistate businesses. However, the increasing availability of state and local investment incentives and the ability to negotiate tailored incentive packages for major expansions can provide significant benefits to growing businesses. As we discuss in Chapter 11, similar multijurisdictional tax and incentive issues arise when businesses also expand beyond national boundaries.

## Key Terms

apportionment  *267*
apportionment
 formula  *267*
economic nexus  *265*
nexus  *263*
payroll factor  *271*
physical presence
 nexus  *265*

property factor  *271*
Public Law 86-272  *265*
reseller exemption  *264*
sales factor  *270*
sales tax  *262*
Streamlined Sales Tax
 Project  *278*

tax increment financing
 (TIF)  *280*
throwback rule  *270*
unitary business  *274*
use tax  *263*
water's edge election  *276*

## Questions and Problems for Discussion

1. Compare the sales tax and the use tax on the following dimensions: (a) collectability, (b) simplicity, (c) equity, and (d) incidence of taxation (i.e., who bears the burden of the tax).

2. Why is the location of the customer rather than the seller the focus of sales tax nexus?

3. Many taxpayers are unaware that use tax exists and is owed on items purchased through the mail. If ignorance of use tax payment requirements is a major issue, do you expect that adding it to state individual income tax returns will increase compliance? Why or why not? Can you suggest other methods that states might use to enforce use tax statutes?

4. What impact would you expect the increase in Internet sales to have on state sales tax revenues? State income tax collections? What activities associated with Internet sales might increase state tax revenues?

5. States that offer substantial tax breaks for new business investment believe that the long-term benefits of such investment far outweigh the tax costs. Name at least five types of potential long-term benefits of new investment for the state.

6. Refer to question 5. What information and assumptions are required to estimate the dollar value of benefits reaped by a state offering tax breaks for business investment?

7. Mr. and Mrs. Parker are starting a new business. They anticipate spending nearly $100,000 in the first few months to acquire equipment, furniture, vehicles, and other tangible equipment to be used by the business. What types of taxes might apply to these purchases? What planning advice would you give the Parkers to minimize the tax costs associated with their asset acquisitions?

8. Do unitary state income tax filing requirements provide any advantages to related corporations? Under what circumstances might this approach be preferred?

9. How might a partnership assist its partners in meeting state income tax compliance burdens when the partnership conducts business in several states?

10. Do you believe that Internet sales should be given preferential tax treatment? Why or why not?

11. How might businesses, consumers, and states benefit from the Streamlined Sales Tax Project?

12. What are the advantages to the tax authority of tax increment financing arrangements? What are the disadvantages to the taxpayer seeking tax location incentives?

## Application Problems

1. Table 10.1 indicates that state and local governments collected over $290 billion in sales tax in 1999 from total tax collections of $816 billion.
   a. If average sales tax rates are 7 percent, what dollar value of consumer sales do these collections represent?
   b. If 10 percent of the sales calculated in part *(a)* are now made online, how much lost sales tax revenue does this represent?
   c. Given your result in part *(b),* what percentage of total state and local tax collections is potentially lost due to Internet sales?

2. Carmen's Luggage is located in Pennsylvania, just a mile north of the Delaware state border. Delaware has no sales tax, but Pennsylvania has a 6 percent sales tax.
   a. Calculate the total after-tax cost to the customer of a $300 luggage set purchased at Carmen's.
   b. Carmen's owner believes that she is losing business since customers can drive to Delaware and buy luggage without paying sales tax and is considering offering a discount on all sales to offset the cost of the sales tax. At what price would the firm need to sell the $300 luggage set so that the after-tax cost to the consumer equals $300?
   c. Given your analysis in parts *(a)* and *(b),* discuss the incidence of sales tax in this situation and the arguments favoring a use tax.

3. Hall Inc. has computed federal taxable income before deduction for state taxes of $3 million. It incurred state income tax in six states of $750,000 and paid $60,000 in state franchise taxes.
   a. Calculate Hall's federal taxable income and tax liability.
   b. Calculate Hall's total federal and state tax burden as a percentage of pretax earnings.

4. Santa Fe Corporation's federal taxable income is $2,100,000 before its deduction for state income taxes. Examination of its books and records reveals the following information.

| | |
|---|---|
| Tax-exempt municipal bond interest income | $ 15,000 |
| Interest income on federal bonds | 25,000 |
| MACRS depreciation deducted on federal return | 400,000 |
| Straight-line depreciation deductible on state return | 320,000 |

   a. On the basis of the common modifications for state income tax purposes discussed in this chapter, calculate state-level taxable income.
   b. If all of Santa Fe's operations are within a single state that assesses state income tax at a rate of 7 percent, calculate its state income tax liability.
   c. Calculate Santa Fe's federal taxable income and federal income tax liability.

5. Vega Inc. conducts business in two states. Its state-level taxable income before apportionment is $1.8 million. Information related to its sales, payroll, and property in each state follows.

|  | State X | State Z | Total |
|---|---|---|---|
| Sales | $4,500,000 | $2,000,000 | $ 6,500,000 |
| Payroll | 600,000 | 300,000 | 900,000 |
| Property | 8,500,000 | 6,500,000 | 15,000,000 |

State X apportions income using a three-factor formula that double-weights the sales factor. State Z uses an equally weighted three-factor apportionment formula. Corporate income tax in State X is 4 percent and in State Z is 6 percent.

*a.* Calculate Vega's apportionment factors for each state and combine these factors as required to determine the percentage of income taxable in each state.

*b.* Calculate Vega's state income tax liability in each state.

*c.* Assume that Vega's federal taxable income before deduction for state income taxes is $2 million. Calculate its federal taxable income, federal income tax liability, and total income tax burden as a percentage of pretax income.

*d.* State Z is considering changing its apportionment formula to a single-factor approach based only on sales. How would this change affect Vega's income tax liability in State Z? How would it affect Vega's federal income tax liability and total income tax burden?

6. Triad Corporation conducts operations in three states. Its state-level taxable income before apportionment is $3 million. Triad has computed the following sales, payroll, and property factors for each state.

| Factor | State A | State B | State C |
|---|---|---|---|
| Sales | 33% | 40% | 27% |
| Payroll | 20 | 65 | 15 |
| Property | 10 | 80 | 10 |

The income tax rate for State A is 7 percent, for State B is 5 percent, and for State C is 10 percent.

*a.* If all three states use the equally weighted three-factor apportionment formula, determine income taxable in each state.

*b.* From your results in part *(a)*, determine Triad's state tax liability in each state.

*c.* How would your results in parts *(a)* and *(b)* change if State B apportions income using a formula that double weights the sales factor?

7. Refer to the facts in application problem 6, part *(c)*. Triad plans to expand its operations by adding $1 million of additional property to its current property of $10 million and $300,000 of additional payroll to its current payroll of $1 million. This expansion will increase overall sales while maintaining the current sales proportions across the states in which Triad operates. *Only* on the basis of state income tax implications, in which state would you recommend that Triad locate its additional property and payroll?

8. Amsalu Corporation sells products in three states. Sales information for each state follows.

|  | State A | State B | State C | Total |
|---|---|---|---|---|
| Gross sales | $400,000 | $300,000 | $200,000 | $900,000 |
| Returns and discounts | (10,000) | (5,000) | (1,000) | (16,000) |

Amsalu ships all products from State A, the location of 100 percent of its property and payroll. Its total state taxable income before apportionment is $300,000. State A assesses income tax of 10 percent. Although State B assesses income tax at 5 percent, Amsalu's activities in State B are insufficient to create nexus. State C assesses no income tax.

a. Assuming that State A does not apply a throwback rule, calculate Amsalu's sales factor for State A.

b. Assuming that State A apportions income using an equally weighted three-factor apportionment formula, calculate Amsalu's taxable income apportioned to State A and tax liability in State A.

c. How would your answers to parts *(a)* and *(b)* change if State A requires throwback of all sales shipped from the state that are not subject to income tax in the destination jurisdiction?

9. Refer to the facts in application problem 8, part *(c)*.

a. How would your answers change if Amsalu's activities in State B were sufficient to establish nexus?

b. If Amsalu's activities in State B were sufficient to establish nexus and State B apportions income using an equally weighted three-factor apportionment formula, calculate the firm's taxable income apportioned to State B and tax liability in State B.

c. Only on the basis of your analysis of state income tax costs, would you recommend that Amsalu establish nexus in State B?

10. Chimera Inc. has operations in two states. Payroll information for both states follows.

| | State A | State B | Total |
|---|---|---|---|
| Officer compensation | $ 200,000 | $100,000 | $ 300,000 |
| Other compensation | 800,000 | 700,000 | 1,500,000 |
| Total | $1,000,000 | $800,000 | $1,800,000 |

a. Calculate payroll factors for States A and B, assuming that both include officer compensation in the payroll factor.

b. How would your answers to part *(a)* change if State B does not include officer compensation in the payroll factor?

11. Wave Corporation has previously conducted all operations in State A. During the current year, however, it has expanded operations into State B. Property information for both states follows.

| | State A | | State B | |
|---|---|---|---|---|
| | Beginning of Year | End of Year | Beginning of Year | End of Year |
| Land | $100,000 | $100,000 | –0– | $200,000 |
| Depreciable assets | 500,000 | 600,000 | –0– | 400,000 |
| Accumulated depreciation | (50,000) | (60,000) | –0– | (20,000) |
| Inventory | 200,000 | 250,000 | –0– | 200,000 |
| Total | 800,000 | 950,000 | | 800,000 |

Wave also leases property in State A for $25,000 annually. In calculating the property factor, assume that both states use average gross book value of assets plus eight times the annual rental cost of leased property.

*a.* Calculate Wave's property factors for States A and B.

*b.* If Wave undertakes no further expansion of its operations, would you expect next year's property factors to be comparable to those for this year? Why or why not?

12. Horizon Inc. conducts business in two states. Its state-level taxable income before apportionment is $250,000. The following information is available for computing its state apportionment factors.

| | State M | State N | Total |
|---|---|---|---|
| Gross sales | $400,000 | $800,000 | $1,200,000 |
| Returns and allowances | (20,000) | (35,000) | (55,000) |
| Executive compensation | 80,000 | 140,000 | 220,000 |
| Other compensation | 100,000 | 250,000 | 350,000 |
| Average inventory | 40,000 | 75,000 | 115,000 |
| Average personal property | 130,000 | 180,000 | 310,000 |
| Average real property | 350,000 | 300,000 | 650,000 |

Horizon also leases property in State M at an annual cost of $50,000.

*a.* Calculate Horizon's sales, payroll, and property factors in each state.

*b.* Assuming that both states use an equally weighted three-factor apportionment formula, calculate Horizon's state taxable income apportioned to each state.

*c.* Calculate Horizon's total state income tax liability if the tax rate in State M is 10 percent and in State N is 8 percent.

*d.* How would your answers to parts *(b)* and *(c)* change if State N uses an apportionment formula that double-weights the sales factor?

13. Parenti Inc. operates entirely within State A. Sub Corporation, its wholly owned subsidiary, operates entirely within State B. During 2004, the taxable income for state purposes for Parenti was $400,000 and for Sub was $250,000. Other information regarding the operations of each entity follows.

| | Parenti | Sub | Total |
|---|---|---|---|
| Sales | $2,000,000 | $1,200,000 | $3,200,000 |
| Payroll | 400,000 | 300,000 | 700,000 |
| Property | 900,000 | 400,000 | 1,300,000 |

*a.* If State A requires unitary reporting, uses an apportionment formula that double weights the sales factor, and has a 7 percent corporate tax rate, calculate taxable income and tax liability in State A.

*b.* If State B requires nonunitary (separate) reporting, uses an equally weighted three-factor apportionment formula, and has a 10 percent corporate tax rate, calculate taxable income and tax liability in State B.

14. Refer to the facts in application problem 13.

*a.* How would your answers change if both States A and B require unitary reporting?

*b.* How would your answers change if both States A and B require separate reporting?

*c.* Under which combination of reporting systems will Parenti and Sub pay the least total state income tax?

15. Gavin Inc. incurred a federal net operating loss during 2004 of $(300,000). After adjusting for differences in the calculation of state and federal taxable income,

$(290,000) remained. Included in this loss is $20,000 of nonbusiness income allocated to State A, Gavin's state of residence. Gavin's business loss must be apportioned between States A and B to determine its state-level net operating losses. Its sales, payroll, and property information follows.

|  | State A | State B | Total |
|---|---|---|---|
| Sales | $1,300,000 | $3,200,000 | $4,500,000 |
| Payroll | 200,000 | 300,000 | 500,000 |
| Property | 500,000 | 600,000 | 1,100,000 |

*a.* If State A applies an apportionment formula that double-weights the sales factor and State B uses an equally weighted three-factor apportionment formula, calculate Gavin's state-level net operating losses.

*b.* If 2004 is the first year in which Gavin conducted business in State B, what are the implications for Gavin's use of its state net operating losses?

## Issue Recognition Problems

Identify the tax issue or issues suggested by the following situations and state each issue in the form of a question.

1. Raisin Inc. sells computer products with a one-year warranty over the Internet to customers in all 50 states. It ships the products from warehouses in Delaware and Oregon. Warranty repair work is performed under contract with independent repair shops located in each state.

2. Latent Inc. wishes to build a new manufacturing facility. Although its corporate headquarters is located in Arkansas, it prefers to locate the new facility somewhere in the southwestern United States, to service customers in that region. Latent projects that the new facility will cost $100 million to build and will employ 2,000 workers.

3. Corporations A, B, and C file a consolidated federal income tax return. Corporation A, the parent corporation, performs market research and product development activities; Corporation B manufactures products that are then distributed to retail customers in 20 different states by Corporation C.

4. Thul Corporation, which is located in a state that assesses income tax, sells its products through mail-order catalogs and does not have nexus in any other state. Since only 10 percent of Thul's sales are made to residents of its state of domicile, it expects its sales factor for state income tax apportionment to be 10 percent.

5. Zenon Inc. incurred a net operating loss for federal income tax purposes in 2004. For federal purposes, it elected to forgo carryback of this loss to its 2002 and 2003 tax years and will carry the loss forward into 2005 and beyond.

6. Luxor Corporation owns, rents, and manages several commercial buildings. During the past two years, real estate prices in its region have increased nearly 25 percent.

7. Mr. Abigail and Mrs. Herman plan to start a new business entity that will sell products to customers in several states. For liability reasons, they are considering forming a corporate entity. To avoid double taxation, however, they might wish to make an S corporation election or to form an LLC.

8. Mr. Geisen runs a small construction business that specializes in home repair and renovation. He buys most of the materials and equipment used in the business at a warehouse-style building supply store that caters to small businesses and do-it-yourselfers.

9. Ms. Hanover and Mr. Jeffers are wine enthusiasts living in a state that assesses sales tax at 9 percent. Every few months, they drive to a neighboring state that has no sales tax to purchase several cases of wine.

10. Mahmud Corporation is a medical services and supply company operating in 10 states in the southwestern United States. It employs sales personnel in each state in which it operates, but all of its corporate officers work at its headquarters in California.

## Research Problems

1. Use the Internet to check the current status of federal legislation regarding Internet taxation and federal authorization allowing states to require out-of-state sellers to collect sales and use tax.

2. Use the Internet to check the current status of the Streamlined Sales Tax Project.

3. Locate the website for the department of revenue of the state in which you reside. Does it assess a corporate income tax? If so, how does it define nonbusiness income and does it apportion such income or tax it to the state of domicile? Does your state allow or require unitary reporting? Does it assess a corporate franchise tax? If so, how is the tax calculated?

## Tax Planning Cases

1. Drosick Corporation is planning to build a new manufacturing facility and must decide whether to locate it in State X or Y. Corporate income tax on profits earned within the state is not assessed in State X, but State Y assesses it at 5 percent. State Y apportions the income of multistate corporations using a three-factor apportionment formula that double-weights the sales factor. Assume that all of Drosick's business operations are within States X and Y and that the following apportionment information is available prior to completion of the new facility:

| | State X | State Y | Total |
|---|---|---|---|
| Gross receipts from sales | $1,000,000 | $1,000,000 | $2,000,000 |
| Payroll expense | 200,000 | 100,000 | 300,000 |
| Property costs | 2,000,000 | 500,000 | 2,500,000 |

Completion of the new manufacturing facility is expected to cost $3,000,000, resulting in increased payroll costs of $250,000 and increased sales of $500,000 in each state. Drosick's projected total taxable income before state income taxes (in both states) will be $2,400,000 following completion of the new facility, which is expected to commence operations in the year following construction and be productive for at least 10 years.

a. Calculate Drosick's apportionment factors, income taxable in each state, and State Y tax liability, assuming that it builds the facility in State X.

b. Calculate Drosick's federal taxable income, federal tax liability, and annual after-tax cash flow, assuming that it builds the facility in State X.

c. Using a 10 percent discount rate, calculate the NPV of after-tax cash flows for the projected 10-year life of the facility and Drosick's projected after-tax return on investment, assuming that it builds the facility in State X.

d. Repeat your calculations in parts *(a), (b),* and *(c),* assuming that Drosick builds the facility in State Y. From your analysis, which location would you recommend?

e. Suppose that the legislature of State Y enacts a new jobs credit that provides a $100 reduction in state corporation income tax for each new job created there. Drosick's new manufacturing facility is expected to employ 500 workers. Also assume that property suitable for the new facility will cost $3,300,000 in State X versus $3,000,000 in State Y. Revise your analysis in parts *(a)*, *(b)*, *(c)*, and *(d)* to reflect these new assumptions. Which location would you now recommend?

*f.* What nontax factors should Drosick consider in making this location decision?

2. Genrick Inc., located in Cheyenne, Wyoming, currently conducts 100 percent of its business in Wyoming using local sales personnel. It is considering expanding into Colorado. All products would continue to be manufactured in and shipped from Wyoming. Genrick could undertake expansion into Colorado by hiring sales personnel residing in Colorado to service customers there or paying travel costs for Wyoming sales personnel to service Colorado customers. If the first alternative is selected, Genrick projects that Colorado sales will total $250,000 per year. If the second alternative is selected, Colorado sales are projected at $230,000, less $20,000 of additional travel costs.

*a.* Ignoring tax costs, which alternative do you think is better?

*b.* If Wyoming assesses no state income tax and Colorado assesses tax only on sales made by Colorado-resident sales personnel, how high would the effective tax rate on Colorado earnings have to be to change your conclusion in part *(a)*?

*c.* What other tax and nontax factors should Genrick consider in making this decision?

# Chapter **Eleven**

# International Business Expansion

## Learning Objectives

*After reading this chapter, you will be able to:*

1. Define U.S. taxing jurisdiction over citizens, residents, domestic corporations, and foreign corporations.

2. Describe the general form of benefits conferred on U.S. taxpayers by tax treaties with foreign governments.

3. Describe the types of taxes assessed in foreign jurisdictions and identify common differences between U.S. and foreign tax systems.

4. Compute the foreign tax credit and the annual limitation on allowable foreign tax credits.

5. Describe the sourcing rules applicable to various types of business income and deductions in determining whether such items are U.S. or foreign source.

6. Identify the alternative legal forms through which a U.S. corporation could choose to conduct business in a foreign jurisdiction.

7. Discuss the tax advantages associated with conducting foreign operations through a controlled foreign subsidiary corporation.

8. Compute the taxable dividend amount and deemed paid foreign tax credit available to a U.S. corporation receiving distributions from a foreign corporation.

9. Describe the rationale underlying the constructive repatriation rules of Subpart F.

10. Discuss the potential for manipulation of income sourcing through transfer pricing. Describe the methods available for computing transfer prices and the issues that arise in identifying comparable uncontrolled transactions.

Multinational taxation is one of the most interesting and exciting areas of tax practice. The typical players in multinational business are large corporations that provide products and services to international customers. These U.S. corporations can produce products in both U.S. and foreign locations to serve international markets, but they face a variety of issues involving the taxation of earnings in multiple jurisdictions. These issues include the pricing of transfers of goods, technology, and know-how between and among countries; the optimal form in which to operate in any given country; and the optimal locations for foreign operations. Many developed countries, particularly in western Europe and Japan, levy taxes at rates higher than the United States assesses. Other countries offer tax-haven opportunities as a way to attract foreign investment. Effective tax planning can identify ways to minimize the costs of doing business in high-tax jurisdictions and maximize the benefits of doing business in low-tax jurisdictions.

This chapter explores many basic tax issues facing multinational businesses and discusses planning opportunities available to these businesses.[1] The focus of the chapter is on **outbound transactions,** in which U.S. citizens, residents, and domestic corporations invest and do business abroad. It does not discuss the variety of special tax rules applicable to **inbound transactions,** in which nonresident aliens and foreign corporations invest and do business in the United States. The chapter first describes the jurisdictional issues that arise when U.S. businesses expand operations into foreign countries. Such expansion creates the potential for double taxation in both the United States and the foreign jurisdiction. Next, it discusses the types of taxes commonly assessed by foreign jurisdictions. A variety of tax rules and planning techniques can alleviate double taxation when it occurs. The chapter reviews basic foreign tax credit rules as a way to relieve double taxation and the use of foreign corporations to avoid U.S. taxation. It also considers the importance of the income sourcing rules in determining U.S. taxing jurisdiction. Finally, it examines the limits on multinational tax planning imposed by Subpart F and the Section 482 transfer pricing rules.[2] The chapter concludes with a multinational planning example that identifies tax issues relevant to international expansion and operating decisions.

# JURISDICTIONAL ISSUES FOR MULTINATIONAL BUSINESSES

**Objective 1**
Define U.S. taxing jurisdiction over citizens, residents, domestic corporations, and foreign corporations.

The U.S. government has jurisdiction to levy federal income tax on the worldwide income of its residents, resident aliens, and domestic corporations.[3] Therefore, all U.S. citizens, even those not residing in the country, are subject to U.S. income tax. Corporations incorporated in one of the 50 states or the District of Columbia are also taxed on worldwide income. To the extent that such worldwide income is subject to tax in other countries, U.S. taxpayers face the potential for double taxation.

**Objective 2**
Describe the general form of benefits conferred on U.S. taxpayers by tax treaties with foreign governments.

Some relief from double taxation might be provided via treaty. The United States has signed **tax treaties** with more than 50 foreign countries. The impact of these treaties is to modify the general tax rules applicable to the income of U.S. taxpayers earned in the treaty country and income earned in the United States by taxpayers from the treaty country. In many cases, treaty provisions relinquish taxing jurisdiction in each country for the other's

---

[1] Many basic multinational tax issues discussed in this chapter were introduced in Chapter 12 of *Principles*. Students familiar with *Principles* can use this chapter as a review and an introduction to additional issues. Students not familiar with *Principles* will find the coverage here sufficient to introduce the important issues in multinational taxation.

[2] For a more detailed discussion of multinational tax issues, see Michael L. Moore and Edmund Outslay, *U.S. Tax Aspects of Doing Business Abroad* (New York: American Institute of Certified Public Accountants, Inc., 2000).

[3] The taxation of resident aliens (non-U.S. citizens residing in the United States) depends on residency status as determined using either a green card or substantial presence test. Discussion of the details of these tests is beyond the scope of this text.

**Tax Talk**

The IRS website provides online access to the current text of all tax treaties between the U.S. and all treaty partners at http://www.irs.gov. The website also provides a detailed technical explanation for each treaty and the text of proposed treaties in current negotiation.

residents if certain criteria are met. Treaty provisions can also take the form of tax credits, lower tax rates, or special exclusions from taxation. Many recent treaties are based in large part on the U.S. Model Income Tax Convention developed in 1996. The Model is intended to facilitate negotiations with potential treaty partners by enabling the negotiators to move quickly to the most important issues that must be resolved. Reconciling these differences often leads to an agreed text that will differ from the Model in numerous respects. Another purpose of the Model is to provide a basic explanation of U.S. treaty policy. The Model is quite detailed, addressing a variety of issues and methods for alleviating double taxation for U.S. taxpayers and citizens of the treaty partner. This discussion of taxation of multinational businesses should be considered a starting point; taxpayers operating in a specific country should always check for special treaty provisions.

| *Income Tax Treaty between the United States and the United Kingdom* | Article 7 of this treaty provides that business profits of a U.S. or U.K. business enterprise are taxed in the other country only if the enterprise conducts business through a permanent establishment. In that case, only business profits attributable to the permanent establishment are taxed by the foreign government. Article 5 of the treaty defines a *permanent establishment* to include a branch, office, factory, workshop, or place of extraction of natural resources. It does not include a place of business used solely for storage, display, delivery, or purchase of merchandise; advertisement; collection of information; or scientific research.[4] |
| --- | --- |

Many U.S. tax treaties contain similar **permanent establishment** provisions enabling a U.S. business to avoid tax liability in a foreign country by ensuring that its level of activity in that jurisdiction does not involve a permanent establishment. This approach is particularly valuable in high-tax foreign jurisdictions in which the U.S. taxpayer sells products by mail or via independent agents. The definition of a permanent establishment varies from treaty to treaty, but generally requires a fixed place of business, a construction site, or a dependent agent of the taxpayer with contracting authority located in the foreign country in order to subject the U.S. business to taxation in the foreign jurisdiction.

# COMMON FOREIGN TAXES

**Objective 3**

Describe the types of taxes assessed in foreign jurisdictions and identify common differences between U.S. and foreign tax systems.

Many business taxes in the United States are common in other countries. Exhibit 11.1 shows the distribution of tax revenues of OECD member countries for 1999.[5] Note that income and profits taxes combined account for 35 percent of tax revenues and that payroll and Social Security taxes represent 26 percent of tax collections. Consumption taxes including sales, excise, and value-added taxes account for 32 percent of total tax revenues. These ratios are in contrast to sources of tax revenue in the United States, where income and profits taxes account for 49 percent of revenues, payroll and Social Security taxes 16 percent, property taxes 10 percent, and consumption taxes 25 percent. These data suggest consumption taxes, like the value-added tax discussed in the next section, play a much larger role in other tax regimes versus the income tax system that dominates U.S. tax collections.

Although many taxes assessed globally are familiar, their form can differ considerably from those in the United States and across foreign jurisdictions. In countries that assess

---

[4] United States–United Kingdom Income Tax Convention, signed at London, December 31, 1975.

[5] *Revenue Statistics of OECD Member Countries, 1965–1999* (Organization for Economic Cooperation and Development, 1999). OECD member countries include Australia, Austria, Belgium, Canada, Czech Republic, Denmark, Finland, France, Germany, Greece, Hungary, Iceland, Ireland, Italy, Japan, Luxembourg, Mexico, Netherlands, New Zealand, Norway, Poland, Portugal, South Korea, Slovak Republic, Spain, Sweden, Switzerland, Turkey, United Kingdom, and the United States.

**EXHIBIT 11.1**
**Types of Tax Collected as a Percentage of Total Tax Revenues for OECD Member Countries, 1999**

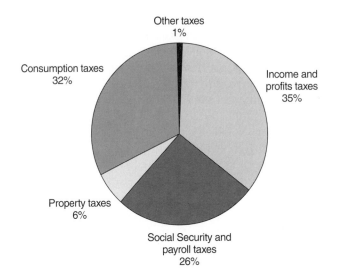

Other taxes 1%

Consumption taxes 32%

Income and profits taxes 35%

Property taxes 6%

Social Security and payroll taxes 26%

income-based taxes, the manner in which "taxable income" is calculated and the rates at which such income is taxed vary. In addition, tax systems such as the value-added tax are common in many developed countries but have not yet been adopted in the United States. The next several examples demonstrate a few possible differences in income tax systems across foreign jurisdictions. This section continues with a brief discussion of value-added taxes. We conclude with a preview of the European Union's attempts to integrate and simplify the tax systems of member countries.

*Imputation Systems to Alleviate Double Taxation of Corporate Earnings*

Double taxation of corporate earnings is a prominent feature of the U.S. income tax system. Corporate earnings are subject to tax at the entity level and are taxed again when they are distributed via dividends to shareholders. Many countries use an imputation system to alleviate this double taxation. Under this system, shareholders reporting dividend income are allowed a tax credit for some portion of the corporate tax paid on distributed earnings. For example, in France, resident individual shareholders receive a 50 percent tax credit against taxes paid on distributions from French corporations. The amount of the dividend included in income must be grossed up by the amount of the credit, as shown in the following example.

| | |
|---|---:|
| Corporate taxable income | $1,000 |
| Corporate tax at 33⅓ percent | (333) |
| After-tax earnings available to distribute | $ 667 |
| Distribution to shareholders (assuming all after-tax earnings are distributed) | $ 667 |
| Gross up equal to 50 percent of corporate tax | 166 |
| Dividend included in shareholder income | $ 833 |
| Individual tax on dividend income at 40 percent | 333 |
| Less: Tax credit equal to gross up amount | (166) |
| Net individual income tax | $ 167 |

Using this approach, the combined tax liability on $1,000 of corporate income is $500 ($167 + 333), or 50 percent. Without the gross-up and credit approaches, the shareholder would pay tax of $267 ($667 × 40 percent) on the dividend distribution, producing a combined tax liability of $600 ($333 + $267), or 60 percent on $1,000 of corporate income.

| *Depreciation of Business Assets* | Although most foreign income tax systems allow some form of deduction related to the cost of business assets, allowable methods, useful lives, and depreciation bases vary considerably. For example, Mexico requires that depreciation be calculated using the straight-line method; Canada prescribes a declining balance method; France, Germany, and Japan permit the use of either the straight-line or declining balance method. Mexican businesses calculate depreciation based on a measure of asset value rather than cost by applying factors derived from the National Consumer Price Index. Canada refers to tax-based depreciation as the *capital cost allowance* (CCA), which is optional and may be forgone in any given year in favor of utilizing loss carryovers. |
|---|---|

| *Corporate Tax Rates* | A January 2003 survey by the accounting firm KPMG finds that the average corporate tax rate for 58 surveyed countries declined during the period 1996 through 2003. The average corporate tax rate of OECD member countries in 2003 was 30.79 percent,[6] of European Union countries was 31.68 percent (see the later section on the European Union), of Central and South American countries was 30.55 percent, and of Asia-Pacific countries was 30.36 percent.[7] Low income tax rate countries include Chile (16.5 percent), Hong Kong (17 percent), Hungary (18 percent), and Ireland (12.5 percent). At the high end of the corporate income tax rate spectrum are Canada (36.6 percent), Germany (39.58 percent), South Africa (37.8 percent), and Japan (42 percent).[8] |
|---|---|

| *Corporate Tax Rate Incentives* | In 1980, legislation in Ireland established a low tax rate of 10 percent for income derived from manufacturing operations, certain projects in the Shannon airport area, and a range of financial services operations in the International Financial Services Centre in Dublin. Ireland's general corporate tax rate (20 percent through 2001) fell to 16 percent effective January 1, 2002, and to 12.5 percent effective January 1, 2003.<br><br>Canada also encourages investment in manufacturing via rate reductions. Beginning in 2000, combined federal and provincial rate reductions for income from manufacturing and processing activities ranged from 7 to 20 percent. |
|---|---|

## Value-Added Tax

As Figure 11.1 shows, consumption taxes represent a large percentage of tax collections by foreign governments. In many developed countries, the primary consumption tax on business activities is a **value-added tax (VAT),** somewhat similar to a sales tax. A sales tax, however, is typically imposed on consumers, whereas a VAT is imposed on producers and distributors of products and services at each stage of the production and distribution process. For each taxpayer, the "value added" equals the difference between the price at which the product or service is sold and the nonlabor costs incurred to produce it.

| *VAT Imposition and Calculation* | Assume a VAT system with a 10 percent tax rate. Suppose that a lumber company harvests and mills trees to be used to produce wood furniture. If the lumber company sells a batch of wood to a furniture manufacturer for $100,000, it owes $10,000 ($100,000 × 10 percent) |
|---|---|

---

[6] See footnote 5 for a list of OECD countries.

[7] The Central and South American countries included in this survey are Argentina, Belize, Bolivia, Brazil, Chile, Colombia, Costa Rica, Dominican Republic, Ecuador, El Salvador, Guatemala, Honduras, Mexico, Panama, Paraguay, Peru, Uruguay, and Venezuela. The Asia-Pacific countries are Australia, Bangladesh, China, Fiji, Hong Kong, India, Indonesia, Japan, Malaysia, New Zealand, Pakistan, Papua New Guinea, Philippines, Singapore, South Korea, Sri Lanka, Taiwan, Thailand, and Vietnam.

[8] Data from KPMG International; *KPMG Corporate Tax Rate Survey—January 2003.*

of VAT tax on this sale. The furniture manufacturer cuts and finishes the wood and assembles it into furniture that it sells to a retailer for $300,000. The furniture manufacturer pays VAT on the difference between its sales price to the retailer and the cost of the trees [i.e., $200,000 ($300,000 − $100,000)], resulting in a $20,000 VAT liability to the manufacturer. Finally, the retailer sells the furniture to consumers for $600,000. The retailer pays VAT of $30,000 on $300,000, the difference between the final consumer sales price of the furniture ($600,000) and its costs to acquire the furniture ($300,000).

Although VAT is borne directly by each participant in the production and distribution process, the real cost of the tax likely is passed on to the next stage—and the ultimate consumer—via higher prices. Thus, in the preceding example, the $600,000 sales price of the furniture includes VAT of $60,000.

VAT rates vary considerably across jurisdictions and products. In Germany, for example, the standard rate is 16 percent with a reduced rate of 7 percent that applies to most agricultural products and some cultural and charitable services. In France, the standard rate is 20.6 percent with reduced rates of 5.5 percent applied to goods for human consumption and certain essential products. Ireland's primary VAT rate is 21 percent with a lower 12.5 percent rate on hotel accommodations, restaurant meals, periodicals, agricultural and veterinary services, fuel, and cinema admissions. Medical, dental, child care, insurance, and educational services are specifically exempt from the Irish VAT system as are passenger transportation and admission to sporting events.

Note that many countries, particularly in Europe, impose both VAT and income taxes on business operations. Thus, the total tax burden under the two systems can be quite high. Although the United States does not impose a VAT on domestic business operations, several proposals to implement this tax nationally (in lieu of the federal income tax) were put forth during the early 1990s. Opponents of a U.S. VAT argued that this fundamentally different tax system would impose high reporting and compliance costs on U.S. businesses without sufficient compensating benefits.

## The European Union

In 1993, the Treaty of Maastricht officially formed the **European Union (EU),**[9] which seeks to create a single, integrated European market that will allow free movement of capital and trade among member countries, resulting in economic growth for the region. As part of a comprehensive development plan, the EU launched the Euro, a common currency for member countries, in 1999 and is working to integrate the banking system of member countries.

As part of the EU's market integration activities, its representatives have been working for several years to harmonize VAT taxation across member countries. VAT taxes would continue to be assessed and paid within each country, but the EU seeks to simplify and modernize the system, increase administrative cooperation among member countries, and increase uniformity of rules across countries. VAT harmonization is appealing to businesses and is critical to the creation of an integrated European market, but progress has been slow.[10] Even less progress has been made toward harmonizing the income tax systems of

---

[9] European Union countries include Austria, Belgium, Cyprus, Czech Republic, Denmark, Estonia, Finland, France, Germany, Greece, Hungary, Ireland, Italy, Latvia, Lithuania, Luxembourg, Malta, Netherlands, Poland, Portugal, Slovenia, Slovakia, Spain, Sweden, and United Kingdom.

[10] For more discussion, see Anne Murrath, "Harmonizing VAT in the EU: The Commissioner's New Strategy," *Journal of International Taxation* 12 (20), February 2001.

EU member countries.[11] Efforts in this direction are ongoing, but in the near term, businesses operating in Europe continue to be confronted with a great diversity in tax rates, tax systems, business incentive provisions, and compliance requirements.

# THE FOREIGN TAX CREDIT

**Objective 4**
Compute the foreign tax credit and the annual limitation on allowable foreign tax credits.

The **foreign tax credit** attempts to alleviate the double taxation that results when businesses are taxed in both the United States and a foreign country.[12] You might recall from your introductory tax course that businesses are allowed a deduction for foreign taxes. However, it usually is more advantageous to forgo this deduction and take the foreign tax credit when it is available. Unfortunately, not all foreign taxes are creditable. A foreign levy must be a tax, in the U.S. sense, to be creditable.[13] Specifically, the levy must be a compulsory, not voluntary, payment not made in exchange for any specific benefit. Second, only income taxes are creditable. Thus, foreign property taxes, value-added taxes, sales taxes, and other levies not based on a measure of taxable income are not eligible for the foreign tax credit but can be deducted as trade or business expenses. Finally, creditable foreign taxes must be assessed in the foreign jurisdiction regardless of whether a U.S. credit is available.

*Creditable versus Noncreditable Foreign Taxes*

The income of foreign corporations doing business in Germany is subject to German corporation tax at a rate of 40 percent and a municipal trade tax at rates ranging from 13 to 20 percent. The trade tax is deductible in computing the corporation tax. Germany also assesses VAT at a standard rate of 16 percent and German municipalities levy real property taxes ranging from 0.6 to 2 percent. Under Articles 2 and 23 of the United States–Federal Republic of Germany Income Tax Treaty, the German corporation tax and trade tax are creditable taxes for purposes of the U.S. foreign tax credit.[14] The VAT and real property taxes are not creditable but can be deducted in computing taxable income.

The maximum foreign tax credit allowed in any given tax year equals the tax assessed by the United States on income from foreign sources.[15] Thus, the allowable foreign tax credit is limited to the extent that the foreign tax rate is higher than the U.S. tax rate. The foreign tax credit limitation is calculated using the following formula:

$$\begin{matrix}\text{Maximum current} \\ \text{foreign tax credit} \\ \text{allowable}\end{matrix} = \frac{\text{Taxable income from foreign sources}}{\text{Worldwide taxable income}} \times \begin{matrix}\text{U.S. tax on worldwide} \\ \text{taxable income} \\ \text{before credits}\end{matrix}$$

The foreign tax credit limit multiplies the ratio of foreign taxable income to worldwide taxable income by U.S. income tax before credits computed on worldwide taxable income. When foreign taxes paid exceed this amount, the current foreign tax credit is limited. Unused foreign tax credits can be carried back two years and forward five years subject to the foreign tax credit limit in such years.[16]

---

[11] See John Hawksworth, "The Slow Process of Business Tax Harmonization in the New Europe," *Journal of International Taxation* 10 (36), September 1999.

[12] Section 901(b)(1) provides the statutory authority for the foreign tax credit.

[13] Treasury Reg. 1.901-2 defines the requirements for a foreign tax to be creditable.

[14] Tax convention between the United States of America and the Federal Republic of Germany, effective January 1, 1990.

[15] Section 904.

[16] Section 904(c).

*Foreign Tax Credit Limitation*

Jefferson Inc., a New York corporation, conducts business in both the United States and Belgium. During 2004, its operations earned taxable income of $300,000 in the United States and $150,000 in Belgium. It paid $60,000 of Belgian income tax. Before the foreign tax credit is considered, Jefferson's U.S. tax liability on its $450,000 of worldwide taxable income is $153,000. Its maximum allowable foreign tax credit is computed as follows.

$$\frac{\$150,000}{\$450,000} \times \$153,000 = \$51,000$$

Thus, Jefferson's 2004 foreign tax credit is limited to $51,000, and its tax liability after the credit is $102,000 ($153,000 − $51,000). The $9,000 excess of foreign taxes paid over the allowable credit can be carried back to 2002 and 2003 if Jefferson had unused credit limit in those years. Any credit not absorbed by carryback can be carried forward up to five years.

*Carryback of Foreign Tax Credit*

Assume that in 2002, Jefferson had $100,000 of foreign-source income and $400,000 of worldwide taxable income, and it paid $27,000 of foreign taxes. Its 2002 federal income tax before foreign tax credit was $136,000. Its maximum allowable foreign tax credit in 2002 was:

$$\frac{\$100,000}{\$400,000} \times \$136,000 = \$34,000$$

Since Jefferson's 2002 foreign taxes were less than the limit, it took a foreign tax credit of $27,000, reducing its 2002 net tax liability to $109,000.

In carrying back its 2004 excess foreign taxes to 2002, Jefferson cannot exceed the $34,000 foreign tax credit limitation computed for that year. Since Jefferson used $27,000 of foreign tax credit in 2002, only $7,000 ($34,000 − $27,000) of its carryback can be applied against its 2002 taxes. Jefferson can apply for a refund of $7,000 of tax paid in 2002. The remaining $2,000 of foreign tax credit will carry to 2003 subject to the applicable limit in that year. Any amount not absorbed in 2003 will be carried forward to 2005.

The examples just considered focus on total foreign income, total worldwide taxable income, and total foreign taxes. However, the actual calculation of the foreign tax credit limitation is more complex. The limitation must be computed for separate categories of income referred to as *baskets*.[17] Then the limit is applied to the foreign taxes paid related to each basket. Included in separate baskets are items such as passive income, high withholding tax interest income, financial services income, shipping income, and certain foreign dividends. To the extent that foreign taxes are assessed at higher rates on some types of income than others, limitations are likely to occur. The intent of the separate limitation rules is to restrict the ability of U.S. taxpayers to average foreign-source income subject to high foreign tax rates with foreign-source income subject to low foreign tax rates to maximize the available foreign tax credit.

The separate basket designations mentioned were chosen to identify the types of income most subject to manipulation. However, most active trade or business income is combined in a single basket and is subject to a general credit limitation. Thus, for taxpayers whose foreign-source income is not subject to separate limitation, cross crediting opportunities still exist.

---

[17] Section 904(d).

| | |
|---|---|
| *Cross Crediting Foreign Taxes Paid in High and Low Tax Rate Jurisdictions* | In Country A, Nova Corporation earned $1 million of foreign-source income on which it paid foreign income taxes of $100,000. It also earned $1.5 million of foreign-source income from Country B on which it paid foreign income taxes of $600,000. Nova's U.S.-source income totaled $3 million. |

In Country A, Nova Corporation earned $1 million of foreign-source income on which it paid foreign income taxes of $100,000. It also earned $1.5 million of foreign-source income from Country B on which it paid foreign income taxes of $600,000. Nova's U.S.-source income totaled $3 million.

Before considering the foreign tax credit, Nova's U.S. income tax liability on worldwide taxable income of $5.5 million is $1.87 million. If all of its foreign-source income is subject to the general credit limitation, its maximum foreign tax credit is $850,000 ($1.87 million × $2.5 million/$5.5 million). Thus, the limitation does not apply, and Nova's foreign tax credit equals $700,000 ($100,000 + $600,000) foreign taxes paid. U.S. tax liability after foreign tax credit is reduced to $1.07 million.

What if Nova's income from Country B were subject to a separate basket limitation? In that case, its total foreign tax credit for Country B taxes would be limited to $510,000 ($1.87 million × $1.5 million/$5.5 million). Nova's total allowable foreign tax credit would be $610,000, and its net U.S. tax liability would increase to $1.26 million.

As this example shows, cross crediting of foreign taxes paid in high-tax countries with those paid in low-tax countries can significantly increase allowable foreign tax credits in a given year with corresponding reductions in worldwide tax liability. In planning for such opportunities, multinational companies must take care to avoid the separate basket limitations imposed on the specific types of foreign-source income previously described.

# SOURCING OF INCOME AND DEDUCTIONS

**Objective 5**
Describe the sourcing rules applicable to various types of business income and deductions in determining whether such items are U.S. or foreign source.

As previously stated, the foreign tax credit is available for foreign taxes paid on foreign-source income. The availability of the credit and the annual limitation on allowable credits depend on income sourcing. In particular, the credit limitation increases when a larger proportion of worldwide income is considered to be from a foreign source. Thus, taxpayers subject to the limitation have an incentive to increase the portion of their total income classified as foreign source. Also note that the sourcing of income rules for U.S. tax purposes might not correspond with those rules applied in foreign jurisdictions to determine foreign tax liability.

Differences in sourcing across jurisdictions can either increase the potential for double taxation or create opportunities to avoid taxation in either jurisdiction. International tax shelter transactions and structures utilizing so-called hybrid entities attempt to capitalize on such opportunities to lower global tax liability. A more in-depth discussion of these transactions is beyond the scope of this text.

Detailed rules define what income constitutes **foreign-source income** versus **U.S.-source income** for U.S. tax purposes.[18] In general, the sourcing of items of gross income depends on the type of income earned and the geographic location in which the economic activity generating it occurred. The following broad sourcing rules apply:

- Income from services is sourced to the geographic location in which the services are performed.
- Income from rental of tangible property is sourced at the property's location.
- Royalty income from intangible property and rights is sourced to the country in which they are used.

[18] Sections 861 through 865 and related regulations provide detailed rules for sourcing income and deductions as either U.S. source or foreign source.

- Interest income is sourced to the debtor's country of residence.
- Dividend income is sourced to the country in which the dividend-paying corporation is incorporated.
- Income from the sale of property and inventory are sourced as discussed in the following two sections.

## Income from the Sale of Property

Income from the sale of property depends on the type sold. Real property sales are sourced to the property's location. In general, sales of personal property are sourced to the seller's country of residence or incorporation. However, two important exceptions to this rule exist for sales of depreciable property and inventory. For sales of depreciable personal property, any portion of the gain on a sale that represents depreciation recapture must be sourced to the location(s) in which income was reduced by prior depreciation deductions. Any additional gain is sourced to the location in which title to the property passes.

*Sourcing of Gain on Sale of Depreciable Property*

Boundary Inc. is located in Detroit, Michigan, and leases construction equipment to customers in both the United States and Canada. During 2004, it sold a piece of used equipment for $30,000 to a Canadian purchaser. Title to the equipment passed in Canada. Boundary originally purchased the equipment for $100,000, and its remaining tax basis was $10,000. While Boundary owned the equipment, it was rented for use 75 percent in the United States and 25 percent in Canada.

During the time that Boundary owned the equipment, depreciation deductions were allocated to the locations in which rental income was earned. Thus, 75 percent of its depreciation deductions were U.S. source, and 25 percent were foreign source. Boundary recognizes a gain of $20,000 on the sale of the equipment ($30,000 amount realized − $10,000 adjusted tax basis). Since all of the gain is depreciation recapture (lesser of gain recognized or prior depreciation of $90,000), $5,000, or 25 percent, of the gain is foreign-source income and $15,000, or 75 percent, is U.S. source income.

## Income from the Sale of Inventory

The sourcing of income from sales of inventory depends on whether the inventory was purchased or manufactured. Income from the sale of purchased inventory is sourced to the location in which the title to it passes. Income from the sale of manufactured inventory is generally sourced to the manufacturing facility's location. However, if the inventory sold is manufactured in the United States for sale abroad, 50 percent of the income is typically treated as foreign source and 50 percent as U.S. source.[19] Given the objective of creating foreign-source income for purposes of the credit limitation, this rule can provide an incentive to U.S. companies for domestic manufacturing. If inventory is manufactured in several stages, some of which occur in the United States and some of which occur abroad, complex allocation rules determine the portion of income sourced to each production location.

*Sourcing of Inventory Sales*

Holzer Inc., a U.S. corporation, recognized $2 million of gross profit on sales of inventory in Mexico. Consider the sourcing of this income under three alternative scenarios.

Alternative 1. If Holzer purchased the inventory for resale, sourcing depends on the country where title is passed when the inventory is sold. Since passage of title is defined by the sales contract, Holzer can effectively choose whether to consider the profit as

[19] Section 863(b) and the temporary regulations thereunder.

sourced in Mexico (foreign source) or the United States. Note that Mexico's jurisdiction to tax this sale is determined by Mexican tax law and the terms of the tax treaty between the United States and Mexico.

Alternative 2.  If Holzer manufactured the inventory in Mexico, all of the profit is considered to be sourced in Mexico (foreign source).

Alternative 3.  If Holzer manufactured the inventory in the United States, 50 percent of the profit is sourced to both Mexico (foreign source) and to the United States.

In addition to income being sourced as either foreign or U.S. source, deductions must be allocated to their related income items. This is a complex area of tax law, and only the most basic rules are discussed here. In general, direct expenses for specific types of income are sourced to the location that generates the income. Indirect expenses that cannot be clearly related to a specific income source must be allocated across business activities and then apportioned between U.S. and foreign source income.[20]

Interest expense is subject to special sourcing rules. Since money is fungible, directly determining how borrowed funds are spent is difficult. As a result, interest expense is allocated between U.S. and foreign activities based on the assets used to support those activities.[21] Finally, **Section 482** gives the IRS broad power to reallocate both income and expenses in a manner that it believes is necessary to "clearly reflect" income.

# TAXATION OF ALTERNATIVE LEGAL FORMS OF FOREIGN OPERATIONS

**Objective 6**

Identify the alternative legal forms through which a U.S. corporation could choose to conduct business in a foreign jurisdiction.

The taxation of foreign income earned by U.S. multinational corporations also depends on the legal form through which the company conducts its foreign operations. A U.S. company can enter foreign markets in a number of ways. Initially, it can simply hire foreign sales representatives to market its products in other countries. It could permit unrelated foreign companies to use patents, processes, or trademarks that it developed through licensing arrangements. These two alternatives involve no physical presence by the U.S. company in the foreign jurisdiction; thus, the income earned might or might not be subject to foreign taxes, depending on the applicable treaty provisions if a treaty exists.

To expand foreign operations, having a physical presence in the foreign country can become necessary. The legal form for establishing this presence has four basic alternatives and is critical to determining the U.S. tax consequences of the resulting foreign income. First, the U.S. corporation can simply establish a branch office in the foreign country. Such a branch is not a legal entity distinct from the U.S. corporation; thus, any income it earns is included in worldwide taxable income. If the U.S. corporation pays taxes in the foreign country on branch earnings, it can claim a foreign tax credit subject to the same rules and limits previously discussed. Second, the U.S. corporation could conduct operations in partnership with others. Its share of partnership income is subject to U.S. taxation in the same manner as discussed in Chapter 7. The corporation's share of any foreign income taxes paid on partnership earnings is passed through to the corporation and is includible in its foreign tax credit. The third and fourth alternatives involve the formation of a controlled subsidiary to conduct foreign operations, incorporated in either the United States or a foreign country.

---

[20] If a business is involved in several activities (manufacturing different products, service activities), indirect expenses are first allocated among the various activities. Then the expenses for each activity are apportioned between U.S.- and foreign-source income on some reasonable basis, often relative income.

[21] Either fair market value or tax basis of assets can be used as the basis for allocation, but once market value is used, it must continue to be used in the future.

## Controlled Subsidiaries

For tax and nontax purposes, the U.S. corporation might wish to establish a controlled subsidiary to engage in foreign operations. Such a subsidiary is a separate legal entity with the U.S. corporation as the controlling (often sole) shareholder. In many foreign countries, legal restrictions exist on foreign ownership of property. Thus, operation through a foreign subsidiary might be the only feasible alternative. In other countries, so-called branch profits taxes could discourage the use of a branch operation and favor the establishment of a subsidiary. The optimal choice varies from country to country and situation to situation.

Taxation of the controlled subsidiary's earnings depends on whether the subsidiary is incorporated in the United States or in a foreign country. A controlled U.S. subsidiary's income is subject to U.S. taxation when earned under general corporate tax rules. If the controlled U.S. subsidiary pays dividends to its parent, such dividends typically qualify for the 100 percent dividends-received deduction and thus produce no U.S. taxation at the time of repatriation. The U.S. parent corporation's consolidated tax return includes the controlled U.S. subsidiary, and the consolidated group claims a foreign tax credit related to the subsidiary's foreign income and foreign taxes paid.

**Objective 7**

Discuss the tax advantages associated with conducting foreign operations through a controlled foreign subsidiary corporation.

A controlled foreign subsidiary is not an eligible corporation for purposes of consolidated return rules and thus cannot be included in the U.S. parent corporation's consolidated tax return. However, the income of a controlled foreign subsidiary is not subject to U.S. taxation when it is earned. Instead, it escapes U.S. taxation until the earnings are repatriated to the United States, meaning when they are paid to the U.S. parent corporation as a dividend. Note that the foreign jurisdiction probably taxes the income when earned and might also assess a tax on any dividend payments to the U.S. parent.

*Taxation of a Controlled Subsidiary*

Kilim Inc. is a wholly owned subsidiary of Southwest Inc., a U.S. corporation. Kilim operates a manufacturing facility in Ireland that makes products for distribution in the United Kingdom and Europe. Under a special incentive provision, the manufacturing facility's profits are subject to Irish income tax at a 10 percent rate. During 2003, Kilim generated $300,000 of taxable income (all from foreign sources), paid $30,000 of Irish corporate income tax, and made no dividend distributions. Southwest generated $400,000 of taxable income from U.S. sources.

If Kilim is incorporated in the United States, the consolidated U.S. income tax return for Southwest and Kilim reports $700,000 of worldwide taxable income. U.S. tax liability prior to credits is $238,000. The group takes a $30,000 foreign tax credit for Kilim's Irish income tax, resulting in net U.S. tax liability of $208,000 and worldwide tax liability of $238,000.

If Kilim is incorporated in Ireland, it does not file a consolidated tax return with Southwest. Since Kilim paid no dividends to Southwest, none of its 2003 income is subject to U.S. tax. Southwest pays U.S. tax liability of $136,000 on its $400,000 of U.S. taxable income. Worldwide tax liability for the group is reduced to $166,000.

**Objective 8**

Compute the taxable dividend amount and deemed paid foreign tax credit available to a U.S. corporation receiving distributions from a foreign corporation.

When a foreign subsidiary pays a dividend to its U.S. parent, it is paying out net earnings after paying foreign taxes. For U.S. tax purposes, the parent corporation recognizes dividend income equal to the gross earnings (before reduction by the foreign taxes paid) and then takes a **deemed paid foreign tax credit** for the applicable tax amount.[22] Taxable dividend income equals the net dividend received plus any foreign withholding tax on the dividend distribution plus foreign taxes paid by the controlled foreign subsidiary on the income from which the dividend is distributed. Note that dividends received from foreign corporations are not eligible for the dividends-received deduction, so the total grossed-up amount of the dividend is subject to U.S. tax.[23]

[22] Sections 902 and 960.

[23] Section 243.

*Taxation of Controlled Subsidiary— Dividend Distributions*

Refer to the previous example involving Southwest and Kilim. During 2004, Kilim generated $200,000 of taxable income (all from non-U.S. sources) and paid $20,000 of Irish corporate income tax. Southwest generated $500,000 of taxable income from U.S. sources. Kilim made dividend distributions to Southwest equal to its Irish after-tax earnings for 2003 and 2004 (i.e., $450,000, or $300,000 − $30,000 + $200,000 − $20,000). Under the income tax treaty between the United States and the United Kingdom, no Irish tax was withheld on the dividend distribution to Southwest.

If Kilim is incorporated in the United States, the 2004 consolidated U.S. income tax return for Southwest and Kilim reports $700,000 of worldwide taxable income. U.S. tax liability prior to credits is $238,000. The group takes a $20,000 foreign tax credit for Kilim's 2004 Irish income tax, resulting in net U.S. tax liability of $218,000 and worldwide tax liability of $238,000. The dividend distribution from Kilim to Southwest is excluded from consolidated taxable income and has no current tax consequences.

If Kilim is incorporated in Ireland, the dividend payment must be grossed up and included in Southwest's U.S. taxable income. The amount of the taxable dividend equals the pretax income from which the dividend was paid (i.e., $500,000, or $450,000 dividend payment + $30,000 Irish tax in 2003 + $20,000 Irish tax in 2004). Southwest reports $1 million total U.S. taxable income for 2004 resulting in U.S. tax liability of $340,000 before credits. Southwest qualifies for a deemed paid foreign tax credit of $50,000, equal to the dividend gross-up amount, producing net U.S. tax liability of $290,000. Worldwide tax liability totals $310,000 for 2004.

Note that the group's worldwide income tax liability over the two-year period is $476,000 regardless of whether the subsidiary is incorporated in the United States or in Ireland. However, incorporation in Ireland defers payment of $72,000 of U.S. tax liability from 2003 until 2004. Using a 7 percent discount rate, the NPV of this deferral is $4,710.[24]

These two examples illustrate the application of two planning variables discussed in Chapter 1, the jurisdiction variable and the time period variable. By investing in low-tax foreign jurisdictions using foreign subsidiaries, U.S. corporations achieve an increase in after-tax value by reinvesting foreign profits rather than currently repatriating them. Although these corporations will owe U.S. tax when they eventually repatriate the foreign profits, deferral of such tax into the future reduces the net present value of this cost.

# SUBPART F INCOME OF CONTROLLED FOREIGN CORPORATIONS

**Objective 9**
Describe the rationale underlying the constructive repatriation rules of Subpart F.

As just demonstrated, a distinct advantage of operating through a foreign subsidiary is the deferral of U.S. taxation until the income is repatriated. If the U.S. parent has no pressing need for the cash and is building its foreign operations, it might delay repatriation indefinitely. If the foreign country in which operations occur has a low tax rate, the income earned by the foreign subsidiary might be subject to very little current taxation. These factors create the incentive for U.S. corporations to source income in so-called tax-haven countries even when the income really is earned elsewhere. Subpart F was enacted to prevent such schemes.

Any income considered **Subpart F income** is **constructively repatriated** and is thus subject to U.S. tax when it is earned by a **controlled foreign corporation (CFC)**.[25] A CFC is any foreign corporation in which U.S. shareholders own more than 50 percent of the total voting power or value of the corporate stock.[26] In applying the 50 percent test, a U.S.

[24] ($72,000 − $72,000/1.07).
[25] Section 951(a).
[26] Section 957(a).

shareholder includes any U.S. individual or corporation owning at least 10 percent of the foreign corporation's voting stock. This 10 percent rule is important because it excludes much of the stock ownership of broadly owned or publicly traded corporations. Thus, if a foreign corporation is owned in equal parts by 11 U.S. shareholders, it is not considered a CFC since no single shareholder owns at least 10 percent.

Subpart F income includes income from sales to related parties when the income is recorded but not really generated by a subsidiary located in a tax-haven country. Subpart F income can occur, for example, when a U.S. manufacturer sells inventory to a CFC. If the CFC sells the inventory in a country other than the one in which it is located, the gross profit from this sale is Subpart F income.

| | |
|---|---|
| *Impact of Subpart F on Sourcing Manipulation* | Suppose that a U.S. distributor wishes to sell its products in Europe. Prior to the enactment of Subpart F, it might have first established a subsidiary in the Cayman Islands, which assess no income tax. It would then have transferred title to the goods to be shipped overseas first to its subsidiary in the Cayman Islands. The distributor would charge the subsidiary a transfer price equal to its cost, resulting in no taxable profit in the United States. Then the subsidiary in the Cayman Islands would sell the goods to a European subsidiary at a transfer price equal to market value. At this transfer price, the European subsidiary would have no profit on eventual sales and owe no tax liability. The group would pay no tax in the Cayman Islands or the United States until it repatriates the profits. Assuming a $1 million gross profit on these sales, tax ranging from $340,000 to $400,000 could be deferred, depending on the applicable European tax rate.<br><br>Under Subpart F, both the subsidiaries in the Cayman Islands and in Europe are considered CFCs. The entire $1 million gross profit on the sales transaction is Subpart F income, constructively repatriated and subject to U.S. tax when earned. |

Note that in this example, the goods in question are shipped directly from the U.S. distributor to its European subsidiary. Thus, the transfer of title to the subsidiary in the Cayman Islands is purely a paper transaction. In this setting, Subpart F applies the "substance-over-form" doctrine, ignoring the form of the transaction in determining its tax consequences.

Subpart F income also includes most types of passive income from foreign sources to discourage the use of a CFC to undertake passive foreign investments.[27] For a variety of public policy reasons, Subpart F income also includes income earned from countries subject to international boycott and from countries with which the U.S. government has severed relations as well as payments of illegal foreign bribes by CFCs. Note that a CFC can earn many types of income not subject to Subpart F and thus not required to be constructively repatriated.

| | |
|---|---|
| *U.S. Taxation of CFC with Both Subpart F and Non-Subpart F Income* | Fuego Inc., a foreign corporation, was formed in 2003 as a wholly owned subsidiary of Firestar Inc., a U.S. corporation. Fuego's 2003 income is $300,000, of which $100,000 is considered Subpart F income. It paid $30,000 of foreign income tax. As a result, $100,000 of Fuego's 2003 income is considered constructively repatriated. Firestar will report constructive dividend income for 2003 grossed up by a proportionate share of Fuego's foreign tax payment. Firestar's taxable dividend amount is $110,000 [$100,000 constructive dividend + $10,000 share of tax payment ($30,000 × $100,000/$300,000)], and it can claim a deemed paid foreign tax credit of up to $10,000. |

---

[27] Subpart F income and other earnings treated as constructively repatriated when earned are defined in Sections 951 through 956 and the related regulations.

Subsequent actual distributions from Subpart F income are not taxed at distribution.[28] As a result, Subpart F simply accelerates taxation but does not cause double taxation. When a CFC earns both Subpart F income and non-Subpart F income, special ordering rules apply to determine the tax treatment of the subsequent distributions. The CFC must separately track its earnings and profits (E&P) from Subpart F sources. Distributions are deemed to be made first from **Subpart F earnings and profits (E&P)** and thus are not taxable when distributed. Additional distributions in excess of Subpart F E&P are deemed to come from non-Subpart F E&P. Because non-Subpart F income of a CFC was not subject to tax when it was earned, such distributions will be taxable to the recipient U.S. corporation.

| *Distribution by CFC with Both Subpart F and Non-Subpart F E&P* | Refer to the example involving Fuego and Firestar. Suppose that in 2004 Fuego earned $200,000 of income that included $50,000 of Subpart F income. Fuego distributed $225,000 to Firestar at the end of 2004. Immediately prior to the distribution, Fuego's Subpart F and non-Subpart F E&P balances were as follows: |
|---|---|

|  | *Subpart F E&P* | *Non-Subpart F E&P* |
|---|---|---|
| 2003 | $100,000 | $200,000 |
| 2004 | 50,000 | 150,000 |
| Total | $150,000 | $350,000 |

Fuego's distribution is deemed to be made first from Subpart F E&P. Thus, the first $150,000 of the distribution is not taxable to Firestar. The remainder of the distribution, $75,000, is made from non-Subpart F E&P and is taxable to Firestar. Firestar is also taxed on Fuego's 2003 Subpart F income since it is considered constructively repatriated. Both taxable distributions are subject to the deemed paid foreign tax credit and related gross-up procedure previously discussed.

# TRANSFER PRICING

**Objective 10**
Discuss the potential for manipulation of income sourcing through transfer pricing. Describe the methods available for computing transfer prices and the issues that arise in identifying comparable uncontrolled transactions.

The IRS uses an important weapon to combat the abuse inherent in the sourcing of foreign trade profits, the **transfer pricing** rules of Section 482. Section 482 applies to transactions between related corporations owned or controlled by the same shareholders. Recall that the tax law requires transactions between related parties to occur at arm's length. The intent of Section 482 is to ensure that the prices of such transactions reflect the arm's-length charges that would occur between independent entities. For example, when product manufacture and distribution involve several stages completed in different locations (particularly different countries with different tax rates), U.S. parent corporations have incentives to manipulate the price at which goods are transferred to controlled foreign corporations to shift profit to low-tax jurisdictions. Complex transfer pricing rules define arm's length for these and other transactions. The following example demonstrates the potential for manipulation of reported income via transfer pricing.

| *Transfer Pricing Manipulation* | Assume that a U.S. shirt manufacturer has a foreign subsidiary in Country X. Cloth to make shirts is woven in the United States for $4 per shirt and is shipped to Country X where it is cut and sewn at a cost of $5 per shirt. These shirts are sold in Europe for $30 per shirt. The profit on each shirt is $21, a portion of which is U.S.-source income and a portion of which is foreign-source income, depending on the price at which the cloth is transferred from the |
|---|---|

[28] Section 959(a).

United States to Country X. If Country X's tax rate is lower than that of the United States, the manufacturer would prefer to recognize profit in Country X and might set a transfer price equal to the cost of the cloth ($4). If the tax rate in Country X is higher than in the United States, the manufacturer would prefer to recognize profit in the United States and might set a transfer price equal to cost plus net profit ($25).

The required transfer price is generally the price at which the cloth could be purchased in an arm's-length transaction between unrelated parties. Rationally, this price is somewhere between $4 and $25. If the arm's-length price were less than $4, the manufacturer would not bother to make the cloth itself but would buy it from the outside source. If the arm's-length price were more than $25, the manufacturer would prefer to sell the raw cloth rather than using it to manufacture shirts.

Section 482 applies not only to transfers of raw materials or inventory but also to any item of income, deduction, credit, or allowance affecting taxable income between controlled entities. In particular, these rules have been applied to transfers of tangible and intangible property, provision of services, rental profits, profits from financial operations, and shifts of expenses. To illustrate the issues involved in complying with these rules, we focus on two areas of common conflict between taxpayers and the IRS, the transfer of tangible inventory and intangible assets.

## Transfer Prices of Tangible Inventory

### Comparable Uncontrolled Transactions

The goal of the transfer pricing rules is to ensure that transactions between related parties are made at the same price (or profit) that would occur in a **comparable uncontrolled transaction** (i.e., a similar transaction between uncontrolled taxpayers). Complexity arises because in many instances a sufficiently comparable uncontrolled transaction is not available from which to determine an arm's-length price. Identifying comparable uncontrolled transactions is particularly difficult for sales of component parts between related corporations. Regulations under Section 482 provide five factors for assessing the comparability of controlled and uncontrolled transactions.

1. Functions performed by controlled and uncontrolled taxpayers.
2. Contractual terms of the controlled and uncontrolled transactions.
3. Risks borne in each transaction.
4. Economic conditions in the markets in which the controlled and uncontrolled transactions take place.
5. The similarity of the property or services transferred.[29]

*Issues in Identifying Comparable Transactions*

Cordovan Corporation is a U.S. computer manufacturer providing products to customers both at home and abroad. It has foreign manufacturing subsidiaries in Countries X and Y and foreign marketing subsidiaries in 10 additional countries. Manufacturing facilities in Country X produce computer components that are shipped to facilities in Country Y and the United States for assembly. Completed products are shipped to the United States and the marketing subsidiaries for sale to customers. To comply with Section 482, Cordovan must identify comparable uncontrolled transactions for pricing the transfer of components from Country X to the United States and Country Y and of completed products from the United States and Country Y to the marketing subsidiaries.

[29] Treasury Reg. 1.482-1(d).

If Cordovan sells its component parts to unrelated parties and uses them in its own production, such sales are potential comparable uncontrolled transactions. However, such sales might not be made under the same contractual terms as related-party sales or in the same markets. In addition, Cordovan might not make such sales. If it is a market leader in the development of new computer technology, sales of components and completed products by other manufacturers might not be sufficiently comparable to guide its pricing.

Once comparable uncontrolled transactions have been identified, the regulations prescribe pricing methods for determining the appropriate arm's-length price for controlled transactions. If the transactions involve transfers of tangible property (such as inventory or its components), six methods are available.

1. Comparable uncontrolled price method
2. Resale price method
3. Cost-plus method
4. Comparable profits method
5. Profit split method
6. Other methods proposed by the taxpayer

In choosing among these methods, the "best method rule" directs taxpayers to choose the method that provides the most accurate measure of an arm's-length result.[30] Not surprisingly, the best method typically produces some profit allocable to both U.S. and foreign locations.

Application of these transfer pricing methods can be quite complex. In addition, the transfer prices produced by each method likely vary considerably and depend on the choice of comparable uncontrolled transactions to which they are applied! We demonstrate each of these methods with simple examples designed primarily to highlight the issues that arise in selecting comparable uncontrolled transactions.

### Comparable Uncontrolled Price Method

When comparable uncontrolled transactions exist without major differences in product or terms of sale, the **comparable uncontrolled price method** is typically considered the best method for determining transfer price.[31]

*Comparable Uncontrolled Price Method*

Refer to the previous example involving Cordovan and its sale of component parts from Country X to Country Y and the United States. Suppose that the Country X subsidiary sells an identical component part to unrelated third parties for $200. Such sales are considered comparable uncontrolled transactions. If the terms of such sales were the same as those of a sale to Cordovan and its Country Y subsidiary, $200 is an appropriate transfer price under the comparable uncontrolled price method.

If the components sold or the terms of the sales to unrelated third parties are not identical, application of this method is possible *only* if the differences are minor and such differences have a reasonably ascertainable effect on price. For example, suppose that sales to third parties require the purchaser to pay freight costs, but the Country X subsidiary pays freight on sales within the Cordovan group. Assuming freight costs of $5 per component, $205 is an appropriate transfer price under the comparable uncontrolled price method.

[30] Treasury Reg. 1.482-1(c).
[31] Treasury Reg. 1.482-3(b).

When multiple uncontrolled transactions exist and produce different arm's-length prices, such transactions establish an arm's-length range of transfer prices. In general, the IRS respects the taxpayer's choice of transfer prices within this range if the related transactions are sufficiently comparable.

| *Range of Arm's-Length Transfer Prices* | Suppose that Cordovan's Country X subsidiary sells the component to 10 different unrelated third parties at prices ranging from $195 to $205. If all of these sales involve the identical component (or one with minor differences having ascertainable effects on price), Cordovan can use any transfer price between $195 and $205 in pricing sales of components from its Country X subsidiary to Country Y and the United States.<br><br>Suppose that Cordovan's marginal tax rate in Country X is 10 percent and in Country Y and the United States is 35 percent. Also assume that Cordovan transfers 2 million components from Country X to Country Y and the United States each year. Setting the transfer price for these transactions at $205 rather than at $195 will produce tax savings of $5 million per year [($205 − $195) × 2 million components × 25 percent rate differential]. |
|---|---|

If sales to unrelated third parties either do not exist or are not sufficiently comparable, transfer prices must be determined using one of the other permissible methods.

### Resale Price Method

The **resale price method** determines transfer prices for controlled transactions by examining the gross profit margin earned in comparable uncontrolled transactions.[32] Ideally, the method considers the gross profit margin that the controlled reseller earns on uncontrolled transactions. If this information is not available, the gross profit margin of other resellers can be used. As with the comparable uncontrolled price method, if application of the method to several comparable uncontrolled transactions produces different transfer prices, an arm's-length range can be identified.

| *Resale Price Method* | Cordovan's marketing subsidiaries sell its computers for $1,500. Suppose that these marketing subsidiaries also sell other computers purchased from unrelated suppliers. The marketing subsidiaries earn a 25 percent average gross profit margin on these other products. If the functions performed by the marketing subsidiaries and the risks and contract terms of these other sales are sufficiently comparable to the sales of Cordovan's computers, the resale price method uses the gross profit margin on these uncontrolled transactions to determine the appropriate transfer price to the marketing subsidiaries. Thus, a transfer price of $1,125 [$1,500 − ($1,500 × 25 percent)] applies to transfers from Cordovan and the Country Y assembly facilities to the marketing subsidiaries. |
|---|---|

### Cost-Plus Method

The **cost-plus method** determines transfer prices for controlled transactions by examining the gross profit markup earned in comparable uncontrolled transactions.[33] Applying this method to several uncontrolled transactions can also produce a range of acceptable arm's-length transfer prices.

| *Cost-Plus Method* | Suppose that Cordovan's Country X subsidiary sells substantially different components to unrelated third parties for $300. These components cost the subsidiary $180 to produce and earn a $120 gross profit. This gross profit represents a 66.7 percent markup on cost. Because these components are substantially different than those transferred within the Cordovan |
|---|---|

[32] Treasury Reg. 1.482-3(c).
[33] Treasury Reg. 1.482-3(d).

group, their price cannot be used to apply the comparable uncontrolled price method. However, the cost-plus method applies the 66.7 percent markup earned on these uncontrolled sales in determining the transfer price for controlled sales. If the cost of goods sold for the controlled sales is $125, the cost-plus method results in a transfer price of $208 ($125 × 1.667).

## Comparable Profits Method

The **comparable profits method** evaluates transfer prices used for controlled transactions based on measures of profitability of uncontrolled taxpayers engaged in similar activities with other uncontrolled taxpayers.[34] Various profit measures are permitted in applying this method, including the rate of return on capital, the ratio of operating profit to sales, and the ratio of gross profit to operating expenses. Taxpayers applying this method must select appropriate uncontrolled taxpayers and an appropriate profitability measure with which to determine transfer prices. In many cases, the method produces an arm's-length range of prices, allowing the taxpayer a choice of price that produces the best tax results.

*Comparable Profits Method*

Suppose that Cordovan's marketing subsidiaries compete with a number of uncontrolled taxpayers engaged in similar activities. Under these circumstances, the profitability of these competitors provides data for applying the comparable profits method. The choice of profitability measure focuses on finding a measure that was relatively stable across several years and several competitors. Suppose that the measure selected is the ratio of operating profit to sales and that average results for five of Cordovan's major competitors are as follows.

| Firm A | Firm B | Firm C | Firm D | Firm E |
|--------|--------|--------|--------|--------|
| 10% | 6.8% | 8.5% | 9% | 7.3% |

In applying the method, assume that one of Cordovan's marketing subsidiaries sold 50,000 computers at $1,500 each, resulting in total sales revenue of $75 million. The subsidiary's operating costs totaled $20 million. If the preceding data provide a range of acceptable operating profit ratios, this subsidiary could report operating profit between $5.1 million ($75 million × 6.8 percent) and $7.5 million ($75 million × 10 percent) after the choice of transfer price for payment to the assembly facilities. Operating profit of $5.1 million implies a cost of goods sold totaling $49.9 million ($75 million sales − $20 million operating costs − $5.1 million operating profit); operating profit of $7.5 million implies a cost of goods sold totaling $47.5 million. Thus, application of the comparable profits method supports a range of transfer prices between $950 ($47.5 million/50,000 computers) and $998 ($49.9 million/50,000 computers) per computer.

## Profit Split Method

The **profit split method** attempts to allocate the combined profit earned on the controlled transactions across members of the group in proportion to the relative value that each member contributes.[35] A number of restrictions are imposed on the use of the profit split method. In issuing the regulations describing this method, the IRS indicated that it is "likely that other methods will provide a more reliable measure of an arm's-length result under the best method rule."[36] Because of its limited use and the computational complexity associated with applying this method, we do not present a numerical example of the profit split method.

[34] Treasury Reg. 1.482-5.
[35] Treasury Reg. 1.482-6.
[36] TD 8552, 07/08/1994.

### Other Methods

Finally, a taxpayer can use a transfer pricing method other than one of the methods described if it provides information regarding the prices or profits the controlled taxpayer could have realized by choosing a realistic alternative to the controlled transaction.[37] The burden falls on the taxpayer to show that this other method provides a better measure of comparability than the methods provided by the regulations.

## Transfer Prices of Intangible Property

Transfer pricing difficulties also abound when the transactions involve the transfer or use of intangible property. For example, developers of new products or production processes typically patent their developments. Allowing a foreign subsidiary to use these patent rights requires the payment of royalties to the developer and the determination of the appropriate arm's-length price for such royalty payments. Established companies also own valuable trademarks, trade names, or brand names. Use of these rights by foreign marketing subsidiaries typically requires a licensing arrangement to which a value must be assigned and priced. Such arrangements often span multiple years, which increases the complexity of the pricing and the identification of comparable uncontrolled transactions for applying the allowable transfer pricing methods.

## Advance Pricing Agreement

Given the difficulties inherent in identifying comparable uncontrolled transactions and the complexity associated with applying the available transfer pricing methods and rules, conflicts frequently occur between taxpayers and the IRS on these issues. IRS audits of taxpayers with transfer pricing issues typically span multiple years and require volumes of supporting data regarding controlled transactions and potential comparable uncontrolled transactions. In addition, the adjustments made by such audits affect not only U.S. tax liability but also the income reported in foreign jurisdictions. If these jurisdictional disagreements about the pricing adjustments or the timing of the adjustment preclude the filing of amended foreign returns, double taxation often results. To mitigate the substantial costs associated with transfer pricing conflicts, advance pricing agreements have been developed.

An **advance pricing agreement (APA)** is an agreement between a taxpayer and the IRS on the transfer pricing method to be used for any set of transactions to which Section 482 applies. In requesting an APA, the taxpayer proposes a pricing method and provides data to support the contention that the proposed method achieves an arm's-length result in allocating income between the related corporations. If the IRS finds the taxpayer's proposal acceptable, it executes an APA. If the United States has a tax treaty in place with the foreign country in which the specified transactions take place, procedures might exist under which the foreign tax authority will also agree to be bound by the APA for these transactions.

# MULTINATIONAL OPERATIONS AND ACCOUNTING FOR INCOME TAXES

As discussed in Chapter 5, temporary differences between financial statement net income and taxable income impact the characterization of tax expense and tax liability as current or deferred. Permanent differences alter overall tax expense and liability and the

---

[37] Treasury Reg. 1.482-3(a).

corporation's effective tax rate. When U.S. corporations and their affiliates operate globally, a variety of income tax accounting issues arise. In particular, overall book tax expense and tax liability include both U.S. and foreign income taxes. Foreign tax credits operate to reduce overall tax liability (by mitigating double taxation). To the extent usage of foreign tax credits is limited, the corporation's overall effective tax rate may exceed the federal statutory rate.

Deferral of taxation achieved through the use of foreign subsidiaries without repatriation of earnings produces a temporary difference between book and taxable income. The related book tax expense and liability is typically deferred until the income is repatriated. However, if the U.S. parent corporation deems such earnings to be permanently invested in the foreign jurisdiction, deferred tax expense need not be recognized. This determination is appropriate only in cases in which the U.S. parent does not expect to repatriate such earnings in the near future.[38]

| *Microsoft Corporation Disclosures* | The following disclosures regarding earnings of foreign subsidiaries were included in the notes to Microsoft Corporation's Annual Report for the year ended June 30, 2003:<br><br>Income tax expense includes U.S. and international income taxes, plus the provision for U.S. taxes on undistributed earnings of international subsidiaries not deemed to be permanently invested. . . . We have not provided for U.S. deferred income taxes or foreign withholding taxes on $1.64 billion of our undistributed earnings for certain non-U.S. subsidiaries, all of which relate to fiscal 2002 and 2003 earnings, because these earnings are intended to be reinvested indefinitely. |
| --- | --- |

## MULTINATIONAL PLANNING EXAMPLE

Hollowell Corporation is a U.S. multinational conducting operations in five countries. It develops and markets computer software for use in a variety of accounting, financial reporting, and management applications. The company's consultants work with each client to customize the software for its individual reporting and business needs. Hollowell's business has grown substantially in recent years, and it is actively exploring new markets in which to distribute its products.

Most of Hollowell's current international operations are conducted through foreign subsidiaries located in Belgium and Singapore. It designs and performs the software development activities in the United States. It then licenses the rights to use the software to the foreign subsidiaries. Consultants employed by either the U.S. parent corporation or a foreign subsidiary generally perform the customization activities in the client's country.

With respect to its existing multinational operations, the Hollowell group pays substantial foreign taxes. Much of the foreign subsidiaries' earnings are reinvested, but some repatriation has occurred, and the U.S. parent corporation earns some foreign source income directly. It has encountered foreign tax credit limitations in some taxable years.

With respect to expansion of its international operations, Hollowell wishes to establish a subsidiary in Central and South America to service clients there. It is also considering moving its Belgian offices to an alternative European location.

Hollowell's international expansion decisions should consider the following relevant tax planning issues:

[38] See *APB 23*, paragraph 12, and *SFAS 109*, paragraph 31.

- For each potential location, it should examine the provisions of existing U.S. treaties to identify protections from double taxation, reductions in withholding rates, and definitions of creditable foreign taxes.
- It must consider the tax burden of all potential taxes, including income taxes, VAT, property, payroll, and other local taxes in each location. When VAT applies, applicability of reduced incentive rates should be explored.
- It should identify tax location incentives in each possible location, including tax credits, lower tax rates, preferential financing options, and so forth.
- It should incorporate its subsidiaries in foreign jurisdictions with lower tax rates to avoid U.S. taxation until repatriation. Care should be taken to avoid Subpart F income when possible.

The following tax planning ideas are relevant to Hollowell's current and future international operations:

- *Cross-crediting opportunities to minimize potential for foreign tax credit limitations.* Hollowell should also reexamine its sourcing of income and deductions and look for ways to increase foreign source income (without a corresponding increase in foreign taxes). If foreign tax credit limitations persist, it might consider deducting foreign taxes in some years rather than taking the credit.
- *Transfer-pricing opportunities.* It should examine the pricing of software licensing rights between the U.S. parent and its foreign subsidiaries. It should identify comparable uncontrolled transactions that support a broader range of potential transfer prices. The firm can then strategically choose prices within this range to shift income from high-tax to low-tax jurisdictions.
- *EU simplification and harmonization.* Given Hollowell's substantial European operations, it should monitor the activities of EU regarding VAT and income tax systems across member countries. Its choice of country in which to relocate its Belgian operations should consider the advantages of locating in the EU or a nonmember country.

## Conclusion

Global expansion of U.S. businesses creates many new opportunities for value maximization. It also creates considerable exposure to new and unfamiliar foreign taxes and increases the complexity of U.S. tax planning and compliance. Planning issues to consider include the existence of tax treaties between the United States and targeted countries, the legal structure through which foreign operations will be conducted, and the transfer pricing requirements for transactions between U.S. corporations and their global subsidiaries. Significant tax implications occur in each of these areas and create new challenges in maximizing after-tax value.

## Key Terms

| | | |
|---|---|---|
| advance pricing agreement (APA)   *308* | constructively repatriated income   *301* | foreign-source income   *297* |
| comparable profits method   *307* | controlled foreign corporation (CFC)   *301* | foreign tax credit   *295* |
| comparable uncontrolled price method   *305* | cost-plus method   *306* | inbound transactions   *290* |
| comparable uncontrolled transaction   *304* | deemed paid foreign tax credit   *300* | outbound transactions   *290* |
| | European Union (EU)   *294* | permanent establishment   *291* |

| Questions and Problems for Discussion | |
|---|---|

**Questions and Problems for Discussion**

1. Discuss at least three reasons why identifying income as either U.S. or foreign source is important for U.S. income tax purposes.

2. Compare the permanent establishment requirement for the taxing jurisdiction of foreign businesses to the nexus rules for state taxing jurisdiction over out-of-state businesses discussed in Chapter 10. Which approach is more likely to establish a jurisdiction to tax?

3. Many foreign countries use imputation systems to avoid double taxation of corporate earnings on distributions to shareholders. What other alternative tax treatments can you propose to alleviate the double taxation of corporate earnings? What are the advantages and disadvantages of each approach?

4. What are the advantages and disadvantages of a VAT system versus a sales tax system? Would you recommend that the United States consider implementing a VAT? Why or why not?

5. If a consumer services provider qualifies for a reduced VAT rate intended to encourage activity in its industry, who will benefit from this incentive?

6. How will harmonization of VAT and income tax systems help the EU meet its goals?

7. Under what conditions would taxpayers have an incentive to manipulate the sourcing of income to recognize proportionately more foreign source income? Under what conditions would proportionately more U.S. source income be desired?

8. Which of the sourcing rules pertaining to inventory sales can the taxpayer most easily manipulate?

9. Given the incentives to shift income into low-tax rate jurisdictions, do you expect such shifting would be easier to accomplish based on the transfer prices applied to tangible goods or those applied to intangible goods and services? Explain your answer.

10. What are the advantages of entering into an advance pricing agreement for a multinational taxpayer? What are the potential disadvantages?

**Application Problems**

1. Country A uses a dividend imputation system to alleviate double taxation of corporation earnings. Resident shareholders receiving dividends from corporations incorporated in Country A report dividend income equal to the cash received plus 100 percent of the corporate tax deemed paid on the dividend distribution. The shareholder is then allowed a tax credit equal to the dividend gross-up amount.

   a. If Corporation X earns $1 million and pays a 25 percent tax in Country A, calculate its net income tax liability and after-tax earnings available for distribution.

   b. Mr. Bennett is a Corporation X shareholder. If he receives a $1,000 cash distribution, calculate his reported dividend income.

   c. If Mr. Bennett's marginal tax rate in Country A is 30 percent, calculate his incremental tax liability as a result of the dividend distribution.

   d. Assuming that all of Corporation X's shareholders have the same marginal tax rate, calculate the combined total tax burden on the corporate taxable income under this system.

2. Consider a production process for the manufacture of baskets. Company A grows and harvests reeds that it sells to Company B for $40,000. Company B weaves the reeds into baskets that it sells to a retailer for $100,000. The retailer sells the baskets to consumers for $130,000. If a VAT of 15 percent applies to these activities, calculate the VAT tax paid by Companies A and B and the retailer and the total VAT assessed on this product.

3. Torres Corporation had the following results for its first three years of operations.

|  | 2002 | 2003 | 2004 |
|---|---|---|---|
| U.S.-source income | $190,000 | $230,000 | $300,000 |
| Foreign-source income | 150,000 | 170,000 | 500,000 |
| Worldwide taxable income | $340,000 | $400,000 | $800,000 |
| Foreign income tax paid | $ 15,000 | $ 35,000 | $200,000 |

   a. Compute Torres's 2002, 2003, and 2004 gross U.S. income tax liability, allowable foreign tax credit, and net U.S. income tax liability.
   b. Compute the refund generated by Torres's carryback of its 2004 excess foreign tax credit and any remaining credit carryforward.

4. Styler Corporation earned income and paid foreign income taxes as follows.

|  | Income Earned | Foreign Taxes Paid |
|---|---|---|
| Foreign-source income, Country A | $1.0 million | $400,000 |
| Foreign-source income, Country B | 2.0 million | 300,000 |
| U.S.-source income | 1.5 million | –0– |
| Total | $4.5 million | $700,000 |

   a. If the income earned in Countries A and B is subject to the general credit limitation, calculate Styler's allowable foreign tax credit, net U.S. income tax liability, and worldwide income tax liability.
   b. How would your answers to part *(a)* change if the income earned in Country A is passive income subject to a separate basket limitation?

5. Grenaker Corporation is located in San Diego, California. It leases vans, buses, and large trucks to customers in both the United States and Mexico. During the current year, Grenaker sold two used buses for $50,000 each for which title passed in the United States. The first bus originally cost $120,000 and had an adjusted tax basis of $40,000 when sold. While Grenaker owned this bus, it rented it for use 20 percent in the United States and 80 percent in Mexico. The second bus originally cost $150,000 and had an adjusted tax basis of $20,000 when sold. Grenaker rented it for use 50 percent in the United States and 50 percent in Mexico.
   a. Calculate Grenaker's gain recognized on each sale.
   b. How much of Grenaker's total gain on sale of the buses is U.S.-source income and how much is foreign-source income?

6. Export Inc., a U.S. corporation, owns 100 percent of the stock of Import Inc., a foreign corporation. For the current year, Export receives a dividend of $30,000 from Import. Import has accumulated E&P (after taxes) of $500,000 before this distribution and has paid foreign taxes on these earnings totaling $300,000. It has made no previous distributions to Export.

*a.* If Export elects to take the deemed-paid foreign tax credit, how much dividend income must it report related to the payment from Import?

*b.* Export has $600,000 U.S.-source income and no other foreign-source income. Calculate its U.S. tax liability before foreign tax credit, allowable deemed paid foreign tax credit, and net tax liability after foreign tax credit.

7. Elmo Inc. is a U.S. corporation with a branch office in Country Z. During 2004, it had $340,000 U.S.-source income and $60,000 foreign-source income from Country Z on which it paid $28,000 of Country Z income tax.

   *a.* Calculate Elmo's U.S. tax liability before foreign tax credit, maximum foreign tax credit allowable, and net U.S. tax liability after foreign tax credit.

   *b.* If Elmo had paid only $10,000 of Country Z income tax, calculate its foreign tax credit allowable and net U.S. tax liability after foreign tax credit.

   *c.* For which situation (foreign tax of $28,000 or $10,000) could Elmo have reduced its worldwide tax burden by operating in Country Z using a foreign subsidiary rather than a branch operation? Explain briefly.

8. Valencia Corporation, a U.S. corporation, has 2004 taxable income from U.S. sources of $300,000 and from foreign sources of $120,000 before considering the impact of foreign taxes. It paid $20,000 of foreign taxes during 2004.

   *a.* If Valencia's foreign taxes are not creditable, calculate its U.S. tax liability for 2004.

   *b.* If Valencia's foreign taxes are creditable, calculate its allowable foreign tax credit and net U.S. tax liability for 2004. Do you recommend that Valencia elect to credit its foreign taxes rather than deduct them?

   *c.* How would your answers to parts *(a)* and *(b)* change if Valencia paid $60,000 of foreign taxes during 2004?

9. Jonus Inc. conducts its European operations through a subsidiary, Jonbel, located in Belgium. During 2004, Jonbel reported net taxable income of $200,000, paid Belgian income tax of $70,000, and made no distributions to Jonus. Assume that Jonus's U.S. source income is $500,000 and that it has no other foreign source income.

   *a.* What are the U.S. tax consequences of Jonbel's 2004 activity if it is a foreign corporation and its income is not considered Subpart F income?

   *b.* What are the U.S. tax consequences of Jonbel's 2004 activity if it is a domestic corporation and files a consolidated tax return with Jonus?

10. Refer to application problem 9. How would your answers change if Jonbel distributed $50,000 to Jonus during 2004? Based on the tax treaty between the United States and Belgium, no taxes were withheld from the distribution.

11. Refer to application problem 9. How would your answer to part *(a)* change if Jonbel's 2004 income were considered Subpart F income?

12. Filigree Inc., a foreign corporation, is a wholly owned subsidiary of Gold Corporation, a U.S. corporation. Filigree's 2004 taxable income of $1 million included $300,000 of Subpart F income. Filigree paid $270,000 of foreign income tax and made no distributions to Gold during 2004. Gold's separate company 2004 taxable income was $2 million, all of which was U.S. source.

    *a.* What are the U.S. tax consequences of Filigree's 2004 activity?

    *b.* Calculate Gold's 2004 taxable income, allowable foreign tax credit, and net U.S. tax liability.

13. Refer to application problem 12. During 2005, Filigree distributed $1 million to Gold. Immediately prior to the distribution, Filigree had Subpart F E&P of $800,000 (after reduction for total foreign taxes of $216,000) and nonsubpart F E&P of $900,000 (after reduction for total foreign taxes of $243,00).

a. What are the U.S. tax consequences of Filigree's distribution to Gold?

b. Calculate Gold's taxable dividend income as a result of the distribution from Filigree.

14. Using the comparable uncontrolled price method, Wyss Corporation has identified a range of potential transfer prices from $400 to $460 for raw materials transferred from its foreign subsidiary to the U.S. corporation for use in its manufacturing operations.

a. If Wyss's marginal U.S. tax rate is 35 percent and the foreign subsidiary's tax rate is 25 percent, what transfer price should Wyss use to price the sale of these raw materials?

b. If 500,000 units of raw material are transferred each year, how much tax savings does your recommended price in part (a) generate?

c. How would your answers to parts (a) and (b) change if the foreign subsidiary's tax rate is 40 percent?

15. Refer to application problem 14. On the assumption of a constant production rate and no change in pricing, what is the present value of the tax savings calculated in part (b) over a 15-year period using a 10 percent discount rate?

16. Mauberry Corporation uses the resale price method to compute transfer prices on sales from its manufacturing subsidiaries to its marketing subsidiaries. Assume that the marketing subsidiaries also sell products purchased from unrelated suppliers. The average gross profit percentage on these other products is 40 percent. Calculate the appropriate transfer price for a product transferred from Mauberry's manufacturing subsidiary and sold by a marketing subsidiary for $600.

17. Danvers Inc. sells raw materials to its foreign subsidiaries for use in manufacturing. It also sells substantially different raw materials to unrelated manufacturers at a price of $400 per unit, earning a gross profit on these sales of $130 per unit. If the materials that Danvers sells to its foreign subsidiaries cost $500 to produce, use the cost-plus method to compute an appropriate transfer price.

18. Spice Corporation distributes its products through marketing subsidiaries in several countries. It has gathered the following data on the ratio of operating profit to sales for competitor marketers to be used in applying the comparable profits method.

| Competitor A | Competitor B | Competitor C |
| --- | --- | --- |
| 14.5% | 12% | 15% |

Assume that one of Spice's marketing subsidiaries sold 400,000 of its products at $200 each. The subsidiary's operating costs totaled $30 million.

a. Calculate the transfer price and operating profit resulting from applying the comparable profits method for each competitor.

b. If the foreign tax rate faced by Spice's marketing subsidiaries is 25 percent and its U.S. marginal tax rate is 34 percent, which of the transfer prices calculated in part (a) would you recommend? How much worldwide tax liability would Spice save annually by using this transfer price rather than each of the alternatives?

## Issue Recognition Problems

Identify the tax issue or issues suggested by the following situations and state each issue in the form of a question.

1. Coleus Corporation, which manufactures paper products, plans to build a new factory in either Country A or Country B. Construction and direct production costs are similar

in each country. Country A assesses no income tax; Country B assesses it at a 20 percent rate.

2. Palmer Inc. is a foreign corporation operating in South America. Its stock is owned by seven shareholders, two U.S. corporations, one U.S. citizen, and four non-U.S. individuals.

3. Moldou Corporation is a foreign subsidiary of a U.S. company. During 2004, it earned $1 million of income from active business operations and $200,000 of interest and dividend income from investments in stocks of other foreign corporations.

4. Global Inc. is a U.S. company with nine foreign subsidiaries. It manufactures products in three countries and sells them via marketing subsidiaries in six additional countries. Of the nine countries in which Global operates, four have income tax rates higher than the U.S. rate and five have lower income tax rates. In the past, Global has recognized very little taxable income in the high–tax rate countries, average taxable income in the United States and considerable taxable income in the low–tax rate countries.

5. Scooter Corporation, a U.S. corporation, ships its products abroad for sale in retail establishments owned by unrelated sellers. Scooter uses independent sales agents to market its products to foreign retailers.

6. Lotus Inc. earns substantial income from foreign sources. Such income is subject to high rates of foreign income tax, and Lotus's use of its foreign tax credits is frequently limited. In the current year, Lotus has also generated foreign-source income from countries with much lower income tax rates.

7. Milne–Fonda Corporation sold $2 million of inventory to customers in foreign countries. Some of the inventory was manufactured in the United States, and some was purchased for resale. On all inventory sales, title passed to the customer in the country in which the customer took delivery.

8. Allen Inc. is a U.S. corporation with foreign subsidiaries in both Canada and Mexico. It licenses proprietary manufacturing processes to its subsidiaries, but the license fee charged to the Canadian subsidiary is substantially higher than one charged to the Mexican subsidiary.

9. Davenport Corporation, a U.S. manufacturer, sells component parts to its foreign subsidiary for assembly and sale to customers abroad. It also sells components that are similar, but not identical, to unrelated manufacturers. Davenport uses the price at which it sells components to unrelated manufacturers as the transfer price for the components it sells to its foreign subsidiary.

# Research Problems

1. Locate an online source for the complete text of all currently effective U.S. income tax treaties. With what Central American countries does the United States have a tax treaty? What Mexican taxes does the tax treaty between the United States and Mexico define to be creditable for purposes of the U.S. foreign tax credit?

2. Fly-by-Night Air operates a regional airline in the northwestern United States. Most of its flights are in the United States, but some flights go to Canada. On average, 80 percent of the tickets on these cross-border flights are sold to passengers who are U.S. residents; the other 20 percent are sold to Canadian passengers. Is Fly-by-Night's revenue from its cross-border flights considered U.S.-source income, foreign-source income, or both? If both, what proportions are U.S. source and foreign source?

3. Alco Corporation is a technology company selling computer peripherals internationally. Its primary market niche is the advancement of new and faster technologies. It invests considerable amounts each year in research and development activities. All of

Alco's research facilities are located in the United States, but 60 percent of revenues from sales of its technology products comes from foreign sources. Should Alco's tax deductions for research and development reduce its U.S.-source income, or must these deductions be allocated between U.S.- and foreign-source income? Describe in general the procedures for any required allocation of these expenses.

## Tax Planning Cases

1. Kaplan Enterprises Inc., a U.S. corporation, wants to expand its business operations into a foreign host country that imposes a 20 percent tax on corporate income earned within its borders. It anticipates that its new foreign operation will generate losses for three years. After the initial loss period, the corporation should be extremely profitable.
   a. Discuss tax and nontax advantages and disadvantages if Kaplan decides to operate the foreign business in either of the following ways:
      (1) Through a U.S. corporate subsidiary.
      (2) Through a corporation created under the laws of the host country.
   b. Assume that Kaplan chooses to form a foreign corporation to conduct its non-U.S. operations. At the end of its fourth year of operations, the foreign corporation distributes $100,000 to Kaplan from its earnings and profits previously taxed by the host country. Under a favorable tax treaty, no taxes are withheld on the dividend payment. Kaplan has U.S. taxable income of $400,000 from other sources. Compute the amount of dividend income Kaplan must recognize as a result of this distribution, as well as its U.S. income tax liability after consideration of any foreign tax credit.

2. Gambler Corporation is a U.S. multinational firm facing a 35 percent U.S. marginal tax rate. Its foreign subsidiary in Country X has a 20 percent tax rate. The subsidiary has $100 million of equity representing earnings and profits that have already been taxed in its home country. Repatriation of these profits to Gambler would trigger taxable income in the United States. Under a favorable tax treaty, Country X imposes no withholding tax on dividends repatriated from it to the United States.
   a. How much U.S. taxable income would Gambler recognize if its foreign subsidiary paid a dividend of $100 million?
   b. How much additional U.S. income tax would Gambler owe on the dividend from part (a) after considering any available foreign tax credit?
   c. Gambler is considering two alternative uses for the funds that have accumulated in its foreign subsidiary. Alternative 1: The $100 million could be reinvested in business activities in Country X producing an annual before-tax return of 13 percent. These activities have a finite investment horizon after which their total accumulated value (including the initial investment of $100 million) in Country X would be repatriated to the United States. Alternative 2: The $100 million could be repatriated currently and the net repatriation (dividend less additional U.S. taxes calculated in part [b]) could be invested in the United States to earn a 15 percent before-tax return.
   Would the U.S. firm prefer to repatriate or to reinvest abroad if its investment horizon is:
      (1) 1 year?
      (2) 5 years?
      (3) 10 years?
   *Hint:* Answer this question by calculating the after-tax accumulation at the end of the investment horizon under each alternative, assuming that each year's after-tax cash flow is reinvested at the same after-tax rate of return.

*d.* How would your calculations in part *(c)* change if the before-tax rate of return in Country X were 11 percent rather than 13 percent?

*e.* Suppose that the only productive investments available in Country X are passive, resulting in Subpart F income. How and when would such income be taxed, and how would your calculations in part *(c)* change?

*f.* What other tax and nontax factors should Gambler consider in making its reinvestment or repatriation decision?

3. Expando Corporation, a U.S. corporation, earned $600,000 of passive foreign source and $4 million of foreign source income in the "other" basket. Expando paid $250,000 of foreign income tax on its passive foreign source income and $1 of foreign income taxes on its other foreign source income. Expando also had $5 million of U.S. source income.

*a.* Compute Expando's separate-basket foreign tax credit limitations.

*b.* Compute Expando's net U.S. tax liability after foreign tax credits.

*c.* Compute Expando's total worldwide tax burden and its worldwide effective tax rate.

*d.* How could Expando have benefited from cross-crediting opportunities in the absence of the separate basket limitations? Specifically, how much current tax savings could it have generated?

*e.* Can you advise Expando on any ways to reduce its foreign-tax credit limitations? Be specific in your recommendations.

## Comprehensive Case for Part Four

### Case Facts

Roadcat Corporation manufactures office supplies—pens, pencils, staplers, binders, etc. Its products have a reputation for durability and reasonable pricing. It distributes these products through office supply retailers primarily in the United States. However, Roadcat has recently begun shipping products to Canada and Central America and is considering additional global expansion of its operations.

Roadcat currently produces its products in one manufacturing facility in the western United States. It plans to continue shipping products from this facility to western Canada. However, it is considering constructing another facility in the eastern United States and additional manufacturing facilities in other parts of the world to serve customers outside North America. It has begun research on the feasibility of construction in the following regions: Central America, South America, and Europe. Given economic and political conditions in the Middle East, Asia, and Africa, Roadcat is not considering expansion into these areas at this time.

Feasible locations for expansion must support the infrastructure needs of Roadcat's manufacturing and shipping operations. Specifically, dependable supplies of electricity, paved roads, an international airport, and access to major port facilities that support container-shipping operations are critical. While highly skilled labor is not a major need, availability of a trainable, reliable employee base is necessary. Each new manufacturing facility would expect to employ 300 workers. Roadcat would likely transfer U.S. management personnel to run any new facilities outside the United States, at least for the first five years of operations. The estimated cost of each new facility, based on U.S. construction costs, is $100 million, incurred over a three-year construction period. This estimate assumes availability of construction materials and construction personnel in the chosen area. If materials and personnel must be imported, construction costs could be as much as $150 million.

Roadcat's marketing personnel have completed initial investigations of the demand for its products in Europe and Central and South America. Projections indicate that expansion into these areas might produce losses in the first several years but would ultimately prove profitable, with payback of expected construction costs over a 10- to 15-year period. These projections assume steady economic growth in the global market for office supplies, a stable political environment in global manufacturing locations, and a flat or slightly expanding U.S. economy.

### Case Requirements

1. Select two states in the eastern United States to research as potential domestic investment locations.

2. Select a region of the world (Europe, Central America, South America). Within that region, select two countries to research as potential international investment locations.

3. Seek out information on the tax and business environments in your four chosen locations. Look for online sources or information available in the library or from accounting firms. Also check whether the U.S. has a tax treaty with each of your chosen countries, and examine the provisions of any treaties that exist. This portion of your research should address the following issues in detail:

   a. The general form of taxation of business investment in each location, including applicable income, value-added, sales, excise, and other forms of taxation.

   b. The rates of tax that apply, available tax credits, and other tax incentive provisions available for new business investment of the type described in the case facts.

   c. Taxation of U.S. citizens working and living in the foreign countries in which Roadcat might construct new facilities.

   d. Other business environmental factors that impact the attractiveness of each location, including general economic and political climate, cost of living, rates of employment/unemployment, education level of the workforce, banking system, conditions of roads, airports, shipping ports, utilities, and so on.

4. Given the information developed in (3) above:

   a. Make a recommendation as to the state in which the domestic facility should be located and the country in which the new international facility should be located.

   b. Indicate the legal form through which the new international operations should be conducted—branch, U.S. subsidiary, or foreign subsidiary—and whether the new domestic operations should be conducted as a division or through a separate subsidiary corporation. Your discussion of these issues should consider the impact of each alternative on Roadcat's consolidated corporate income tax liability, including the deductibility of any losses incurred in the early years of the new operations.

   c. Explain and justify your recommendations.

# Part Five

# Business Capital Transactions

# Chapter Twelve

# Dispositions of Equity Interests in Business Entities

### Learning Objectives

*After reading this chapter, you will be able to:*

1. Describe the situations in which a shareholder adjusts the basis in C corporation stock.

2. Compute the Section 1202 exclusion.

3. Characterize the loss recognized on sale or exchange of Section 1244 stock as ordinary or capital.

4. Determine the tax consequences of a stock redemption to the shareholder.

5. Compute the reduction in E&P and AAA from a stock redemption.

6. Characterize the gain or loss recognized on sale or exchange of a partnership interest.

7. Determine the tax consequences of a liquidating distribution from a partnership.

8. Contrast the treatment of suspended losses under the basis, at-risk, and passive activity loss limitations.

Part Five of *Advanced Strategies* consists of three chapters that examine the tax consequences of **capital transactions,** defined as transactions that change the ownership of a business entity. This chapter focuses on the dispositions of equity interests in business entities, Chapter 13 introduces the challenging topic of corporate acquisitions, mergers, and divisions, and Chapter 14 explores the tax consequences of liquidations and terminations that mark the end of an entity's existence.

Owners can dispose of equity interests through various methods. They can transact with a third party by selling or exchanging an interest for cash or other property. Sales and exchanges are generally taxable transactions that result in gain or loss recognition for the seller.[1] As an alternative to a sale or exchange, the owner can surrender the interest back to the entity in exchange for a cash or property distribution. This chapter addresses the tax consequences of both alternatives, first by discussing dispositions of stock in both C and S corporations and then by discussing dispositions of partnership interests. The last part of this chapter summarizes the effect of the dispositions of interests in passthrough entities on the owner's suspended losses with respect to the interest.

Regardless of the disposition method, an owner wants to receive the highest possible price for an equity interest. The price at which an interest changes hands depends on the underlying FMV of the business. Professional appraisers who specialize in business valuations consider all relevant facts, including the value of both recorded and unrecorded assets (such as goodwill) and the future earning capacity of the business as a going concern. Even when the FMV of a business is determined, the FMV of a *part interest* in that business is negotiable. If the interest does not give the owner control of the business, the interest's FMV might reflect a **minority interest discount.** If the interest does give the owner control, its FMV may reflect a **control premium.**

| | |
|---|---|
| *Valuing an Equity Interest* | Mrs. Wayne is negotiating the sale of her 35 percent equity interest in WTP Company to Pemberton LLC. Two professional appraisers conclude that WTP's business has a $10 million FMV. Pemberton already owns a 20 percent interest, and the acquisition of Mrs. Wayne's interest would give it control of WTP's business policies. After intense bargaining, Pemberton finally agrees to Mrs. Wayne's asking price of $4.25 million, which includes a $750,000 control premium [$4.25 million − (35 percent × $10 million FMV of business)]. |

# SALES AND EXCHANGES OF CORPORATE STOCK

A classic characteristic of the corporate form of business is the free transferability of equity interests. Stock in publicly held corporations is traded on an established securities market, such as the New York Stock Exchange (NYSE) or Nasdaq. Consequently, the stock is a highly liquid asset that the owner can convert to cash almost instantly. Stock in closely held corporations is much less liquid, and its sale is a private market transaction, the terms of which must be negotiated between seller and buyer.

Closely held stock is often subject to a **buy-sell agreement** restricting the shareholder's right to dispose of the stock. This agreement might require the shareholder to obtain approval from the board of directors or to offer the stock to the other shareholders or to the corporation itself before the shareholder can sell the stock to a third party. These types of restrictions are particularly important for S corporations as safeguards against stock dispositions to impermissible shareholders that would terminate the S election. Buy-sell agreements often include a formula (such as capitalization of earnings or discounted cash flow) to fix the value of the stock. Such formulas are intended to minimize shareholder disputes and eliminate the need for costly professional appraisals.

## Corporate Stock as a Capital Asset

For federal tax purposes, the ownership of corporate stock is an investment activity. Even in the case of a sole shareholder who completely controls corporate policy, the corporation's business activities are not attributed to the shareholder. In other words, the shareholder is an investor in a separate and distinct entity that operates a business. This

---

[1] Nontaxable exchanges of equity interests are discussed in Chapter 13.

distinction between the shareholder's investment and the corporation's business is reflected by the fact that corporate stock is a capital asset. When a shareholder sells or exchanges stock in a taxable transaction, the gain or loss is capital regardless of the fact that the stock represents an equity interest in noncapital business assets.

| *Capital Gain on Stock Sale* | Mr. Farkas recently sold 300 shares of stock in Gregson Inc., which operates a manufacturing business. On date of sale, Gregson had the following balance sheet: |
| --- | --- |

|  | Tax Basis |
| --- | --- |
| Cash | $     20,000 |
| Accounts receivable | 100,000 |
| Inventory | 1,500,000 |
| Plant and equipment | 8,000,000 |
|  | $9,620,000 |
| Paid-in capital (1,000 shares) | $   100,000 |
| Retained earnings | 9,520,000 |
|  | $9,620,000 |

Mr. Farkas was one of the original investors who founded Gregson in 1986, and the tax basis in his 300 shares was only $30,000. The selling price for the 300 shares was $3,100,000, so he recognized a $3,070,000 long-term capital gain on sale.

Mr. Farkas's gain is primarily a result of Gregson's reinvestment of its after-tax earnings in operating assets. If Gregson had distributed these earnings, its shareholders (including Mr. Farkas) would have recognized dividend income. Instead, Mr. Farkas recognized the enhanced stock value resulting from Gregson's accumulation of business earnings as capital gain.

## Basis Issues

**Objective 1**
Describe the situations in which a shareholder adjusts the basis in C corporation stock.

Gain or loss recognized on the taxable disposition of corporate stock equals the difference between the amount realized and the owner's adjusted basis. The owner's initial basis, determined when the stock is acquired, equals either the cost or the substituted basis of property contributed to the corporation in a nontaxable Section 351 exchange. If the owner acquired blocks of stock at different times, she must keep track of the basis of each block.[2]

The initial basis of stock in a taxable corporation is not adjusted unless the shareholder makes a capital contribution to the corporation or the corporation distributes a return of capital to the shareholder.[3]

| *Stock Basis Adjustments* | Mrs. Echol purchased 1,000 shares of Olean stock for $89,000. Three years after the purchase, Olean's shareholders made a pro rata cash contribution to provide emergency working capital. Mrs. Echol's share of the capital contribution was $10,000. Last year, Olean distributed both a dividend and a return of capital to its shareholders. Mrs. Echol's return of capital was $3,400. Currently, the adjusted basis in her 1,000 shares is $95,600 ($89,000 cost + $10,000 capital contribution − $3,400 return of capital). |
| --- | --- |

[2] If a shareholder elects a dividend reinvestment option to purchase additional shares, the dividend amount becomes the cost basis in the additional shares.

[3] Section 301(c)(2).

If a shareholder sells only some of his shares of a particular stock and can identify the specific shares sold, the basis of those shares determines the gain or loss on sale. If the specific shares cannot be identified, the shareholder is deemed to have sold the shares with the earliest acquisition date.[4]

| *Determination of Stock Basis* | Mr. Hull purchased his 6,000 shares of Curtiz stock in the following transactions: |
|---|---|

| | June 2, 1990 | 2,200 shares at $16 per share |
|---|---|---|
| | November 13, 1995 | 800 shares at $24 per share |
| | December 8, 1999 | 3,000 shares at $43 per share |

This year, he sold 2,000 shares for $50 per share ($100,000 amount realized) and delivered a stock certificate to the purchaser for 2,000 of the 3,000 shares purchased on December 8, 1999. Because Mr. Hull could specifically identify the 2,000 shares, his basis is $86,000 (2,000 shares × $43), and his capital gain on sale is $14,000.

If Mr. Hull could not identify the specific Curtiz shares, he is deemed to have sold 2,000 of the shares purchased on June 2, 1990. His basis would be $32,000 (2,000 shares × $16), and his capital gain on sale would be $68,000.

## Tax Costs and Savings from Stock Sales

Individuals pay tax on their net long-term capital gain at a preferential rate. Currently, the preferential rates range from 5 to 28 percent, depending on the individual's marginal rate on ordinary income and certain characteristics of the capital gain. Unless otherwise noted, this text uses the 15 percent rate to compute the individual tax cost of a long-term capital gain. Corporations have no preferential rate on capital gains. Even so, corporate taxpayers prefer capital gains to ordinary income because their capital losses are deductible only to the extent of their capital gains.

### *Qualified Small Business Stock*

**Objective 2**
Compute the Section 1202 exclusion.

Most individuals who recognize capital gains are aware of the preferential tax rates. They should also be aware of an additional tax preference for gain recognized on sale or exchange of qualified small business stock. Section 1202 provides that if the individual held the stock for more than five years, 50 percent of the gain is excluded from gross income.[5] The gain eligible for the **Section 1202 exclusion** from the sale of stock *in any one corporation* is limited to the *greater* of (1) $10 million less any eligible gains recognized in prior years or (2) 10 times the basis of the corporation's qualified small business stock disposed of by the individual during the year.

| *Limit on Eligible Gain* | In 1995, Mrs. Broussard paid $55 per share for 50,000 shares of Traybone stock, which was qualified small business stock for federal tax purposes. Last year, she sold 15,000 shares for $260 per share, thereby recognizing a $3,075,000 gain ($205 gain per share × 15,000 shares). The entire gain was eligible for exclusion because it did not exceed $10 million (greater of $10 million or 10 × $825,000 basis of 15,000 shares). Consequently, Mrs. Broussard's Section 1202 exclusion last year was $1,537,500 (50 percent × $3,075,000). |
|---|---|

This year, Mrs. Broussard sold her 35,000 remaining Traybone shares for $670 per share, thereby recognizing a $21,525,000 gain ($615 gain per share × 35,000 shares). The gain

[4] Reg. 1.1012-1(c).
[5] Section 1202.

eligible for exclusion is limited to $19,250,000 (greater of $10 million − $3,075,000 eligible gain last year or 10 × $1,925,000 basis of 35,000 shares). Consequently, Mrs. Broussard's Section 1202 exclusion this year was $9,625,000 (50 percent × $19,250,000).

Use of the Section 1202 exclusion has two major drawbacks. First, the preferential rate on the taxable half of the eligible gain is 28 percent instead of 15 percent.[6] A 28 percent rate on one-half of a gain is equivalent to a 14 percent rate on the entire gain. Consequently, the Section 1202 exclusion results in 1 percent rate reduction. Second, 7 percent of the excluded gain is an AMT tax preference item that the seller must include in alternative minimum taxable income.[7] If the seller must actually pay AMT, the incremental AMT attributable to the exclusion eliminates almost the entire benefit of the 1 percent rate reduction.

| | | |
|---|---|---|
| ***Benefit of Exclusion*** | This year, Mr. Lee recognized a $200,000 capital gain on the sale of qualified small business stock, all of which is eligible for the Section 1202 exclusion. Unfortunately, his alternative minimum taxable income is high enough that he must pay AMT in addition to his regular tax. Here is a comparison of Mr. Lee's tax on the gain with and without use of the exclusion. | |

| | *With Exclusion* | *Without Exclusion* |
|---|---|---|
| Total gain | $200,000 | $200,000 |
| Exclusion | (100,000) | |
| Taxable gain | $100,000 | $200,000 |
| Preferential rate | .28 | .15 |
| Regular tax | $ 28,000 | $ 30,000 |
| | | |
| AMT preference | $ 7,000  *7% of 100,000* | |
| AMT marginal rate | .28 | |
| AMT | $ 1,960 | |
| | | |
| Total tax on gain | $ 29,960 | $ 30,000 |

If Mr. Lee had not been in an AMT position, the Section 1202 exclusion would have saved him $2,000 tax on a $200,000 gain. But because he was required to pay AMT, his tax savings from the exclusion is $40.

**Qualified small business stock** is issued after August 10, 1993, by a qualified small business in exchange for a contribution of money, property, or services. (Individuals cannot acquire qualified small business stock *from another shareholder.*) A qualified small business is a domestic C corporation with not more than $50 million gross assets immediately after the stock issuance. The corporation must conduct an active business other than a financial, leasing, real estate, farming, mining, hospitality, or professional service business.

[6] Section 1(h)(5).
[7] Section 57(a)(7).

### Section 1244 Stock

**Objective 3**
Characterize the loss recognized on sale or exchange of Section 1244 stock as ordinary or capital.

The preferential capital gain tax rates and the Section 1202 exclusion can reduce the tax cost of gains recognized on stock sales. The tax law contains another preference that works in the opposite direction by increasing the tax savings from losses recognized on stock sales. Section 1244 provides that the loss recognized by an individual on the sale or exchange of Section 1244 stock is ordinary rather than capital loss. As a result, the individual can deduct the loss against any source of income rather than against only capital gain. The annual ordinary loss limit for unmarried individuals or married individuals filing separately is $50,000 and for married individuals filing jointly is $100,000. Any recognized loss in excess of these limits is capital loss.

---

*Character of Loss on Sale of Section 1244 Stock*

In 1997, Mrs. Jett paid $18 per share for 15,000 shares of Wooster stock, which was Section 1244 stock for federal tax purposes. This year, she sold 10,000 shares for $4.50 per share, thereby recognizing a $135,000 loss ($13.50 loss per share × 10,000 shares). She filed a joint return on which she reported $100,000 ordinary loss and $35,000 long-term capital loss.[8] Mr. and Mrs. Jett recognized $53,800 of long-term capital gain on other security transactions, so the $35,000 capital loss was completely deductible. Assuming a 35 percent marginal rate on ordinary income, their tax savings from the Wooster loss was $40,250.

| | |
|---|---:|
| $100,000 ordinary loss × 35 percent | $35,000 |
| $35,000 capital loss × 15 percent | 5,250 |
| | $40,250 |

---

**Section 1244 stock** is the first $1 million of stock issued by a domestic corporation in exchange for a contribution of money or property. (Individuals cannot acquire Section 1244 stock in exchange for services performed for the corporation *or* from another shareholder.) In addition, the issuing corporation must derive more than 50 percent of its aggregate gross receipts from the active conduct of a business.

## Stock in S Corporations

The rules governing the tax consequences of stock dispositions apply regardless of whether the corporation is a C or an S corporation. Even though the owner of S corporation stock must recognize a pro rata share of the corporation's ordinary business income, the stock is still a capital asset. Accordingly, the sale or exchange of the stock generates capital gain or loss. The gain on sale of S corporation stock is not eligible for the Section 1202 exclusion because only C corporations can be qualified small business corporations. However, S corporation stock can qualify as Section 1244 stock so that the seller can characterize a limited amount of loss as an ordinary loss.

At each year-end, shareholders adjust the basis in their S corporation stock by their allocations of income and loss and distributions with respect to the stock. A shareholder who sells stock during the year must adjust the stock basis through the date of sale to compute gain or loss.

---

[8] The ordinary loss is reported as a loss from the sale of a noncapital asset on Form 4797, and the capital loss is reported on Schedule D.

| *Basis Adjustment through Date of Sale* | On January 1, Mr. Roth owned 50 shares in Slimrex, a calendar year S corporation. His adjusted basis in the stock was $77,400. He sold the stock to another shareholder on August 15 for $125,000. Mr. Roth could not determine his stock basis on the date of sale until Slimrex issued his Schedule K-1 for the year, which reported that his share of income from January 1 through August 15 was $18,800 and that he received no distributions. Consequently, Mr. Roth's stock basis on August 15 was $96,200 ($77,400 + $18,800), and his long-term capital gain was $28,800 ($125,000 amount realized − $96,200 adjusted basis). |
|---|---|

# STOCK REDEMPTIONS

**Tax Talk**
Silver Diner, a corporation that operates a popular chain of restaurants in the Washington, D.C., area, paid 32 cents per share to redeem the stock of every shareholder owning 5,000 shares or less. The redemption reduced the total number of shareholders to fewer than 200 and converted Silver Diner from a publicly held to a private company.

A **stock redemption** is a capital transaction in which a corporation acquires shares of its own stock in exchange for cash or property. It can then retire the shares or hold them as treasury stock. Corporations redeem stock for a variety of business reasons; these are some of the more common.

- A corporation might be obligated under a buy-sell agreement to purchase the stock of any shareholder who offers it for sale.
- A publicly held corporation might repurchase its own shares to stabilize the market price at which the shares are trading or to increase earnings per share reported on its financial statements.[9]
- A publicly held corporation might go private by redeeming all shares traded on a securities market, thereby concentrating the corporate ownership in the hands of a private group of investors.
- A corporation with outstanding employee stock options might purchase its own shares to use when the options are exercised.
- A corporation with preferred stock outstanding might redeem the stock to eliminate its financial obligation to pay fixed annual dividends.
- A corporation with dissident minority shareholders might redeem the dissidents' stock to restore harmony to the corporate governance.

## Shareholder Tax Consequences

**Objective 4**
Determine the tax consequences of a stock redemption to the shareholder.

When a shareholder surrenders stock in a corporate redemption, the surrender could significantly decrease the shareholder's equity interest relative to that of the other shareholders. Alternatively, the surrender could have little or no effect on the shareholder's relative equity interest. The next two examples illustrate these contrasting situations.

| *Stock Redemption: Decrease in Relative Equity* | At the beginning of the year, Nokia had six classes of common stock outstanding. Its board of directors voted to redeem all 100,000 shares of Class D nonvoting common for $85 per share. Pursuant to this redemption, Mrs. Loker surrendered 750 shares for $67,150 cash. After the redemption, she owned no Nokia stock and had no equity interest in the corporation. |
|---|---|

[9] For example, IBM spent almost $39 billion repurchasing shares from 1995 through 2000.

| | |
|---|---|
| *Stock Redemption: No Decrease in Relative Equity* | At the beginning of the year, Paylow had 5,000 outstanding shares of its single class of common stock. Ms. Hermes owned 1,000 shares. Paylow's board of directors voted to redeem 10 percent of the common stock for $1,850 per share. Pursuant to this redemption, Ms. Hermes surrendered 100 shares for $185,000 cash. Before and after the redemption, she owned 20 percent of Paylow's outstanding stock, so her surrender of 100 shares had no effect on her relative equity interest in the corporation. |

According to Subchapter C, a stock redemption is treated as a sale of stock if it significantly decreases the shareholder's equity relative to that of the other shareholders.[10] In this case, the shareholder recognizes capital gain or loss equal to the difference between the redemption payment and the adjusted basis in the surrendered shares. If a stock redemption does not significantly decrease the shareholder's relative equity, the surrender of shares is ignored, and the redemption payment is treated as a distribution.[11] Consequently, the shareholder recognizes dividend income to the extent the distribution is paid from corporate E&P.

| | |
|---|---|
| *Redemption Treated as Sale* | Because Nokia's redemption of 750 shares from Mrs. Loker significantly reduced her equity interest, she could treat the redemption as a stock sale. If the adjusted basis in her 750 Nokia shares was $43,000, she recognized a $24,150 long-term capital gain ($67,150 redemption payment −$43,000 stock basis) on the redemption. |

| | |
|---|---|
| *Redemption Payment Treated as Distribution* | Because Paylow's redemption of 100 shares from Ms. Hermes did not significantly reduce her relative equity, she had to treat the $185,000 redemption payment as a distribution. Because Paylow had sufficient E&P, she recognized a $185,000 dividend. The redemption had no effect on the aggregate basis in her Paylow investment. The aggregate basis in her 1,000 shares simply became the aggregate basis in her 900 remaining shares (same investment, fewer shares). |

## Redemptions Treated as Stock Sales

Section 302 contains two objective tests under which a redemption is treated as a sale. Under the first test, a redemption is treated as a sale if it terminates the shareholder's entire interest in the corporation.[12] (Note that Nokia's redemption of Mrs. Loker's stock met this test.) Under the second test, a redemption is treated as a sale if it is substantially disproportionate.[13] A substantially disproportionate redemption must satisfy two arithmetic requirements:

1. Immediately after the redemption, the shareholder owns less than 50 percent of the total voting power represented by the corporation's outstanding stock.
2. The shareholder's percentage interest in voting stock *after* the redemption is less than 80 percent of his percentage interest *before* the redemption.[14]

---

[10] Section 302(a).

[11] Section 302(d).

[12] Section 302(b)(3).

[13] Section 302(b)(2).

[14] If the corporation has nonvoting common stock, the shareholder's percentage ownership of the total FMV of common stock must also meet this 80 percent test.

| *Substantially Disproportionate Redemption* | At the beginning of the year, Mr. Rooker owned 21,000 (42 percent) of the 50,000 outstanding shares of Rutherford voting stock. On June 1, Rutherford paid $118 per share to redeem 10,000 of his shares. Immediately after the redemption, he owned 11,000 (27.5 (11/40) percent) of Rutherford's 40,000 remaining voting shares. The redemption was substantially disproportionate because Mr. Rooker owned less than 50 percent of the voting power of Rutherford's stock after the redemption, and his interest *after* the redemption was less than 80 percent of his interest *before* the redemption (27.5 percent/42 percent = 65.5 percent). Consequently, Mr. Rooker could treat the redemption as a sale of stock. If the adjusted basis in his Rutherford shares was $85 per share, he recognized a $330,000 long-term capital gain ($33 gain per share × 10,000 shares) on the redemption. |
| --- | --- |

If a stock redemption cannot be treated as a sale under either the complete termination test or the substantially disproportionate test, the shareholder can still make a subjective argument that the redemption should be treated as a sale because it is "not essentially equivalent to a dividend."[15] The IRS and the courts have accepted this argument when the facts and circumstances show that the redemption caused a "meaningful reduction" in the shareholder's economic interest.[16] Because of the uncertainty of the outcome, shareholders usually make this argument as a last resort to avoid dividend treatment.[17]

### Stock Ownership Attribution Rules

The two key factors in determining the tax treatment of a redemption are the shareholder's percentage ownership of stock before and after the redemption. These crucial percentages include the stock directly owned by the shareholder as well as any stock indirectly owned. Indirect ownership is determined under the four attribution rules of Section 318(a). These rules can be summarized as follows.

Rule 1. An individual indirectly owns any shares of stock directly owned by the individual's spouse, parents, children, and grandchildren. Rule 1 is described as the family attribution rule.

| *Family Attribution* | Mr. King directly owns 20 shares of Acme stock. His father directly owns 12 Acme shares, his wife directly owns 50 Acme shares, and his daughter directly owns 27 Acme shares. Because of Rule 1, Mr. King indirectly owns the 89 shares owned by his family members. Thus, he owns a total of 109 shares. |
| --- | --- |

Rule 2. A partner, LLC member, or shareholder indirectly owns a proportionate number of shares of stock owned by a partnership, LLC, or S corporation. A shareholder *who owns 50 percent or more in value of the stock in a C corporation* indirectly owns a proportionate number of shares of stock owned by the C corporation. Rule 2 is described as the attribution-from-an-entity rule.

| *Attribution from an Entity* | Ms. Schmidt owns a 15 percent interest in an LLC that owns 200 shares of Beta stock. Because of Rule 2, Ms. Schmidt indirectly owns 30 shares of Beta stock (15 percent × 200 shares). |
| --- | --- |

[15] Section 302(b)(1).

[16] *United States v. Davis,* 397 U.S. 301 (1970).

[17] Redemptions that qualify as partial liquidations of the corporation and redemptions of stock to pay death taxes are treated as sales under Section 302(b)(4) and Section 303. Any discussion of these specialized redemption transactions is beyond the scope of this text.

Mr. Nathan owns 25 percent of the value of the stock in DK Inc., a C corporation that owns 700 shares of Beta stock. He also owns 63 percent of the value of the stock in PN Inc., a C corporation that owns 1,250 shares of Beta stock. Because of Rule 2, Mr. Nathan indirectly owns 787.5 shares of Beta stock (63 percent × 1,250 shares owned by PN). Since Mr. Nathan does not own 50 percent or more of DK Inc., none of DK's Beta shares are attributed to him.

Rule 3.  A partnership, LLC, or S corporation indirectly owns the stock owned by a partner, member, or shareholder. A C corporation indirectly owns the stock owned by a shareholder *who owns 50 percent or more in value of the stock in such C corporation*. Rule 3 is described as the attribution-to-an-entity rule.

*Attribution to an Entity*

Mr. Bank owns 87 shares of Gamma stock and is a partner is LJH Partnership. Because of Rule 3, LJH indirectly owns 87 shares of Gamma stock. Note that Mr. Bank's percentage ownership of LJH is irrelevant in the application of Rule 3.

Mrs. Cardoza owns 810 shares of Gamma stock and is a 75 percent shareholder in CDT, a C corporation. Because of Rule 3, CDT indirectly owns 810 shares of Gamma stock. Mrs. Cardoza is also a 42 percent shareholder in BBR, a C corporation, but none of her Gamma shares are attributed to BBR because she owns less than a 50 percent interest in BBR.

Rule 4.  A person who has an option to acquire stock indirectly owns such stock.

*Option Attribution*

Luling Inc. owns an option to purchase 20,000 shares of Delta stock from Mr. Biggs. Because of Rule 4, Luling indirectly owns the 20,000 shares of Delta stock.

The examples given for each attribution rule demonstrate only the simplest, first-order effect of the rule. Section 318 also includes a set of operating rules governing how the four rules work together in combination. The indirect ownership resulting from such combinations can be extremely complicated to determine. Instead of addressing these complications, it is more useful to focus on the role that the attribution rules play in determining the tax consequences of a stock redemption.

*Family Attribution*

Refer to the example under Rule 1 in which Mr. King directly and indirectly owns 109 shares of Acme stock. Acme has 500 shares outstanding, so Mr. King owns a 21.8 percent interest. Assume that Acme redeems 10 of the 20 shares directly owned by Mr. King. After this redemption, Mr. King owns 10 shares directly and the 89 shares attributed to him from his family. Consequently, he owns a 20.2 percent interest (99 shares/490 shares outstanding) after the redemption. This interest is not less than 80 percent of his interest before the redemption (20.2 percent/21.8 percent = 92.6 percent). Consequently, the redemption is not substantially disproportionate, even though Acme redeemed half of the shares that Mr. King owned directly.

In this example, the family attribution rule blocked redemption treatment for Mr. King. What would be the result if Acme were to redeem all 20 of Mr. King's shares? This redemption would terminate his entire direct interest in Acme. However, it would not terminate his indirect ownership of 89 shares. After the redemption, he would still own an 18.5 percent interest (89 shares/480 shares outstanding). This interest is 84.9 percent of his interest before the redemption, so the redemption of his 20 shares is still not substantially disproportionate!

Luckily for individuals like Mr. King, Section 318 includes an extremely useful waiver of the family attribution rule. If a stock redemption terminates an individual's *entire direct interest* in a corporation, the family attribution rule is waived if three conditions are met. First, the individual must have no relationship with the corporation (other than a relationship as a creditor) immediately after the redemption. This condition means that the individual cannot continue to serve as an officer, director, or employee of the corporation. Second, the individual cannot acquire any interest in the corporation (other than stock acquired by inheritance) for 10 years after the redemption. Third, the individual must file a written agreement with the IRS to notify it of any prohibited acquisition of an interest within this 10-year period.[18]

| | |
|---|---|
| *Waiver of Family Attribution* | Acme paid Mr. King $6,500 per share for his 20 shares of Acme stock. After this redemption, Mr. King has no relationship of any kind with Acme. He files an agreement to notify the IRS if he acquires any interest in Acme during the next 10 years. Because Mr. King prospectively has complied with the three conditions, the family attribution rule is waived, and he owns no Acme stock either directly or indirectly after the redemption. Consequently, he can treat the $130,000 received from Acme as an amount realized on sale of his Acme stock rather than a dividend. |
| *Attribution to an Entity* | Refer to the first example under Rule 3 in which LJH Partnership indirectly owns the 87 shares of Gamma stock owned by Mr. Bank. LJH owns 8 shares of Gamma directly with a $5,000 basis per share, and Gamma has 150 shares outstanding. Assume that Gamma redeems all 8 of LJH's shares for $7,250 per share. The redemption is not a complete termination of LJH's interest because it still owns 87 shares indirectly. The redemption is not substantially disproportionate because LJH indirectly owns more than a 50 percent interest in Gamma after the redemption. So LJH must treat the $58,000 received from Gamma as a dividend. This treatment raises a very interesting question: What happens to LJH's $40,000 tax basis in the redeemed shares? According to Reg. 1.302-2(c), this basis is not lost but instead attaches to the 87 shares owned by Mr. Bank. |

## Corporate Tax Consequences

**Objective 5**
Compute the reduction in E&P and AAA from a stock redemption.

If a corporation pays cash to redeem stock, the redemption has no effect on its taxable income. If a corporation distributes property to redeem stock, it must recognize gain (but not loss) as if it had sold the property for FMV.[19] The redemption payment itself does reduce the corporation's E&P, but the amount of reduction depends on the treatment of the payment to the recipient shareholder. If the shareholder treats the payment as an amount realized on sale of the redeemed shares, the E&P reduction is limited to the ratable portion of E&P attributable to the redeemed shares.[20] If the shareholder treats the redemption payment as a dividend, E&P is reduced by the entire payment.

| | |
|---|---|
| *E&P Reduction* | On March 23, BVR paid $690,000 to redeem 150 (15 percent) of its 1,000 shares of outstanding stock. This payment was BVR's only distribution to shareholders during the year. Before considering the payment, BVR had E&P of $3,400,000. If the recipient shareholders treated the redemption as a sale of their stock, the E&P reduction is limited to $510,000 (15 percent × |

[18] Section 318(c)(2).

[19] Section 311(a) and (b). See the discussion of corporate property distributions in Chapter 8.

[20] Section 312(n)(7).

$3,400,000). In this case, the stock redemption eliminated 15 percent of BVR's dividend-paying capacity although it did not result in dividend income to any shareholder. If the recipient shareholders treated the redemption payment as a dividend, BVR's E&P is reduced by $690,000.

## Stock Redemptions by S Corporations

Because Subchapter S provides no special rule for stock redemptions, Subchapter C applies in determining whether the redemption is treated as a sale or distribution to the shareholder. If a redemption is treated as a sale, the shareholder recognizes a capital gain or loss equal to the difference between the redemption payment and the adjusted basis in the surrendered shares. If the redemption payment is treated as a distribution, the Subchapter S distribution rules (discussed in Chapter 8) apply.

*Redemption of S Corporation Stock*

Myers, which has been an S corporation since it was formed, paid $100,000 cash to redeem 85 shares owned by Ms. Slovin, whose basis in the shares (adjusted through date of redemption) was $67,800. If the redemption is treated as a sale under Section 302, she recognizes a $32,200 capital gain ($100,000 amount realized − $67,800 adjusted basis). If the redemption is not treated as a sale, the $100,000 payment is a nontaxable distribution to the extent of Ms. Slovin's $67,800 stock basis. She must recognize the $32,200 excess distribution as capital gain, so she is indifferent as to whether the redemption is treated as a sale or a distribution.

S corporations with accumulated E&P from years in which they were C corporations must keep track of their S corporation earnings in an accumulated adjustment account (AAA). If an S corporation with an AAA makes a redemption payment to a shareholder, the payment reduces AAA. The amount of reduction depends on the treatment of the redemption to the shareholder. If the shareholder treats the redemption as a sale of the redeemed shares, the AAA reduction is proportionate to the reduction in the number of shares outstanding.[21] If the shareholder treats the redemption payment as a distribution, AAA is reduced (but not below zero) by the distribution.

*AAA Reduction*

On December 31, FJL, an S corporation with a history as a C corporation, paid $280,000 to redeem 100 of its 300 outstanding shares from Mr. Frisch. The amount of the payment was based on an independent appraisal of the FMV of a one-third interest in FJL's business. Because the redemption completely terminated his interest in FJL, Mr. Frisch could treat the redemption as a sale of his stock. Immediately before the redemption, FJL had a $450,000 balance in its AAA and $108,000 accumulated E&P. The redemption payment reduced these tax accounts as follows.

|  | AAA | E&P |
| --- | --- | --- |
| Balance before redemption | $450,000 | $108,000 |
| Redemption payment | (150,000) | (36,000) |
| Balance after redemption | $300,000 | $ 72,000 |

The one-third reduction in AAA is proportionate to the one-third reduction in the number of shares outstanding. Similarly, the reduction in E&P is limited to the one-third attributable to the 100 redeemed shares.

[21] Section 1368(e)(1)(B).

# SALES AND EXCHANGES OF PARTNERSHIP INTERESTS

Partners in business partnerships usually want to protect the business from disruption if a partner decides to leave. They especially want to prevent any partner from transferring an interest to a third party who is unqualified to participate in the business or who is unacceptable to the remaining partners. Partners can accomplish this objective by entering into buy-sell agreements under which any partner wanting to dispose of an interest must either sell it to the remaining partners or surrender it to the partnership. Because buy-sell agreements are the rule rather than the exception, partnership interests are considered highly illiquid assets.

When a partner sells or exchanges a partnership interest, the gain or loss recognized equals the difference between the amount realized and the partner's outside basis in the interest adjusted through date of sale. The amount realized includes cash, the FMV of any property received by the seller, and the relief of the seller's share of partnership liabilities.[22]

*Computation of Gain or Loss on Sale*

Mr. Tilly sold his interest in TKS Partnership on December 31. The adjusted basis in his interest through date of sale was $18,400, which included a $1,200 share of TKS's liabilities. He received $25,000 cash from the purchaser. Mr. Tilly's amount realized was $26,200 (cash + relief of liability), and his recognized gain on sale was $7,800.

## Character of Recognized Gain or Loss

**Objective 6**
Characterize the gain or loss recognized on sale or exchange of a partnership interest.

Subchapter K includes a general rule that gain or loss recognized on sale or exchange of a partnership interest is characterized as capital gain or loss. This rule suggests the entity theory of partnerships under which a partner's interest is treated as an investment asset, much like a share of corporate stock. However, the general rule is subject to a major exception. Under Section 751(a), the sale or exchange of a partnership interest results in ordinary gain or loss to the extent of the partner's share of ordinary gain or loss inherent in partnership assets. This exception clearly embraces the aggregate theory of partnerships under which a partner's interest represents a proportionate interest in each asset owned by the partnership.

Assets with the potential to generate ordinary gain or loss for the partnership are nicknamed **hot assets.** The two types of hot assets are inventory items and unrealized receivables. Inventory items include the partnership's stock of merchandise and any other property held primarily for sale to customers.[23] The partnership's sale of an inventory item always generates ordinary gain or loss. **Unrealized receivables** include the partnership's trade accounts receivable (rights to payment for goods or services) to the extent not previously included in income under the partnership's method of accounting.[24] If a partnership uses the accrual method, its receivables have already been included in income. These realized receivables have a tax basis equal to face value and are not hot assets. If a partnership uses the cash method, its receivables have not been included in income. These unrealized receivables have a zero tax basis and are hot assets.

*Realized versus Unrealized Receivables*

At the end of its taxable year, Gillain Partnership has $83,900 uncollected receivables from its clients. If it is an accrual basis partnership, it recognized $83,900 ordinary income when the clients were billed, and the receivables have a $83,900 tax basis. Collection of the receivables

---

[22] Section 752(d).

[23] Section 751(d) includes the complete definition of inventory items.

[24] Section 751(c).

will not result in additional partnership income. If Gillain is a cash basis partnership, it did not recognize income when the clients were billed, and the receivables have a zero tax basis. It will recognize ordinary income when it collects the receivables.

Unrealized receivables also include the ordinary gain potential in a partnership's operating assets. This potential equals any gain that the partnership would recapture as ordinary income if it sold the assets for FMV. This potential gain is treated as a separate hot asset with a zero tax basis.[25]

| | |
|---|---|
| *Ordinary Gain Potential as Unrealized Receivable* | Gillain owns furniture with a $144,000 adjusted tax basis ($312,000 initial cost − $168,000 accumulated depreciation). The furniture is currently worth $250,000. If Gillain sold the furniture for FMV, it would recognize a $106,000 gain. Because the gain is less than accumulated depreciation, the entire gain would be characterized as ordinary under the Section 1245 full depreciation recapture rule. Consequently, Gillain has a $106,000 unrealized receivable with respect to its furniture. |

A partner who sells an interest in a partnership that owns hot assets must recognize ordinary gain or loss equal to the ordinary gain or loss that would be allocated to him if the partnership sold all of its assets for FMV immediately before the partner's sale. Once the partner's ordinary gain or loss from this hypothetical asset sale is determined, the difference between this gain or loss and the seller's total gain or loss from sale of the interest is characterized as capital gain or loss.

| | |
|---|---|
| *Character of Recognized Gain* | Ms. Owen recognized a $57,000 gain ($200,000 amount realized − $143,000 outside basis) on the sale of her 20 percent interest in the accrual basis MJO Partnership. On the date of sale, MJO owned the following assets: |

| | | Book/Tax Basis | FMV |
|---|---|---|---|
| Cash | | $ 30,000 | $ 30,000 |
| Accounts receivable | | 45,000 | 45,000 |
| Inventory | | 282,000 | 345,000 |
| Equipment: | | | |
| Cost | $570,000 | | |
| Accumulated depreciation | (212,000) | | |
| | | 358,000 | 380,000 |
| Unrecorded goodwill | | –0– | 200,000 |
| | | $715,000 | $1,000,000 |

MJO owns two hot assets: a $22,000 unrealized receivable (ordinary gain potential in its equipment) and inventory. If it had sold all of its assets for FMV immediately before Ms. Owen's sale, it would recognize $22,000 ordinary gain on sale of its equipment and $63,000 ordinary gain on sale of its inventory. Because Ms. Owen would be allocated $17,000 of this hypothetical gain (20 percent × $85,000), she must recognize $17,000 ordinary gain and only $40,000 capital gain on sale of her interest.

[25] Reg. 1.751-1(c)(5).

*Ordinary Gain and Capital Loss*

Mr. Proada recognized a $26,800 gain ($160,000 amount realized − $133,200 outside basis) on the sale of his 40 percent interest in the cash basis Acama Partnership. On date of sale, Acama owned the following assets:

|  |  | Book/Tax Basis | FMV |
|---|---|---|---|
| Cash |  | $ 38,000 | $ 38,000 |
| Accounts receivable |  | –0– | 75,000 |
| Equipment: |  |  |  |
| Cost | $215,000 |  |  |
| Accumulated depreciation | (180,000) |  |  |
|  |  | 35,000 | 35,000 |
| Investment assets |  | 260,000 | 252,000 |
|  |  | $333,000 | $400,000 |

Acama owns one hot asset: its zero basis accounts receivables. If it had sold all of its assets for FMV, it would recognize $75,000 ordinary gain on the sale of the receivables. Because Mr. Proada would be allocated $30,000 of this hypothetical gain (40 percent × $75,000), he must recognize $30,000 ordinary gain and $3,200 capital *loss* ($26,800 total gain − $30,000 ordinary gain) on the sale of his interest.

## Tax Consequences to Purchaser

The tax consequences of the sale of a partnership interest reflect the aggregate theory because the partner is treated as *selling* a proportionate share of partnership assets. If Subchapter K was theoretically consistent, the purchaser of the interest should be treated as *buying* a proportionate share of partnership assets, and the cost of the interest should become the inside basis in the purchaser's share of the assets. Subchapter K is not consistent, however. As a general rule, the purchaser's cost becomes the outside basis in the partnership interest, and the inside basis of partnership assets is unchanged.[26]

*Purchase of Partnership Interest*

Refer to the previous example in which Ms. Owen sold her 20 percent interest in MJO Partnership. The purchaser, Kemp Inc., paid $200,000 cash for the interest. Recall that MJO owned the following assets:

|  | Book/Tax Basis | FMV |
|---|---|---|
| Cash | $ 30,000 | $ 30,000 |
| Accounts receivable | 45,000 | 45,000 |
| Inventory | 282,000 | 345,000 |
| Equipment | 358,000 | 380,000 |
| Goodwill | –0– | 200,000 |
|  | $715,000 | $1,000,000 |

Kemp's cost basis in its new partnership interest is $200,000, which equals 20 percent of the FMV of MJO's assets. Under the general rule, this cost basis does not attach to the partnership assets. Thus, the inside basis of Kemp's proportionate share of MJO's assets remains unchanged at $143,000 (20 percent × $715,000 total tax basis).

[26] Section 743(a).

### Special Basis Adjustment for Purchaser

Partnerships can override the general rule by electing to adjust the inside basis of their assets when a purchaser buys an interest in the partnership. The result of this **Section 754 election** is a special basis adjustment to the purchaser's share of assets.[27] The total adjustment equals the difference between the purchaser's outside basis in the interest and a proportionate share of inside basis. The total adjustment is allocated to specific assets based on the purchaser's interest in the unrealized gain or loss in each asset.[28]

| | | | |
|---|---|---|---|
| *Special Basis Adjustment for Purchaser* | If MJO Partnership has a Section 754 election in effect for the year in which Kemp purchased its 20 percent interest, Kemp has a $57,000 special basis adjustment ($200,000 outside basis − $143,000 proportionate share of inside basis). The portion of the adjustment allocated to each asset equals Kemp's 20 percent interest in any unrealized gain or loss in the asset. | | |

| | Book/Tax Basis | Kemp's Basis Adjustment | FMV |
|---|---|---|---|
| Cash | $ 30,000 | –0– | $ 30,000 |
| Accounts receivable | 45,000 | –0– | 45,000 |
| Inventory | 282,000 | $12,600 | 345,000 |
| Equipment | 358,000 | 4,400 | 380,000 |
| Goodwill | –0– | 40,000 | 200,000 |
| | $715,000 | $57,000 | $1,000,000 |

(FMV-BV) * % interest

A special basis adjustment belongs only to the purchasing partner and has no effect on the common inside basis of partnership property.[29] The partnership uses the special adjustment to compute the purchaser's distributive share of income, gain, deduction, and loss with respect to partnership assets.

| | |
|---|---|
| *Tax Consequences of Special Basis Adjustment* | Kemp's special basis adjustments in MJO's assets have the following tax consequences:<br><br>• When MJO sells its inventory, it will recognize $63,000 ordinary gain ($345,000 FMV − $282,000 inside basis). Kemp's share of this gain is $12,600. However, Kemp has $12,600 additional basis in its share of MJO's inventory, so its ordinary gain is reduced to zero.<br>• MJO treats Kemp's $4,400 special basis adjustment in the equipment as new depreciable property. The annual MACRS deduction with respect to this property is allocated entirely to Kemp.<br>• MJO treats Kemp's $40,000 special basis adjustment in goodwill as a purchased intangible. The 15-year amortization deduction with respect to this goodwill is allocated entirely to Kemp. |

Because the tax consequences of a Section 754 election are so favorable to Kemp, why would MJO hesitate to make the election? One reason is that the election is permanent and applies not only to Kemp's purchase but also to future purchases of partnership interests. Accordingly, if a future purchaser's outside cost basis is *less* than a proportionate share of

[27] Section 743(b).
[28] Reg. 1.755-1(b)(1).
[29] Reg. 1.743-1(j).

inside basis, the purchaser would be forced to accept a *negative* basis adjustment with unfavorable tax consequences. A second reason is that Kemp's special basis adjustment confers no tax benefit on MJO's other partners, but these partners must share in the additional cost of keeping the tax records necessary to track the basis adjustment. Because Section 754 elections can create an administrative burden, many partnership agreements state explicitly that the partnership will *not* make the election.

# LIQUIDATIONS OF PARTNERSHIP INTERESTS

It is not unusual for a partnership agreement to provide that the only way a partner can dispose of an equity interest is to surrender it back to the partnership in exchange for a liquidating distribution. The distribution decreases the withdrawing partner's capital account to zero and extinguishes the partner's equity interest. A well-drafted partnership agreement specifies how to determine the amount of the distribution. The agreement could simply provide that liquidating distributions are based on the book capital account balance adjusted through the date of withdrawal. In this case, the distribution equals the partner's equity in the net book value of the partnership's recorded assets.

*Liquidating Distribution Based on Net Book Value*

Ms. Valdez withdrew from GreenHill LLC on December 31. According to the GreenHill operating agreement, members are entitled to receive any positive balance in their book capital accounts upon withdrawal. Immediately before Ms. Valdez's withdrawal, GreenHill had the following balance sheet.

|  | Book/Tax Basis |
| --- | --- |
| Cash | $   250,000 |
| Accounts receivable | 370,000 |
| Inventory | 790,000 |
| Equipment | 715,000 |
|  | $2,125,000 |
|  |  |
| Liabilities | $   832,000 |
| Capital:  Ms. Valdez (10 percent) | 129,300 |
| Other members | 1,163,700 |
|  | $2,125,000 |

Pursuant to its operating agreement, GreenHill distributed $129,300 cash to Ms. Valdez in complete liquidation of her 10 percent interest.

A liquidating distribution based on net book value disregards any differences between book value and FMV of partnership assets. Moreover, net book value fails to include the partner's interest in unrecorded intangible assets such as goodwill. Because net book value can be such an inaccurate economic indicator, partnership agreements often require liquidating distributions to equal the FMV of a partner's capital account. In this case, the partnership must revalue its property *for book purposes* and adjust the book capital accounts to reflect the revaluation.[30]

[30] Reg. 1.704-1(b)(2)(iv)(f).

*Liquidating Distribution Based on FMV*

Assume that the GreenHill operating agreement provides that members will receive the FMV of their capital accounts upon withdrawal. Furthermore, FMV must be determined by an independent appraisal and must include unrecorded goodwill. Immediately before Ms. Valdez's withdrawal, a professional appraiser provided the following valuation.

|  | Book/Tax Basis | FMV |
|---|---|---|
| Cash | $ 250,000 | $ 250,000 |
| Accounts receivable | 370,000 | 370,000 |
| Inventory | 790,000 | 790,000 |
| Equipment | 715,000 | 775,000 |
| Goodwill | –0– | 750,000 |
|  | $2,125,000 | $2,935,000 |
|  |  |  |
| Liabilities | $ 832,000 | $ 832,000 |
| Capital: Ms. Valdez (10 percent) | 129,300 | 210,300 |
| Other members | 1,163,700 | 1,892,700 |
|  | $2,125,000 | $2,935,000 |

On the basis of the appraisal, GreenHill wrote up its assets and capital accounts to FMV and then distributed $210,300 cash to Ms. Valdez in complete liquidation of her 10 percent interest. This $810,000 write-up is for book purposes only and *has no effect on the inside tax basis* of assets. Here is GreenHill's balance sheet after the distribution.

|  | Tax Basis | Book Basis |
|---|---|---|
| Cash | $ 39,700 | $ 39,700 |
| Accounts receivable | 370,000 | 370,000 |
| Inventory | 790,000 | 790,000 |
| Equipment | 715,000 | 775,000 |
| Goodwill | –0– | 750,000 |
|  | $1,914,700 | $2,724,700 |
|  |  |  |
| Liabilities | $ 832,000 | $ 832,000 |
| Capital: Other members | 1,082,700 | 1,892,700 |
|  | $1,914,700 | $2,724,700 |

## Tax Consequences of Liquidating Distributions

**Objective 7**
Determine the tax consequences of a liquidating distribution from a partnership.

Partnerships typically distribute cash to liquidate the interest of a withdrawing or retiring partner. (The tax consequences of current and liquidating *property* distributions to partners are discussed in Chapters 8 and 14.) As a general rule, partners who receive liquidating cash distributions do not recognize gain or loss unless the amount is more or less than the outside basis in their partnership interest. The amount of the distribution includes both actual cash and any decrease in the withdrawing partner's share of partnership liabilities.[31] Any gain or loss recognized is characterized as capital gain or loss.[32]

[31] Section 752(b).
[32] Section 731(a).

| | | |
|---|---|---|
| *Tax Consequences to Partner* | Assume that Ms. Valdez's outside basis in her 10 percent LLC interest immediately before she received the liquidating distribution was $212,500 (including an $83,200 share of LLC liabilities). | |

- If the cash distribution was $129,300 (book value of capital account), the total distribution was $212,500 (cash + $83,200 decrease in share of liabilities). Because the distribution equaled her outside basis, she recognized no gain or loss.
- If the cash distribution was $210,300 (FMV of capital account), the total distribution was $293,500 (cash + $83,200 decrease in share of liabilities). Ms. Valdez must recognize the $81,000 excess of the distribution over her outside basis as capital gain.

Regardless of the tax consequences to the withdrawing partner, a liquidating distribution does not trigger gain or loss recognition to the remaining partners. If their shares of partnership liabilities increase because of the withdrawal, the outside basis in their partnership interests reflects this increase.[33] In the case of Ms. Valdez's withdrawal from GreenHill LLC, the other members increased their aggregate outside bases in their LLC interests by $83,200.

### Partnership Consequences

As a general rule, a partnership does not make any adjustment to the tax basis in its assets because of a liquidating distribution to a partner. This rule can cause a problem for the remaining partners. Refer to GreenHill's balance sheet *after* it distributed $210,300 cash to liquidate Ms. Valdez's interest. Note that the LLC paid $81,000 for her share of unrealized appreciation in its assets. Under the general rule, the LLC *cannot* capitalize this payment to the inside basis of its appreciated assets (equipment and goodwill). GreenHill can correct this problem by making a Section 754 election to adjust the inside basis by the $81,000 capital gain that Ms. Valdez recognized on the distribution.[34]

| | | | |
|---|---|---|---|
| *Special Basis Adjustment for Partnership* | If GreenHill LLC makes a Section 754 election, it can increase the inside basis of its assets by $81,000. The adjustment results in the following adjusted tax basis balance sheet: | | |

| | Tax Basis after Distribution | Basis Adjustment | Adjusted Tax Basis |
|---|---|---|---|
| Cash | $ 39,700 | –0– | $ 39,700 |
| Accounts receivable | 370,000 | –0– | 370,000 |
| Inventory | 790,000 | –0– | 790,000 |
| Equipment | 715,000 | $ 6,000 | 721,000 |
| Goodwill | –0– | 75,000 | 75,000 |
| | $1,914,700 | $81,000 | $1,995,700 |
| Liabilities | $ 832,000 | –0– | $ 832,000 |
| Capital | 1,082,700 | $81,000 | 1,163,700 |
| | $1,914,700 | $81,000 | $1,995,700 |

[33] Section 752(a).
[34] Section 734(b). According to Reg. 1.755-1(c)(1)(ii), the adjustment must be made to the basis of capital assets and Section 1231 property.

GreenHill can treat the $6,000 basis adjustment to equipment as new MACRS property and the $75,000 basis adjustment to goodwill as a purchased intangible amortizable over 15 years.

As the GreenHill example illustrates, a Section 754 election allows a partnership with appreciated property to make a positive basis adjustment when it makes a liquidating distribution to a partner. Once a partnership makes a Section 754 election, the election is permanent and applies to all future partnership distributions. If a partnership with *devalued* property (FMV less than tax basis) makes a liquidating distribution, a Section 754 election could force it to make a *negative* basis adjustment with unfavorable tax consequences.

## Payment for Zero Basis Accounts Receivable

Subchapter K provides a special rule for liquidating distributions to general partners by cash basis partnerships in which capital is not a material income-producing factor (service partnerships). The portion of the distribution in payment for the partner's interest in accounts receivable is treated as a guaranteed payment instead of a distribution.[35] The partner must recognize the guaranteed payment as ordinary income, and the partnership can deduct the payment in computing its business income.

*Distribution as Guaranteed Payment*

Dr. Bell, a 25 percent general partner, withdrew from B&T Partnership this year. B&T is a professional partnership providing medical services, and capital is not a material income-producing factor. Immediately before Dr. Bell's withdrawal, B&T had the following balance sheet:

|  | Book/Tax Basis |
|---|---|
| Cash | $135,000 |
| Accounts receivable ($260,000 face value) | –0– |
| Furniture and fixtures | 5,000 |
|  | $140,000 |
| Capital: Dr. Bell (25 percent) | $ 35,000 |
| Other partners | 105,000 |
|  | $140,000 |

The B&T agreement provides that withdrawing partners are entitled to a cash distribution equal to any positive balance in their capital account plus their share of accounts receivables. On the basis of this provision, B&T paid $100,000 ($35,000 capital account balance + $65,000 share of accounts receivable) to Dr. Bell to liquidate her interest.

The $65,000 distribution for Dr. Bell's interest in unrealized accounts receivable is treated as a guaranteed payment. Thus, she recognized $65,000 ordinary income, and B&T was allowed a $65,000 ordinary deduction. The tax consequences of the $35,000 remaining distribution are determined under the general rule. If Dr. Bell's outside basis in her interest was $35,000, she recognized no capital gain or loss on the liquidation of her interest.

[35] Section 736(b)(2).

This special rule reflects the aggregate theory under which the disposition of a partnership interest represents the disposition of a proportionate share of partnership assets. Because B&T's accounts receivable represent unrealized ordinary income earned while Dr. Bell was a partner, she should recognize her $65,000 (25 percent) share when she disposes of her partnership interest. Although B&T will recognize $260,000 ordinary income on collection of the receivables, it also has a $65,000 ordinary deduction. As a result, the other partners will recognize only $195,000 (75 percent) of the ordinary income represented by the accounts receivable.[36]

# EFFECT OF DISPOSITIONS ON SUSPENDED LOSSES

**Objective 8**
Contrast the treatment of suspended losses under the basis, at-risk, and passive activity loss limitations.

As you learned in Chapter 7, owners of passthrough entities may be allocated business losses that they cannot entirely deduct. The loss deduction could be limited because the owner does not have enough basis or at-risk amount or because the owner's interest is a passive activity. The nondeductible portion of a passthrough loss is called a **suspended loss.** Suspended losses are carried forward as potential deductions against future taxable income. What happens to these suspended losses if the owner disposes of the interest? We will address this question in the final section of the chapter.

## Suspended Losses under the Basis Limitation

Subchapter K and Subchapter S have similar rules limiting a partner's or a shareholder's deduction of losses. Partners can deduct their share of partnership losses only to the extent of the outside basis in their partnership interest. Shareholders can deduct their share of S corporation losses only to the extent of the basis in their stock plus the basis in any debt obligation from the S corporation. Under both rules, suspended losses can be deducted in future taxable years to the extent that the partner or shareholder restores basis.[37]

If an owner has a suspended loss because of the basis limitation, the basis in the passthrough interest is necessarily zero. A taxable disposition of the interest triggers a gain equal to any amount realized on the disposition. After the disposition, the former owner no longer has any opportunity to restore basis. Consequently, any suspended losses with respect to that interest are permanently disallowed.[38]

| | |
|---|---|
| *Permanent Loss Disallowance* | On January 1, Mrs. Jerolt owned 29 shares of stock in JRT, an S corporation. Her basis in the stock was zero, and she had a $4,300 suspended ordinary loss because of the basis limitation. Mrs. Jerolt sold her stock to another shareholder for $5,000 on May 1. Her pro rata share of income for January 1 through May 1 was $1,600.[39] Because this income allocation increased Mrs. Jerolt's stock basis to $1,600, she could deduct $1,600 of her suspended loss. As a result, she had no ordinary business income from JRT to include in taxable income. The deduction of the loss reduced her stock basis back to zero, so she recognized a $5,000 capital gain on sale. Her $2,700 remaining suspended loss is permanently disallowed. |

[36] Subchapter K includes another rule that applies when a partner receives a liquidating cash distribution in payment for the interest in other hot assets (substantially appreciated inventory and ordinary income recapture potential). Under Section 751(b), the partner must recognize ordinary income as if the partner had sold the interest in these assets for cash. The application of this rule is enormously difficult and beyond the scope of this text.

[37] Sections 704(d) and 1366(d).

[38] *Sennett,* 80 TC 825 (1983) and Reg. 1.1366-2(a)(5).

[39] A shareholder who disposes of stock in an S corporation is treated as the owner for the day of disposition. Reg. 1.1377-1(a)(2)(ii).

## Suspended Losses under the At-Risk Limitation

Partners and shareholders subject to the at-risk limitation can deduct their share of the entity's losses only to the extent of their at-risk amount in the entity. Any disallowed loss is suspended and can be deducted in future taxable years to the extent that the partner or shareholder increases the at-risk amount. An owner's at-risk amount is increased by any allocation of income from the entity. When an owner disposes of the interest in a taxable transaction, any gain recognized is treated as income *from the entity*.[40] This rule allows the owner to deduct the suspended loss to the extent of the gain.

| | |
|---|---|
| *Deduction Allowed on Disposition of Interest* | Mr. Schuman had a $6,100 outside basis in his Alcott LLC interest. The basis equaled his $8,000 *negative* capital account plus his $14,100 share of LLC liabilities. Because the liabilities were nonrecourse, Mr. Schuman could not include his share in his at-risk amount. Thus, his at-risk amount was zero, and he had an $8,000 suspended ordinary loss because of the at-risk limitation. Mr. Schuman sold his LLC interest to another member for $1,000 cash. His amount realized was $15,100 (cash + $14,100 relief of liability), and his recognized gain was $9,000 ($15,100 amount realized − $6,100 outside basis). This recognized gain increased Mr. Schuman's at-risk amount to $9,000, thereby allowing him to deduct his $8,000 suspended loss under the at-risk limitation. |

The fact that Mr. Schuman's gain on the disposition of his LLC interest was sufficient to allow the deduction of his entire suspended loss is not just a happy coincidence. As discussed in Chapter 7, the difference between an owner's basis and at-risk amount is usually the share of nonrecourse liabilities included in basis. If the owner's share of nonrecourse liabilities *exceeds* basis, the at-risk amount necessarily is zero, and an amount of loss equal to the excess has been disallowed. When the owner disposes of the interest, the relief of nonrecourse liabilities is included in the amount realized. Therefore, the gain recognized must be at least as much as the excess of nonrecourse liabilities over basis—at least as much as the suspended loss. Because of the math, the taxable disposition of an interest in a business entity usually triggers the deduction of all suspended losses under the at-risk limitation.

## Suspended Passive Activity Losses

Even if an owner has sufficient basis and at-risk amount to deduct losses from a passthrough entity, the owner might have to contend with the passive activity loss limitation. If the interest in the entity is a passive activity, the owner can deduct losses only to the extent of income generated by other passive activities. Any disallowed loss is suspended and can be deducted in future taxable years to the extent of future passive activity income. If the owner disposes of the entire interest in a taxable transaction, the entire suspended loss is deductible in the year of disposition.[41]

| | |
|---|---|
| *Deduction Allowed on Disposition of Interest* | Mr. Nuncy had a $65,000 outside basis in his HNV Partnership interest. This interest was a passive activity, and he had a $4,800 suspended ordinary loss because of the passive activity loss limitation. Mr. Nuncy received a $53,200 liquidating distribution from HNV and recognized the $11,800 excess of his outside basis over the amount of the distribution as a capital loss. Because the liquidation was a taxable disposition of his entire HNV interest, he could deduct his $4,800 suspended loss this year. |

[40] Prop. Reg. 1.465-66(a).
[41] Section 469(g)(1).

## Conclusion

Owners planning to dispose of an interest in a business entity want to maximize the after-tax proceeds from the disposition. To do so, they must compute any tax costs or savings from the disposition. These costs or savings depend on both the amount of taxable gain or loss triggered by the disposition and the characterization of the gain or loss as capital or ordinary. Exhibit 12.1 provides a chart that compares these factors as they pertain to interests in corporations and interests in partnerships and LLCs. If owners have suspended losses with respect to an interest in a passthrough entity, the tax effect of the disposition depends on the extent to which they can deduct these losses in the year of disposition.

**EXHIBIT 12.1 Comparison Chart**

| Tax Issue | Corporation | Partnership/LLC |
|---|---|---|
| What is the character of gain or loss recognized on the sale of an equity interest in an entity? | Capital gain or loss. | Ordinary income or loss based on the partner's interest in hot assets; remaining gain or loss is capital. |
| Does an entity adjust the tax basis of its property when an owner sells an equity interest? | No. | No, unless the partnership has a Section 754 election in effect. |
| Can an owner dispose of an equity interest by surrendering it back to the entity? | Yes, through a stock redemption. | Yes, through a liquidating distribution. |
| Can a surrender of equity result in ordinary income to the owner? | Yes. A redemption that is not treated as a sale can result in dividend income to the shareholder. | Yes, to the extent that a distribution is payment for a general partner's share of unrealized receivables of a service partnership. |
| Can a surrender of equity result in capital gain or loss to the owner? | Yes. A redemption that is treated as a sale results in capital gain or loss. | No, unless cash received is more or less than the partner's outside basis. |
| Does an entity adjust the tax basis of its property when an owner recognizes capital gain or loss on the surrender of equity? | No. | No, unless the partnership has a Section 754 election in effect. |

## Key Terms

buy-sell agreement *322*
capital transactions *321*
control premium *322*
hot assets *333*
minority interest discount *322*
qualified small business stock *325*
Section 754 election *336*
Section 1202 exclusion *324*
Section 1244 stock *326*
stock redemption *327*
suspended loss *341*
unrealized receivables *333*

## Questions and Problems for Discussion

1. To what extent does the market price received on the sale of publicly traded stock reflect the FMV of the corporation's business?
2. If a parent corporation owns a controlling interest in a subsidiary and both corporations operate the same business, is the subsidiary stock a business asset or a capital asset to the parent corporation?
3. Mr. Trevino contributed $40,000 cash to TOP in exchange for 4,000 shares of TOP stock. Could this stock be both qualified small business stock (for purposes of the Section 1202 exclusion) and Section 1244 stock? Discuss briefly.

4. Four years ago, Mrs. Kirkland paid $15,000 for 30 shares of stock in BWP, an S corporation. This year, she sold the stock for $43,000. Identify Mrs. Kirkland's possible error if she computes her capital gain by reference to her original cost basis in the BWP stock.

5. Contrast the character of the gain or loss recognized by a shareholder on sale of S corporation stock with the character of the gain or loss recognized by a partner on sale of a partnership interest.

6. Explain why the tax consequences of a stock redemption depend on the economic substance rather than the legal form of the redemption.

7. MSL Inc. recently paid $250,000 cash to redeem all 12,500 shares of common stock owned by Ms. Morley. What other information does she need to determine the tax consequences of the redemption payment?

8. Explain why the accounts receivable of a cash basis partnership are hot assets, but the accounts receivable of an accrual basis partnership are not.

9. Do the tax consequences to a partner who sells a partnership interest reflect the aggregate or the entity theory of partnerships? What about the tax consequences to the purchaser of the interest?

10. An owner's share of loss from a business entity might be disallowed under the basis limitation, the at-risk limitation, or the passive activity loss limitation. Discuss whether these limitations result in a permanent or temporary loss disallowance.

## Application Problems

Assume that the entities in the following problems use the calendar year for federal tax purposes.

1. Jessup Corporation, which is publicly held, purchased 13,000 shares of ABC stock as a short-term investment for $85,000. At year-end, FMV of the ABC stock was $93,000. For financial reporting purposes, Jessup uses the mark-to-market method to account for its ABC investment. Consequently, it wrote up the book value of the stock to $93,000 and recorded $8,000 book income.
   a. Does Jessup have a difference in its book and tax income with respect to the ABC stock?
   b. Next year, Jessup sells the 13,000 ABC shares for $105,250 cash. Does this transaction result in a book/tax difference?

2. Four years ago, Hobson contributed property ($25,000 FMV and $18,000 basis) to Mhairi Inc. in exchange for 100 shares of stock. During the past four years, Hobson received $8,900 cash distributions from Mhairi ($7,800 dividends and $1,100 return of capital). What is Hobson's basis in its 100 shares assuming that its contribution:
   a. Qualified as a Section 351 exchange. 18,000 carryover - 1,100
   b. Did not qualify as a Section 351 exchange. 25,000 - 1,100

3. This year, Mrs. Asada sold 1,000 shares of qualified small business stock for $500 per share. She purchased 750 of the shares in 1995 for $71 each and another 250 in 2000 for $398 each. Assuming that Mrs. Asada does not pay AMT this year, compute her after-tax cash flow from the stock sale.

4. Mr. Randall, a single taxpayer, sold 600 shares of Section 1244 stock for $90 per share. Determine the amount and character of his gain or loss assuming that he purchased the stock for:
   a. $85 per share.
   b. $152 per share.
   c. $200 per share.

5. Mrs. Kaufman sold 3,000 shares of Sinese stock for $72 per share. She purchased the shares in 1994 for $15 per share. Compute her capital gain or loss under each of the following assumptions.

   a. Sinese is a C corporation. She received $38,000 cash distributions ($35,000 dividends and $3,000 return of capital) since 1994.

   b. Sinese is an S corporation. She was allocated a $46,900 pro rata share of income and received $27,000 cash distributions since 1994.

   c. Sinese is an S corporation. She was allocated a $46,900 pro rata share of income and received $9,000 cash distributions since 1994.

6. Mr. Jenkins received $100,000 cash in redemption of 500 shares of KWQ common stock. His basis in the shares was $47,300. KWQ has E&P in excess of $5 million. What are the tax consequences to Mr. Jenkins under each of the following assumptions?

   a. He is KWQ's sole shareholder. After the redemption, he owns all 4,500 outstanding shares of its common stock. *dividend*

   b. The 500 shares represented his entire equity interest, and he has no indirect ownership of any KWQ stock. *sale*

7. HJJ Inc., which has a 35 percent marginal tax rate, received $50,000 cash in redemption of 150 shares of Manuel stock. HJJ's basis in the shares was $8,800. Manuel has E&P in excess of $5 million. Compute HJJ's after-tax cash flow under each of the following assumptions.

   a. The 150 shares represented HJJ's entire equity interest in Manuel, and it has no indirect ownership of any Manuel stock.

   b. After the redemption, HJJ still owns 58 percent of Manuel's outstanding voting stock.

8. At the beginning of the year, Mrs. Dashell owned 3,000 of the 10,000 shares of BDF's only class of outstanding stock. Her basis per share was $310. BDF had E&P in excess of $15 million. On June 1, BDF paid $750,000 to redeem 700 shares from Mrs. Dashell.

   a. Compute her after-tax cash flow assuming that she is in a 35 percent tax bracket and has no indirect ownership of any BDF shares.

   b. What is her basis per share in her 2,300 remaining BDF shares?

9. On December 31, Pembrook distributed $800,000 cash to redeem 250 of the 1,000 shares of its only class of stock. Before considering this distribution, Pembrook's E&P was $1,940,000. Determine the reduction to E&P from the redemption assuming that:

   a. The stock redemption was treated as a sale of Pembrook stock by the participating shareholders.

   b. The stock redemption was treated as a dividend to Pembrook's shareholders.

   c. How would your answers to parts (a) and (b) change if E&P before consideration of the distribution was $3,479,000?

10. On December 31, Mayfield, an S corporation since its formation, distributed $50,000 cash to redeem 10 of its 100 outstanding shares of stock. Before considering the distribution, Mayfield had a $420,000 balance in its AAA. Determine the AAA balance after the distribution assuming that:

    a. The stock redemption was treated as a sale of Mayfield stock by the participating shareholders.

    b. The stock redemption was treated as a distribution to the participating shareholders.

    c. How would your answers to parts (a) and (b) change if the AAA balance before consideration of the distribution was $595,000?

11. Bultona Corporation sold its 8 percent interest in Skiles LLC for $90,000 cash. On date of sale, Skiles owned no hot assets. Compute Bultona's capital gain or loss on the sale assuming that:

a. Its outside basis in its LLC interest was $41,000 (including an $11,000 share of LLC liabilities).

b. Its outside basis in its LLC interest was $125,000 (including no share of LLC liabilities).

12. Mrs. Story sold her 10 percent interest in accrual basis ABC Partnership for $50,000 cash. At date of sale, her outside basis in the interest was $40,000. ABC had no liabilities and owned the following assets:

|  | Book/Tax | FMV |
|---|---|---|
| Cash | $ 8,000 | $ 8,000 |
| Accounts receivable | 22,000 | 22,000 *Accrual* |
| Inventory | 175,000 | 154,000 |
| Equipment: | | *116,000* |
| Cost | $200,000 | |
| Acc. depr. | (109,000) | |
| | 91,000 | 91,000 |
| Investment assets | 104,000 | 225,000 *200,000* |
| | $400,000 | $500,000 |

Determine the amount and character of Mrs. Story's gain or loss on sale of her ABC interest.

13. Refer to the facts in application problem 12, but assume that FMV of the equipment was $116,000 and FMV of the investment assets was $200,000. Determine the amount and character of Mrs. Story's gain or loss on sale of her ABC interest.

14. A partnership owns the following items of depreciable equipment. Identify the <u>hot</u> asset represented by each item.

|  | Cost | Accumulated Depreciation *book* | FMV | Hot Asset |
|---|---|---|---|---|
| Item 1 | $10,000 | $ 5,500 *4,500* | $ 7,000 | *2,500* |
| Item 2 | 24,000 | 3,000 *21,000* | 25,000 | *4,000* |
| Item 3 | 50,000 | 21,000 *29,000* | 29,000 | *0* |
| Item 4 | 16,250 | 14,000 *2,250* | 2,000 | *0* |

15. United Product Corporation sold its 50 percent interest in Varley LLC to Elson Inc. for $500,000 cash. Immediately before the transaction, Varley had the following balance sheet:

|  | Book/Tax | FMV |
|---|---|---|
| Cash | $ 40,000 | $ 40,000 |
| Accounts receivable | 180,000 | 180,000 *indicate accrual* |
| Inventory | 300,000 | 380,000 |
| Plant and equipment | 360,000 | 360,000 |
| Unrecorded goodwill | –0– | 120,000 |
| | $880,000 | $1,080,000 |

| | | |
|---|---|---|
| Liabilities | $ 80,000 | $  80,000 |
| Capital: | | |
| United Product | 400,000 | 500,000 |
| Other members | 400,000 | 500,000 |
| | $880,000 | $1,080,000 |

a. Determine the amount and character of United Product's gain or loss on sale if its outside basis in its LLC interest was $440,000.

b. How would your answer change if its outside basis was only $370,000?

c. Determine Elson's initial outside basis in its LLC interest.

d. Varley has a Section 754 election in effect. Compute Elson's special basis adjustment and allocate it to the LLC assets.

16. On May 15, Mr. Rosa sold his 40 percent general interest in cash basis Surefire LLP for $125,000 cash. Immediately before the sale, his outside basis in his interest was $22,000 (including a $15,000 share of LLP liabilities), and Surefire had the following balance sheet:

| | | Book/Tax | FMV |
|---|---|---|---|
| Cash | | $55,000 | $ 55,000 |
| Accounts receivable | | –0– | 175,000 |
| Equipment: | | | |
| Cost | $148,000 | | |
| Acc. depr. | (148,000) | | |
| | | –0– | 20,000 |
| Unrecorded goodwill | | –0– | 100,000 |
| | | $55,000 | $350,000 |
| | | | |
| Liabilities | | $37,500 | $ 37,500 |
| Capital:  Mr. Rosa | | 7,000 | 125,000 |
| Other partners | | 10,500 | 187,500 |
| | | $55,000 | $350,000 |

Determine the amount and character of Mr. Rosa's gain or loss on sale of his Surefire interest.

17. Ms. Damon was a 40 percent general partner in Quarto LLP, a cash basis service partnership in which capital is not a material income-producing factor. Quarto distributed $238,000 cash to Ms. Damon in liquidation of her interest. At date of liquidation, Quarto's accounts receivable totaled $511,000, and it had no liabilities.

a. What are the tax consequences of the distribution to Ms. Damon if her outside basis was $25,000?

b. What are the tax consequences of the distribution to Quarto?

18. Taylor LLC liquidated Mrs. Beard's interest by paying her $75,000 cash. Compute her gain or loss on the distribution assuming that her outside basis in her interest was:

a. $77,000 (including a $2,000 share of LLC liabilities).

b. $26,000 (including a $2,000 share of LLC liabilities).

c. $89,000 (including a $2,000 share of LLC liabilities).

√19. Refer to the facts in problem 18. Assume that Mrs. Beard's interest in Taylor LLC was a passive activity, and she had a $14,500 suspended ordinary loss on the date of liquidation. How much loss can Mrs. Beard deduct because of the liquidation of her interest under the assumptions in parts *(a)*, *(b)*, and *(c)*?

20. Ms. LaShelle sold her five shares of stock in XYZ, an S corporation, for $10,000. Her stock basis adjusted through date of sale was zero. She had a $2,300 suspended loss because of the basis limitation and a $4,410 suspended passive activity loss. What is the net effect of the sale on Ms. LaShelle's adjusted gross income?

√21. Mr. Schultz recognized an $8,200 ordinary gain and a $22,900 capital gain on sale of his interest in Hathaway LLC. He had a $10,000 suspended loss under the at-risk limitation and a $3,750 suspended passive activity loss. What is the net effect of the sale on Mr. Schultz's adjusted gross income?

## Issue Recognition Problems

Identify the tax issue or issues suggested by the following situations and state each issue in the form of a question.

1. Mr. and Mrs. King purchased 2,000 MapleLeaf shares in 1996. The shares were qualified small business stock within the meaning of Section 1202. Last year, the Kings made a gift of 500 MapleLeaf shares to their daughter. Fourteen months after receiving the gift, she recognized a $32,000 gain on sale of her shares.

2. Eight years ago, Mr. McHale contributed cash and property to RPC Inc. in exchange for 500 shares of Section 1244 stock. His initial basis in the 500 shares was $10,000. Three years ago, Mr. McHale made a $2,500 capital contribution to RPC. Because he did not receive any additional shares, the contribution increased the basis in his 500 shares to $12,500. This year, RPC declared bankruptcy, and Mr. McHale's 500 shares became worthless.

3. Mr. Arturo, a single taxpayer, owns 10,000 shares of Section 1244 stock with a $24 basis per share. Jamestown LLC has offered to buy his stock for $15 per share, and he plans to sell 5,500 shares on December 31 and the 4,500 remaining shares on January 1.

4. Four years ago, Mr. Abbot paid $20 per share for 1,000 Cheever shares. The shares have steadily declined in value and are now trading at only 40 cents per share. Mr. Abbot just mailed his stock certificate to Cheever's corporate office with a letter announcing his formal abandonment of his shares.

5. Revely Inc. distributed $200,000 cash to Mrs. Silva to redeem her 300 Revely shares. Although she is a good friend of the six remaining shareholders, she does not indirectly own any of their stock. The appraised FMV of her shares was only $170,000, but she is in ill health, and the board of directors wanted to be generous.

6. On May 1, RP Inc. distributed $200,000 cash to Mr. Roper in redemption of a portion of his RP shares. His ownership percentage before and after the redemption was 45 percent and 35 percent, respectively. On December 1, RP redeemed shares from other shareholders, increasing Mr. Roper's ownership percentage to 41 percent.

7. Six years ago, Boyd Corporation contributed investment land ($300,000 FMV and $50,000 basis) to BVR Partnership in exchange for a 30 percent interest. BVR did not have a Section 754 election in effect. This year, Boyd sold its interest to an unrelated purchaser. BVR still owns the contributed land, which now has a $450,000 FMV.

8. Last year, Mr. Wong sold all his shares in Bayland, an S corporation, to another shareholder. At the date of sale, he had a $3,300 suspended loss because of the basis limitation. This year, he inherited 50 Bayland shares from his mother. Mr. Wong's initial basis in these shares was $40,000.

9. Ms. Horton sold all her shares in Dempsy, an S corporation, to her son. At the date of sale, she had a $14,900 suspended passive activity loss with respect to her Dempsy stock.

10. Two years ago, Mr. Uber contributed his interest in TUV Partnership to Yardley Inc. in exchange for stock. The exchange was nontaxable under Section 351. At the date of contribution, he had a $10,000 suspended passive activity loss with respect to his TUV interest. This year, Mr. Uber recognized a $12,000 capital gain on sale of all his Yardley stock. Yardley still owns the TUV interest.

## Research Problems

1. CGJ Inc. is a closely held corporation with 5,000 shares of outstanding stock owned as follows.

| | |
|---|---|
| Mrs. Lauren Casey | 1,000 |
| Mr. Manuel Munoz | 2,050 |
| C&M Partnership | 850 |
| Ms. Kay Lenz | 1,100 |
| | 5,000 |

None of the three individual shareholders have any family ties. However, Mrs. Casey and Mr. Munoz are the two equal partners in C&M Partnership. The partnership owns an option to purchase the 1,100 CGJ shares from Kay Lenz.

Mrs. Casey would like to dispose of her 1,000 CGJ shares through a stock redemption. If CGJ redeems all 1,000 shares for their current FMV, will the redemption be treated as a sale for federal tax purposes?

2. On January 15, Ms. Sack contributed $20,000 cash and investment property (FMV $20,000 and $2,000 basis) to Dylan LLC in exchange for a 10 percent interest. She had acquired the investment property in 1991. On December 3, she sold the interest for $55,500. On the date of sale, Dylan had no hot assets, so Ms. Sack's entire $33,500 gain was capital gain. How much of the gain is short term and how much is long term?

## Tax Planning Cases

1. Mr. Burton owns 58,000 of the 100,000 outstanding shares of Mirkwood stock with a $50 basis per share. He wants to retire from business, and Mirkwood's board of directors has offered to redeem any number of his shares for FMV ($120 per share). Mr. Burton wants to surrender enough shares so that the redemption will be treated as a sale instead of a dividend distribution.

   a. Determine the *minimum* number of whole shares that Mirkwood can redeem from Mr. Burton.

   b. Compute Mr. Burton's after-tax cash flow from the redemption and compare it to his after-tax cash flow if Mirkwood redeemed *one share less* than the minimum number. Assume that his marginal tax rate on ordinary income is 35 percent.

2. DeVore Inc. must decide whether to purchase an interest in Alpha Partnership or Zeta Partnership. In both cases, $1,250,000 of the purchase price is attributable to the partnership's unrecorded (zero basis) goodwill. Alpha has agreed to make a Section 754 election if DeVore purchases the Alpha interest, but Zeta will not make the election if DeVore purchases the Zeta interest. DeVore needs to know the value of the election with respect to Alpha's goodwill. Provide this information by computing the NPV of the tax savings from the Section 754 election. DeVore has a 35 percent marginal tax rate and uses a 9 percent discount rate to compute NPV.

# Corporate Acquisitions, Mergers, and Divisions

**Learning Objectives**

*After reading this chapter, you will be able to:*

1. Explain how an acquiring corporation can benefit from a tax-deferred acquisition.

2. Describe the four quadrants in the corporate acquisitions matrix.

3. Allocate a lump-sum purchase price to the assets in a taxable acquisition.

4. Determine the tax consequences of tax-deferred asset acquisitions.

5. Determine the tax consequences of tax-deferred stock acquisitions.

6. Describe the status of the target's tax attributes in each quadrant of the corporate acquisitions matrix.

7. Compute the Section 382 limitation on a target's NOL carryforwards.

8. Determine the tax consequences of corporate divisions.

The decades of the 1980s and 1990s witnessed an unprecedented number of capital transactions involving the purchase and sale of corporate businesses. Private companies went public, publicly held companies were taken private, and both successful and thwarted takeovers of multibillion dollar corporations made front-page news. This chapter introduces the fascinating topic of corporate acquisitions, mergers, and divisions. It opens with an overview of the different ways in which corporate acquisitions can be structured, and then it examines the tax consequences of the various structures. This discussion leads to an analysis of the effect of an acquisition on a corporation's tax attributes. The chapter concludes with a summary of the tax consequences of corporate divisions. The two appendices provide additional technical information on the topics of leveraged buyouts and corporate reorganizations.

# OVERVIEW OF CORPORATE ACQUISITIONS

When one corporation decides to acquire a business operated by another corporation, the acquirer must make many legal and financial decisions. The next two sections of this chapter focus on two fundamental decisions. First, should the acquiring corporation purchase the targeted corporation's assets or its stock? Second, should the acquisition be structured as a taxable or a tax-deferred transaction? Both decisions have tax implications that can dramatically affect the after-tax value of the transaction to both parties.

## Acquisition of Assets or Stock?

### Asset Acquisition

In an asset acquisition, the acquirer can be selective as to which business assets to buy (a selection process described as *cherry picking*). The purchase contract can stipulate the price for each specific asset, or the acquirer and seller can agree on a lump-sum price for all assets. Legal title to the assets must be transferred from the seller to the acquirer. This "titling over" procedure can be both time consuming and costly. The purchase contract should clearly specify which, if any, of the target's liabilities are legally assumed by the acquiring corporation as consideration for the assets. Any liabilities that the acquirer does not assume remain the responsibility of the target corporation and its shareholders.

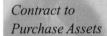
*Contract to Purchase Assets*

Primo Inc. and Carter Inc. entered into a contract under which Primo paid $5 million to Carter for all operating assets of Carter's cattle feedlot business. The contract indemnified Primo against any liability associated with Carter's operation of the business. Consequently, Primo acquired Carter's business assets but none of its liabilities.

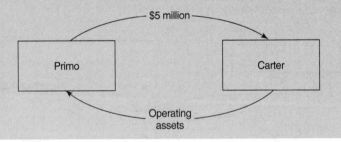

A corporation can acquire a target's assets indirectly by structuring a merger of the two corporations. A **merger** is the absorption of one corporation into another corporation under state law. The acquiring corporation becomes the owner of all the target's assets by operation of law, and the cost of titling over specific assets is avoided. After the merger, the acquirer is responsible for all known and contingent liabilities of the target, which no longer exists as a legal entity. State merger statutes generally require that shareholders owning either a majority or two-thirds of the voting stock of the acquiring corporation and the target corporation approve the merger. If the merger is approved, all target shareholders must participate in the merger. As a result, the merger squeezes out any target shareholders that dissented to the acquisition.

*Merger*

Assume that Primo acquired the cattle feedlot business through a merger of Carter into Primo under Oklahoma law. On the date of merger, Carter's operating assets were valued at $5 million, and its accounts payable totaled $200,000. Pursuant to the merger, Primo paid

$4.8 million to Carter's shareholders. After the merger, Carter no longer exists, and Primo is liable for Carter's accounts payable as well as any unrecorded liabilities.

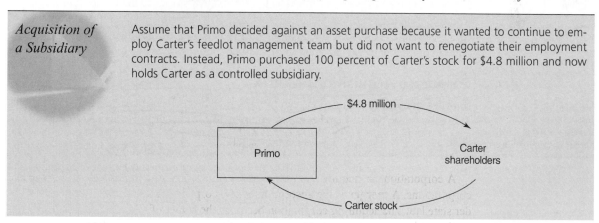

### Stock Acquisition

A corporation might prefer to acquire a targeted business by acquiring a controlling interest in the target's stock. After the acquisition, the acquiring corporation can operate the business indirectly as the parent of a controlled subsidiary. If the parent eventually wishes to operate the business directly, it can simply liquidate the subsidiary.[1] Through a stock acquisition, a corporation can buy a business already neatly packaged in corporate form. The purchase of a corporate package could have many advantages. For instance, the target could own nontransferable property rights such as copyrights, patents, licenses, or franchises that the purchaser could not buy directly. The target could be a party to favorable leases or contracts that the purchaser does not want to renegotiate. The target could have an established management structure or a high level of employee loyalty that the purchaser wishes to preserve. Finally, public recognition of the target corporation's name or other aspects of its goodwill might be obtainable only by acquiring the entity itself rather than just its assets.

*Acquisition of a Subsidiary*

Assume that Primo decided against an asset purchase because it wanted to continue to employ Carter's feedlot management team but did not want to renegotiate their employment contracts. Instead, Primo purchased 100 percent of Carter's stock for $4.8 million and now holds Carter as a controlled subsidiary.

One negative aspect of a stock acquisition is that the target's disclosed, undisclosed, and contingent liabilities are part of the corporate package. Like any shareholder, a parent corporation has limited legal liability to a subsidiary corporation's creditors. Therefore, the risk represented by the target's undisclosed or contingent liabilities is minimized if the acquirer keeps the target alive as a subsidiary. Another negative aspect is the presence of minority shareholders if the parent corporation fails to acquire every share of the target's outstanding stock. Minority shareholders can be troublesome because of their claim on the target's earnings and assets and their right to participate in certain management decisions.

[1] The liquidation of a controlled subsidiary is a nontaxable event under Sections 332 and 337. See the discussion beginning on page 389, Chapter 14.

## Taxable or Tax-Deferred Acquisition?

**Objective 1**
Explain how an acquiring corporation can benefit from a tax-deferred acquisition.

In addition to weighing the relative merits of an asset acquisition or a stock acquisition, a corporation must also consider whether the acquisition should be structured in a taxable or tax-deferred form. The distinction refers to the income tax consequences of the transaction to the selling party (the target corporation that is selling assets or the target shareholders that are selling stock). From the acquiring corporation's perspective, a *purchase* of property is not a taxable event. So why should the acquirer care whether a proposed transaction is taxable or tax deferred? Part of the answer lies in the possibility that the sellers might accept a lower price for the business if they will not recognize a current gain on sale.

*Taxable versus Tax-Deferred Acquisition*

Assume that the Carter shareholders in the previous example had a $650,000 aggregate basis in their stock. Because they sold the stock to Primo for $4.8 million, they recognized a $4,150,000 capital gain. Even at a 15 percent preferential rate, the tax on the gain is $622,500, and the shareholders' after-tax cash is $4,177,500 ($4.8 million cash − $622,500 tax). If Primo had structured a tax-deferred acquisition of Carter's stock, the shareholders' tax cost would have been postponed indefinitely. Because of the reduced tax cost, the shareholders might have been willing to accept a lower price that nevertheless increased the transaction's after-tax value.

As we will discuss later in this chapter, the dominant characteristic of a tax-deferred acquisition is that a major portion of the purchase price consists of equity (i.e., stock) in the acquiring corporation. To the extent that a corporation can use its own stock rather than cash or debt to acquire property, it can minimize the cash drain associated with the purchase. The use of stock is tax efficient because a corporation does not recognize a gain or loss when it acquires any type of property in exchange for its own stock.[2] (This broad nonrecognition rule applies to the use of newly issued stock as well as treasury stock.) Of course, the use of equity certainly is not without economic cost. The acquirer's existing shareholders suffer a dilution of their equity when new stock is issued to purchase a targeted business.

## Corporate Acquisitions Matrix

**Objective 2**
Describe the four quadrants in the corporate acquisitions matrix.

Both asset and stock acquisitions can be structured as taxable or tax-deferred transactions. These four basic choices can be organized in the following corporate acquisitions matrix illustrated in Exhibit 13.1.

The selection of one of the four types of acquisitions depends on the legal, political, financial, accounting, and tax objectives of both the acquiring and target corporations and their shareholders. The objectives of the various parties in a **friendly takeover** of a business are in relative harmony, and the parties can negotiate to achieve these objectives at the lowest tax cost. In a **hostile takeover,** the target corporation's management spurns the advances

**EXHIBIT 13.1**
**Corporate Acquisitions Matrix**

| Taxable asset acquisitions | Taxable stock acquisitions |
|---|---|
| Tax-deferred asset acquisitions (Type A or C reorganizations) | Tax-deferred stock acquisitions (Type B reorganizations) |

[2] Section 1032(a).

of the purchaser and might be willing to incur any cost to prevent the acquisition. In either case, the corporations involved incur professional and investment banking fees as well as other expenditures related to the acquisition. The IRS and the courts have taken the position that these expenditures cannot be deducted but must be capitalized for tax purposes.[3]

| *Acquisition Expenditures* | Manua Inc. paid $8 million to the shareholders of Grissom Inc. to acquire a controlling stock interest. Manua paid $210,000 legal fees directly relating to this acquisition, which it had to capitalize as part of the Grissom stock cost. Because corporate stock is not an amortizable asset, Manua will not recover the $210,000 expenditure until it disposes of the Grissom stock. |
|---|---|

An extensive body of literature deals with the economic ramifications of both friendly and hostile acquisitions of corporate businesses. This chapter concentrates on the important tax issues, beginning with the consequences of taxable acquisitions of either the target corporation's assets or its stock.

# TAXABLE ACQUISITIONS

## Purchase of Target's Assets

A corporation that purchases assets in a taxable transaction takes a cost basis in each asset. The acquirer can recover the cost of any purchased inventory item when it sells or consumes the item. Similarly, the acquirer can recover the cost of most operating assets over time as depreciation or amortization deductions. When a corporation contracts to purchase assets, the buyer and seller can negotiate the price of each specific asset. Alternatively, they can agree on a lump-sum purchase price for all assets to be transferred. In the latter case, the acquirer wants to allocate as much of the purchase price as possible to inventory items and depreciable or amortizable assets to maximize its future cost recovery deductions.

**Objective 3**
Allocate a lump-sum purchase price to the assets in a taxable acquisition.

Section 1060 provides the rules of this allocation game. The portion of a lump-sum price allocable to a specific asset cannot exceed its FMV. Furthermore, the price allocation must be consistent between buyer and seller so that the acquiring corporation's cost basis in each asset is the same as the target corporation's amount realized on that asset's sale. If the lump-sum purchase price exceeds the aggregate FMV of the target's operating assets, the excess price is allocated to goodwill, which is amortizable over 15 years.[4]

| *Allocation of Lump-Sum Purchase Price* | LaCroix paid $10 million ($9.75 million cash + $250,000 assumption of liabilities) to purchase Shelby's manufacturing business. The purchase contract stipulated the following FMVs for Shelby's balance sheet assets. |
|---|---|

|  | FMV |
|---|---|
| Merchandise inventory | $1,200,000 |
| Material and supplies inventory | 720,000 |
| Machinery and equipment | 2,400,000 |
| Long-term lease | 365,000 |
| Depreciable buildings | 2,835,000 |
| Land | 750,000 |
|  | $8,270,000 |

[3] *Indopco Inc. v. Commissioner*, 503 U.S. 79 (1992).
[4] Section 197(a).

LaCroix must allocate $8,270,000 of the lump-sum purchase price to these assets. The price allocated to each asset (and LaCroix's cost basis) equals its stipulated FMV. LaCroix must capitalize the $1,730,000 remaining price to purchased goodwill.

Shelby must use the stipulated FMV as the amount realized on sale of each balance sheet asset and must compute taxable gain or loss accordingly. Shelby must also recognize a $1,730,000 gain on the sale of unrecorded goodwill. Because Shelby created this goodwill through the development of its successful business, the goodwill was a capital asset to Shelby, and the gain is a capital gain.[5]

A target corporation that sells its entire business has two choices. It can remain in existence as a corporate entity and invest its after-tax proceeds in a new business or financial venture. Alternatively, it can liquidate by distributing the after-tax proceeds to its shareholders. As a general rule, the liquidation is a taxable event to the shareholders, who must recognize gain or loss equal to the difference between the liquidating distribution and their stock basis. The tax consequences of corporate liquidations are covered in detail in Chapter 14. Note that a target corporation's sale of its business can result in a double tax: a corporate tax on the sale itself and a shareholder tax when the after-tax proceeds are distributed to the shareholders.

## Cash Mergers

If an asset acquisition is structured as a taxable merger (commonly called a **cash merger**) of the target corporation into the acquiring corporation, the target must recognize gain or loss as if it had sold all its assets for FMV. The target's shareholders must also recognize gain or loss equal to the difference between the payment received for their target stock and their stock basis.[6] This double tax can make the merger quite costly.

*Cash Merger*

Yorgen plans to acquire the business operated by Lerner through a cash merger. Lerner's business assets are worth $6 million, and their aggregate tax basis is only $2.3 million. The required number of Lerner's shareholders have approved the merger and accepted Yorgen's offer of $45 per Lerner share. If the acquisition is structured as a merger of Lerner into Yorgen, Lerner must report a $3.7 million taxable gain ($6 million FMV of assets − $2.3 million tax basis) on its final corporate tax return. Each Lerner shareholder must report gain or loss based on the $45 amount realized on the surrender of each Lerner share. The merger transaction is diagrammed as follows:

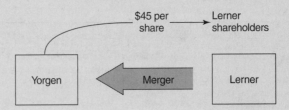

Yorgen and Lerner can avoid the double tax resulting from a straightforward merger of Lerner into Yorgen by structuring the acquisition as a **reverse cash merger,** in which the acquiring corporation forms a new subsidiary for the sole purpose of accomplishing the

[5] Section 197(c)(2).
[6] Rev. Rul. 69-6, 1969-1 CB 104.

merger. The subsidiary is then merged *into the target*, and the original target shareholders are bought out with cash. The target survives the merger as a controlled subsidiary of the acquiring corporation. If the acquirer chooses to liquidate its subsidiary, it can do so at no tax cost.[7]

**Reverse Cash Merger**

To reduce the tax cost of the merger, Yorgen forms Subco by contributing cash in exchange for 100 percent of Subco's stock. Subco is then merged into Lerner under Kentucky law. Subco uses the cash contributed by Yorgen to pay $45 for each Lerner share. The merger is a taxable event to the Lerner shareholders, *but it does not trigger a corporate tax to Lerner.* After the merger, Yorgen holds Lerner as a controlled subsidiary. The following is a diagram of this reverse merger.

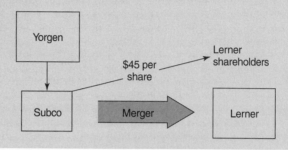

Reverse cash mergers are more tax efficient than straightforward cash mergers because they result in only a single tax at the shareholder level. However, in a straightforward merger, the acquirer's tax basis in the target's assets is stepped up to FMV (cost basis). In a reverse merger, the tax basis of the target's assets does not change.

## Purchase of Target's Stock

A corporation that purchases a controlling interest in a target's stock takes a cost basis in the stock. The purchase generally has no effect on the target's tax basis in its assets.[8] If the target becomes a member of an affiliated group filing a consolidated tax return, the acquiring corporation will adjust the basis in the target's stock as required by the consolidated regulations. (These stock basis adjustments are discussed in Chapter 9.) If the acquiring corporation and its new subsidiary file separate tax returns, the acquirer's cost basis will not change over time.

**Stock Basis**

Gemini Inc. purchased 70 percent of IFG's stock in 1988 for $675,000. Several individuals and a tax-exempt foundation own the 30 percent minority interest. Gemini has never contributed any additional capital to IFG. Although IFG has paid dividends to its shareholders every year, it has never distributed a return of capital. Thus, Gemini's tax basis in its IFG stock is still $675,000.

---

[7] See footnote 1 and Rev. Rul. 90-95, 1990-2 CB 67.

[8] Section 338(a) and (g) allow an acquiring corporation to elect to treat the purchase of a controlling stock interest as an asset purchase to get a stepped-up basis in the target's assets. However, the target must recognize taxable gain to the extent of the step-up. The election is seldom used unless the target has NOL carryforwards to offset the recognized gain or is a member of a consolidated group. See the discussion of Section 338 (h)(10) elections in Chapter 9.

# TAX-DEFERRED ACQUISITIONS

**Objective 4**
Determine the tax consequences of tax-deferred asset acquisitions.

As the matrix in Exhibit 13.1 shows, only asset and stock acquisitions that qualify as corporate reorganizations are tax deferred. This section analyzes the tax rules that permit this deferral and identifies the defining characteristics of these reorganizations.

## Asset Acquisition

In an asset acquisition that qualifies as a reorganization, the acquiring corporation issues its own stock to the target corporation's shareholders, the target's assets and liabilities transfer to the acquirer, and the target goes out of existence. After the reorganization, the former target shareholders are shareholders in the acquiring corporation, which owns the target's business. This sequence of transactions is diagrammed in Exhibit 13.2.

In a reorganization, the target corporation does not recognize gain or loss on the transfer of its assets to the acquiring corporation.[9] Nor do the target shareholders recognize gain or loss on the exchange of their target stock for stock in the acquiring corporation.[10] Instead, each shareholder's basis in the target stock becomes the substituted basis in the acquirer's stock.[11]

---

*Tax-Deferred Asset Acquisition*

Autry Inc. negotiated with the Dumfrey shareholders to acquire Dumfrey's business through a reorganization. Immediately before the acquisition, Dumfrey's tax basis balance sheet showed the following assets.

| | |
|---|---:|
| Merchandise inventory | $ 740,000 |
| Material and supplies inventory | 90,000 |
| Machinery and equipment | 1,100,000 |
| Copyrights and patents | 480,000 |
| | $2,410,000 |

The parties agreed that the FMV of Dumfrey's business was $4 million. Consequently, Autry issued $4 million of its own stock to Dumfrey's shareholders in proportion to their equity interests in Dumfrey. Dumfrey transferred its assets and liabilities to Autry and dissolved as a legal entity.

Dumfrey does not recognize taxable gain on its transfer of appreciated assets to Autry. Therefore, the parties to the reorganization avoid the cost of a corporate-level tax. Moreover, the shareholders avoid any shareholder-level tax on the exchange of their Dumfrey shares for Autry shares.

---

**EXHIBIT 13.2**
**Acquisitive Asset Reorganization**

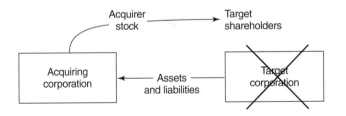

[9] Section 361(a).
[10] Section 354(a)(1).
[11] Section 358(a)(1).

| *Substituted Basis in Acquiring Corporation's Stock* | Mr. Janeway owned 390 Dumfrey shares with a $248,000 basis. Pursuant to the reorganization, he received 1,850 Autry shares worth $351,200. Although Mr. Janeway realized a $103,200 gain on the exchange ($351,200 FMV of Autry stock − $248,000 basis of Dumfrey stock), he did not recognize any gain. His basis in his new Autry stock is $248,000. Because of this substituted basis, Mr. Janeway's $103,200 realized gain is tax deferred. |
|---|---|

If an asset acquisition qualifies as a reorganization, the acquiring corporation does not take a cost basis in the target's assets but must take a carryover basis equal to the target's basis.

| *Carryover Basis in Acquired Assets* | Although Autry issued $4 million of stock to acquire Dumfrey's assets, it does not take a $4 million cost basis in the assets. Instead, Autry takes a $2,410,000 carryover basis, and the unrealized gain in Dumfrey's assets is preserved in the reorganization. |
|---|---|

**Tax Talk**

The largest merger in history occurred in 2001 when Internet giant AOL acquired Time Warner by issuing over $156 billion of stock to the Time Warner shareholders. The merger proved to be a troubled marriage. The AOL Time Warner stock has lost about two-thirds of its value since the merger, the main architects of the merger no longer are in active management positions, and the board of directors finally decided to drop AOL from the corporate name.

In acquisitions in which the target's assets are worth more than their tax basis, the carryover basis rule is detrimental to the acquiring corporation. The rule prevents the acquirer from recovering the entire cost of the assets through future cost recovery deductions (cost of goods sold, depreciation, or amortization). An acquirer must weigh this detriment against the benefits of using stock rather than cash to pay for the assets.

### Type A Reorganization

An asset acquisition is tax deferred if it qualifies as either a type A or a type C reorganization.[12] A **type A reorganization** must be structured as a merger or consolidation of two corporations. In a merger, the acquiring corporation is the surviving legal entity. In a consolidation, the acquiring and the target corporations combine to form a new legal entity. The business statutes of the state or states in which the acquirer and target are incorporated establish the legal requirements for mergers and consolidations.

According to Treasury regulations, a merger or consolidation does not qualify as a reorganization unless the target shareholders continue their proprietary interest in the target's business. Target shareholders satisfy this **continuity of interest requirement** to the extent that they receive the acquiring corporation's stock in exchange for their target stock.[13] It is not necessary, however, for *every* target shareholder to receive *only* stock. The IRS has ruled that a merger or consolidation satisfies the continuity of interest requirement if at least 50 percent of the total payment to the target shareholders consists of stock in the acquiring corporation.[14] The balance of the payment can consist of cash, other corporate property, or corporate debt.

| *Type A Reorganization* | Revalon Inc. acquired the business operated by TBM Inc. by merging TBM into Revalon under Arizona law. Revalon paid $900,000 to TBM's shareholders, consisting of $400,000 Revalon voting common stock, $100,000 Revalon nonvoting common stock, $300,000 |
|---|---|

---

[12] Section 368(a)(1) defines seven types of corporate reorganization. Tax professionals have labeled these reorganizations by reference to the subparagraph describing each one. Section 368(a)(1)(A) describes a type A reorganization, Section 368(a)(1)(B) describes a type B reorganization, and so on. Only the first three of these seven types of reorganizations involve the acquisition of a target corporation's assets or stock by another corporation.

[13] Reg. 1.368-1(e).

[14] Rev. Proc. 77-37, 1977-2 CB 568.

Revalon long-term bonds, and $100,000 cash. Because 55.5 percent of the payment ($500,000 common stock/$900,000 total payment) consisted of Revalon stock, the merger qualified as a type A reorganization.

Target shareholders that do not receive any stock in the acquirer must recognize any gain or loss realized on the exchange of their target stock. Any shareholders that receive a mixture of stock and other consideration must treat the other consideration as *boot*. The receipt of boot triggers the recognition of gain (but not loss) to the extent of the FMV of the boot.[15]

| *Receipt of Boot in a Type A Reorganization* | Thirty-two TBM shareholders exchanged their stock pursuant to TBM's merger into Revalon. According to the merger agreement, each shareholder could choose to receive any combination of stock, bonds, or cash from Revalon. Here are the tax consequences to four of the TBM shareholders. |
|---|---|

- Mr. Pearson exchanged his 200 shares (basis $49,000) for Revalon stock ($180,000 FMV). Because he did not receive any boot, he did not recognize any of his $131,000 realized gain. Mr. Pearson's basis in the Revalon stock is $49,000 (substituted basis).
- Bolle Company exchanged its 200 shares (basis $86,000) for Revalon stock ($145,000 FMV) and Revalon bonds ($35,000 FMV). Because Bolle received $35,000 boot, it recognized $35,000 of its $94,000 realized gain. Bolle's basis in the Revalon stock is $86,000 (substituted basis), and its basis in the Revalon bonds is $35,000 (FMV).
- Mrs. Compton exchanged her 80 shares (basis $16,000) for Revalon bonds ($72,000 FMV). Because she did not receive any Revalon stock, she recognized the entire $56,000 realized gain. Mrs. Compton's basis in her Revalon bonds is $72,000 (FMV).
- Salton LLC exchanged its 40 shares (basis $40,000) for $36,000 cash. Because Salton did not receive any Revalon stock, it recognized the entire $4,000 realized loss.

### Forward Triangular Merger

Recall from the earlier discussion that the shareholders of both the acquiring and target corporations must approve a merger or consolidation. If one or both of the corporations are publicly held, obtaining the necessary shareholder approval can be both time consuming and costly. An acquiring corporation can avoid obtaining the approval of *its own* shareholders by using a type A reorganization called a **forward triangular merger** in which the acquirer contributes its own stock to a new subsidiary in exchange for the subsidiary's stock. The target corporation merges into the subsidiary, which distributes its parent's stock as payment to the target's shareholders.[16] Because the acquiring parent is the sole shareholder of the subsidiary participating in the merger, the parent's shareholders are not required to give their approval. After the triangular merger is complete, the parent corporation owns the target as a controlled subsidiary.

| *Forward Triangular Merger* | Mistford is a publicly held corporation with thousands of shareholders. It wanted to acquire the business operated by Dunstan Corporation in a merger under Virginia law. According to Virginia law, shareholders representing two-thirds of the voting power in both corporations must approve a merger. To avoid the cost of obtaining the approval of its own shareholders, Mistford contributed 80,000 Mistford shares in exchange for the stock in newly incorporated |
|---|---|

---

[15] Section 356(a)(1). If the exchange of target stock for stock in the acquiring corporation completely terminates the shareholder's equity interest in the target, the recognized gain is capital gain under Section 356(a)(2).

[16] Section 368(a)(2)(D). The subsidiary does not recognize gain on the distribution of parent stock to the target shareholders. Reg. 1.1032-2(b).

MD, which was formed to accomplish the Dunstan merger. Once Mistford obtained approval from two-thirds of Dunstan's shareholders, MD distributed the 80,000 Mistford shares to the shareholders, and Dunstan merged into MD. After the merger, Mistford can either operate Dunstan's business through MD or liquidate MD and operate the business directly. A diagram of the merger transaction follows.

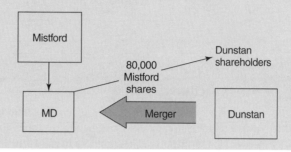

The majority of tax-deferred asset acquisitions are structured as mergers or consolidations that qualify as type A reorganizations. Occasionally, state law prevents a merger between the acquiring corporation and its target. In these unusual cases, the corporations have no choice but to accomplish the asset acquisition through a type C reorganization.

### Type C Reorganization

In a **type C reorganization,** often described as a *practical merger,* the acquiring corporation enters into a contract to purchase the target's business assets. For the purchase to qualify as a type C reorganization, the acquirer must obtain substantially all the target's assets solely in exchange for voting stock.[17] (The acquirer's assumption of target liabilities does not violate this requirement.) Thus, a type C reorganization is inflexible as to the type of consideration the acquirer may use.[18] Another requirement is that the target corporation must liquidate after exchanging its assets for the acquirer's stock; the target shareholders do not have the option to keep their corporate entity alive as a holding company.

| *Type C Reorganization* | Hauck Inc. and Tempo Inc. entered into a contract under which Hauck purchased Tempo's business assets. The entire $3 million payment for the assets consisted of Hauck's voting common stock. Immediately after the exchange of its assets, Tempo liquidated by distributing the Hauck stock proportionately to its shareholders. Because the series of transactions qualified as a type C reorganization, Tempo did not recognize any gain or loss on the exchange of its assets, and the Tempo shareholders did not recognize any gain or loss on the exchange of their Tempo stock for Hauck stock. |
|---|---|

One of the key differences between type A and type C reorganizations is the effect on the target corporation's liabilities. In a type A reorganization, the acquirer becomes responsible for all the target's liabilities—even undisclosed liabilities that may have originated long before the acquisition date. In a type C reorganization, the acquirer can select the specific liabilities (if any) that it will assume as part of the purchase agreement. Any liabilities that the acquirer does not assume by contract remain the legal responsibility of the target corporation and its shareholders. In today's litigious business climate, this important difference is generating renewed interest in the practical merger as a strategy for minimizing risk.

---

[17] Section 368(a)(1)(C).

[18] Section 368(a)(2)(B) allows a minimal amount of other consideration to be paid by the acquiring corporation, but this "boot relaxation" rule is very narrow.

**EXHIBIT 13.3**
**Acquisitive Stock**
**Reorganization**

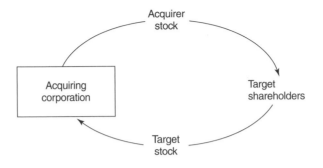

## Stock Acquisition

**Objective 5**
Determine the tax
consequences of
tax-deferred stock
acquisitions.

In stock acquisitions that qualify as reorganizations, the acquiring corporation issues stock
to the target shareholders in exchange for their stock. After the reorganization, the former
target shareholders are shareholders in the acquiring corporation, which owns the target as
a controlled subsidiary. Note that the target itself does not participate in the reorganization
transaction. The exchange between the acquiring corporation and the target shareholders is
diagrammed in Exhibit 13.3.

 If a stock acquisition qualifies as a reorganization, the target shareholders do not recognize gain or loss on the exchange of their stock.[19] Instead, each shareholder's basis in the
target stock becomes the substituted basis in the acquirer's stock.[20]

*Tax-Deferred*
*Stock Acquisition*

Moby issued 100,000 shares in exchange for 100 percent of the stock in Tudor. Ms. Kwan received 35,000 Moby shares ($782,000 FMV) in exchange for her 4,600 Tudor shares
($135,000 basis). Because the stock acquisition qualified as a reorganization, she did not recognize any of her $647,000 realized gain. Ms. Kwan's basis in her Moby shares is $135,000.
Because of this substituted basis, her $647,000 realized gain is tax deferred.

 If a stock acquisition qualifies as a reorganization, the acquiring corporation does not
take a cost basis in the target stock. Instead, the acquirer must take a carryover basis equal
to the stock basis in the hands of the target shareholders.[21] In the Moby example, Moby's
tax basis in the 4,600 Tudor shares acquired from Ms. Kwan is only $135,000 (carryover
basis from Ms. Kwan) instead of the $782,000 cost of the shares.

 The carryover basis rule could cause a practical problem when the target corporation is
publicly held or has a large number of shareholders. Although each shareholder's basis in
each share of target stock technically becomes the acquirer's basis, the basis information
might be impossible to obtain with any accuracy. In acknowledgment of this problem, the
IRS permits the acquiring corporation to use a statistical sampling technique to estimate a
reasonable aggregate carryover basis in the target's stock.[22]

### Type B Reorganization

A stock acquisition is tax deferred if it qualifies as a **type B reorganization** in which the
acquirer uses only voting stock to pay for the target stock. Immediately after the stock-for-
stock exchange, the acquirer must own at least 80 percent voting control of the target and
80 percent of any nonvoting class of target stock. Note that 80 percent control does not have
to be acquired *in* the exchange so long as control exists *after* the exchange.

---

[19] Section 354(a)(1).
[20] Section 358(a)(1).
[21] Section 362(b).
[22] Rev. Proc. 81-70, 1981-2 CB 729.

| *Type B Reorganization* | In 1997, Anchor exchanged 35,000 shares of its voting stock for 110,000 shares of Gerhard stock. Immediately after this exchange, Anchor owned 55 percent of Gerhard's stock. This stock acquisition did not qualify as a type B reorganization and was a taxable exchange for the participating Gerhard shareholders. This year, Anchor exchanged 24,700 shares of its voting stock for another 60,000 shares of Gerhard stock. Immediately after this exchange, Anchor owned 85 percent of Gerhard's stock. Therefore, this stock acquisition qualified as a type B reorganization and was a nontaxable exchange for the participating Gerhard shareholders. |
|---|---|

Because the acquiring corporation can use *nothing but voting stock* as payment, type B reorganizations are dangerously inflexible. An insignificant amount of boot paid to the target shareholders disqualifies the entire acquisition as a tax-deferred reorganization.

| *Violation of the Voting Stock Requirement* | In Yarnell's bid to acquire Twinning, it offered 10 shares of its voting stock for every share of Twinning stock. A group of 38 shareholders who collectively owned 98 percent of Twinning's stock accepted this offer, but one shareholder (who owned the remaining 2 percent) demanded cash in payment for her shares. Consequently, Yarnell used voting stock worth $784,000 and $16,000 cash to acquire 100 percent of Twinning's stock. This acquisition failed to qualify as a type B reorganization because the payment did not consist solely of voting stock. Accordingly, all 39 shareholders recognized gain or loss on the taxable disposition of their Twinning stock. |
|---|---|

Yarnell could have prevented this outcome by refusing to buy out the obstinate 2 percent shareholder. It could have tolerated the minority interest until the stock-for-stock exchange was "old and cold," then purchased the interest for cash in a separate transaction.[23] Through this simple strategy, Yarnell could have deferred any tax cost of the stock-for-stock exchange for Twinning's 38 other shareholders.

## Business-Related Requirements for Reorganizations

According to Treasury regulations, the purpose of the highly beneficial reorganization provisions is to allow shareholders to readjust their corporate structures "as required by business exigencies" at no tax cost.[24] An acquisitive reorganization must result in a continuation of the target's business enterprise in a modified corporate form. To satisfy this **continuity of business enterprise requirement,** the acquiring corporation must either continue the target's historic business or use a significant portion of its assets in the acquirer's own business. If facts and circumstances show that the acquiring corporation violated the requirement by promptly dismantling the target's business, the IRS can disqualify the acquisition as a reorganization.[25]

Similarly, the IRS might challenge the status of any reorganization not motivated by a valid business purpose. According to the courts, capital transactions with no purpose other than tax avoidance should not qualify as reorganizations.[26] If the various parties cannot demonstrate a persuasive legal, political, financial, or accounting reason for their corporate restructuring, they run the risk that the IRS will disqualify the restructuring as a tax-deferred reorganization.

---

[23] Reg. 1.368-2(c) suggests that Yarnell should wait at least 12 months after the stock-for-stock type B reorganization before cashing out the minority shareholder.

[24] Reg. 1.368-1(b)

[25] Reg. 1.368-1(d).

[26] *Gregory v. Helvering*, 293 U.S. 465 (1935).

## Book/Tax Differences Resulting from Reorganizations

For financial reporting purposes, corporations must account for the acquisition of a target business using the **purchase method of accounting** prescribed by GAAP.[27] Under the purchase method, the acquirer records the target's assets at cost: the amount of cash plus the FMV of any property (including the acquirer's stock) paid for the assets. The purchase method applies regardless of whether the acquisition is taxable or tax deferred. In a tax-deferred acquisition, the tax basis of the target's assets is not stepped up (or down) to reflect their cost to the acquirer. Consequently, the acquirer's book basis and tax basis in the assets could differ. This difference is temporary and will reverse as basis is recovered through amortization or depreciation or when the acquirer disposes of the assets.

| | |
|---|---|
| *Book/Tax Difference in Basis* | Clairon acquired O'Hara's business assets in a merger under Delaware law. Clairon paid $18 million for the assets ($13 million common stock and $5 million long-term bonds). The merger qualified as a type A reorganization. As a result, O'Hara's $7.6 million aggregate tax basis in the assets carried over to become Clairon's tax basis. For financial reporting purposes, Clairon used the purchase method to account for the acquisition. As a result, its aggregate book basis in its new assets was $18 million. |

# SURVIVAL OF THE TARGET CORPORATION'S TAX ATTRIBUTES

One major consideration in a corporate acquisition is the extent to which the target corporation's tax attributes survive. *Tax attributes* are the various items associated with a specific corporate entity, such as its accumulated E&P and the various accounting methods and conventions used to compute taxable income. The most valuable tax attributes (as far as the acquiring corporation is concerned) are usually the target's loss or credit carryforwards. These carryforwards represent future tax savings, and their survival could be an important goal in structuring the acquisition.

| | |
|---|---|
| *Value of Target's NOL Carryforward* | Tussman Inc. operates a business valued at $6 million and has a $1 million net operating loss (NOL) carryforward. A corporation interested in acquiring Tussman should be willing to pay $6 million for the business alone. If it can also acquire Tussman's NOL carryforward to deduct against future income, it should be willing to pay a premium equal to the NPV of the future tax savings from the NOL deductions. |

## Tax Attributes in the Acquisitions Matrix

**Objective 6**
Describe the status of the target's tax attributes in each quadrant of the corporate acquisitions matrix.

By referring to the corporate acquisitions matrix introduced in Exhibit 13.1, we can address the status of a target corporation's tax attributes in each of the four quadrants. In the two right-hand quadrants (taxable and tax-deferred stock acquisitions), the survival of the target's tax attributes is a nonissue. In a stock acquisition, the target maintains its corporate identity with its tax attributes intact. In the upper left-hand quadrant (taxable asset acquisitions), the acquiring corporation can purchase all of the target's tangible and intangible assets but not its tax attributes. In other words, these attributes remain with the selling corporation.[28]

---

[27] According to the Financial Accounting Standards Board (FASB), the pooling-of-interest method is no longer permitted in accounting for business acquisitions. See FASB, *Business Combinations and Intangible Assets,* 1999 Exposure Draft reconfirmed on January 24, 2001.

[28] In a straightforward cash merger, the target's tax attributes do not survive. In a reverse cash merger, the target itself survives the merger as a controlled subsidiary. If the acquiring corporation eventually liquidates the target, the acquiring corporation succeeds to the target's tax attributes under Section 381(a)(1).

**EXHIBIT 13.4**
**Corporate Acquisitions Matrix Including Tax Attributes**

| Taxable asset acquisitions | Taxable stock acquisitions |
|---|---|
| • Acquirer cannot purchase target's tax attributes | • Target's tax attributes are intact |
| Tax-deferred asset acquisitions (Type A or C reorganization) | Tax-deferred stock acquisitions (Type B reorganization) |
| • Acquirer succeeds to target's tax attributes | • Target's tax attributes are intact |

In the lower left-hand quadrant of Exhibit 13.4 (tax-deferred asset acquisitions), the acquiring corporation does, in fact, "succeed to and take into account" the target's tax attributes.[29] Remember that the acquisitions in this quadrant must qualify as type A or type C reorganizations. Reorganizations are corporate restructurings characterized by a continuity of both the target shareholders' proprietary interest and the target's business enterprise. These characteristics justify the survival of the target's accumulated E&P, accounting methods, and loss and credit carryforwards, even though the target itself disappears in the reorganization.

*Survival of the Target's Tax Attributes*

Jacobi acquired Taubert's business in a merger of Taubert into Jacobi under Illinois law. Both corporations were calendar year taxpayers. The effective date of the merger was July 1, 2005, and Taubert's last taxable year was the short period from January 1 through June 30, 2005. On this date, Taubert had $923,000 accumulated E&P and a $48,000 capital loss carryforward that originated in 2002. If the merger was a taxable asset acquisition, these tax attributes did not survive, but if it qualified as a type A reorganization, Jacobi succeeded to these tax attributes.

An acquiring corporation that succeeds to the target's loss and credit carryforwards can take the losses and credits into account on a "go-forward" basis. In other words, the acquirer can deduct the losses only against postacquisition income and can use the credits only against the tax on this income.

*Use of Loss Carryforward by the Acquiring Corporation*

Assume that Taubert's merger into Jacobi qualified as a type A reorganization so that Jacobi succeeded to Taubert's E&P, capital loss carryforward, and other tax attributes as of July 1, 2005. Jacobi could not use Taubert's $48,000 capital loss as a carryback to its own previous taxable years,[30] but it could deduct Taubert's capital loss against net capital gains attributable to the 184 days from July 1 through December 31, 2005. Jacobi's net capital gain for the year was $62,800, of which $31,358 was attributable to the 184-day postacquisition period.[31]

$62,800 net capital gain × (184 days/365 days) = $31,658

Accordingly, Jacobi deducted only $31,658 of Taubert's capital loss in 2005 and carried the $16,342 remaining capital loss into 2006.

[29] Section 381(a)(2).
[30] Section 381(b)(3).
[31] Section 381(c)(3)(C)

The carryforward period for a capital loss is five taxable years after the year in which the loss originated. The carryforward schedule for Taubert's 2002 capital loss follows.

|  | Taubert | Jacobi |
|---|---|---|
| First year | 2003 | |
| Second year | 2004 | |
| Third year* | short year ended 6/30/2005 | |
| Fourth year | | 2005 |
| Fifth year | | 2006 |

*A short year resulting from the closing of a target corporation's taxable year counts as a full year in the carryforward period. (Reg. 1.381(c)(3)-1(d)(3).)

If Jacobi cannot deduct the carryforward against capital gains in 2006, the unused carryforward will expire.

## Limitations on the Use of the Target's Loss Carryforwards

The fact that a target corporation's loss carryforwards survive so many types of corporate acquisitions raises a tax policy concern: an acquiring corporation might find a target attractive *only* because of its loss carryforwards. In this case, tax avoidance might be the acquirer's sole motive. Consider the following extreme example of this possibility:

*Acquisition Motivated by Tax Avoidance*

Mega, a profitable manufacturing company with several operating divisions, purchased a controlling stock interest in Luma. Luma operated a chain of retail clothing stores and had NOL carryforwards in excess of $15 million. Immediately after the purchase, Mega replaced Luma's management team, closed its stores, fired its employees, and sold the assets used in its retail business. Mega then transferred one of its operating divisions into Luma so that Luma can deduct the NOL carryforwards from the defunct retail business against the future income generated by the manufacturing division.

Section 269, added to the tax law in 1943, gives the IRS the authority to disallow a target's loss or credit carryforwards if the principal purpose of the acquisition is to evade or avoid federal income tax. The IRS can apply Section 269 to a corporate acquisition only if the facts and circumstances support a conclusion that the acquisition was tax motivated. Acquiring corporations have often challenged this conclusion in court, and many have won their cases because they could demonstrate credible nontax reasons for the acquisition. Because the application of Section 269 is so subjective, it has never been a reliable deterrent against tax-motivated acquisitions.

Section 382, enacted in 1986, is also intended to discourage tax-motivated corporate acquisitions. This section establishes an annual limitation on the NOL carryforwards deductible against taxable income in any year following a significant change in a target corporation's ownership.[32] A technical discussion of the statutory definition of *ownership change* is beyond the scope of this text. Suffice it to say that all the corporate acquisitions described in this chapter cause a Section 382 ownership change.

---

[32] Section 383 extends the concept of the Section 382 annual limitation to capital loss and tax credit carryforwards.

| | |
|---|---|
| *Acquisitions Causing an Ownership Change* | Each of the following acquisitions causes an ownership change in the target corporation.<br><br>• ABC purchased 92 percent of Targett stock in a taxable stock acquisition.<br>• DEF exchanged its voting stock for 100 percent of Targett II stock in a type B reorganization.<br>• GHI acquired the business operated by Targett III in a merger that qualified as a type A reorganization.<br><br>If Targett, Targett II, or Targett III had NOL carryforwards from taxable years ending before the ownership change, Section 382 limits the NOL deduction in taxable years ending after the ownership change. |

| | |
|---|---|
| **Objective 7**<br>Compute the Section 382 limitation on a target's NOL carryforwards. | The **Section 382 limitation** equals the long-term tax-exempt federal rate (an interest rate published monthly by the IRS) multiplied by the FMV of the target corporation's stock immediately before the ownership change. This limitation represents the maximum deduction of *prechange NOLs* against the taxable income for a *postchange* year. |

| | |
|---|---|
| *Computation of the Section 382 Limitation* | ABC's purchase of 92 percent of Targett stock occurred on December 31, 2003, the last day of Targett's taxable year. Targett had a $986,000 NOL carryforward into 2004. On December 31, the long-term tax-exempt federal rate was 5.24 percent, and the FMV of Targett's stock was $4 million. The Section 382 limitation on Targett's annual NOL deduction for 2004 and subsequent years is $209,600 (5.24 percent $\times$ $4 million). |

| | |
|---|---|
| *Application of the Section 382 Limitation* | During 2004, ABC revitalized Targett's business with an infusion of cash and managerial talent. Consequently, Targett earned $1,322,000 net income for the year. Even though it had a $986,000 NOL carryforward, it could deduct only $209,600 because of the Section 382 limitation. Targett's 2004 taxable income was $1,112,400 ($1,322,000 net income − $209,600 NOL deduction).<br><br>In 2005, Targett earned $1,896,000 net income. Its NOL carryforward was $776,400 ($986,000 prechange NOL carryforward − $209,600 deducted in 2004). Because Targett's NOL deduction was limited to $209,600, its 2005 taxable income was $1,686,400 ($1,896,000 net income − $209,600 NOL deduction). |

As the Targett example illustrates, the Section 382 limitation can significantly reduce the value of a target's NOL carryforwards. Without the Section 382 limitation, Targett could have deducted its entire $986,000 prechange NOL in 2004. The tax savings from the deduction at a 34 percent rate would have been $335,240. Because of the Section 382 limitation, Targett's annual NOL deduction is limited to $209,600 in 2004 through 2007 and $147,600 in 2008. At a 10 percent discount rate, the 2004 NPV of the annual tax savings from this series of deductions is only $282,702.

One additional feature of the Section 382 limitation can eliminate any value of a target corporation's prechange NOL carryforwards. If the new owners do not continue the target's historic business at all times during the two-year period following the ownership change, the Section 382 limitation drops to zero for every postchange year.[33]

---

[33] Section 382(c)(1).

# CORPORATE DIVISIONS

So far in the chapter, we have analyzed capital transactions in which one corporation acquires another corporation's assets or stock. The final sections of the chapter consider the reverse: capital transactions that result in corporate divisions.

### Spin-Offs, Split-Offs, and Split-Ups

As discussed in Chapter 9, parent corporations typically operate different business activities through controlled subsidiaries. Although the parent and its subsidiaries are separate legal entities, they represent one economic unit. This unit's owners are the parent corporation's shareholders. These shareholders do not own stock in the subsidiaries, but the value of their investment in the parent is a function of the value of the businesses operated by the subsidiaries.

The shareholders of a parent-subsidiary group can restructure their ownership through a divisive transaction called a **spin-off,** in which a parent corporation distributes subsidiary stock proportionally to the parent's shareholders. After the distribution, the shareholders directly own the stock of both corporations.

*Spin-Off*

MacKeon Inc. owned all 1,000 shares of SouthMac stock. MacKeon spun off the subsidiary by distributing the stock to its shareholders. After the spin-off, each shareholder owned the same proportionate interest in both MacKeon and SouthMac. The following diagram illustrates the ownership structure before and after this corporate division.

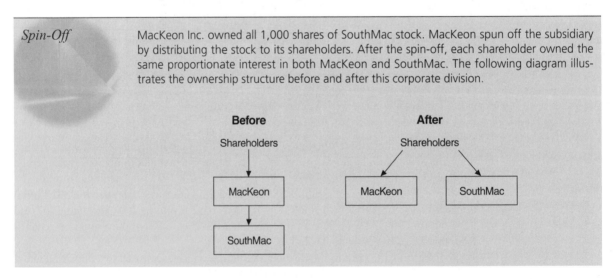

A parent-subsidiary group's shareholders could decide that one set of shareholders should retain ownership of the parent and a different set should acquire ownership of the subsidiary. This division is accomplished by a **split-off,** in which the parent distributes subsidiary stock to one set of shareholders in exchange for their parent stock. After this exchange, the participating shareholders own the former subsidiary but no interest in the parent.

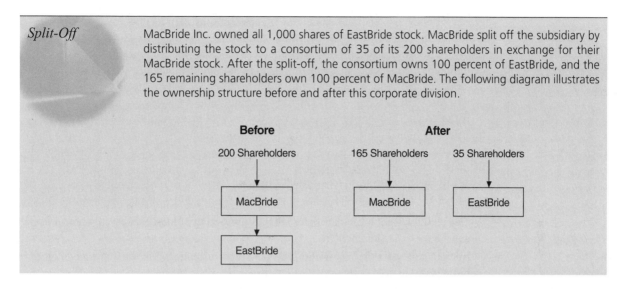

*Split-Off*

MacBride Inc. owned all 1,000 shares of EastBride stock. MacBride split off the subsidiary by distributing the stock to a consortium of 35 of its 200 shareholders in exchange for their MacBride stock. After the split-off, the consortium owns 100 percent of EastBride, and the 165 remaining shareholders own 100 percent of MacBride. The following diagram illustrates the ownership structure before and after this corporate division.

A third type of restructuring involves a nonoperating parent corporation that functions as a holding company for multiple operating subsidiaries. The shareholders could eliminate the holding company through a divisive transaction called a **split-up,** in which the parent liquidates by distributing the stock of its subsidiaries to its shareholders. After the liquidation, the shareholders directly own the subsidiaries.

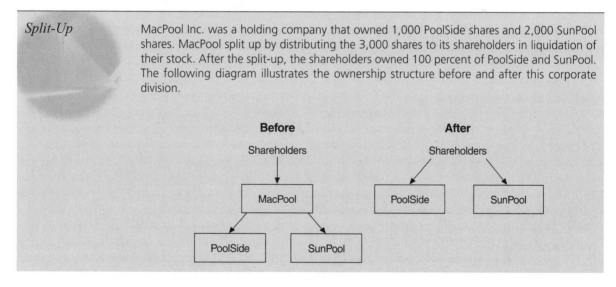

*Split-Up*

MacPool Inc. was a holding company that owned 1,000 PoolSide shares and 2,000 SunPool shares. MacPool split up by distributing the 3,000 shares to its shareholders in liquidation of their stock. After the split-up, the shareholders owned 100 percent of PoolSide and SunPool. The following diagram illustrates the ownership structure before and after this corporate division.

## Tax Consequences of Corporate Divisions

**Objective 8**
Determine the tax consequences of corporate divisions.

Without a special tax provision, the three varieties of corporate divisions would be taxable transactions at both the corporate and the shareholder levels. The parent's distribution of subsidiary stock is a property distribution, and a corporation generally must recognize gain to the extent that the FMV of distributed property exceeds its basis.[34] In a spin-off, the proportionate distribution of subsidiary stock to the shareholders is equivalent to a

---

[34] Section 311(b).

property dividend. Generally, shareholders recognize ordinary income equal to the FMV of a property dividend. In a split-off, the exchange of subsidiary stock for parent stock is equivalent to a stock redemption. Shareholders generally recognize gain or loss on the redemption of their stock.[35] In a split-up, the distribution of subsidiary stock is equivalent to a liquidating distribution. As you will learn in Chapter 14, shareholders generally recognize gain or loss on the receipt of a liquidating distribution.

If the general Subchapter C rules apply, the tax cost of a corporate division could be extraordinarily high. Fortunately for the corporate community, Subchapter C contains a provision that can eliminate the tax cost of corporate divisions. Section 355 provides that neither the parent corporation nor the participating shareholders recognize current gain or loss if a corporate division meets all requirements listed in the code section. Unfortunately, these requirements are dauntingly complex. In summary, a corporate division is nontaxable only if:

- The parent corporation distributes stock representing at least 80 percent control of the subsidiary to its shareholders.
- Immediately after the distribution, the subsidiary is engaged in the active conduct of a business.
- Immediately after a spin-off or split-off, the parent is engaged in the active conduct of a business. (The parent no longer exists after a split-up.)
- The subsidiary and the parent have actively conducted these businesses throughout the five-year period ending on the date of distribution.
- The division was performed for one or more corporate business purposes and was not principally a device for the distribution of the parent's E&P.

Because Section 355 is so technically difficult, its successful application requires the services of a tax expert. Even considering the compliance cost, the tax savings offered by the section can be enormous.

| | |
|---|---|
| *Tax Benefit of Section 355* | Jellico Inc. owns all 50,000 shares of Kelli stock ($8 million FMV and $1 million basis). Jellico's accumulated E&P exceeds $50 million. For an urgent legal reason, it must divest itself of the Kelli stock, and its board of directors wants to spin off the stock to Jellico's shareholders. |
| | If the spin-off does not meet the requirements of Section 355, Jellico will recognize a $7 million gain ($8 million FMV − $1 million basis) on the distribution of its Kelli stock, and its shareholders will recognize an $8 million dividend. If the spin-off meets the requirements of Section 355, Jellico will not recognize gain on the distribution of the Kelli stock, and its shareholders will not recognize dividend income. |

### Shareholder's Stock Basis

Shareholders who receive a distribution of subsidiary stock pursuant to a *taxable* corporate division take a basis in the stock equal to its FMV. In contrast, shareholders who receive a distribution pursuant to a *nontaxable* corporate division must allocate some or all of the tax basis in their parent stock to the subsidiary stock received.

| | |
|---|---|
| *Basis Allocation In a Spin-Off* | Refer to the facts of Jellico's spin-off of Kelli stock in the preceding example. Ms. Haig is a Jellico shareholder who received 310 Kelli shares (FMV $49,600) pursuant to this corporate division. If the spin-off was taxable, Ms. Haig must recognize $49,600 dividend income and take a $49,600 basis in the Kelli shares. If the spin-off was nontaxable, she must allocate the |

---

[35] Section 302(a).

original tax basis in her Jellico shares between her Jellico shares and her Kelli shares based on their relative FMVs after the spin-off.[36]

If the original basis in Mrs. Haig's Jellico shares was $92,200 and these shares had a $350,000 FMV after the spin-off, she must allocate the $92,200 basis as follows.

$$\frac{\$350,000 \text{ FMV Jellico stock}}{\$399,600 \text{ FMV both stocks}} \times \$92,200 \text{ original basis} = \$80,756 \text{ Jellico basis}$$

$$\frac{\$49,600 \text{ FMV Kelli stock}}{\$399,600 \text{ FMV both stocks}} \times \$92,200 \text{ original basis} = \$11,444 \text{ Kelli basis}$$

| | |
|---|---|
| *Basis Allocation In a Split-Off* | Lester LLC owned 497 shares of MSP Inc. stock with a $8,500 basis. MSP recently split off a controlled subsidiary, Cavel Inc., by distributing all 10,000 shares of Cavel stock to a minority group of MSP shareholders in exchange for their MSP stock. Pursuant to this corporate division, Lester received 216 Cavel shares (FMV $39,100). If the split-off was taxable, Lester must recognize a $30,600 capital gain ($39,100 FMV of Cavel shares received − $8,500 basis of MSP shares surrendered). In this case, the LLC's basis in the Cavel shares is $39,100. If the split-off was nontaxable (so that Lester does not recognize gain), the LLC's basis in the Cavel shares is $8,500, which is the basis of the MSP shares surrendered.[37] |

## Type D Reorganizations

To this point, all our examples of corporate divisions have involved parent-subsidiary groups. The shareholders of a single corporation might have a business reason for dividing it into two or more corporations. The division can be accomplished in a two-step process. First, the corporation transfers a portion of its assets to a new corporation in exchange for stock. Then the parent distributes the stock to its own shareholders. After the dust settles, the shareholders own the stock of both the original corporation and the new corporation. If the distribution meets the requirements of Section 355, the entire process qualifies as a **type D reorganization.** As a result, none of the parties recognizes gain or loss because of the corporate division.

| | |
|---|---|
| *Type D Reorganization* | Kingston, a Maryland corporation, operated 17 retail stores, 10 on the east coast and 7 in the southwest. To improve managerial efficiency, Kingston's board of directors divided the original corporation into two corporations. As the first step, Kingston contributed the seven southwest stores to a new corporation, KingsWest, in exchange for 100 percent of its stock. As the second step, Kingston distributed the KingsWest stock to its shareholders. Because the distribution met the requirements of Section 355, the corporate division qualified as a type D reorganization, and neither Kingston nor Kingston's shareholders recognized any gain or loss. |

## Conclusion

This chapter has introduced the rules governing the taxation of corporate acquisitions, mergers, and divisions. It discussed the fact that different acquisition structures have strikingly different tax consequences even if they have the same economic outcome. Thus, the purchaser and seller want to choose the structure with the best after-tax result to each party.

[36] Reg. 1.358-2(a)(2).
[37] Reg. 358(a)(1).

Depending on the circumstances, the optimal structure could be an asset or a stock acquisition and could be taxable or tax deferred to the seller. The acquisition structure determines how the purchaser computes the tax basis in its new assets as well as the extent to which any valuable tax attributes of the business survive the acquisition.

## Key Terms

acquisitive type D reorganization   *379*
cash merger   *356*
continuity of business enterprise requirement   *363*
continuity of interest requirement   *359*
forward triangular merger   *360*
friendly takeover   *354*

hostile takeover   *354*
junk bonds   *378*
leveraged buyout (LBO)   *378*
merger   *352*
purchase method of accounting   *364*
reverse cash merger   *356*
Section 382 limitation   *367*
spin-off   *368*

split-off   *368*
split-up   *369*
type A reorganization   *359*
type B reorganization   *362*
type C reorganization   *361*
type D reorganization   *371*
type E reorganization   *379*
type F reorganization   *379*
type G reorganization   *379*

## Questions and Problems for Discussion

1. Russo Inc. wants to acquire the restaurant business operated by D'Arcole Inc. Each of ten shareholders owns 100 shares of D'Arcole's 1,000 shares of outstanding stock. Seven shareholders want to sell D'Arcole to Russo, but the other three are adamantly opposed. Is there a way for Russo to structure an acquisition to force the three shareholders to sell?

2. Duncan Inc. agreed to pay a $5 million lump-sum price to purchase Firth Inc.'s business. Duncan plans to allocate $1 million of the price to Firth's inventory, but Firth plans to allocate only $750,000 of the price to its inventory. Since the two unrelated corporations are dealing at arm's length, can each make its planned allocation?

3. Identify any tax or nontax factors that might cause a shareholder in a target corporation to prefer a taxable acquisition to a tax-deferred acquisition.

4. Explain why publicly held corporations use forward triangular mergers instead of straightforward mergers to acquire target corporations.

5. Since type A reorganizations and type C reorganizations have the same tax-deferred results to the target shareholders, why are type A reorganizations so much more common than type C reorganizations?

6. White Inc. wants to acquire Black Inc.'s business. White's board of directors believes that Black could have major undisclosed and contingent liabilities. Black's owners are adamant that they will sell their business only in a tax-deferred transaction. Which type of reorganization would you recommend to the board of directors? Explain briefly.

7. Jumbo Inc. acquired 100 percent of Little Inc. stock in exchange for $7.5 million Jumbo voting stock and $2.5 million cash. After the acquisition, Jumbo operated Little as a controlled subsidiary.
   a. Was the stock-for-stock exchange nontaxable for the participating Little shareholders?
   b. Would your answer to part *(a)* change if the payment to the Little shareholders consisted of $9.99 million Jumbo voting stock and only $10,000 cash?

8. What is the difference between the continuity of interest requirement and the continuity of business enterprise requirement for reorganizations?

9. Ruggers Inc. recently acquired all operating assets used in Jason Inc.'s business. Why does the tax law permit Ruggers to acquire Jason's tax attributes if the acquisition was a reorganization but not if it was a taxable asset purchase?

10. Differentiate between a spin-off, a split-off, and a split-up.

11. Explain why a Section 355 distribution can occur without a type D reorganization, but a type D reorganization cannot occur without a Section 355 distribution.

## Application Problems

Unless otherwise stated, the business entities in the following problems are calendar year taxable corporations.

1. Stookey Inc. is negotiating with the shareholders of Nolan Inc. to acquire Nolan's business through a cash merger under Tennessee law. Nolan's aggregate tax basis in its assets is $310,000, it has no liabilities, and its marginal tax rate is 34 percent. The shareholders' aggregate basis in their stock is $92,000, and their capital gains tax rate is 15 percent. Compute the after-tax cash available to Nolan's shareholders under the following alternatives:
   a. Stookey will pay $1 million cash for Nolan's assets. Nolan will distribute its after-tax cash to its shareholders and merge directly into Stookey (straightforward merger).
   b. Stookey will contribute $1 million cash to a new corporation in exchange for 100 percent of its stock. The new corporation will distribute the cash to the Nolan shareholders and merge into Nolan (reverse merger).

2. Refer to the facts in application problem 1.
   a. What is Stookey's tax basis in Nolan's assets if Stookey acquires them in a straightforward cash merger?
   b. What is Stookey's tax basis in Nolan's assets if Stookey acquires them in a reverse cash merger?

3. Fowler plans to acquire MLP's business through a merger under Missouri law. Explain whether the merger will be taxable or tax deferred to the MLP shareholders under the following assumptions.
   a. Fowler will pay $4 million cash and $1 million short-term notes.
   b. Fowler will pay $1 million cash, $2.5 million short-term notes, and $1.5 million Fowler stock.
   c. Fowler will pay $250,000 cash, $2 million short-term notes, and $2.75 million Fowler stock.
   d. Fowler will pay $1 million short-term notes and $4 million Fowler stock.

4. Omandi acquired TriState's business in a straightforward merger under Colorado law. On the merger date, TriState's assets had a $920,000 FMV and a $146,000 tax basis, and its liabilities totaled $100,000. Determine Omandi's basis in TriState's assets assuming that the merger:
   a. Qualified as a type A reorganization.
   b. Did not qualify as a type A reorganization.

5. Mr. Conway surrendered his Bentley stock (basis $31,600) upon Bentley's merger into Tellco, which qualified as a type A reorganization. How much gain did he recognize, and what is his basis in the Tellco stock in each of the following cases?
   a. Mr. Conway received 200 shares of Tellco stock worth $60,000.
   b. Mr. Conway received 150 shares of Tellco stock worth $47,500 and $12,500 cash.
   c. Mr. Conway received 100 shares of Tellco stock worth $30,000 and $30,000 cash.

6. Beta acquired Tomassini's business for $3,575,000 cash and the assumption of $200,000 of its liabilities. On the date of acquisition, Tomassini owned the following recorded assets.

| | Tax Basis | FMV |
|---|---|---|
| Accounts receivable | $ 160,000 | $ 160,000 |
| Inventory | 550,000 | 640,000 |
| Plant and equipment | 400,000 | 500,000 |
| Investment land | 1,700,000 | 2,000,000 |
| | $2,810,000 | $3,300,000 |

   a. How much gain did Tomassini recognize on the sale of its business?
   b. Allocate Beta's lump-sum purchase price to the various assets acquired in the transaction.

7. Refer to the acquisition described in application problem 6. Assume that Beta used $3,575,000 of its voting stock instead of cash to pay for Tomassini's business, and Tomassini liquidated immediately after titling over its assets to Beta. The Tomassini shareholders' aggregate basis in their stock was $921,000.
   a. Did the acquisition qualify as a type C reorganization? Briefly explain your conclusion.
   b. Assuming that the acquisition qualified as a type C reorganization, how much gain did Tomassini recognize on the sale of its business?
   c. Assuming that the acquisition qualified as a type C reorganization, how much gain did Tomassini's shareholders recognize on receipt of the Beta stock?
   d. What is their tax basis in this stock?
   e. What is Beta's tax basis in the assets acquired from Tomassini?

8. Parnell acquired all 10,000 shares of Abbot's outstanding stock in three separate transactions occurring four years apart. Determine which (if any) of the transactions qualified as a type B reorganization.
   a. In the first transaction, Parnell exchanged 14,900 shares of voting stock for 6,000 Abbot shares.
   b. In the second transaction, Parnell exchanged 6,390 shares of voting stock for 2,500 Abbot shares.
   c. In the third and final transaction, Parnell exchanged 4,900 shares of voting stock and 100 shares of nonvoting stock for 1,500 Abbot shares.

9. Mrs. Howell exchanged her 600 PTV shares ($50,000 FMV and $22,300 basis) for 11,800 shares of Muncy stock ($50,000 FMV) as part of Muncy's acquisition of PTV. How much gain does she recognize and what is her basis in her Muncy shares assuming that the acquisition:
   a. Qualified as a type B reorganization?
   b. Did not qualify as a type B reorganization?

10. Borlano issued 1,500,000 shares of voting stock ($12.3 million FMV) in exchange for 920,000 shares of Grissom stock, which was publicly traded on Nasdaq.
   a. If this transaction qualified as a type B reorganization, how much gain does Borlano recognize on the issuance of stock in exchange for the Grissom stock, and what is its basis in the Grissom stock?
   b. If this transaction failed to qualify as a type B reorganization, how much gain does Borlano recognize on the issuance of stock in exchange for the Grissom stock, and what is its basis in the Grissom stock?

11. This year, Charlton acquired commercial real estate ($1 million FMV and $771,000 tax basis) as part of its acquisition of HSK. What is Charlton's book basis and tax basis in the real estate assuming that the acquisition:
    *a.* Was a taxable asset acquisition?
    *b.* Was a type C reorganization?

12. On January 1, VKZ acquired Sterling's business. VKZ's accumulated E&P was $200,000, and Sterling's accumulated E&P was $92,000. VKZ distributed $300,000 cash to its shareholders on June 30, and its current E&P this year was $18,000. How much of the cash distribution was a dividend assuming that VKZ's acquisition of Sterling's business:
    *a.* Was a taxable asset acquisition?
    *b.* Was a type C reorganization?

13. On December 31 of last year, Zeron merged into Parton under Ohio law. Because of overlapping ownership of the two corporations, the merger was not an ownership change that triggered the application of Section 382. Among its other tax attributes, Zeron had a $200,000 NOL carryforward. This year, Parton had $715,000 taxable income before any NOL deduction. Compute its taxable income if:
    *a.* The merger with Zeron qualified as a type A reorganization.
    *b.* The merger with Zeron did not qualify as a type A reorganization.

14. On December 31 of last year, a consortium of investors paid $1.8 million for 100 percent of Brio's stock. Among its other tax attributes, Brio had a $1,270,000 NOL carryforward. The long-term tax-exempt federal interest rate was 5.5 percent on the date of Brio's ownership change.
    *a.* Compute Brio's taxable income for this year if taxable income before any NOL deduction was $680,000.
    *b.* How would your computation in part *(a)* change if the investors paid $8.9 million instead of $1.8 million for Brio's stock?
    *c.* How would your computation in part *(a)* change if Brio sold its entire business operation on May 29 and invested the proceeds in residential real estate?

15. On December 31 of last year, Emetech acquired Franklin's business in a type A reorganization. The FMV of Franklin's stock was $750,000, the long-term tax-exempt federal interest rate was 4.9 percent, and Franklin had a $200,000 NOL carryforward. This year, Emetech had $612,000 taxable income before any NOL deduction.
    *a.* Compute Emetech's taxable income if the reorganization was not an ownership change under Section 382.
    *b.* Compute Emetech's taxable income if the reorganization was an ownership change under Section 382.
    *c.* How would your answer to part *(b)* change if Franklin's NOL carryforward was $30,000 instead of $200,000?

16. On June 30, Waylon distributed the stock in a controlled subsidiary to its shareholders in proportion to their Waylon ownership. The stock's FMV was $900,000, and Waylon's basis was only $340,000. Waylon's accumulated E&P exceed $20 million. What are the tax consequences to Waylon and its shareholders if:
    *a.* The spin-off meets the requirements of Section 355?
    *b.* The spin-off does not meet the requirements of Section 355?

17. On December 31, IPC distributed the stock in a controlled subsidiary ($800,000 FMV and $500,000 basis) to Mr. Raimey in exchange for his 150 IPC shares ($800,000 FMV and $245,000 basis). After the exchange, Mr. Raimey owned 100 percent of the subsidiary stock and no IPC stock.

a. How much gain does IPC recognize if the split-off meets the requirements of Section 355?

b. How much gain does Mr. Raimey recognize on the exchange of his IPC stock for subsidiary stock if the split-off meets the requirements of Section 355? What is his basis in his subsidiary stock?

c. How would your answers to parts *(a)* and *(b)* change if the split-off does not meet the requirements of Section 355?

18. Mrs. Cox received 1,000 shares of RPO stock ($100 FMV per share) as a distribution from Trilex. She owns 8,000 Trilex shares ($50 FMV and $13 basis per share).

a. Assuming that Trilex has sufficient E&P, how much dividend income did Mrs. Cox recognize if the distribution was part of a spin-off that met the requirements of Section 355?

b. What is Mrs. Cox's basis per share in her RPO and Trilex stock after the spin-off?

c. How would your answers to parts *(a)* and *(b)* change if the spin-off did not meet the requirements of Section 355?

## Issue Recognition Problems

Identify the tax issue or issues suggested by the following situations, and state each issue in the form of a question.

1. Newport Inc. just purchased Jenson Inc.'s business for $20 million cash. Jenson's assets had an appraised FMV of $25 million. Newport got a bargain price for the business because Jenson had negative goodwill caused by the public disclosure of appalling animal rights violations in its product testing.

2. On July 14, CPQ issued 40,000 voting shares in exchange for 54 percent of the stock in Lubley. On August 29, CPQ issued 20,000 additional voting shares to a different group of Lubley shareholders in exchange for their 27 percent stock interest.

3. On May 1, PRX merged into Harrold Inc. under Alabama law. The PRX shareholders received Harrold stock worth $12 million, bonds worth $4 million, and $1 million cash. On June 3, a group of former PRX shareholders sold $9.3 million of their newly acquired Harrold stock to an unrelated Canadian corporation for cash.

4. Mr. and Mrs. Wicam were the sole shareholders of Wicam Products. Mega, a publicly held corporation, issued $3 million nonvoting, nonparticipating, 7.5 percent preferred stock to the Wicams pursuant to a merger of Wicam into Mega under Oregon law. After selling their family corporation, the Wicams retired to Florida.

5. On January 1, Lumus paid $5 million of its own stock and $350,000 cash to Sternhagen's shareholders pursuant to a merger of Sternhagen into Lumus under Wisconsin law. On the date of merger, Sternhagen operated three separate businesses. Six months after the merger, Lumus discontinued two of these businesses.

6. DelMarva was incorporated under Virginia law in 1955. Its board of directors recently decided to reincorporate under Delaware law to take advantage of the state's favorable tax climate. DelMarva's shareholders will receive 10 shares in the new corporation (renamed DelMarDel) in exchange for each share in the old corporation.

7. Gannon Inc. has operated a restaurant since the Gannon family formed the corporation in 1973. In recent years the restaurant became unprofitable, and the corporation has a $385,000 NOL carryforward. The family plans to close the restaurant, sell all assets, and offer early retirement to its employees. The corporation will move into the real estate management business, which should be profitable in the very near future.

8. Pearson Inc. operates a service business and also owns commercial rental property. Mr. Tinque, who owns 35 percent of Pearson's stock, needs a source of passive activity

income so he can deduct substantial suspended passive activity losses. He has proposed that Pearson contribute the commercial rental property to a new corporation and then distribute the new corporation's stock to him in complete redemption of his Pearson stock. After this split-off, Mr. Tinque will make an S election for his new corporation so that the rental income will flow through to him as passive activity income.

9. Kochard Inc. recently went through a type D reorganization in which it transferred an extremely profitable operating division to a new corporation and then distributed the new corporation's stock to its shareholders. Immediately before the reorganization, Kochard had $12.7 accumulated E&P. Nine months after the reorganization, the new corporation distributed $500,000 cash to its shareholders.

## Research Problems

1. Banbury Corporation offered to acquire the business operated by Luttrell Inc. in a type C reorganization. In addition to its business, Luttrell owns residential rental property ($420,000 FMV and $270,000 adjusted basis) that Banbury does not want. According to the reorganization plan, Banbury will issue voting stock in exchange for Luttrell's business assets and immediately after this exchange, Luttrell will liquidate by distributing the stock and rental property to its shareholders. The FMV of the distribution will exceed the Luttrell shareholders' aggregate basis in their stock by $2 million. What tax consequences result from the fact that Banbury is not acquiring the rental property in the type C reorganization?

2. Romano, a publicly held corporation, plans to change its capital structure to include newly issued nonvoting common stock and preferred stock. Mr. Morenez, who owns 4,800 shares of Romano voting common ($92,600 basis), has agreed to exchange these shares for 4,800 shares of nonvoting common ($158,000 FMV) and 25 shares of preferred stock ($25,000 FMV). The preferred stock's dividend rate equals the federal prime interest rate plus 1.5 percent and is adjusted semiannually. Will Mr. Morenez's exchange of his original Romano stock for new stock cause any gain recognition?

## Tax Planning Cases

1. Ninety-three percent of Bonanza's shareholders approved a merger of their corporation into Keystone Inc. that qualifies as a type A reorganization. Mrs. Olmos owns 51,000 Bonanza shares with a $2.75 tax basis per share. She can choose to receive a cash payment of $14.00 per share or two Keystone shares for each Bonanza share. Keystone's market price is $6.70 per share. If Mrs. Olmos accepts the cash, she plans to reinvest the after-tax proceeds in marketable securities with the same investment risk as the Keystone stock. She plans to stay in the stock market for five more years and then to sell her equities and invest in U.S. government bonds. Given this five-year plan, should Mrs. Olmos choose the cash or the Keystone stock to maximize the after-tax value of the payment for her Bonanza stock? In making your calculations, assume that the preferential rate on long-term capital gain in five years will be 15 percent, and the NPV of the capital gains tax is based on a 9 percent discount rate (.708 discount factor).

2. Mr. and Mrs. Truman are the sole shareholders in TPN Corporation, which has a $398,000 aggregate tax basis in its assets and a 34 percent tax rate. Acme Inc. has offered to buy TPN's assets for $820,000 cash. Zelda Inc. has offered to buy Mr. and Mrs. Truman's stock ($450,000 basis) for $700,000 cash. Regardless of which offer they accept, the Trumans plan to invest the proceeds in residential rental property that they can manage during retirement and transfer to their children at death. Which offer do you think the Trumans should accept, and what tax strategies must they implement to facilitate their long-term investment plan?

# Leveraged Buyouts

Many corporate acquisitions are structured as **leveraged buyouts (LBOs).** An LBO's defining characteristic is the substantial amount of debt used as payment. One of the most highly publicized LBOs was the $24.7 billion buyout of RJR Nabisco by Kohlberg Kravis Roberts in 1988. This LBO had a dramatic effect on RJR Nabisco's financial statements. Its debt-to-equity ratio increased from approximately 1 to 1 to more than 12 to 1, and its annual debt service payments increased sixfold.

A second characteristic of an LBO is the use of junk bonds to finance the acquisition. A **junk bond** is an unsecured obligation bearing a high yield and subordinated to senior debt obligations. Because of their high risk, institutional investors do not consider junk bonds to be investment grade. As part of the RJR Nabisco acquisition, $4 billion of junk bonds in the newly structured corporation were sold to the public.[38]

LBOs can be either taxable asset purchases or taxable stock purchases. Let's use a stock purchase to describe the steps involved in a typical LBO. The first step is for a purchaser (or consortium of purchasers) to identify a target corporation whose stock seems to be undervalued by the market but whose business is fundamentally sound. (In other words, the purchaser is hunting for a bargain!) The purchaser then forms a corporate shell by contributing cash in exchange for 100 percent of the shell's stock. The shell proceeds to purchase the target's stock, financing the acquisition by issuing new debt (some combination of short-term notes, investment-grade bonds, and junk bonds). After the shell has acquired a controlling equity interest in the target, the target is liquidated into the shell, and the LBO is complete.

[38] Individual investors can buy junk bonds through mutual funds concentrating in high-yield corporate debt obligations.

### Acquiring a Corporate Business through an LBO

Homestead Inc. decided to acquire the business operated by PTM Inc. through an LBO. Homestead contributed $500,000 cash to a new subsidiary (Takeover Inc.) in exchange for 100 percent of Takeover's stock. Takeover raised $1 million additional cash by issuing long-term bonds through the capital markets. It used its $1.5 million cash to purchase PTM voting stock. As soon as Takeover acquired a controlling stock interest, it liquidated PTM and absorbed its business.

In this example, Homestead borrowed $1 million to acquire PTM stock. As a result of this leverage, $1 million of corporate equity was replaced by an equal amount of corporate debt, and nondeductible dividend payments were supplanted by deductible interest payments. For this reason, PTM's new capital structure should result in a significant tax savings and a corresponding improvement in cash flow.

Because LBOs can represent a major shift from equity to debt financing, they may increase a corporation's exposure to cash flow problems, insolvency, and bankruptcy. As yet, no empirical evidence indicates that this increased financial risk is detrimental to the U.S. economy. Moreover, proponents of LBOs argue that some degree of leverage in a corporation's capital structure is healthy. The federal government subsidizes corporate debt through the interest expense deduction, and the pressure to make the required debt service payments should keep the corporation's management on its toes.

# Other Types of Corporate Reorganizations

This chapter discussed three types of reorganizations (type A, type B, and type C) by which one corporation acquires another corporation's assets or stock. In addition to these acquisitive reorganizations, the chapter also discussed type D reorganizations by which one corporation divides into two or more corporations. Section 368(a)(1) defines four more types

of reorganizations in which corporate shareholders exchange their original stock for new stock. In each case, the exchange is tax deferred. The shareholders do not recognize gain or loss, and the basis of the original stock becomes the substituted basis of the new stock. The following is a brief description of these reorganizations and an example of each.

# ACQUISITIVE TYPE D REORGANIZATION

In certain corporate acquisitions, the acquirer has a business reason to preserve the target's legal identity. To accomplish this objective, the acquirer transfers all of its assets and liabilities to the target in exchange for target stock representing control of the target. The acquirer then liquidates by distributing the target stock to its shareholders. After this **acquisitive type D reorganization,** the surviving target owns the acquirer's business, and the former shareholders in the acquirer (which no longer exists) have control of the target. For purposes of an acquisitive type D reorganization, control is defined as at least 50 percent of the total voting power or at least 50 percent of the total value of the target's stock.[39]

### A Minnow Swallows a Shark

Shark Corporation wants to acquire Minnow Inc. Although its business is three times larger than Minnow's business, Shark's board of directors wants Minnow to be the surviving entity for public relations purposes. Consequently, Shark transfers its business to Minnow in exchange for 75,000 shares of new Minnow stock. After the transfer, Minnow has 100,000 shares outstanding. Shark liquidates by distributing the 75,000 Minnow shares to its shareholders, thereby giving them a 75 percent controlling interest in Minnow. Because the entire transaction qualifies as a reorganization, the transfer of Shark's assets to Minnow is nontaxable, and the exchange of Shark stock for Minnow stock is tax deferred.

# TYPE E REORGANIZATION

A corporation could have a business reason to modify its capital structure by issuing new stock to its shareholders in exchange for their original stock. This recapitalization is a **type E reorganization.**

### Creating Preferred Stock

Since its formation in 1977, Jenson Family Inc.'s capital structure has consisted of 500 shares of voting common stock. Grandpa Jenson is ready to retire as CEO and has agreed to exchange his 260 voting common shares for 100,000 shares of newly issued nonvoting

preferred stock. Because the recapitalization qualifies as a reorganization, his exchange of common stock for preferred stock is tax deferred.[40]

# TYPE F REORGANIZATION

A corporation could have a business reason to change its name, form, or place of organization by issuing new stock to its shareholders in exchange for their original stock. Such a mere change in identity is a **type F reorganization.**

### What's in a Name?

Chemical Sludge Inc. has been in the waste disposal business for 35 years. Its marketing department has finally persuaded the board of directors to legally change the corporation's name to EarthOnly. To accomplish the name change, the corporation will issue one share of EarthOnly stock for each outstanding share of Chemical Sludge stock. Because the name change qualifies as a reorganization, the exchange of Chemical sludge stock for EarthOnly stock is tax deferred.

# TYPE G REORGANIZATION

When a corporation files for bankruptcy under Title 11 (Federal Bankruptcy Code) or a similar state proceeding, the shareholders, creditors, employees, and other interested parties can agree to a court-supervised plan to revitalize the corporation. The capital restructuring resulting from the bankruptcy is a **type G reorganization.**

### Rising from the Ashes

When Moribund Corporation filed for bankruptcy protection, it had $10 million of long-term debt. The bankruptcy judge approved a plan to transfer Moribund's assets to newly formed Phoenix Inc. Moribund's shareholders will receive 5 percent of the Phoenix stock in exchange for their Moribund stock, and Moribund's creditors will receive 95 percent of the Phoenix stock in discharge of their debt. Because the restructuring qualifies as a reorganization, the transfer of Moribund assets to Phoenix is a nontaxable event, and the exchange of Moribund stock for Phoenix stock is tax deferred.

[39] Sections 368(a)(2)(H) and 304(c).

[40] Section 354(a)(2)(C)(ii) provides that preferred stock is not treated as boot in the recapitalization of a family-owned corporation.

# Chapter **Fourteen**

# Business Liquidations and Terminations

**Learning Objectives**

*After reading this chapter, you will be able to:*

1. Apply the bankruptcy and insolvency exceptions for discharge of debt income.
2. Describe the effect of the bankruptcy and insolvency exceptions on tax attributes.
3. Distinguish between the tax consequences of business and nonbusiness bad debts.
4. Identify the corporate tax consequences of liquidating distributions.
5. Compute the gain or loss recognized by a shareholder on receipt of a liquidating distribution.
6. Summarize the tax consequences of the liquidation of a controlled subsidiary.
7. Compute the gain or loss recognized by a partner on receipt of a liquidating distribution.
8. Determine whether a sale or exchange of a partnership interest terminates the partnership.

This chapter examines the tax consequences of transactions that occur during the last stage of a business entity's existence. For legal, financial, or even personal reasons, the owners no longer want to conduct their business in its current form and take the steps necessary to close the business and dissolve the entity. The decision to close a business is often based on the fact that the owners are losing money. Accordingly, the first section of the chapter addresses the particular tax issues faced by financially distressed businesses. The second section focuses on corporate liquidations and the tax consequences at both the corporate and the shareholder levels. The final section focuses on partnership terminations and their tax consequences to the partners. The appendix examines two special cases involving the discharge of debt in connection with the ownership of property.

# TAX ISSUES FOR FINANCIALLY DISTRESSED BUSINESSES

A healthy business must generate enough cash flow to meet its financial obligations. Cash flow is the lifeblood that enables a business to pay its employees and suppliers, service its debts, replace its operating assets, and make distributions to its owners. Because cash is so critical, financial analysts are often more interested in a company's statement of cash flows than its income statement.

If a business cannot generate enough cash flow to pay its debts, it could be forced to file for **bankruptcy,** a legal process through which a debtor petitions a federal court to restructure or discharge its debt. The process not only gives the debtor a fresh financial start but also provides a fair method to satisfy the competing claims of the creditors. The Bankruptcy Code (Title 11 of the United States Code) offers two choices to financially distressed businesses. The first choice is a **Chapter 11 reorganization** in which the owners and a majority of the creditors agree to a court-approved plan to restructure the business's debt. The second choice is a **Chapter 7 liquidation** in which the business assets are sold and the proceeds are distributed to the creditors according to a priority established by the court. Chapter 11 gives the owners a chance to turn a struggling business around; Chapter 7 marks the end of the road for a failed business.

*The End of TWA*

Trans World Airlines Inc. (TWA) was forced into bankruptcy in 2000. According to its chief executive officer, the company had not earned a profit for 12 years and was "bleeding" cash at the rate of $3 million a day.[1] After long negotiations involving TWA's shareholders, employees, and creditors, the bankruptcy judge approved American Airlines' offer to buy the ailing airline for $742 million and to assume TWA's $3.5 billion secured debt. The offer did not include any funds to pay TWA's unsecured creditors.

## Discharge of Debt Income

Long before a business is forced into bankruptcy, it can approach its creditors about restructuring its debt obligations. The creditors may be willing to extend the maturity date or reduce the interest rate on their loans to a financially distressed business. They might even be willing to discharge some portion of the debt to help the business survive. The general tax rule is that the business must recognize the discharged debt as gross income.[2]

*Discharge of Debt Income*

Horton Inc. has been experiencing cash flow problems for the last year and is six weeks overdue in paying a $65,000 bill. The creditor has agreed to accept $55,000 as full payment if Horton can make the payment within the week. If Horton pays only $55,000 to satisfy a $65,000 debt, it must recognize $10,000 **discharge of debt income**.

**Objective 1**
Apply the bankruptcy and insolvency exceptions for discharge of debt income.

Section 108 provides several useful exceptions to the general recognition rule. A business can exclude a discharge of debt from gross income if the discharge occurs pursuant to a Title 11 bankruptcy case.[3] Because of the bankruptcy exception, businesses that have been relieved of their debt burden by a bankruptcy court avoid an immediate tax cost from the relief.

---

[1] "Bankruptcy Judge Postpones TWA Decision until Monday," *Washington Post,* p. B-2, March 10, 2001.

[2] Section 61(a)(12).

[3] Section 108(a)(1)(A).

| *Bankruptcy Exception* | Early this year, TPK Industries filed for bankruptcy with the federal court. Under a Chapter 11 plan of reorganization, the court discharged $900,000 of TPK's unsecured liabilities. TPK excluded the entire $900,000 discharge of debt from its gross income under the bankruptcy exception. |
|---|---|

A business that is not yet in bankruptcy but is insolvent can exclude a discharge of debt from gross income, but the exclusion cannot exceed the amount of insolvency.[4] The **insolvency** equals the excess of the business's liabilities over the FMV of its assets immediately before the discharge. Because of the insolvency exception, a business recognizes income on the discharge of debt only to the extent that the discharge increases its net worth. If a business has no net worth even after the discharge, it does not recognize income.

| *Insolvency Exception* | McVaney Company paid $40,000 cash in full settlement of a $47,500 debt. Before the payment, its assets were worth $65,000, and its liabilities totaled $82,000. Therefore, McVaney was insolvent by $17,000. After the payment, its assets were worth $25,000 ($65,000 − $40,000 cash payment), it had $34,500 of liabilities ($82,000 − $47,500 discharge), and it was still insolvent by $9,500. Because McVaney had no net worth before or after the discharge, it could exclude the entire $7,500 discharge of debt from gross income. |
|---|---|
| | Now assume that McVaney's liabilities before the payment totaled only $70,000, so that it was insolvent by only $5,000 ($65,000 FMV of assets − $70,000 of liabilities). After the $40,000 payment in settlement of a $47,500 debt, McVaney's assets were worth $25,000, and it had only $22,500 of liabilities. Thus, it was solvent with a $2,500 net worth. In this case, McVaney can exclude only $5,000 of the $7,500 discharge of debt and must include $2,500 in gross income. |

### Reduction of Tax Attributes

**Objective 2**
Describe the effect of the bankruptcy and insolvency exceptions on tax attributes.

A business that excludes a discharge of debt from gross income under the bankruptcy or insolvency exception must pay a price: The exclusion must be applied to reduce the following tax attributes.[5]

- Net operating loss carryforwards
- General business credit carryforwards
- Minimum tax credit carryforwards
- Capital loss carryforwards
- Tax basis in property
- Passive activity loss and credit carryforwards
- Foreign tax credit carryforwards

These attributes are reduced in the order listed (NOL carryforwards first, general business credit carryforwards second, etc.), and the reduction occurs on the first day of the tax year *following* the year of discharge.[6] Attributes that result in a deduction against future taxable income (loss carryforwards and tax basis in property) are reduced dollar-for-dollar by the amount of the exclusion. Attributes that reduce future tax liability (credit carryforwards)

---

[4] Section 108(a)(1)(B) and (a)(3).

[5] Section 108(b).

[6] Taxpayers can elect to apply the reduction to the tax basis of property (fifth on the list) before any other attributes. Section 108(b)(5).

are reduced by 33.3 cents for every dollar of exclusion. Application of the attribute reduction rules can be quite complex, but their point is simple: A business that enjoys a current tax benefit because of the bankruptcy or insolvency exception must sacrifice some future tax benefit.

---

**Reduced Tax Attributes**

McKenna, a calendar-year corporation, excluded a $25,000 discharge of debt from 2004 gross income under the insolvency exception. Before the exclusion, it had an $8,800 NOL carryforward and a $19,000 general business credit carryforward into 2005. McKenna must apply $8,800 of the exclusion to reduce the NOL carryforward to zero. The $16,200 remaining exclusion reduces the general business credit carryforward by $5,400 ($16,200/3). Accordingly, its credit carryforward into 2005 is only $13,600.

---

Corporate taxpayers have their own tax attributes, and any reduction of the attributes occurs at the entity level. S corporations are not taxable entities and have no tax attributes such as loss or credit carryforwards. Section 108 surmounts this difficulty with an interesting twist. Although the bankruptcy and insolvency exceptions apply at the entity level, the attribute reduction is applied to loss carryforwards at the shareholder level.[7] Specifically, if a shareholder has a suspended loss because of the basis limitation, the suspended loss is treated as a corporate NOL and must be reduced by a pro rata share of the S corporation's excluded discharge of debt income.

---

**S Corporation Discharge of Debt**

Mr. Slater is the sole shareholder in SMS, a calendar year S corporation. His stock basis on January 1, 2004, was $8,000. In 2004, SMS excluded a $10,000 discharge of debt from gross income because it was insolvent. SMS's ordinary loss for 2004 was $31,600. The corporation's discharge of debt has no effect on Mr. Slater's stock basis.[8] Consequently, Mr. Slater could deduct only $8,000 of SMS's loss on his 2004 Form 1040.

| | |
|---|---|
| Stock basis on January 1, 2004 | $ 8,000 |
| Decrease for deductible loss | (8,000) |
| Stock basis on January 1, 2005 | –0– |

Because of the basis limitation, Mr. Slater had a $23,600 suspended loss ($31,600 allocated loss − $8,000 deductible loss), which must be reduced by the $10,000 corporate exclusion of discharge of debt income. Consequently, Mr. Slater's loss carryforward into 2005 is only $13,600.

---

Partnerships, like S corporations, are nontaxable entities with no loss or credit carryforwards at the entity level. Consistent with the aggregate theory, Section 108 does not apply to the partnership itself but applies to each partner.[9] If a partnership debt is discharged, the discharge is treated as a separately stated item of income allocated among the partners. A partner must include his share in gross income unless the *partner* is in bankruptcy or insolvent.

---

[7] Section 108(d)(7).

[8] Section 108(d)(7)(A).

[9] Section 108(d)(6).

| *Partnership Discharge of Debt* | MCV Partnership paid $85,000 cash to settle a $100,000 account payable, thereby recognizing $15,000 discharge of debt income. It allocated $5,000 of the income to each of its three individual partners. Because Mr. Mullins was involved in a bankruptcy proceeding, he could exclude his $5,000 share from gross income. Because Mrs. Coil was insolvent, she could exclude her $5,000 share from gross income. Because Mrs. Verne was neither in bankruptcy nor insolvent, she had to include her $5,000 share of MCV's discharge of debt income in gross income. Mr. Mullins and Mrs. Coil must reduce their individual tax attributes (NOL carryforwards, etc.) by their $5,000 exclusion of MCV's discharge of debt income. |

## Tax Consequences to Creditors

**Objective 3**
Distinguish between the tax consequences of business and nonbusiness bad debts.

As a general rule, a creditor is allowed an ordinary deduction for any portion of a debt that is discharged or becomes worthless during the taxable year.[10] In the case of noncorporate creditors, the deduction is available only for bad debts related to the creditor's business. If debt is not business related, the creditor can recognize a loss only if the debt becomes totally worthless. Moreover, the **nonbusiness bad debt** is treated as a short-term capital loss.[11]

| *Business versus Nonbusiness Bad Debt* | Youngblood LLC, a software development firm, declared bankruptcy this year. Pursuant to the bankruptcy proceeding, the court discharged a $20,000 debt to NyLar Inc., which took a $20,000 ordinary deduction for the bad debt. The court also discharged a $4,500 debt to Dr. Harold, who had loaned the money to Youngblood as an investment and not in connection with his professional medical practice. Consequently, Dr. Harold recognized a $4,500 short-term capital loss for his nonbusiness bad debt. |

Shareholders often lend money to their closely held corporations in return for the corporation's debt obligation. For noncorporate shareholders, such loans represent an additional investment in the corporation, and the debt obligation is a nonbusiness asset. If the corporation becomes financially distressed and unable to repay the debt, the shareholder recognizes a capital loss rather than an ordinary deduction.

| *Shareholder Nonbusiness Bad Debt* | Mr. Coltrane owns 40 percent of the stock in Cree Inc., which operates a construction business. Several years ago, Mr. Coltrane loaned the corporation $35,000 in return for an unsecured interest-bearing note. This year, Cree declared bankruptcy, and the court discharged the $35,000 debt to Mr. Coltrane. Because the bad debt is unrelated to any business activity of Mr. Coltrane, he must recognize it as a short-term capital loss. |

**Tax Talk**
Enron's plan for emerging from bankruptcy received a New York court's initial blessing and will be sent to creditors to either accept or reject a proposal that will pay them about 20 percent of the $66.4 billion they are owed. Enron's interim chief executive said the company could emerge from Chapter 11 by 2005.

Shareholders often work as corporate employees, and their *employment* is considered a business activity. A shareholder/employee who has a bad debt from the corporation often argues that the loan was made to protect her employment rather than her stock investment. Therefore the shareholder/employee should be allowed an ordinary deduction for a business bad debt instead of a capital loss for a nonbusiness bad debt. This argument is tough to sell in federal court. The courts acknowledge that an individual who is both an employee and a shareholder could have mixed motives for loaning money to a corporation. However, unless the facts and circumstances clearly show that the individual's *dominant* motive in making the loan was to protect employment, the loan represents a nonbusiness debt.[12]

[10] Section 166(a). This rule does not apply to worthless securities as defined in Section 165(g)(2)(c).
[11] Section 166(d).
[12] *United States v. Generes*, 405 U.S. 93 (1972).

*Shareholder/*
*Employee Debt*

Ten years ago, Mr. Froehlich formed a corporation through which to operate an automobile dealership. As its CEO, he received an annual salary that ranged from $100,000 to $200,000. Several years ago, the car dealership began experiencing financial problems, and Mr. Froehlich loaned the corporation $400,000 to keep it afloat. In spite of his best efforts, the dealership went bankrupt. He reported his $400,000 bad debt as an ordinary business deduction. Upon audit, the IRS reclassified the debt as a short-term capital loss. In its evaluation of the facts and circumstances, the Tax Court noted that Mr. Froehlich "knew that with his experience and background in the automobile sales field, he would be able to obtain employment and commensurate levels of compensation elsewhere." Accordingly, the court concluded that he made the loan primarily to protect his stock investment instead of his salary and that the IRS was correct in classifying the $400,000 loss as a nonbusiness bad debt.[13]

# CORPORATE LIQUIDATIONS

A **corporate liquidation** is a process in which the corporation ceases any business activity, sells its marketable assets, pays its liabilities, distributes any remaining cash and assets to its shareholders, and dissolves under state law. Thus, a liquidation marks the end of its life as a business entity.

## Corporate Tax Consequences

**Objective 4**
Identify the corporate tax consequences of liquidating distributions.

As part of the typical liquidation process, a corporation sells as many assets as possible for cash. The gains and losses recognized on these dispositions are included in the corporation's income for its last taxable year. The corporation can also distribute assets to its shareholders pursuant to the liquidation. In this case, the corporation recognizes gains and losses on the distribution as if it had sold the assets for FMV.[14] A corporation can have capitalized costs on its balance sheet that have no independent value, such as unamortized goodwill. Because the corporate business is no longer a going concern, such costs have no future benefit and can be written off in the year of liquidation.

*Corporate Tax*
*Consequences*

Ganaway is a calendar year corporation that has operated a manufacturing business since 1981. On January 1, its board of directors voted to liquidate the corporation. It ceased daily operations on April 30 after generating $68,400 operating income for the first four months of the year. During May and June, Ganaway recognized $12,000 ordinary income on the bulk sale of its remaining merchandise and supplies inventories and a $8,300 Section 1231 loss on the sale of its equipment. After paying its liabilities, Ganaway had the following tax basis balance sheet.

| | |
|---|---:|
| Cash on hand | $295,000 |
| Investment land | 100,000 |
| Unamortized goodwill | 6,000 |
| | $401,000 |
| | |
| Paid in capital (5,000 shares) | $   5,000 |
| Retained earnings | 396,000 |
| | $401,000 |

---

[13] *Froehlich*, TC Memo 1996-487.

[14] Section 336(a). Losses from distributions of devalued property to controlling shareholders are not disallowed under Section 267(a)(1).

The unamortized goodwill is attributable to Ganaway's purchase of a competitor's business in 1994. Because it discontinued all business operations, Ganaway can write off the $6,000 unrecovered cost as an ordinary loss. Ganaway plans to distribute its cash and land to its shareholders. The land's FMV is $175,000, so Ganaway will recognize a $75,000 capital gain on the distribution.

Ganaway's taxable income for the year of liquidation is computed as follows.

| | |
|---|---|
| Net income from operations | $ 68,400 |
| Ordinary income on bulk sale of inventories | 12,000 |
| Section 1231 loss on sale of equipment | (8,300) |
| Write-off of unamortized goodwill | (6,000) |
| Capital gain on distribution of land | 75,000 |
| Taxable income | $141,100 |

Based on the corporate rate schedule, Ganaway's federal income tax for its last year is $38,279.[15] It must satisfy this liability before making a final distribution to its shareholders. As a result, the liquidating distribution will consist of $256,721 cash ($295,000 cash on hand − $38,279 tax) and investment land worth $175,000, for a total distribution of $431,721.

When a corporation liquidates and ceases to exist as a taxable entity, its tax attributes usually vanish. For instance, Ganaway's accumulated E&P will vanish when it liquidates. If a corporation has loss or credit carryforwards, these valuable attributes do not survive the liquidation and are not available to the shareholders.

## Shareholder Tax Consequences

**Objective 5**
Compute the gain or loss recognized by a shareholder on receipt of a liquidating distribution.

According to Section 331, shareholders that receive a liquidating distribution can treat the distribution as payment in exchange for their stock. Thus, the shareholders recognize capital gain or loss equal to the difference between the amount of the liquidating distribution and the tax basis in their stock. If the liquidating distribution includes property, the amount of the distribution includes the property's FMV, which becomes the shareholder's tax basis in the property.

*Shareholder Tax Consequences*

Mr. Elliot owns 2,250 (45 percent) of Ganaway's 5,000 shares of stock and is entitled to a $194,274 liquidating distribution (45 percent × $431,721 total distribution). The shareholders have agreed that Mr. Elliot will receive the investment land worth $175,000 and $19,274 cash. His basis in his stock is $55,800, so he will recognize a $138,474 capital gain ($194,274 liquidating distribution − $55,800 stock basis) on Ganaway's liquidation. His basis in the investment land will be $175,000.

As the Ganaway example illustrates, a liquidating distribution can result in capital gain recognition for the recipient shareholders. On the bright side, a liquidating distribution does not result in dividend income regardless of the amount of the corporation's accumulated E&P. In this respect, a corporate liquidation is an opportunity for shareholders to convert potential dividend income into capital gain.

[15] If Ganaway liquidates before December 31, it will have a short taxable year. It is not required to annualize short-period income to compute its tax because it was not in existence for the entire taxable year. Reg. 1.443-1(a)(2).

If a liquidating corporation is insolvent, it does not have enough assets to pay its creditors. Although the shareholders are not liable for unpaid corporate liabilities, they are not entitled to any cash or property upon liquidation. Consequently, their stock is worthless. For tax purposes, they are treated as if they sold their worthless stock for a zero amount realized on the last day of the taxable year.[16] Because of this constructive sale, the shareholders generally recognize the unrecovered basis in their stock as a capital loss.

| | |
|---|---|
| *Worthless Stock* | PRT Inc. is liquidating pursuant to a Chapter 7 bankruptcy. After selling its marketable assets, it has $458,500 cash and $610,000 unsecured liabilities. The bankruptcy court has ordered the cash to be paid proportionally to PRT's creditors (about 75 cents on the dollar). Its $151,500 unpaid liabilities will be discharged. Mr. and Mrs. Coogan own 100 percent of PRT's stock with a $39,500 basis. They will receive nothing for their PRT equity and can recognize their unrecovered basis as a loss. The $39,500 loss is characterized as a capital loss unless the stock qualifies as Section 1244 stock. In such case, the entire loss is ordinary. |

*[Handwritten margin notes: first 1 million of stock issued by company domestic, active business — treat ordinary loss up to 50,000 single 100,000 joint]*

## High Tax Cost of Corporate Liquidations

Under the general Subchapter C rules, a corporate liquidation is a taxable event at both the corporate and the shareholder levels. The corporation must recognize gain or loss on the distribution of any property, and the shareholders must treat the liquidation as a taxable sale of their stock. Thus, the final transaction in a corporation's life can have a high tax cost. Business owners who decide to operate in the corporate form should be aware of the potential tax costs of liquidation. They must remember that the corporate form can be compared to a lobster trap: easy to get in but hard to get out.

| | |
|---|---|
| *No Exit* | Four years ago, Mr. and Mrs. Bernard incorporated their family business by contributing assets in a nontaxable exchange for stock. The assets had a $1 million FMV and a $174,000 basis. Because the corporate formation was nontaxable, the Bernards' basis in the assets carried over to become the corporation's basis. Moreover, the basis of the assets became the Bernards' substituted basis in their stock. Because the Bernards have grown increasingly unhappy with the double tax regime on corporate earnings, they consulted their tax adviser about liquidating the corporation and restructuring their business as an LLC. The corporate assets have a $1.2 million FMV and a $100,000 basis. The Bernards were horrified to learn that the total tax cost of liquidation would be $471,800, computed as follows. |

| | |
|---|---:|
| Corporate gain on liquidating distribution of assets ($1.2 million FMV − $100,000 basis) | $1,100,000 |
| | .34 |
| Corporate tax | $ 374,000 |
| After-tax distribution to Mr. and Mrs. Bernard ($1.2 million FMV of assets − $374,000 tax cost) | $ 826,000 |
| Mr. and Mrs. Bernards' stock basis | (174,000) |
| Capital gain recognized on liquidation | $ 652,000 |
| | .15 |
| Shareholder tax | $ 97,800 |
| Total tax cost ($374,000 + $97,800) | $ 471,800 |

[16] Section 165(g).

Given the prohibitive tax cost of liquidation, what strategies are available to the Bernards? If their corporation is eligible, they could make a Subchapter S election, converting it to a passthrough entity. The election would eliminate the double tax on future corporate earnings but not the double tax on past earnings. Chapter 7 discussed the fact that an S corporation that was once a C corporation is subject to the built-in gains tax.[17] If the corporation disposes of property during its first 10 years as an S corporation, it must pay a 35 percent corporate-level tax on its net recognized built-in gain.

If the Bernards make an S election, their corporation will have a net unrealized built-in gain of $1.1 million (excess of FMV of assets over tax basis at date of conversion). If the corporation liquidates within 10 years of the conversion, $1.1 million of the corporate gain recognized on the distribution of assets will be subject to the built-in gains tax. The after-tax gain will be allocated to the Bernards for inclusion in their income, and they will pay a shareholder-level tax. Because of the built-in gains tax, the total tax cost of the liquidation will approximate the cost if the Bernards had not made the S election.[18]

## Liquidation of a Controlled Subsidiary

**Objective 6**
Summarize the tax consequences of the liquidation of a controlled subsidiary.

The general Subchapter C rules governing liquidations do not apply to the liquidation of a controlled subsidiary into a parent corporation. A **controlled subsidiary** is one in which the parent owns at least 80 percent of the total voting power and value of the stock. (This is the same control requirement that permits a parent and subsidiary to file a consolidated tax return.) Subchapter C treats the liquidation of a subsidiary as a nonevent in which the subsidiary is simply absorbed into the parent. The subsidiary does not recognize gain or loss on the distribution of its assets, and the parent does not recognize gain or loss on receipt of the liquidating distribution.[19] The subsidiary's basis in the distributed assets carries over to become the parent's basis, and the subsidiary's tax attributes survive to become the parent's tax attributes.[20]

*Liquidation of a Subsidiary*

Immediately before its liquidation, HTL had the following tax basis balance sheet.

| | |
|---|---:|
| Cash on hand | $ 260,000 |
| Accounts receivable | 440,000 |
| Inventory | 945,000 |
| Plant and equipment | 2,360,000 |
| | $4,005,000 |
| | |
| Accounts payable | $ 112,000 |
| Shareholders' equity: | |
| Paid in capital (1,000 shares) | 10,000 |
| Retained earnings | 3,883,000 |
| | $4,005,000 |

Pursuant to the liquidation, HTL paid $112,000 to its creditors and distributed its remaining cash and assets to Harling Inc., which owned all 1,000 shares of HTL stock. Regardless of the FMV of its assets, HTL recognized no gain or loss on the distribution. Regardless of the basis

[17] Section 1374.
[18] Because the Bernards can increase their stock basis by the allocated gain, they will not recognize any gain on receipt of the liquidating distribution.
[19] Sections 337 and 332.
[20] Sections 334(b) and 381(a)(1).

in its HTL stock, Harling recognized no gain or loss on the receipt of the cash and assets. (The basis in its HTL stock vanishes in the liquidation.) HTL's basis in the accounts receivable, inventory, and plant and equipment carries over to Harling, which succeeds to HTL's tax attributes, such as accumulated E&P, methods of accounting, and loss and credit carryforwards.

### Insolvent Subsidiary

If a liquidating subsidiary is insolvent, it must distribute all of its assets as payment to its creditors; the parent corporation receives nothing. As a result, the parent's stock is worthless. In this case, the parent is allowed to recognize a loss equal to its basis in the stock.[21] If the subsidiary derived more than 90 percent of its gross receipts for all taxable years from the active conduct of a business, the parent's loss is characterized as ordinary loss.[22] If the subsidiary fails the gross receipts test, the loss is characterized as a capital loss.

### Distributions to Minority Shareholders

The nonevent status of the liquidation of a corporate subsidiary does not extend to distributions to minority shareholders. The subsidiary must recognize a gain (but not a loss) if it distributes property to a minority shareholder.[23] This rule prevents subsidiaries from intentionally distributing devalued assets to minority shareholders to trigger loss recognition. The liquidation is taxable to the minority shareholders who must recognize capital gain or loss equal to the difference between the amount of the liquidating distribution and their stock basis.

**Minority Distributions**

Change the facts in the HTL example by assuming that Harling owned 950 of HTL's 1,000 shares, and Burdine Inc. owned the 50 remaining shares. As a minority shareholder, Burdine was legally entitled to receive 5 percent of the liquidating distribution; assume that Burdine's distribution had to be worth $210,000. Because HTL would recognize gain on the distribution of appreciated property but could not recognize loss on the distribution of devalued property, it distributed $210,000 cash to Burdine. Because Burdine's basis in its HTL stock was $238,000, it recognized a $28,000 capital loss on the liquidation.

The fact that a controlled subsidiary has minority shareholders does not affect the parent corporation's tax consequences of the liquidation. The parent's receipt of its share of the distribution is nontaxable, it takes a carryover basis in any property received from the subsidiary, and it succeeds to all the subsidiary's tax attributes. In the HTL example, Harling succeeded to 100 percent of HTL's tax attributes, even though it received only 95 percent of the liquidating distribution.

# PARTNERSHIP TERMINATIONS

Although partnerships (including LLCs) are not taxable entities, they have an identity for federal tax purposes. A partnership must have a federal employer identification number (EIN) that it includes on its Form 1065 and Schedule K-1s. A partnership keeps its own books and records, has its own taxable year and methods of accounting, and makes most of the elections necessary to compute annual taxable income. Certain of these elections (such as the Section 754 election) are permanent and remain in effect for all taxable years in which the partnership continues to exist.

[21] Reg. 1.332-2(b).
[22] Section 165(g)(3).
[23] Section 336(d)(3).

For Subchapter K purposes, a partnership continues to exist unless it is terminated. A partnership termination for tax purposes is not synonymous with a dissolution of the partnership under state or local law.[24] A partnership can terminate for tax purposes but not dissolve for legal purposes, and vice versa. Section 708 provides for two types of partnership termination: natural terminations and automatic terminations.

## Natural Terminations

A **natural termination** occurs if a partnership discontinues all business and financial operations conducted by its partners. Note that a natural termination can occur because the partnership's business ends or because the business is no longer conducted in the partnership form.

| | |
|---|---|
| *Discontinuance of Partnership Form* | Triad, a calendar year partnership, has operated a chain of movie theaters since 1990. On June 1, Mr. Harris, who had been a 35 percent partner since 1997, purchased the entire interests of the other six partners. Because Triad no longer had more than one owner, the partnership terminated on May 31, and Mr. Harris became the sole proprietor of the theater business. |

If a partnership decides to discontinue business, it winds down its daily operations, sells its marketable assets, and pays its liabilities (the same sequence of events that occurs in a corporate liquidation). The partnership terminates when it distributes all remaining cash and property to the partners in liquidation of their interests. The partnership's final taxable year closes on the date of termination.

| | |
|---|---|
| *Closing the Taxable Year of a Terminated Partnership* | Yates LLC, which used the calendar year for tax purposes, discontinued business on August 15 after generating $31,700 operating income for the first seven and one-half months of the year. In September, Yates recognized $4,800 recaptured ordinary income and a $1,300 Section 1231 gain on sale of its operating assets. After paying all its liabilities and writing up the members' book capital accounts to reflect the FMV of its remaining assets, Yates had the following balance sheet. |

|  | Tax Basis | Book Basis (FMV) |
|---|---|---|
| Cash on hand | $108,000 | $108,000 |
| Closely held corporate stock | 23,900 | 42,000 |
| Investment land | 100,000 | 200,000 |
| | $231,900 | $350,000 |
| Capital: Ms. Philby | $ 46,380 | $ 70,000 |
| Mrs. Yates | 139,140 | 210,000 |
| Ms. Lorch | 46,380 | 70,000 |
| | $231,900 | $350,000 |

Yates distributed its cash and property to the three members on September 30. Its final Form 1065 for the short year ending September 30 reported $36,500 ordinary business income ($31,700 operating income + $4,800 recaptured ordinary income) and $1,300 Section 1231 gain.

---

[24] Reg. 1.706-1(c)(1).

# Tax Consequences of Liquidating Distributions

**Objective 7**
Compute the gain or loss recognized by a partner on receipt of a liquidating distribution.

In marked contrast to corporate liquidations, partnership terminations are generally nontaxable events. A partnership never recognizes gain or loss on the distribution of cash or property to its partners.[25] A partner who receives a liquidating distribution reduces outside basis in the partnership interest by any cash received and then substitutes the remaining outside basis as the basis of any property received.[26] This benign result reflects the aggregate theory under which the partnership entity is transparent, and the partners are considered to own a proportionate interest in partnership property. In certain situations, however, the aggregate theory cannot hold, and a liquidating distribution does trigger gain or loss recognition to the partner.

## Recognition of Gain by a Partner

If a partner receives a cash distribution that exceeds outside basis, the partner must recognize the excess as capital gain.[27] In this situation, the partner's basis in any property received is zero.

*Gain Recognition*

Refer to the example on page 391 concerning the termination of Yates LLC. The three LLC members agreed to the following liquidating distributions of cash and property.

Ms. Philby:   $28,000 cash and stock (FMV $42,000)
Mrs. Yates:   $10,000 cash and investment land (FMV $200,000)
Ms. Lorch:   $70,000 cash

As required by the capital account maintenance rules, the distributions were based on each member's book capital account.

- Ms. Philby's $46,380 outside basis was reduced by the $28,000 cash distribution, and the $18,380 remaining basis became her basis in the distributed stock. (The LLC's $23,900 inside basis in the stock vanishes.) Ms. Philby recognized no gain or loss on the distribution.
- Mrs. Yates's $139,140 outside basis was reduced by the $10,000 cash distribution, and the $129,140 remaining basis became her basis in the distributed land. (The LLC's $100,000 inside basis in the land vanishes.) Mrs. Yates recognized no gain or loss on the distribution.
- Ms. Lorch's outside basis in her LLC interest was $46,380, so she had to recognize a $23,620 capital gain ($70,000 cash − $46,380 outside basis) on the distribution.

As the Yates example demonstrates, partnership property included in a liquidating distribution takes a substituted basis. As a general rule, the substituted basis is flexible: It could be less than the partnership's inside basis (as in the case of the stock distributed to Ms. Philby) or more than the partnership's inside basis (as in the case of the land distributed to Mrs. Yates).

## Distributions of Ordinary Income Property

Subchapter K includes a more rigid basis rule for distributions of partnership unrealized receivables or inventory items (property with ordinary gain potential). The partner's substituted basis in these items can never be *more than* the partnership's inside basis.[28] This basis ceiling ensures that any unrealized ordinary gain does not vanish when the property is

---

[25] Section 731(b).
[26] Section 732(b).
[27] Section 731(a)(1).
[28] Section 732(c)(1)(A).

distributed to a partner. A partner who receives an unrealized receivable must recognize ordinary income upon its eventual collection or disposition. A partner who receives an inventory item must recognize ordinary gain or loss if the partner sells or exchanges the item within five years from the date of distribution.[29] These characterization rules prevent the unrealized ordinary gain in the unrealized receivables or inventory from converting to a capital gain for a partner.

| | |
|---|---|
| *Basis Ceiling for Ordinary Income Property* | Celeste Inc. received a liquidating distribution from CDE Partnership consisting of $3,000 cash, an inventory item ($5,500 FMV and $4,100 inside basis), and equipment ($1,000 FMV and $1,000 inside basis). Celeste's outside basis in its partnership interest before the distribution was $10,000. It reduced this basis by the $3,000 cash and allocated the $7,000 remaining basis to the distributed properties. Because of the basis ceiling, Celeste could allocate only $4,100 basis to the inventory item and had to allocate $2,900 basis to the equipment.<br><br>  Celeste did not use the distributed inventory item in its business and sold it for $6,000 six months after the distribution. Even though the item was a capital (nonbusiness) asset in its hands, Celeste recognized a $1,900 ordinary gain ($6,000 amount realized − $4,100 basis) on sale. If Celeste had waited for more than five years to sell the distributed item, it would have recognized a capital gain or loss. |

### Recognition of Loss by a Partner

A partner that receives a liquidating distribution consisting only of cash can recognize a capital loss to the extent that the cash is less than outside basis. If the distribution includes partnership property, the partner generally does not recognize a loss because the outside basis becomes the substituted basis in the property. However, if the property consists *only* of unrealized receivables or inventory items, the basis ceiling could prevent the entire outside basis from attaching to the property. In this case, the partner can recognize a capital loss equal to the unattached outside basis.

| | |
|---|---|
| *Loss Recognition* | Immediately before its termination, EHF Real Estate Partnership had the following balance sheet: |

| | Tax Basis | Book Basis (FMV) |
|---|---|---|
| Cash on hand | $150,000 | $150,000 |
| Land held as inventory: | | |
| Tract 1 | 132,000 | 105,000 |
| Tract 2 | 60,000 | 105,000 |
| | $342,000 | $360,000 |
| | | |
| Capital:  EnRex Inc. | $114,000 | $120,000 |
| Mr. Hansell | 114,000 | 120,000 |
| Ms. Freese | 114,000 | 120,000 |
| | $342,000 | $360,000 |

The three partners agreed to the following liquidating distributions based on their book capital accounts:[30]

---

[29] Section 735(a).

[30] The distribution is not disproportionate within the meaning of Section 751(b) because the partnership's inventory items are not substantially appreciated.

> EnRex: $120,000 cash
>
> Mr. Hansell: $15,000 cash and Tract 1 (FMV $105,000)
>
> Ms. Freese: $15,000 cash and Tract 2 (FMV $105,000)

- EnRex's outside basis was $127,500, which was more than its one-third share of inside basis because EHF did not make a Section 754 election when EnRex purchased its interest several years ago. Therefore, EnRex recognized a $7,500 capital loss ($127,500 outside basis − $120,000 cash) on the distribution.
- Mr. Hansell's outside basis was $114,000. This basis was reduced by the $15,000 cash distribution, and the $99,000 remaining basis became his basis in Tract 1. Note that the basis ceiling did not prevent Mr. Hansell's substituted basis from being *less than* EHF's $132,000 inside basis in this inventory item.
- Ms. Freese's outside basis, also $114,000, was reduced by the $15,000 cash distribution. Because of the basis ceiling, only $60,000 (EHF's inside basis) of the remaining basis could attach to Tract 2. Because Ms. Freese did not receive any other property, she recognized her $39,000 unattached outside basis as a capital loss.

In this example, Ms. Freese could have been the victim of poor tax planning. She recognized a $39,000 capital loss (with limited deductibility) because of the receipt of property with a $45,000 built-in gain ($105,000 FMV of Tract 2 − $60,000 substituted basis). She will recognize this gain as ordinary income if she sells Tract 2 within the next five years. Contrast these tax consequences to those of Mr. Hansell, who recognized no gain or loss on the receipt of property with only a $6,000 built-in gain ($105,000 FMV of Tract 1 − $99,000 substituted basis) to be recognized as ordinary income within the next five years.

## Termination of an Insolvent Partnership

If a terminating partnership is insolvent, it does not have enough assets to pay its creditors. Typically, partners who are personally liable for partnership debts must restore any deficit balance in their capital accounts by contributing funds to the partnership. The partnership uses the contributed funds to pay its debts and liquidate the interests of any partners with positive capital account balances.

*Insolvent Partnership*

Immediately before its termination, VTY Partnership had the following balance sheet:

|  | Tax/Book Basis |
| --- | --- |
| Cash on hand | $ 82,800 |
| | |
| Liabilities | $109,100 |
| Capital: Vitali Inc. | (36,300) |
| Mr. Tomkin | 10,000 |
| Mr. Yarrow | –0– |
| | $ 82,800 |

The VTY agreement requires Vitali, the sole general partner, to restore its deficit capital account prior to termination. After Vitali contributed $36,300, VTY had enough cash to pay its creditors and distribute $10,000 to Mr. Tomkin.

- Before Vitali contributed the cash, its outside basis was $72,800 ($36,300 *negative* capital account + $109,100 share of partnership liabilities). After Vitali contributed the cash and VTY paid its liabilities, Vitali's outside basis was zero ($72,800 + $36,300 cash contribution − $109,100 decrease in share of liabilities). Consequently, Vitali recognized no gain or loss on the partnership's termination.
- Mr. Tomkin's outside basis was $10,000, so he recognized no gain or loss on the receipt of the $10,000 liquidating distribution.
- Mr. Yarrow's outside basis was zero. He did not receive any liquidating distribution and did not recognize any gain or loss on the partnership's termination.

## Automatic Termination

**Objective 8**
Determine whether a sale or exchange of a partnership interest terminates the partnership.

Section 708 provides that a partnership terminates if a sale or exchange of 50 percent or more of the total interest in partnership capital and profits occurs within a 12-month period. This **automatic termination** happens regardless of the fact that the partners have no intention of discontinuing their partnership business. Only sales or exchanges of partnership interests can trigger an automatic termination. Other dispositions of partnership interests, such as gifts or transfers at death, are irrelevant. Changes in the partners' interests resulting from contributions or distributions of cash or property are also irrelevant.

The 50 percent threshold for termination is based on the cumulative total of percentage interests sold or exchanged during any consecutive 12-month period.[31] The partnership terminates on the day the cumulative total equals or exceeds 50 percent.

*Terminating Sale of Interest*

Mrs. Bourne, Mr. Krantz, Mrs. Lopiano, and Osaka Inc. formed BKLO Partnership in 1995 and held equal interests until May 12, 2004.

- On May 12, 2004, Mrs. Lopiano sold her 25 percent interest to Devon LLC.
- On July 8, 2004, Mrs. Bourne sold one-half of her 25 percent interest (12.5 percent interest) to Devon LLC.
- On November 22, 2004, Mr. Krantz made a gift of his 25 percent interest to his daughter Kate.
- On April 15, 2005, Kate Krantz exchanged the interest received from her father for common stock in newly formed Lapin Inc. This exchange was nontaxable under Section 351.

Neither the May 12 nor the July 8 sale terminated BKLO because they represented a cumulative sale of only a 37.5 percent interest. The November 22 gift was irrelevant. The April 15 exchange terminated BKLO because it represented a cumulative sale or exchange of a 62.5 percent interest within the period May 12, 2004, through April 15, 2005.

The cumulative total of percentage interests sold or exchanged within a 12-month period does not include successive transfers of the same interest.[32] For instance, if Devon LLC (which purchased a 25 percent interest from Mrs. Lopiano on May 12 and a 12.5 percent interest from Mrs. Bourne on July 8) sold its 37.5 percent interest on December 15, 2004, the sale would not have terminated BKLO.

An automatic termination closes the partnership's taxable year on the date of termination. This closing could result in a bunching of income for any partner with a taxable year different than the partnership year.

[31] Reg. 1.708-1(b)(2).
[32] Ibid.

*Closing the Partnership Year on Termination*

Refer to the facts in the BKLO Partnership example on page 395. BKLO used a calendar year for tax purposes. As a result of its automatic termination, its final taxable year ended on April 15, 2005. Osaka Inc., which owned a 25 percent interest in BKLO from 1985 through the date of termination, uses a June 30 fiscal year-end. Two partnership taxable years (calendar year 2004 and the short year ending April 15, 2005) ended within Osaka's fiscal year ending June 30, 2005. Accordingly, Osaka must include its 25 percent share of 15.5 months of partnership income on its Form 1120.

Partnerships can protect against an automatic termination by including a buy-sell provision in the partnership agreement. These provisions typically prevent partners from selling, exchanging, or otherwise disposing of a partnership interest without the approval of the other partners. If a partner requests approval for a sale or exchange that would cause a termination, the other partners can disapprove or require the partner to delay the transaction until the critical 12-month period has elapsed. If BKLO Partnership could have required Kate Krantz to delay the exchange of her partnership interest until after May 12, 2005, her exchange would not have terminated the partnership.

An automatic termination has no effect on the daily operation of the partnership business. For federal tax purposes, however, the termination marks the end of the existence of the old partnership and the beginning of a new one. This transformation is deemed to occur through a two-step process. First, the old partnership contributes all its assets and liabilities to a new partnership in exchange for a 100 percent interest. Second, the old partnership distributes interests in the new partnership to its partners in liquidation of their interests in the old partnership.[33] The transformation generally does not change either the inside basis of the partnership assets or the outside basis of the partners' interests. Any tax elections in effect for the old partnership (such as a Section 754 election) expire, and the new partnership is free to make (or not make) its own elections.

## Conclusion

Transactions that occur at the end of a business entity's existence can have significant tax consequences for its owners. The owners of a financially distressed business might try to salvage their situation by negotiating with creditors or filing for bankruptcy. Through careful tax planning, the owners can minimize the tax cost of any discharge of business debt. Shareholders must be aware of the potentially high tax cost of corporate liquidations, which can trigger gain recognition at both the corporate and shareholder levels. In contrast, partners and LLC members might be able to unwind their partnership business at little or no tax cost. Exhibit 14-1 provides a chart that summarizes the major issues introduced in Chapter 14 and compares the answers pertaining to corporations with the answers pertaining to partnerships and LLCs.

[33] Reg. 1.708-1(b)(4).

**EXHIBIT 14.1 Comparison Chart**

| Tax Issue | Corporation | Partnership/LLC |
| --- | --- | --- |
| Can an entity exclude discharge of debt income from gross income? | Yes, if the corporation is insolvent or in bankruptcy. | No. The insolvency and bankruptcy exclusions apply at the partner level. |
| Does an entity that excludes discharge of debt income reduce its tax attributes? | Yes, for C corporations. No, for S corporations; tax attributes are reduced at the shareholder level. | Tax attributes of the partners are reduced. |

**EXHIBIT 14.1 Comparison Chart—*continued***

| Tax Issue | Corporation | Partnership/LLC |
|---|---|---|
| Does an entity recognize gain or loss on liquidating property distributions to owners? | Yes, unless the corporation is a controlled subsidiary. | No. |
| What is the owner's tax basis in distributed property? | FMV. | Partner's outside basis limited to carryover basis for inventory and unrealized receivables. |
| Do owners recognize gain or loss on receipt of liquidating distributions? | Yes, unless the shareholder is the parent of a controlled subsidiary. | No, unless cash received is more or less than outside basis or the partner receives only inventory or unrealized receivables. |

## Key Terms

automatic termination of a
   partnership   *395*
bankruptcy   *382*
Chapter 11
   reorganization   *382*

Chapter 7 liquidation   *382*
controlled subsidiary   *389*
corporate liquidation   *386*
discharge of debt
   income   *382*

insolvency   *383*
natural termination of a
   partnership   *391*
nonbusiness bad
   debt   *385*

## Questions and Problems for Discussion

1. Discuss the financial circumstances that cause a business to file for bankruptcy protection in federal court. Must a business be insolvent to do so?
2. What is the difference between a Chapter 11 bankruptcy and a Chapter 7 bankruptcy?
3. Does a corporation's balance sheet provide enough information to determine whether it is insolvent for tax purposes?
4. Do the insolvency and bankruptcy exclusions for discharge of debt income result in tax-exempt income or tax-deferred income?
5. Discuss the reason that a business would elect to reduce the tax basis of its assets by the amount of its excluded discharge of debt income before reducing its NOL carryforward.
6. What facts and circumstances indicate that a shareholder/employee made a loan to the corporation with the dominant motive to protect her employment rather than her stock investment?
7. Can a corporation distribute its goodwill to its shareholders when it liquidates?
8. On April 15 and June 15, Largo distributed $20,000 to each of its six individual shareholders. Largo liquidated on October 1. Can the shareholders treat the April and June distributions as liquidating distributions? Why would this treatment benefit the shareholders? What facts and circumstances would support this treatment?
9. In the liquidation of a controlled subsidiary, minority shareholders typically receive cash rather than corporate property. Can you explain why?
10. New partners can be admitted and existing partners can leave without terminating a partnership for federal tax purposes. Does this fact reflect the entity or the aggregate theory of partnerships?

11. On May 1, TKL Partnership terminated by distributing its assets to the partners based on their book capital accounts. Mr. Thornton did not recognize gain or loss on the receipt of his liquidating distribution. He had a $1,200 suspended passive activity loss with respect to his TKL interest. Can he deduct the loss this year?

## Application Problems

1. Noland Inc. owed a $50,000 unsecured business debt to Wainwright LLC. Wainwright accepted $35,000 cash in full settlement of the debt. What are the tax consequences of this settlement to Noland and Wainwright in each of the following cases?
   a. Noland was not insolvent or in bankruptcy at the date of the settlement.
   b. The settlement was pursuant to Noland's bankruptcy case in federal court.
   c. Noland was not in bankruptcy, but the total FMV of its assets was $60,000 less than its total liabilities before the settlement.
   d. Noland was not in bankruptcy, but the total FMV of its assets was $8,000 less than its total liabilities before the settlement.

2. Merida Corporation had a $132,800 NOL carryforward into this taxable year. During the year, it had a $75,000 discharge of debt and generated $100,000 net income from operations. Compute Merida's taxable income under each set of facts.
   a. It excluded the discharge of debt from gross income under the insolvency exception.
   b. It was neither insolvent nor in bankruptcy this year.

3. This year, QVO, an S corporation, excluded $4,420 discharge of debt from its gross income under the insolvency exception. Mrs. Quinn, the sole shareholder who manages QVO's business, received a Schedule K-1 showing the following items.

| | |
|---|---|
| Ordinary business loss | $5,050 |
| Long-term capital gain | 2,715 |

   Before consideration of these items, Mrs. Quinn's basis in her QVO stock was zero, and she had a $1,100 suspended ordinary loss from last year.
   a. How much ordinary loss can Mrs. Quinn deduct this year?
   b. How much suspended loss can Mrs. Quinn carry forward to deduct next year?

4. Ms. Sandridge and Ms. Sosa each own a 50 percent interest in calendar year SanSosa LLC. This year, one of SanSosa's creditors discharged a $14,000 unsecured debt. As a result, each member's Schedule K-1 included $7,000 discharge of debt income. The LLC was insolvent at the date of discharge by $22,000. However, neither member was insolvent or in bankruptcy.
   a. To what extent do Ms. Sandridge and Ms. Sosa include their share of discharge of debt income in gross income?
   b. What is the effect of the discharge of debt income on each member's outside basis in her LLC interest?

5. Creditor C holds a $12,500 unsecured note receivable ($12,500 basis) from General Corporation and just learned that General is bankrupt without any funds to pay any liabilities. Identify the tax consequences of the bad debt to Creditor C assuming that it is:
   a. A corporate taxpayer that sold supplies to General on credit.
   b. A partnership that sold supplies to General on credit.
   c. A corporate taxpayer that loaned $12,500 to General as a short-term investment.
   d. An individual shareholder in General.

6. Reid, a calendar year corporation, discontinued business on August 31. Its taxable income through this date was $392,000, and it had made two $55,000 installment payments of federal income tax. Reid plans to liquidate on October 15 by distributing

all available cash plus investment securities ($188,000 FMV and $50,000 basis) to its shareholders. How much cash should Reid retain to pay the balance due of its federal income tax for its final year?

7. Immediately before its liquidation, Sayer Corporation had the following balance sheet. *[handwritten: not partnership]*

| | Tax Basis | FMV |
|---|---|---|
| Cash | $440,000 | $440,000 |
| Business equipment | 18,000 | 10,000 *(8000)* |
| Office furnishings | 7,500 | 10,000 *2,500* |
| Unamortized leasehold costs *[handwritten: can write off unamort. intang.]* | 5,600 | –0– *(5,600)* |
| | $471,100 | $460,000 |
| Paid in capital | $ 10,000 | $ 10,000 |
| Retained earnings | 461,100 | 450,000 |
| | $471,100 | $460,000 |

Sayer liquidated by distributing its cash, equipment, and office furnishings to its shareholders. If its operating income through date of liquidation was $116,900, compute Sayer's taxable income for its final year.

8. Refer to the facts in application problem 7. In each of the following cases, compute the shareholders' capital gain or loss recognized and the tax basis of any property received in Sayer's liquidation.
   a. Mr. McCone received $25,000 cash in liquidation of stock with a $33,400 basis.
   b. Mrs. Christie received $5,000 cash and the office furnishings in liquidation of stock with an $11,000 basis.
   c. Mr. Andersen received the business equipment in liquidation of stock with a $2,400 basis.

9. Wilton Inc. is in the process of liquidation. It discontinued business two months ago and paid its creditors. It plans to pay its federal and state income tax for its final year and then distribute all remaining cash ($100,000) and corporate assets ($350,000 FMV and $210,000 basis) to its sole shareholder. The shareholder's basis in the Wilton stock is $163,000. Determine the gain recognized by Wilton and the shareholder and the shareholder's basis in the distributed assets assuming that the shareholder is:
   a. An individual.
   b. A corporate taxpayer.

10. Immediately before its liquidation, Charles Inc. had the following balance sheet:

| | Tax Basis | FMV |
|---|---|---|
| Cash | $ 48,000 | $ 48,000 |
| Marketable securities | 18,000 | 6,200 |
| Inventories | 100,000 | 130,000 |
| Business equipment | 500,000 | 675,000 |
| | $666,000 | $859,200 |
| Accounts payable | $ 19,000 | $ 19,000 |
| Shareholders' equity: | | |
|   Paid in capital (10,000 shares) | 10,000 | 10,000 |
|   Retained earnings | 637,000 | 830,200 |
| | $666,000 | $859,200 |

GKP Inc. owns 9,500 Charles shares ($215,000 basis), and Mr. Grayling owns the remaining 500 shares ($8,000 basis).

   *a.* Charles plans to distribute cash to liquidate Mr. Grayling's minority interest. How much cash should he receive? What are his tax consequences?

   *b.* Charles plans to transfer its remaining assets and liabilities to GKP. How much gain or loss will Charles recognize on the distribution?

   *c.* How much gain or loss will GKP recognize on receipt of the liquidating distribution?

   *d.* Determine GKP's basis in the marketable securities, inventories, and business equipment.

   *e.* On the date of liquidation, Charles had $458,500 accumulated E&P. How much of it transfers to GKP?

11. Carmel Corporation owns 100 percent of CDE stock ($84,000 basis) and a $50,000 note receivable from CDE, which derives 98 percent of its gross receipts from its manufacturing business. Carmel plans to liquidate CDE, which is insolvent. CDE's unsecured creditors (including Carmel) should receive 40 cents for every dollar of CDE debt. Describe the tax consequences of CDE's liquidation to Carmel.

12. Mrs. Gillis, Mr. Wagner, and Mrs. Harriet, the three equal partners in calendar year Hartwell LLP, ended their professional association and ceased conducting business as Hartwell LLP on June 30. Hartwell's balance sheet on July 1 follows.

|  | Book/Tax Basis |
|---|---|
| Cash | $ 96,700 |
| Operating assets | 200,000 |
|  | $296,700 |
| Liabilities | $ 17,700 |
| Capital: Mrs. Gillis | 93,000 |
| Mr. Wagner | 93,000 |
| Mrs. Harriet | 93,000 |
|  | $296,700 |

On July 22, the partners sold the operating assets for $185,000 cash, paid the liabilities, and distributed the cash in the LLP bank account to themselves.

   *a.* On what date does Hartwell LLP terminate for federal tax purposes?

   *b.* How much cash did each partner receive as a liquidating distribution?

   *c.* Immediately before receiving the cash distribution, Mrs. Gillis and Mr. Wagner each had an $88,000 outside basis, and Mrs. Harriet had a $95,000 outside basis. How much capital gain or loss does each partner recognize?

13. Each of the following independent cases describes a liquidating distribution to a partner. Compute the partner's recognized gain or loss and basis in any property received.

   *a.* Hobson Corporation received $30,000 cash. Its outside basis was $37,500.

   *b.* Mrs. Chang received $30,000 cash. Her outside basis was $22,000.

   *c.* Ms. Mallory received $18,000 cash and a partnership capital asset ($10,000 FMV and $1,200 inside basis). Her outside basis was $22,000.

   *d.* Dowling Inc. received $6,300 cash and a partnership capital asset ($50,000 FMV and $45,000 inside basis). Its outside basis was $30,000.

   *e.* Ms. Anitra received a partnership capital asset ($100,000 FMV and $70,000 inside basis). Her outside basis was $40,000.

*f.* Lincoln Corporation received $20,000 cash and a partnership capital asset ($3,000 FMV and $2,200 inside basis). Its outside basis was $19,000.

14. Each of the following independent cases describes a liquidating distribution to a partner. Compute the partner's recognized gain or loss and basis in any property received.

   *a.* Ms. Kobe received a partnership inventory item ($5,000 FMV and $6,000 inside basis). Her outside basis was $4,810.

   *b.* ECM Inc. received a partnership inventory item ($14,000 FMV and $10,000 inside basis). Its outside basis was $12,500.

   *c.* Mrs. Drew received $20,000 cash and a partnership inventory item ($50,000 FMV and $28,500 inside basis). Her outside basis was $55,000.

   *d.* Holland Company received a partnership capital asset ($20,000 FMV and $9,000 inside basis) and a partnership inventory item ($50,000 FMV and $28,500 inside basis). Its outside basis was $55,000.

15. Mr. Molokai received a distribution from Wallace Company in liquidation of his equity interest, which had a $40,000 basis. The distribution consisted of an item of Wallace's merchandise inventory ($50,000 FMV and $36,000 basis). Determine Mr. Molokai's basis in the inventory item assuming that Wallace is:

   *a.* A taxable corporation.

   *b.* An S corporation.

   *c.* An LLC.

16. Immediately before its liquidation, GBS Partnership had the following balance sheet:

|  | Book/Tax Basis |
|---|---|
| Cash on hand | $163,700 |
|  |  |
| Liabilities | $129,000 |
| Capital:  Mr. Gingrich | (5,800) |
| Mrs. Bradley | 43,400 |
| Mrs. Steger | (2,900) |
|  | $163,700 |

State law requires Mr. Gingrich and Mrs. Steger to restore their deficit capital accounts on liquidation.

   *a.* Mr. Gingrich's outside basis was $80,200 (including an $86,000 share of partnership liabilities). Describe the tax consequences of the liquidation to him.

   *b.* Mrs. Bradley's outside basis was $43,400 (including no share of partnership liabilities). Describe the tax consequences of the liquidation to her.

17. Refer to the facts in application problem 16. Assume that GBS is an LLC instead of a partnership and that no member has a deficit restoration obligation. How do these facts change the tax consequences of the liquidation to Mr. Gingrich and Mrs. Bradley?

18. Myron, Michele, and Martin Johnson formed calendar year MMM Partnership on July 1, 2001. On April 1, 2004, Martin Johnson sold his 33.3 percent interest to Coen Inc. On November 15, 2004, Coen sold this 33.3 percent interest to Stuart Lynch.

   *a.* Does Coen's sale cause an automatic termination of MMM Partnership?

   *b.* Now assume that Michele Johnson sold her 33.3 percent interest to Stuart Lynch on November 15, 2004. Would this sale cause an automatic termination of MMM Partnership?

19. On January 1, 2003, four members (Mrs. Apple, Bruen Inc., Mr. Crenshaw, and Mr. Deetz) owned equal interests in calendar year Windsor LLC. These four members created Windsor in 1995.
    - On June 8, 2003, Mrs. Apple sold her interest to Mr. Crenshaw.
    - On November 19, 2003, Ms. Gale became a member by contributing cash in exchange for a 40 percent interest in capital and profits. After Ms. Gale's admission, Bruen and Mr. Deetz each owned a 15 percent interest, and Mr. Crenshaw owned a 30 percent interest.
    - On March 2, 2004, Mr. Crenshaw died, and his estate became the new owner of his Windsor interest.
    - On May 14, 2004, Ms. Gale contributed her entire Windsor interest (along with other assets) to GM Inc. in exchange for 85 percent of GM's stock.
    a. Do any of these transactions terminate Windsor LLC for federal tax purposes?
    b. What is the effect of any termination on Windsor's taxable year?

20. Refer to the facts in application problem 19. Corporate partner Bruen Inc. uses a June 30 fiscal year-end for federal tax purposes. According to Windsor's books, it earned the following taxable income during the following periods of time:

| | |
|---|---|
| January 1–June 8, 2003 | $200,000 |
| June 9–November 19, 2003 | 119,000 |
| November 20–December 31, 2003 | 76,200 |
| January 1–March 2, 2004 | 70,000 |
| March 3–May 14, 2004 | 141,300 |
| May 15–December 31, 2004 | 199,800 |

   a. How much LLC income must Bruen include in taxable income for fiscal year-end June 30, 2004?
   b. How would your answer to part (a) change if Mrs. Gale had delayed the formation of GM for one month (until June 14, 2004)?

## Issue Recognition Problems

Identify the tax issue or issues suggested by the following situations and state each issue in the form of a question.

1. Mr. Rappaport recently discharged a $150,000 debt from ROR Inc. which was not insolvent or in bankruptcy. He is the sole shareholder and discharged the debt to improve ROR's debt-equity ratio on its balance sheet.

2. Mrs. Bao's four children are the equal members of Bao Bakery LLC. Three years ago, she helped them start their business by lending $40,000 to the LLC in return for an interest-bearing demand note. On Christmas day, Mrs. Bao tore up the note and announced to her children that she was discharging the LLC's debt to her.

3. Two years ago, Mrs. Null wrote off a $4,000 nonbusiness debt owed to her by Sterne LLC because she believed the LLC was hopelessly insolvent. Much to her amazement, Sterne honored the debt this year by paying her $4,000 plus interest.

4. Howell Inc. liquidated several years ago by distributing $1 million cash proportionally to its 12 individual shareholders. The IRS recently completed its audit of Howell's final two corporate tax returns and assessed an additional $27,900 corporate income tax for those years.

5. Mr. and Mrs. Tenorio are the sole shareholders in Tenorio Inc., which discontinued all business activities three years ago but has not been dissolved under state law. Its only

assets are $625,000 of tax-exempt municipal bonds. Mr. and Mrs. Tenorio are delaying the corporate liquidation until they need to cash in the bonds.

6. Littleton Corporation liquidated on February 28. It distributed land ($100,000 basis) to one of its individual shareholders and used a $300,000 FMV to compute a $200,000 recognized gain on the distribution. Because of NOL carryforwards, Littleton reported no taxable income and income tax liability on its final Form 1120. The individual shareholder developed and subdivided the land and sold the lots to the public. His total amount realized was $298,000.

7. PZN Inc. purchased 70 percent of Paccioli's stock 14 years ago. On May 1 of this year, it purchased an additional 11 percent. Paccioli liquidated on May 31.

8. ADB Partnership terminated by distributing its cash and operating assets to its 16 partners. At the date of termination, it had $1,200 unamortized organization costs and $3,500 syndication costs on its balance sheet.

9. On January 18, Mr. Denzel offered to buy Mrs. Tyler's 55 percent interest in TK Partnership for $55,000. Mrs. Tyler agreed to sell a 49.5 percent interest for $49,500 on January 18 and the remaining 5.5 percent interest for $5,500 on January 19 of the following year.

10. Four years ago, Lamont LLC made a Section 754 election that has become a tremendous administrative burden. Three of Lamont's members, who collectively own 79 percent of the LLC, plan to contribute their Lamont interests to a new LLC in exchange for a proportionate interest in the LLC. The only asset in the new LLC will be a 79 percent interest in Lamont.

## Research Problems

1. Pursuant to its complete liquidation, Ripon Inc. distributed Blackacre, a tract of investment land, to Mr. Lukart. Ripon's basis in Blackacre was $153,500, and the land was subject to a $320,000 nonrecourse mortgage. Two independent appraisers determined that Blackacre's FMV was only $275,000. In addition to Blackacre, Mr. Lukart received marketable securities worth $81,000. His basis in his Ripon stock was $73,000. How much gain did Ripon recognize on the distribution of Blackacre? How much gain did Mr. Lukart recognize because of his liquidating distribution? What is his basis in Blackacre?

2. Alpha Inc. and Beta Inc. own equal interests in AB Partnership, which has a $1,600,000 net worth and uses a March 31 fiscal year-end. Mr. O'Toole, Mr. Bishop, and Mrs. Erwin own equal interests in Northshore LLC, which has an $800,000 net worth and uses a calendar year. The two groups of owners have decided to merge their businesses into newly formed AB North LLC. Alpha and Beta will each receive a 33.5 percent interest and Mr. O'Toole, Mr. Bishop, and Mrs. Erwin will each receive an 11 percent interest. The owners want to use a March 31 fiscal year-end for the new LLC. Can they do so without permission of the IRS?

## Tax Planning Cases

1. Mr. Howard is the sole shareholder and CEO of EFH Inc., a taxable corporation in financial trouble. The FMV of EFH's assets is about $50,000 less than its liabilities. Mr. Howard is negotiating with EFH's major creditor, who might be willing to accept $75,000 in full settlement of a $115,000 short-term note from EFH. Mr. Howard is prepared to invest an additional $75,000 to fund the settlement, but he is uncertain as to whether he should contribute the $75,000 to EFG's capital or loan the $75,000 in return for a long-term note. Advise Mr. Howard as to which option is the better tax strategy.

2. Mr. Smitovich (age 68) and his daughter Grace Pelton (age 32) are equal partners in Shore Realty Partnership. They plan to discontinue Shore's business and divide the partnership's $14,000 cash and two remaining inventory items between them. The inventory items are tracts of undeveloped land: Greenacre (FMV $100,000 and inside basis $60,000) and Sunnyacre (FMV $100,000 and inside basis $92,500). Because the two tracts have the same value, the partnership could distribute an undivided half interest in each tract to father and daughter. Alternatively, it could distribute one tract to Mr. Smitovich and the other tract to Ms. Pelton. Advise the partnership as to which tract of land should go to which partner on the basis of the following information.

- Both partners have a $91,250 outside basis in their partnership interest.
- Mr. Smitovich owns an investment portfolio of marketable securities that generates significant capital gain income each year. Ms. Pelton's only other investment is her Roth IRA.
- Mr. Smitovich plans to hold the land that he receives from the partnership as a long-term investment. Ms. Pelton plans to sell the land that she receives as soon as possible and use the proceeds to build a new personal residence.

## Comprehensive Cases for Part Five

1. Hubburd Inc. is a calendar year, cash basis C corporation, and Ms. Sharon Atwater has owned 500 of Hubburd's 1,000 outstanding shares of common stock since 1997. Her tax basis in the shares is $10,000. Sharon plans to dispose of her entire interest in Hubburd this year. Here is Hubburd's balance sheet immediately before the disposition.

|  | Tax Basis | FMV |
|---|---|---|
| Cash | $26,000 | $ 26,000 |
| Accounts receivable | –0– | 58,200 |
| Furniture and fixtures | 63,800 | 63,800 |
| Goodwill | –0– | 250,000 |
|  | $89,800 | $398,000 |
| Paid-in capital (1,000 shares) | $20,000 | $ 20,000 |
| Retained earnings | 69,800 | 378,000 |
|  | $89,800 | $398,000 |

*a.* Assume that Sharon disposes of her Hubburd stock by selling it to an unrelated purchaser for $199,000 cash. Compute Sharon's capital gain recognized on sale.

*b.* Assume that Hubburd redeems Sharon's stock by distributing $20,000 cash and a seven-year, interest-bearing note for $179,000. Sharon will not receive the first principal payment on the note until next year. After the redemption, Sharon will have no indirect ownership in any of Hubburd's 500 outstanding shares. How much capital gain must Sharon recognize this year, and what is her tax basis in the Hubburd note?

*c.* Assume that Megolux Inc., a publicly held corporation, acquires Hubburd through a merger under Oregon law that qualifies as a type A reorganization for federal tax purposes. Sharon receives Megolux short-term bonds worth $50,000 and Megolux common stock worth $149,000. Both the bonds and stock are readily tradable through the securities market. How much capital gain must Sharon recognize this year, and what is her tax basis in the Megolux bonds and stock?

Suggested research aid: Section 453

2. Foursquare is a calendar year, cash basis partnership that operates a service business in which capital is not a material income-producing factor. Mr. Don Phan has been a general partner since 1997. His tax basis in his 10 percent LLC interest is $17,960. Don plans to dispose of his entire interest in Foursquare this year. Here is Foursquare's balance sheet immediately before the disposition.

| | Tax Basis | FMV | |
|---|---|---|---|
| Cash | $ 57,850 | $ 57,850 | |
| Accounts receivable | –0– | 157,400 | Hot asset. |
| Furniture and fixtures | 71,750 | 71,750 | |
| Stock in Proctor Inc.* | 50,000 | 250,000 | |
| | $179,600 | $537,000 | |
| | | | |
| Accounts payable | $ 20,000 | $ 20,000 | |
| Partners' capital:  Don Phan | 15,960 | 51,700 | |
| Others | 143,640 | 465,300 | |
| | $179,600 | $537,000 | |

\* Proctor Inc. is a closely held C corporation.

a. Assume that Don disposes of his interest by selling it to an unrelated purchaser for $51,700 cash. Compute Don's ordinary income and capital gain recognized on sale.

b. Assume that Foursquare liquidates Don's entire interest by distributing $51,700 cash to him. Compute Don's ordinary income and capital gain recognized on receipt of the distribution.

c. Assume that Foursquare terminates by paying off its liabilities and distributing its remaining cash and assets proportionally among its members. Don receives $3,785 cash, $15,740 accounts receivable, furniture and fixtures ($7,175 FMV and inside basis), and Proctor stock ($25,000 FMV and $5,000 inside basis). Compute Don's ordinary income and capital gain recognized on receipt of the distribution and determine his tax basis in the accounts receivable, furniture and fixtures, and Proctor stock.

# Appendix **14–A**

# Special Cases Involving Discharge of Debt in Connection with Property

If neither the bankruptcy nor insolvency exception applies, a discharge of debt generally results in gross income. However, Section 108 includes two provisions that allow businesses to reduce the basis of property by the amount of the discharge instead of recognizing income. The first provision applies if the purchaser of property owed the discharged debt to the seller. In this case, the purchaser can treat the *purchase-money debt reduction* as a reduction in the purchase price rather than as income.[34]

[34] Section 108(e)(5).

### Purchase Price Reduction

Two years ago, Brantley Inc. purchased investment land from Martin Company for $1 million. Brantley paid $200,000 cash and gave Martin its five-year note secured by the real estate for the $800,000 balance of the purchase price. Although Brantley is solvent, it has cash flow problems and is in arrears on its note payments. Martin does not want to foreclose on the land, so it agrees to reduce the principal balance of the note by $150,000 and extend the payment schedule. Because the discharge of debt occurs between a purchaser and a seller of property, both Brantley and Martin treat the discharge as a purchase price reduction. Brantley reduces its tax basis in the land by $150,000, and Martin recomputes its taxable gain or loss on the sale.

The second provision for a basis adjustment applies if the discharged debt is *qualified real property business indebtedness*, which is debt incurred in connection with real property used in a business and secured by the property.[35] The discharge of

[35] Section 108(c). If the debt was incurred or assumed before January 1, 1993, it must simply be secured by the property. If it was incurred on or after January 1, 1993, the debt must have been incurred or assumed to acquire, construct, reconstruct, or substantially improve the property.

this debt is excluded from gross income but only to the extent that the debt's principal balance immediately before the discharge exceeds the property's FMV. (In real estate terms, such property is described as *underwater.*) The basis of the property is reduced by the amount of the exclusion.

### Qualified Real Property Business Indebtedness

Six years ago, Dumfree LLC purchased real property for $750,000 to use in its business. It financed the purchase by obtaining a $625,000 mortgage from First State Bank. The mortgage's principal balance is now $540,000. Because of a severe downturn in the real estate market, the property's FMV is only $500,000. Dumfree and First State Bank agree that Dumfree will continue to pay off the mortgage, and the bank will reduce the principal balance to $500,000. Because the amount of the discharge is not more than the $40,000 excess of the mortgage over FMV, Dumfree can exclude the discharge from gross income and reduce its basis in the property by $40,000.

# Personal Wealth Planning

# Chapter **Fifteen**

# The Transfer Tax System

## Learning Objectives

*After reading this chapter, you will be able to:*

1. Discuss the policy issues underlying transfer taxation, the integration of the gift and estate taxes, and the cumulative nature of the transfer tax system.

2. Calculate gift tax liability.

3. Identify the characteristics of a *gift,* describe items specifically excluded from gift treatment, and apply the annual exclusion from taxable gifts.

4. Calculate estate tax liability.

5. Identify items included in the *gross estate* and items deductible in calculating the *taxable estate.*

6. Discuss the rationale behind the generation-skipping transfer tax and the importance of the exemption.

7. Identify important interactions between the income and transfer tax systems.

Investors and businesspeople who practice effective strategies for maximizing after-tax value often accumulate substantial personal wealth. Although these earnings have already been subject to income tax, the threat of additional taxation looms via the federal transfer tax system. In Part Six of this text, we begin by discussing the policy rationale underlying the transfer tax system and recent legislation substantially altering these taxes. We then describe the federal transfer tax system and its three parts: gift tax, estate tax, and generation-skipping transfer tax. Most of the discussion focuses on the two main components of the transfer tax system, the gift and estate tax. Our consideration of the generation-skipping transfer tax is brief because of its limited applicability. We also describe the transfer taxes assessed at the state level and the impact of state death taxes on federal estate tax liability. We conclude the chapter with a discussion of interactions between the income and transfer tax systems. Chapter 16 discusses income and transfer tax issues associated with trusts as a vehicle for family wealth planning and briefly describes the income taxation of estates. Chapter 17 discusses strategies for reducing the transfer tax burden to maximize family wealth available to future generations. Thus, Chapter 17 explores a variety of planning ideas associated with the tax issues introduced in Chapters 15 and 16.

*[handwritten: history/issues of start of transfer tax]*

# TRANSFER TAX POLICY ISSUES

**Objective 1**
Discuss the policy issues underlying transfer taxation, the integration of the gift and estate taxes, and the cumulative nature of the transfer tax system.

The intent of the transfer tax system is **wealth redistribution** from the private to the public domain. One study by a New York University economist estimates that in 1998, 38.1 percent of this nation's net wealth was concentrated in the hands of 1 percent of households, and more than 59 percent of net wealth was held by 5 percent of households.[1]

Consistent with the objective of wealth distribution, the transfer tax system applies only to those taxpayers with significant wealth to redistribute! Specifically, only taxpayers with transferable wealth in excess of a threshold amount ($1 million in 2003) are potentially subject, and many exclusions reduce exposure of these individuals to such taxes. Thus, transfer taxation is not an issue for the vast majority of taxpayers. In 1997, only 1.9 percent of deaths triggered estate taxes, with 5 percent of this group paying one-half of the taxes assessed.[2]

In spite of the limited number of taxpayers subject to estate and gift taxes, calls for the repeal of the transfer tax system have become frequent and politically popular. In particular, small business owners and family farmers argue that heirs are often forced to sell to generate sufficient cash to pay the estate tax. On June 7, 2001, President George W. Bush signed into law the **Economic Growth and Tax Relief Reconciliation Act of 2001 (EGTRRA).** This legislation gradually reduces the estate tax for taxpayers dying after 2001 and before 2010, by reducing estate tax rates and increasing the amount of estate assets exempt from taxation. EGTRRA repeals the estate tax for individuals dying after 2009. However, this repeal is subject to an important caveat: Under a "sunset" provision included to meet budgetary restrictions, none of EGTRRA's transfer tax provisions apply after 2010! As a result, unless Congress passes additional legislation to extend the estate tax repeal, the transfer tax system currently in place for 2001 will be reinstated in 2011. EGTRRA does not repeal the gift tax, although the maximum gift tax rates are substantially reduced by the act, for years prior to 2011. The generation-skipping transfer tax is also repealed in 2010, but reinstated in 2011 under the sunset provisions.

**Tax Talk**
In late 2003, Senator Jon Kyl (Republican, Arizona), one of the Senate's staunchest opponents of the estate tax, drafted a tax reform proposal that would keep it intact in modified form. This move broke a long-held Republican taboo against any plan that does not fully repeal the "death tax." Kyl's actions indicate a deep concern among estate tax opponents that surging budget deficits might jeopardize their chances of achieving full repeal.

EGTRRA introduces considerable new complexity into an area of the law already regarded by tax practitioners as a challenging set of tax rules. Although some tax and political commentators believe that full reinstatement of the estate tax in 2011 is unlikely, future Congressional action will be required to avoid reinstatement, and the ultimate timing and form of such legislation cannot be predicted. As a result, planning efforts must contend with this tax law uncertainty. Taxpayers should continue to pursue wealth transfer planning strategies that reduce the cost of the gift tax and the cost of the estate tax during the phase-out period and after reinstatement. As the law is currently written, only taxpayers dying in 2010 will owe no estate tax; however, the tax basis of property received by their heirs will be reduced. Planning strategies specific to the period affected by EGTRRA are discussed in Chapter 17.

## OVERVIEW OF TRANSFER TAXATION

Several aspects distinguish the transfer tax system from taxes such as the federal income tax. First, note that transfer taxes are assessed on the transferor rather than the recipient

---

[1] Statistics from Gene Koretz, "Death Knell for Death Taxes? Estate Levies May Bite the Dust," *Business Week,* July 31, 2000.

[2] Ibid.

**TABLE 15.1**
**Federal Transfer Tax Rates for Transfers after 1983, before 2002, and after 2010**
The following rate schedule can be used to compute the federal gift or estate tax before any reduction for the unified credit.

| If the Taxable Transfer Is | | The Tax Is | |
|---|---|---|---|
| Over | But Not Over | | Of the Amount Over |
| –0– | $   10,000 | 18% | –0– |
| $   10,000 | 20,000 | $   1,800 + 20% | $   10,000 |
| 20,000 | 40,000 | 3,800 + 22% | 20,000 |
| 40,000 | 60,000 | 8,200 + 24% | 40,000 |
| 60,000 | 80,000 | 13,000 + 26% | 60,000 |
| 80,000 | 100,000 | 18,200 + 28% | 80,000 |
| 100,000 | 150,000 | 23,800 + 30% | 100,000 |
| 150,000 | 250,000 | 38,800 + 32% | 150,000 |
| 250,000 | 500,000 | 70,800 + 34% | 250,000 |
| 500,000 | 750,000 | 155,800 + 37% | 500,000 |
| 750,000 | 1,000,000 | 248,300 + 39% | 750,000 |
| 1,000,000 | 1,250,000 | 345,800 + 41% | 1,000,000 |
| 1,250,000 | 1,500,000 | 448,300 + 43% | 1,250,000 |
| 1,500,000 | 2,000,000 | 555,800 + 45% | 1,500,000 |
| 2,000,000 | 2,500,000 | 780,800 + 49% | 2,000,000 |
| 2,500,000 | 3,000,000 | 1,025,800 + 53% | 2,500,000 |
| 3,000,000 | | 1,290,800 + 55% | 3,000,000 |

A 5 percent surtax applies to taxable transfers in excess of $10 million but not in excess of the amount at which the average transfer tax rate is 55 percent. This surtax recaptures the benefit of the progressive rates on the first $3 million of taxable transfers. See Section 2001(c)(2).

of transferred property. Thus, the giver of the gift, not the recipient, pays the gift tax; the estate pays the estate tax, not the heirs. Although the gift tax is computed on an annual basis, it is cumulative in nature. The gift tax due in any given year depends on taxable gifts in the current year and total taxable gifts in prior years. This cumulative feature is also apparent in the integration of the gift and estate taxes. Thus, the total taxable gifts of an individual during his or her lifetime affect the estate tax due on death. Finally, transfer tax rates are steeply progressive. The maximum rate can be as high as 55 percent; thus, without proper planning more than one-half of a large estate could be lost to the government. Note that state and local inheritance taxes could also apply, depending on the decedent's residence and the location of estate assets.

Table 15.1 presents transfer tax rates applicable before and after EGTRRA. Table 15.2 presents the transfer tax rates for 2004. Note the reduction in the top marginal rate from 55 to 48 percent, under the provisions of EGTTRA. The act also eliminates the 5 percent surtax described at the bottom of Table 15.1. Between 2005 and 2009, EGTRRA continues to gradually reduce the top marginal transfer tax rate, as follows:

- 47 percent in 2005
- 46 percent in 2006
- 45 percent in 2007, 2008, and 2009

These rate reductions do not affect the lower brackets of the transfer tax schedule. Thus, in 2005 (2006), if taxable transfers exceed $2 million, the tax is $780,800 plus 47 (46) percent of the amount over $2 million. In 2007 through 2009, if taxable transfers exceed $1.5 million, the tax is $555,800 plus 45 percent of the amount over $1.5 million.

**TABLE 15.2**
**Federal Transfer Tax Rates for Transfers during 2004**
The following rate schedule can be used to compute the federal gift or estate tax before any reduction for the unified credit.

| If the Taxable Transfer Is | | The Tax Is | |
|---|---|---|---|
| Over | But Not Over | | Of the Amount Over |
| –0– | $   10,000 | 18% | –0– |
| $   10,000 | 20,000 | $   1,800 + 20% | $   10,000 |
| 20,000 | 40,000 | 3,800 + 22% | 20,000 |
| 40,000 | 60,000 | 8,200 + 24% | 40,000 |
| 60,000 | 80,000 | 13,000 + 26% | 60,000 |
| 80,000 | 100,000 | 18,200 + 28% | 80,000 |
| 100,000 | 150,000 | 23,800 + 30% | 100,000 |
| 150,000 | 250,000 | 38,800 + 32% | 150,000 |
| 250,000 | 500,000 | 70,800 + 34% | 250,000 |
| 500,000 | 750,000 | 155,800 + 37% | 500,000 |
| 750,000 | 1,000,000 | 248,300 + 39% | 750,000 |
| 1,000,000 | 1,250,000 | 345,800 + 41% | 1,000,000 |
| 1,250,000 | 1,500,000 | 448,300 + 43% | 1,250,000 |
| 1,500,000 | 2,000,000 | 555,800 + 45% | 1,500,000 |
| 2,000,000 | | 780,800 + 48% | 2,000,000 |

In 2010, the top marginal gift tax rate drops to 35 percent; thus for taxable transfers over $500,000 the tax is $155,800 plus 35 percent of the amount over $500,000. The estate and generation-skipping transfer tax rates drop to zero for 2010. In 2011, under the sunset provisions of EGTRRA, the estate and generation-skipping taxes are reinstated and the unified transfer tax rates return to those specified in Table 15.1.

Although the rate schedules in Tables 15.1 and 15.2 appear to subject all taxable transfers to gift and estate tax, the unified credit reduces tax liability to zero for cumulative lifetime transfers up to the exemption equivalent amount. The unified credit represents a lifetime exemption from transfer tax.[3] It is first used to absorb gift tax on transfers during the person's life. The unified credit available in any given year is reduced by the unified credit used to absorb gift taxes in prior years.[4] Any unused credit remaining at death reduces the estate's tax liability. Thus, the unified credit is so named because it applies to (unifies) both the gift and estate tax systems.

The **unified credit** is defined as the amount of transfer tax computed on the exemption equivalent. The **exemption equivalent amount** is the wealth allowed to be transferred free of any transfer taxes. For the 10 years ending in 1997, the exemption equivalent was fixed at $600,000, resulting in a unified credit of $192,800. Since that time, the exemption equivalent has increased each year, as shown in Table 15.3.

EGTRRA gradually increases the exemption equivalent amount for estate tax purposes as shown in Table 15.4.

For gift tax purposes, EGTRRA fixes the exemption equivalent amount at $1 million for 2002 and beyond resulting in a unified credit of $345,800. Thus, for 2004 through 2009, the exemption equivalent and unified credit amounts for gift and estate tax purposes are different. Finally, after 2010, the exemption equivalent amount for both gift and estate tax purposes is $1 million, under the sunset provisions.

The application of the unified credit in reducing gift and estate tax, including the cumulative nature of the credit, is discussed in the following sections.

[3] Sections 2505 and 2010.

[4] Section 2505(a)(2).

**TABLE 15.3**
**Phase In of Unified Credit**

| Year of Transfer | Unified Credit | Exemption Equivalent |
|---|---|---|
| 1987–1997 | $192,800 | $600,000 |
| 1998 | 202,050 | 625,000 |
| 1999 | 211,300 | 650,000 |
| 2000 and 2001 | 220,550 | 675,000 |

**TABLE 15.4**
**Estate Tax Unified Credit and Exemption Equivalent Amounts under EGTTRA**

| Year of Transfer | Unified Credit | Exemption Equivalent |
|---|---|---|
| 2002 and 2003 | $  345,800 | $1,000,000 |
| 2004 and 2005 | 555,800 | 1,500,000 |
| 2006, 2007, and 2008 | 780,800 | 2,000,000 |
| 2009 | 1,455,800 | 3,500,000 |

# GIFT TAX

**Objective 2**
Calculate gift tax liability.

Exhibit 15.1 presents the formula for calculating the annual gift tax. A brief inspection of this formula reveals its cumulative nature. The tax base on which a gift tax is initially calculated is the sum of current and prior year taxable gifts. The tax computed on **cumulative taxable gifts** is then reduced by the gift tax applicable to taxable gifts in prior years. If the gift tax were assessed at a constant (proportional) rate, this cumulative approach would produce the same final tax liability as an annual assessment on current taxable gifts. Given the progressive nature of the transfer tax rates, however, the cumulative approach ensures that successive gifts are taxed at higher rates than prior gifts.

---

*Cumulative Taxable Transfers*

In 2004, Mr. Cameron, who had made no prior taxable gifts, transfers current taxable gifts of $100,000. The gift tax computed on these transfers, using Table 15.1, is $23,800. In 2005, he also transfers current taxable gifts of $100,000, so his 2005 cumulative taxable gifts total $200,000, producing a gross transfer tax of $54,800. Mr. Cameron can reduce this tax liability by the $23,800 tax computed on his 2004 taxable transfers, resulting in a 2005 precredit gift tax liability of $31,800.[5] Although Mr. Cameron's annual transfer amounts are identical, the related gift tax liability increases.

---

## Transfers Considered Gifts

**Objective 3**
Identify the characteristics of a *gift*, describe items specifically excluded from gift treatment, and apply the annual exclusion from taxable gifts.

Before a gift tax can be determined, a decision must be made as to which transfers during the year are considered *gifts*. The code defines a gift as a transfer for less than adequate consideration in money or money's worth.[6] Although donative intent is not required, transfers occurring in a business context generally do not result in a gift. Thus, a forced sale at less than FMV, necessitated by a need for speedy cash flow, does not result in a gift. Sales for less than FMV occurring in a personal context (such as between family members), however, likely result in gift treatment for the difference between the FMV and the stated sales price. Gift treatment occurs in this context because the transfer was for less than adequate consideration.

[5] As depicted in Exhibit 15.1, the *precredit gift tax* is the tax computed before reduction for the unified credit.

[6] Section 2512(b).

**EXHIBIT 15.1**
**Calculation of Annual Gift Tax**

Fair market value of total gifts during the year
− Annual exclusions and deductions
Current year taxable gifts
+ Prior year taxable gifts
Cumulative taxable gifts
× Transfer tax rates
Tax on cumulative gifts
− Tax computed on prior year gifts
Precredit gift tax
− Unified credit
Gift tax payable

---

*Sale with Partial Gift Treatment*

Mrs. Garet sold a house to her niece, Ms. Jennings, for $50,000. If the house has an FMV of $150,000, Mrs. Garet has made a gift to her niece of $100,000, the difference between its FMV and the price for which it was sold.

---

To be considered a gift, a transfer must be complete, which means that the transferor retains no rights to the transferred property. In particular, the transferor cannot retain the right to take back the property and negate the transfer. Intuitively, an **incomplete transfer** is not really a gift since the transferor retains control of the property. For example, if individual A writes a will naming individual B as heir to all of A's property, a gift has not occurred. Individual A retains the right to change the will at any time prior to death. Thus, B could ultimately receive nothing. A similar result occurs if individual A purchases a life insurance policy naming individual B as beneficiary. Incomplete transfers often occur in the creation of certain types of trusts such as Crummey trusts and qualified trusts to benefit a minor. These trusts are described in Chapter 17 as part of the discussion of the role of trusts in family wealth planning.

## Valuing Gift Transfers

For completed transfers considered gifts, the FMV of the transferred property is potentially subject to gift tax. FMV is defined as the price at which property would change hands between a willing buyer and a willing seller, neither being under any compulsion to buy or sell and both having reasonable knowledge of the relevant facts.[7] For items such as stocks and bonds of publicly traded corporations, a ready market value exists. For other items, such as interests in closely held businesses, real estate, artwork, and personal assets, it could be necessary to obtain appraisals to accurately value the transfer. The burden of proving the value assigned for gift tax purposes rests with the transferor, and appropriate documentation is critical. Valuation issues and planning strategies are discussed in more detail in Chapter 17.

Special valuation issues arise on transfers of partial interests in property. For example, a transferor could gift the income arising from a piece of property to one individual for the person's lifetime and specify that ownership of the property passes to a second individual on the death of the recipient of the income. In this case, two gifts have been made: (1) the **income interest** has been given to one recipient and (2) the **remainder interest** has been given to a second recipient.[8] For gift tax purposes, the total value of the property must be

---

[7] Reg. 20.2031-1(b).

[8] Such gifts are typically made using a trust to hold the property during the income recipient's lifetime. Trusts of this type are discussed in more detail in Chapter 16.

allocated between the two gifts. Treasury regulations provide guidance on the valuation of these interests, which depends on the projected annual income of the property and the life expectancy of the income interest recipient. The total value of the two interests cannot exceed the FMV of an undivided interest in the property.

## Exclusions from Gift Treatment

Certain items are specifically excluded from gift tax treatment, including political contributions,[9] payments of medical expenses on another's behalf, and tuition payments to an educational institution on another's behalf. Note that tuition payments must be made directly to the educational institution to qualify for this exclusion. Similarly, medical expenses must be paid to the medical provider.[10] Transfers of property pursuant to divorce are also exempt from the gift tax.[11]

### Annual Gift Tax Exclusion

The **annual gift tax exclusion** omits many small transfers from gift tax treatment. Up to $11,000 of gifts made to any individual during a taxable year are excluded from gift tax.[12] From a practical standpoint, the annual exclusion avoids complex record-keeping and filing requirements from applying to birthday and holiday gifts and other transfers of insignificant economic value. A transferor who makes gifts to multiple individuals qualifies for multiple annual exclusions. Thus, if Individual A gives $100,000 to Individual B, $11,000 of this gift is excluded, and $89,000 is subject to gift tax. If Individual A gives $11,000 each to 10 different individuals, 10 annual exclusions are available, and none of the transfers are subject to gift tax. If Individual A gives $5,000 to Individual B and $15,000 to Individual C, all of the gift to B is excluded; $11,000 of the gift to C is excluded but $4,000 of the gift to Individual C is subject to gift tax.

For married couples, an important special rule allows a doubling of the available annual exclusion amount. The **gift-splitting election** allows married couples to treat all gifts made by either spouse as being made jointly by both spouses.[13] As a result, each spouse can use the annual exclusion on his or her portion of each gift, and the maximum total amount excluded from gift tax treatment increases to $22,000 per recipient. The gift-splitting election seeks to equalize tax treatment for married couples not residing in community property states with that of couples residing in such states and for whom gifts from marital assets would automatically be considered as made by both spouses. Note that married couples do *not* file joint gift tax returns regardless of their income tax reporting choice. Gift and estate tax returns apply only to the gifts and estates of the individuals owning the subject property.

| | |
|---|---|
| *Gift Splitting and the Annual Exclusion* | Mr. George gives $30,000 cash to his niece and $15,000 cash to his nephew. If Mr. George is single, he can exclude $11,000 of each gift. His taxable gifts equal $23,000 ($30,000 + $15,000 − $11,000 − $11,000). If he is married and he and his wife elect gift splitting, Mr. George is deemed to have made a $15,000 gift to his niece and a $7,500 gift to his nephew. He can exclude $11,000 of the gift to his niece and all ($7,500) of the gift to his nephew; his |

[9] Section 2501(a)(5).

[10] Section 2503(e).

[11] These transfers must be made under a written agreement between spouses, and a final divorce decree must be obtained within a three-year period beginning one year before the agreement becomes effective. Section 7516.

[12] Section 2503(b). The exclusion amount is indexed for inflation, with inflation adjustments rounded to the next lowest multiple of $1,000. Prior to 2002, the exclusion was $10,000.

[13] Section 2513.

taxable gifts equal $4,000 ($15,000 + $7,500 − $11,000 − $7,500). Mrs. George is deemed to have made identical gifts with the same exclusions and taxable gift amounts. Thus, taxable gifts for the couple are reduced in total from $23,000 to $8,000.

In most circumstances, gift splitting is clearly beneficial for married couples, but the election might not be optimal in limited circumstances. For example, if one spouse has used all of his or her unified credit and owes current gift tax on any additional gifts, splitting large gifts made by the other spouse could accelerate the gift tax.

The annual exclusion applies only to gifts of a present interest, not to gifts of a future interest.[14] A **present interest** is an unrestricted right to the immediate use, possession, or enjoyment of property or income from property.[15] A **future interest** provides use, possession, or enjoyment of property or income at some future date.[16] Thus, a gift of an income interest in property is considered a present interest and qualifies for the annual exclusion. However, a gift of a remainder interest in property that does not transfer the property ownership until the death of the income interest holder is considered a future interest and does not qualify for the annual exclusion. This transfer is still considered a gift, however, and is subject to gift tax at the date transferred (not in the future when use, possession, or enjoyment occurs).

| | |
|---|---|
| *Present and Future Interest Gifts* | Mrs. Wingfield owns rental real estate that provides significant rental income. She gives the right to all future rental income to her daughter, Laura, for Laura's lifetime. Mrs. Wingfield also provides that the ownership of the property will pass to her grandson, Tom, on Laura's death. The current total market value of the real estate is $400,000. Using the methods specified in the regulations, the value of the income interest given to Laura is $175,000; the value of the remainder interest given to Tom is $225,000. The gift to Laura is a gift of a present interest and qualifies for the annual exclusion. The gift to Tom is a gift of a future interest and does not qualify for the annual exclusion. Mrs. Wingfield's taxable gifts from this transaction total $389,000 ($175,000 − $11,000 + $225,000). |

A recent exception to the present interest rule has been created for gifts to educational IRAs[17] and qualified state tuition programs.[18] These programs allow taxpayers to contribute money to the equivalent of a savings account for future educational expenses of minor children. Earnings in the account are exempt from income tax, and distributions from the account are not taxable if used for qualifying educational expenses. For transfer tax purposes, contributions to these accounts are considered a gift of a present interest qualifying for the annual exclusion.

## Gift Tax Deductions

Two important deductions reduce the total amount of transfers subject to gift tax. First, an unlimited **marital deduction** eliminates all transfers to the taxpayer's spouse.[19] This deduction essentially treats a married couple as a single economic unit for gift tax purposes. Second, a deduction is allowed for transfers to qualified charitable and other nonprofit organizations, such as religious, scientific, literary, or educational institutions.[20] In general,

---

[14] Section 2503(b)(1).

[15] Reg. Section 20.2503-3(b).

[16] Reg. Section 20.2503-3(a).

[17] Section 530.

[18] Section 529.

[19] Section 2523(a).

[20] Section 2522(a).

these are the same organizations for which individuals are allowed a **charitable deduction** for income tax purposes. This deduction acknowledges that gifts to charity accomplish the wealth redistribution goals of the transfer tax system without requiring the government to act as an intermediary.

## Calculating the Gift Tax Liability

The FMV of all transfers during the current year reduced by allowable annual exclusions, the marital deduction, and any charitable deductions determines total current **taxable gifts.** To this current total must be added taxable gifts from all prior years as computed under the same rules applied in calculating current taxable gifts. The sum of all current and prior taxable gifts forms the tax base for calculating the gift tax.

*Cumulative Taxable Gifts*

Ms. Marion, a single individual, made five gifts during 2004, giving $20,000 cash to each of her three grandchildren, land with a market value of $100,000 to her son, and stock with a value of $50,000 to Villanova University. In prior years, she made taxable gifts totaling $400,000. Her current and cumulative taxable gifts follow:

| | |
|---|---|
| Cash gifts | $ 60,000 |
| Land | 100,000 |
| Stock | 50,000 |
| Total current gifts | $210,000 |
| Less: | |
| Charitable deduction | (50,000) Villanova |
| Four annual exclusions | (44,000) 3 grandchildren & son |
| Current taxable gifts | $116,000 |
| Prior years taxable gifts | 400,000 |
| Cumulative taxable gifts | $516,000 |

The next step in calculating the gift tax applies the rates found in Table 15.2 to cumulative taxable gifts. This approach produces a cumulative gift tax amount, which is then reduced by tax computed on taxable gifts in prior years.[21] The remainder represents the tax on current gifts prior to the unified credit.

The maximum lifetime unified credit for gifts prior to 2002 is defined in Table 15.3. After 2001, the unified gift tax credit is $345,800. The unified credit allowable in any given year is reduced by amounts used in previous years. After reduction for the unified credit, any remaining tax liability must be paid currently. In years in which the unified credit amount increases, taxpayers benefit by excluding additional gifts from taxation, even if available unified credit in prior years had been fully utilized. Any unified credit not used to offset gift tax liability during a person's life reduces the estate tax liability after his or her death.

*Using the Unified Credit*

In 1998, Mr. Anthony made his first taxable gifts totaling $250,000. The precredit tax on such gifts, using Table 15.1, is $70,800. Mr. Anthony's available unified credit for 1998, from Table 15.3, is $202,050. Thus, his gift tax liability is reduced to zero, and his unified credit will be reduced by $70,800 in future periods.

[21] The reduction is calculated using current transfer tax rates regardless of the rates actually in effect in the years in which prior gifts were made. This approach is appropriate because the reduction applies against the tax on cumulative taxable gifts, computed using current rates.

*[handwritten: unitedcredithnow 211,300 −70,800 = 140,500 / already used]*

In 1999, Mr. Anthony made additional taxable gifts of $450,000. His 1999 gift tax liability is computed as follows:

*[handwritten: (200,000×.37) + 155,800]*

| | |
|---|---|
| Current taxable gifts | $450,000 |
| Plus: Prior taxable gifts | 250,000 |
| Cumulative taxable gifts | $700,000 |
| Tax computed on cumulative taxable gifts | $229,800 |
| Less: Tax computed on prior taxable gifts | (70,800) |
| Precredit gift tax | $159,000 |
| Less: Unused unified credit | (140,500) |
| 1999 gift tax payable | $ 18,500 |

From Table 15.3, the maximum unified credit available for 1999 is $211,300. Since Mr. Anthony used $70,800 of unified credit in 1998, his 1999 gift tax liability can be reduced by the unified credit of $140,500 ($211,300 − $70,800).

In 2000, Mr. Anthony made additional taxable gifts of $100,000. His 2000 gift tax liability is computed as follows:

*[handwritten: Unified 220,550]*

*[handwritten: [248,300 + (50,000×.37)]]*

| | |
|---|---|
| Current taxable gifts | $ 100,000 |
| Plus: Prior taxable gifts | 700,000 |
| Cumulative taxable gifts | $800,000 |
| Tax computed on cumulative taxable gifts | $267,300 |
| Less: Tax computed on prior taxable gifts | (229,800) |
| Precredit gift tax | $ 37,500 |
| Less: Unused unified credit* | (9,250) |
| 2000 gift tax payable | $ 28,250 |

*$9,250 equals $220,550, 2000 unified credit − $211,300 unified credit used in prior years. *[handwritten: Additional credit given]*

Notice that Mr. Anthony is allowed to reduce his 2000 gift tax liability by the increase in the unified credit in 2000 relative to 1999. Even though he used all of the unified credit available in 1999 to reduce his gift tax liability in that year, he benefits from the phase in of the additional exemption equivalent amount.

## Comprehensive Gift Tax Example

Mr. and Mrs. Burton, a married couple, made the following gratuitous transfers during 2003:

- Cash of $300,000 to each of their four children.
- Cash of $30,000 to each of their six grandchildren.
- Tuition payments of $20,000 paid to each of three universities for their three oldest grandchildren.
- Stock with a value of $10,000, contributed to UNICEF.
- Cash of $5,000 contributed to their church.
- Political contributions totaling $2,000.

In prior years, each had reported the following taxable gifts and gift tax payments.

| Year | Taxable Gifts | Gift Tax Paid | Unified Credit Used |
|------|---------------|---------------|---------------------|
| 1990 | $200,000 | –0– | $ 54,800 |
| 1995 | 250,000 | –0– | 84,000 |
| 1997 | 100,000 | –0– | 35,500 |
| 1998 | 175,000 | $37,000 | 27,750 |
| Total | $725,000 | $37,000 | $202,050 |

Assume that the Burtons elect gift splitting for 2003. Each spouse reports the following 2003 gift tax liability.

| | |
|---|---:|
| Current year gifts | $ 697,500 |
| Less: | |
|    Charitable contribution deduction | (7,500) |
|    Annual exclusions | (110,000) |
| Total current taxable gifts | $ 580,000 |
| Plus:   Prior taxable gifts | 725,000 |
| Cumulative taxable gifts | $1,305,000 |
| Tax computed on cumulative taxable gifts | $ 470,850 |
| Less:   Tax computed on prior taxable gifts | (239,050) |
| Precredit gift tax | $ 231,800 |
| Less:   Unused unified credit* | (143,750) |
| 2002 gift tax payable | $ 88,050 |

*The $143,750 equals 2003 unified credit ($345,800) less unified credit previously used by each spouse to reduce tax liability on prior taxable gifts ($202,050).

In computing current year taxable gifts, note that the tuition payments and the political contributions are excluded from gift treatment. The remaining transfers total $1,395,000 ($300,000 × 4 + $30,000 × 6 + $10,000 + $5,000). With gift splitting, one-half of these transfers, $697,500, is deemed to be made by each spouse. Each spouse then takes a charitable contribution deduction for one-half of the transfers to UNICEF and the church [$7,500 = 50 percent × ($10,000 + $5,000)]. Each spouse takes a full annual exclusion for the gifts to the four children and six grandchildren ($11,000 × 10).

Note that the tax on cumulative taxable gifts is reduced by the tax computed on prior taxable gifts ($239,050), *not* the tax actually *paid*. Although it might seem that this approach reduces current gift tax, note that the unified credit available in the current year has been reduced by credits used to absorb prior gift tax liability. Finally, notice that additional unified credit is available this year because of the increase in the exemption equivalent amount from 1998 (the year in which the Burtons first paid gift tax) to 2003. Exhibit 15.2 illustrates page 1 of the 2003 gift tax return filed by Mr. Burton.

## Gift Tax Filing Requirements

Not all individuals making gifts are required to file a gift tax return. However, they are required to file in many instances in which no actual gift tax will be paid.[22] Form 709 must be

---

[22] Section 6019 defines the circumstances under which a gift tax return must be filed.

**EXHIBIT 15.2**
**Gift Tax Return**

Form **709**

Department of the Treasury
Internal Revenue Service

**United States Gift (and Generation-Skipping Transfer) Tax Return**

(For gifts made during calendar year 2003)

▶ **See separate instructions.**

OMB No. 1545-0020

**2003**

| 1 Donor's first name and middle initial | 2 Donor's last name | 3 Donor's social security number |
|---|---|---|
| AL | BURTON | 123 45 6789 |

| 4 Address (number, street, and apartment number) | 5 Legal residence (domicile) (county and state) |
|---|---|
| 999 FREEDOM WAY | ADAMS CTY / NE |

| 6 City, state, and ZIP code | 7 Citizenship |
|---|---|
| MAYFIELD, NE 68900 | U.S. |

**Part 1—General Information**

| | | Yes | No |
|---|---|---|---|
| 8 | If the donor died during the year, check here ▶ ☐ and enter date of death | | |
| 9 | If you received an extension of time to file this Form 709, check here ▶ ☐ and attach the Form 4868, 2688, 2350, or extension letter | | |
| 10 | Enter the total number of donees listed on Schedule A—count each person only once. ▶ 10 | | |
| 11a | Have you (the donor) previously filed a Form 709 (or 709-A) for any other year? If "No," skip line 11b | X | |
| 11b | If the answer to line 11a is "Yes," has your address changed since you last filed Form 709 (or 709-A)? | | X |
| 12 | Gifts by husband or wife to third parties.—Do you consent to have the gifts (including generation-skipping transfers) made by you and by your spouse to third parties during the calendar year considered as made one-half by each of you? (See instructions.) (If the answer is "Yes," the following information must be furnished and your spouse must sign the consent shown below. If the answer is "No," skip lines 13–18 and go to Schedule A.) | X | |
| 13 | Name of consenting spouse ZELDA BURTON | **14** SSN 987-65-4321 | |
| 15 | Were you married to one another during the entire calendar year? (see instructions) | X | |
| 16 | If the answer to 15 is "No," check whether ☐ married ☐ divorced or ☐ widowed, and give date (see instructions) ▶ | | |
| 17 | Will a gift tax return for this year be filed by your spouse? (If "Yes," mail both returns in the same envelope.) | | |
| 18 | **Consent of Spouse**—I consent to have the gifts (and generation-skipping transfers) made by me and by my spouse to third parties during the calendar year considered as made one-half by each of us. We are both aware of the joint and several liability for tax created by the execution of this consent. | | |

Consenting spouse's signature ▶ _____ Date ▶ _____

**Part 2—Tax Computation**

| | | | |
|---|---|---|---|
| 1 | Enter the amount from Schedule A, Part 4, line 11 | **1** | 580,000 |
| 2 | Enter the amount from Schedule B, line 3 | **2** | 725,000 |
| 3 | Total taxable gifts (add lines 1 and 2) | **3** | 1,305,000 |
| 4 | Tax computed on amount on line 3 (see Table for Computing Tax in separate instructions) | **4** | 470,850 |
| 5 | Tax computed on amount on line 2 (see Table for Computing Tax in separate instructions) | **5** | 239,050 |
| 6 | Balance (subtract line 5 from line 4) | **6** | 231,800 |
| 7 | Maximum unified credit (nonresident aliens, see instructions) | **7** | 345,800 00 |
| 8 | Enter the unified credit against tax allowable for all prior periods (from Sch. B, line 1, col. C) | **8** | 202,050 |
| 9 | Balance (subtract line 8 from line 7) | **9** | 143,750 |
| 10 | Enter 20% (.20) of the amount allowed as a specific exemption for gifts made after September 8, 1976, and before January 1, 1977 (see instructions) | **10** | 0 |
| 11 | Balance (subtract line 10 from line 9) | **11** | 143,750 |
| 12 | Unified credit (enter the smaller of line 6 or line 11) | **12** | 143,750 |
| 13 | Credit for foreign gift taxes (see instructions) | **13** | 0 |
| 14 | Total credits (add lines 12 and 13) | **14** | 143,750 |
| 15 | Balance (subtract line 14 from line 6) (do not enter less than zero) | **15** | 88,050 |
| 16 | Generation-skipping transfer taxes (from Schedule C, Part 3, col. H, Total) | **16** | 0 |
| 17 | Total tax (add lines 15 and 16) | **17** | 88,050 |
| 18 | Gift and generation-skipping transfer taxes prepaid with extension of time to file | **18** | 0 |
| 19 | If line 18 is less than line 17, enter **balance due** (see instructions) | **19** | 88,050 |
| 20 | If line 18 is greater than line 17, enter **amount to be refunded** | **20** | |

**Sign Here**

Under penalties of perjury, I declare that I have examined this return, including any accompanying schedules and statements, and to the best of my knowledge and belief, it is true, correct, and complete. Declaration of preparer (other than donor) is based on all information of which preparer has any knowledge.

▶ Signature of donor _____ Date _____

**Paid Preparer's Use Only**

| Preparer's signature ▶ | Date | Check if self-employed ▶ ☐ |
|---|---|---|
| Firm's name (or yours if self-employed), address, and ZIP code ▶ | | Phone no. ▶ ( ) |

For Disclosure, Privacy Act, and Paperwork Reduction Act Notice, see page 12 of the separate instructions for this form. Cat. No. 16783M Form **709** (2003)

*Attach check or money order here.*

filed for any year in which gifts made exceed the annual exclusion amount.[23] In addition, a gift tax return is required for gifts of a future interest and to elect gift splitting. A gift tax return is not required for spousal gifts qualifying for the unlimited marital deduction. If the only gifts made during the year are to charities, no gift tax return is required so long as an entire interest in property is transferred. A return is required for charitable transfers of partial interests. The gift tax return is always filed on a calendar year basis and is due on the

[23] Note that filing a gift tax return, even if not required, might be a wise strategy so that the statute of limitations begins to run (Section 2002(f)).

**EXHIBIT 15.3**
**Calculation of Estate Tax**

Fair market value of gross estate
− Deductions
Taxable estate
+ Post-1976 cumulative taxable gifts
Cumulative taxable transfers
× Transfer tax rates
Precredit estate tax
− Gift taxes paid or deemed paid
− Estate tax credit
Estate tax payable

following April 15. An extension of the filing deadline can be obtained for sufficient reason. For most individuals reporting on a calendar year for income tax purposes, an extension of time to file Form 1040 also automatically extends the filing deadline for Form 709.

# ESTATE TAX

**Objective 4**
Calculate estate tax liability.

An **estate** is formed on the death of an individual to manage, conserve, and distribute property to specified individuals. Exhibit 15.3 presents the formula for calculating the estate tax. The cumulative nature of the transfer tax system is again evident through the inclusion of lifetime taxable gifts in the tax base. The tax calculated on cumulative transfers (during life and at death) is then reduced by the gift tax paid during life and the unified credit.

## Gross Estate

**Objective 5**
Identify items included in the *gross estate* and items deductible in calculating the *taxable estate*.

The estate tax calculation begins with the FMV of the gross estate (defined later). As a general rule, value is determined on the date of the decedent's death. With large estates, appraisals of nonliquid assets are critical to establishing a defensible valuation. One exception to date-of-death valuation is allowed at the election of the estate executor. If lower, the estate can be valued at an **alternate valuation date** six months after the decedent's death.[24] The choice is made by valuing the estate as a whole rather than each asset individually.[25] Any assets disposed of by the estate during this six-month period are valued on the date of disposition. Thus, the alternate valuation date for each estate asset is the last date the property is held, up to six months after death.

*Determining Estate Value*

Mr. Marcos died on January 31, 2004. The alternate valuation date is July 31, 2004. His estate included three assets with date-of-death and alternate-valuation-date values as follows:

| Asset | Value on 1/31/04 | Value on 7/31/04 |
|---|---|---|
| Real estate | $1,500,000 | $1,450,000 |
| Stock in ABC Corp. | 500,000 | 600,000 |
| Stock in XYZ Inc. | 750,000 | 500,000 |
| Total | $2,750,000 | $2,550,000 |

[24] The alternate valuation date election is available only if the estate must file an estate tax return and if making the election reduces both the value of the gross estate and the final estate tax liability. Section 2032(c).

[25] Section 2032(a).

In this case, the alternate valuation date election reduces the taxable gross estate by $200,000. If the XYZ stock were sold by the estate for $600,000 on June 1, 2004, its value on the sale date is included for purposes of the alternate valuation date, resulting in a taxable gross estate of $2,650,000.

The **gross estate** includes the following items:

- Property owned at date of death.[26]
- Life insurance proceeds from policies owned by the decedent or benefiting the estate.[27]
- A portion of jointly owned property.[28]
- Transfers with retained life estate.[29]
- Certain gifts made within three years of death.[30]
- Gift tax paid on gifts made within three years of death.[31]
- Survivorship annuity benefits.[32]

All property owned by the decedent on the date of death is typically included in the **probate estate.** The probate estate includes all property passing to the decedent's heirs under terms of the will or state intestacy laws (for those dying without a will). The probate estate is subject to administration by the estate executor, whose responsibilities include settling estate liabilities, managing and disposing of assets, and preparing estate tax returns. Significant probate costs, including attorney, accountant, and appraisal fees, could be incurred in administering the estate.

For estate tax purposes, the taxable gross estate is typically larger than the probate estate since several of the items listed earlier pass to beneficiaries or new owners outside the operation of the decedent's will or state intestacy laws. The probate estate does not include property passing outside the will by operation of law. For example, death benefits paid on life insurance policies on the life of the decedent are paid directly to the beneficiaries named in the policies. However, if the decedent possessed any incidents of ownership of the policies, the proceeds are included in the gross estate.[33] Incidents of ownership include the right to name or change policy beneficiaries and any other economic benefits of ownership.[34] The proceeds of life insurance policies payable to or benefiting the estate are also included in the gross estate for transfer tax purposes.[35]

An important category of assets (often overlooked by individuals attempting to assess their estate tax exposure without professional tax advice) involves pension and retirement benefits. The value of accumulated benefits in Individual Retirement Accounts and qualified employer-provided pension and retirement accounts is included in the taxable gross estate. For many individuals, the combined value of retirement and life insurance benefits is

[26] Section 2033.
[27] Section 2042.
[28] Section 2040.
[29] Section 2036.
[30] Section 2035.
[31] Section 2035.
[32] Section 2039.
[33] Section 2042.
[34] Reg. 20.2042-1(a)(1).
[35] Section 2042.

sufficient to produce a taxable gross estate in excess of the exemption equivalent amount, regardless of other property ownership.[36]

Joint ownership of property can occur in several forms: joint tenancy, tenancy by the entirety, tenancy in common, and community property. The first two ownership forms (joint tenancy and tenancy by the entirety) provide rights of survivorship. This means that on the death of one tenant, ownership automatically passes to the surviving owner or owners. **Joint tenancy** means joint ownership, with rights of survivorship, by two or more individuals regardless of their relationship. In some states, joint tenancy between husband and wife is referred to as **tenancy by the entirety.**

The remaining two forms of joint ownership (tenancy in common and community property) do *not* confer rights of survivorship. If one joint owner dies, his or her property rights pass to the estate or heirs. **Tenancy in common** means joint ownership, without rights of survivorship, by two or more individuals regardless of their relationship. **Community property** interests arise from the acquisition of property by a married couple residing in a community property state.[37] Generally, any property acquired after marriage, except by gift or inheritance, is considered community property for such couples.

The form of joint ownership determines the portion of jointly owned property included in the gross estate.[38] For jointly owned property with rights of survivorship, the decedent's interest in the property terminates at death and ownership automatically passes to the other owner(s). A portion of the value of the property, however, is included in the gross estate. The value included generally depends on the decedent's relative contribution to the property's original purchase. For property owned jointly with the decedent's spouse, 50 percent of the value is included in the gross estate regardless of which spouse provided the initial funds.

For jointly owned property without rights of survivorship (community property and property owned as tenants in common), the decedent's ownership rights are determined under state law. Community property is generally considered owned 50 percent by each spouse.

---

*Joint Ownership*   Ms. Candinski and Mr. Williams each contributed $50,000 to purchase a piece of land. If the form of ownership is joint tenancy and he dies, she automatically owns 100 percent of the property. If the form of ownership is tenants in common, ownership of Mr. Williams's 50 percent interest in the property is transferred in accordance with his will or state intestacy laws. If the property is worth $180,000 at the time of his death, $90,000 is included in his gross estate under either joint tenancy or tenancy in common ownership.

Now suppose that Ms. Candinski and Mr. Williams are married. If Mr. Williams acquired the property during their marriage and they live in a community property state, only 50 percent of the value, or $90,000, will be included in his estate. If the couple does not reside in a community property state, the amount included in his estate depends on whether title is held in his name alone or with Ms. Candinski as either tenants by the entirety or tenants in common. If titled to him, 100 percent of the value of the property is included in his estate. If titled jointly with Ms. Candinski, 50 percent of the value is included in his estate regardless of whether she contributed to the purchase of the property.

---

[36] Distributions from these accounts are also likely to result in taxable income to either the estate or the account beneficiaries. *Income in respect of a decedent* (IRD) is discussed in more detail in Chapter 16.

[37] Arizona, California, Idaho, Louisiana, New Mexico, Nevada, Texas, Washington, and Wisconsin are the community property states.

[38] Section 2040.

Previously, we discussed splitting property rights into an income interest and a remainder interest. If a taxpayer gifts a remainder interest in property during his or her life but retains the rights to income from the property until death, the entire value of the property is included in the decedent's gross estate.[39] The retained income interest, commonly referred to as a **retained life estate,** ensures that the decedent enjoys the economic benefits of property ownership until death and that the transfer tax system captures the value of that economic benefit.

Certain other gifts made within three years of death also increase the gross estate. These rules exist to prevent deathbed transfers that would reduce the cumulative tax base by the amount of any gift taxes paid on such transfers. In general, the gross estate includes gift tax paid on transfers within three years of death. In limited cases, however, the value of the property itself (rather than the gift tax) is included in the gross estate. The most important of these inclusions are (1) the ownership of life insurance policies transferred within three years of death and (2) the transfer of a retained life estate in property within three years of death.[40]

| | |
|---|---|
| *Adjustment for Gifts within Three Years of Death* | During the three years prior to his death, Mr. Josef made the following taxable gifts: |

| Asset | Value on Date of Gift | Value on Date of Death | Gift Tax Paid |
|---|---|---|---|
| Life insurance policy | $ 20,000 | $500,000 | –0– |
| Land | 200,000 | 250,000 | $78,000 |
| Stock | 50,000 | 100,000 | 19,500 |

His gross estate includes the $500,000 proceeds of the insurance policy and the gift tax paid on the other two gifts totaling $97,500.[41]

The final significant item included in the gross estate involves survivorship benefits associated with the decedent's annuity rights. If the decedent owned an interest in an annuity that after the decedent's death continues to provide benefits to another person, such as the decedent's spouse, the value of these survivorship benefits is included in the gross estate.[42]

## Taxable Estate

The following deductions are allowed to reduce the gross estate in calculating the **taxable estate.**

- Funeral expenses
- Estate administration costs
- Estate casualty and theft losses
- Certain liabilities
- Charitable deduction
- Marital deduction

[39] Section 2036.

[40] Section 2035.

[41] Because the proceeds of the life insurance policy are included in Mr. Josef's gross estate, the value of the gift is not included in the addition for cumulative taxable gifts required to calculate the final transfer tax base.

[42] Section 2039.

The deductions allowed for funeral and estate administrative costs recognize that these expenses reduce the value of the estate available for distribution to the heirs.[43] Similarly, if estate property suffers losses due to casualty or theft during the period of estate administration, such losses are deductible against the gross estate.

Various liabilities are deductible in determining the taxable estate.[44] A deduction is allowed for mortgage liabilities on property included in the gross estate. A deduction is also allowed for the decedent's outstanding debts at the time of death. A deduction is allowed for unpaid property, income, and gift taxes incurred but unpaid at the decedent's death. The deduction for liabilities recognizes that payment of these amounts prior to the decedent's death would have reduced the value of the taxable gross estate.

A deduction is also allowed for the value of the property specifically willed by the decedent to a qualified nonprofit organization.[45] This deduction is consistent with the intent of the transfer tax system to redistribute wealth from private individuals to the public sector.

Often the most significant deduction allowed in calculating the taxable estate is the marital deduction. Consistent with the treatment of spousal gifts discussed previously, an unlimited marital deduction is allowed for transfers at death to the decedent's spouse.[46] The deduction applies to all transfers of property included in the gross estate and passing to the spouse as the decedent's heir, as the surviving tenant for property owned in joint tenancy or tenants by the entirety, or as the beneficiary of insurance on the life of the decedent. To the extent that property transferred to the spouse is encumbered by a mortgage, only the net value of the property (FMV less the mortgage) is allowed as a marital deduction. Chapter 17 discusses important planning issues involving the marital deduction, including the use of a QTIP election for certain transfers.

*Estate Tax Deductions and the Taxable Estate*

Assume that Mr. Alfredo's gross estate of $2,000,000 included assets encumbered by mortgages totaling $400,000. Of these totals, assets of $1 million are willed to his spouse, including a house subject to a $200,000 mortgage. His will also made a $100,000 bequest to a specified charity. At Mr. Alfredo's death, he had other outstanding debts totaling $25,000. His estate paid funeral costs of $10,000 and fees totaling $50,000 to the accountant, attorney, and appraiser. His taxable estate is determined as follows.

| | |
|---|---|
| Gross estate | $2,000,000 |
| Less: | |
| Outstanding debts* | (425,000) |
| Charitable deduction | (100,000) |
| Funeral costs | (10,000) |
| Administrative costs | (50,000) |
| Marital deduction† | (800,000) |
| Taxable estate | $ 615,000 |

*$400,000 + $25,000. The mortgage on the house willed to Mr. Alfredo's wife is included in the $400,000 of total mortgage liabilities.
†$1,000,000 value of property left to Mr. Alfredo's wife less the $200,000 mortgage included in the liability deduction.

[43] Section 2053. The estate can elect to deduct administrative expenses on the estate income tax return rather than on the estate tax return if it is more beneficial. This choice is discussed further in Chapter 16.
[44] Section 2053.
[45] Section 2055.
[46] Section 2056.

## Calculating the Estate Tax

As Exhibit 15.3 indicates, the tax base for calculating the estate tax (i.e., cumulative taxable transfers) is the sum of the taxable estate and post-1976 cumulative taxable gifts made during the decedent's lifetime.[47] The same transfer tax rates found in Tables 15.1 and 15.2 are applied to cumulative taxable transfers to derive the gross estate tax liability before credits. Several credits allowed to reduce this gross liability result in the final estate tax payable.

First, a credit is allowed for the lesser of gift taxes actually paid on post-1976 cumulative taxable gifts or gift taxes that would have been paid on such gifts under the current transfer tax rates.[48] The **deemed paid gift tax credit** is less than the actual gift tax paid for gifts from 1977 through 1983 when the transfer tax rates were higher than the current rates.

The full amount of the unified credit available in the year of death reduces estate tax liability. The available unified credit is not reduced by such credit previously used to offset gift taxes.[49] Although this approach might seem to provide a double benefit, recall that cumulative gifts are included in the tax base but that the deemed paid gift tax credit reduces estate tax liability only by the amount of the gift tax actually paid or deemed paid (after reduction for the unified credit).

A credit is also allowed for state death taxes paid on property included in the gross estate and for death taxes paid to foreign countries.[50] The credit for foreign death taxes is limited to the lesser of the foreign tax paid or the federal estate tax assessed on the property subject to foreign tax.

The credit for state death taxes is also subject to a maximum limitation. The maximum credit is computed using a graduated rate table with credit rates varying from 0 to 16 percent. The credit limitation is computed on the basis of the taxable estate reduced by $60,000.[51] Given this approach, adjusted taxable gifts have no impact on the state credit allowed. As a result of the $60,000 threshold, small estates receive no federal credit, although state death taxes are still paid. Many states have adopted a simplified death tax system in which the state tax paid at least equals the federal credit allowed. As a result, larger estates could get a full credit for state death taxes, effectively shifting tax revenue from the federal government to the state. The types of state death taxes assessed are discussed in more detail in the final section of this chapter.

| *State Death Tax Credit* | Mr. Colby died in the current year with a taxable estate of $30,000. Although no federal estate tax was owed, his state of residence assessed death taxes of $3,000. |
|---|---|
| | If Mr. Colby's taxable estate were $1 million instead, the maximum allowable credit for state death taxes would be $33,200. If state death taxes paid totaled $40,000, the credit would be limited to $33,200. If state death taxes paid totaled $30,000, the credit would equal the actual taxes paid. |

[47] The unified transfer tax system was enacted in 1976. Prior to that time, separate gift and estate taxes were assessed at much lower rates than those of the current system.

[48] Section 2012.

[49] Section 2010.

[50] Sections 2011 and 2014.

[51] The credit is computed using a schedule contained in Section 2011(b). The actual calculation of the credit is beyond the scope of this text. EGTRRA reduces the amount of the credit allowable after 2001, and replaces the credit with a deduction beginning in 2005.

Finally, a credit is allowed to the extent that property included in the gross estate has passed through another estate during the last 10 years.[52] If this property was assessed an estate tax within two years, a full credit is allowed for the lesser of the estate tax paid by the prior estate or the estate tax assessed in the current estate. If greater than two years have elapsed since the property was taxed in another estate, the credit is reduced by 20 percent for every two-year increment.

| *Credit for Estate Tax on Prior Transfers* | Mrs. Natalie died in 1999, leaving property valued at $200,000 to her sister, Mrs. Lana. Mrs. Natalie's estate paid $82,000 of estate tax attributable to this property. In 2003, Mrs. Lana died, leaving the property received from her sister to her daughter. Prior to the credit, this property increased the gross estate tax on Mrs. Lana's estate by $90,000.[53] Her estate is allowed a credit for $65,600 ($82,000 × 80 percent). |
| --- | --- |

## Comprehensive Estate Tax Example

Refer to the facts in the comprehensive gift tax example beginning on page 418. In 2004, Mr. Burton died owning the following assets.

| Assets | Fair Market Value |
| --- | --- |
| Stocks and bonds | $1,000,000 |
| Cash in joint bank accounts with Mrs. Burton | 90,000 |
| House owned as tenants in the entirety with Mrs. Burton | 450,000 |
| Other real estate | 500,000 |
| Life insurance policy naming Mr. Burton's two children as equal beneficiaries | 2,000,000 |

At the time of his death, Mr. Burton had the following liabilities outstanding:

| | |
| --- | --- |
| Mortgage on house owned with Mrs. Burton | $200,000 |
| Mortgages on other real estate | 150,000 |
| Miscellaneous personal debts | 15,000 |

Mr. Burton's will leaves stocks worth $200,000 to his sister, Mrs. Janinz, stocks worth $100,000 and the other real estate to his wife, and bonds worth $50,000 to Harvard University. All remaining assets, after payment of all personal liabilities, estate taxes, administration fees, and funeral expenses, are to pass to his two children in equal shares. Note that the house and cash in joint bank accounts automatically pass to Mrs. Burton outside of the will by virtue of their joint ownership. Thus, Mr. Burton's children receive the life insurance proceeds and all stocks and bonds remaining after satisfaction of estate costs and the bequests to his wife, his sister, and Harvard University.

Mr. Burton's gross estate includes the following.

[52] Section 2013.

[53] Assuming that Mrs. Lana's estate is in a 45 percent marginal estate tax bracket ($90,000 = $200,000 × 45 percent).

| | |
|---|---|
| Stocks and bonds | $1,000,000 |
| Mr. Burton's share of the cash in joint bank accounts with his wife | 45,000 |
| Mr. Burton's share of the house owned as tenants in the entirety with his wife | 225,000 |
| Other real estate | 500,000 |
| Life insurance policy naming Mr. Burton's two children as equal beneficiaries | 2,000,000 |
| Gift tax paid on gifts within 3 years of death | 143,750 |
| Total gross estate | $3,913,750 |

Note that Mr. Burton's gross estate includes only 50 percent of the two assets owned jointly with Mrs. Burton. Also note that gift taxes paid on 2003 gifts, from the Comprehensive Gift Tax Example, are included in the gross estate since these gifts occurred within three years of his death.

Mr. Burton's funeral expenses totaled $15,000. In addition, his estate incurred $25,000 of attorney, accountant, and appraisal fees. His taxable estate and cumulative taxable transfers are calculated as follows.

| | |
|---|---|
| Total gross estate | $3,913,750 |
| Less: | |
| Funeral expenses | (15,000) |
| Estate administration costs | (25,000) |
| Liabilities | (265,000) |
| Charitable contribution deduction | (50,000) |
| Marital deduction | (620,000) |
| Taxable estate | $2,938,750 |
| Plus: Post-1976 cumulative taxable gifts | 1,305,000 |
| Cumulative taxable transfers | $4,243,750 |

The deduction for liabilities includes the miscellaneous personal debts outstanding at Mr. Burton's death, 50 percent of the mortgage on the house owned jointly with Mrs. Burton, and the mortgages outstanding on the other real estate. The marital deduction is calculated as follows.

| | |
|---|---|
| Mr. Burton's share of the joint bank account | $ 45,000 |
| Mr. Burton's share of the house | 225,000 |
| Other real estate | 500,000 |
| Stocks bequeathed to Mrs. Burton | 100,000 |
| Less: | |
| Mortgage on Mr. Burton's share of house | (100,000) |
| Mortgages on other real estate | (150,000) |
| Total marital deduction | $620,000 |

Mr. Burton's state of residence assesses inheritance tax at a rate of 2 percent of the federal taxable estate. His final federal estate tax liability is calculated as follows.

|---|---|
| Tax on cumulative taxable transfers | $1,857,800 |
| Less: | |
| Tax paid on cumulative taxable gifts* | (180,750) |
| Unified credit for 2004 (Table 15.4) | (555,800) |
| State inheritance taxes† | (58,775) |
| Estate tax payable | $1,062,475 |

*$143,750 paid on 2003 gifts + $37,000 paid on 1998 gifts.
†$58,775 = 2 percent × $2,938,750. This simplified approach to state death taxes is used to illustrate the credit; it is not representative of the tax assessed in most states. State death taxes are discussed in more detail later in this chapter.

Exhibit 15.4 (on page 430) illustrates page 1 of the estate tax return filed by Mr. Burton's estate.

### Estate Tax Filing Requirements

Only estates with potential tax liability are required to file an estate tax return. Specifically, Form 706 must be filed if the *gross estate* plus *post-1976 cumulative taxable gifts* exceed the exemption equivalent amount shown in Table 15.4 for the year of death ($1.5 million in 2004). Form 706 is due nine months after the date of death,[54] with an extension possible at the request of the estate executor.[55]

## GENERATION-SKIPPING TRANSFER TAX

**Objective 6**
Discuss the rationale behind the generation-skipping transfer tax and the importance of the exemption.

The **generation-skipping transfer tax (GSTT)** is assessed on transfers by gift or bequest that skip a generation (e.g., grandparent to grandchild). The intent of this tax is to prevent the avoidance of estate and gift tax liability due on each generational transfer. The tax is assessed at the maximum transfer tax rate. Two important exemptions limit the application of the GSTT: (1) the annual gift exclusion of $11,000 per recipient reduces the amount subject to the GSTT and (2) every transferor is entitled to an exemption equal to the estate tax exemption equivalent amounts shown in Table 15.4. For years prior to 2002, the GSTT exemption amount is $1,060,000. The GSTT is repealed for 2010, but will be reinstated in 2011 under the sunset provisions. The GSTT is an area in which tax planning seeks to avoid the tax by appropriate structuring of transfers to maximize the use of the exemption and the annual exclusion.

## STATE DEATH TAXES

All 50 states in the United States impose some form of death tax. The three primary forms are (1) inheritance taxes, (2) estate taxes, and (3) pick-up taxes. An **inheritance tax** is levied on the recipient of property bequests based on the property's value and the relationship between the decedent and the beneficiary. In many states, exemptions from inheritance tax or lower rates apply on gifts to immediate family members. Inheritance tax rates vary tremendously from state to state. For example, the marginal rates on nonrelative bequests in South Dakota range from 6 to 30 percent and tax rates on bequests to surviving children

[54] Section 6075(a).
[55] Section 6081.

**EXHIBIT 15.4**
Estate Tax Return

Form **706**
(Rev. August 2003)

Department of the Treasury
Internal Revenue Service

### United States Estate (and Generation-Skipping Transfer) Tax Return

Estate of a citizen or resident of the United States (see separate instructions).
To be filed for decedents dying after December 31, 2002, and before January 1, 2004.
For Paperwork Reduction Act Notice, see the separate instructions.

OMB No. 1545-0015

| | | |
|---|---|---|
| **1a** Decedent's first name and middle initial (and maiden name, if any) *AL* | **1b** Decedent's last name *BURTON* | **2** Decedent's Social Security No. *123:45:6789* |
| **3a** Legal residence (domicile) at time of death (county, state, and ZIP code, or foreign country) *ADAMS CTY/NE  68900* | **3b** Year domicile established *1961*  **4** Date of birth *4/17/1938* | **5** Date of death *3/13/04* |
| **6a** Name of executor (see page 3 of the instructions) *ZELDA BURTON* | **6b** Executor's address (number and street including apartment or suite no. or rural route; city, town, or post office; state; and ZIP code) *999 FREEDOM WAY  MAYFIELD, NE  68900* | |
| **6c** Executor's social security number (see page 3 of the instructions) *987:65:4321* | | |
| **7a** Name and location of court where will was probated or estate administered *ADAMS COUNTY COURT, HASTINGS, NE* | | **7b** Case number *04-212* |

**8** If decedent died testate, check here ▶ ☐ and attach a certified copy of the will. **9** If Form 4768 is attached, check here ▶ ☐

**10** If Schedule R-1 is attached, check here ▶ ☐

*Part 1.—Decedent and Executor*

| | | |
|---|---|---|
| **1** Total gross estate less exclusion (from Part 5, Recapitulation, page 3, item 12) | **1** | 3,913,750 |
| **2** Total allowable deductions (from Part 5, Recapitulation, page 3, item 23) | **2** | 975,000 |
| **3** Taxable estate (subtract line 2 from line 1) | **3** | 2,938,750 |
| **4** Adjusted taxable gifts (total taxable gifts (within the meaning of section 2503) made by the decedent after December 31, 1976, other than gifts that are includible in decedent's gross estate (section 2001(b))) | **4** | 1,305,000 |
| **5** Add lines 3 and 4 | **5** | 4,243,750 |
| **6** Tentative tax on the amount on line 5 from Table A on page 4 of the instructions | **6** | 1,857,800 |
| **7** Total gift tax payable with respect to gifts made by the decedent after December 31, 1976. Include gift taxes by the decedent's spouse for such spouse's share of split gifts (section 2513) only if the decedent was the donor of these gifts and they are includible in the decedent's gross estate (see instructions) | **7** | 180,750 |
| **8** Gross estate tax (subtract line 7 from line 6) | **8** | 1,677,050 |
| **9** Maximum unified credit (applicable credit amount) against estate tax **9** 555,800 | | |
| **10** Adjustment to unified credit (applicable credit amount). (This adjustment may not exceed $6,000. See page 5 of the instructions.) **10** 0 | | |
| **11** Allowable unified credit (applicable credit amount) (subtract line 10 from line 9) | **11** | 555,800 |
| **12** Subtract line 11 from line 8 (but do not enter less than zero) | **12** | 1,121,250 |
| **13** Credit for state death taxes (cannot exceed line 12). **Attach credit evidence** (see instructions). Figure the credit by using the amount on line 3 less $60,000. See Table B in the instructions. Enter the amount here from Table B ▶ .................. x .50 ▶ | **13** | 58,775 |
| **14** Subtract line 13 from line 12 | **14** | 1,062,475 |
| **15** Credit for Federal gift taxes on pre-1977 gifts (section 2012) (attach computation) **15** 0 | | |
| **16** Credit for foreign death taxes (from Schedule(s) P). (Attach Form(s) 706-CE.) **16** 0 | | |
| **17** Credit for tax on prior transfers (from Schedule Q) **17** 0 | | |
| **18** Total (add lines 15, 16, and 17) | **18** | 0 |
| **19** Net estate tax (subtract line 18 from line 14) | **19** | 1,062,475 |
| **20** Generation-skipping transfer taxes (from Schedule R, Part 2, line 10) | **20** | 0 |
| **21** Total transfer taxes (add lines 19 and 20) | **21** | 1,062,475 |
| **22** Prior payments. Explain in an attached statement **22** 0 | | |
| **23** United States Treasury bonds redeemed in payment of estate tax **23** 0 | | |
| **24** Total (add lines 22 and 23) | **24** | 0 |
| **25** Balance due (or overpayment) (subtract line 24 from line 21) | **25** | 1,062,475 |

*Part 2.—Tax Computation*

Under penalties of perjury, I declare that I have examined this return, including accompanying schedules and statements, and to the best of my knowledge and belief, it is true, correct, and complete. Declaration of preparer other than the executor is based on all information of which preparer has any knowledge.

Signature(s) of executor(s)                                         Date

Signature of preparer other than executor        Address (and ZIP code)        Date

Cat. No. 20548R

### Tax Talk

As a result of the reduction and scheduled repeal of the federal estate tax, states with pick-up taxes tied to the federal credit for state death taxes stand to lose revenue. To combat this loss, 18 states and the District of Columbia have passed new legislation separating their estate tax from the federal system. The latest estate planning advice from some estate tax planners? Move to another state!

range from 0 to 7.5 percent. In Pennsylvania, lineal descendents are taxed at 6 percent and nonrelatives at 15 percent.

The estate, not the heirs, pays state estate taxes. In most states, a progressive rate system applies that does not vary based on the relationship between the decedent and the beneficiaries. Estate tax rates also vary from state to state. For example, estate tax rates range in Ohio from 2 to 7 percent and in New York from 2 to 21 percent.

All 50 states impose a **pick-up tax,** often in addition to an inheritance or estate tax.[56] The pick-up tax equals any excess of the allowable federal credit for state death taxes over any inheritance or estate tax already imposed by the state. As a result, the state "picks up" tax revenue that would otherwise be paid to the federal government.

| | |
|---|---|
| *State Pick-Up Tax* | Mr. Melvin's heirs and estate paid state inheritance and estate taxes totaling $200,000. If the maximum federal credit for state death taxes allowed to his estate is $240,000, the state of his residence assesses a pick-up tax of $40,000. If the maximum federal credit allowed is $180,000, no pick-up tax is owed, and Mr. Melvin's estate is allowed a credit of only $180,000. |

# INTERACTIONS BETWEEN THE INCOME TAX AND TRANSFER TAX SYSTEMS

## Charitable Contributions

**Objective 7**
Identify important interactions between the income and transfer tax systems.

As previously discussed, transfers by gift or bequest to qualified charitable organizations are not subject to transfer taxation. To understand the rationale for such exemption, recall that the goal of the transfer tax system is to redistribute wealth to the public sector. If individuals voluntarily undertake wealth redistribution through charitable giving, transfer taxation is unnecessary. Incentives for charitable giving are also provided through the income tax system. Two important income tax rules encourage private charitable support: (1) taxpayers are allowed a deduction for charitable contributions and (2) contributions of capital gain property are deductible at FMV, with any related appreciation exempt from income tax.

| | |
|---|---|
| *Tax Incentives for Charitable Giving* | Mr. Norman wishes to contribute to the American Cancer Society. He owns stock with a tax basis of $10,000 and a market value of $15,000. If he sells the stock and contributes the proceeds to charity, he recognizes a taxable gain of $5,000 and takes a charitable contribution deduction of $15,000. Overall, his taxable income decreases by $10,000. The contribution is exempt from transfer taxation. If instead he contributes the stock to charity, he is not required to report any gain, and (assuming that the stock has been held at least one year) takes a charitable contribution deduction of $15,000, decreasing his taxable income by $15,000. Again, the contribution is exempt from transfer taxation. |

## Tax Basis Issues

The transfer of property via a gift or bequest has important income tax consequences to the property's recipient. First, if the property produces income, the recipient is taxed on that income beginning on the date of the transfer. Second, the recipient's initial tax basis in the asset must be calculated using special rules.

EGTRRA fundamentally changes the calculation of tax basis for inherited property following repeal of the estate tax. This section first discusses the calculation of tax basis for property inherited in tax years prior to 2010 and subsequent to the reinstatement of the estate tax in 2011. Next, we describe the calculation of tax basis for gifted property. Finally, we discuss the special rules applicable to tax basis of property inherited from decedents dying in 2010.

---

[56] The pick-up tax is also often referred to as a *soak-up tax.*

If property is inherited upon the death of the transferor (in any year other than 2010), the recipient's tax basis equals the FMV of the property included in the transferor's gross estate. Thus, if the property is valued on the date of the decedent's death, that value becomes the recipient's tax basis. If the estate elected the alternate valuation date, the value on that date becomes the recipient's tax basis.[57]

*Tax Basis of Inherited Property*

Two assets in Mr. DeLong's estate have the following valuations.

|  | Date-of-Death Value | Alternate Valuation Date Value |
|---|---|---|
| Asset 1 | $800,000 | $1,000,000 |
| Asset 2 | 500,000 | 350,000 |

Mr. DeLong willed Asset 1 to his daughter and Asset 2 to his son. If Mr. Delong's executor elects the alternate valuation date, his daughter will have an initial tax basis of $1 million in Asset 1 and his son will have an initial tax basis of $350,000 in Asset 2. If Mr. DeLong's executor does not elect the alternate valuation date, his daughter will have an initial tax basis of $800,000 in Asset 1 and his son will have an initial tax basis of $500,000 in Asset 2.

Given the integrated nature of the transfer tax system, we might expect the tax basis of gifted property to be the same as the tax basis of inherited property. Unfortunately, that is not so. The tax basis of property acquired by gift is complicated and depends on whether the property's value is greater or less than the donor's tax basis on the date of the gift. If the FMV of the asset exceeds the donor's tax basis on the date of the gift, a carryover basis rule applies. The recipient's tax basis in the gifted property equals the donor's tax basis.[58] If the asset's FMV is less than the donor's tax basis on the date of gift, a split basis rule applies. The recipient's tax basis in this case depends on whether he or she ultimately sells the property at a gain or at a loss. The tax basis for determining a gain on the disposition is equal to the donor's tax basis on the date of the gift. The tax basis for determining a loss on the disposition is the (lower) FMV of the asset on the date of the gift. The effect of these basis rules is to capture any unrealized gains existing when property is gifted but to disallow any unrealized losses.

*Tax Basis of Gifted Property*

Mrs. Florenz gave stock to her son, Leon Florenz, in 2000. On the date of the gift, her tax basis in the stock was $5,000.

**Alternative 1**
Suppose that the market value of the stock on the date of gift was $12,000. If Mr. Florenz sells the stock in 2003 for $15,000, he recognizes a $10,000 long-term capital gain. If he sells the stock for $3,000, he recognizes a $2,000 long-term capital loss.

[57] Note from our prior discussion that the alternate valuation date can be elected only if the total value of all estate assets (and tax liability) is lower on that date. Although total value might be lower, the value of some individual estate assets might actually be higher on the alternate valuation date than on the date of death.

[58] Tax basis of appreciated property received by gift could also be increased by a portion of any gift tax paid. The increase equals the proportion of the gift tax attributable to the unrealized appreciation of the property. See Section 1015(d)(2).

**Alternative 2**

Now suppose that the market value of the stock on the date of gift was $4,000. If Mr. Florenz sells the stock in 2003 for $3,000, he recognizes only a $1,000 long-term capital loss since the tax basis for determining loss in this case is the FMV on the date of the gift (because that value is less than the donor's tax basis).

**Alternative 3**

Now suppose that the FMV of the stock on the date of gift was $2,000. If Mr. Florenz sells the stock in 2003 for $3,000, he recognizes neither a gain nor a loss. To understand this result, recall that the tax basis for determining gain is Mrs. Florenz's tax basis of $5,000. In this case, he does not have a gain since he sold the stock for less than $5,000. However, the tax basis for determining loss is $2,000 (value on the date of the gift, since it is lower than his mother's tax basis). Now Mr. Florenz has no loss since he sold the stock for more than $2,000!

When the estate tax is repealed in 2010, the tax basis of inherited property is determined under a modified carryover basis system. With two important exceptions discussed in the next paragraphs, the tax basis determined under this system is the same as the tax basis of property acquired by gift. Thus, the recipient's initial tax basis is the lesser of the decedent's tax basis or the FMV of the property on the date of the decedent's death.

EGTRRA allows two basis increases for property included in the estate of individuals dying in 2010.[59] The **aggregate basis increase** provides an increase in basis of up to $1,300,000, allocated to estate property as determined by the executor. The increase allocated to any piece of property cannot exceed the excess of the property's FMV over the decedent's tax basis.

*Aggregate Basis Increase for 2010 Decedent*

Mrs. Lomax dies in 2010. Her estate includes four assets with the following basis and FMV information:

| Asset | Mrs. Lomax's Tax Basis | FMV on Date of Death |
|---|---|---|
| Asset 1 | $2,000,000 | $1,900,000 |
| Asset 2 | 1,000,000 | 1,200,000 |
| Asset 3 | 500,000 | 3,000,000 |
| Asset 4 | 400,000 | 500,000 |
| Total | $3,900,000 | $6,600,000 |

Because Asset 1 has a FMV less than the decedent's tax basis, none of the aggregate basis adjustment can be allocated to this asset. The maximum aggregate basis adjustment allocable to the remaining assets is as follows: Asset 2, $200,000 ($1,200,000 − $1,000,000); Asset 3, $2,500,000 ($3,000,000 − $500,000); and Asset 4, $100,000 ($500,000 − $400,000). Because the sum of these maximum adjustments exceeds $1,300,000, the executor must decide how much adjustment to allocate to each asset.

The **spousal basis increase** permits a second basis adjustment for property transferred to the decedent's surviving spouse. The maximum amount of this basis increase is $3 million,

---

[59] Certain types of property are excluded from these basis adjustments. See new Section 1022(c) and (d) for details of these exclusions.

allocated to estate property as determined by the executor. The increase allocated to any piece of property cannot exceed the excess of the property's FMV over the decedent's tax basis after adjustment for the aggregate basis increase.

| *Spousal Basis Increase for 2010 Decedent* | Refer to the example involving Mrs. Lomax. Suppose that the estate executor elects to allocate all of the aggregate basis increase of $1,300,000 to Asset 3. As a result, the new tax basis of the estate property prior to the spousal basis increase is as follows: Asset 1, $1,900,000; Asset 2, $1,000,000; Asset 3, $1,800,000 ($500,000 carryover basis + $1,300,000 aggregate basis increase); and Asset 4, $400,000. If Mrs. Lomax's will leaves all property to her surviving spouse, the maximum spousal basis increase allocable to these assets is as follows: Asset 1, zero (since FMV < decedent's tax basis); Asset 2, $200,000 ($1,200,000 FMV − $1,000,000 decedent's tax basis); Asset 3, $1,200,000 ($3,000,000 FMV − $1,800,000 tax basis after aggregate basis increase); and Asset 4, $100,000 ($500,000 FMV − $400,000 decedent's tax basis). In total, the spousal basis increase results in $1,500,000 of additional tax basis to Mr. Lomax. |
|---|---|

The tax basis rules described here have important implications when selecting assets to be given away during the donor's lifetime versus assets to be held until the donor's death. As a general rule, business and investment assets that have declined in value should not be gifted or held until death since the unrealized loss inherent in these assets will be lost when the recipient's tax basis is set at their FMV. These assets should be sold prior to death if possible to recognize the tax loss and maximize possible deductions.[60] When assets have appreciated in value, the step up to FMV allowed at death (for years other than 2010), without subjecting the appreciation to income taxation by either the decedent or the heir, creates an incentive to hold appreciated assets until death. However, as the length of time between a proposed transfer by gift and expected transfer at death increases, the incentive to gift property that might increase in value substantially prior to death exists. We address strategies for gifting assets in more detail in Chapter 17.

## Conclusion

Although recent calls for repeal of the transfer tax system have raised its political profile, in reality only a small percentage of Americans are at risk to pay gift or estate taxes. A thorough understanding of the application of these taxes to transfers by gift or bequest is necessary before exploring effective planning strategies for preserving family wealth. This chapter identified the transactions subject to gift tax, the assets subject to estate tax, and the manner in which those taxes are assessed. It also discussed important interactions between the transfer tax system and the income tax system that could impact planning. Chapter 16 discusses the use of trusts for family planning and the taxation of trusts and estates for income tax purposes. Chapter 17 applies the knowledge gained in this chapter and Chapter 16 to develop tax planning strategies for preserving family wealth in the face of both income and transfer taxation.

[60] Realized losses on personal assets are not deductible for income tax purposes.

# Key Terms

aggregate basis
increase *433*

alternate valuation
date *421*

annual gift tax
exclusion *415*

charitable deduction *417*

community property *423*

cumulative taxable
gifts *413*

deemed paid gift tax
credit *426*

Economic Growth and Tax
Relief Reconciliation Act
of 2001 (EGTRRA) *410*

estate *421*

exemption equivalent
amount *412*

future interest *416*

generation-skipping transfer
tax (GSTT) *429*

gift-splitting election *415*

gross estate *422*

income interest *414*

incomplete transfer *414*

inheritance tax *429*

joint tenancy *423*

marital deduction *416*

pick-up tax *431*

present interest *416*

probate estate *422*

remainder interest *414*

retained life estate *424*

spousal basis
increase *433*

taxable estate *424*

taxable gift *417*

tenancy by the
entirety *423*

tenancy in common *423*

unified credit *412*

wealth redistribution *410*

# Questions and Problems for Discussion

1. A transfer is considered a gift only if it is "complete." Why is this restriction necessary? What difficulties would arise in assessing transfer taxes if incomplete transfers were subject to gift tax?

2. If an interest in property is split between income and remainder interests and both are given away, is it necessary to value both interests separately? Explain your answer.

3. Given the general attitude of the transfer tax system toward married couples, why is the exclusion of transfers pursuant to divorce appropriate or equitable?

4. What rationale justifies the annual exclusion from gift tax?

5. If a taxpayer gives or bequeaths items for which a ready market price does not exist (such as personal assets or unique items like artwork), what methods or types of information can be used to determine the FMV?

6. How does the gradual increase of the unified credit between 1998 and 2002 affect the timing of gift transfers? Which tax planning maxim discussed in Chapter 1 applies to this situation?

7. Comment on the following assertion: "Without gift tax requirements, no estate tax would ever need to be paid."

8. What rationale justifies the rule that 50 percent of property owned jointly with the decedent's spouse is included in the gross estate regardless of the contribution toward its purchase?

9. What rationale justifies the deductions allowed for funeral and estate administrative expenses, casualty and theft losses, and liabilities in computing the taxable estate?

10. Without the generation-skipping transfer tax, what type of tax planning would maximize the long-term preservation of family wealth?

11. Why is it equitable to limit the credit for taxes on prior gifts, allowed in computing the estate tax, to the *lesser* of taxes paid or the amount deemed paid?

# Application Problems

1. During the current year, Mrs. Wilhemina gives property with a tax basis of $75,000 and a market value of $100,000 to her daughter. She also gives cash of $100,000 to her son and of $15,000 to each of her four grandchildren.
   a. Calculate Mrs. Wilhemina's current taxable gifts.
   b. If Mrs. Wilhemina and her husband elect gift-splitting, calculate her current taxable gifts.

2. Mr. Travis owns rental real estate that generates sizable monthly cash flow. His mother is retired and living on a fixed income. To assist her to meet expenses, Mr. Travis gives her an income interest in his rental property for her lifetime. He retains the remainder interest so that on her death, all rights to the property revert back to him. Based on her life expectancy and IRS-prescribed valuation methods, the gift of the income interest has a value of $50,000.

   a. Is the gift of the income interest to Mr. Travis's mother considered complete for gift tax purposes?

   b. Is the gift to Mr. Travis's mother a gift of a present interest or a future interest?

   c. Calculate Mr. Travis's taxable gift as a result of this transaction.

3. In 2003, Mrs. Juhle made her first gratuitous transfers, giving cash of $100,000 to her sister and property worth $20,000 to Villanova University. In 2004, she gives $40,000 to her brother and pays tuition to four universities on behalf of her nieces and nephews. Calculate Mrs. Juhle's cumulative taxable gifts to be reported on her 2004 gift tax return.

4. Referring to application problem 3, calculate Mrs. Juhle's 2004 gift tax prior to utilization of the unified credit.

5. Mr. Adams makes taxable gifts in 2001 totaling $400,000. If his cumulative taxable gifts for years prior to 2001 totaled $500,000, calculate his 2001 gift tax payable.

6. Referring to application problem 5, if Mr. Adams makes taxable gifts of $50,000 in 2002, calculate his 2002 gift tax payable.

7. For each of the following independent situations, indicate whether a gift tax return, Form 709, must be filed. In each case, assume that the gifts mentioned are the only ones the donor makes in the current year.

   a. Mr. Frank makes gifts of $3,000 to each of his four children and 10 grandchildren.

   b. Mr. and Mrs. Carl make gifts totaling $15,000 to each of their three children. To avoid the gift tax, they wish to make the gift-splitting election.

   c. Mr. Grant makes a gift of an income interest in property to his daughter for her lifetime and of the remainder interest to his grandson. The value of the income interest is $10,000 and of the remainder interest is $5,000.

   d. Mrs. Madeline gifts property worth $1 million to her new husband.

   e. Mr. Barry gives all of his shares of Microsoft Corporation stock valued at $40,000 to the United Way.

8. Mr. and Mrs. Jones made the following gratuitous transfers during 2003:
   - Cash of $200,000 to their son.
   - Land with a FMV of $200,000 (adjusted tax basis of $80,000) to their daughter.
   - College tuition of $20,000 for their grandson, paid directly to Villanova University, and rent of $10,000 on his apartment paid directly to the landlord.
   - Securities with an FMV of $30,000 (adjusted basis of $15,000) to United Way.
   - Medical expenses of $5,000 for their maid paid directly to the local hospital.

   a. If Mr. and Mrs. Jones elect gift-splitting and have not made any taxable gifts in previous years, calculate Mr. Jones's 2003 taxable gifts and any gift tax liability.

   b. How would your answer to part *(a)* change if Mr. Jones had previously made taxable gifts totaling $500,000?

9. Refer to the facts in application problem 8, part *(b)*. In 2004, Mr. Jones died. When he died, he owned the following assets:
   - Land with an FMV of $1,000,000.
   - Stock investments with an FMV of $500,000.

½

- House with an FMV of $400,000 owned jointly with Mrs. Jones as joint tenants with <u>right of survivorship</u>. The house was purchased for $100,000, with Mr. Jones providing 100 percent of the consideration.
- Life insurance policy with a death benefit of $2,000,000, naming the couple's children as equal beneficiaries.

Mr. Jones's will bequeathed 50 percent of his stock portfolio to his only brother, the other 50 percent of the portfolio and <u>the house to Mrs. Jones, and</u> residual assets (after the payment of estate taxes and expenses) to his children equally. The estate incurred $10,000 of funeral costs. His state of residency assessed an inheritance tax at a flat rate of 3 percent of the federal taxable estate.

  Calculate Mr. Jones's gross estate, taxable estate, precredit estate tax, estate tax payable, and state inheritance tax payable.

 10. At the time of Ms. Naomi's death on January 5, 2004, her estate included four assets with date-of-death and alternate-valuation-date values as follows.

| Asset | Value | |
|---|---|---|
| | *January 5, 2004* | *July 5, 2004* |
| Various household items | $ 50,000 | $ 50,000 |
| Personal residence | 500,000 | 550,000 |
| Other real estate | 600,000 | 620,000 |
| Stocks and bonds | 800,000 | 700,000 |

  a. Should the executor of Mrs. Naomi's estate elect to use the alternate valuation date? If so, at what value will her assets be included in her gross estate?
  b. Would your answer to part *(a)* change if the executor had sold all of the stocks and bonds on March 1, 2004, for $780,000? What total value would apply to the alternate valuation date election in this case?

11. In 1990, Ms. Lin, Mr. Han, and Mr. Kutz each contributed $50,000 toward the purchase of a piece of real estate owned as joint tenants. When Ms. Lin dies in 2004, the property is valued at $360,000. How much is included in her gross estate with respect to this property?

12. In 1995, Mr. Avram gave a remainder interest in property to his daughter and retained the income interest for his life. At the time of the gift, the property's total value was $500,000, with $100,000 assigned to the income interest and $400,000 assigned to the gifted remainder interest. In 2004, he dies. At the time of his death, the property is valued at $650,000.
  a. In 1995, what was the impact of this transaction on Mr. Avram's taxable gifts?
  b. In 2004, what is included in Mr. Avram's gross estate with respect to this property?

13. Mrs. Verona died on October 1, 2004. In the years preceding her death, she made several taxable gifts. For each of the following, indicate the value included in her gross estate:
  a. In 1990, Mrs. Verona transferred a remainder interest in property and retained the income interest (retained life estate). In 2003, she gifted the income interest to her son. At the time of the second gift, the total value of the property was $1 million and the income interest was worth $300,000. She paid a gift tax of $97,500 in 2003 on the gift of the income interest.
  b. On December 1, 2001, Mrs. Verona gave land valued at $200,000 to her daughter. Because of the unified credit, she paid no gift tax on this gift.

c. In 2002, Mrs. Verona made taxable gifts of cash totaling $100,000 and paid a gift tax of $27,750 on these gifts.

14. When Mr. Donelle died, his will left real estate valued at $1,500,000 to his wife. The property was encumbered by a mortgage with a balance of $1,000,000.

   a. Calculate the marital deduction allowed to Mr. Donelle's estate.

   b. By what amount does Mr. Donelle's taxable estate increase as a result of this property? Explain briefly.

15. At Mr. Peter's death, he owned a 50 percent interest in property with a total value of $1 million subject to a mortgage of $750,000. His other assets totaled $2,000,000 on the date of his death. Mr. Peter bequeathed $100,000 to charity, $500,000 to his wife, and the remainder of his estate to his children. The estate incurred $15,000 of funeral costs and $20,000 of administrative costs.

   a. Calculate Mr. Peter's gross estate.

   b. Calculate Mr. Peter's taxable estate.

16. For each of the following situations, indicate whether an estate tax return, Form 706, must be filed.

   a. Mr. Norton's gross estate totaled $1 million, his taxable estate totaled $500,000, and he made no taxable gifts during his lifetime.

   b. Mr. Quentin's gross estate totaled $500,000 on his death in 2001. He made post-1976 cumulative taxable gifts totaling $200,000.

   c. Refer to the information in part *(b)* and assume that Mr. Quentin dies in 2004.

17. Mr. Antonio sells land for $100,000, which he had received as a gift from his mother, Maria Antonio.

   a. If Mrs. Antonio's tax basis in the land was $50,000 and its market value on the date of the gift was $80,000, how much gain must her son recognize?

   b. How would your answer to part *(a)* change if the value of the land on the date of the gift was $40,000?

   c. How would your answer to part *(a)* change if Mrs. Antonio's tax basis in the land was $120,000 and its value on the date of gift was $110,000?

   d. How would your answer to part *(a)* change if Mrs. Antonio's tax basis in the land was $120,000 and its value on the date of gift was $80,000?

   e. How would yours answers to parts *(a)* through *(d)* change if Mr. Antonio received the land by bequest on his mother's death?

18. Ms. Camila, a single individual, made the following transfers during 2004:
   - To her niece, $100,000 cash.
   - To her nephew, stock with an FMV of $50,000 (adjusted tax basis $10,000).
   - To her longtime friend Mr. Charles, $10,000 cash.
   - To Villanova University, $20,000 tuition paid on behalf of another niece

   Ms. Camila had made cumulative taxable gifts in prior years totaling $580,000. However, because of the unified credit, she has never paid a gift tax. Calculate her current taxable gifts and gift tax liability.

19. Mr. Jordan's estate and heirs paid state inheritance and estate taxes of $160,000.

   a. If Mr. Jordan's estate is allowed a federal credit for state death taxes of $200,000, how much pick-up tax will his state of residence assess on his estate?

   b. How would your answer to part *(a)* change if the maximum allowable federal credit is $150,000?

   c. If Mr. Jordan's estate and heirs paid only $5,000 of state inheritance and estate taxes on a taxable estate of $35,000, will his estate be allowed a federal credit for state death taxes? Will any pick-up taxes be assessed? Why or why not?

## Issue Recognition Problems

Identify the tax issue or issues suggested by the following situations, and state each issue in the form of a question.

1. Mr. Kembo purchases an insurance policy on his life, naming his children as beneficiaries. He then transfers ownership of the policy to his wife. Six years later, he dies.

2. Mr. Harold sells stock to his brother for $5,000. On the day of the sale, the stock traded on the New York Stock Exchange for $12,000. Mr. Harold's tax basis in the stock was $2,000.

3. Mr. and Mrs. Jenks divorce in 2004. Pursuant to their divorce decree, he transfers ownership of their house to her. He also gives her sole ownership of their car even though he is not required to do so under the divorce decree.

4. Mr. Kendall gifts cash of $20,000 to his son. To avoid any gift tax, Mrs. Kendall agrees to make the gift-splitting election. Since no taxable gift remains after the annual exclusion, Mr. and Mrs. Kendall believe that they do not need to file gift tax returns.

5. When Mr. Oliver died, his primary asset was stock in a publicly traded corporation of which he was CEO. In the months following his death, the stock price plummeted as the company searched for a new CEO.

6. Mr. and Mrs. Brendan were married for 30 years prior to her death in 2004. Both were highly successful entrepreneurs and accumulated substantial wealth during their marriage. The couple resided in Arizona throughout their marriage.

7. Mrs. Shen owns rental property that she wishes to give to her son. The property has a tax basis to her of $150,000 and a FMV of $120,000, and it generates net rental income of $1,000 per month.

8. Mr. and Mrs. Cindas are concerned about saving for future college expenses of their three minor children. Their parents have offered to make annual contributions to educational IRAs to be established for each child.

9. Mrs. Borden, age 75, transfers ownership of her personal residence to her son. She continues to live in the house and pays for all maintenance of the property but pays no rent to her son.

10. Mr. Raymond recently retired after working 50 years in management for a large automobile manufacturer. His pension income is sufficient for him to live comfortably, but he has few personal or investment assets other than his home. He is not concerned about estate tax liability when he dies since he believes that the value of his potential estate is less than the exemption equivalent amount.

11. Mr. Kramer dies owning real property located in seven different states.

## Research Problems

1. To reduce future estate tax liability, Mrs. Madden adopted a plan of systematic giving by which she transfers $10,000 per year to each of her children and grandchildren. She normally makes these transfers in early December. For most of December 2003, however, she was traveling abroad. She returned home on December 30, quickly wrote checks to all of her children and grandchildren, and distributed them to each recipient at their family New Year's Eve party. The recipients cashed the checks in January 2004. Are these transfers considered completed gifts in 2003?

2. Mr. Jacksmith died when the commercial jet on which he was a passenger crashed during an emergency landing. His estate sued the airline and aircraft manufacturer for wrongful death when the cause of the crash was determined to be a mechanical failure. The plaintiffs settled the lawsuit for $2 million payable to the estate for the benefit of Mr. Jacksmith's widow and children. Is the $2 million settlement included in his gross estate for purposes of the estate tax?

## Tax Planning Cases

1. Mr. Hollis, age 93, has accumulated substantial assets during his life. Among his investments are the following stocks, which he is considering giving to his grandson.

| Stock | Adjusted Basis | Fair Market Value |
|---|---|---|
| Green Corporation | $ 50,000 | $700,000 |
| Red Corporation | 70,000 | 71,000 |
| Blue Corporation | 200,000 | 50,000 |

He has been in ill health for the past five years, and his physician has predicted that he probably will not live for more than six months. Advise Mr. Hollis which stocks should be transferred as gifts, which should be transferred as bequests, and whether any stocks should be sold. Explain the rationale behind your recommendations.

2. Mr. and Mrs. Lopez are a retired couple in their 60s. They jointly own the following assets.

| Asset | Fair Market Value |
|---|---|
| Stock and bond portfolio | $800,000 |
| Personal residence | 500,000 |
| Other real estate | 300,000 |
| Other miscellaneous assets | 100,000 |

In addition, the current value of their retirement accounts is $1 million for Mr. Lopez and $500,000 for Mrs. Lopez.

a. Mr. Lopez's will bequeaths his one-half of the personal residence to Mrs. Lopez. His interest in all other assets passes to their children. He previously made taxable gifts totaling $250,000. If he were to die today, calculate his estate tax liability (ignoring state death taxes).

b. Mrs. Lopez's will provides that if Mr. Lopez predeceases her, all of her assets (including the residence) pass to their children on her death. She previously made taxable gifts totaling $100,000. Assuming that Mrs. Lopez were to die shortly after Mr. Lopez (with no change in the asset values listed), calculate her estate tax liability (ignoring state death taxes).

c. Mr. and Mrs. Lopez are shocked by the results of your calculations in parts *(a)* and *(b)*. They would like to begin transferring their assets during life to reduce any future estate tax. If they have four children and eight grandchildren, how much of their estate value could they transfer over the next 10 years using gift-splitting and annual transfers equal to the gift tax exclusion? Which assets do you recommend they use for these annual transfers?

d. Recalculate Mr. and Mrs. Lopez's estate tax liability, assuming that the transfers calculated in part *(c)* are made and that both live until 2012. Also assume no change in the values of their assets listed. How much estate tax is saved through the program of systematic giving?

# Chapter **Sixteen**

# Income Taxation of Trusts and Estates

## Learning Objectives

*After reading this chapter, you will be able to:*

1. Identify nontax reasons for establishing trusts to manage property.

2. Differentiate between revocable, nonrevocable, simple, and complex trusts; explain the importance of these distinctions.

3. Describe the application of the modified conduit approach to taxation of trust and estate earnings.

4. Calculate trust accounting income and explain the economic significance of its definition.

5. Calculate trust taxable income, distributable net income, and the trust distribution deduction.

6. Explain the tax treatment of trust and estate distributions to beneficiaries.

7. Describe the important differences in calculating estate taxable income and trust taxable income.

Trusts are an important tool often used as part of a comprehensive plan for the transfer and preservation of family wealth. A trust is generally a separate legal entity subject to income taxation, although it might have been created for transfer tax reasons. Thus, trust planning must encompass both transfer and income tax implications. This chapter focuses on the income tax consequences of trusts and estates. Like trusts, estates hold assets to facilitate eventual transfer to beneficiaries and are subject to both transfer and income taxation. We also discuss nontax considerations that could motivate the use of trusts to manage and preserve transferred assets.

Chapter 15 described the application of the estate and gift transfer taxes. With the background provided by Chapter 15 and this chapter, Chapter 17 presents planning strategies for wealth preservation aimed at minimizing the income and transfer tax costs associated with generational transfers.

# NONTAX TRUST CONSIDERATIONS

**Objective 1**
Identify nontax reasons for establishing trusts to manage property.

A trust is created when a transferor, called the **donor,** transfers property to a trust **fiduciary** or **trustee** to be managed for the benefit of one or more **beneficiaries.**[1] The trust property is referred to as trust **corpus** or **principal.** The trust can be created during the donor's lifetime (an *inter vivos* **trust**) or upon the donor's death as directed in the donor's will (a **testamentary trust**). The terms of the trust are dictated by the trust document written by the donor to designate the trustee and beneficiaries. The trust document describes the manner in which the donor wishes the property to be managed, how and when trust property or income will be distributed to the beneficiaries, and when the trust will terminate.

The trustee can be an individual or a corporation, such as a bank. Most large banks have professional trust departments that manage trust property and assess an annual fee for their services. One advantage of using a corporate trustee is expertise in the investment and management of trust property. In addition, designation of a corporate trustee avoids issues that could arise when a named individual trustee dies or becomes unable to fulfill his or her fiduciary duties. However, a noncorporate trustee with a personal interest in the welfare of the beneficiaries might devote more time and energy to investing and managing trust property.

Why use a trust to hold property rather than transferring that property directly to the individuals designated as trust beneficiaries? In many cases, trusts are formed to hold property whose income will support individuals not capable of managing the property directly, such as minor children or aging relatives. For example, a single parent might provide in his or her will for the formation of a testamentary trust holding assets whose income will support minor children following his or her death. This trust might terminate when the children reach adulthood with remaining trust assets distributed into the children's direct control at that time.

Trusts are also useful when the income from property is to be used to support specified individuals (income interest) while the property's ultimate ownership will pass to other individuals (remainder interest). The property is transferred into trust, and the trust document defines how and when income is to be paid to the income beneficiaries and the circumstances under which the trust will terminate and the property pass to the remainder beneficiaries.

Other trusts are created specifically for estate tax planning purposes (credit shelter or bypass trusts, for example), to avoid estate probate costs (living trusts), or to shield the assets of well-known individuals from public scrutiny (blind trusts). Exhibit 16.1 summarizes some common trusts and their intended usage. Many of these trusts are used for family wealth planning purposes and are discussed in more detail in Chapter 17.

The preceding examples are relatively straightforward, but a trust's terms can be as complex as needed to accomplish the donor's objectives for the property and the beneficiaries. The trust document is critical to successful implementation of the donor's wishes with regard to the trust property. It should be drafted by an attorney with transfer tax experience and familiarity with the relevant laws of the donor's state of residence. In defining the terms of the trust, the donor must carefully consider possible future events (such as the death of a trust beneficiary) and provide for all conceivable contingencies affecting the property, the trustee, and the beneficiaries.

**Objective 2**
Differentiate between revocable, nonrevocable, simple, and complex trusts; explain the importance of these distinctions.

In most cases, once the trust document has been signed and the property transferred, the donor gives up all future control over the trust, considered an **irrevocable trust.** In other cases, the donor retains the right to revoke the transfer of property to the trust and regain control and title. The establishment of such a **revocable trust** is not considered a complete

---

[1] Regulation 301.7701-4(a).

| Type of Trust | Common Objectives |
|---|---|
| Blind trust | Holds and manages assets of the grantor, typically while the grantor holds political office or some other sensitive position |
| Bypass (credit shelter) trust | Used in estate planning, to ensure maximum use of the unified credit (see Chapter 17) |
| Crummey trust | Used in gift tax planning, to ensure that a gift in trust qualifies for the annual exclusion (see Chapter 17) |
| Life insurance trust | Used in estate planning, to ensure that life insurance proceeds are not subject to estate tax (see Chapter 17) |
| Living (revocable) trust | Manages assets of the grantor and beneficiary during life and to reduce probate costs after death (see Chapter 17) |
| Retirement trust | Manages assets contributed to a qualified retirement plan |

**EXHIBIT 16.1**
**Examples of Common Trusts**

transfer for gift and estate tax purposes (see Chapter 15) and is similarly ignored for income tax purposes.[2]

In some circumstances, a trust arrangement can be irrevocable while continuing to provide the grantor with substantial benefits from the trust property or control over its disposition. Such a trust is labeled a **grantor trust,** which exists if the grantor retains (1) beneficial enjoyment of the trust principal or (2) the power to dispose of trust income without the approval or consent of an adverse party.[3] A grantor trust is also ignored for tax purposes, and any income from trust property is taxed to the grantor. However, the grantor is allowed to retain a number of powers without causing trust income to be taxed to the grantor, including the following.[4]

- The power to allocate trust income or principal among charitable beneficiaries.
- The power to invade principal on behalf of a designated beneficiary.
- The power to withhold income from a minor or disabled beneficiary.
- The power to allocate receipts and disbursements between income and principal.
- The power to apply trust income toward support of the grantor's dependents. However, to the extent trust income is actually used for this purpose, the grantor is taxed on the income.

Irrevocable trusts are also classified as either simple or complex. For any given year, a **simple trust** is required to distribute all of its accounting income to its beneficiaries and makes no charitable contributions or distributions of underlying trust property. A **complex trust** is any trust not qualifying as a simple trust.[5] The trust classification is made each year. Thus, any trust is considered complex in its final year when trust property is distributed and the trust terminates. The distinction between a simple and a complex trust is important in determining trust taxable income and the trust distribution deduction, as discussed later.

[2] Section 676.
[3] Section 672(a) and (b), and Section 674. An adverse party is an individual whose economic interests are not necessarily aligned with those of the grantor.
[4] Sections 674(b) and 677(b).
[5] Regulation 1.651(a)-1.

The next section of this chapter describes the basic concepts surrounding the income taxation of trusts and estates. The general approach to taxing these two entities is the same, although some important differences exist. The focus is first on taxation of trusts and then on additional issues unique to estates. The chapter also describes the taxation of distributed fiduciary income to the recipient beneficiaries.

# BASIC CONCEPTS OF FIDUCIARY INCOME TAXATION

**Objective 3**
Describe the application of the modified conduit approach to taxation of trust and estate earnings.

The taxation of fiduciary entities (trusts and estates) follows a modified conduit entity approach. Recall from Chapter 7 that partnerships and S corporations are considered conduit entities in the sense that their partners or shareholders pay tax on the income the entity earns. In fiduciary taxation, the conduit approach is modified to tax trust and estate beneficiaries on income distributed to them while taxing the entity on any income retained by the trust or estate. Fiduciary entities are allowed a deduction for amounts distributed and taxed to their beneficiaries. As a result of this deduction, the income of fiduciary entities is not subject to the double taxation of the corporate income tax system. Since trusts and estates are temporary entities intended merely to hold property for the benefit of individuals, the approach to taxing these entities treats them almost as an extension of the individual taxpayers whom they benefit rather than as truly separate taxpayers.

# INCOME TAXATION OF TRUSTS

Exhibit 16.2 presents six steps for determining trust taxable income and the amount of any trust distributions taxable to the beneficiaries. As noted later in this chapter, these same steps are used to determine the income tax consequences for an estate.

## Conceptual Overview

Before describing each step in Exhibit 16.2 in detail, let's consider the intuition behind trust taxation and the need for each element of the calculation. As previously mentioned, a *simple trust* is required to distribute all of its accounting income to its beneficiaries annually. Thus, the calculation in step 1 defines the economic rights of simple trust beneficiaries to receive distributions from the trust. Given the modified conduit approach to fiduciary taxation, trust accounting income is also important in determining the amount of trust income taxed to the beneficiaries and the amount of the trust's distribution deduction.

Trust taxable income before the distribution deduction is computed in step 2 using the same basic principles of taxation that apply to individual taxpayers. Gross income includes the same income items that are earned by and taxable to individuals; the trust is entitled to similar deductions and subject to similar limitations on allowable deductions.

The trust **distribution deduction** (step 4) captures the modified conduit approach to fiduciary taxation. The distribution deduction reduces the trust's tax base by an amount

**EXHIBIT 16.2**
**Calculation of Trust Taxable Income and Tax Liability**

**Step 1** Calculate trust accounting income.
**Step 2** Calculate trust taxable income before the distribution deduction.
**Step 3** Compute distributable net income (DNI) and the distribution deduction.
**Step 4** Subtract the distribution deduction from the amount in step 2 to determine trust taxable income.
**Step 5** Calculate trust tax liability.
**Step 6** Allocate DNI and the distribution deduction to the beneficiaries to determine the amount and character of income taxed to each beneficiary.

**TABLE 16.1**
**UPIA Allocations between Accounting Income and Principal**

| Allocated to Accounting Income | Allocated to Principal |
|---|---|
| • Interest, dividends, rents, and royalties | • Capital gains and losses on investment assets |
| • Operating income from trust assets | • Casualty gains and losses and related insurance recoveries |
| • Operating expenses and depreciation related to trust assets | • Extraordinary repairs and capital improvements |
| • Taxes levied on accounting income | • Taxes levied on items allocated to principal |

equal to the trust income that will be taxed to the beneficiaries. In addition to sharing in current income, complex trust beneficiaries might also receive distributions of trust property or distributions from prior year earnings taxed to and accumulated by the trust. Distributions from these sources should not be taxed to the beneficiaries to the extent that they exceed current income. To achieve this result, **distributable net income (DNI)** (step 3) provides a measure of the maximum current income that could be distributed and limits the trust distribution deduction and the beneficiaries' taxable income, so as not to exceed DNI.

## Trust Accounting Income

**Objective 4**
Calculate trust accounting income and explain the economic significance of its definition.

The computation of trust **accounting income** is not a simple determination for an important reason: The trust document controls which items of income and expense of the trust are considered part of trust accounting income and which are allocated to or against trust principal. Let's consider a simple example. Suppose that Individual A creates a trust by transferring ownership of $200,000 worth of stocks and bonds. Individual A designates her nieces as the beneficiaries of income from the trust during A's lifetime and provides that on A's death, the trust assets pass to her sister. Suppose that, during the current year, the trustee sells one stock held by the trust at a gain and reinvests the sales proceeds in other stocks. Is the gain a part of trust accounting income? Since it arose from the sale of trust assets and was reinvested in new trust assets, should it be allocated to principal? Should the trustee's fee for managing the trust reduce the annual income available for distribution to A's nieces, or should it be paid out of principal? These issues must be addressed in drafting trust documents.

If the trust document is silent with respect to the allocation of any item of income or expense, state law controls. Most states have adopted the **Uniform Principal and Income Act (UPIA)** to define allocations of trust items between principal and accounting income. Table 16.1 lists several common allocations between principal and accounting income under UPIA. However, allocations specified in the trust document supercede state law. Thus, the donor has complete power to define whatever allocations are needed to meet his or her objectives. In particular, the trust document should designate the allocation of trust administration fees between income and principal.

*Calculating Accounting Income*

Trotter Trust is a simple trust with Ms. Trudeau as its only income beneficiary and Mr. Matthews as its only remainder beneficiary. During 2003, Trotter earned $10,000 of dividend income, recognized a $5,000 capital gain, and paid $2,000 of trustee fees.

**Alternative 1**
Suppose that the trust document allocates all receipts, including capital gains, to income and trustee fees to principal. Trust accounting income is $15,000, and Ms. Trudeau receives that amount as a distribution. Trust principal (and the amount eventually to be received by Mr. Matthews) decreases by $2,000.

**Alternative 2**

Suppose that the trust document follows UPIA in its allocations and specifies that trustee fees are to be divided equally between income and principal. Then trust accounting income is $9,000 [$10,000 dividend income − (50 percent × $2,000 trustee fees)]. Ms. Trudeau receives $9,000 as a distribution. Trust principal increases by $4,000 [$5,000 capital gain − (50 percent × $2,000 trustee fees)].

Note that the cash flow received by Ms. Trudeau from the trust can differ substantially, depending on the definition of accounting income. Assuming that this trust terminates in 10 years and that it earns the same amount of income each year and using a 7 percent discount rate, the present value of before-tax cash flows to Ms. Trudeau from the trust is $105,360 under Alternative 1 and $63,216 under Alternative 2.[6]

## Trust Taxable Income before the Distribution Deduction

**Objective 5**
Calculate trust taxable income, distributable net income, and the trust distribution deduction.

The discussion of corporate taxation in Chapter 5 noted that frequent differences arise between *taxable income*, determined under the Internal Revenue Code, and *accounting income*, determined under Generally Accepted Accounting Principles. Similar differences arise between trust accounting income and trust taxable income. Whether an item is included in trust accounting income or allocated to principal does not determine whether it is included in trust taxable income.

**Trust taxable income** is computed in a manner similar to the taxable income of individuals. Trust receipts are included in gross income under the same rules that apply to individuals. Trust expenditures qualifying as business or investment expenses are deductible by the trust with no distinction between deductions *for* and *from* adjusted gross income.[7] Although the standard deduction has no trust equivalent, trusts are entitled to a personal exemption as discussed subsequently. Finally, trust taxable income is reduced by the distribution deduction for which there is no individual equivalent.

*Trust Gross Income*

Compass Trust has the following receipts:

| | |
|---|---:|
| Dividend income | $ 5,000 |
| Interest income from municipal bonds | 3,000 |
| Capital gain | 10,000 |

The trust document allocates all dividend and interest income to the trust's income beneficiaries, and capital gains are allocated to principal. Ignoring any related expenses, trust accounting income is $8,000 ($5,000 dividend income + $3,000 interest income). For tax purposes, the interest income on municipal bonds is tax exempt. The capital gain, although allocated to principal for trust accounting purposes, is included in taxable gross income. Thus, gross income for tax purposes is $15,000 ($5,000 dividend income + $10,000 capital gain).

---

[6] The $105,360 equals $15,000 × 7.024, the annuity factor for a 10-year annuity at 7 percent. The $63,216 from Alternative 2 equals $9,000 × 7.024.

[7] Trusts are technically subject to the 2 percent-of-adjusted-gross-income floor on the deductibility of miscellaneous itemized deductions. However, trustee fees and trust tax return preparation fees are not included in this category and are not subject to the floor. Trust AGI for this purpose is computed as for an individual except that trust administration expenses, the personal exemption, and the distribution deduction are considered deductible for AGI (Section 67(e)). As a result of these rules, the 2 percent-of-AGI floor typically has an immaterial impact for most trusts.

Expenses incurred by a trust generally fall into one of the following categories: (1) depreciation, (2) other expenses for the production of income, (3) charitable contributions, and (4) trust administration expenses. Trusts are allowed to deduct most of these expenses for tax purposes under the same rules as those applying to individual taxpayers. However, several special rules apply in determining the deductibility of depreciation and indirect expenses associated with tax-exempt income.

Depreciation on trust property is deductible by the trust or by its income beneficiaries or apportioned partially to both, depending on the terms of the trust document.[8] The ability to specify who will deduct depreciation provides an important planning opportunity in drafting trust documents since this tax deduction can reduce the net tax cost of trust income without reducing trust cash flow. If no allocation is specified in the trust document, depreciation is apportioned to the recipients of trust accounting income. As a result, depreciation on the assets of a simple trust is deducted entirely by the income beneficiaries. In a complex trust, a portion of the depreciation might be deducted by the trust to the extent that it retained part of the trust accounting income.

---

*Depreciation Apportionment*

JR Trust is a complex trust with one income beneficiary, Ms. Monicia. The trust document does not specify an allocation of depreciation deductions. During 2004, the trust had $40,000 of accounting income, and the trustee distributed $25,000 to Ms. Monicia. Depreciation on trust assets equaled $6,000 and is apportioned as follows.

$$\text{Depreciation apportioned to income beneficiary} \qquad \$6,000 \times \frac{\$25,000}{\$40,000} = \$3,750$$

$$\text{Depreciation apportioned to JR Trust} \qquad \$6,000 \times \frac{\$15,000}{\$40,000} = \$2,250$$

JR Trust deducts $2,250 of depreciation in calculating its taxable income, and Ms. Monicia deducts $3,750 of depreciation on her individual income tax return. If JR Trust had been a simple trust, all of its accounting income would be required to be distributed to Ms. Monicia, and she would also deduct all of the depreciation on the trust assets.

---

If a trust earns tax-exempt income, no expenses directly associated with the production of such income are deductible.[9] In addition, a portion of the trust's indirect expenses must also be allocated to tax-exempt income and are not deductible. Indirect expenses are those not directly related to the production of particular items of trust income. For example, depreciation and operating expenses on rental property owned by a trust are considered direct expenses of that item of trust income. However, trust administration fees are typically considered indirect expenses and must be allocated between taxable and tax-exempt income, as follows.

$$\frac{\substack{\text{Tax-exempt income} \\ \text{(net of direct expenses)}}}{\substack{\text{Trust accounting income} \\ \text{(net of all direct expenses)}}} \times \substack{\text{Indirect} \\ \text{expenses}} = \substack{\text{Indirect expenses allocated} \\ \text{to tax-exempt income}}$$

---

[8] Section 167(h) and Section 611(b)(3) and (4).
[9] Section 265.

*Indirect Expense Allocation*

Horner Trust earned the following items of income:

| | |
|---|---|
| Interest income from municipal bonds | $ 5,000 |
| Rental income | 50,000 |
| Capital gains | 10,000 |

The trust also incurred the following expenses:

| | |
|---|---|
| Rental expenses | $15,000 |
| Trust administration fees | 4,000 |

The trust document defines accounting income to include interest and net rental income; capital gains and trust administration expenses are to be allocated to principal. The rental expenses are considered direct expenses of producing the rental income and reduce trust accounting income. The trust administration fees are indirect expenses and must be allocated to tax-exempt income as follows:

$$\$5,000/\$40,000 \times \$4,000 = \$500$$

Trust accounting income is $40,000 ($5,000 interest income + $50,000 rental income − $15,000 rental expenses). As a result of the allocation, $500 of trust administration fees are not deductible. Trust taxable income before the distribution deduction and the personal exemption is computed as follows:

| | |
|---|---|
| Rental income | $50,000 |
| Capital gains | 10,000 |
| Less: | |
| Rental expenses | (15,000) |
| Deductible portion of trust administration fees | (3,500) |
| Trust taxable income before distribution deduction and personal exemption | $41,500 |

Trusts are entitled to a personal exemption in every year of their existence except the final year. The amount of the exemption varies, depending on the trust terms. If the trust is required to distribute all income annually, a $300 exemption is allowed. Otherwise, the exemption amount is $100. Under these rules, every simple trust receives a $300 exemption. In addition, complex trusts that are required to distribute all income also qualify for a $300 exemption.[10] All other complex trusts are limited to the $100 exemption amount.[11]

## Distributable Net Income and the Distribution Deduction

Conceptually, *distributable net income (DNI)* defines the maximum amount of (1) the trust distribution deduction and (2) the income from the trust taxable to the trust beneficiaries.[12] DNI attempts to measure the current increase in trust value available for distribution to income

---

[10] A trust that is required to distribute all income currently could be considered a complex trust rather than a simple trust because of charitable contributions or principal distributions.

[11] Section 642(b).

[12] Sections 652 and 662.

beneficiaries. To the extent that the trust makes distributions in excess of this curre[...] in value (by distributing underlying trust property or prior year earnings retained by th[...] such distributions are not captured by DNI and thus should not be taxed to the recipients. calculate DNI, taxable income before the distribution deduction is adjusted as follows:[13]

- Add the personal exemption.
- Subtract capital gains allocated to principal.
- Add capital losses allocated to principal.
- Add tax-exempt interest.
- Subtract expenses allocated to tax-exempt interest.

The adjustments made in calculating DNI recognize that taxable income is not an appropriate measure of the current increase in economic value of the trust available for distribution. The personal exemption is added back because it is a statutory deduction rather than an economic expenditure. The adjustments for capital gains and losses allocated to principal acknowledge that these amounts have been defined in the trust document as part of underlying trust property. The adjustment for net tax-exempt interest recognizes that these amounts are economic income available for distribution even though they are not subject to tax.[14]

For a simple trust with no tax-exempt income, the distribution deduction equals the lesser of trust accounting income or DNI. For a simple trust with tax-exempt income, the otherwise allowable distribution deduction must be reduced by the amount of tax-exempt income net of allocated expenses.

*Calculating DNI and the Distribution Deduction for a Simple Trust*

Austin Trust is a simple trust with the following income and expenditures:

| | Amounts Allocable to | |
| --- | --- | --- |
| | *Income* | *Principal* |
| Corporate bond interest income | $25,000 | |
| Capital gains on sales of stock | | $12,000 |
| Capital losses on sales of stock | | (5,000) |
| Trustee fees | 2,000 | 2,000 |

Trust accounting income is $23,000 ($25,000 corporate bond interest − $2,000 one-half of trustee fees). Taxable income before the distribution deduction is calculated as follows:

| | |
| --- | --- |
| Corporate bond interest income | $25,000 |
| Capital gains on sales of stock | 12,000 |
| Less: | |
|    Capital losses on sales of stock | (5,000) |
|    Trustee fees | (4,000) |
|    Personal exemption | (300) |
| Trust taxable income before distribution deduction | $27,700 |

[13] Section 643.

[14] Note that the calculation of DNI prescribed by the Code takes an indirect approach by starting with taxable income before the distribution deduction and adding or subtracting needed adjustments. A more direct approach could also be taken, by recognizing that DNI includes all trust accounting income, reduced by all trust expenses including those allocated to principal.

...NI is calculated as follows:

| | |
|---|---:|
| Trust taxable income before distribution deduction | $27,700 |
| Plus: Capital losses on sales of stock | 5,000 |
| Personal exemption | 300 |
| Less: Capital gains on sales of stock | (12,000) |
| DNI | $21,000 |

The distribution deduction for Austin Trust is $21,000, the lesser of trust accounting income ($23,000) or DNI ($21,000).

In a complex trust, the distribution deduction cannot exceed the taxable portion of amounts actually distributed to trust beneficiaries. The starting point for calculating the distribution deduction of a complex trust is the lesser of (1) the sum of required distributions under the trust agreement plus discretionary distributions or (2) DNI. If distributions exceed DNI, the allowed distribution deduction equals DNI reduced by net tax-exempt income. If DNI exceeds total distributions, the distribution deduction equals total distributions reduced by a proportionate share of net tax-exempt income, calculated as follows:

$$\text{Reduction in distribution deduction} = \text{Total distributions} \times \frac{\text{Net tax-exempt income}}{\text{DNI}}$$

*Calculating the Distribution Deduction for a Complex Trust*

Kramer Trust has DNI of $50,000, including $10,000 of net tax-exempt income.

**Alternative 1**

If Kramer distributes $20,000 to its beneficiaries, the trust is entitled to a distribution deduction of $16,000, calculated as follows:

| | |
|---|---:|
| Lesser of total distributions ($20,000) or DNI ($50,000) | $20,000 |
| Less: Proportion of distribution from tax-exempt income ($20,000 × $10,000/$50,000) | (4,000) |
| Distribution deduction | $16,000 |

**Alternative 2**

If Kramer distributes $60,000 to its beneficiaries, it is entitled to a distribution deduction of $40,000, calculated as follows:

| | |
|---|---:|
| Lesser of total distributions ($60,000) or DNI ($50,000) | $50,000 |
| Less: Portion of DNI from tax-exempt income | (10,000) |
| Distribution deduction | $40,000 |

## Trust Taxable Income and Tax Liability

Step 4 of the process described in Exhibit 16.2 calculates trust taxable income as taxable income before the distribution deduction (step 2) minus the distribution deduction from

**TABLE 16.2**
2004 Income Tax
Rates for Estates
and Trusts

| If Taxable Income Is | | The Tax Is | |
|---|---|---|---|
| Over | But Not Over | Of the Amount Over | |
| –0– | $1,950 | 15% | –0– |
| $1,950 | 4,600 | $ 292.50 + 25% | $1,950 |
| 4,600 | 7,000 | 955.00 + 28% | 4,600 |
| 7,000 | 9,550 | 1,627.00 + 33% | 7,000 |
| 9,550 | | 2,468.50 + 35% | 9,550 |

**Tax Talk**
The 2003 enactment of preferential rates on dividend income adds a new factor for trustees to consider in making investment and distribution decisions. Under prior law, if a trust retained dividend income, it was often taxed at higher rates than if distributed to lower tax rate beneficiaries. Under the new law, both the trust and the beneficiaries qualify for preferential rates.

Trustees may also change investment strategy, choosing investments producing less interest income (still taxed at ordinary tax rates) and more dividend income (now taxed at preferential rates).

step 3. Positive taxable income indicates that the trust has retained taxable receipts or gains rather than distributing them to its beneficiaries.

Trust (and estate) taxable income is subject to regular income tax at steeply progressive tax rates. See Table 16.2 for the rates applicable for 2004. Trusts are allowed to reduce regular tax liability by a variety of credits that are generally computed in the same manner as for individuals. To the extent that capital gains and losses are allocated to principal, the trust qualifies for the same preferential capital gains rates available to individuals. Trusts also qualify for the reduced tax rates on dividend income enacted in 2003, to the extent such income is taxed to the trust. Finally, trusts might be subject to the alternative minimum tax computed in a manner similar to the individual alternative minimum tax.

Although the maximum fiduciary tax rate is the same as that applicable to individuals (35 percent), this rate is reached at much lower income levels. As a result, in many cases, trusts are not an effective vehicle for using the entity variable to lower overall tax liability. If trust income beneficiaries have lower marginal tax rates than the donor, however, a transfer into a trust with income distributed might subject the income from trust property to lower tax rates.

*Trust versus Beneficiary Tax Liability*

Gordon Trust is a complex trust with one income beneficiary, Ms. Gabbe. The trustee has discretion to determine how much trust income to distribute to her and how much to retain in the trust. Assume that the trust has $100,000 of ordinary taxable income before the distribution deduction, and Ms. Gabbe is single with a marginal income tax rate of 33 percent. Then 2004 tax liability attributable to trust income varies as follows, depending on the amount of income distributed.

| | Trust Income Taxed to | | | Ms. Gabbe's | |
|---|---|---|---|---|---|
| Distribution Amount | Gordon Trust | Ms. Gabbe | Trust Tax Liability | Incremental Tax Liability | Total Tax Liability |
| –0– | $100,000 | –0– | $34,126 | –0– | $34,126 |
| $ 50,000 | 50,000 | $ 50,000 | 16,626 | $16,500 | 33,126 |
| 100,000 | –0– | 100,000 | –0– | 33,000 | 33,000 |

Notice that the combined tax liability is lowest when all income is distributed and taxed to Ms. Gabbe, the trust beneficiary. Combined tax liability is highest when the trust retains all income.

Although the donor might consider the differential tax cost of distributing versus retaining trust income in writing the trust document, nontax considerations also influence distribution decisions.

# Taxation of Trust Beneficiaries

**Objective 6**
Explain the tax treatment of trust and estate distributions to beneficiaries.

Our initial discussion of fiduciary tax concepts noted that fiduciary income is not subject to double taxation. The distribution deduction allowed to a trust ensures that it is not taxed on income distributed to its beneficiaries. Conversely, the total amount taxable to all trust beneficiaries in any given year equals the distribution deduction allowed to the trust.

In many cases, however, total distributions to trust beneficiaries can exceed the trust distribution deduction. This is true for a simple trust if its accounting income exceeds DNI or if a portion of DNI is tax exempt. In a complex trust, distributions of principal (underlying trust assets) also cause total distributions to exceed the trust distribution deduction. As a result, an allocation process is needed to determine the amount of trust income taxed to each beneficiary. In addition, the character of the income taxable to trust beneficiaries depends on the character of the income earned by the trust.

The trustee of a simple trust is required to distribute all accounting income annually. If total trust accounting income exceeds the trust distribution deduction, the amount taxable to trust beneficiaries is limited to the trust distribution deduction.[15] If the trust has more than one income beneficiary, each is taxed proportionately on its share of taxable amounts distributed.

| | |
|---|---|
| *Taxable Distributions from a Simple Trust* | Stewart Trust is a simple trust with two income beneficiaries, Mr. Davis and Ms. Lao. For 2004, Stewart had trust accounting income of $42,000 and DNI of $40,000. DNI included $10,000 of net tax-exempt income, resulting in a trust distribution deduction of $30,000. If the beneficiaries are equal income beneficiaries, each is entitled to receive a distribution of $21,000 (50 percent of the $42,000 trust accounting income). The taxable portion of such distribution is $15,000 (50 percent of the $30,000 trust distribution deduction). |

For complex trusts, allocation issues arise when the trust is not required to distribute all accounting income and more than one beneficiary receives trust distributions. In this case, distributions must be classified as either first-tier or second-tier distributions.[16] **First-tier distributions** are required distributions from income; all other distributions are considered **second-tier distributions.**[17]

If all distributions are from the same tier (either all first tier or all second tier), the taxable amount to each beneficiary is determined in the same manner described earlier for a simple trust. Each recipient beneficiary is taxed on a proportionate share of a total taxable amount equal to the trust distribution deduction. If both first- and second-tier distributions are made in a given year, an ordering process assigns taxability, in the following manner:

- When total first-tier distributions exceed DNI, each first-tier beneficiary is taxed on a proportionate share of taxable DNI (equal to the trust distribution deduction). None of the second-tier distributions are taxable to the recipients.
- When total first-tier distributions do not exceed DNI but the total of first- and second-tier distributions exceeds DNI, DNI is first absorbed by first-tier distributions. Each first-tier beneficiary is taxed as follows.

---

[15] Note that state-level taxable income for a trust and its beneficiaries is computed under state laws. In particular, if the trust earns municipal bond interest income that is taxed at the state level, income reported for state purposes might be greater than federal taxable income.

[16] Section 662(a)(1) and (2).

[17] Regulation 1.662(a)-2 and -3.

$$\text{First-tier distributions} \atop \text{to the beneficiary} \times \frac{\text{Taxable DNI}}{\text{Total DNI}} = {\text{Income taxable to the} \atop \text{first-tier beneficiary}}$$

Remaining DNI is allocated to second-tier beneficiaries, each of whom is taxed as follows.

$$\frac{\text{Second-tier distributions} \atop \text{to the beneficiary}}{\text{Total of second-tier} \atop \text{distributions}} \times {\text{Remaining DNI after} \atop \text{first-tier distributions}} = {\text{Beneficiary's} \atop \text{share of DNI}}$$

$${\text{Beneficiary's} \atop \text{share of DNI}} \times \frac{\text{Taxable DNI}}{\text{Total DNI}} = {\text{Income taxable to the} \atop \text{second-tier beneficiary}}$$

- Finally, when the total of all distributions is less than DNI, each beneficiary is taxed on a proportionate share of the trust distribution deduction.

---

*Taxable Distributions from a Complex Trust*

Gorman Trust is a complex trust with two beneficiaries, Ms. Belk and Mrs. O'Dell. The trustee of Gorman Trust is required to distribute $10,000 of trust income each year to each of them. In addition, the trustee has the power to make other distributions at his discretion. During 2003, the trust has accounting income of $100,000 and DNI of $90,000. DNI includes $15,000 of net tax-exempt income.

**Alternative 1**

In addition to the required distributions, the trustee makes discretionary distributions of $42,000 to each beneficiary. Thus, total distributions of $104,000 exceed DNI. The amount of first-tier distributions taxable to each beneficiary is $8,333 [$10,000 × ($75,000/$90,000)]. The amount of second-tier distributions taxable to each beneficiary follows:

$$\frac{\$42,000}{\$84,000} \times (\$90,000 - \$20,000) \times \frac{\$75,000}{\$90,000} = \$29,167$$

Thus, each beneficiary reports $37,500 ($8,333 + $29,167) of taxable income as a result of distributions from the Gorman Trust. Of the additional $14,500 ($52,000 − $37,500) each received, $7,500 is considered a distribution from trust tax-exempt income and retains its tax-exempt character in the hands of the beneficiaries. The remaining $7,000 distributed to each beneficiary is a nontaxable distribution of trust principal.

**Alternative 2**

Suppose instead that the trustee makes discretionary distributions to each beneficiary totaling $3,500 in addition to the required distributions. In this case, total distributions of $27,000 are less than trust DNI. The trust distribution deduction is $22,500 [$27,000 − $27,000 × ($15,000/$90,000)]. Each beneficiary is taxed on $11,250 [$22,500 × ($13,500/$27,000)].

---

To the extent that taxable amounts earned by the trust differ in character, the character of amounts taxed to the beneficiaries must also be determined. In general, *character* is assigned proportionately to taxable distribution amounts using the same ordering described for first-tier and second tier-distributions.

---

*Character of Distributions from a Complex Trust*

Refer to the example for Gorman Trust, Alternative 1. Suppose that of the trust's $75,000 of taxable DNI ($90,000 DNI − $15,000 tax-exempt income), $50,000 is ordinary income and $25,000 is dividend income eligible for prefential tax rates. Each beneficiary therefore reports $25,000 of ordinary income [$37,500 total taxable distribution × ($50,000/$75,000)] and $12,500 of dividend income [$37,500 × ($25,000/$75,000)].

For some trusts, the **separate share rule** overrides these allocation procedures for determining the amount and character of distributions taxed to beneficiaries.[18] The separate share rule applies when a trust has multiple beneficiaries and each is entitled to substantially separate and independent shares of trust income or assets. The determination of whether separate shares exists is complex but depends on whether distributions from the trust are made as though separate trusts had been established for each beneficiary.[19]

Consideration of the character of trust income and the marginal tax rates of trust beneficiaries relative to the marginal tax rates of the trust and the donor might create planning opportunities in defining income to be distributed to the beneficiaries versus retained by the trust.

---

*Income Shifting with Trusts*

Ms. Bever wishes to create a trust to benefit Mr. Huang. Her marginal tax rate on ordinary income is 35 percent; his is 25 percent. Ms. Bever plans to contribute investment assets to the trust and expects it to generate approximately $10,000 of ordinary income and $6,000 of long-term capital gains annually.

If Ms. Bever continued to own these assets, her after-tax cash flow from this income stream is determined as follows:

| | |
|---|---:|
| Ordinary income | $10,000 |
| Tax on ordinary income at 35 percent | (3,500) |
| Capital gain | 6,000 |
| Tax on capital gain at 15 percent | (900) |
| After-tax cash flow | $11,600 |

If the trust distributes all income (including capital gains) to Mr. Huang, his after-tax cash flow from this income stream is:

| | |
|---|---:|
| Ordinary income | $10,000 |
| Tax on ordinary income at 25 percent | (2,500) |
| Capital gain | 6,000 |
| Tax on capital gain at 15 percent | (900) |
| After-tax cash flow | $12,600 |

Finally, if the trust retains all income, its after-tax cash flow is calculated as follows:

| | |
|---|---:|
| Ordinary income | $10,000 |
| Tax on ordinary income using Table 16.2 | (2,626) |
| Capital gain | 6,000 |
| Tax on capital gain at 15 percent | (900) |
| After-tax cash flow | $12,474 |

Note that all differential cash flow effects are due to the tax rate on ordinary income. If Ms. Bever did not wish the trust to distribute all income to Mr. Huang, she might choose to allocate to principal any item of income whose tax cost was not higher when the trust retained it (i.e., capital gains).

---

[18] Section 663(c).

[19] A more detailed discussion of the separate share rule is beyond the scope of this text.

## Trust Property Distributions

The preceding discussion of trust distributions does not distinguish distributions of cash from distributions in the form of trust property. As a general rule, property distributed to trust beneficiaries passes from the trust at its adjusted tax basis. The trust does not recognize a gain or loss for any difference between adjusted basis and the FMV of this property distributed. If a trust distributes property to meet required income distributions, the distribution absorbs DNI and qualifies for the distribution deduction to the extent of the lesser of adjusted tax basis or FMV on the date of the distribution.[20] The beneficiary receiving the property takes a carryover basis equal to the property's adjusted tax basis to the trust. In addition, the beneficiary's holding period for the property includes the period of time it was held by the trust.

At the trustee's option, a trust might elect to recognize a gain on distributions of appreciated trust property. If the election is made, the distribution absorbs DNI and qualifies for the distribution deduction to the extent of the property's FMV on the distribution date. The beneficiary's new tax basis in the distributed property also equals its FMV, and the beneficiary's holding period in the property begins on the date of distribution. A trustee might wish to make the election if the distribution involves capital gain property and the trust has unused capital losses to offset the gain.

*Distribution of Appreciated Property*

Maxwell Trust distributed a piece of property with an adjusted tax basis of $10,000 to one of its beneficiaries.

**Alternative 1**
Assume that the property's FMV on the distribution date is $15,000. If the trustee does not elect to recognize gain on the distributed property, the distribution potentially absorbs $10,000 of DNI and qualifies for a $10,000 distribution deduction. The recipient beneficiary takes a $10,000 tax basis in the property received.

**Alternative 2**
Assume that the property's FMV on the distribution date is $8,000. The distribution potentially absorbs $8,000 of DNI and qualifies for an $8,000 distribution deduction. The recipient beneficiary takes a $10,000 tax basis in the property received.

**Alternative 3**
Assume that the property's FMV on the distribution date is $15,000 and the trustee elects to recognize gain on the distributed property. The distribution then potentially absorbs $15,000 of DNI and qualifies for a $15,000 distribution deduction. The recipient beneficiary takes a $15,000 tax basis in the property received.

## Trust Filing Requirements

All trusts must use a calendar year for tax reporting purposes. This requirement eliminates any potential for deferral of taxation by adopting a trust taxable year that differs from the trust beneficiaries' taxable year. A trust is required to file Form 1041 if it has positive taxable income or gross income of $600 or more. Form 1041 is due on April 15 following the trust year-end. In addition, trusts are required to make quarterly estimated tax payments.

## Comprehensive Trust Income Taxation Example

West Trust was formed to hold rental property and other investment assets. It has two income beneficiaries, Mr. Alt and Mrs. Chima. During 2004, the trust had the following receipts and expenses:

[20] Section 643(d).

| | |
|---|---|
| Corporate bond interest income | $20,000 |
| Municipal bond interest income | 10,000 |
| Capital gain on sale of investments | 2,000 |
| Capital loss on sale of investments | (6,000) |
| Rental income | 60,000 |
| Rental operating expenses | 15,000 |
| Depreciation on rental property | 5,000 |
| Trustee fees | 3,000 |

The trust document provides that items of income and expense be allocated between principal and income using the guidelines of UPIA (see Table 16.1) and that trustee fees be divided equally between income and principal. The trust document also requires annual distributions of $15,000 to each beneficiary from trust income with additional distributions possible at the trustee's discretion. During 2004, the trustee made discretionary distributions of $5,000 and $10,000 to Mr. Alt and Mrs. Chima, respectively.

*Step 1.* Trust accounting income is calculated as follows:

| | |
|---|---|
| Corporate bond interest income | $20,000 |
| Municipal bond interest income | 10,000 |
| Rental income | 60,000 |
| Rental operating expenses | (15,000) |
| Depreciation on rental property | (5,000) |
| One-half of trustee fees | (1,500) |
| Trust accounting income | $68,500 |

*Step 2.* Trust taxable income before the distribution deduction is calculated as follows:

| | |
|---|---|
| Corporate bond interest income | $20,000 |
| Capital gain | 2,000 |
| Deductible portion of capital loss | (5,000) |
| Rental income | 60,000 |
| Rental operating expenses | (15,000) |
| Trust share of depreciation on rental property | (1,715) |
| Deductible portion of trustee fees | (2,571) |
| Trust personal exemption | (100) |
| Trust taxable income before the distribution deduction | $57,614 |

Three issues arise in the calculation of trust taxable income before the distribution deduction. First, note that the trust capital loss is deductible in excess of the capital gain up to $3,000 under the same capital loss rules that apply to individual taxpayers. Second, the trust's share of the depreciation deduction is $1,715 [$5,000 − $5,000 × ($45,000 distributions/$68,500 accounting income)]. Third, a portion of trustee fees must be allocated to tax-exempt income as follows: $3,000 × ($10,000 tax-exempt income/$70,000 trust accounting income before reduction for trustee fees) or $429 nondeductible trustee fees.

*Step 3.*    DNI for the West Trust is calculated as follows:

| | |
|---|---|
| Trust taxable income before distribution deduction | $57,614 |
| Plus: | |
|   Capital loss | 5,000 |
|   Personal exemption | 100 |
|   Tax-exempt interest income | 10,000 |
| Less: | |
|   Expenses allocated to tax-exempt income | (429) |
|   Capital gains on sales of stock | (2,000) |
| DNI | $70,285 |

The trust distribution deduction follows:

| | |
|---|---|
| Lesser of total distributions ($45,000) or DNI ($70,285) | $45,000 |
| Less:  Proportion of distribution from net tax-exempt | |
|     income [$45,000 × ($10,000 − $429)/$70,285] | (6,128) |
| Distribution deduction | $38,872 |

*Step 4.*    Trust taxable income is $18,742 ($57,614 − $38,872).

*Step 5.*    Trust tax liability, using Table 16.2, is $5,686.

*Step 6.*    Total trust distributions of $45,000 are less than trust DNI of $70,285. Each beneficiary is taxed on a proportionate share of the trust distribution deduction, as follows:

**Taxable Distribution to Mr. Alt**

$$\$17,276 = \$38,872 \times \frac{\$20,000}{\$45,000}$$

**Taxable Distribution to Mrs. Chima**

$$\$21,576 = \$38,872 \times \frac{\$25,000}{\$45,000}$$

All of the taxable distribution to both beneficiaries is considered ordinary income.

# INCOME TAXATION OF ESTATES

As defined in Chapter 15, an *estate* is formed on the death of an individual to manage, conserve, and distribute property to beneficiaries specified in the decedent's will or by state intestacy laws. Chapter 15 discussed the application of transfer taxation to estates. During the time between the decedent's death and the final distribution of assets to the estate's beneficiaries, any income earned by estate assets is subject to income taxation. This time period could be a matter of months or several years should the will be contested or difficulties exist in identifying assets or locating heirs.

**Objective 7**
Describe the important differences in calculating estate taxable income and trust taxable income.

In general, the income taxation of estates and their beneficiaries follows the same steps as outlined for trusts in Exhibit 16.1. The computations and allocation rules discussed for each of these steps apply to estates as to trusts. In particular, the calculation of estate taxable income is similar to that of a complex trust since estates typically have no required distributions to income beneficiaries. If the decedent's will specifies an allocation of estate income between principal and income beneficiaries, that allocation is respected in computing estate accounting income. In many cases, however, state law controls such allocations. In addition, several issues unique to estates deserve further discussion to complete the presentation of the income tax consequences of estate activities.

## Income and Deductions in Respect of a Decedent

The decedent's final individual income tax return includes all income recognized under the decedent's method of accounting up to the date of death. To the extent that the decedent earned income prior to death that is not reported on the decedent's final tax return, such income is considered **income in respect of a decedent (IRD).**[21] The estate collects many IRD items after the decedent's death and must report them on the estate income tax return. In some cases, beneficiaries other than the estate collect IRD, which must be reported on the beneficiaries' individual income tax returns.

For cash basis decedents, IRD includes salary, interest, dividends, and other items of income earned but not collected prior to death. It also includes items such as death benefits from qualified retirement plans and other deferred compensation arrangements as well as unrecognized gains on installment sale receivables.

Because IRD represents a receivable of the decedent at death, it is an asset subject to estate tax.[22] When the estate collects the IRD, it is also subject to income tax. This dual taxation might seem harsh, but it is consistent with the treatment of income reported by the decedent prior to death and invested in assets held at death.

| | |
|---|---|
| *Income and Estate Taxation of IRD* | On September 30, 2004, Mr. Mannix received and deposited his monthly paycheck for $7,000. On October 5, 2004, he died. In November, his estate received $1,000 from his employer representing his final paycheck for the first five days of October. The estate also received two dividend payments. A $2,000 payment represented dividends declared in September to owners of record on October 1, 2004. A $5,000 payment represented dividends declared in October to owners of record on November 1, 2004. Finally, at his death, Mr. Mannix was entitled to $200,000 of retirement benefits under his employer's qualified retirement plan. Mrs. Mannix received a check for these benefits as his named beneficiary under the plan. |

**Income Tax Reporting**
Mr. Mannix's final individual income tax return reports the $7,000 salary payment. The $1,000 salary payment and the $2,000 dividend payment are considered IRD taxable to the estate. The $5,000 dividend payment is also taxable to the estate but is not IRD since he was not the owner of record on November 1. The $200,000 payment of retirement benefits is also IRD but will be taxed to Mrs. Mannix, not the estate, since it was paid directly to her.

**Estate Tax**
Mr. Mannix's gross estate includes $203,000 of IRD ($1,000 salary + $2,000 dividends + $200,000 retirement benefits). The value of the two dividend-paying stocks and the balance in his bank accounts (including any portion of the September 30 paycheck remaining) are also included in the gross estate.

[21] Section 691 and related regulations.
[22] Section 2033.

Deductible expenses associated with IRD not claimed on the decedent's final tax return are referred to as **deductions in respect of a decedent (DRD).** These deductions are allowed to reduce the estate income tax when paid. They also represent the decedent's liabilities and thus reduce the taxable estate for transfer tax purposes. Common DRD items include business- or investment-related interest expense, property taxes, and state income taxes that the decedent owed at the date of death.

| | |
|---|---|
| *IRD and DRD* | Ms. Colette, a cash basis taxpayer, died on November 10, 2004. On that date, she was owed $10,000 in wages earned but not yet paid. On December 1, 2004, her employer sent her estate the final paycheck reduced by $2,000 of state income tax. The $10,000 salary payment is considered IRD and is included in the estate's gross income. The $2,000 of state income tax withholding is considered DRD and is deductible in computing estate taxable income. |

## Estate Administration Expenses

As discussed in Chapter 15, costs associated with estate administration (executor expenses, accounting and appraisal fees) are deductible against the gross estate in computing estate tax. These costs cannot be claimed again as income tax deductions unless the estate does not claim them in calculating the transfer tax. The estate fiduciary can choose to allocate these expenses between the estate tax and the income tax in whatever manner is most beneficial. Given the filing requirements for estate income tax (discussed later), many estates that pay no estate tax due to the unified credit could still owe income tax.

| | |
|---|---|
| *Deducting Estate Administration Expenses* | Mr. Herald died in 2004 with a gross estate of $2 million, a taxable estate of $500,000, and cumulative taxable transfers of $650,000 before consideration of estate administration expenses. Because the unified credit reduced Mr. Herald's estate tax liability to zero, the estate executor elected to deduct all estate administration expenses on the estate income tax return. If such expenses totaled $15,000 and the estate's taxable income before the deduction was $200,000, this election would save $5,250 ($15,000 × 35 percent) of estate income tax. |

## Estate Personal Exemption and Filing Requirements

All estates are allowed a $600 personal exemption. Any estate with gross income of $600 or more is required to file Form 1041 by the 15th day of the fourth month following the close of the estate's taxable year.[23] Unlike trusts, estates are not required to use a calendar year for tax reporting purposes but may select any fiscal year for filing the first estate income tax return. Estate (and trust) beneficiaries report their share of fiduciary taxable income for estate (trust) years ending with or within the beneficiaries' tax year. Thus, if an estate has a June 30 year-end and its beneficiaries have calendar year-ends, a six-month time lag exists between the dates on which the estate reports its taxable income and on which the beneficiaries report their share of taxable distributions. This potential deferral presents a planning opportunity for the estate when selecting its year-end.

Estates are exempt from estimated tax payment requirements for tax years ending less than two years after the date of the decedent's death. This exemption recognizes the liquidity problems that could exist in the early months of an estate's existence. If the estate has not distributed all property and terminated within the two-year exemption period, quarterly estimated tax payments are then required.

---

[23] Section 6012(a).

## Comprehensive Estate Income Tax Example

Mrs. Leonis died on June 1, 2003. Her estate included investment assets, life insurance, retirement benefits, and her personal residence. For income tax reporting purposes, the executor of her estate elected a May 30 taxable year. The estate recognized the following income items during its first taxable year:

- Mrs. Leonis's final paycheck, received by the estate, showed gross wages of $10,000 and state income tax withholding of $1,500.
- Mrs. Leonis's investments earned $13,000 of taxable interest income.
- The executor sold some of the estate's investment assets, producing long-term capital gains of $12,000 and long-term capital losses of $3,000.

The estate executor incurred $6,000 of estate administration expenses and elected to deduct them on the estate income tax return. On May 30, 2004, Mrs. Leonis's estate has not distributed its assets to her beneficiaries. However, the executor has distributed $20,000 of estate income to the beneficiaries.

Assume that Mrs. Leonis's will did not specify an allocation of items between income and principal. Her state of residence generally follows UPIA for these allocations with administration expenses allocable to principal.

*Step 1.* Estate accounting income is calculated as follows.

| | |
|---|---:|
| Income in respect of decedent (final paycheck) | $10,000 |
| Interest income | 13,000 |
| Deductions in respect of decedent (payroll taxes) | (1,500) |
| Estate accounting income | $21,500 |

*Step 2.* Estate taxable income before the distribution deduction is calculated as follows.

| | |
|---|---:|
| Income in respect of decedent (final paycheck) | $10,000 |
| Interest income | 13,000 |
| Capital gains | 12,000 |
| Capital losses | (3,000) |
| Deductions in respect of decedent (payroll taxes) | (1,500) |
| Estate administration expenses | (6,000) |
| Estate personal exemption | (600) |
| Taxable income before the distribution deduction | $23,900 |

*Step 3.* DNI for the estate is calculated as follows.

| | |
|---|---:|
| Taxable income before the distribution deduction | $23,900 |
| Plus: | |
| Capital loss | 3,000 |
| Personal exemption | 600 |
| Less: Capital gain | (12,000) |
| DNI | $15,500 |

*Step 4.* The estate distribution deduction and estate taxable income are as follows.

| | |
|---|---:|
| Lesser of total distributions ($20,000) or DNI ($15,500) | $15,500 |
| Estate taxable income ($23,900 − $15,500) | $ 8,400 |

Note that all of the estate's taxable income is attributable to net capital gains. As a result, the estate will owe capital gains tax of $1,260 (15 percent of $8,400). The estate beneficiaries will recognize ordinary income equal to the estate distribution deduction of $15,500.

# LOSSES IN THE TERMINATION YEAR OF A TRUST OR ESTATE

If a trust or estate incurs a net operating loss or net capital losses, such losses do not flow through to the beneficiaries as they would in a partnership or S corporation. Instead, such losses carry back or forward within the trust or estate, for possible deduction in other years.[24] However, if a trust or estate incurs negative taxable income in the year it terminates, this excess loss flows through to the beneficiaries. The net loss is an itemized deduction in the beneficiary's tax year with or within which the entity's tax year ends. The amount allocable to each beneficiary is in proportion to the relative amount of assets received by the beneficiary upon termination of the entity. If the trust or estate has capital loss carryovers unused at the time of its termination, these losses also flow through to the beneficiaries in proportion to the relative amount of assets received by each upon termination of the entity. These losses carryovers will be deductible by the beneficiaries subject to the usual limitations on capital loss carryovers.

*Loss Flowthrough on Termination of an Estate*

The Williams estate terminates on August 31, 2004. In the termination year, the estate incurred $10,000 of negative taxable income and has $15,000 of net long-term capital loss carryovers. Mr. Johnson received $500,000 of assets on termination of the estate, and Ms. Green received $300,000.

The amount of negative taxable income allocable to each beneficiary is:

Mr. Johnson:    $6,250 = $10,000 × ($500,000/$800,000)
Ms. Green:    $3,750 = $10,000 × ($300,000/$800,000)

Mr. Johnson and Ms. Green will be allowed an itemized deduction for these allocated losses on their 2004 individual income tax returns.

The amount of capital loss carryover allocated to each beneficiary is:

Mr. Johnson:    $9,375 = $15,000 × ($500,000/$800,000)
Ms. Green:    $5,625 = $15,000 × ($300,000/$800,000)

Mr. Johnson and Ms. Green will combine these capital loss allocations with their other capital gains and losses to determine their potential deduction.

## Conclusion

Trusts often provide a useful tool for meeting asset management goals regardless of income and transfer tax considerations. A comprehensive plan for the preservation and transfer of family wealth can utilize a variety of trust arrangements and must consider the income tax

[24] Loss carrybacks and carryforwards of a trust or estate are subject to the same rules applicable to individuals. Thus a net operating loss would be carried back 2 years and forward 20 years. Excess capital losses would carry forward indefinitely.

consequences of trust earnings to both trusts and their beneficiaries. Trusts can also be formed at death as part of a comprehensive estate plan. Since trusts and estates are subject to income tax under similar rules, testamentary trusts are typically formed for nontax reasons. Given the filing requirements for estates, many small estates might owe income tax on estate earnings even though no estate tax is due as a result of the unified credit. Chapter 16 explores a variety of planning ideas surrounding the timing and manner of transferring assets to future generations.

## Key Terms

| | | |
|---|---|---|
| accounting income 445 | donor 442 | revocable trust 442 |
| beneficiary 442 | fiduciary 442 | second-tier |
| complex trust 443 | first-tier | distributions 452 |
| corpus 442 | distributions 452 | separate share rule 454 |
| deductions in respect of a | grantor trust 443 | simple trust 443 |
| decedent (DRD) 459 | income in respect of a | testamentary trust 442 |
| distributable net income | decedent (IRD) 458 | trustee 442 |
| (DNI) 445 | *inter vivos* trust 442 | trust taxable income 446 |
| distribution | irrevocable trust 442 | Uniform Principal and |
| deduction 444 | principal 442 | Income Act (UPIA) 445 |

## Questions and Problems for Discussion

1. When creating a trust, why might the donor prefer to designate a friend or family member as the trustee rather than a bank trust department or other corporate trustee?

2. What arguments support the allocation of depreciation on trust assets to income rather than to principal for purposes of calculating trust accounting income? What arguments might support the allocation of depreciation to principal rather than income?

3. Why do ignoring grantor trusts for income tax reasons and taxing any trust earnings to the grantor make sense?

4. Mr. Gary plans to establish a testamentary trust to provide for his minor children in the event of his death. He is confused about the distinction between a simple trust and a complex trust and wonders which would be more appropriate in these circumstances. Explain the difference to him, and advise him of the issues he should consider in making this choice.

5. Discuss the similarities and differences between the conduit approach to the taxation of partnerships and the modified conduit approach to the taxation of fiduciary entities.

6. The trustee of Allen Trust, a simple trust, is required to distribute all accounting income (defined under UPIA) to the income beneficiaries annually. The trust principal is composed of stocks and bonds, and the trustee has discretion over investment decisions. What impact will the trustee's discretion have on the required distributions to the income beneficiaries?

7. How does the definition of trust accounting income impact the calculation of DNI and the trust distribution deduction?

8. Mrs. Andrews is a wealthy widow in her 60s. She wishes to establish a simple trust to benefit her granddaughter, a 22-year-old graduate student. She will transfer investments to the trust to produce current cash flow from dividends and interest. She plans to define accounting income consistent with UPIA. Which tax planning maxim from Chapter 1 guides the income tax consequences of this trust arrangement?

9. Do the steeply progressive tax rates that apply in calculating trust income tax liability remove all incentive to use trusts as an income-shifting device? Under what conditions would income shifting still be viable using a trust?

10. If income in respect of a decedent were not subject to estate income tax, what incentives would be created for the deferral of income?

11. Why is it necessary to assess income tax on estates? What incentives would be created if this tax were not assessed?

12. In what ways do the estate income tax rules encourage a speedy distribution of estate assets and liquidation of the estate?

## Application Problems

1. Indicate which trusts in each of the following situations are classified as simple or complex.

   a. The trustee of Anderson Trust is <u>required</u> to distribute all trust accounting income to Mrs. Bruce, the trust income beneficiary. In addition, the trustee has discretion to make additional distributions to her. During 2004, the trustee makes the required income distributions and no discretionary distributions.

   b. The trustee of Conrad Trust has discretionary control over all of its distributions. During 2004, the trustee distributes 100 percent of the trust accounting income to its beneficiaries.

   c. Draper Trust has two income beneficiaries, Elridge College and Mr. Fallon. The trustee is required to distribute all of the trust's accounting income in equal shares to the two income beneficiaries. *If qualified charity, then complex*

   d. Galant Trust is required to distribute all accounting income to its beneficiaries annually. During 2004, Galant terminates and distributes all income and remaining trust property. *complex.*

2. Refer to application problem 1. Indicate whether the trust in each situation qualifies for a $100 or $300 personal exemption. *finaly of trust $ exempt*

3. Indicate whether the trust in each of the following situations is *(a)* revocable or *(b)* irrevocable, and, if so, indicate whether the <u>trust is a grantor trust.</u>

   *Situation 1.* Mrs. Collins establishes a trust to benefit her elderly mother of which she and her sister are cotrustees, with discretion over all distributions and the ability to change the beneficiary at any time. The trust is to terminate on the death of their mother or at any earlier time designated by the trustees. At termination, the trust property reverts to Mrs. Collins.

   *Situation 2.* Mr. Tonorio establishes a living trust to hold title to his assets. He is the trustee and the beneficiary of the trust for his lifetime. At his death, the trust assets are distributable to his children.

   *Situation 3.* Mr. Marty transfers assets into a simple trust, naming himself as income beneficiary, his children as remainder beneficiaries, and his attorney as trustee. The trust terminates on Mr. Marty's death.

4. Mayberry Trust has the following receipts and expenses for 2004.

| | |
|---|---|
| Dividend income | $10,000 |
| Municipal bond interest income | 5,000 |
| Rental income | 80,000 |
| Rental operating expenses | 25,000 |
| Capital improvements to rental property | 10,000 |
| Royalty income | 7,000 |
| Capital gains from sale of investments | 9,000 |
| Trust administration fees | 8,000 |

If Mayberry follows UPIA in allocating items between income and principal and requires the trust administration fees to be divided equally between income and principal, calculate trust accounting income.

5. Longwood Trust is a simple trust with two income beneficiaries each entitled to one-half of the trust's annual accounting income. For 2004, the trust has ordinary income of $50,000, a long-term capital gain of $18,000 (allocable to <u>principal</u>), and trustee fees of $6,000 (allocable to <u>principal</u>).

    *a.* Calculate the trust's accounting income. How much income is each beneficiary entitled to receive?

    *b.* What is the trust's DNI?

    *c.* What is the trust's taxable income?

    *d.* How much is taxed to each beneficiary?

6. The trustee of the Windfall Trust has the discretion to make distributions. During 2004, the trust distributed $15,000 to each of its three beneficiaries. The trust had taxable interest income of $80,000 and tax-exempt interest income of $20,000 and paid a trustee fee of $10,000 (one-half allocable to principal, one-half allocable to income).

    *a.* Calculate trust accounting income.

    *b.* Calculate trust taxable income before the distribution deduction.

    *c.* Calculate DNI, the trust distribution deduction, and trust taxable income.

    *d.* How much is taxed to each beneficiary?

7. Daniels Trust has two equal income beneficiaries, Mr. Charleston and Ms. Jackson. For 2004, Daniels had $100,000 of accounting income and $20,000 of depreciation.

    *a.* If Daniels is a simple trust, determine the amount of depreciation deductible by the trust and each beneficiary.

    *b.* Now assume that Daniels is a complex trust and that Mr. Charleston and Ms. Jackson both receive distributions of $40,000 during 2004. Determine the amount of depreciation deductible by the trust and each beneficiary.

8. Fielding Trust had the following receipts and expenses for 2004.

| | |
|---|---:|
| Royalty income | $15,000 |
| Royalty expenses | (5,000) |
| Dividend income | 1,000 |
| Municipal bond interest income | 4,000 |
| Capital gain | 3,000 |
| Trust administration fees | (2,000) |

The trust document provides that <u>trust administration fees be allocated to principal</u>.

    *a.* Following UPIA, calculate trust accounting income.

    *b.* Determine the portion of indirect expenses allocated to tax-exempt income.

    *c.* Calculate trust taxable income before the distribution deduction.

9. Refer to application problem 8. If Fielding is a simple trust, calculate DNI, the trust distribution deduction, trust taxable income, and trust tax liability.

10. Refer to application problem 8 and assume that Fielding is a complex trust with one income beneficiary receiving $10,000 during 2004. Calculate DNI, the trust distribution deduction, trust taxable income, and trust tax liability.

11. Refer to application problem 10 and assume that Fielding distributes $25,000 during 2004. Recalculate with this change.

12. Lansing Trust is a simple trust with one income beneficiary, Mr. Alonso. For 2004, Lansing reported the following.

| | |
|---|---:|
| Accounting income | $100,000 |
| DNI | 90,000 |
| Distribution deduction | 80,000 |
| Taxable income | 5,700 |

    *a.* How much is the trust required to distribute to Mr. Alonso during 2004?
    *b.* How much of the required distribution is taxable to Mr. Alonso?
    *c.* To what would you attribute any nontaxable distribution to Mr. Alonso?

13. Felipe Trust has two beneficiaries, Mr. Molina and Mrs. Calderon. Felipe's trustee is required to distribute $10,000 of trust income annually to each beneficiary and can make additional discretionary distributions. During 2004, the trustee distributed $5,000 in discretionary distributions to Mr. Molino.
    *a.* If Felipe Trust has DNI of $15,000 and takes a distribution deduction of $12,000, determine the amount taxable to each beneficiary.
    *b.* If DNI is $23,000 and the trust distribution deduction is $18,000, determine the amount taxable to each beneficiary.
    *c.* If DNI is $30,000 and the trust distribution deduction is $24,000, determine the amount taxable to each beneficiary.

14. Ms. Johnna's estate incurred $20,000 of administration expenses. The estate's taxable income before the deduction of these expenses is $300,000. For estate tax purposes, Ms. Johnna had cumulative taxable transfers of $2.5 million before any deduction for administration expenses.
    *a.* Calculate the potential estate income tax savings from deducting the administration expenses on the income tax return.
    *b.* Calculate the potential estate tax savings from deducting the administration expenses on the estate tax return.
    *c.* Given your answers to parts *(a)* and *(b),* what would you recommend to the estate's executor?

15. Mr. Williams died on October 21, 2004. For the year ended December 31, 2004, he or his investments earned the following items of income:
- Salary income of $175,000. Of this total, $165,000 was paid to him prior to his death. The remaining $10,000 represents Mr. Williams's earnings from October 1 through October 21, paid to his estate on November 1, 2004.
- Dividend income totaling $20,000. Of this total, he received $17,000 prior to his death. Mr. Williams's estate received the remaining $3,000; $2,000 of this balance related to dividends declared in September payable to owners of record on October 15, 2004. The remaining $1,000 related to dividends declared in October payable to owners of record on November 1, 2004.
- Mr. Williams had a $350,000 balance in his employer's qualified retirement plan. His two children each received 50 percent of these benefits as his named beneficiaries.
    *a.*   Which of the preceding income items will be reported on Mr. Williams's final individual income tax return?
    *b.*   Which of the preceding income items are considered income in respect of a decedent, included in Mr. Williams's gross estate?

    *c.*   Which of the preceding items are taxable on the estate income tax return?

    *d.*   Are the items in parts *(b)* and *(c)* the same? If not, why not?

16. Ms. Paul died on July 1, 2003. The executor of her estate elected a June 30 taxable year. For the period ended June 30, 2004, the estate incurred the following items of income and expense.

| | |
|---|---|
| Dividend income | $30,000 *inc* |
| Interest income | 10,000 *inc* |
| Capital gains | 1,000 *prin* |
| Capital losses | (4,000) *prin* |
| Royalty income | 20,000 *inc* |
| Estate administration expenses | (5,000) |

Assume that Ms. Paul's state of residence follows UPIA in allocating items to income and principal with administration expenses allocated to principal. The executor of Ms. Paul's estate distributed $25,000 of cash (from current receipts) to her beneficiaries during the year and made no property distributions. The executor also elects to deduct all estate administration expenses on the estate tax return rather than the estate income tax return.

    *a.*  Calculate estate accounting income and estate taxable income before the distribution deduction.

    *b.*  Calculate estate distributable net income and the estate distribution deduction.

    *c.*  Calculate estate taxable income and tax liability.

    *d.*  How much estate tax could have been saved if the executor had elected to deduct the administration expenses on the estate income tax return? Assuming that the executor made the value-maximizing choice, what does this choice indicate about the marginal estate tax rate that must apply to Ms. Paul's estate?

17. Alcott Estate terminated on November 30, 2004. In the termination year, the estate incurred $40,000 of negative taxable income and has $10,000 of net long-term capital loss carryovers. Mr. Bennett received $1 million of assets on termination of the estate, and Ms. Charles received $3 million.

    *a.*  Calculate the amount of negative taxable income allocated to Mr. Bennett and Ms. Charles. What are the tax consequences of these allocations to each beneficiary?

    *b.*  Calculated the amount of capital loss carryover allocated to Mr. Bennett and Ms. Charles. What are the tax consequences of these allocations to each beneficiary?

## Issue Recognition Problems

Identify the tax issue or issues suggested by the following situations, and state each issue in the form of a question.

1. As Mr. Martin ages, he is becoming concerned about preserving his assets for his children. He plans to establish a trust into which he will place most of his income-producing assets. He will be the income beneficiary of the trust, with his children as remainder beneficiaries to receive the trust assets on his death. Mr. Martin has not yet selected a trustee for the trust. He is considering naming himself as trustee until such time as he can no longer manage the assets and then will name a successor trustee.

2. Halloway Trust owns rental property. Most of its principal is invested in depreciable assets, producing large annual depreciation deductions.

3. Kaufman Trust is a simple trust whose primary investments have been in corporate bonds producing taxable interest income. Kaufman's trustee is considering shifting a portion of trust investments into municipal bonds and growth stocks.

4. Connelly Trust was formed by Mr. Timberlake for the benefit of his elderly father. Connelly is required to distribute all trust income to his father annually. In addition, the Connelly trustee has discretion to make distributions of trust property if and when the elder Mr. Timberlake needs it.

5. Boston Trust is a new trust whose provisions require that 100 percent of trust accounting income be distributed annually to its beneficiaries. The Boston Trust trustee expects the trust to have zero taxable income each year since all income will be taxed to the beneficiaries.

6. Morgan Trust is a complex trust whose trustee has discretion to distribute trust property to its beneficiaries. During 2004, the trust distributes several investment assets to Ms. Donnell. The FMV of these assets exceeds their tax basis to the trust at the time of the distribution.

7. At the time of Mrs. Hansen's death, she had received but not yet paid credit card bills totaling $4,000 and property tax assessments totaling $25,000.

8. Mr. Allan died on March 1, 2000. One of his heirs contested his will. As of December 31, 2004, the estate had still not distributed its assets or liquidated.

9. Mrs. Stavros created a trust with a transfer of investment property. She named her younger brother as the income beneficiary and the family attorney as the trustee. The trust terminates when her brother reaches the age of 40, at which time the trust property reverts back to Mrs. Stavros.

10. Mr. Ericson died on January 15, 2004. On February 1, 2004, his widow received the final paycheck from his employer for the period January 1, 2004, through the date of his death. In March, his widow received Mr. Ericson's Form W-2 from his employer showing his taxable wages and withholding for the year ended December 31, 2003.

**Research Problems**

1. At the time of his death, Mr. Aaron held notes receivable from Mr. Davidson. The notes arose as part of an installment sale transaction four years before Mr. Aaron's death. He has been reporting gain on the sale using the installment method. At the time of his death, $50,000 of deferred gain remained to be recognized. Mr. Davidson still has two additional payments of $45,000 each to make over the next two years under the sales agreement.

   a. At what value should the installment receivable be included in Mr. Aaron's estate for estate tax purposes?

   b. Is the $50,000 of deferred gain remaining on the sale at the time of Mr. Aaron's death considered income in respect of a decedent? Will his estate report the income on the estate income tax return, or will his heirs report it when the payments are received from Mr. Davidson?

2. Amigo Trust is a simple trust with one income beneficiary, Ms. Luces. The trust has existed for 10 years, and each year on December 26, the trustee has sent her a check for the required income distributions. The trust assets are invested in stocks, bonds, and mutual funds, with automatic reinvestment of dividends and capital gains. In late 2004, the stock market experienced sharp declines. Because of automatic reinvestments, the trust did not have enough available cash on December 26, 2004, to pay Ms. Luces's required distribution. The trustee did not wish to sell assets at their market price on that

date and therefore waited until early January when the market experienced some re-bound to sell sufficient investments to make Ms. Luces's 2004 income distribution. Is Amigo Trust entitled to a distribution deduction on its 2004 tax return? Must Ms. Luces report on her 2004 individual tax return the amount of the distribution she was entitled to receive, or is this amount reportable in 2005 when she actually received the cash?

## Tax Planning Cases

1. As part of a comprehensive estate plan, Mr. Wesley intends to establish a trust naming his sister, Mrs. Chelsea, as income beneficiary and her two children as remainder beneficiaries on her death. Mr. Wesley will form the trust with an initial transfer of assets valued at $300,000. He is trying to decide what type of assets to place in the trust: ordinary income-producing assets, assets expected to appreciate in value to generate capital gains on sale but little current income, or a combination of such assets. Mr. Wesley intends that ordinary income items such as rents and interest be included in accounting income and distributed currently to Mrs. Chelsea but that capital gains would be allocated to principal. Although he wishes the trust to generate some current income for Mrs. Chelsea, he would also like to see the trust principal grow during her lifetime to increase the value ultimately available to her children.

   To assist Mr. Wesley in making his transfer choices, he has asked you to analyze three benchmark cases. For each of the following, assume (1) an 8 percent discount rate in calculating present value, (2) a trust term of 20 years, (3) annual trustee fees of $3,000 payable out of principal, and (4) a marginal income tax rate on ordinary income of 30 percent for Mrs. Chelsea.

   *Case 1:* Assume that all trust assets are invested to produce annual ordinary income of $30,000 that is distributed annually to Chelsea.

   *Case 2:* Assume that all trust corpus is invested in capital gain–producing assets. Trust assets are expected to appreciate at a rate of 9 percent annually. At the time of the transfer into the trust, the assets have an adjusted tax basis equal to their FMV. In the final year of the trust, it will sell all assets and pay any required taxes prior to distributing the net proceeds to the remainder beneficiaries.

   *Case 3:* Assume that 50 percent of trust assets are invested to produce annual ordinary income of $15,000. All such income is distributed annually to Mrs. Chelsea. The remaining trust assets are invested to produce capital gain. For this portion of trust assets, make the same appreciation and disposition assumptions as stated for Case 2.

   *a.* For each of the three cases just described, determine the following:
   1. The net present value of the stream of after-tax income available to Mrs. Chelsea.
   2. The net present value of remaining trust assets to be distributed to Mrs. Chelsea's children on termination of the trust.
   3. The total net present value of the trust income and corpus.

   *b.* Given Mr. Wesley's stated goals and your analysis in part (a), what would you recommend to him? Explain your recommendation.

2. Mr. Dikembe plans to form a trust for the benefit of his nephew. It will provide cash flow to the boy during his high school, college, and graduate school education and terminate when he turns 25. Mr. Dikembe's sister (the boy's mother) is named as the remainder beneficiary. He plans to fund the trust with investment assets and expects the trust to generate approximately the following types and amounts of income annually from the assets initially contributed to the trust.

| Ordinary income | $17,000 |
|---|---|
| Long-term capital gain | 6,000 |
| Tax-exempt income | 5,000 |
| Total | $28,000 |

Mr. Dikembe would like to provide his nephew $20,000 of after-tax cash flow each year. His nephew has little other income; his marginal tax rate on ordinary income is 15 percent. Mr. Dikembe would like to designate the source of such distributions to maximize the sum of after-tax cash flow to his nephew plus after-tax cash flow remaining in the estate. This way, designation will preserve the value of the remainder interest to his sister. Mr. Dikembe estimates that the trust will incur $4,000 of administration costs per year allocable to principal.

a. If Mr. Dikembe specifies that distributions from the trust be made first from ordinary income sources, second from capital gains, and third from tax-exempt income, how much cash must the trust distribute for the nephew to have $20,000 of annual after-tax cash flow?

b. At the distribution level determined in part *(a)*, compute the trust's taxable income, tax liability, and after-tax cash flow.

c. What are the potential alternative ordering choices that Mr. Dikembe could use to specify the source of cash distributions? For each alternative identified, calculate the distributed amount in accordance with part *(a)* and results for part *(b)*.

d. Given the results of your analysis in parts *(a)*, *(b)*, and *(c)*, make a recommendation to Mr. Dikembe regarding the specification of distributed amounts that you believe maximizes the sum of after-tax value to the nephew and the value of the trust remainder interest.

e. What factors would you recommend that the trustee consider in determining how to invest the trust's after-tax cash flow remaining following distributions? How are your recommendations affected by the distribution ordering that you recommended in part *(d)?*

# Chapter **Seventeen**

# Wealth Transfer Planning

### Learning Objectives

*After reading this chapter, you will be able to:*

1. Develop a plan to maximize the benefit of the annual gift tax exclusion.

2. Describe the use of trusts to make gifts to minors that are eligible for the annual exclusion.

3. Select appropriate assets to be transferred by gift.

4. Explain the techniques for removing life insurance proceeds from the taxable gross estate.

5. Describe the factors affecting the valuation of closely held business interests for transfer tax purposes.

6. Discuss the trade-off inherent in the optimal use of the unified credit versus the marital deduction.

7. Describe the options for deferring payment of estate tax liability.

8. Discuss strategies for reducing estate probate costs.


Our discussions thus far in Part Six of *Strategies* have described the substantial tax costs often imposed by the transfer and income tax systems on transfers of accumulated personal wealth by gift or at death. This chapter focuses on strategies to reduce these tax burdens. Some techniques described here are quite simple and easily implemented by any forward-thinking taxpayer. Others are more complex and could require the assistance of a qualified tax attorney to draft necessary documents. Any taxpayer with substantial exposure to transfer taxation should seek the advice of tax specialists in crafting a comprehensive estate plan to maximize after-tax wealth available to his or her heirs.

As discussed in Chapter 15, the Economic Growth and Tax Relief Reconciliation Act of 2001 (EGTRRA) gradually phases out the estate tax from 2002 through 2009, with repeal of the tax in 2010. Had EGTRRA permanently repealed the estate tax, transfer tax planning would be limited to minimizing gift taxes during life and protecting the estates of decedents dying during the phase-out period. However, the sunset provisions of EGTRRA reinstate the estate tax in its 2001 form for decedents dying after 2010. Absent future legislation to extend the estate tax repeal, only the assets of decedents dying in 2010 escape estate taxation.

While taxpayers might be tempted to assume that the estate tax repeal will be extended, doing so is a bit like playing Russian roulette with a loaded gun! The cost of such an assumption to the taxpayer's heirs could be disastrous. Responsible estate planning must address the tax law as currently written. Thus, wealthy individuals should consider planning strategies to minimize transfer taxes under the assumption that the estate tax will apply to decedents dying after 2010. Transfer tax planning also remains important for decedents dying before 2010 whose estate values exceed the increased exemption amounts described in Chapter 15. At several points in this chapter, we highlight planning strategies applicable to the 2002 through 2009 phaseout period of EGTRRA.

This chapter begins with strategies for gifting assets during the taxpayer's lifetime. These strategies include the maximization of annual gift tax exclusions, the use of serial gifts, family limited partnerships, trusts for minors, the use of gifts to shift income to low-bracket family members, and the choice of assets to be gifted. We then consider planning ideas for minimizing estate taxes. In particular, we consider strategies for reducing the value of the gross estate, the optimal use of the unified credit and the marital deduction, provisions for deferring payment of estate tax liability, and the use of a variety of trusts as estate planning tools. The chapter concludes with a discussion of planning to reduce probate costs.

# GIFT TAX PLANNING ISSUES

**Objective 1**
Develop a plan to maximize the benefit of the annual gift tax exclusion.

The simplest strategy for avoiding gift tax is to maximize the use of the annual exclusion. As discussed in Chapter 15, the annual exclusion allows up to $11,000 of present interest gifts to be made annually to each recipient free of gift tax. In addition, married taxpayers who elect gift splitting can double their annual tax-free transfers to $22,000 per recipient. Through a systematic plan for annual giving, each taxpayer can transfer substantial wealth over a period of years without incurring gift tax and without utilizing any unified credit.

*annual exclusion for future interest*

| *Maximizing Annual Gifts* | Mr. Samir is 50 years old and has four children and six grandchildren. If he gives $11,000 to each child and grandchild each year for 15 years, he will have transferred $1.65 million ($11,000 × 10 recipients × 15 years) without incurring transfer tax. If he is married and elects gift splitting, he and his spouse can transfer $3.3 million ($22,000 × 10 recipients × 15 years) tax free. |
|---|---|

Effective utilization of the annual exclusion not only avoids gift tax but also reduces the value of property remaining in the taxpayer's estate at death. The estate is reduced by both the amounts gifted and any earnings or appreciation in value attributable to the gifted property. In some cases, the combination of systematic giving during life and the unified credit at death can completely eliminate transfer taxation. Of course, the larger the potential estate, the earlier a systematic giving plan must begin to maximize estate tax savings.

| *Giving to Reduce Estate Tax* | Ms. Day is 60 years old, expects to live at least 10 more years, and estimates that at her death, her estate will be worth $2 million. If she undertakes no transfer tax planning, estate taxes of $435,000[1] will be due at her death, leaving net assets of $1,565,000 for her heirs. If she makes annual gifts of $11,000 to each of her five children and five grandchildren for the next |
|---|---|

[1] Using Table 15.1 from Chapter 15, the tax on an estate of $2 million is $780,800. Assuming that Ms. Day dies after 2010, her unified credit amount will be $345,800 (tax on $1 million exemption amount, using Table 15.1), resulting in a net tax liability of $435,000.

10 years, her taxable estate will be reduced to $900,000 [$2 million − ($11,000 × 10 recipients × 10 years)]. Estate tax on $900,000 will be completely offset by the unified credit, and no estate tax will be owed. Ms. Day's heirs will receive $2 million free of any transfer taxation. Using a 7 percent discount rate, the present value of the estate tax savings (assuming that she dies in 10 years) is $221,132.

In spite of the tax advantages of annual giving, various nontax considerations often discourage taxpayers from taking full advantage of this planning strategy. Taxpayers could be unwilling to give away the bulk of their assets because of the uncertainty over their life expectancy and the potential for high costs of medical care and assisted living. In other cases, the taxpayer's assets might be noncash illiquid investments (such as real estate or stock in closely held businesses) not easily divisible into $11,000 increments. How might such assets be transferred to utilize the annual exclusion? Two primary options exist. First, joint ownership of an asset could be given to several individuals so that the value given to each does not exceed the annual exclusion. For example, a taxpayer with four children could gift each of them an equal interest in property valued at $44,000 and utilize four annual exclusions to avoid transfer tax.

Alternatively, ownership of property could be transferred in fractions over time using a serial gift technique. One approach to serial gifts is to "sell" the asset to the recipient on an installment basis under terms requiring annual installment and interest payments not in excess of $11,000. The transferor can then "forgive" the payment of the required annual installments each year. Caution should be exercised in using this technique, however, since the IRS may use "substance-over-form" arguments to characterize the entire transfer as a gift in the year of the sale which would negate the benefits of multiple annual exclusions.

The family limited partnership is another alternative for transferring ownership of fractional interests in property over time. As typically structured, a **family limited partnership** is established by parents or grandparents who transfer property (such as a family business) into a partnership in exchange for general partner interests. Over time, the partnership creators give limited partner interests in the partnership to their children and grandchildren. These gifts are considered a present interest qualifying for the annual exclusion. However, since the gifts are limited partner interests, the recipients do not share in the management of the property. The creators, as general partners, retain control over the partnership assets. Because of the lack of control and marketability, the valuation of the limited partner interests typically warrants substantial discounts (often 25 to 60 percent) in relation to the value of the underlying property.[2] Throughout the remaining life of the partnership, each partner recognizes his or her allocable share of partnership income and loss in the manner described in Chapter 7. When the partnership creators die, only the value of their remaining general partner interests are included in their gross estates.

**Tax Talk**

In a recent U.S. Tax Court case, the court included 100 percent of the value of assets transferred to a family limited partnership in the transferor's gross estate on death, arguing that the transferor's retention of control over the assets did not impair his ability to possess and enjoy such assets until the time of his death. This case is currently under appeal; in the interim, estate tax planners are advising donors to reduce their control over partnerships to which they've contributed substantial assets (*Estate of Albert Strangi et al.,* TC Memo 2003-145).

*Gifts of Family Limited Partnership Interests*

Mr. and Mrs. Berkman own and operate a small retail business. The couple wishes to begin transferring partial ownership of it to their children and grandchildren. The Berkmans create a partnership by transferring the business assets in exchange for general partner interests.[3] The Berkmans then give 1 percent limited partner interests to each of their four children and six grandchildren. If the value of the underlying business assets is $2.5 million, the maximum value attributable to a 1 percent interest would be $25,000. However, a minority discount

[2] Additional issues associated with valuing family-owned businesses are discussed later in this chapter as part of the section on Reducing the Taxable Gross Estate.

[3] As discussed in Chapter 3, the original transfer is not taxable under Section 721.

of 25 percent would reduce the gift's value to $18,750. With gift splitting, each gift is fully offset by the annual exclusion. With additional annual gifts, the Berkmans could transfer most of the ownership of the business to their heirs in just a few years while retaining control as general partners of the family limited partnership.

Another factor that often inhibits the early adoption of an annual giving plan is the age of potential recipients. For a gift to be *complete*, legal ownership, including related rights and responsibilities, must be transferred to the recipient. Parents and grandparents are often understandably reluctant to make these transfers to minor children. In these circumstances, use of a trust with a trustee to manage trust property could be desirable. However, one limitation of using trusts for gift tax purposes is that transfers into a trust might not be considered a gift of a present interest since the trust beneficiary does not always have an immediate right to income and enjoyment of the trust property.[4] If the gift is not of a present interest, the $11,000 annual exclusion is not available. Fortunately, this limitation is waived in circumstances involving qualified trusts to benefit minors and Crummey trusts.

**Objective 2**
Describe the use of trusts to make gifts to minors that are eligible for the annual exclusion.

What type of trust is considered a **qualified trust to benefit a minor**? First, the trust must be irrevocable for transfers into it to qualify as complete gifts. Both income and principal of the trust can be expended by or for the benefit of a minor child under age 21. Any portion of the trust property or income not expended by the time the minor reaches 21 must pass to the minor at that time. If the minor dies before age 21, the trust assets must be payable to the minor's estate or the minor's designated beneficiary. If all of these conditions are met, transfers of property into the trust are considered gifts of a present interest and qualify for the annual exclusion.[5] This type of trust could be established with an initial gift of $11,000 and additional transfers made on an annual basis. If the trustee distributes income to the minor, recall from Chapter 16 that this income is taxed to the recipient beneficiary at the beneficiary's tax rate.[6] If the trustee accumulates trust income, it is taxed to the trust. Also note that if the minor's parent is the trustee, the trust assets are included in the parent's estate if he or she dies before the child reaches age 21. Since this result likely negates the planning objective of removing the trust assets from the parent's estate, the choice of another trustee is desirable.

*Qualified Trusts to Benefit a Minor*

Mr. and Mrs. Mahendra form a qualified trust for the benefit of their five-year-old daughter. They name her brother as trustee of the trust and grant him discretion to accumulate trust income or distribute it for her benefit. Mr. and Mrs. Mahendra plan to transfer $22,000 to the trust each year for the next 15 years. Using the gift-splitting election, each transfer qualifies for two annual exclusions. Over the 15-year transfer period, Mr. and Mrs. Mahendra will transfer $330,000 free of transfer taxation. Trust income will be taxed to either their daughter or the trust, depending on discretionary distributions. When the daughter turns 21, the trust will dissolve and trust property plus any accumulated income will be transferred to her.

The **Crummey trust** is another solution for qualifying gifts to a trust as a present interest for purposes of the annual exclusion. The technique is named after a court case holding that certain demand powers available to each trust beneficiary qualified as a

---

[4] Recall from Chapter 15 that gifts of an income interest in property with rights to immediate possession and enjoyment of income are considered present interest gifts but gifts of a remainder interest in property are not considered present interest gifts.

[5] Section 2503(c).

[6] For minors under the age of 14, the kiddie tax, discussed shortly, can increase the tax rate applicable to income distributed from the trust.

present interest.[7] These trusts are generally written to provide beneficiaries the right to demand distributions of trust income equal to the lesser of the annual gift exclusion ($11,000 or $22,000 with gift splitting) or the amount gifted into the trust that year.[8] Even if the beneficiary does not exercise the demand power, the courts have held that the annual exclusion is available for current transfers. Of course, the donor hopes that the beneficiary will not exercise the demand right and that annual contributions to the trust will accumulate. Once a beneficiary has demanded a distribution, the donor often ceases to make additional contributions. A Crummey trust is generally more flexible than a qualified trust for a minor since it can terminate at whatever point the donor specifies and can be established for beneficiaries of any age.

| *Using a Crummey Trust* | Mr. Torvall establishes a trust for the benefit of his niece by transferring investment assets worth $100,000. He also plans to transfer assets to the trust each year and grants the trustee discretionary power to make distributions of trust income to his niece. The trust will terminate when she is 30 years of age, and all remaining trust assets will be distributed to her at that time. Without a Crummey provision, Mr. Torvall's annual gifts to this trust will not qualify for the annual exclusion since annual distributions are not required but are discretionary. A Crummey power would provide his niece the right to demand annual distributions not exceeding the lesser of $11,000 or the amount transferred into the trust by Mr. Torvall in any given year. For example, suppose that in 2004 he gifts $11,000 into the trust. With a Crummey provision, the gift qualifies for the annual exclusion, whether or not his niece exercises the demand power. |
| --- | --- |

**Objective 3**
Select appropriate assets to be transferred by gift.

In choosing property to give, the best choice for tax purposes might depend on the relative marginal income tax rates of the donor and recipient. For example, gifts of income-producing property can be used to reduce income tax burden when gifted from a taxpayer in a high marginal tax bracket to a taxpayer in a low marginal tax bracket. Recall that this approach was discussed in Chapter 1 as an illustration of tax planning using the entity variable. This planning technique is subject to an important limitation for gifts to children under 14. Unearned income of a child under 14 is taxed at the parents' highest marginal tax rate.[9] One strategy for avoiding the so-called **kiddie tax** is to gift investment property generating little current income but expected to appreciate in value. As long as these assets are held until after the child's 14th birthday, any gain on their disposition is taxed at the lesser of the child's marginal tax rate or the applicable capital gains rate.

| *Entity Variable Gifts and the Kiddie Tax* | Mr. and Mrs. Randall are in the 35 percent marginal tax bracket. They are considering gifting property worth $20,000 to their son who is in the 15 percent marginal tax bracket. With gift splitting, the transfer qualifies for the annual exclusion and produces no gift tax. If the property earns $4,000 of income annually and their son is at least 14 years of age, the family unit saves $800 [$4,000 × (35 percent − 15 percent)] of annual tax liability. Assuming that the property generates the same earnings each year for the next 20 years, the present value of total income tax savings from this single gift, using a 7 percent discount rate, is $8,475. However, if their son is under 14, the income earned on the property will continue to be taxed at 35 percent until he reaches the age of 14. In this case, the Randalls might prefer to transfer assets not producing current income but expected to appreciate in value. As long as the property is held until their son turns 14, any gain is not subject to the kiddie tax. |
| --- | --- |

[7] *D. Clifford Crummey v. CIR,* AFTR 2d 6023 (9th Cir., 1968).
[8] The beneficiary must be advised of his or her demand rights and each year decline to demand any distribution.
[9] Sec. 1(g).

In choosing assets to give, the donor should also consider whether the property's FMV is greater or less than the donor's tax basis at the time of the gift. A gift of appreciated property has an income tax advantage because the donor is not taxed on the gift's appreciation in value. If the gift recipient sells the property, the appreciation is taxed at the recipient's (possibly lower) tax rate, given the carryover basis rules discussed in Chapter 15. A gift of appreciated property also removes value from the donor's future gross estate but subjects the transfer to gift tax if the value of the property given exceeds the annual exclusion.

The primary disadvantage of giving appreciated property is the carryover of the donor's lower tax basis to the recipient. If appreciated property is instead held until death (except for decedents dying in 2010), the recipient beneficiary is allowed to step up the basis of the property to its FMV on the date of death, and its appreciation in value in the hands of the decedent is never subject to income tax. However, the value of the property on the date of death is subject to estate tax.[10]

---

*Gifts of Appreciated Property*

Mr. Wayne plans to transfer property with a fair market value of $100,000 to his son, who is 15 years old and in the 15 percent marginal income tax bracket. The property produces annual income of $10,000. If Mr. Wayne's tax basis in the property is $25,000 and his marginal income tax rate is 35 percent, the transfer will reduce the family's annual income tax liability by $2,000 [$10,000 × (35 percent − 15 percent)]. He will not pay income tax on the $75,000 of appreciation in value at the date of the gift, but the excess of the gift's value over the annual exclusion ($89,000) will absorb unified credit.

Suppose that his son continues to hold the property when Mr. Wayne dies 10 years after the gift, at which time the property is valued at $180,000. The postgift appreciation escapes transfer taxation. If Mr. Wayne's marginal estate tax rate is 55 percent, the tax savings attributable to such appreciation is $44,000 ($80,000 × 55 percent). His son's tax basis in the property is $25,000, and he must pay income tax on both pre- and postgift appreciation when he sells the property. Assuming that the property is a capital asset, the tax cost of this sale is $23,250 [15 percent capital gains rate × ($180,000 − $25,000)]. The present value of total family tax savings from gifting this asset (assuming that Mr. Wayne dies and his son sells the property in 10 years) is determined as follows:

| | |
|---|---|
| Estate tax savings on appreciation of property | $44,000 |
| Capital gains tax on sale of property | (23,250) |
| Net tax savings in 10 years | $20,750 |
| Present value of future tax savings at 7 percent | $10,541 |
| Present value of stream of tax savings on income from the property ($2,000 per year for 10 years) at 7 percent | 14,048 |
| Total net present value of tax savings from gift | $24,589 |

If Mr. Wayne bequeathed the property to his son at his death, the entire $180,000 value is subject to transfer tax, and his son's tax basis in the asset is $180,000.

---

Property that has declined in value should not be gifted or held until death since the value decline will never be deductible for income tax purposes. As discussed in Chapter 15, the recipient of this type of property takes a tax basis equal to the donor's FMV on the date

---

[10] If the size of the estate is such that the unified credit will eliminate estate tax liability, the step up in basis allowed at death makes holding appreciated or appreciating assets until death optimal in many circumstances.

of gift if the value is less than the donor's tax basis.[11] The best tax strategy is to sell property that has declined in value prior to death to recognize the loss and maximize its potential deductibility.

An optimal gift strategy is to give property that has appreciated or is expected to appreciate substantially in the future. Although this gift can produce some current gift tax (if in excess of the annual exclusion), no future estate tax is owed and future appreciation is taxed to the recipient if and when the property is sold. Any gift tax paid also decreases the value of the giver's future estate.

| *Choosing Property to Give* | Mr. Saul has the following assets, one of which he wants to give to his daughter: |
|---|---|

| Asset Description | Adjusted Basis | Fair Market Value |
|---|---|---|
| Corporate stock in ABC Inc. | $10,000 | $15,000 |
| Corporate stock in XYZ Corporation | 20,000 | 15,000 |
| Corporate bonds | 14,000 | 15,000 |
| Land | 5,000 | 15,000 |

The ABC stock pays current dividends of $1,000 per year, and the corporate bonds pay interest of $1,500 per year. Mr. Saul expects the land to appreciate in value substantially over the next 10 years.

Which asset should Mr. Saul give to his daughter? The best choice depends on both the current and expected future appreciation, and the relative marginal income tax rates for father and daughter. The stock in XYZ Corporation is clearly a poor choice because of its decline in value unless he believes that its value will increase in the future while his daughter owns it. If her marginal income tax rate is lower than her father's, a gift of either the corporate bonds or the ABC Inc. stock would achieve an entity variable income shift. Because of the expected future appreciation of the land, a gift of that asset would reduce future estate tax liability. Since the corporate bonds are unlikely to appreciate substantially, the best choice is either the ABC stock or the land, depending on the relative expected future appreciation of these assets.

For tax years prior to 2004 and after 2010, a single exemption equivalent amount applies for both gift and estate tax purposes. As discussed in Chapter 15, this exemption equivalent amount excludes from transfer taxation cumulative wealth transfers made during life and at death not exceeding the exemption. EGTRRA fixes the lifetime gift tax exemption amount at $1 million; however, the estate tax exemption increases to $1.5 million for 2004 and 2005, $2 million for 2006 through 2008, and $3.5 million for 2009. During this period, taxpayers might prefer to limit cumulative taxable gifts to $1 million, to avoid gift tax. If death occurs during the phaseout period, additional transfers will qualify for the increased estate tax exemption.

| *Gift Strategies during Estate Tax Phaseout Period* | Mr. Farrell is in poor health, and expects to live no longer than five years. He has previously made no taxable transfers and his estate is currently valued at $5 million. He expects several of his assets to appreciate substantially during the next five years and would like to give those assets to his children now. If Mr. Farrell transfers all of his assets to his children in 2004, $1 million of such transfers will qualify for the gift tax exemption. The remaining $4 million will |
|---|---|

[11] If the property later increases in value, the split basis rule allows the gift recipient to calculate the gain using the donor's tax basis. See Chapter 15.

be subject to gift tax, with a top marginal rate of 48 percent. Alternatively, if Mr. Farrell transfers only $1 million of assets to his children in 2004, no current gift tax is owed. If Mr. Farrell's remaining assets appreciate to $4.5 million at his death in 2009, an additional $2.5 million estate exemption amount ($3.5 million 2009 estate exemption equivalent amount reduced by $1 million cumulative lifetime gift exemption) applies and only $2 million is subject to estate tax, with a top marginal rate of 45 percent.

# ESTATE TAX PLANNING ISSUES

Estate tax planning strategies typically fall into one of three categories: (1) reducing the value of the taxable gross estate, (2) maximizing the value of estate tax deductions and credits, or (3) deferring payment of estate tax liability. The remainder of this chapter describes planning options in each category and also considers strategies for reducing estate probate costs to maximize after-tax value available to the heirs.

## Reducing the Taxable Gross Estate

We have previously discussed in depth one important strategy for reducing the taxable gross estate: maximizing lifetime transfers eligible for the annual exclusion. In some circumstances, it is also advisable to transfer assets in excess of the annual exclusion prior to death. These transfers initially absorb unified credit, effectively deferring transfer taxation into the future. In addition, postgift appreciation is not subject to transfer taxation, as discussed previously. Finally, any gift taxes paid during the transferor's life reduce estate assets and thus estate tax at death.

### Life Insurance Trusts

**Objective 4**
Explain the techniques for removing life insurance proceeds from the taxable gross estate.

Life insurance represents one of the most valuable assets at death for many taxpayers. A simple planning technique transfers ownership of life insurance policies to someone other than the decedent with named beneficiaries other than the estate. If the taxpayer retains no **incidents of ownership,** a transfer of this type avoids inclusion of the insurance proceeds in the gross estate. Prohibited incidents of ownership include the power to change the beneficiary of the policy, cancel the policy, borrow against the policy, pledge the policy for a loan, or revoke the policy's assignment. If the taxpayer retains any of these powers, the policy proceeds are included in the decedent's gross estate.

The ownership of life insurance policies can be transferred into a trust that terminates on death. This transfer must be irrevocable to qualify as a completed transfer for gift and estate tax purposes. A trustee other than the grantor is necessary to avoid estate tax on the trust property, and the grantor must not retain any of the prohibited powers described earlier. Also note that this transfer must be made more than three years before death to be effective in removing the insurance proceeds from the taxable estate.[12] Although the transfer of life insurance is considered a gift, its value subject to transfer tax is based on the cost to purchase a comparable policy at the time of the gift. This cost is considerably smaller than the future death benefit that the policy provides. The trust document must be drafted carefully since the grantor must relinquish all power over the policy. For example, if the policy names the grantor's spouse as a beneficiary, the trust document might wish to direct the trustee regarding changes in beneficiary designation in the event of divorce or death of the original beneficiary.

[12] This three-year window is inflexible and applies even if the death of the insured is accidental or unexpected.

| *Transferring Ownership of Life Insurance* | Mrs. Martin purchases a whole-life policy on her own life with a death benefit of $2 million. She names her two young children as equal beneficiaries of the policy. Shortly after the purchase, she transfers the policy into a trust naming her brother as trustee. Mrs. Martin has made a gift equal to the cost of the policy. As long as she retains no incidents of ownership and lives at least three years beyond the date of the gift, the $2 million death benefit is not included in her gross estate. |
|---|---|

### Asset Valuation Issues

**Objective 5**
Describe the factors affecting the valuation of closely held business interests for transfer tax purposes.

As mentioned in Chapter 15, the valuation of assets subject to transfer taxation is a critical aspect of tax determination. In some cases, such as marketable securities, estate assets can be easily valued when a ready market exists for them. In other cases, valuation could be difficult. For example, if a primary asset of the estate is an interest in a closely held business, no ready market for the asset necessarily exists. Typically, the estate argues for a lower value than that asserted by the IRS to reduce transfer taxation. Revenue Ruling 59-60[13] lists the factors to be considered in valuing stock of closely held corporations for transfer tax purposes, including the following:

- Nature and history of the business.
- General economic outlook and economic condition of the industry in which the business operates.
- Book value of the stock.
- The company's financial condition, earning capacity, and dividend-paying capacity.
- Existence of goodwill or other intangible value in the company.
- Previous sales of company stock and the size of the ownership interest to be valued.
- The market price of similar corporations whose stock is publicly traded.

Although all of these factors should be carefully considered in valuing closely held business interests, arguments in favor of lower valuations have often focused on goodwill, marketability, and the size of the ownership interest included in the estate.

In valuing an interest in an established business with a solid earnings record, the IRS is likely to argue that goodwill exists to increase the value of the business beyond that of its identifiable tangible assets. If such goodwill can be attributed to the decedent's efforts, however, the estate might argue that goodwill value has been impaired following the decedent's death.

In many cases, the courts have allowed **marketability discounts** in the valuation of closely held business interests. These discounts acknowledge the costs that would be incurred in creating a market to dispose of closely held stock, including underwriting costs and other expenses of going public. With respect to the size of the estate's ownership interest, valuation discounts have been allowed related to both minority interests and controlling interests. A **minority interest discount** reflects the lack of control that minority owners can exercise, particularly with respect to dividend payment policies.

| *Minority Discounts and Related Valuation Allowances* | Ms. Kosman owned a substantial stock interest in a closely held banking business. She gifted portions of her holdings to her children. In a dispute with the IRS over the appropriate value of the gifted stock, the Tax Court allowed a 10 percent minority interest discount in addition to a 15 percent discount for lack of marketability and a 4 percent discount for lack of voting control.[14] |
|---|---|

[13] 1959-1 C.B. 237.
[14] Jane Kosman, (1996), TC Memo 1996-112.

Given the rationale for minority interest discounts, one might expect controlling interests to be valued at a premium. An alternative theory argues, however, that the disposition of a large controlling interest in the stock of a single corporation within a short period of time could depress stock price. This **blockage rule** allows a discount on the per share price at which smaller blocks of stock are expected to trade in valuing a large block of stock.

The **special use valuation method** provides an opportunity to reduce the value of business property included in the gross estate.[15] This method applies when the primary asset in a family business is real estate. In particular, this valuation method applies to family farming or ranching operations. This technique differentiates between the property's FMV under its "current use"—farming or ranching—versus its "best" or "highest" use—such as developed commercial real estate. Typically the value under current use is lower, and this lower value is allowed for estate tax purposes if the estate meets the requirements described in the following discussion. The reduction in the estate value due to this method is limited to $850,000 in 2004. Thus, if the difference in value between the current use and the highest use is greater than $850,000, an intermediate value (highest use − $850,000) is used for estate tax purposes.

| | |
|---|---|
| *Reduction in Estate Tax Value under the Special Use Valuation Method* | Ms. Itol's estate includes property qualifying for special use valuation. It is valued at $1.5 million under its current use. If the property value under its highest use is $2 million, a reduction in estate value of $500,000 is permitted, and the property is included in her gross estate at a $1.5 million value. However, if the property value under its highest use is $2.5 million, the reduction in estate value is limited to $850,000, and the property is included in Ms. Itol's gross estate at a value of $1.65 million ($2.5 million − $850,000). |

The special use valuation method is elective and requires that (1) at least 50 percent of the adjusted gross estate be property (real and personal) devoted to the qualifying use and (2) at least 25 percent of the adjusted gross estate be real property devoted to the qualifying use. In applying these percentages, the property is valued at its best or highest use. Thus, the adjusted gross estate for this purpose is the decedent's gross estate calculated without reduction for the special use valuation method.

| | |
|---|---|
| *Qualification for Special Use Valuation* | Mr. Harmon's estate includes a cattle ranch. At the time of his death, the real property associated with the ranch is valued at $1.8 million under its current use and $2.2 million under its highest use. Personal property used in the ranching business is valued at $500,000. His estate also includes other property valued at $2 million. To determine qualification for the special use valuation method, his adjusted gross estate value is $4.7 million ($2.2 million + $500,000 + $2 million). The first requirement for use of the method is satisfied since the value of the real and personal property devoted to ranching, $2.7 million ($2.2 million + $500,000), exceeds $2.35 million (50 percent × $4.7 million). The second requirement is also satisfied since the value of the real property devoted to ranching, $2.2 million, exceeds $1.175 million (25 percent × $4.7 million). The reduction allowed under the special use valuation method is $400,000 ($2.2 million − $1.8 million), and Mr. Harmon's taxable gross estate totals $4.3 million ($2.2 million − $400,000 + $500,000 + $2 million). |

The special use valuation method also requires the decedent and members of his or her family to have owned the real property for five of eight years prior to the decedent's death

---

[15] Section 2032A.

and that the decedent and members of his or her family have materially participated in the operation of the business during that period.

Finally, the property subject to special use valuation must pass to qualifying heirs—ancestors, spouse, lineal descendents, and their spouses. The heirs must continue to use the property in a qualifying manner for at least 10 years following the decedent's death. If they fail to do so, the estate tax savings are recaptured, and the IRS seeks repayment from the heirs.

The special use valuation election is available in addition to the family-owned business exclusion previously discussed. From a planning perspective, note that both the family-owned business exclusion and the special use valuation election apply to transfers at death to reduce estate tax liability but are not available for transfers by gift during life. This distinction does not mean that partial transfers prior to death are not desirable; certainly to the extent of the annual exclusion, these transfers can reduce overall transfer tax potential.

## Maximizing Estate Tax Deductions and Credits

**Objective 6**
Discuss the trade-off inherent in the optimal use of the unified credit versus the marital deduction.

The *marital deduction* provides a very powerful estate tax–planning opportunity for married couples. Of course, if all assets are left to the surviving spouse, no estate tax is owed. However, this approach suffers from two important deficiencies. First, the bequest of all assets to the surviving spouse wastes the unified credit available to the first spouse to die. When the second spouse dies, the assets of both spouses are fully subject to estate tax reduced by only one unified credit. Second, the direct bequest of assets to the surviving spouse means that the survivor has complete control of all assets, including determining to whom they will be left on that spouse's death. If each spouse brings significant assets into the marriage, each might wish to control the ultimate disposition of premarital property. Fortunately, planning techniques can be used to address both of these issues while obtaining value from the marital deduction.

Effective planning must consider the optimal use of the marital deduction versus the unified credit. A typical strategy is to leave at least the exemption equivalent amount ($1.5 million in 2004) to someone other than the surviving spouse. For example, assets of this value could be left in trust for minor children or transferred in trust or directly to other heirs designated by the will of each spouse. The remaining assets could be left to the surviving spouse, resulting in zero estate tax liability after the marital deduction and unified credit.

Other factors to consider are the expected future appreciation of the estate property. If the property is expected to increase in value dramatically before the probable death of the surviving spouse, transferring it to the children or other heirs and paying some estate taxes on the lower FMV at the death of the first spouse might be better than waiting until the surviving spouse dies. In particular, in choosing assets to absorb the unified credit, appreciating assets are a good option.

*Sacrificing the Unified Credit of One Spouse*

Mr. and Mrs. Ulysses both own substantial assets individually. When Mrs. Ulysses dies in 2004, she leaves her entire estate valued at $2 million to her husband. The marital deduction reduces her taxable estate to zero, and no estate tax is owed. When Mr. Ulysses dies in 2014, his estate includes assets received from his wife then valued at $3 million plus $1 million of additional assets for a total taxable estate of $4 million. After reduction for Mr. Ulysses's unified credit, his estate tax liability is $1,495,000.[16] If Mrs. Ulysses had left assets equal to her unified credit to other heirs, $1.5 million of her estate would have passed to those heirs, and

[16] Using Table 15.1 from Chapter 15, the gross estate tax on a taxable estate of $4 million is $1,840,800. The unified credit in 2014 is $345,800 (the tax on $1 million from Table 15.1), reducing the estate tax liability to $1,495,000.

her husband would have received the remaining $500,000. At the same rate of appreciation assumed previously, these assets would be worth $750,000 at Mr. Ulysses's death. His taxable estate would total $1.75 million, resulting in net estate tax liability after unified credit of $322,500. Utilizing his wife's unified credit rather than leaving all of her assets to him saves $1,172,500 of estate tax for their heirs. The 2004 present value of this estate tax savings, using a 6 percent discount rate, is $654,255.

Although leaving assets in excess of the unified credit to the taxpayer's spouse could be an effective tax planning strategy, it eliminates the taxpayer's control over the ultimate disposition of those assets. Consider a scenario involving Mr. and Mrs. Betts, each of whom was married previously and came into this marriage with considerable individual personal wealth. They have no children together. Each wishes to bequeath assets to his or her children from previous marriages, but also wishes to minimize estate tax and provide for his or her spouse when he or she dies. If Mrs. Betts dies first, leaving assets equal to the exemption equivalent amount to her children and the rest to her husband, no estate tax will be owed on her death. However, Mr. Betts can then choose to leave all of his assets, as well as everything he received from his wife, to his children and ignore her children! This result is probably not what Mrs. Betts wanted.

A taxpayer who wishes to provide for a surviving spouse while controlling the ultimate disposition of assets upon the spouse's death can will a portion of his or her assets to a trust. Income from the trust can be paid to the surviving spouse for his or her lifetime with the remainder interest in trust assets passing to designated beneficiaries at the time of the surviving spouse's death. The treatment of such a trust for estate tax purposes depends on the terms of the trust and something called a qualified terminable interest property (QTIP) election.

The granting of an income interest in property is considered a **terminable interest** because it terminates after the passage of time or the occurrence of a specified event (such as the death of the surviving spouse). In general, a terminable interest does not qualify for the marital deduction if the remainder interest in the property passes to someone other than the surviving spouse. In this case, a trust granting an income interest to the surviving spouse and a remainder interest to other beneficiaries is called a **bypass trust**. The term refers to the fact that the trust property bypasses the estate of the second spouse to die since that spouse's interest terminates at death. The transfer of property into the bypass trust on the death of the first spouse, however, does not qualify for the marital deduction and is included in the taxable estate of the first spouse to die. In most cases, the amount of property transferred to a bypass trust equals the decedent's available unified credit to avoid estate tax on the trust assets. This trust is also referred to as a **credit shelter trust** since it ensures the utilization of the unified credit of the first spouse to die.

*Use of a Bypass Trust*

Mr. Orson dies in 2004 with a gross estate valued at $2 million. His will transfers $500,000 of his assets outright to his spouse and the remaining $1.5 million into a bypass trust. Mrs. Orson is granted an income interest in the trust for her lifetime with the remainder interest in trust assets passing to Mr. Orson's children from a prior marriage upon her death. The $500,000 direct bequest qualifies for the marital deduction, but the $1.5 million transfer into trust does not. The tax on Mr. Orson's taxable estate of $1.5 million is fully offset by the unified credit, and no estate tax is due. When Mrs. Orson dies, the FMV of the assets remaining in the bypass trust is not included in her taxable gross estate since her interest in these assets terminates at death. The assets pass to Mr. Orson's children under the terms of the trust. Her gross estate includes any remaining assets from the direct bequest received from her husband, and any separate property that she owned.

What if a taxpayer wishes to provide his or her surviving spouse an income interest in assets in excess of the unified credit? The terminable interest rule generally subjects the excess assets to estate tax. Two options exist to qualify this transfer for the marital deduction. However, the cost of these options is that the transferred assets are included in the estate of the surviving spouse at his or her death. This approach could represent an effective use of the time period variable for tax planning since the tax cost is deferred until the death of the second spouse. If the assets appreciate in value substantially during the deferral period, however, the increased tax cost could outweigh the value of the deferral.

The first approach to qualifying a terminable interest for the marital deduction is referred to as a **qualified terminable interest property (QTIP)** election.[17] QTIP is defined as property passing from one spouse to another by gift or at death, in which the recipient spouse has a qualifying income interest for life. A *qualifying income interest* requires that (1) the recipient be entitled to income from the property for life annually or at more frequent intervals and (2) no portion of the qualifying property can be appointed to anyone other than the recipient spouse during his or her lifetime. If these conditions are met and the QTIP election is made, the entire value of property transferred into a QTIP trust qualifies for the marital deduction. On the death of the surviving spouse, the FMV of the trust property is included in that decedent's gross estate.[18]

| QTIP Election | Mrs. Estevez dies in 2004 with a taxable estate of $4 million before considering the QTIP election. Her will transfers property with a value equal to her exemption equivalent amount ($1.5 million in 2004) directly to her children. All remaining estate property is transferred into a QTIP trust, leaving a qualifying income interest to her husband for life. The remainder interest in trust property will pass to her children on Mr. Estevez's death. The $2.5 million of property transferred into the trust qualifies for the marital deduction as a result of the QTIP election. Mrs. Estevez's taxable estate equals $1.5 million. All tax on her estate is offset by her unified credit, resulting in zero estate tax liability. When her husband dies, the FMV of the trust assets remaining in the QTIP trust is included in his taxable gross estate, even though these assets pass directly to Mrs. Estevez's children under the terms of the trust. |
|---|---|
| | If Mrs. Estevez's estate does not make the QTIP election for the trust, her taxable estate is $4 million, producing estate tax liability of $1,185,000.[19] The trust property is not included in her husband's estate on his death. If his marginal estate tax rate is 55 percent and he lives for 10 years after his wife's death, the present value of the tax savings from not including the property in his estate (assuming a value of $2.5 million when he dies and a 7 percent discount rate) is $698,500. Thus, the QTIP election results in present value estate tax savings of $486,500 for the combined estates of Mr. and Mrs. Estevez. |

When is the QTIP election advisable? The deferral value of the election is greater the longer the life expectancy of the surviving spouse but is reduced when assets in the QTIP trust are expected to increase in value during the surviving spouse's remaining lifetime. This trade-off should be considered in determining which assets to transfer into a QTIP trust and which to transfer directly to other beneficiaries. Between 2004 and 2009, deferral also takes advantage of the increase in unified credit that could occur between the deaths of the spouses.

---

[17] Section 2056(b)(7).

[18] Section 2044.

[19] Tax on $4 million, using Table 15.2 from Chapter 15, is $1,740,800. The tax is reduced by the 2004 unified credit of $555,800 (Table 15.4, Chapter 15), leaving net liability of $1,185,000.

*Choice of Assets for a QTIP Trust*

Mr. Fong owns undeveloped real estate valued at $1 million and stock investments valued at $1 million. He expects the real estate to appreciate substantially in value over the next 20 years. His portfolio of stock investments is structured to produce current income at the expense of future appreciation. He plans to transfer half of his estate to his children outright and half into a QTIP trust for the benefit of his much younger second wife. The stock investments would be the best choice for the QTIP trust; these assets will provide income for Mrs. Fong's support and will achieve deferral of estate tax until her death without substantial appreciation in value to offset the benefits of deferring the tax.

Another option to qualify a terminable interest for the marital deduction is to grant the surviving spouse a general power of appointment over trust assets. This power causes the trust assets to be included in the estate of the surviving spouse upon his or her death but also qualifies the original transfer for the marital deduction, resulting in only a single estate tax. If the surviving spouse exercises the general power of appointment to consume the trust assets, however, the planning objective of allowing the transferor spouse to control asset disposition is not met!

## Deferring Payment of Estate Tax Liability

**Objective 7**
Describe the options for deferring payment of estate tax liability.

As discussed in Chapter 15, the estate tax return and any related tax liability are generally due nine months after the decedent's death. Meeting this payment deadline could be difficult for estates composed largely of closely held business interests or other illiquid assets. Although effective predeath planning seeks to minimize estate taxes, two options exist to defer payment of any remaining liability after death. The estate executor can request an extension of time for paying estate taxes for a period of up to 10 years. The IRS has discretion to grant such extensions upon showing of "reasonable cause."[20] For this purpose, reasonable cause includes cases in which the estate's liquid assets are not readily accessible, in which the assets that would be liquidated to pay the tax would have to be sold at a discount or in a depressed market, or in which the estate is composed primarily of assets for which payments will be received in the future (such as annuity contracts or receivables). Interest will accrue on the unpaid tax balance during the extension period at the normal rate on tax underpayments.

When a large portion of the estate consists of closely held business interests, an additional option exists for deferring the payment of estate tax. Under this option, payment could be extended as much as 15 years beyond the filing of the estate tax return.[21] To qualify for this extension, closely held business interests must exceed 35 percent of the adjusted gross estate. For this purpose, the adjusted gross estate is defined as the gross estate less allowable deductions for estate expenses, debts of the decedent, taxes, and casualty and theft losses. A closely held business interest includes (1) a sole proprietorship, (2) a partnership interest representing a 20 percent or greater capital interest in a partnership, (3) any interest in a partnership with 45 or fewer partners, (4) corporate stock representing a 20 percent or greater voting interest in the corporation, or (5) stock in a corporation with 45 or fewer shareholders.[22] The deferral of tax payment available to closely held businesses is an addi-

---

[20] Section 6161.

[21] Section 6166.

[22] EGTRRA expands the definition of a closely held business interest after 2001 to include certain lending and finance businesses. These businesses are allowed a maximum five-year estate tax deferral. Because this change applies to a limited number of taxpayers, it is not discussed in detail. See Section 6166(b)(10)(A).

tional attempt by Congress to ensure that heirs need not sell such business interests to pay estate taxes.

| | |
|---|---|
| *Qualification for Tax Deferral* | Mr. Popov's estate includes assets of a sole proprietorship valued at $1.8 million. His adjusted gross estate (including the sole proprietorship) totals $4 million. The estate qualifies to defer payment of tax attributable to the sole proprietorship since $1.8 million exceeds $1.4 million (35 percent 3 $4 million). |

For qualifying estates, the allowable deferral of payment of estate tax is as follows:

- Total estate tax liability is partitioned to identify the portion attributable to the closely held business interest. The portion not so attributed is payable at the normal due date.
- No payments of tax are required for 5 years on the portion of estate tax attributable to the closely held business interest. Thereafter, annual installment payments are made over a period no longer than 10 years.
- Interest on the unpaid estate tax is assessed at a rate of 2 percent.[23] This rate is limited to $1 million of estate value attributable to the closely held business interest in excess of the exemption equivalent amount. Interest on additional unpaid tax is assessed at 45 percent of the rate payable on tax underpayments. No deduction is allowed for this interest for either income or estate tax purposes.
- If the estate or the heirs dispose of the closely held business interest, any remaining deferred estate tax payments are accelerated.[24]

| | |
|---|---|
| *Tax Deferral for Closely Held Business Interests* | Refer to the previous example in which Mr. Popov's qualified small business interest equals $1.8 million of his total gross estate of $4 million. Also assume that his taxable estate totals $3 million and that he died during 2004. Gross estate tax liability of $1,260,800[25] is reduced by a unified credit of $555,800,[26] leaving net tax liability of $705,000. This tax liability is allocated to the closely held business interest based on the ratio of the value of this interest to the total gross estate, as follows. $$\$705,000 \times \frac{\$1.8 \text{ million}}{\$4 \text{ million}} = \$317,250$$ Based on this allocation, payment of $317,250 of Mr. Popov's estate tax can be deferred. The remaining $387,750 must be paid at the normal due date.<br><br>Interest on the deferred tax is assessed at a rate of 2 percent on tax related to the first $1 million of value attributed to the closely held business interest in excess of the exemption equivalent amount. For 2004, the exemption equivalent amount is $1.5 million. The excess value is $300,000 ($1.8 million − $1.5 million). Thus, all of the deferred liability accrues interest at the 2 percent rate. |

## Reducing Probate Costs

**Probate** is the process of administering and disposing of estate assets under the terms of a decedent's will or in accordance with state intestacy laws. Costs of probate include attorney and accountant fees, appraisal costs, expenses associated with disposing of assets, and court costs. Although probate costs depend on the value and type of estate assets, a conservative

---

[23] Section 6601(j)(1).

[24] Section 6166(g).

[25] Calculated using Table 15.2 in Chapter 15.

[26] See Table 15.4 in Chapter 15.

**Objective 8**
Discuss strategies for reducing estate probate costs.

estimate of total costs is 5 to 15 percent of the probate estate. Thus, a large estate could incur hundreds of thousands of dollars in probate costs. A number of strategies can be employed to remove assets from the probate estate and reduce related costs. Most of these strategies involve designating the recipients of property during life by means other than the will. For example, property owned as joint tenants with rights of survivorship automatically passes to the surviving owner on the death of one joint tenant. Such property might be included in the decedent's taxable gross estate but is not included in the probate estate and thus avoids probate costs.

| | |
|---|---|
| *Probate Costs for Real Property* | Ms. Somersby owns a house in Tennessee, a vacation condominium in Florida, and rental property in South Carolina. When she dies and these properties are included in her estate, probate courts in each of these states will control the granting of clear title to these properties. The estate will thus incur additional legal fees and court costs related to these proceedings. To avoid these costs, she could gift partial ownership in these properties to her intended heirs to establish joint ownership with rights of survivorship. Then title and full ownership of the properties would automatically pass to the survivors at Ms. Somersby's death and probate costs would be reduced. |

Another strategy for avoiding probate costs is the use of a **living trust.** This trust holds title to all assets that an individual owns, and the trust document specifies how these assets will be transferred on the grantor's death. As a result, the trust assets avoid probate. In this case, the taxpayer's will is very simple, designating treatment only of what few assets might not be included in the trust and referring to the trust document for disposition of all other assets. Typically, the grantor is also the trustee of a living trust, and the trust is ignored for income tax purposes. Another advantage of the living trust is the privacy afforded the decedent's family. In contrast to a will, which is considered a public document available for all to inspect, a trust document is not subject to public disclosure.

## Conclusion

The planning ideas discussed in this chapter have illustrated the considerable tax savings that can be achieved through advance planning for the transfer of personal wealth. Through a systematic plan for lifetime gifts, significant wealth can be transferred to many heirs over time with no transfer tax consequences. Additional planning strategies focus on reducing the value of the taxable gross estate. For closely held business interests, a number of valuation discounts could be appropriate to reduce the taxable value. In addition, the family-owned business exclusion and special use valuation method apply in some circumstances to reduce value subject to estate tax. Effective use of the marital deduction and the unified credit can reduce and defer the estate tax of a married couple. Finally, opportunities exist to defer payment of estate tax due in some circumstances. The critical message of this chapter is that planning to avoid transfer taxation is well worth the investment.

## Key Terms

| | | |
|---|---|---|
| blockage rule *480* | kiddie tax *475* | qualified terminable |
| bypass trust *482* | living trust *486* | interest property |
| credit shelter trust *482* | marketability | (QTIP) *483* |
| Crummey trust *474* | discount *479* | qualified trust to benefit a |
| family limited | minority interest | minor *474* |
| partnership *473* | discount *479* | special use valuation |
| incidents of | probate *485* | method *480* |
| ownership *478* | | terminable interest *482* |

**Questions and Problems for Discussion**

1. This chapter discussed the tax advantages associated with annual gifts of assets. Name four nontax reasons for taxpayers to hesitate to give away the bulk of their assets prior to death.

2. Mr. McDonald wishes to give a piece of real estate valued at $100,000 to his daughter. To maximize the use of the gift tax exclusion on this transfer, he has proposed that she purchase the property from him on an installment basis. He will then forgive each annual installment as it comes due. From his daughter's perspective, what are the risks associated with this plan?

3. The demand power available to the beneficiary of a Crummey trust qualifies transfers to these trusts for the annual gift tax exclusion. In most cases, the grantor hopes that the power will not be exercised. If the trust beneficiary exercises the demand power each year, however, is there any advantage to using a Crummey trust rather than making a direct gift?

4. Mr. Lyle is 40 years old. He and his wife have two young children. He recently purchased a life insurance policy with a death benefit of $2 million, naming his wife as its beneficiary. His tax adviser has suggested that he transfer the policy into a life insurance trust to remove the death benefit from his estate. The tax adviser explained to Mr. Lyle that he would have to relinquish all incidents of ownership over the policy for the transfer to be effective for estate tax purposes. Mr. Lyle is hesitant to make the transfer and has proposed that he wait to do so until he is at least 50 years old. Can you suggest some reasons why he might hesitate to relinquish all incidents of ownership over the insurance policy? Also discuss the costs and benefits of transferring ownership now versus waiting until Mr. Lyle is older.

5. What are the income tax consequences of a family limited partnership arrangement with gifts of limited partner interests? Specifically, how is the taxable income of the givers and recipients affected? Is the family limited partnership technique an effective use of the entity variable for income shifting?

6. In valuing closely held business interests, some have argued that a controlling interest should be valued at a premium; others argue for a discount under the blockage rule theory. Explain the arguments in support of each alternative valuation approach.

7. The special use valuation method allows a reduction in estate value where a difference exists between the "current use" and "highest use" value of real estate. As this difference in value increases, would you expect the heirs to be more or less likely to elect special use valuation? Explain your reasoning.

8. The IRS has the discretion to grant extensions of time to pay estate tax upon the showing of "reasonable cause." In consideration of the liquidity of estate assets as part of predeath planning, is it a good idea to rely on this extension provision? Discuss.

9. A special estate tax payment deferral is allowed for tax attributable to qualified closely held business interests. Discuss three reasons that the use of this provision is preferable to requesting a discretionary extension of time to pay estate tax.

10. Mr. Stein has taken steps to reduce his probate estate by placing most of his assets in joint ownership with his wife and children. Since he believes the value of his probate estate is less than $300,000, he sees no need to do further estate planning. Advise him.

11. Which tax planning maxim discussed in Chapter 1 applies to the benefits of a QTIP election? Explain briefly.

12. Given that probate costs are deductible as estate administration expenses for either estate or estate income tax purposes, explain how reducing probate costs can actually increase tax liability.

**Application Problems**

1. Mr. Trevor expects to accumulate assets valued at $3 million during his lifetime and wishes to leave his estate to his six children. On the basis of family history, he expects to live until 2040 at age 75.
   a. So that his estate will pay zero estate tax after the unified credit, at what age will Mr. Trevor need to begin making annual gifts of $11,000 to each of his children?
   b. If Mr. Trevor is married and elects gift splitting with his spouse, at what age will he need to begin making annual gifts to each of his children so that his estate pays zero estate tax after the unified credit?

2. Mrs. Harrison is 50 years old today and has just begun to think about transfer tax planning. She is divorced, with two children and five grandchildren. She expects to live to age 70 and projects that her estate will total $5 million. Calculate the expected savings in estate tax if Mrs. Harrison transfers $11,000 annually to each of her children and grandchildren from now until her death.

3. George and Isaac Kowalski are brothers who own and operate a business conducted through a general partnership. As they get older they wish to begin transferring ownership of the business to their children. They are considering revising the partnership agreement to allow for the admission of limited partners. Each brother could then gift a portion of his 50 percent interest in the partnership to his children as limited partners. The brothers would retain control of the business as general partners. The total value of the business assets is currently estimated at $3 million. The brothers believe that a 30 percent discount for lack of marketability and lack of control should be applied in valuing the gifted limited partner interests.
   a. George Kowalski would like to restrict his gifts each year to the annual exclusion amount. If he has six children and elects gift splitting with his wife, what percentage interest in the partnership could he transfer to his children annually?
   b. George Kowalski intends to gift limited partner interests to his children up to 40 percent of total ownership. He would then retain a 10 percent general partner interest until his death. At the rate of giving determined in part *(a)*, how many years will it take him to meet this goal?
   c. Isaac Kowalski, a widower, has four children. Apply the same questions asked in parts *(a)* and *(b)* for George to Isaac.

4. Refer to application problem 3. After five years of gifts, what percentage of total partnership ownership will belong to the Kowalski brothers? Assume that the partnership earns $750,000 of ordinary income per year. If they are in a 35 percent tax bracket and their children's average marginal tax rate is 25 percent, how much income tax will the family save in the fifth year as a result of the ownership transfers?

5. Mr. and Mrs. Hopewell transfer property worth $90,000 to their daughter. The property produces ordinary income of $6,000 annually. The Hopewells' marginal tax rate is 35 percent.
   a. If their daughter is 21 with a marginal tax rate of 25 percent, calculate the annual income tax savings of this gift.
   b. How would your answer to part *(a)* change if their daughter is 13?

6. Mr. Gordon wishes to give to his grandson property that produces no current income but is expected to appreciate in value. On the date of the gift, the property's FMV is $150,000 and Mr. Gordon's tax basis in the property is $10,000.
   a. Mr. Gordon projects that the property will be worth $400,000 in 2012. If his grandson sells the property at that time, calculate his gain recognized on the sale and related tax costs. Using an 8 percent discount rate, calculate the net present value of after-tax cash flow to his grandson from the sale.

*b.* Now suppose that Mr. Gordon kept the property until his death in 2012. If his taxable estate including this property is $3.5 million, calculate the estate tax due.

*c.* Recalculate Mr. Gordon's estate tax due, assuming that the gift to his grandson is made in 2004.

*d.* Given your results from parts *(b)* and *(c)*, calculate the net present value of estate tax savings from the gift using an 8 percent discount rate.

*e.* Does the gift increase after-tax value for the family unit? Explain briefly.

7. Refer to application problem 6. How would your answer to part *(e)* change if Mr. Gordon's taxable estate in part *(b)* were only $1 million?

8. Mr. Lowe's estate includes property qualifying for the special use valuation method. Calculate the allowable valuation reduction for each of the following independent situations.

| Situation | Current Use Value | Highest Use Value |
|-----------|-------------------|-------------------|
| Situation A | $3,000,000 | $4,000,000 |
| Situation B | 1,000,000 | 1,250,000 |
| Situation C | 500,000 | 600,000 |
| Situation D | 500,000 | 1,300,000 |

9. Mr. Pierre's estate includes real property used for farming valued at $1 million under its current use and $1.7 million under its highest use. In addition, personal property used in the farming operation is valued at $300,000. His estate also includes other property valued at $2 million.

*a.* Apply the percentage tests to determine whether Mr. Pierre's estate can elect special use valuation.

*b.* How would your answer to part *(a)* change if the value of the real property under its highest use were $1.5 million?

*c.* As part of predeath planning, what recommendations would you make to Pierre to ensure the availability of special use valuation?

10. When Mr. Cameron dies in 2004, his gross estate is valued at $2.5 million. His will transfers $1 million directly to his children, $500,000 to his wife and places $1 million in trust. Mrs. Cameron is granted an income interest in the trust for her lifetime with the remainder interest in trust property passing to the children upon her death.

*a.* If the trust is not a QTIP trust, determine the amount of the marital deduction allowable to Mr. Cameron's estate.

*b.* If the trust is not a QTIP trust, determine the amount of trust property included in Mrs. Cameron's taxable estate on her death.

*c.* How would your answers to parts *(a)* and *(b)* change if the trust is a QTIP trust?

11. Refer to application problem 13. Assume that Mrs. Cameron's taxable estate at death includes only the property received from Mr. Cameron and that the trust assets are valued at $1.5 million when she dies in 2014.

*a.* Calculate Mr. Cameron's and Mrs. Cameron's taxable estates and estate tax liabilities if the trust is a QTIP trust. Calculate the net present value of total estate tax liability for the couple, using a 9 percent discount rate.

*b.* How would your answer to part *(a)* change if the trust is not a QTIP trust?

*c.* On the basis of the results of your analysis in parts *(a)* and *(b)*, do you recommend that Mr. Cameron's estate make the QTIP election?

12. Ms. Delias owned real estate worth $1 million at her death.
    a. Calculate the potential probate costs associated with this property, assuming that in Mrs. Delias's state of residence these costs average 5 percent of value.
    b. Now assume that Mrs. Delias gave her son a 10 percent interest in the real estate 15 years before her death, conveying joint ownership with rights of survivorship. At the time of the gift, the property was worth $500,000. Mrs. Delias did not pay gift tax on this gift, but the excess over the annual exclusion reduced her available unified credit. If Mrs. Delias's marginal estate tax rate is 48 percent, calculate the estate tax savings attributable to the prior gift of property ownership to her son, and the increase in estate tax attributable to the reduction in deductible probate costs as a result of the ownership change.

## Issue Recognition Problems

Identify the tax issue or issues suggested by the following situations, and state each issue in the form of a question.

1. Mrs. Hannah dies owning 70 percent of the stock of a closely held corporation in which the primary asset is land used for cattle ranching.

2. The son of Mr. and Mrs. Marcus wishes to purchase a house. He believes that his income is sufficient to afford the annual payments, but he does not have enough cash for the down payment. His parents have offered to give him part of the needed amount and lend him the rest interest free for five years.

3. Mr. Royce establishes a trust naming his six-year old son as beneficiary. During 2004, Mr. Royce transfers property valued at $11,000 into the trust.

4. Ms. Seth plans to make annual gifts to each of her children. For 2004, she is considering whether to give $11,000 cash or $11,000 worth of corporate bonds to each child. The bonds have a tax basis below FMV and generate annual interest income of approximately 8 percent.

5. Mr. Haynes owns an insurance policy on his own life with a death benefit of $2 million. In 2004, he transfers the policy to an insurance trust. At the time of the transfer, the cost to purchase a comparable policy is $30,000. Two years later, he dies.

6. Mrs. Lynn creates an insurance trust to hold a policy on her life with a death benefit of $1 million. The policy names her husband as beneficiary. Mrs. Lynn designates her brother as trustee of the trust but retains the right to change the beneficiary of the policy if she and her husband divorce.

7. At his death, Mr. Blake owns 90 percent of the stock of a closely held business. He started the business 20 years ago and worked there 50 to 60 hours per week until his death. The IRS has asserted that the estate tax value of the business interest should be $1.5 million based on the value of comparable businesses whose stock is publicly traded.

8. Ms. Ochoa is a wealthy widow contemplating marriage to a much younger man. As part of their prenuptial agreement, she promises that at her death her prospective husband will be named the income beneficiary of a trust holding $5 million of investment assets.

9. Mr. Yakima's will stipulates that $2 million of his assets be placed in a QTIP trust for the benefit of his wife. His estate includes a variety of stock investments, real estate, limited partnership investments, and part ownership of a local car dealership that he managed until his death.

10. Ms. Chevalier lived in New Jersey for 70 years until retiring to Arizona five years ago. At her death, she still owned a house in New Jersey occupied by her son and a condominium in Tucson.

**Research Problems**

1. When Mr. Jolson died in January 2004, his will provided for the establishment of a QTIP trust. Mrs. Jolson was named to receive income from the trust for her lifetime with their children named as remainder beneficiaries. Because she has substantial other assets and income sources, she does not believe that the QTIP trust is necessary and prefers that the assets of the trust pass directly to their children instead. Is it possible for her to disclaim or renounce her interest in the trust? Would this renunciation or disclaimer result in the trust assets passing to the children from Mr. Jolson's estate? What would be the impact of the disclaimer on the marital deduction allowable to his estate?

2. Mr. Keith and Mr. Lars were business partners for 30 years. Under their partnership agreement, at the death of one partner, the survivor is granted the right to purchase the deceased partner's interest in the business from the estate. To ensure the availability of funds to make this purchase, each partner purchased a life insurance policy on the life of the other with the purchaser named as beneficiary. The partnership agreement provided that each partner had the power to veto any changes in the beneficiary designation of the policy on his life.

   In 2004, Mr. Keith died. Mr. Lars received $500,000 of insurance proceeds from his policy on his partner's life and used this money to purchase Mr. Keith's interest in their business. Did Mr. Keith's veto right over the beneficiary designation give him "incidents of ownership" that would require the proceeds of the policy to be included in his gross estate?

**Tax Planning Cases**

1. As part of an annual giving plan, Ms. Olivia must select one of the following assets to give to her 25-year-old grandson.

| Asset Description | Adjusted Basis | Fair Market Value |
|---|---|---|
| Cash | $10,000 | $10,000 |
| Corporate stock | 2,000 | 10,000 |
| Limited partnership interest | 15,000 | 10,000 |
| Interest in commercial real estate | 7,000 | 10,000 |

   The corporate stock generates no current dividends but has increased in value 50 percent each year that she has owned it. The limited partnership interest has produced losses in the past several years. The real estate interest generates $1,000 of ordinary income annually.

   a. Discuss the transfer and income tax advantages and disadvantages of each asset as a potential gift for Mrs. Olivia and her grandson.

   b. Recommend to Mrs. Olivia which asset she should give her grandson. Support your choice.

   c. Which asset would the grandson prefer to receive? Explain your answer.

2. Mr. Zinder is 60 years old and married with three children and seven grandchildren. He has never done any wealth transfer tax planning. His current assets include (but are not limited to) the following:

   • Personal residence in Wayne, Pennsylvania. The house and the land on which it sits are currently valued at $1 million. He bought the house 30 years ago for $100,000. The house is owned jointly with Mrs. Zinder (as joint tenants with rights of survivorship).

- Stock portfolio valued at $400,000. Mr. Zinder's tax basis in these investments totals $350,000. The portfolio produces approximately $25,000 of interest and dividend income annually.
- A 50 percent interest in a law partnership in which Mr. Zinder is a general partner. The practice has been very successful, and his interest is valued at $2 million. His tax basis in the partnership interest is $500,000. Two of his children are practicing attorneys who work for the partnership. The partnership agreement provides that all partners must approve admission of any new partners to the firm.
- A life insurance policy on Mr. Zinder's own life with a death benefit of $1 million. Current replacement cost of the policy is estimated at $40,000. Mrs. Zinder and their three children are named as equal beneficiaries of the insurance policy.

Given the assets described here, make three detailed wealth transfer–planning recommendations to Mr. Zinder. You should discuss how your recommendations could reduce his future estate tax liability, any gift tax implications, and any income tax implications.

3. Mr. and Mrs. Sondheim are rewriting their wills. He is not in good health and expects to die before his wife. He wishes to leave all of his assets to her to ensure that she is taken care of for the rest of her life. Mrs. Sondheim wants her will to specify that all assets remaining on her death go to their three children.
   a. If Mr. Sondheim were to die in 2004 with a total estate before the marital deduction of $5 million and no lifetime taxable transfers, calculate the total estate tax that would be saved by leaving all of his assets to Mrs. Sondheim.
   b. If Mrs. Sondheim lives 10 more years (until 2014) and her taxable estate at death (including the assets received from her late husband) is $6 million, calculate her estate tax liability. Assume that she had no taxable transfers during life.
   c. Using a 7 percent discount rate, calculate the net present value of total estate taxes paid by Mr. Sondheim and Mrs. Sondheim in parts *(a)* and *(b)* and the net present value of after-tax assets remaining for their children.
   d. How would your answers to parts *(a)*, *(b)*, and *(c)* change if Mr. Sondheim leaves $2 million of his assets directly to their children rather than to Mrs. Sondheim? In this case, assume that her taxable estate at death is reduced to $3.5 million minus taxes paid on Mr. Sondheim's estate. Thus, the $2 million of assets left to the children by Mr. Sondheim are worth $2.5 million in 10 years.
   e. Is the net present value of after-tax assets remaining for the Sondheim children greater in part *(d)*? By how much?
   f. Explain to Mr. and Mrs. Sondheim the source of the tax savings in part *(e)*.

# Comprehensive Case for Part Six

Marvin Brown is 50 years old and has recently experienced some health problems. As a result, he has begun thinking more about family wealth planning and the potential bite of the estate tax. Marvin is married to Nicole, his second wife, who is 38 years old. They have a 4-year old daughter, Gwen. Marvin also has two children, David and Abigail, from his first marriage. David is 26 years old, married, and has two young children. Abigail is 20 years old, single, and a junior in college.

Marvin has approached you for some estate planning advice. As a preliminary step, he has compiled the following list of assets, their tax basis, current value, and projected value in 10 years (his life expectancy if his current health problems persist).

| | Tax Basis | Current Value | Projected Future Value |
|---|---|---|---|
| Personal residence | $400,000 | $ 700,000 | $1,000,000 |
| Rental real estate | 900,000 | 1,600,000 | 2,200,000 |
| Undeveloped land | 300,000 | 500,000 | 600,000 |
| Stock investments | 500,000 | 600,000 | 1,000,000 |
| Mutual funds | 250,000 | 200,000 | 350,000 |

Marvin also owns an insurance policy on his life with a death benefit of $1.5 million dollars. Nicole, David, and Abigail are equal beneficiaries under the policy. The rental real estate is an office building Marvin inherited from his parents 10 years ago. He devotes much of his time to managing the property and hopes that Abigail will join him in the business following graduation from college. The undeveloped land is farmland originally owned by Marvin's grandparents. The land is 300 miles away from Marvin's residence and is rented to local farmers; Marvin and his family are not actively involved in farming operations. The Browns' personal residence is owned jointly by Marvin and Nicole, as joint tenants with rights of survivorship. The other assets are Marvin's separate property; Nicole waived all rights to these assets in their prenuptial agreement. Nicole's remaining personal assets have a current value of approximately $300,000.

Marvin's will currently bequeaths 50 percent of his stock investment portfolio to Nicole. Their personal residence will also pass to Nicole under her survivorship rights. All other assets pass in equal parts to David, Abigail, and Gwen. Marvin has agreed to make any revisions to his will necessary to implement your estate planning ideas.

1. To date, Marvin has made no gifts in excess of the annual exclusion amount. If Marvin's value estimates are correct and he undertakes no gift or estate planning, makes no changes to his will, and dies in 10 years, what would his taxable estate and estate tax liability be?

2. Marvin is considering establishing a trust for Gwen's benefit by immediately transferring $300,000 of stock investments into a qualified trust to benefit a minor. The trust would make no distributions during Marvin's lifetime. If Marvin dies before Gwen reaches the age of 21, the trust would distribute annual income to Gwen. Remaining accumulated income and trust principal would be distributed to Gwen on her 21st birthday.

   a. If the trust earns a 10 percent pretax return on investment each year (ordinary income), what would trust taxable income and tax liability be in the first year of the trust's existence? Calculate the trust's after-tax cash flow and rate of return on investment.

   b. If the trust maintains the same average after-tax rate of return calculated in part *(a)* and reinvests this return each year, what would its total projected value be in 10 years?

   c. Given the value determined in part *(b)*, if Marvin dies in 10 years, what would the expected annual income distribution to Gwen be?

3. Marvin would like to begin making annual gifts of property to Abigail, David, and David's children. He is considering establishing a family limited partnership by transferring the rental real estate to the partnership and gifting limited partnership interests to Abigail, David, and David's children.

   a. Suppose that a conservative discount for lack of control and marketability of the partnership interests is 30 percent. What percentage interest in the partnership could Marvin transfer each year to each recipient so as to take advantage of the annual exclusion? To make this determination, assume that the amount given each year is based on the projected future value of the real estate, so that all gifts are less than or equal to the annual exclusion.

   *b.* How much of his future estate value could Marvin transfer via these gifts in the next 10 years?

4. Make two additional estate planning recommendations to Marvin, aimed at reducing the value of his gross estate. Be specific and explain the benefits and any potential costs of your recommendations.

5. Suppose that Marvin implements the plans specified in (2) and (3), and all of your recommendations in (4). These actions successfully reduce the expected value of his taxable estate in 10 years to $2 million. Calculate his expected estate tax liability under this plan and the NPV of expected estate tax savings as a result of these planning efforts.

# Glossary

## A

**accounting income**   Items of income and expense allocable to trust income beneficiaries as the trust document specifies.

**accrual method of accounting**   The overall method of accounting under which revenues are realized in the year that the earnings process is complete and expenses are matched against revenues when the liability for the expenses is incurred.

**accumulated adjustments account (AAA)**   The portion of an S corporation's retained earnings on which the shareholders have paid tax.

**accumulated earnings and profits (E&P)**   A corporation's undistributed E&P for all taxable years preceding the current year.

**accumulated earnings tax**   A penalty tax levied on corporations accumulating income beyond the reasonable needs of the business to avoid paying dividends to shareholders. The tax is levied in addition to the regular corporate income tax.

**acquisitive type D reorganization**   A tax-deferred exchange of substantially all the assets of one corporation for a controlling stock interest in another corporation followed by the liquidation of the transferring corporation.

**adjusted current earnings (ACE)**   The measurement of earnings conceptually similar to a corporation's economic income for the year; used in calculating the ACE adjustment for corporate alternative minimum tax.

**administrative authority**   Interpretations of the Internal Revenue Code issued by the Department of the U.S. Treasury.

**advance pricing agreement (APA)**   An agreement between a taxpayer and the IRS on the transfer pricing method to be used for any set of transactions to which Section 482 applies.

**affiliated group**   A parent corporation and its 80 percent or more controlled subsidiaries that are eligible to file a federal consolidated income tax return.

**aggregate basis increase**   Provision in EGTRRA allowing an increase in tax basis of estate property up to $1,300,000.

**aggregate theory of partnerships**   The theory that a partnership is transparent, with no separate and distinct identity from that of its partners. Under the aggregate theory, a partner's interest in a partnership represents a proportionate interest in partnership property.

**all-events test**   The test for determining whether an accrued expense is deductible, which is satisfied if (1) all events that establish the fact of the liability have occurred, (2) the amount of the liability can be determined with reasonable accuracy, and (3) economic performance has occurred with respect to the liability.

**alternate valuation date**   Generally, the date six months after the date of a decedent's death. Any assets disposed of by the estate during this six-month period are valued on the date of disposition.

**alternative minimum tax (AMT)**   A second federal tax system parallel to the regular income tax system enacted by Congress to ensure that every individual and corporation pays at least a nominal amount of tax each year.

**alternative minimum taxable income (AMTI)**   The tax base for the AMT: regular taxable income increased or decreased by AMT adjustments and increased by AMT tax preferences.

**AMT adjustments**   The increases or decreases to regular taxable income in the computation of AMTI.

**AMT exemption**   The minimum AMTI on which AMT is not assessed; $40,000 for corporations with AMTI not in excess of $150,000 but phased out above this threshold at a rate of 25 cents for every dollar of excess AMTI.

**AMT preferences**   Certain items increasing regular taxable income in the computation of AMTI.

**annual gift tax exclusion**   An annual inflation-adjusted amount of gifts made to one donee that is excluded from total taxable gifts to such donee.

**annuity**   A cash flow consisting of a constant dollar amount for a specific number of periods.

**apportionment**   A method of dividing a firm's taxable income among the various states with jurisdiction to tax the firm's business activities.

**apportionment formula**   A mathematical formula combining sales, payroll, and property factors to determine the percentage of an entity's taxable income to be reported for state tax purposes.

**arm's-length transaction**   A transaction occurring between unrelated parties who are dealing in their own self-interests.

**assignment of income doctrine**   A judicial doctrine that income must be taxed to the entity that renders the service or owns the capital with respect to which the income is paid.

**at-risk amount**   The dollar amount that a taxpayer would lose with respect to an investment in a business if the business failed.

**attribution rules**   The various sets of statutory rules for determining a person's indirect ownership of corporate stock or a partnership interest.

**automatic termination of a partnership**   The partnership termination that occurs because of sale or exchange of 50 percent or more of the total interest in partnership capital and profits within a 12-month period.

# B

**bankruptcy**   The legal process through which a debtor petitions a federal court to restructure or discharge its debt.

**bargain element**   The excess of the FMV of optioned shares of corporate stock over the strike price at the date of exercise.

**basic research credit**   The tax credit equal to 20 percent of cash payments to a qualified basic research organization, such as a college or university, to support basic research.

**beneficiary**   The party to whom trust income or property is to be distributed and for whose benefit the trust property is managed.

**blockage rule**   The valuation rule that allows a discount on the per share price at which smaller blocks of stock would be expected to trade in valuing a large block of stock for estate tax purposes.

**boot**   Any cash or other nonqualifying property included as part of a nontaxable exchange of property.

**brother-sister group**   A type of controlled group in which the same individual shareholders have common ownership of two or more corporations.

**built-in gain or loss**   The difference between FMV and carryover basis of property contributed to an entity by an owner.

**built-in gains tax**   The tax imposed on any net recognized built-in gain of an S corporation during the 10-year period after its conversion from a C corporation.

**business purpose doctrine**   The judicial doctrine that a transaction should not be effective for tax purposes unless it is intended to achieve a genuine and independent business purpose other than tax avoidance.

**buy-sell agreement**   A binding agreement restricting the conditions and terms under which owners can dispose of equity interests in business entities.

**bypass trust**   A trust granting an income interest to the surviving spouse and a remainder interest to other beneficiaries.

# C

**capital account**   The financial record of each partner's equity interest in partnership property.

**capital account maintenance rules**   The regulatory accounting rules by which a partnership must determine and maintain each partner's capital account.

**capital transactions**   Transactions that change the ownership of a business entity.

**carryover basis**   The tax basis of property in the hands of a transferee determined by reference to the tax basis of the property in the hands of the transferor.

**cash merger**   A taxable acquisition in which both the target corporation and the target's shareholders recognize gain or loss.

**cash method of accounting**   The overall method of accounting under which revenue is accounted for when payment is received and expenses are accounted for when payment is made.

**ceiling rule**   Under the traditional Section 704(c) allocation method, the rule that the tax allocation of income, gain, deduction, or loss to a partner cannot exceed the actual taxable income, gain, loss, or deduction recognized by the partnership.

**Chapter 11 reorganization**   The bankruptcy proceeding in which the owners and creditors of a business agree to a court-approved plan to restructure the business debt.

**Chapter 7 liquidation**   The bankruptcy proceeding in which the assets of a business are sold and the proceeds are distributed to the business creditors according to a priority established by the court.

**charitable deduction**   The deduction allowed in computing gift and estate tax for transfers to qualified charitable and other nonprofit organizations, such as religious, scientific, literary, or educational institutions.

**Citator**  A research tool used to determine the status of tax judicial decisions, revenue rulings, and revenue procedures. For each decision, the Citator provides a list of subsequent rulings that have referenced the decision and a brief indication of the nature of the subsequent reference.

**combined group**  A type of controlled group that includes both parent-subsidiary and brother-sister corporations.

**community development entities (CDEs)**  A corporation or partnership whose primary mission is serving or providing investment capital for low-income communities or low-income individuals.

**community property**  The property acquired after marriage, except by gift or inheritance, by a married couple residing in a community property state.

**comparable profits method**  The method for determining the transfer price for controlled transactions based on measures of profitability of uncontrolled taxpayers engaged in similar activities.

**comparable uncontrolled price method**  The method for determining the transfer price for controlled transactions based on the price for comparable uncontrolled transactions.

**comparable uncontrolled transaction**  The transaction between uncontrolled taxpayers used as a benchmark to price similar transactions between related parties.

**complex trust**  Any trust not qualifying as a simple trust.

**consolidated group**  An affiliated group of corporations in any year in which the group files a consolidated tax return.

**consolidated taxable income (CTI)**  The taxable income reported by a consolidated group of corporations.

**constructive dividend**  A distribution by a corporation to a shareholder that the corporation classifies as salary, interest, rent, or some other type of payment but that the IRS classifies as a dividend.

**constructively repatriated income**  The income of a controlled foreign corporation subject to U.S. income tax when earned regardless of whether such income is actually repatriated to U.S. shareholders.

**continuity of business enterprise requirement**  The requirement for a reorganization under which the acquiring corporation must continue the target's historic business or use a significant portion of the target's assets in its own business.

**continuity of interest requirement**  The requirement for a reorganization under which target shareholders must receive

stock in the acquiring corporation as a major part of the consideration for their target stock.

**control premium**  The portion of the FMV of a part interest in a business attributable to the fact that the interest gives the owner control of the business.

**controlled foreign corporation (CFC)**  Any foreign corporation in which U.S. shareholders own more than 50 percent of the total voting power or value of the corporate stock.

**controlled group**  Two or more corporations that must share the progressive corporate tax brackets and other tax benefits limited to a dollar amount.

**controlled subsidiary**  For tax purposes, any subsidiary corporation in which the parent corporation owns at least 80 percent of the total voting power and value of the stock.

**corporate liquidation**  The process by which a corporation ceases its business activity and distributes all remaining cash and property to its shareholders in cancellation of their stock.

**corporate welfare**  The criticism of tax incentives for business as providing tax savings to special interests and large corporations at the expense of middle and working-class families.

**corporation**  An organization formed under the corporation laws of a state or national government. For federal tax purposes, a corporation is a taxable entity unless it has a Subchapter S election in effect; referred to as a *regular* or a *C corporation.*

**corpus**  The trust property.

**cost-plus method**  The method for determining the transfer price for controlled transactions by examining the gross profit markup earned in comparable uncontrolled transactions.

**credit shelter trust**  See *bypass trust.*

**Crummey trust**  A trust providing its beneficiaries the right to demand distributions of trust income equal to the lesser of the annual gift exclusion or the amount gifted into the trust that year. Transfers into such trusts qualify as a gift of a present interest for purposes of the annual gift tax exclusion.

**cumulative taxable gifts**  The sum of current and prior year taxable gifts.

**current distribution**  Any distribution by a partnership to a partner that does not extinguish the partner's equity interest.

**current earnings and profits (E&P)**  The annual taxable income of a corporation reduced by federal income tax and adjusted for certain statutory and regulatory items.

# D

**deductions in respect of a decedent (DRD)**   The expenses associated with income in respect of a decedent not allowed on the decedent's final tax return.

**deemed paid foreign tax credit**   The credit available to U.S. corporations that receive dividends from a foreign subsidiary; based on the foreign tax that the subsidiary pays.

**deemed paid gift tax credit**   The credit allowed against the estate tax for the lesser of gift taxes actually paid on post-1976 cumulative taxable gifts or gift taxes that would have been paid on such gifts under the current transfer tax rates.

**deferred compensation**   Any arrangement in which an employee performs current services in exchange for the promise of a future compensatory payment.

**deferred tax asset**   The excess of tax payable over tax expense per books resulting from a temporary difference between book income and taxable income.

**deferred tax liability**   The excess of tax expense per books over tax payable resulting from a temporary difference between book income and taxable income.

**deficiency dividend**   The cash distribution made by a corporation within 90 days after the determination that it is liable for the personal holding company tax for a previous year. The distribution is treated as a dividend paid during the previous year.

**deficit restoration obligation**   A partner's legal obligation to contribute an amount equal to the negative balance in the partner's capital account to the partnership immediately before the partnership liquidates.

**defined-benefit plan**   A qualified plan under which the employer promises participating employees a targeted benefit, usually in the form of a pension, when they retire.

**defined-contribution plan**   A qualified plan under which the employer promises to make an annual contribution to each participating employee's retirement account.

**disabled access credit**   The tax incentive for small businesses to remove existing barriers to handicapped access; equals 50 percent of qualified expenditures in excess of $250 with a maximum annual credit of $5,000.

**discharge of debt income**   The gross income resulting from the satisfaction (discharge) of a debt for less than its face amount.

**discount rate**   The rate of interest used to calculate the present value of future cash flows.

**disguised sale**   A contribution of property by a partner to a partnership and a related distribution from the partnership to the partner treated as the taxable sale of a part interest in the property.

**disregarded entity**   An entity that has no identity for federal tax purposes.

**distributable net income (DNI)**   The maximum amount of both the trust distribution deduction and the income from the trust taxable to the beneficiaries; DNI attempts to measure the current increase in trust value available for distribution to income beneficiaries.

**distribution deduction**   The income tax deduction equal to the lesser of (1) the taxable portion of DNI or (2) the taxable portion of actual or required distributions.

**distributive share**   A partner's share of any item of taxable income, gain, deduction, or loss recognized by a partnership.

**dividend**   Any distribution of cash or property made by a corporation to its shareholders to the extent the distribution is paid from E&P.

**donor**   An individual who makes a gift.

# E

**earnings and profits (E&P)**   The measure of a corporation's financial capacity to pay a return on the shareholders' invested capital without returning the capital itself.

**Economic Growth and Tax Relief Reconciliation Act of 2001 (EGTRRA)**   Tax bill signed into law by President George W. Bush on June 7, 2001.

**economic nexus**   The taxing jurisdiction established by the use of intangible assets, such as trademarks or licenses, within a state.

**economic performance**   The third requirement of the all-events test that generally occurs when all activities required to be performed in connection with a liability have been completed.

**effective tax rate**   The corporation's total income tax expense per books divided by pretax book income.

**employer identification number (EIN)**   The number assigned to an employer by the IRS to identify the employer for employment tax purposes.

**empowerment zone**   A government-designated distressed area qualifying for special tax incentives for new business investment.

**empowerment zone employment credit**   The tax credit of up to $3,000 per employee for hiring employees who both live and work in an empowerment zone.

**enterprise community**   A government-designated distressed area qualifying for special tax incentives for new business investment.

**entity theory of partnerships** The theory that partners and their partnership are separate and distinct entities for federal tax purposes, and a partner's interest is an equity interest in the partnership as a whole.

**estate** A fiduciary entity formed on the death of an individual to manage, conserve, and distribute property to specified individuals.

**European Union (EU)** The alliance of European countries seeking to create a single, integrated European market to allow free movement of capital and trade among member countries and to result in economic growth for the region.

**excess loss account** A negative basis in the stock of a member of a consolidated group.

**excess net passive income tax** The tax imposed on an S corporation's excess net passive income if it has accumulated E&P on the last day of the taxable year.

**exemption equivalent amount** The total amount of wealth allowed to be transferred by an individual free of any transfer tax.

# F

**fair market value (FMV)** The price at which property would change hands between a willing buyer and a willing seller in an arm's-length transaction in which neither party is under any compulsion to transact and in which both parties have reasonable knowledge of the relevant facts.

**family limited partnership** A partnership established by parents or grandparents who transfer property (such as a family business) into a partnership in exchange for general partner interests. Over time, the partnership creators give limited interests in the partnership to their children and grandchildren.

**favorable M-1 adjustments** The adjustments that decrease book income in the reconciliation of book to taxable income on Schedule M-1 including nontaxable income or gain items included in book income and deductible items not included in book income.

**fiduciary** The party designated in the trust document to manage trust property in accordance with the donor's instructions.

**52–53 week year** The taxable year consisting of either 52 or 53 weeks and ending on the same day of the week each year.

**first-tier distributions** The required distributions from trust accounting income.

**foreign-source income** The taxable income attributable to a U.S. firm's business activities in a foreign jurisdiction.

**foreign tax credit** The credit against U.S. tax based on foreign income tax paid or accrued during the year.

**forward triangular merger** A type A reorganization in which the target is merged into a subsidiary of the acquiring corporation.

**friendly takeover** An acquisition of a target business that is regarded favorably by the target's existing management and owners.

**fringe benefit** Any indirect or noncash form of compensation in addition to an employee's base salary or wage.

**future interest** The right to use, possession, or enjoyment of property or income from property at some future date.

# G

**general business credit** The aggregate of 12 different tax credits available to business enterprises.

**general business credit limitation** The total general business credit usable in any tax year that cannot exceed the net income tax before the credit less the greater of (1) the tentative minimum tax or (2) 25 percent of net regular tax liability in excess of $25,000.

**general partnership** A partnership in which all partners have unlimited personal liability for debts incurred by the partnership.

**Generally Accepted Accounting Principles (GAAP)** The set of accounting rules developed by the Financial Accounting Standards Board and adhered to by the public accounting profession in preparing financial statements.

**generation-skipping transfer tax (GSTT)** The tax assessed on transfers by gift or bequest that skip a generation (e.g., grandparent to grandchild).

**gift-splitting election** The election that allows married couples to treat all gifts made by either spouse as made jointly by both spouses, allowing each spouse to use the annual gift tax exclusion.

**grantor trust** An irrevocable trust that provides the grantor with either substantial benefits from the trust property or control over its disposition.

**gross estate** The FMV of all property owned by the decedent at the date of death (or on the alternate valuation date) plus life insurance proceeds from policies owned by the decedent or benefiting the estate, a portion of jointly owned property, transfers with a retained life estate, certain gifts made within three years of death, gift tax paid on gifts made within three years of death, and survivorship annuity benefits.

**guaranteed payment** The payment from a partnership to a partner to compensate the partner for regular services performed for the partnership.

# H

**hostile takeover**   An acquisition of a target business that is regarded unfavorably and is resisted by the target's existing management and owners.

**hot assets**   Partnership assets that generate ordinary gain or loss including unrealized receivables and inventory.

# I

**implicit tax**   The reduction in the before-tax rate of return that investors are willing to accept because of the tax-favored characteristics of an investment.

**inbound transactions**   Business or investment activities in the United States by nonresident aliens or foreign corporations.

**incentive stock option (ISO)**   A qualified stock option for federal tax purposes. Individuals do not recognize the bargain element as taxable income on the exercise of an ISO.

**incidents of ownership**   With respect to life insurance policies, the power to change the policy's beneficiary, cancel it, borrow against it, pledge it for a loan, or revoke its assignment.

**includible corporation**   A corporation that can be included in an affiliated group. Tax-exempt corporations, foreign corporations, insurance companies, and S corporations are not includible corporations.

**income in respect of a decedent (IRD)**   The income earned by the decedent prior to death that is not reported on the decedent's final tax return.

**income interest**   The right to receive the income generated by a specific property interest, usually for life.

**incomplete transfer**   A transfer in which the transferor retains rights to the transferred property and that is not considered a gift for gift tax purposes.

**increased limited expensing election**   The election to expense $20,000 in addition to the expensing amount allowed under Section 179 for tangible personal property placed in service in an empowerment zone by a qualified business.

**incremental research activities credit**   The tax credit equal to 20 percent of qualified current expenditures in excess of a base amount that considers the taxpayer's prior history of research expenditures.

**inheritance tax**   The tax levied on the recipient of property bequests and based on the FMV of the property and the relationship between the decedent and the beneficiary.

**initial public offering (IPO)**   The first offering of corporate stock on a securities market that converts the corporation from a closely held to a publicly held corporation.

**inside basis**   The adjusted tax basis in property owned by a partnership.

**insolvency**   The excess of a business's debts over the FMV of its assets.

**intangible drilling costs (IDCs)**   Expenditures incident to the drilling and preparation of wells for the production of oil and gas such as wages, fuel, repairs, and supplies.

***inter vivos* trust**   A trust created during the donor's lifetime.

**intercompany dividend**   A dividend paid by one member to another member of a consolidated group.

**intercompany transaction**   A transaction between corporations that are members of the same consolidated group immediately after the transaction.

**Internal Revenue Code**   The compilation of statutory tax laws written and enacted by the Congress of the United States.

**irrevocable trust**   A trust in which the donor gives up all future control over the trust property.

# J

**joint tenancy**   The joint ownership of property with the right of survivorship by two or more individuals regardless of their relationship.

**judicial authority**   The decisions of federal courts interpreting the tax law.

**junk bonds**   Unsecured corporate debt obligations bearing a high yield and a high degree of risk.

# K

**Keogh plan**   A qualified retirement plan for self-employed individuals and their employees.

**kiddie tax**   The tax on a child's unearned income based on the marginal rate of the child's parents.

# L

**leveraged buyout (LBO)**   The taxable acquisition of a target in which the acquiring corporation uses a substantial amount of new debt to finance the acquisition.

**limited expensing election** The election under which firms can expense a limited dollar amount of the cost of tangible personalty placed in service during the taxable year.

**limited liability company (LLC)** The form of unincorporated business organization in which the members have limited liability for business debt. LLCs are generally treated as partnerships for federal tax purposes.

**limited liability partnership (LLP)** A partnership in which the individual partners have limited liability for malpractice-related claims resulting from the professional misconduct of any other individual partner.

**limited partnership** A partnership in which one or more partners are not personally liable for partnership debt. A limited partnership must have at least one general partner with personal liability.

**liquidating distribution** A distribution by a partnership to a partner that extinguishes the partner's equity interest.

**living trust** A grantor trust holding title to all assets owned by an individual that specifies how to transfer such assets on the death of the grantor and that allows the assets to avoid probate on the grantor's death.

**low-income housing credit** The tax incentive to construct or substantially renovate multiunit housing for low-income residents.

# M

**majority interest taxable year** The partnership taxable year corresponding to the taxable year of one or more partners who own more than 50 percent of capital and profits.

**marginal tax rate** The tax rate that applies to the next dollar of taxable income.

**marital deduction** The deduction allowed in calculating gift and estate tax for transfers to the spouse of the donor or decedent.

**marketability discount** The valuation discount for estate tax purposes acknowledging the costs that would be incurred in creating a market to dispose of closely held stock, including underwriting costs and other expenses of going public.

**matching rule** The accounting rule for intercompany transactions under which the effect of the transaction on a separate entity basis must match the effect on a single entity basis.

**material participation** A business owner's regular, continuous, and substantial involvement in the daily operation of the business.

**merger** The absorption of one corporate entity into another corporate entity under state law.

**minimum tax credit** The AMT liability carried forward indefinitely as a credit against future regular tax liability.

**minority interest discount** The valuation discount for a part interest in a business reflecting the lack of control that can be exercised by minority owners.

# N

**natural termination of a partnership** The termination that occurs when a partnership discontinues all business and financial operations conducted by its partners.

**net cash flow** The difference between cash received and cash disbursed.

**net operating loss (NOL)** The excess of a taxpayer's allowable business deductions over gross income for the taxable year.

**net present value (NPV)** The sum of the present values of all cash inflows and outflows relating to a transaction.

**net recognized built-in gain** The recognized portion of an S corporation's net unrealized built-in gain on which it must pay the built-in gains tax.

**net unrealized built-in gain** The amount by which the FMV of an S corporation's assets exceeds the aggregate adjusted basis immediately following its conversion from a C corporation.

**new markets tax credit** The credit for equity investments in community development entities that provides an incentive for investment in low-income communities.

**nexus** The degree of contact between a business and a state necessary to establish the state's jurisdiction to tax the business.

**nonbusiness bad debt** A totally worthless debt held by an individual creditor and unrelated to the creditor's business that the individual can recognize as a short-term capital loss.

**nonqualified plan** A retirement plan that consists of an employer's promise (usually unfunded) to pay employee compensation at a future date.

**nonrecourse liability** A liability secured only by specific collateral for which no individual or entity is personally liable for repayment.

**nonseparately computed income or loss** The ordinary business income or loss of an S corporation disregarding any separately stated items.

# O

**outbound transactions**   Business or investment activities in foreign jurisdictions by U.S. citizens, residents, or domestic corporations.

**outside basis**   The adjusted tax basis of a partner or LLC member in the partnership or LLC interest.

# P

**parent-subsidiary group**   A type of controlled group consisting of a chain of corporations headed by a parent corporation.

**partnership**   The unincorporated association of two or more persons to conduct business as co-owners.

**passive activity loss**   The nondeductible excess of aggregate losses from passive activities over aggregate income from passive activities.

**passthrough entity**   A business entity that is not a taxpayer for federal income tax purposes and whose income, gain, deduction, and loss are reported by the entity's owners.

**payment liabilities**   The liabilities for which economic performance does not occur until the liability is paid.

**payroll factor**   One of three factors measuring the degree of business activity within a state. The payroll factor is generally the ratio of the payroll for in-state employees to total payroll.

**percentage depletion**   An annual deduction based on the gross income generated by a depletable property multiplied by a statutory depletion rate.

**permanent difference**   A difference between book income and taxable income that affects only one year and does not reverse in a future year or years.

**permanent establishment**   A tax treaty term referring to a fixed location at which an entity conducts business within a treaty country and which establishes the country's taxing jurisdiction over the entity.

**personal holding company tax**   The penalty tax levied on personal holding companies that fail to distribute their entire after-tax income to their shareholders.

**phantom stock plan**   The arrangement in which an employee's deferred compensation is hypothetically invested in employer stock so that the amount of compensation is indexed to the appreciation in the FMV of the stock.

**physical presence nexus**   The taxing jurisdiction established by a taxpayer maintaining a physical presence within a state.

**pick-up tax**   The tax equal to any excess of the allowable federal estate tax credit for state death taxes over any inheritance or estate tax already imposed by the state.

**premature withdrawal**   The withdrawal from a qualified retirement plan made before the owner of the plan reaches age 59½ or satisfies other statutory conditions.

**present interest**   The unrestricted right to the immediate use, possession, or enjoyment of property or income from the property.

**primary authorities**   The original sources of tax law including statute, regulations, IRS pronouncements, and judicial authority.

**principal**   See *corpus.*

**principal partner**   Any partner who owns at least 5 percent of partnership capital or profits.

**private activity bonds**   The tax-exempt bonds issued by state or local governments for nongovernmental purposes such as industrial development.

**private letter ruling (PLR)**   The IRS's written response to a taxpayer's written inquiry as to how the tax law applies to a proposed transaction.

**probate**   The process of administering and disposing of estate assets under the terms of the decedent's will or in accordance with state intestacy laws.

**probate estate**   The property owned by a decedent and disposed of according to the terms of a valid will or state intestacy laws.

**profit split method**   The transfer pricing method that allocates the combined profit earned on a controlled transaction among members of the group in proportion to the relative value that each member contributes to the transaction.

**profits interest**   A partner's right to a share of income, gain, loss, or deduction generated by partnership transactions.

**property factor**   One of three factors measuring the degree of business activity within a state; generally, the ratio of property located within the state to total property.

**pro rata share**   The share of S corporation items of income, gain, deduction, or loss based on the shareholder's stock ownership throughout the year.

**Public Law 86-272**   The federal statute prohibiting states from assessing income tax on businesses whose only activity within the state is the solicitation of orders for tangible personal property if such property is shipped to the customer from outside the state.

**publicly traded partnership (PTP)**   An active business partnership with interests traded on an established securities market or readily tradable on a secondary market.

**purchase method of accounting**   A GAAP method of accounting for corporation acquisitions under which the acquirer of a target business records the target's assets at the cost paid for the assets.

# Q

**qualified nonrecourse financing**   A nonrecourse liability incurred with respect to the holding of real property, secured by such property, and borrowed from a commercial lender or a government.

**qualified plan**   A retirement plan that allows participants to defer income recognition on vested plan contributions and earnings until the year in which they receive distributions from the plan.

**qualified small business stock**   Stock in a qualified small business issued after August 10, 1993. Gain recognized on sale of qualified small business stock is eligible for the Section 1202 exclusion.

**qualified Subchapter S subsidiary (QSub)**   A wholly owned subsidiary of an S corporation that is a disregarded entity for federal tax purposes.

**qualified terminable interest property (QTIP)**   Any property passing from one spouse to another by gift or at death in which the recipient spouse has a qualifying income interest for life.

**qualified trust to benefit a minor**   An irrevocable trust in which income and principal may be expended by or for the benefit of a minor child under the age of 21. Any portion of trust property or income not expended by the time the minor reaches 21 must pass to the minor at that time. If the minor dies before age 21, trust property must be payable to the minor's estate or the minor's designated beneficiary.

# R

**Rabbi trust**   A nonqualified deferred compensation arrangement in which the employer transfers cash or property to a trust for the benefit of the employee. The employer cannot reclaim the trust assets, but the assets are subject to claim by the employer's creditors.

**recourse liability**   A liability for which one or more persons is personally liable for repayment.

**recurring item exception**   An exception to the economic performance requirement under which a liability is considered incurred in a taxable year in which it meets the first two requirements of the all-events test and economic performance occurs within 8.5 months after year-end.

**related parties**   Persons presumed by the tax law to share common economic interests or objectives who cannot deal at arm's length in a transaction.

**related-party transaction**   A transaction between parties who share a common economic interest or objective and who presumably cannot deal at arm's length.

**remainder interest**   The right to receive ownership of property upon termination of the income interest.

**remedial method**   A regulatory method for making Section 704(c) allocations that eliminates distortions caused by the ceiling rule under the traditional method.

**renewal community**   A government-designated distressed area qualifying for special tax incentives for new business investment.

**resale price method**   The method for determining the transfer price for controlled transactions based on the gross profit margin earned in comparable uncontrolled transactions.

**reseller exemption**   The exemption from sales and use tax for goods purchased for resale or used in the manufacture of products for resale.

**restricted stock**   Any stock received as compensation by a corporate employee that is nontransferable or subject to a substantial risk of forfeiture.

**retained life estate**   The right reserved by a donor of property to receive the income from the property or to otherwise enjoy the property until the donor's death.

**revenue procedures**   Published pronouncements explaining administrative procedures that taxpayers must follow in reporting transactions or filing tax returns.

**revenue rulings**   Published pronouncements explaining how the IRS applies current tax law to a particular set of facts and circumstances.

**reverse cash merger**   A taxable acquisition in which a subsidiary formed by the acquiring corporation merges into the target corporation. The target survives the merger so that only its shareholders recognize gain or loss on the transaction.

**revocable trust**   A trust in which the donor retains the right to revoke the transfer of property to the trust and regain control and title.

# S

**S corporation**   A domestic corporation with a Subchapter S election in effect that is a passthrough entity for federal income tax purposes.

**sales factor** One of three factors measuring the degree of business activity within a state; generally, the ratio of sales within the state to total sales.

**sales tax** A consumption tax based on the sales price of tangible personal property or services, assessed state, county, and city governments.

**Schedule M-1** The schedule on Form 1120, Form 1120S, or Form 1065 on which the entity must reconcile book income to taxable income.

**secondary authorities** The sources of tax information, such as textbooks, treatises, professional journals, and commercial tax services that explain and interpret the tax law.

**second-tier distributions** All trust distributions other than first-tier distributions.

**Section 338(h)(10) election** The joint election made by the seller and purchaser of a controlling interest in the stock of a target corporation. The seller and the target must be members of the same consolidated group immediately before the sale. The effect of the election is that the sale is treated as a taxable sale of the target's assets rather than the target's stock.

**Section 382 limitation** The annual limitation on NOL carryforwards deductible against taxable income in any year following a corporate ownership change.

**Section 482** The transfer pricing rules applied to transactions between business entities owned or controlled directly or indirectly by the same interests, the intent of which is to ensure that the price charged on these transactions reflects the arm's-length price that would be charged between independent entities.

**Section 754 election** The partnership election that results in a special adjustment to the inside basis of partnership property for the purchaser of a partnership interest.

**Section 1202 exclusion** The exclusion of 50 percent of the gain recognized on sale of qualified small business stock that the seller owned for at least five years.

**Section 1244 stock** The first $1 million of stock issued by certain corporations in exchange for cash or property. Some portion of the loss recognized on sale of Section 1244 stock is characterized as ordinary rather than capital loss.

**self-rental rule** The regulatory rule that disqualifies rental income as passive income if the property is rented for use by a business in which the owner of the property materially participates.

**separate share rule** The statutory rule that applies when a trust has multiple beneficiaries who are each entitled to a substantially separate and independent share of trust income or property.

**separate taxable income** The intermediate calculation of net income or loss made by each member of a consolidated group as part of the calculation of consolidated taxable income.

**separately stated items** The items of income, gain, deduction, or loss that a passthrough entity cannot include in the computation of ordinary business income or loss and that must be accounted for independently in the computation of the owners' taxable income.

**simple trust** Any trust required to distribute all accounting income to its beneficiaries and that makes no charitable contributions or distributions of property during the year.

**single-member LLC** Any LLC owned by one person and generally disregarded as an entity for federal tax purposes.

**sole proprietorship** An unincorporated business owned by one individual.

**special use valuation method** The valuation method that differentiates between a property's FMV under its "current use" versus its "best" or "highest" use.

**spin-off** The distribution of a controlling stock interest in a subsidiary by a parent corporation to its shareholders.

**split-off** The distribution of a controlling stock interest in a subsidiary by a parent corporation in redemption of the parent's stock.

**split-up** The distribution of a controlling stock interest in two or more subsidiaries by a parent corporation pursuant to the liquidation of the parent.

**spousal basis increase** Provision in EGTRRA allowing an increase in tax basis of estate property transferred to the decedent's surviving spouse up to $3 million.

**statutory authority** The tax law as codified in the Internal Revenue Code of 1986.

**step transaction doctrine** The judicial doctrine under which the IRS can collapse a series of intermediate transactions into a single transaction to determine the tax consequences of the arrangement in its entirety.

**stock appreciation right (SAR)** The right of an employee to receive deferred compensation equal to the appreciation in the value of one share of employer stock between the date of grant and the date of exercise.

**stock basis adjustments** The adjustments made by each member of a consolidated group to the tax basis of stock in another member.

**stock dividend** The distribution from a corporation to its shareholders of additional shares of corporate stock.

**stock option** The right to purchase a stated number of shares of corporate stock for a stated price (strike price) for a stated period of time.

**stock redemption** The acquisition by a corporation of its own stock in exchange for a distribution of cash or property.

**Streamlined Sales Tax Project** The joint effort by 30 states to simplify and integrate the assessment and collection of sales and use taxes.

**strike price** The price at which an employee can purchase employer stock under a stock option.

**Subchapter C** The portion of the Internal Revenue Code (Sections 301 through 385) governing the tax consequences of transactions between corporations and shareholders.

**Subchapter K** The portion of the Internal Revenue Code (Sections 701 through 777) governing the operation of partnerships and the tax treatment of their partners.

**Subchapter S** The portion of the Internal Revenue Code (Sections 1361 through 1379) governing the operation of S corporations and the tax treatment of their shareholders.

**Subpart F earnings and profits (E&P)** Accumulated E&P of a controlled foreign corporation (CFC) representing undistributed Subpart F income.

**Subpart F income** Foreign source income earned by a controlled foreign corporation (CFC) that is taxed to the U.S. shareholders in the year earned instead of the year in which the CFC pays a dividend; conceptually, income with no commercial or economic connection to the country in which the CFC is incorporated.

**substance over form doctrine** The judicial doctrine that the IRS can look through the legal formalities to determine the economic substance of a transaction and to base the tax consequences on the substance instead of the form.

**substantial economic effect** The economic benefit or burden corresponding to a tax allocation of income, gain, deduction, or loss; determined by reference to the effect of the allocation on a partner's book capital account.

**substituted basis** The tax basis of property received in a transaction determined by reference to the tax basis of other property disposed of in the transaction.

**suspended loss** The nondeductible portion of an owner's share of a passthrough entity's loss.

# T

**taxable estate** The FMV of a decedent's gross estate minus allowable deductions.

**taxable gift** The FMV of property transferred for less than adequate consideration in money or money's worth reduced by allowable exclusions and deductions.

**taxable year** The annual 12-month period for which a taxpayer determines taxable income.

**tax basis books** The financial records of a business reflecting the tax rules for income measurement.

**tax benefit** A decrease in tax liability for any period resulting from a transaction.

**tax cost** An increase in tax liability for any period resulting from a transaction.

**tax credit and deduction for clean-fuel-burning vehicles** The tax incentives to encourage the use of vehicles powered by alternative energy sources including a tax credit of 10 percent of the cost of electric vehicles, with a maximum credit of $4,000 per vehicle, and a deduction for a portion of the cost of clean-fuel-burning vehicles in the year placed in service.

**tax incentives** The tax provisions enacted to encourage actions that have desirable economic or social consequences.

**tax increment financing (TIF)** The technique used by state and local jurisdictions to link the tax incentives granted to a business directly to the economic benefits that the business provides to the locality and to provide an incentive payment based on the increase in a specific tax base resulting from the presence of the business in the locality.

**tax planning** The structuring of transactions to reduce tax costs or increase tax savings to maximize net present value.

**tax treaties** The bilateral treaties between the United States and more than 50 foreign countries that modify the statutory tax rules applicable to income of U.S. persons earned in the treaty country and U.S. income earned by persons from the treaty country.

**technical advice memorandum (TAM)** The technical advice requested by a revenue agent or appeals officer during the examination or appeal of a taxpayer's return representing the IRS position on a disputed item and applying only to the taxpayer for whom it was issued.

**temporary difference** A difference between book income and taxable income in one year that reverses in a future year or years.

**tenancy by the entirety** The ownership of property in joint tenancy between husband and wife.

**tenancy in common** The joint ownership of property without right of survivorship by two or more individuals regardless of their relationship.

**terminable interest** An interest in property that terminates after the passage of time or the occurrence of a specified event.

**testamentary trust** A trust created upon the donor's death as directed in the donor's will.

**throwback rule**   A rule that includes a sale of goods in the sales factor of the state from which the goods are shipped if the destination state lacks jurisdiction to tax the income from the sale.

**time value of money**   The concept that a dollar available today is worth more than a dollar available tomorrow because the current dollar can be invested immediately.

**traditional Section 704(c) method**   The basic regulatory method for making Section 704(c) allocations with respect to property contributed to a partnership.

**transfer pricing**   The pricing of goods or services exchanged in the international area between controlled corporations operating in different taxing jurisdictions.

**Treasury regulations**   Official interpretations of statutory tax rules written by the U.S. Treasury.

**trustee**   See *fiduciary*.

**trust taxable income**   Trust income subject to federal taxation under Subchapter J of the Internal Revenue Code.

**type A reorganization**   A tax-deferred acquisition accomplished through a merger or consolidation.

**type B reorganization**   A tax-deferred acquisition accomplished through a stock-for-stock exchange.

**type C reorganization**   A tax-deferred acquisition accomplished through a stock-for-assets exchange.

**type D reorganization**   A tax-deferred transaction in which one corporation divides into two or more corporations.

**type E reorganization**   A tax-deferred exchange of stock pursuant to the recapitalization of a corporation.

**type F reorganization**   A tax-deferred exchange of stock to accomplish a corporation's mere change in identity, form, or place of organization.

**type G reorganization**   A tax-deferred exchange of securities pursuant to the reorganization of a corporation in bankruptcy.

# U

**unfavorable M-1 adjustments**   The adjustments that increase book income in the reconciliation of book to taxable income on Schedule M-1 including taxable income or gain items not included in book income and nondeductible expenses and losses.

**unified credit**   A lifetime exemption from transfer tax for each individual.

**Uniform Principal and Income Act (UPIA)**   The legislation adopted by most states to allocate trust items between principal and accounting income.

**unitary business**   Related corporations whose operations are integrated and interdependent.

**unrealized receivables**   The zero-basis accounts receivable of a cash basis partnership and ordinary gain potential in partnership operating assets.

**use tax**   The tax levied on the ownership, possession, or consumption of goods if the owner did not pay the jurisdiction's sales tax when the goods were purchased.

**U.S.-source income**   Taxable income attributable to business activities conducted in the United States.

**U.S. Circuit Courts of Appeals**   Thirteen federal courts that hear appeals of trial court decisions.

**U.S. Court of Federal Claims**   A federal trial court located in Washington, D.C., in which taxpayers can sue the government for a refund of tax.

**U.S. District Courts**   Federal trial courts in which taxpayers can sue the government for a refund of tax.

**U.S. Supreme Court**   The highest federal court. The Supreme Court hears appeals of circuit court decisions.

**U.S. Tax Court**   A federal court that tries only federal income, gift, and estate tax cases.

# V

**value-added tax (VAT)**   The tax levied on firms engaged in any phase of the production or manufacture of goods and based on the incremental value the firm adds to the goods.

**varying interest rule**   The statutory rule that each partner's distributive share of partnership items must take into account any changes in the partners' capital interests during the year.

# W

**water's edge election**   The election by multinational corporate groups to confine unitary state income tax reporting to activities within the United States.

**wealth redistribution**   The intent of the transfer tax system to redistribute private wealth to the public domain.

# Appendix A

# Present Value of $1

| Periods | 3% | 4% | 5% | 6% | 7% | 8% | 9% |
|---------|------|------|------|------|------|------|------|
| 1 | .971 | .962 | .952 | .943 | .935 | .926 | .917 |
| 2 | .943 | .925 | .907 | .890 | .873 | .857 | .842 |
| 3 | .915 | .889 | .864 | .840 | .816 | .794 | .772 |
| 4 | .888 | .855 | .823 | .792 | .763 | .735 | .708 |
| 5 | .863 | .822 | .784 | .747 | .713 | .681 | .650 |
| 6 | .837 | .790 | .746 | .705 | .666 | .630 | .596 |
| 7 | .813 | .760 | .711 | .665 | .623 | .583 | .547 |
| 8 | .789 | .731 | .677 | .627 | .582 | .540 | .502 |
| 9 | .766 | .703 | .645 | .592 | .544 | .500 | .460 |
| 10 | .744 | .676 | .614 | .558 | .508 | .463 | .422 |
| 11 | .722 | .650 | .585 | .527 | .475 | .429 | .388 |
| 12 | .701 | .625 | .557 | .497 | .444 | .397 | .356 |
| 13 | .681 | .601 | .530 | .469 | .415 | .368 | .326 |
| 14 | .661 | .577 | .505 | .442 | .388 | .340 | .299 |
| 15 | .642 | .555 | .481 | .417 | .362 | .315 | .275 |
| 16 | .623 | .534 | .458 | .394 | .339 | .292 | .252 |
| 17 | .605 | .513 | .436 | .371 | .317 | .270 | .231 |
| 18 | .587 | .494 | .416 | .350 | .296 | .250 | .212 |
| 19 | .570 | .475 | .396 | .331 | .277 | .232 | .194 |
| 20 | .554 | .456 | .377 | .312 | .258 | .215 | .178 |

| Periods | 10% | 11% | 12% | 13% | 14% | 15% | 20% |
|---------|------|------|------|------|------|------|------|
| 1 | .909 | .901 | .893 | .885 | .877 | .870 | .833 |
| 2 | .826 | .812 | .797 | .783 | .769 | .756 | .694 |
| 3 | .751 | .731 | .712 | .693 | .675 | .658 | .579 |
| 4 | .683 | .659 | .636 | .613 | .592 | .572 | .482 |
| 5 | .621 | .593 | .567 | .543 | .519 | .497 | .402 |
| 6 | .564 | .535 | .507 | .480 | .456 | .432 | .335 |
| 7 | .513 | .482 | .452 | .425 | .400 | .376 | .279 |
| 8 | .467 | .434 | .404 | .376 | .351 | .327 | .233 |
| 9 | .424 | .391 | .361 | .333 | .308 | .284 | .194 |
| 10 | .386 | .352 | .322 | .295 | .270 | .247 | .162 |
| 11 | .350 | .317 | .287 | .261 | .237 | .215 | .135 |
| 12 | .319 | .286 | .257 | .231 | .208 | .187 | .112 |
| 13 | .290 | .258 | .229 | .204 | .182 | .163 | .093 |
| 14 | .263 | .232 | .205 | .181 | .160 | .141 | .078 |
| 15 | .239 | .209 | .183 | .160 | .140 | .123 | .065 |
| 16 | .218 | .188 | .163 | .141 | .123 | .107 | .054 |
| 17 | .198 | .170 | .146 | .125 | .108 | .093 | .045 |
| 18 | .180 | .153 | .130 | .111 | .095 | .081 | .038 |
| 19 | .164 | .138 | .116 | .098 | .083 | .070 | .031 |
| 20 | .149 | .124 | .104 | .087 | .073 | .061 | .026 |

# Appendix B

# Present Value of Annuity of $1

| Periods | 3% | 4% | 5% | 6% | 7% | 8% | 9% |
|---|---|---|---|---|---|---|---|
| 1 | .971 | .962 | .952 | .943 | .935 | .926 | .917 |
| 2 | 1.913 | 1.886 | 1.859 | 1.833 | 1.808 | 1.783 | 1.759 |
| 3 | 2.829 | 2.775 | 2.723 | 2.673 | 2.624 | 2.577 | 2.531 |
| 4 | 3.737 | 3.630 | 3.546 | 3.465 | 3.387 | 3.312 | 3.240 |
| 5 | 4.580 | 4.452 | 4.329 | 4.212 | 4.100 | 3.993 | 3.890 |
| 6 | 5.417 | 5.242 | 5.076 | 4.917 | 4.767 | 4.623 | 4.486 |
| 7 | 6.230 | 6.002 | 5.786 | 5.582 | 5.389 | 5.206 | 5.033 |
| 8 | 7.020 | 6.733 | 6.463 | 6.210 | 5.971 | 5.747 | 5.535 |
| 9 | 7.786 | 7.435 | 7.108 | 6.802 | 6.515 | 6.247 | 5.995 |
| 10 | 8.530 | 8.111 | 7.722 | 7.360 | 7.024 | 6.710 | 6.418 |
| 11 | 9.253 | 8.760 | 8.306 | 7.887 | 7.499 | 7.139 | 6.805 |
| 12 | 9.954 | 9.385 | 8.863 | 8.384 | 7.943 | 7.536 | 7.161 |
| 13 | 10.635 | 9.986 | 9.394 | 8.853 | 8.358 | 7.904 | 7.487 |
| 14 | 11.296 | 10.563 | 9.899 | 9.295 | 8.745 | 8.244 | 7.786 |
| 15 | 11.938 | 11.118 | 10.380 | 9.712 | 9.108 | 8.559 | 8.061 |
| 16 | 12.561 | 11.652 | 10.838 | 10.106 | 9.447 | 8.851 | 8.313 |
| 17 | 13.166 | 12.166 | 11.274 | 10.477 | 9.763 | 9.122 | 8.544 |
| 18 | 13.754 | 12.659 | 11.690 | 10.828 | 10.059 | 9.372 | 8.756 |
| 19 | 14.324 | 13.134 | 12.085 | 11.158 | 10.336 | 9.604 | 8.950 |
| 20 | 14.877 | 13.590 | 12.462 | 11.470 | 10.594 | 9.818 | 9.129 |

| Periods | 10% | 11% | 12% | 13% | 14% | 15% | 20% |
|---|---|---|---|---|---|---|---|
| 1 | .909 | .901 | .893 | .885 | .877 | .870 | .833 |
| 2 | 1.736 | 1.713 | 1.690 | 1.668 | 1.647 | 1.626 | 1.528 |
| 3 | 2.487 | 2.444 | 2.402 | 2.361 | 2.322 | 2.283 | 2.106 |
| 4 | 3.170 | 3.102 | 3.037 | 2.974 | 2.914 | 2.855 | 2.589 |
| 5 | 3.791 | 3.696 | 3.605 | 3.517 | 3.433 | 3.352 | 2.991 |
| 6 | 4.355 | 4.231 | 4.111 | 3.998 | 3.889 | 3.784 | 3.326 |
| 7 | 4.868 | 4.712 | 4.564 | 4.423 | 4.288 | 4.160 | 3.605 |
| 8 | 5.335 | 5.146 | 4.968 | 4.799 | 4.639 | 4.487 | 3.837 |
| 9 | 5.759 | 5.537 | 5.328 | 5.132 | 4.946 | 4.772 | 4.031 |
| 10 | 6.145 | 5.889 | 5.650 | 5.426 | 5.216 | 5.019 | 4.192 |
| 11 | 6.495 | 6.207 | 5.938 | 5.687 | 5.453 | 5.234 | 4.327 |
| 12 | 6.814 | 6.492 | 6.194 | 5.918 | 5.660 | 5.421 | 4.439 |
| 13 | 7.103 | 6.750 | 6.424 | 6.122 | 5.842 | 5.583 | 4.533 |
| 14 | 7.367 | 6.982 | 6.628 | 6.302 | 6.002 | 5.724 | 4.611 |
| 15 | 7.606 | 7.191 | 6.811 | 6.462 | 6.142 | 5.847 | 4.675 |
| 16 | 7.824 | 7.379 | 6.974 | 6.604 | 6.265 | 5.954 | 4.730 |
| 17 | 8.022 | 7.549 | 7.120 | 6.729 | 6.373 | 6.047 | 4.775 |
| 18 | 8.201 | 7.702 | 7.250 | 6.840 | 6.467 | 6.128 | 4.812 |
| 19 | 8.365 | 7.839 | 7.366 | 6.938 | 6.550 | 6.198 | 4.843 |
| 20 | 8.514 | 7.963 | 7.469 | 7.025 | 6.623 | 6.259 | 4.870 |

# Index